THE PROBABILITY PROBLEM SOLVER ®

REGISTERED TRADEMARK

A Complete Solution Guide to Any Textbook

Vance Berger, Ph.D.
Former Adjunct Professor
Rutgers University
New Brunswick, New Jersey

Research and Education Association
61 Ethel Road West
Piscataway, New Jersey 08854

THE PROBABILITY PROBLEM SOLVER ®

Printed in the United States of America

Library of Congress Catalog Card Number 96-67687

International Standard Book Number 0-87891-839-6

PROBLEM SOLVER is a registered trademark of
Research and Education Association, Piscataway, New Jersey

WHAT THIS BOOK IS FOR

Students have generally found probability a difficult subject to understand and learn. Despite the publication of hundreds of textbooks in this field, each one intended to provide an improvement over previous textbooks, students continue to remain perplexed as a result of the numerous conditions that must often be remembered and correlated in solving a problem. Various possible interpretations of terms used in probability also contributed to much of the difficulties experienced by students.

In a study of the problem, REA found the following basic reasons underlying students' difficulties with probability taught in schools:

(a) No systematic rules of analysis have been developed which students may follow in a step-by-step manner to solve the usual problems encountered. This results from the fact that the numerous different conditions and principles which may be involved in a problem, lead to many possible different methods of solution. To prescribe a set of rules to be followed for each of the possible variations, would involve an enormous number of rules and steps to be searched through by students, and this task would perhaps be more burdensome than solving the problem directly with some accompanying trial and error to find the correct solution route.

(b) Textbooks currently available will usually explain a given principle in a few pages written by a professional who has an insight in the subject matter that is not shared by students. The explanations are often written in an abstract manner which leaves the students confused as to the application of the principle. The explanations given are not sufficiently detailed and extensive to make the student aware of the wide range of applications and different aspects of the principle being studied. The numerous possible variations of principles and their applications are usually not discussed, and it is left for the students to discover these for themselves while doing exercises. Accordingly, the average student is expected to rediscover that which has been long known and practiced, but not published or explained extensively.

(c) The examples usually following the explanation of a topic are too few in number and too simple to enable the student to obtain a thorough grasp of the principles involved. The explanations do not provide sufficient basis to enable a student to solve problems that may be subsequently assigned for homework or given on examinations.

The examples are presented in abbreviated form which leaves out much material between steps, and requires that students derive the omitted material themselves. As a result, students find the examples difficult to understand— contrary to the purpose of the examples.

Examples are, furthermore, often worded in a confusing manner. They do not state the problem and then present the solution. Instead, they pass through a general discussion, never revealing what is to be solved for.

Examples, also, do not always include diagrams/graphs, wherever appropriate, and students do not obtain the training to draw diagrams or graphs to simplify and organize their thinking.

(d) Students can learn the subject only by doing the exercises themselves and reviewing them in class, to obtain experience in applying the principles with their different ramifications.

In doing the exercises by themselves, students find that they are required to devote considerably more time to probability than to other subjects of comparable credits, because they are uncertain with regard to the selection and application of the theorems and principles involved. It is also often necessary for students to discover those "tricks" not revealed in their texts (or review books), that make it possible to solve problems easily. Students must usually resort to methods of trial-and-error to discover these "tricks," and as a result they find that they may sometimes spend several hours to solve a single problem.

(e) When reviewing the exercises in classrooms, instructors usually request students to take turns in writing solutions on the boards and explaining them to the class. Students often find it difficult to explain in a manner that holds the interest of the class, and enables the remaining students to follow the material written on the boards. The remaining students seated in the class are, furthermore, too occupied with copying the material from the boards, to listen to the oral explanations and concentrate on the methods of solution.

This book is intended to aid students in probability overcome the difficulties described, by supplying detailed illustrations of the solution methods which are usually not apparent to students. The solution methods are illustrated by problems selected from those that are most often assigned for class work and given on examinations. The problems are arranged in order of complexity to enable students to learn and understand a particular topic by reviewing the problems in sequence. The problems are illustrated with detailed step-by-step explanations, to save the students the large amount of time that is often needed to fill in the gaps that are usually found between steps of illustrations in textbooks or review/outline books.

The staff of REA considers probability a subject that is best learned by allowing students to view the methods of analysis and solution techniques themselves. This approach to learning the subject matter is similar to that practiced in various scientific laboratories, particularly in the medical fields.

In using this book, students may review and study the illustrated problems at their own pace; they are not limited to the time allowed for explaining problems on the board in class.

When students want to look up a particular type of problem and solution, they can readily locate it in the book by referring to the index which has been extensively prepared. It is also possible to locate a particular type of problem by glancing at just the material within the boxed portions. To facilitate rapid scanning of the problems, each problem has a heavy border around it. Furthermore, each problem is identified with a number immediately above the problem at the right-hand margin.

To obtain maximum benefit from the book, students should familiarize themselves with the section, "How To Use This Book," located in the front pages.

MAX FOGIEL, PH.D.
Program Director

HOW TO USE THIS BOOK

This book can be an invaluable aid to students in probability as a supplement to their textbooks. The book is subdivided into 12 chapters, each dealing with a separate topic. The subject matter is developed beginning with definitions and basic concepts, discrete random variables, continuous random variables, extends through moments, joint distributions, conditional probability, independence, and random samples. It then moves on to some famous results of probability theory, Markov stochastic processes, random walks and martingales, and ends with a comprehensive glossary and references list.

TO LEARN AND UNDERSTAND
A TOPIC THOROUGHLY

1. Refer to your class text and read the section pertaining to the topic. You should become acquainted with the principles discussed there. These principles, however, may not be clear to you at that time.

2. Then locate the topic you are looking for by referring to the Table of Contents in front of this book, *The Probability Problem Solver*.

3. Turn to the page where the topic begins and review the problems under each topic, in the order given. For each topic, the problems are arranged in order of complexity, from the simplest to the more difficult. Some problems may appear similar to others, but each problem has been selected to illustrate a different point or solution method.

To learn and understand a topic thoroughly and retain its contents, it will be generally necessary for students to review the problems several times. Repeated review is essential in order to gain experience in recognizing the principles that should be applied, and in selecting the best solution technique.

TO FIND A PARTICULAR PROBLEM

To locate one or more problems related to particular subject matter, refer to either the index, located at the back of the book or the indexes found at the beginning of each chapter. In using the indexes, be certain to note that the numbers given refer to problem numbers, not page numbers. This arrangement of the indexes is intended to facilitate finding a problem more rapidly, since two or more problems may appear on a page.

If a particular type of problem cannot be found readily, it is recommended that the student refer to the Table of Contents in the front pages, and then turn to the chapter which is applicable to the problem being sought. By scanning or glancing at the material that is boxed, it will generally be possible to find problems related to the one being sought, without consuming considerable time. After the problems have been located, the solutions can be reviewed and studied in detail. For the purpose of locating problems rapidly, students should acquaint themselves with the organization of the book as found in the Table of Contents.

In preparing for an exam, locate the topics to be covered on the exam in the Table of Contents, and then review the problems under those topics several times. This should equip the student with what might be needed for the exam.

CONTENTS

CHAPTER 1

DEFINITIONS AND BASIC CONCEPTS

Basic Attacks and Strategies for Solving Problems in this Chapter. See pages 4 to 83 for step-by-step solutions to problems.

Probability has been defined in several ways by different authors. For our purposes the probability of an event will be taken as the limit of the ratio of the number of successes (defined as the occurrence of the event) to the number of trials or experiments (in which the event may or may not occur) as the number of experiments becomes larger and larger. For example, we may consider tossing a "fair" coin and consider the probability of obtaining a result of heads, meaning that the coin lands heads up. By virtue of being fair we are assigning equal probabilities to the events heads and tails. If we assume that the coin never gets lost and never lands on its side, then we accept the premise that the probability of either heads or tails is one (we are certain that either one or the other of these outcomes will occur). We define a success as heads and a failure as tails. Denote the probability of heads by $P(H)$ and the probability of tails by $P(T)$. As these two events are equally likely and sum to one, these events are related by the equations

$$P(H) + P(T) = 1$$

(the probabilities of the two events sum to one)

and $P(H) = P(T)$

(the two events are equally likely).

Since $P(H) = P(T)$, we may substitute the second equation into the first, obtaining

$$P(H) + P(H) = 1,$$

or $\quad 2P(H) = 1.$

The solution to this equation is $P(H) = 0.5$. Thus, $P(T) = P(H) = 0.5$. Again, we may ask what this means. There is no guarantee that ten tosses of the coin will result in five heads and five tails. But as the number of tosses of this coin increases, the relative proportion of heads will become closer and closer to 0.5. In general, to say that an event A has probability p means that as the experiment is repeated over and over again, say n times, A will occur in about $100p\%$ of these experiments and will not occur in about $100(1 - p)\%$ of these experiments. For example, if $p = 0.6$, then we would expect event A to occur in about 60% of the experiments. If $p = 1.0$, then we would expect event A to occur in 100%, or all of the experiments. Thus, the proportion of trials favorable to event A will be approximately pn/n, or p, the true probability. The proportion of trials not favorable to event A will be approximately

$$\frac{(1 - p)n}{n}$$

or $(1 - p)$, the probability of event A not occurring. A number of concepts have been alluded to, and these will be considered in more detail in the remainder of Chapter 1.

REVIEW OF SET THEORY

Set theory is a useful tool in the study of probability theory. Sets are defined as collections of points. Points may be objects, items, numbers, or anything else. For example, the set of states in the USA but outside the Continental USA is {Alaska, Hawaii}. The set of positive integers under five is {1, 2, 3, 4}.

Set B is a subset of set A if each element of B also belongs to A. Every set is a subset of itself. Set B is a proper subset of set A if it is a subset of A and A is not a subset of B. Two sets, A and B, are equivalent, written $A = B$, if each is a subset of the other. The empty (or null) set contains no elements and is a subset of every set. The universal set contains all elements. Therefore, every set is a subset of the universal set.

The four most common set functions are the complement, the intersection, the union, and the set difference. The complement of set A is everything other than A, and is denoted A^C. There is an implicit notion of a universal set, required for the definition of the complement of a set. For example, if the universal set is the set of 50 states, then the complement of {Alaska, Hawaii} would be the remaining 48 states. If the universal set is the set of positive integers under 10, then the complement of $\{1, 2, 3, 4\}$ is $\{5, 6, 7, 8, 9\}$. Notice that $(A^C)^C = A$.

The intersection of sets A and B is the set of points which belong to both A and B, and is denoted $A \cap B$. That is, a point is in $A \cap B$ if it is in both A and B. Notice that for any sets A and B, $A \cap B = B \cap A$. The union of sets A and B is the set of points which lie in either A or B, and is denoted $A \cup B$. That is, a point is in $A \cup B$ if it is in either A or B, or both. Notice that for any sets A and B, $A \cup B = B \cup A$.

The set difference between sets A and B, written $A - B$, is the set of points in A but not in B. That is, $A - B = A \cap B^C$. Notice that the complement of A is the set difference between the universal set and A.

We may define an experiment as any action which results in an outcome, the result of which may not be entirely predictable prior to performing the experiment. The set of possible outcomes associated with an experiment is called the sample space. For example, if the experiment is the toss of a coin, then the sample space is $\{H, T\}$, where H denotes that the coin fell heads up, and T denotes that the coin fell tails up. If two coins are tossed, then the sample space is $\{HH, HT, TH, TT\}$. We may define event A by the condition that there were no heads, event B by one head, and event C by two heads. One may wish to find the probability of B. Set theory helps in this endeavor, because $A = \{TT\}$ (two tails is tantamount to no heads), $B = \{HT \cup TH\}$ (exactly one head), and $C = \{HH\}$ (two heads), showing that B is the union of two outcomes in the sample space. If we wanted to know the probability of at least one head (call this event D), then we would need to consider $D = B \cup C$ (at least one head may be written as exactly one head or exactly two heads). If we already knew the probability of D and wanted to find the probability of A, we would need to recognize that $A = D^C$, because there is no overlap between A and D and they exhaust the entire sample space. That is, there are no heads (A) if and only if there were not at least one head (D). It is true in general that $A \cap A^C$ is the null (empty) set, and $A \cup A^C$ is the universal set containing all elements.

Step-by-Step Solutions to Problems in this Chapter, "Definitions and Basic Concepts."

✓ • **PROBLEM 1–1**

Let the sample space (universal set) be $\{0, 1, 2, 3, 4\}$, and let $A = \{0, 1, 2\}$ and $B = \{2, 3, 4\}$. Find the complement of each set, the union of these sets, the intersection of these, and the complement of the union and of the intersection.

SOLUTION:

First $A^C = \{0, 1, 2, 3, 4\} - \{0, 1, 2\} = \{3, 4\}$ and $B^C = \{0, 1, 2, 3, 4\} - \{2, 3, 4\} = \{0, 1\}$. Now $A \cap B = \{2\}$, as this is the only element common to both sets. Also $A \cup B = \{0, 1, 2, 3, 4\}$, because each of these elements is contained in either A or B, or both. Finally, $(A \cap B)^C = \{0, 1, 2, 3, 4\} - A \cap B = \{0, 1, 2, 3, 4\} - \{2\} = \{0, 1, 3, 4\}$ and $(A \cup B)^C = \{0, 1, 2, 3, 4\} - A \cup B = \{0, 1, 2, 3, 4\} - \{0, 1, 2, 3, 4\} = \{\}$, or the empty set, because there are no elements which are not in the union.

? • **PROBLEM 1–2**

Consider tossing a pair of dice and define events E_1, E_2, and E as an even number on the first die, an even number on the second die, and an even number for the total of the two dice. Express E and E^C as unions and intersections of E_1 and E_2.

SOLUTION:

Since the sum of even numbers is even, we know that if both E_1 and E_2 occur, then E will occur. Also, the sum of two odd numbers is even, so if neither E_1 nor E_2 occur, then again E will occur. But the sum of one even and one odd number is odd, so any other combination will result in E^C. Thus, $E = (E_1 \cap E_2) \cup (E_1{}^C \cap E_2{}^C)$ (either both dice are even or both dice are odd) and $E^C = (E_1 \cap E_2{}^C) \cup (E_1{}^C \cap E_2)$ (one die is even and the other is odd).

✓ • PROBLEM 1-3

Consider tossing three coins. What is the sample space? For which outcomes will there be exactly two heads?

SOLUTION:

If there are three coins, then the sample space is {*TTT, TTH, THT, THH, HTT, HTH, HHT, HHH*}. The event exactly two heads will occur if any of the outcomes {*HHT, HTH, THH*} occur. Therefore, this event can be written as *HHT* ∪ *HTH* ∪ *THH*.

• PROBLEM 1-4

Prove that $(A \cap B)^C = A^C \cup B^C$ and $(A \cup B)^C = A^C \cap B^C$.

SOLUTION:

A general method of proving two sets equal is to prove that each is a subset of the other. Let $E_1 = (A \cap B)^C$, $E_2 = A^C \cup B^C$, $E_3 = (A \cup B)^C$, and $E_4 = A^C \cap B^C$. We must show that E_1 is a subset of E_2, E_2 is a subset of E_1, E_3 is a subset of E_4, and E_4 is a subset of E_3.

Consider an element in E_1, say x. Then x is in $(A \cap B)^C$, so consequently x is not in $(A \cap B)$. That is, x is not in both A and B, so x must be in either A^C or in B^C. That is, x is in $A^C \cup B^C$, and we have proven that E_1 is a subset of E_2. Now consider x in E_2. By definition of union, x is either in A^C or in B^C (or both), so x is in at least one of the complements and hence cannot be in both A and B. That is, x is not in $A \cap B$, so x is in E_1, and E_2 is a subset of E_1. Now $E_1 = E_2$.

If x is in E_3, then x is not in the union of A and B, so x cannot be in either A or B. That is, x must be in the complement of each, so x is in E_4 and E_3 is a subset of E_4. Now let x be in E_4. Then x is in the complement of both A and B, so x is in neither A nor B. Thus, x is not in $A \cup B$, so x is in E_3. Then E_4 is a subset of E_3, and $E_3 = E_4$.

• PROBLEM 1–5

Prove that for any set E, $E \cup E^C$ is the universal set.

SOLUTION:

A general method for establishing the equivalence of two sets is to show that each is a subset of the other. Since any set is a subset of the universal set, it remains to show that the universal set is a subset of $E \cup E^C$. It would suffice to show that any element in the universal set is in $E \cup E^C$. Consider, then, any given element in the universal set, and denote this element by x. If x is in E, then x is also in $E \cup E^C$, because E is contained in this larger set by definition of union. If x is not in E, then by definition of complement x must be in E^C. But now $E \cup E^C$ also contains E^C, again by definition of union. Either way, then, x must belong to $E \cup E^C$.

• PROBLEM 1–6

Prove that for any set E, $E \cap E^C$ is the empty set.

SOLUTION:

A general method for establishing the equivalence of two sets is to show that each is a subset of the other. Since the empty set is a subset of any set, it remains to show that $E \cap E^C$ is a subset of the empty set, or that it contains no elements. Assume, to the contrary, that some element x belongs to $E \cap E^C$. If x is in E, then x is not in E^C, so it cannot be in any subset of E^C, including $E \cap E^C$. If x is not in E, then it cannot be in any subset of E, including $E \cap E^C$. Either way, then, x cannot belong to $E \cap E^C$.

• PROBLEM 1-7

Prove, for any sets E_1 and E_2, that E_1 is a subset of $E_1 \cup E_2$.

SOLUTION:

To show that E_1 is a subset of $E_1 \cup E_2$, we must show that any element of E_1 also belongs to $E_1 \cup E_2$. Consider, then, an arbitrary element x of E_1. To belong to $E_1 \cup E_2$, an element would need to belong to either E_1 or to E_2. Since x belongs to E_1, it must be an element of $E_1 \cup E_2$.

• PROBLEM 1-8

Prove, for any sets E_1 and E_2, that $E_1 \cap E_2$ is a subset of E_1.

SOLUTION:

To show that $E_1 \cap E_2$ is a subset of E_1, we must show that any element of $E_1 \cap E_2$ also belongs to E_1. Consider, then, an arbitrary element x of $E_1 \cap E_2$. Since x belongs to $E_1 \cap E_2$, it must belong to both E_1 and E_2 by definition of intersection. Since x is an element of E_1, our proof is complete.

• PROBLEM 1-9

Prove, for any sets E_1 and E_2, that $E_1 \cap E_2$ is a subset of $E_1 \cup E_2$.

SOLUTION:

If a set A is a subset of a set B, which in turn is a subset of a set C, then by the transience property of containment A is a subset of C. The previous two problems showed that $E_1 \cap E_2$ is a subset of E_1, which is a subset of $E_1 \cup E_2$. Thus, $E_1 \cap E_2$ must also be a subset of $E_1 \cup E_2$, and this completes the proof.

There are three red balls, two blue balls, and one yellow ball in an urn. Two balls are selected at random without replacement. Let A denote the event that at least one ball is red, and let B denote the event that at least one ball is blue. Use set notation to describe the event that both balls are yellow.

SOLUTION:

If both balls are yellow, then no balls can be either red or blue. Thus, neither event A nor event B can occur. Conversely, if neither event A nor event B occurs, then there are no red or blue balls, and consequently both balls must be yellow. Thus, the event we are looking to describe is the same as the event which specifies that neither A nor B occurs. This is just $A^c \cap B^c$.

Using the same urn and sampling scheme as in Problem 1–10, describe the event that there is one red ball and one blue ball.

SOLUTION:

The event we wish to describe specifies that there is one red ball and one blue ball, so events A and B both must occur. Conversely, if events A and B both occur, then our sample will contain at least one red ball and at least one blue ball. Since there are only two balls in the sample, the sample must contain one red ball and one blue ball. Thus, the event we wish to describe is the same as the event which specifies that events A and B both occur. This is $A \cap B$.

✓ • **PROBLEM 1-12**

Using the same urn model and sampling scheme as in Problem 1–10, describe, in words, the events $A \cap B^C$, $A \cup B$, and $A \cup B^C$.

SOLUTION:

The event $A \cap B^C$ specifies that event A occurs but event B does not. Thus, the sample would have at least one red ball but no blue balls. The possible outcomes (without regard to order) are {red, red} and {red, yellow}.

The event $A \cup B$ specifies that either event A occurs or event B occurs (or both events A and B occur). In other words, they cannot both fail to occur. If they did both fail to occur, then there would be no red or blue balls in the sample, so both balls would need to be yellow. This is the complement of the event we wish to describe. Thus, the event is that at least one ball is not yellow, and the possible outcomes (without regard to order) are {red, red}, {red, blue}, {red, yellow}, {blue, blue}, and {blue, yellow}. But notice that there is but one yellow ball, so these outcomes are the only possible ones. In this case the event is the universal event.

The event $A \cup B^C$ specifies that either event A occurs or event B does not occur (or event A occurs and event B does not occur). In other words, it is impossible for event B to occur if event A does not also occur. The event in which event B occurs and event A does not specifies that there are no red balls but there is at least one blue ball in the sample. The possible outcomes for this event are {blue, blue} and {blue, yellow}. We want the complement of this event, so the outcomes which are favorable to the event we wish to describe are {red, red}, {red, blue}, and {red, yellow}. {y,y} ? Notice that this is precisely event A, or at least one ball is red. This is because the other component of our event, B^C, implies that event A occurs because if there are no blue balls in the sample, then there must be at least one red ball (since there is but one yellow ball).

Let $A = \{1, 2, 3, 4\}$ and $B = \{3, 4, 5, 6\}$. What is the set difference between A and B? What is the set difference between B and A? Are these two differences the same?

SOLUTION:

The set difference between A and B is the set of elements in A but not in B, or $\{1, 2\}$. The set difference between B and A is the set of elements in B but not in A, or $\{5, 6\}$. These differences are not the same.

******

REVIEW OF EVENTS AND OUTCOMES

Events and outcomes, along with random variables, are the basic units essential to the study of probability theory. Events and outcomes also form the link between sets and random variables, as events are sets of outcomes, and thus the set theory developed in the previous section can be fruitfully applied to events and outcomes in the study of random variables, providing a deeper insight into the workings of probability.

As an example of an outcome, consider selecting a state at random from the 50 states in the United States of America. There are 50 outcomes, each corresponding to a given state. For example, {New Jersey} is an outcome, as is {Oregon}. An event is a collection of outcomes, or in this case, a collection of states. For example, we may describe the West Coast as an event consisting of the union of three outcomes, namely {Washington, Oregon, California}. Likewise, New England is an event consisting of the union of {Maine, Vermont, New Hampshire, Massachusetts, Rhode Island, and Connecticut}. Each of the 50 outcomes is also a particular event.

There will, in general, be more events than there will be outcomes. In fact, if there are k outcomes, then there will be 2^k events, including the null event which includes none of the k outcomes. This may be seen by considering each possible inclusion or exclusion of a given outcome. With only one outcome, there are $2^1 = 2$ events, namely the event consisting of the outcome and the event not consisting of the outcome. As each outcome may either be included or excluded in a given set, each additional outcome doubles the previous number of events. Induction on k gives the general formula of 2^k events when there are k outcomes.

A general definition of an event is an arbitrary set of unions and/or intersections of the outcomes. It may not be intuitive to think of the empty set as an event. After all, if this event obtains (occurs), then nothing has transpired. Nevertheless, in most developments the empty (or null) set is given event status. The class of sets to which a probability is assigned must be closed under various set operations (unions, intersections, and complements, for example). Since the null set is the intersection of any pair of disjoint (mutually exclusive) sets, including different outcomes, it must be included in the class.

It will often be important to generate all events given the set of outcomes. As an example of how to attack this type of exercise, consider the four years in which an undergraduate student in a four-year degree program can be enrolled. The outcomes are {freshman, sophomore, junior, senior}. As there are four outcomes, we know that there are $2^4 = 16$ events. We may list them as

1. {} ϕ Note this as being the null (or empty) event (which cannot occur)

2. {freshman}

3. {sophomore}

4. {junior}

5. {senior}

6. {freshman, sophomore}

7. {freshman, junior}

8. {freshman, senior}

9. {sophomore, junior}

10. {sophomore, senior}

11. {junior, senior}

12. {freshman, sophomore, junior}

13. {freshman, sophomore, senior}

14. {freshman, junior, senior}

15. {sophomore, junior, senior}

16. {freshman, sophomore, junior, senior}

A systematic method for generating all events given the set of possible outcomes is to think of each outcome as a light switch. Start with each switch turned off. This corresponds to a set which contains none of the outcomes, or the empty set. Now turn on the first switch only. This set contains only the first outcome. Replace this switch with the next switch, and continue until each switch was turned on. This results in the set of events consisting of one outcome each. To generate the events which contain two events each, turn off all switches and then turn on the first two switches only. Then replace the second with the third, and continue.

This type of exercise would be important to answer questions such as "What proportion of students are upperclassmen?". This question would be answered by finding the probability of event number 11, {junior, senior}, when randomly selecting students from the school under study. Of course the probability of the null set is zero in any context. Likewise, the probability of the universal set is always one. The universal set is the complement of the null set, and in fact it is true in general that the probabilities of complementary events must sum to one.

In this example, the universal set is event number 16, {freshman, sophomore, junior, senior}. The probability is one that a given undergraduate student can be classified as one of these four outcomes under the model we are considering. Since events 8 and 9 are complementary to each other, their intersection is event 1 (the null set) and their union is event 16 (the universal set). Consequently,

$$P\{\text{event 8} \cap \text{event 9}\} = 0$$

and $P\{\text{event 8} \cup \text{event 9}\} = 1.$

We are typically concerned with finding the probabilities of various events. This is often facilitated by first finding the probabilities of the component outcomes which comprise the event, and then adding these up.

It is always true that the probability of an event is equal to the sum of the probabilities of its component outcomes. It is not always true, however, that the probability of an event can be written as the sum of probabilities of other events whose union is the given one. Why is this true in general for outcomes but not for events? The salient feature of outcomes which makes this true is the fact that they are mutually exclusive. That is, they decompose the universal set. There is no overlap among them. The intersection of any set of outcomes with more than a single outcome is necessarily the empty set. In light of this, we may state that it is true, in general, that the sum of the probabilities of mutually exclusive events is equal to the probability of the union of these events.

For example, consider tossing three fair coins. The sample space, defined as the set of outcomes, is {HHH, HHT, HTH, HTT, THH, THT, TTH, TTT}. Since the coin is fair, the eight outcomes are all equally likely, and thus have probability $1/8$. There are 2^3 events which can be defined. Some of these events will be mutually exclusive, and some will not. The probability of tossing a heads on the first toss is $1/2$, since the coin is fair. But we can also find this by considering those outcomes for which the first toss resulted in heads. These outcomes are {HHH, HHT, HTH, HTT}. There are four such outcomes, and each has probability $1/8$. Inspection of these four outcomes reveals that they are, in fact, mutually exclusive. That is, the occurrence of any one precludes the others. For example, if we observe HHT, then we could not have also observed HTH on the same three rolls, because if the last roll resulted in heads, then it could not have also resulted in tails.

Since these outcomes are mutually exclusive (as outcomes always are), the probability of their union is the sum of their individual probabilities. The union of these four outcomes is the event that the first toss results in heads, and its probability is

$$\frac{1}{8} + \frac{1}{8} + \frac{1}{8} + \frac{1}{8} = \frac{4}{8} = \frac{1}{2}.$$

This agrees with our previous answer.

For a more complicated example, consider the probability of tossing

1. a heads on the first toss, or

2. a tails on the second toss, or

3. both a heads on the first toss and a tails on the second toss.

There are six (mutually exclusive) outcomes which comprise this event (HHH, HHT, HTH, HTT, TTH, and TTT). We therefore know that the answer is $6/8 = 3/4$. In a larger example we would not be so willing to enumerate the outcomes which comprise this event. Another approach is require. If we define E as the event (heads on the first toss or tails on the second toss or both), E_1 as the event (heads on the first toss), and E_2 as the event (tails on the second toss), then we see that E may be expressed as $E_1 \cup E_2$. From the previous example we know that the probability of E_1 is $P(E_1) = 1/2$. Likewise, $P(E_2) = 1/2$. If E_1 and E_2 were mutually exclusive, then $P(E)$ would be

$$P(E_1) + P(E_2) = \frac{1}{2} + \frac{1}{2} = 1.$$

This is, of course, not the case.

What went wrong is that E_1 and E_2 are not mutually exclusive. In other words, their intersection is not zero. In fact,

$$P(E_1 \cap E_2) = P(\text{HTH, HTT})$$

$$= \frac{2}{8} > 0.$$

We may split E_1 into two portions, one which is mutually exclusive of E_2 (HHH and HHT) and one which is not (HTH and HTT). Call these events E_11 and E_22, respectively. We can likewise decompose E_2 into $E_22 = \{\text{TTH, TTT}\}$ and $E_21 = \{\text{HTH, HTT}\}$. We see that $E_12 = E_21$ and that $E_11 \cup E_12 \cup E_22 = E$, and E_11, E_12, and E_22 are mutually exclusive. Thus,

$$P(E) = P(E_11) + P(E_12) + P(E_22) = \frac{2}{8} + \frac{2}{8} + \frac{2}{8} = \frac{6}{8} = \frac{3}{4}.$$

Now we have the right answer.

It is not required to solve this problem by finding a partition of the event which is mutually exclusive. A more general formula allows for the solution of this problem based only on E, E_1, and E_2. Notice that the formula for mutually exclusive events would say that

$$P(E) = P(E_1) + P(E_2).$$

With our finer partition we see that this would imply that

$$P(E) = [P(E_11) + P(E_12)] + [P(E_21) + P(E_22)]$$

$$= [P(E_1 1) + P(E_1 2) + P(E_2 2)] + P(E_2 1).$$

Thus, we are off by $P(E_2 1)$, since this is being counted twice. This set, $E_1 2$ $= E_2 1$, is included in both E_1 and E_2, since it is the common component of the two. If we wish to find $P(E)$, then we must compensate for counting $E_1 2$ twice by subtracting it away. The general formula is therefore

$$P(E_1 \cup E_2) = P(E_1) + P(E_2) - P(E_1 \cap E_2).$$

In this example,

$$P(E) = P(E_1) + P(E_2) - P(E_1 2)$$

$$= \frac{1}{2} + \frac{1}{2} - \frac{1}{4}$$

$$= \frac{3}{4}$$

Notice that if E_1 and E_2 are mutually exclusive, then $E_1 \cap E_2 = 0$ and the general formula reduces to the simpler one.

✓ • PROBLEM 1–14

Consider the set of primary colors, {red, blue, yellow}. If these are the possible outcomes resulting from an experiment in which a subject is asked to specify his or her favorite primary color, then how many events are there? Describe and interpret each event.

SOLUTION:

Since there are three outcomes, there are $2^3 = 8$ events. These are as follows.

1. {}

This is the null event which, by assumption, cannot occur.

2. {red}

This is the event in which the subject specifies red.

3. {blue}

This is the event in which the subject specifies blue.

4.   {yellow}

This is the event in which the subject specifies yellow.

5.   {red, blue}

This is the event in which the subject either specifies red or specifies blue.

6.   {red, yellow}

This is the event in which the subject either specifies red or specifies yellow.

7.   {blue, yellow}

This is the event in which the subject either specifies blue or specifies yellow.

8.   {red, blue, yellow}

This is the universal event, in which the subject specifies red, specifies blue, or specifies yellow. This event must occur, by assumption.

✓ **• PROBLEM 1–15**

> Two fair coins are tossed. What is the probability of either HH or TT?

SOLUTION:

Since these two outcomes are mutually exclusive, we may use the simpler formula. There are four outcomes, HH, HT, TH, and TT, and each is equally likely. The probability of each is $1/4$. Thus,

$$P(\text{HH} \cup \text{TT}) = P(\text{HH}) + P(\text{TT})$$

$$= \frac{1}{4} + \frac{1}{4}$$

$$= \frac{1}{2}$$

✓ • **PROBLEM 1-16**

A single die is rolled. What is the probability that it shows either an even number or a number under four (or both)?

SOLUTION:

We first must address the issue of whether or not these two events are mutually exclusive. The outcomes are (1, 2, 3, 4, 5, 6), and are equally likely. There are six equally likely outcomes, so the probability of any one outcome is $1/6$. Let us define event E as an even number showing or a number less than four showing (or both), and event E_1 as an even number showing. Then E_1 consists of (2, 4, and 6). If we call E_2 the event that the die shows less than four, then $E_2 = (1, 2, 3)$, $E = E_1 \cup E_2$, and $E_1 \cap E_2 = \{2\}$, which is not the null set. Thus, E_1 and E_2 are not mutually exclusive and

$$P\{E\} = P\{E_1 \cup E_2\}$$
$$= P\{E_1\} + P\{E_2\} - P\{E_1 \cap E_2\}$$
$$= P\{2, 4, 6\} + P\{1, 2, 3\} - P\{2\}$$
$$= \frac{3}{6} + \frac{3}{6} - \frac{1}{6}$$
$$= \frac{5}{6}$$

This problem could have been solved by enumeration. The favorable outcomes are {1, 2, 3, 4, 6}. There are five favorable (mutually exclusive) outcomes, each with probability $1/6$, so the probability we seek is $5/6$.

✓ • **PROBLEM 1-17**

A card is drawn from a deck of cards and is observed to be an ace. How many outcomes are there? What are these outcomes? How many events are there? What are these events? Interpret each event.

SOLUTION:

There are four outcomes. These are the four suits, or {spades, hearts, diamonds, clubs}. Since there are four outcomes, there are $2^4 = 16$ events. These are

1. {}

This is the empty event, which cannot occur.

2. {spades}

This is the event that the ace of spades was selected.

3. {hearts}

This is the event that the ace of hearts was selected.

4. {diamonds}

This is the event that the ace of diamonds was selected.

5. {clubs}

This is the event that the ace of clubs was selected.

6. {spades, hearts}

This is the event that either the ace of spades or the ace of hearts was selected.

7. {spades, diamonds}

This is the event that either the ace of spades or the ace of diamonds was selected.

8. {spades, clubs}

This is the event that either the ace of spades or the ace of clubs was selected.

9. {hearts, diamonds}

This is the event that either the ace of hearts or the ace of diamonds was selected.

10. {hearts, clubs}

This is the event that either the ace of hearts or the ace of clubs was selected.

11. {diamonds, clubs}

This is the event that either the ace of diamonds or the ace of clubs was selected.

12. {spades, hearts, diamonds}

This is the event that the ace of spades or the ace of hearts or the ace of diamonds was selected. This can be expressed as the ace of clubs was not selected.

13. {spades, hearts, clubs}

This is the event that the ace of diamonds was not selected.

14. {spades, diamonds, clubs}

This is the event that the ace of hearts was not selected.

15. {hearts, diamonds, clubs}

This is the event that the ace of spades was not selected.

16. {spades, hearts, diamonds, clubs}

This is the universal event.

✓ • PROBLEM 1–18

Patients entering a hospital are classified both by gender (male/female) and by age (under 30, between 30 and 50, over 50). How many outcomes are there? What are these outcomes? How many events are there?

SOLUTION:

There are two categories to describe gender and three categories to describe age. Thus, there are $2 \times 3 = 6$ outcomes. These are

1. under-30 male

2. middle-aged male

3. over-50 male

4.   under-30 female

5.   middle-aged female

6.   over-50 female

Since there are six outcomes, there are $2^6 = 64$ events.

∨ • PROBLEM 1-19

Using the model described in Problem 1–18, describe the events {male} and {male or over-50} in terms of the outcomes listed.

SOLUTION:

The six outcomes are listed in the solution to Problem 1–18. The first three of these outcomes are favorable to the event {male}. Thus, the solution is $E_1 \cup E_2 \cup E_3$, where

$E_1 = \{$under 30, male$\}$,

$E_2 = \{$30-50, male$\}$,

and $E_3 = \{$over-50, male$\}$.

Each of these outcomes is favorable to the event {male or over-50}, but in addition the outcome {over-50, female} is also favorable. Thus, the solution is $E_1 \cup E_2 \cup E_3 \cup E_4$, where E_1, E_2, and E_3 are as previously defined and $E_4 = \{$over-50, female$\}$.

✳✳✳✳✳✳

REVIEW OF COUNTING

Counting is important to the study of probability in that many models use the classical approach of defining a probability of an event as the number of outcomes favorable to the event divided by the total number of outcomes. Of course this is only applicable when each outcome is equally likely. Two concepts which will facilitate counting will be permutations and combinations. The distinction between these two concepts often causes confusion among students new to the field.

A permutation is a rearrangement of the same elements. No change to the elements has occurred. The only change is to the order in which the elements appear. A combination, on the other hand, is a particular way to combine elements to form a set. Different combinations contain different elements. Different permutations do not.

As a simple example, consider three colors; red, blue, and yellow. If we list these in order, then we may specify six different orders. These are

1. {red, blue, yellow}

2. {red, yellow, blue}

3. {blue, red, yellow}

4. {blue, yellow, red}

5. {yellow, red, blue}

6. {yellow, blue, red}

The goal is to develop methods for finding the number of permutations of a given number of elements without resorting to a complete enumeration. When there are only three elements, complete enumeration presents no difficulties. When the number of elements gets large, however, this is not the case. The formula for the number of permutations may not be obvious, but the following thought process will help to clarify.

As the elements are to be ordered, there must be a first element. In our example there were three elements, namely red, blue, and yellow. Any of these could be the first element, and thus there are three possible choices of a first element. Having chosen a first element, the task becomes to choose a second. One of the three elements already appears as the first element, so there are only two left. Either of these two can be the second element. Having chosen both a first and a second element, there remains only one element left, and this one must necessarily be the third element in the order. If we multiply the number of options, we obtain $3 \times 2 \times 1 = 3! = 6$. The expression "3!" is read as "three factorial," and is used to denote $3 \times 2 \times 1$.

If instead of three elements we had an arbitrary number, say k elements, then we would have k elements to choose as the first. Having picked the first, there would be $(k - 1)$ elements left to occupy the second position, $(k - 2)$ for the third, and so forth. Multiplying yields $k \times (k - 1) \times (k - 2) \times ... \times 3 \times 2 \times 1 = k!$ permutations of k elements. This formula holds true in general. For example, if we had been dealing with four elements, then there would have been $4! = 4 \times 3 \times 2 \times 1 = 24$ permutations.

A typical problem involving permutations might ask how many ways a president, vice president, and treasurer can be selected out of three officers. The answer would be $3 \times 2 \times 1 = 3! = 6$, since there are six permutations of the three officers. Suppose, instead, that we were asked how many ways we could select three officers out of five candidates. Here the order would not matter (we are not specifying any particular titles beyond the fact that all three chosen will be officers). Since the numbers are small, we can resort to complete enumeration in this case. Suppose the candidates are named Jefferson, Johnson, Jones, Smith, and Taylor. The possibilities are

1. Jefferson, Johnson, Jones

2. Jefferson, Johnson, Smith

3. Jefferson, Johnson, Taylor

4. Jefferson, Jones, Smith

5. Jefferson, Jones, Taylor

6. Jefferson, Smith, Taylor

7. Johnson, Jones, Smith

8. Johnson, Jones, Taylor

9. Johnson, Smith, Taylor

10. Jones, Smith, Taylor.

There are 10 such combinations. This is in contrast to the six permutations of three officers. In fact, the number of permutations did not depend on the fact that there were five candidates. It only depended on the fact that there were three officers.

We must find a general formula for the number of combinations of k items from a set of n items. We know that the value of this formula must be 10 when k is three and n is five, as in the previous example. The formula comes from binomial coefficients, and for the interested reader, can be proven by induction (a proof, however, is beyond the scope of this book). In particular, the formula is

$$C(n, k) = \frac{n!}{[k!(n-k)!]}.$$

This is the number of ways of selecting k items out of n items. As a check, notice that

$$C(5, 3) = \frac{5!}{[3! \times 2!]} = \frac{120}{6 \times 2} = 10.$$

As another check, notice that in the previous example we could have rephrased the question to ask how many ways we could select two candidates out of five NOT to be selected as officers. Clearly this is the same question as the original one, since any set of three officers leaves two candidates who are not officers, and vice versa. Thus, we would expect to obtain the same answer. If we calculate the number of ways of selecting two candidates not to be officers out of five candidates, then we compute

$$C(5, 2) = \frac{5!}{[2! \times 3!]} = \frac{120}{2 \times 6} = 10.$$

Careful inspection of the formula reveals that this phenomenon is not a coincidence. For general n and k,

$$C(n, k) = \frac{n!}{[k!(n-k)!]} = \frac{n!}{[(n-k)!k!]} = C(n, n-k). \qquad *$$

We may generalize the concept of combinations by asking a question such as in how many ways can n items be grouped into n_1 items of a certain type, n_2 items of another type, and so on, with k types of items (and $n_1 + n_2 + ... + n_k = n$). For example, in a pick-up football game four new players show up. It is decided that two players will be added to each team. This can be accomplished in

$$C(4, 2) = \frac{4!}{[(2!)\,(2!)]} = 6 \text{ ways.}$$

But if there are four teams, so each team receives one new player, then this can be accomplished in

$$\frac{4!}{[(1!)\,(1!)\,(1!)\,(1!)]} = 24 \text{ ways,}$$

since any of the four can be assigned to the first team, any of the remaining three to the second team, and so on.

But what if there are four teams, one of which has fewer players than the others, and five new players show up. It may be decided to add two players to the short-sided team and one to each of the other teams. This can be accomplished in

$$\frac{4!}{[(2!)\,(1!)\,(1!)\,(1!)]} \text{ ways.}$$

This suggests the general formula that n items can be partitioned into n_1, n_2, ..., n_k items in

✳ $$\frac{n!}{[(n_1!)\,(n_2!)\dots(n_k!)]} \text{ ways.}$$

This formula is derived from the multinomial coefficients.

✓ • **PROBLEM 1–20**

What is $5!$?

SOLUTION:

By definition,

$$5! = 5 \times 4 \times 3 \times 2 \times 1 = 120.$$

✓ • **PROBLEM 1-21**

What is $(1,000!/999!)$?

SOLUTION:

This may seem like a very difficult problem, and indeed it would be if one were required to evaluate both the numerator and the denominator to solve it. Fortunately, however, there is a simpler way. We recognize that we may factor, for any value of k, the quantity $k!$ as $k \times (k - 1)!$. For example, $5! = 5 \times 4!$, each being 120. In this case,

$$1,000! = 1,000(999!),$$

so the ratio is 1,000.

✓ • **PROBLEM 1-22**

What is $C(5, 2)$?

SOLUTION:

By definition,

$$C(5,2) = \frac{5!}{[(2!)\,(5-2)!]}$$

$$= \frac{5!}{[2!\,3!]}$$

$$= \frac{5 \times 4 \times 3 \times 2 \times 1}{[(2 \times 1)\,(3 \times 2 \times 1)]}$$

$$= \frac{5 \times 4}{2 \times 1}$$

$$= \frac{20}{2}$$

$$= 10$$

✓ • **PROBLEM 1–23**

What is $C(1,000, 1)$?

SOLUTION:

By definition,

$$C(1,000, 1) = \frac{1,000!}{[(999!)\,(1!)]} = 1,000$$

(as in Problem 1–21).

✓ • **PROBLEM 1–24**

Prove that $C(k, 1) = k$ for any value of K.

SOLUTION:

By definition,

$$C(k, 1) = \frac{k!}{[(1!)\,(k-1)!]}$$

$$= \frac{k!}{[(1)\,(k-1)!]}$$

$$= \frac{k \times (k-1)!}{(k-1)!}$$

$$= k$$

This is in accord with common sense because there are k ways to select one item from k (each item corresponds to a choice).

What is $C(1,000, 999)$?

SOLUTION:

By definition,

$$C(1,000, 999) = \frac{1,000!}{[(999!)\,(1!)]} = 1,000.$$

Prove that $C(k, k-1) = k$ for any value of k.

SOLUTION:

By definition,

$$C(k, k-1) = \frac{k!}{\{(k-1)![k-(k-1)]!\}}$$

$$= \frac{k!}{\{(k-1)![k-k+1]!\}}$$

$$= \frac{k!}{\{(k-1)![1]!\}}$$

$$= \frac{k!}{(k-1)!}$$

$$= k$$

This is in accord with common sense, because picking $(k-1)$ items out of k items is equivalent to picking, from the k items, the one item NOT to be included. Clearly there are k ways to make such a choice.

✓ • **PROBLEM 1–27**

What is $C(1,000, 1,000)$?

SOLUTION:

By definition,

$$C(1,000, 1,000) = \frac{1,000!}{[(1,000)!\,(0)!]}$$

By convention 0! is taken to be 1. Thus, the ratio is one.

✓• **PROBLEM 1–28**

Prove that $C(k, k) = 1$ for any value of k.

SOLUTION:

By definition,

$$C(k, k) = \frac{k!}{[(k!)\,(0!)]} = \frac{k!}{k!} = 1.$$

This is in accord with common sense, because there is but one way to select k items out of k items.

✓ • **PROBLEM 1–29**

How many ways are there to arrange four books on a shelf?

SOLUTION:

This problem involves permutations, so the answer is $4! = 24$.

√ • PROBLEM 1-30

There are four officers, of which one will be president, one vice president, one secretary, and one treasurer. In how many ways can the officers be matched to the titles?

SOLUTION:

This problem involves permutations. There are four possible choices for president. Having selected a president, there are then three remaining possible choices for vice president. There are then two possible choices for secretary, and one choice for treasurer. The solution is then

$$4 \times 3 \times 2 \times 1 = 4! = 24.$$

The particular order of the titles is of no consequence. That is, had we selected the treasurer first, for example, the answer would have remained the same.

√ • PROBLEM 1-31

Four couples (eight people total) have tickets to a soccer game. In how many ways can these eight people be seated? In how many ways can they be seated if they require that each couple be seated together?

SOLUTION:

Without restriction there are eight seats to be allocated to eight people, so this can be accomplished in $8! = 40,320$ ways. If, however, we require each couple to sit together, then the problem becomes more complicated. There are four locations, one for each couple. These can be allocated to the couples in $4! = 24$ ways. But then within each couple there are two seating arrangements (namely man-woman and woman-man). Thus, there are

$$(24) (2) (2) (2) (2) = (24) (16) = 388 \text{ ways.}$$

✓ • **PROBLEM 1–32**

Suppose that four couples (eight people) are to have dinner together at a round table. How many possible seating arrangements are there? How many seating arrangements are there if each couple must sit together?

SOLUTION:

The fact that the table is round means that there is no head of the table. In other words, rotating the table will not alter the seating arrangement. Likewise, shifting each person a specified number of seats to the left will result in an equivalent seating arrangement. In the unconstrained problem, we may "anchor" one person by specifying this person as the head of the table, regardless of where he or she sits. Now there are seven additional seats and seven additional people to be seated. There are therefore 7! = 5,040 possible seating arrangements.

We solve the constrained problem in similar fashion by anchoring a given couple and declaring this couple to be the head of the table, regardless of where they sit. There are now three pairs of adjacent seats and three couples to be assigned to these pairs of seats. This can be accomplished in 3! = 6 possible ways. Each couple can be seated as male-female or female-male. For our purposes the mirror reflection of a given seating arrangement will not be considered to be equivalent to the given seating arrangement. Thus, there are

$$(3!)\,(2)\,(2)\,(2)\,(2) = (6)\,(16) = 96$$

possible seating arrangements.

∨ • **PROBLEM 1–33**

In how many ways may a party of four women and four men be seated at a round table if the women and men are to occupy alternate seats?

SOLUTION:

If we consider the seats indistinguishable, then this is a problem in circular permutations, as opposed to linear permutations. In the standard linear permutation approach, each chair is distinguishable from the others. Thus, if a woman is seated first, she may be chosen four ways, then a man seated next to her may be chosen four ways, the next woman can be chosen three ways and the man next to her can be chosen three ways...Our diagram to the linear approach shows the number of ways each seat can be occupied.

4	4	3	3	2	2	1	1

By the Fundamental Principle of Counting, there are thus $4 \times 4 \times 3 \times 3 \times 2 \times 2 \times 1 \times 1 = 576$ ways to seat the people.

However, if the seats are indistinguishable, then so long as each person has the same two people on each side, the seating arrangement is considered the same. Thus, we may suppose one person, say a woman, is seated in a particular place, and then arrange the remaining three women and four men relative to her. Because of the alternate seating scheme, there are three possible places for the remaining three women and four possible places for the four men. Hence, the total number of arrangements is $(3!) \times (4!) = 6 \times 24 = 144$. In general, the formula for circular permutations of n items and n other items which are alternating is $(n - 1)! \, n!$. In our case we have

$$(4 - 1)! \, 4! = 3! \, 4! = 3 \times 2 \times 4 \times 3 \times 2 = 144.$$

$$\left(n-1\right)! \, n!$$

• PROBLEM 1-34

A soccer team has 11 players, of which one is a goalkeeper, four are defenders, three are midfielders, and three are forwards. In how many ways can a team be formed?

SOLUTION:

By the general formula there are

$$\frac{11!}{[(1!)\,(4!)\,(3!)\,(3!)]}\text{ ways.}$$

✓ • **PROBLEM 1–35**

Some soccer coaches prefer to play a 4-4-2 alignment, in which there are four midfielders and only two forwards. In how many ways can such a team be formed?

SOLUTION:

As in the last problem, we use the general formula to find that there are

$$\frac{11!}{[(1!)\,(4!)\,(4!)\,(2!)]}$$

ways to form such a team.

✓ • **PROBLEM 1–36**

A soccer coach holds tryouts for a soccer team, and 30 players show up. The coach can only keep 20 players, of which nine will be substitutes. The other 11 may be aligned either as a 4-3-3 team or as a 4-4-2 team. In how many ways can the coach form his team?

SOLUTION:

There are two possible partitions of the 30 players corresponding to the two alignments the coach may choose. In addition to positioning the 11 starters the coach must now also pick his starters, as well as the ten players he will cut. Thus, the partitions are as follows:

	Team 4-3-3	Team 4-4-2
cut	10	10
substitutes	9	9
keeper	1	1
defenders	4	4
midfielders	3	4
forwards	3	2
total	30	30

so there are

$$\frac{30!}{[(10!)\,(9!)\,(1!)\,(4!)\,(3!)\,(3!)]}$$

ways to form a 4-3-3 team, and

$$\frac{30!}{[(10!)\,(9!)\,(1!)\,(4!)\,(4!)\,(2!)]}$$

ways to form a 4-4-2 team. Adding these together results in the total number of teams which can be formed.

• PROBLEM 1-37

How many baseball teams of nine members can be chosen from among 12 boys, without regard to the position played by each member?

SOLUTION:

Since there is no regard to position, this is a combinations problem (if order or arrangement had been important, it would have been a permutations problem). The general formula for the number of combinations of n items taken r at a time is

$$C(n, r) = \frac{n!}{r!(n-r)!} \; .$$

We have to find the number of combinations of 12 items taken nine at a time. Hence, we have

$$C(12, 9) = \frac{12!}{9!(12-9)!} = \frac{12!}{9!3!} = \frac{12 \times 11 \times 10 \times 9!}{3 \times 2 \times 1 \times 9!} = 220.$$

Therefore, there are 220 possible teams.

******

REVIEW OF RANDOM VARIABLES

A random variable is a real-valued (numerical) function of the outcomes. In other words, a random variable maps the set of outcomes (the sample space) into the real line. A simple example of a random variable is a function tied into the toss of a coin in such a way that if the coin lands heads, then the function takes on the value one, and if the coin lands tails, then the function takes on the value zero. This is known as a Bernoulli random variable and is a special case of the more general binomial random variable.

Random variables are often described in terms of their probability mass functions (or densities when the random variables are continuous) or in terms of their cumulative distribution functions. Different random variables may have the same probability mass function (and consequently the same cumulative distribution function); this does not make them the same random variable. It only means that they are equally likely to take on the same values, but there need be no correspondence as to when they take on these values. For example, consider tossing a fair coin. That is, the probability of heads is 0.5 and the probability of tails is 0.5. Let X be zero if the coin lands heads and one if the coin lands tails. Let Y be one if the coin lands heads and zero if the coin lands tails. Then the probability mass function of each random variable is as follows:

$$P\{X = k\} = 0.5 \text{ for } k = 0, 1,$$

$$P\{X = k\} = 0 \text{ for other values of } k,$$

$$P\{Y = k\} = 0.5 \text{ for } k = 0, 1,$$

and $P\{Y = k\} = 0$ for other values of k.

These formulas describe the probability mass functions of X and Y, and they convey what was just discussed, namely that the random variable X can take on the values zero and one with probability 0.5 each, and that there is zero probability that X will take on any other value. The same can be said for Y. Thus, X and Y have the same probability mass functions and cumulative distribution functions, but they are always different (i.e., if the coin lands tails, then $X = 1$ and $Y = 0$, while if the coin lands heads, then $X = 0$ and $Y = 1$).

Random variables may be either discrete (finite or countably infinite) or continuous (combinations of both are called mixed distributions). The random variables we have discussed so far have all been discrete, and in fact finite. Other finite random variables are the number of teeth with cavities at a given visit to the dentist, the number showing on a randomly drawn card, and the sum of the numbers showing when a pair of dice is tossed. Examples of countably infinite random variables are the number of cars passing a given point of the highway within an hour, the number of cavities in a given visit to the dentist, and the number of phone calls received in a week.

While the actual number observed for any of these random variables must necessarily be finite, the range of these random variables prior to observing them is infinite. That is, no upper limit can be established. For example, it is highly unlikely that anybody, no matter how popular, would receive 10,000,000,000 phone calls in any given week. But if we were prepared to rule this out as an impossibility, then we would need to further specify any other impossible values. Is it possible to receive 1,000,000 phone calls in a week? What about 1,000? What about 100? Clearly it is not feasible to specify a maximum number of phone calls which could be received in a week, and thus it is mathematically convenient to allow the range to be infinite, or to have no upper limit. The distinction between the number of teeth with cavities and the number of cavities is that the number of cavities, like the number of phone calls received, has no theoretical upper limit, since any given tooth may have more than one cavity. The number of teeth with cavities, however, is limited by the number of teeth in the mouth.

The support of a random variable is the set of points for which its probability mass function is positive. This function is everywhere non-negative, but it may be zero at some points. These points would not be in the support of the random variable.

The probability mass function of a discrete random variable is a set of numbers, each specifying the probability that the random variable takes on a certain value. To qualify as a probability mass function, the probabilities must sum to one. The density of a continuous random variable is a con-tinuous non-negative function to be interpreted as the probability that the random variable assumes a value between two numbers, say a and b, is the integral from a to b of the density function. This is equivalent to saying that the probability that the random variable assumes a value between a and b is the area, between a and b, under the curve of the density function. Since the total probability must be one, the integral of this density function over the entire real line must be one.

Since the values taken on by random variables are real-valued num-bers, and since real-valued numbers can be completely ordered, we may completely order the values taken on by a random variable. This enables us to define the cumulative distribution function of a random variable X. Denoted $F_X(k)$, the cumulative distribution function of X evaluated at k is the probability that X takes on a value no larger than k, or $P\{X \le k\}$.

Looked at as a function of k, $F_X(k)$ has several properties that are worth noting. It is non-decreasing over its entire range. It is also bounded from below by zero and bounded from above by one. That is, it only takes values between zero and one (by virtue of representing probabilities). The function is right-continuous, so that

$$\lim_{d \text{ tends to zero}} F_X(k + d) = F_X(k)$$

for $d > 0$. As k gets small, F tends to 0, so

$$\lim_{k \text{ tends to negative infinity}} F_X(k) = 0,$$

because for small enough k the probability is zero that X will be no greater than k. Also

$$\lim_{k \text{ tends to positive infinity}} F_X(k) = 1$$

because for large enough k the probability is one that X will be no greater than k.

An equivalent definition of the support of a random variable X is the set of points on which the cumulative distribution function is increasing, in the sense that its right-hand limit differs from its left-hand limit. When this occurs, the right-hand limit will always be equal to the actual value of the cumulative distribution function at the point in question (by right-continuity), and this value will exceed the left-hand limit (since the cumulative distribution function is non-decreasing).

The cumulative distribution function provides the same information as the probability mass function (as seen by summing or taking differences for discrete random variables, and integrating or differentiating for continuous random variables), but in certain situations one may be more useful than the other.

For example, if the probability mass function of a discrete random variable X is given by

$$P\{X = k\} = \frac{1}{3} \text{ for } k = 0, 1, \text{ and } 2;$$

$$P\{X = k\} = 0 \text{ for other } k,$$

then the cumulative distribution function of X, denoted $F_X(k)$, is given by

$$F_X(k) = 0 \text{ for } k < 0;$$

$$F_X(k) = \frac{1}{3} \text{ for } 0 \le k < 1;$$

$$F_X(k) = \frac{2}{3} \text{ for } 1 \le k < 2; \text{ and}$$

$$F_X(k) = 1 \text{ for } 2 < k.$$

These values can be found by summing the probabilities of the individual outcomes. For example,

$$F_X(1.5) = P\{X \le 1.5\} \quad \text{(by definition of the cumulative distribution function)}$$

$$= P\{X = 0 \text{ or } X = 1\}$$

$$= P\{X = 0 \cup X = 1\} \qquad \text{(by definition of the union)}$$

$$= P\{X = 0\} + P\{X = 1\} \quad \text{(by the mutual exclusivity of these outcomes)}$$

$$= \frac{1}{3} + \frac{1}{3} \qquad \text{(as given by the probability mass function of } X)$$

$$= \frac{2}{3}$$

Conversely, had we been given the cumulative distribution function of X and we were asked to find the probability mass function of X, then we would take differences. For example, if we were asked to find $P\{X = 1\}$, then we would proceed by writing

$$P\{X = 1\} = P\{X \le 1 \text{ and not } X < 1\}$$

$$= P\{X \le 1\} - P\{X < 1\} \qquad \text{(by mutual exclusivity)}$$

$$= P\{X \le 1\} - P\{X \le 0\}$$

$$= F_X(1) - F_X(0)$$

$$= \frac{2}{3} - \frac{1}{3}$$

$$= \frac{1}{3}$$

Notice that we may define random variables as real-valued functions of other random variables, and these derived random variables will also have probability mass functions and cumulative distribution functions. To find these probability mass functions and cumulative distribution functions, it is prudent to revert to the definitions, because short cuts will usually be wrong. For example, some may be tempted to state that the probability mass function or cumulative distribution function of a function, $Y = g(X)$, of a random variable, X, is the same function, g, applied to the probability mass function and cumulative distribution function of X. This will almost never be correct.

✓ • **PROBLEM 1–38**

A fair coin is tossed. The random variable is defined as $X = 0$ if tails is observed, and $X = 1$ if heads is observed. Let $Y = 2X$. What is the cumulative distribution function of X? What is the probability mass function of Y? What is the cumulative distribution function of Y?

SOLUTION:

We previously derived the probability mass function of X as

$$P\{X = 0\} = \frac{1}{2} = P\{X = 1\}.$$

Now $F_X(k) = P\{X \leq k\} = 0$ for $k < 0$,

since for such a (negative) k, the probability is zero that X (non-negative) will be less than or equal to such a k. Likewise,

$$F_X(k) = \frac{1}{2} \text{ for } 0 \leq k < 1,$$

because for such k the probability of X being less than or equal to such k is the probability that $X = 0$, which is $\frac{1}{2}$. Finally, $F_X(k) = 1$ for $k > 1$, because for such k

$$P\{X \leq k\} = P\{X = 0 \text{ or } X = 1\}$$
$$= P\{X = 0 \cup X = 1\} \quad \text{(by definition of union)}$$
$$= P\{X = 0\} + P\{X = 1\} \quad \text{(by mutual exclusivity)}$$
$$= \frac{1}{2} + \frac{1}{2} \quad \text{(since the coin is fair)}$$
$$= 1$$

Now $Y = 2X$, so when $X = 0$, Y is also zero. This happens with probability $\frac{1}{2}$. When $X = 1$, $Y = 2$, and this also happens with probability $\frac{1}{2}$. Thus,

$$P\{Y = k\} = \frac{1}{2} \text{ for } k = 0 \text{ or } 2,$$

and $P\{Y = k\} = 0$ for other k.

This is the probability mass function of Y.

To find the cumulative distribution function of Y, we compute

$$P\{Y \le k\} = 0 \text{ for } k < 0,$$

$$P\{Y \le k\} = \frac{1}{2} \text{ for } 0 \le k < 2,$$

and $P\{Y \le k\} = 1 \text{ for } 2 \le k.$

Thus, $F_Y(k) = 0 \text{ for } k < 0;$

$$= 1 \text{ for } k \ge 2;$$

and $= \frac{1}{2} \text{ in between.}$

This is the cumulative distribution function of Y.

$\checkmark$ • **PROBLEM 1–39**

Calculate the number of permutations of the letters a, b, c, d taken two at a time.

SOLUTION:

The first of the two letters may be taken in four ways (a, b, c, d). The second letter may therefore be selected from the remaining three letters in three ways. By the Fundamental Principle the total number of ways of selecting two letters is equal to the product of the number of ways of selecting each letter, hence

$$p\,(4, 2) = 4 \times 3 = 12.$$

The list of these permutations is:

ab	ba	ca	da
ac	bc	cb	db
ad	bd	cd	dc.

✓ • **PROBLEM 1-40**

Let X be as in Problem 1–38, and let $Z = X + Y + 1$. What is the probability mass function of Z? What is the cumulative distribution function of Z? What is the probability that Z is larger than two?

SOLUTION:

When

$$X = 0,\ Y = 2X = 0 \text{ and } Z = X + Y + 1 = 0 + 0 + 1 = 1.$$

This happens with probability $1/2$. When

$$X = 1,\ Y = 2X = 2 \text{ and } Z = X + Y + 1 = 1 + 2 + 1 = 4.$$

This also happens with probability $1/2$. Thus, the probability mass function of Z is

$$P\{Z = k\} = \frac{1}{2} \text{ for } k = 1 \text{ or } 4,$$

and $P\{Z = k\} = 0$ for other k.

The cumulative distribution function of Z is

$$F_Z(k) = P\{Z \le k\} = 0 \text{ for } k < 1;$$

$$= \frac{1}{2} \text{ for } 1 \le k < 4;$$

and $= 1$ for $4 \le k$.

Consequently,

$$P\{Z > 2\} = 1 - P\{Z \le 2\} = 1 - F_Z(2) = 1 - \frac{1}{2} = \frac{1}{2}.$$

✓ • **PROBLEM 1-41**

Calculate the number of permutations of the letters a, b, c, d taken four at a time.

SOLUTION:

The number of permutations of the four letters taken four at a time equals the number of ways the four letters can be arranged or ordered. Consider four places to be filled by the four letters. The first place can be filled in four ways, choosing from the four letters. The second place may be filled in three ways, selecting one of the three remaining letters. The third place may be filled in two ways with one of the two still remaining. The fourth place is filled one way with the last letter. By the Fundamental Principle, the total number of ways of ordering the letters equals the product of the number of ways of filling each ordered place, or $4 \times 3 \times 2 \times 1 = 24 = P(4, 4) = 4!$ (read "four factorial").

In general, for n objects taken r at a time,

$$P(n, r) = n\,(n-1)\,(n-2)\ldots(n-r+1) = \frac{r!}{(n-r)!}\,(r < n).$$

For the special case where $r = n$,

$$P(n, n) = n\,(n-1)\,(n-2)\ldots(3)\,(2)\,(1) = n!,$$

since $(n-r)! = 0!$ which equals one by definition.

• PROBLEM 1-42

A pair of dice are thrown. Let X be the sum of the two outcomes, and let Y be the product of the two outcomes. Find the probability mass function of X, the cumulative distribution function of X, the probability mass function of Y, and the cumulative distribution function of Y. Also find $P\{X > Y\}$, $P\{2X > Y\}$, and $P\{X < Y < 2X\}$.

SOLUTION:

There are six possible outcomes per die, and hence $6 \times 6 = 36$ possible outcomes. These are enumerated in the following table.

	1	2	3	4	5	6
1	$X=2$	$X=3$	$X=4$	$X=5$	$X=6$	$X=7$
	$Y=1$	$Y=2$	$Y=3$	$Y=4$	$Y=5$	$Y=6$
	$X>Y$	$X>Y$	$X>Y$	$X>Y$	$X>Y$	$X>Y$
	$2X>Y$	$2X>Y$	$2X>Y$	$2X>Y$	$2X>Y$	$2X>Y$
2	$X=3$	$X=4$	$X=5$	$X=6$	$X=7$	$X=8$
	$Y=2$	$Y=4$	$Y=6$	$Y=8$	$Y=10$	$Y=12$
	$X>Y$	$X=Y$	$Y>X$	$Y>X$	$Y>X$	$Y>X$
	$2X>Y$	$2X>Y$	$2X>Y$	$2X>Y$	$2X>Y$	$2X>Y$
			$X<Y<2X$	$X<Y<2X$	$X<Y<2X$	$X<Y<2X$
3	$X=4$	$X=5$	$X=6$	$X=7$	$X=8$	$X=9$
	$Y=3$	$Y=6$	$Y=9$	$Y=12$	$Y=15$	$Y=18$
	$X>Y$	$X=Y$	$Y>X$	$Y>X$	$Y>X$	$Y>X$
	$2X>Y$	$2X>Y$	$2X>Y$	$2X>Y$	$2X>Y$	$2X=Y$
		$X<Y<2X$	$X<Y<2X$	$X<Y<2X$	$X<Y<2X$	
4	$X=5$	$X=6$	$X=7$	$X=8$	$X=9$	$X=10$
	$Y=4$	$Y=8$	$Y=12$	$Y=16$	$Y=20$	$Y=24$
	$X>Y$	$Y>X$	$Y>X$	$Y>X$	$Y>X$	$Y>X$
	$2X>Y$	$2X>Y$	$2X>Y$	$2X=Y$	$Y>2X$	$Y>2X$
		$X<Y<2X$	$X<Y<2X$			
5	$X=6$	$X=7$	$X=8$	$X=9$	$X=10$	$X=11$
	$Y=5$	$Y=10$	$Y=15$	$Y=20$	$Y=25$	$Y=30$
	$X>Y$	$Y>X$	$Y>X$	$Y>X$	$Y>X$	$Y>X$
	$2X>Y$	$2X>Y$	$2X>Y$	$Y>2X$	$Y>2X$	$Y>2X$
		$X<Y<2X$	$X<Y<2X$			

6	X = 7	X = 8	X = 9	X = 10	X = 11	X = 12
	Y = 6	Y = 12	Y = 18	Y = 24	Y = 30	Y = 36
	X > Y	Y > X	Y > X	Y > X	Y > X	Y > X
	2X > Y	2X > Y	2X = Y	Y > 2X	Y > 2X	Y > 2X
		X < Y < 2X				

Each of the 36 outcomes is equally likely, so each has probability $1/36$. The probability mass function of X is found by counting the occurrences of each value of X. Doing so reveals that X takes on the value 2 once; the value 3 twice; the value 4 three times; the value 5 four times; the value 6 five times; the value 7 six times; the value 8 six times; the value 9 five times; the value 10 four times; the value 11 twice; and the value 12 once. Then

$$P\{X = k\} = \frac{1}{36} \text{ for } k = 2 \text{ or } 12;$$

$$= \frac{2}{36} \text{ for } k = 3 \text{ or } 11;$$

$$= \frac{3}{36} \text{ for } k = 4 \text{ or } 10;$$

$$= \frac{4}{36} \text{ for } k = 5 \text{ or } 9;$$

$$= \frac{5}{36} \text{ for } k = 6 \text{ or } 8;$$

and

$$= \frac{6}{36} \text{ for } k = 7.$$

The cumulative distribution function of X is found by summing, and is

$$F_X(k) = 0 \text{ for } k < 2;$$

$$= \frac{1}{36} \text{ for } 2 \le k < 3;$$

$$= \frac{3}{36} \text{ for } 3 \le k < 4;$$

$$= \frac{6}{36} \text{ for } 4 \leq k < 5;$$

$$= \frac{10}{36} \text{ for } 5 \leq k < 6;$$

$$= \frac{15}{36} \text{ for } 6 \leq k < 7;$$

$$= \frac{21}{36} \text{ for } 7 \leq k < 8;$$

$$= \frac{26}{36} \text{ for } 8 \leq k < 9;$$

$$= \frac{30}{36} \text{ for } 9 \leq k < 10;$$

$$= \frac{33}{36} \text{ for } 10 \leq k < 11;$$

$$= \frac{35}{36} \text{ for } 11 \leq k < 12;$$

and $$= \frac{36}{36} \text{ for } 12 \leq k.$$

The probability mass function of Y is found in a similar fashion and is found to be

$$P\{Y = k\} = \frac{1}{36} \text{ for } k = 1, 9, 16, 25, \text{ and } 36$$

(the squares which have no other factors under seven);

$$= \frac{2}{36} \text{ for } k = 2, 3, 5, 8, 10, 15, 18, 20, 24, \text{ and } 30;$$

$$= \frac{3}{36} \text{ for } k = 4;$$

and $$= \frac{4}{36} \text{ for } k = 6 \text{ and } 12.$$

The cumulative distribution function of Y is seen to be

$$F_Y(k) = 0 \text{ for } k < 1;$$

$$= \frac{1}{36} \text{ for } 1 \le k < 2;$$

$$= \frac{3}{36} \text{ for } 2 \le k < 3;$$

$$= \frac{5}{36} \text{ for } 3 \le k < 4;$$

$$= \frac{8}{36} \text{ for } 4 \le k < 5;$$

$$= \frac{10}{36} \text{ for } 5 \le k < 6;$$

$$= \frac{14}{36} \text{ for } 6 \le k < 8;$$

$$= \frac{16}{36} \text{ for } 8 \le k < 9;$$

$$= \frac{17}{36} \text{ for } 9 \le k < 10;$$

$$= \frac{19}{36} \text{ for } 10 \le k < 12;$$

$$= \frac{23}{36} \text{ for } 12 \le k < 15;$$

$$= \frac{25}{36} \text{ for } 15 \le k < 16;$$

$$= \frac{26}{36} \text{ for } 16 \le k < 18;$$

$$= \frac{28}{36} \text{ for } 18 \le k < 20;$$

$$= \frac{30}{36} \text{ for } 20 \le k < 24;$$

$$= \frac{32}{36} \text{ for } 24 \le k < 25;$$

$$= \frac{33}{36} \text{ for } 25 \le k < 30;$$

$$= \frac{35}{36} \text{ for } 30 \le k < 36;$$

and $$= \frac{36}{36} \text{ for } 36 \le k.$$

To find

$$P\{X > Y\},$$

$$P\{2X > Y\},$$

and $P\{X < Y < 2X\},$

we must count the number of boxes (outcomes) favorable to each of these events. The first event occurs in 11 of the 36 boxes, so

$$P\{X > Y\} = \frac{11}{36} .$$

The second event occurs in 25 boxes, so

$$P\{2X > Y\} = \frac{25}{36}.$$

The third event occurs in 13 boxes, so

$$P\{X < Y < 2X\} = \frac{13}{36}.$$

✓ • **PROBLEM 1–43**

There are two roads between towns A and B. There are three roads between towns B and C. How many different routes may one travel between towns A and C?

SOLUTION:

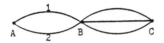

If we take road 1 from town A to town B and then any road from B to C, there are three ways to travel from A to C. If we take road 2 from A to B and then any road from B to C, there are again three ways to travel from A to C. These two possibilities are the only ones available to us. Thus, there are 3 + 3 = 6 ways to travel from A to C.

This problem illustrates the Fundamental Principle of Counting. This principle states that if an event can be divided into k components, and there are n_1 ways to carry out the first component, n_2 ways to carry out the second, n_i ways to carry out the ith, and n_k ways to carry out the kth, then there are $n_1 \times n_2 \times n_3 \times \ldots \times n_k$ ways for the original event to take place.

• **PROBLEM 1–44**

A random variable, X, has cumulative distribution function F as follows:

$F_X(k) = 0$ for $k \leq 4$, and

$F_X(k) = 1$ for $k > 4$.

What is the support of X?

SOLUTION:

The support of X is the set of points on which the cumulative distribution function increases. Clearly in this example {4} is the only such point.

? • **PROBLEM 1-45**

A random variable, X, takes on the values $\{2, 4, 6, 8\}$ with equal probability, and takes on no other values with positive probability. At what points does the cumulative distribution function take on the value 1.2?

SOLUTION:

The support of X is $\{2, 4, 6, 8\}$. The probability mass function of X is

$$P\{X = k\} = \frac{1}{4} \text{ for } k = 2, 4, 6, \text{ and } 8;$$

and $P\{X = k\} = 0$ for other k.

Thus, the cumulative distribution function is

$$F_X(k) = 0 \text{ for } k < 2;$$

$$= \frac{1}{4} \text{ for } 2 \leq k < 4;$$

$$= \frac{1}{2} \text{ for } 4 \leq k < 6;$$

$$= \frac{3}{4} \text{ for } 6 \leq k < 8;$$

and $= 1$ for $8 \leq k$.

The solution is thus seen to be any values between 4 (inclusive) and 6 (exclusive), or $[4, 6)$.

✓ • **PROBLEM 1-46**

How many sums of money can be obtained by choosing two coins from a box containing a penny, a nickel, a dime, a quarter, and a half dollar?

SOLUTION:

The order makes no difference here, since a selection of a penny and a dime is the same as a selection of a dime and a penny insofar as the sum is concerned. This is a case of combinations, then, rather than permutations. The number of combinations of n different objects taken r at a time is equal to:

$$\frac{n(n-1)\ldots(n-r+1)}{1\times 2\ldots r}$$

In this example, $n = 5$, $r = 2$, therefor,e

$$C\,(5,\,2) = \frac{5\times 4}{1\times 2} = 10.$$

✓ • **PROBLEM 1–47**

A fair coin is tossed four times. Let X represent the number of heads. What is the support of X?

SOLUTION:

The possible values X can take on are $\{0,\,1,\,2,\,3,\,4\}$. This is the support. Notice, however, that these events are not equally likely.

✓ • **PROBLEM 1–48**

In medical studies patients are typically classified by their gender, age, weight, and height. Which of these are random variables?

SOLUTION:

Since age, weight, and height are numerical variables, they are random variables. Since gender is not numerically valued, it is not a random variable. It is, however, often coded so that $X = 0$ for males and $X = 1$ for females. This X would be a random variable.

✓ • PROBLEM 1–49

Of the four random variables in Problem 1–48 (including the gender code), which are finite, which are countably infinite, and which are uncountable?

SOLUTION:

Age, weight, and height are uncountable, as they may assume an uncountably infinite number of possible values. If, however, we limit age to be recorded to the nearest year, weight to the nearest pound, and height to the nearest inch, then these all become countably infinite (because we cannot presuppose an upper limit). The gender code is finite.

• PROBLEM 1–50

Why must probability mass functions, density functions, and cumulative distribution functions be non-negative?

SOLUTION:

The probability mass function and the cumulative distribution functions each represent probabilities. Since probabilities cannot be negative, these functions cannot be negative. The density function specifies probabilities through its integrals over various regions. If the density function is negative over any region, then its integral over this region will also be negative, and this would lead to a negative probability.

Which of the following are probability mass functions?

1. $f(k) = \dfrac{1}{4}$ for $k = 3, 7, 89, 114$ yes

2. $f(k) = k$ for $k = \dfrac{1}{2}, \dfrac{1}{4}, \dfrac{1}{8}, \dfrac{1}{16}, \ldots$ yes

3. $f(k) = k$ for $k = 1, 2$ no

4. $f(k) = \dfrac{1}{k}$ for $k = 2, 3$ no

5. $f(k) = \dfrac{1}{k}$ for $k = 2, 4, 8, 16, \ldots$ yes

6. $f(k) = \dfrac{1}{5}$ for $k = 0, 1, 2, 3, 4, 5$ no

7. $f(k) = \dfrac{1}{2}$ for $k = 1, 2, 3; f(k) = -\dfrac{1}{2}$ for $k = 4$ no

SOLUTION:

The first function is non-negative, and its sum is $=1$

$$\left(\frac{1}{4}\right) + \left(\frac{1}{4}\right) + \left(\frac{1}{4}\right) + \left(\frac{1}{4}\right) = 1,$$

so this function qualifies as a probability mass function. The second function is non-negative and its sum is

$$\left(\frac{1}{2}\right) + \left(\frac{1}{4}\right) + \left(\frac{1}{8}\right) + \left(\frac{1}{16}\right) + \ldots = 1,$$

so this also qualifies as a probability mass function (this is an example of a countably infinite probability mass function). The ~~third~~ function is non-negative but its sum is   fourth

$$\frac{1}{2} + \frac{1}{3} = \frac{5}{6} < 1,$$

so this is not a probability mass function. The ~~fourth~~ function is non-negative and its sum is *fifth*

$$\left(\frac{1}{2}\right) + \left(\frac{1}{4}\right) + \left(\frac{1}{8}\right) + \left(\frac{1}{16}\right) + \dots = 1,$$

so this is a probability mass function. The ~~fifth~~ function is non-negative and its sum is *sixth*

$$\left(\frac{1}{5}\right) + \left(\frac{1}{5}\right) + \left(\frac{1}{5}\right) + \left(\frac{1}{5}\right) + \left(\frac{1}{5}\right) + \left(\frac{1}{5}\right) = \frac{6}{5} > 1,$$

so this is not a probability mass function. The ~~sixth~~ function sums to *seventh*

$$\left(\frac{1}{2}\right) + \left(\frac{1}{2}\right) + \left(-\frac{1}{2}\right) = 1,$$

but this function is not non-negative so it cannot be a probability mass function.

$\vee$ • **PROBLEM 1-52**

Which of the following functions are density functions?

1. $f(k) = k$ for $-1 < k < 1$ *no*

2. $f(k) = 2$ for $0 < k < \dfrac{1}{2}$ *yes*

3. $f(k) = 3$ for $0 < k < 1$ *no*

4. $f(k) = 1$ for $1 < k < 4$ *no*

5. $f(k) = 3k^2$ for $0 < k < 1$ *yes*

SOLUTION:

The first function is not non-negative, so it cannot be a density function. The second function is non-negative and its integral is

$$(2)(\frac{1}{2} - 0) = (2)\,(\frac{1}{2}) = 1,$$

so this is a density function. The third function is non-negative and its integral is

$$(3) (1 - 0) = (3) (1) = 3 > 1,$$

so this is not a density function. The fourth function is non-negative and its integral is

$$(1) (4 - 1) = (1) (3) = 3 > 1,$$

so this is not a density function. The fifth function is non-negative and its integral is

$$1^3 - 0^3 = 1 - 0 = 1,$$

so this is a density function.

• PROBLEM 1–53

Which of the following functions are cumulative distribution functions?

1. $f(k) = k$ for $0 < k < 1$ yes

2. $f(k) = k - 1$ for $\dfrac{1}{2} < k < 2$ no

3. $f(k) = k^{4.5}$ for $0 < k < 1$ yes

4. $f(k) = 0$ for $k < 6.7$, $f(k) = 1$ for $k \geq 6.7$ yes

5. $f(k) = 0$ for $k \leq 6.7$, $f(k) = 1$ for $k > 6.7$ no

SOLUTION:

The first function is non-decreasing and right-continuous, and it ranges between zero and one. It is, therefore, a cumulative distribution function. The second function takes on negative values, so it cannot be a cumulative distribution function. The third function is non-decreasing and right-continuous, and it ranges between zero and one. It is, therefore, a cumulative distribution function. The fourth function is non-decreasing and right-continuous, and it ranges between zero and one. It is, therefore, a cumulative distribution function. The fifth function is left-continuous, but not right-continuous, so it cannot be a cumulative distribution function.

REVIEW OF MEASURES OF CENTRAL TENDENCY

Random variables are often described by simple summary measures. Perhaps the most frequently quoted summary measures are measures of central tendency. These measures propose to answer, in various ways, the question "Approximately where is the distribution centered?"

The most common measure of central tendency is the mean, as it has come to be known, but more accurately we should call it the unweighted arithmetic mean (to distinguish it from other types of means). The mean is sometimes referred to as the average, but this is ambiguous because there are different types of averages.

Consider a set of numbers, say {2, 3, 8, 11}. If someone were to ask, on average, how large these numbers are, we may report the mean by adding these numbers and dividing by the total number count. If we add these numbers, we obtain

$$2 + 3 + 8 + 11 = 24.$$

The number count is four, as there are four numbers. Thus, the mean is $^{24}/_4$ = 6.

The mean has a number of appealing properties as a summary measure of central tendency. It is the unique number for which the sum of deviations is zero. In our example, the deviations from the mean are

$$2 - 6 = -4, 3 - 6 = -3, 8 - 6 = 2, \text{ and } 11 - 6 = 5.$$

If we add these deviations, we obtain $(-4) + (-3) + (2) + (5) = 0$, so the mean is "right on average." There is compensation, in some sense between its underrepresentation of large values and its overrepresentation of small values. A second property of the mean is that it uniquely minimizes the sum of squared deviations. That is, if we define

$$g(z) = (2 - z)^2 + (3 - z)^2 + (8 - z)^2 + (11 - z)^2,$$

then $g(z)$ is uniquely minimized by selecting $z = 6$.

In terms of linear algebra the mean can be justified as a perpendicular projection onto the subspace in which all coordinates are equal. This is essentially the same property as minimizing the sum of squared deviations.

Another property of the mean is that it weights each observation equally. For example, in our case the mean is

$$\frac{(2+3+8+11)}{4} = \left(\frac{1}{4}\right)(2) + \left(\frac{1}{4}\right)(3) + \left(\frac{1}{4}\right)(8) + \left(\frac{1}{4}\right)(11)$$

so the weights (or coefficients, or multipliers) are $1/4$ for each observation. This may be considered to be a good property to some, but it is considered a bad property by others.

Suppose the data had been (−7, −5, 2, 3, 5, 7, 10, 113). Then the mean would be

$$\frac{[(-7)+(-5)+(2)+(3)+(5)+(7)+(10)+(113)]}{8} = \frac{128}{8} = 16$$

Some may argue that the number 113 represents an outlier, or that it is not representative of the population from which it was drawn, because it is so far away from the other numbers in the sample. These people may further argue that less weight should be given to that observation. To be fair, of course, if we decide to give less weight to the largest observation, then we should give the same small weight to the smallest observation. For example, we may decide to only consider the middle two observations and completely ignore the smallest and the largest. We would then take the mean of the middle six numbers and obtain

$$\frac{[(-5)+(2)+(3)+(5)+(7)+(10)]}{6} = \frac{22}{6}$$

as an answer. This type of mean is called a trimmed mean. In general, one must specify the trimming fraction. In our case two of eight observations were trimmed, so the trimming fraction was $2/8 = 25\%$.

The trimmed mean is a special case of the weighted mean. A weighted mean takes the form

$$\Sigma_{i=1 \text{ to } n} w(i)X(i),$$

with $w(i) \geq 0$

and $\Sigma_{i=1 \text{ to } n} w(i) = 1$.

The X's are the data and the w's are the non-negative weights. If $w(i) = 1/n$ for all i, then this weighted mean reduces to the unweighted mean. If $w(i) = 0$ for the largest $p\%$ of the observations and for the smallest $p\%$ of the observations, and

$$w(i) = \frac{1}{[(n)(1-2p\%)]}$$

for the remaining observations, then this weighted mean reduces to a trimmed mean with trimming fraction $2p\%$.

The median is the middle observation. That is, if one were to order the observations from smallest to largest, then the median would be the observation in the middle. If there were an odd number of observations, then the median would be the middle value. If there were an even number of observations, then the median would be the mean of the middle two observations. It is readily seen that the median is a special case of a trimmed mean, with a (large) trimming fraction depending on the number of observations. The median is useful when there is a high degree of variability in the data, because it limits the influence of any one observation. In contrast, the unweighted mean can be made arbitrarily large or arbitrarily small by varying any one observation.

The mode is the most frequently occurring observation. For example, in the data set {2, 3, 5, 6, 6, 9}, six is the mode because it occurs twice, and no other observation occurs more than once. The mode need not be unique.

The midrange is the mean of the largest and the smallest observations. The usefulness of this summary measure depends on the particular distribution being studied.

The harmonic mean is the inverse of the mean of the inverses, and cannot be defined if any observations take on the value zero. It is used most frequently with proportions. For example, if we observe proportions of

$$\left\{\frac{1}{2}, \frac{1}{3}, \frac{1}{6}\right\},$$

then to calculate the harmonic mean we would first compute the inverse of each observation. These are 2, 3, and 6, respectively. Then we would average these, obtaining

$$\frac{(2+3+6)}{3} = \frac{11}{3}$$

Finally, we would invert this result, obtaining $3/11$. Compare this to the mean, which is

$$\frac{(\frac{1}{2}+\frac{1}{3}+\frac{1}{6})}{3} = \frac{(\frac{3}{6}+\frac{2}{6}+\frac{1}{6})}{3} = \frac{(\frac{6}{6})}{3} = \frac{1}{3}$$

The harmonic mean is $3/11$, or $9/33$. The mean is $1/3$, or $11/33$. Thus, the harmonic mean is smaller. Trimmed harmonic means are defined in a similar fashion to trimmed means, except based on inverses.

The geometric mean substitutes multiplication for addition, and thus is most useful with non-negative data. In fact, the geometric mean is undefined if there are an even number of observations and the product of these observations is negative.

The geometric mean is the nth root of the product of the n observations, or

$$\pi_{i=1 \text{ to } n}X(i)^{1/n}. \quad \left(\prod x(i)\right)^{1/n}$$

More formally, this is the unweighted geometric mean. Weighted geometric means can also be defined as

$$\pi_{i=1 \text{ to } n}X(i)^{w(i)},$$

again with

$$w(i) \geq 0 \text{ and } \Sigma_{i=1 \text{ to } n}w(i) = 1.$$

If $w(i) = 1/n$ for each i, then this weighted geometric mean reduces to the unweighted geometric mean. The geometric mean is tied in with the logarithmic function by virtue of the fact that

$$\Sigma_{i=1 \text{ to } n}w(i)\log[X(i)] = \Sigma_{i=1 \text{ to } n}\log[X(i)^{w(i)}] = \log[\pi_{i=1 \text{ to } n}X(i)^{w(i)}],$$

so the weighted mean of the logarithms is the logarithm of the weighted geometric mean.

✓ • **PROBLEM 1–54**

A sample consists of the observations {2, 7, 13, 19, 24}. Find the unweighted arithmetic mean, the 40% trimmed mean, the median, and the mode.

SOLUTION:

The unweighted arithmetic mean is

$$\frac{(2+7+13+19+24)}{5} = \frac{65}{5} = 13.$$

The 40% trimmed mean is the mean of the middle 60% of the observations, or in this case, the mean of {7, 13, 19}. This is

$$\frac{(7+13+19)}{3} = \frac{39}{3} = 13.$$

The median is the middle, or in this case the third, ordered observation, or 13.

✓ • PROBLEM 1–55

Using weights of (0.1, 0.1, 0.1, 0.1, 0.6), find the weighted average of the observations given in Problem 1-55.

SOLUTION:

The weighted average is

$$\Sigma_{i=1 \text{ to } 5} w(i)X(i),$$

or $(0.1)\,(2) + (0.1)\,(7) + (0.1)\,(13) + (0.1)\,(19) + (0.6)\,(24).$

First we must verify that this is a proper set of weights. Each is non-negative and the sum is

$$0.1 + 0.1 + 0.1 + 0.1 + 0.6 = 1,$$

so we may proceed. The weighted average is

$$(0.1)\,(2 + 7 + 13 + 19) + (0.6)\,(24) = \left(\frac{41}{10}\right) + \left(\frac{144}{10}\right)$$

$$= \frac{185}{10}$$

$$= 18.5$$

√ • **PROBLEM 1-56**

What is the unweighted geometric mean of {4, 9, 6}? What is the unweighted arithmetic mean?

SOLUTION:

The unweighted geometric mean is

$$(4 \times 6 \times 9)^{1/3} = 216^{1/3} = 6.$$

The unweighted arithmetic mean is

$$\frac{(4+6+9)}{3} = \frac{19}{3} = 6.33.$$

√ • **PROBLEM 1-57**

What is the unweighted arithmetic mean of {1, 2, 6}? What is the median? What happens if the 6 becomes 96? What happens if 90 is added to each observation so the data becomes {91, 92, 96}?

SOLUTION:

The mean is

$$\frac{(1+2+6)}{3} = \frac{9}{3} = 3.$$

The median is the middle observation, or 2. The mean of {1, 2, 96} is

$$\frac{(1+2+96)}{3} = \frac{99}{3} = 33.$$

The median of this data is still 2. The mean of {91, 92, 96} is

$$\frac{(91+92+96)}{3} = \frac{279}{3} = 93$$

The median of this data is 92.

$\sqrt{}$ • **PROBLEM 1–58**

Four proportions are observed. These are $\{1/8, 1/4, 1/4, 1/2\}$. Find the mean, the 50% trimmed mean, the median, the harmonic mean, and the 50% trimmed harmonic mean.

SOLUTION:

The mean is

$$\frac{(\frac{1}{8} + \frac{1}{4} + \frac{1}{4} + \frac{1}{2})}{4} = \frac{(\frac{1}{8} + \frac{2}{8} + \frac{2}{8} + \frac{4}{8})}{4}$$

$$= \left(\frac{\frac{9}{8}}{4}\right)$$

$$= \frac{9}{32}.$$

The 50% trimmed mean, which is also the median, is

$$\frac{(\frac{1}{4} + \frac{1}{4})}{2} = \frac{1}{4}.$$

The inverse of the harmonic mean is

$$\frac{(8 + 4 + 4 + 2)}{4} = \frac{18}{4} = \frac{9}{2}.$$

Thus, the harmonic mean is $2/9$. The inverse of the 50% trimmed harmonic mean is

$$\frac{(4 + 4)}{2} = \frac{8}{2} = 4.$$

Thus, the 50% trimmed harmonic mean is $1/4$.

Four proportions are observed. These are $\{1/2, 1/2, 1/4, 1/8\}$. Find the mean, the 50% trimmed mean, the harmonic mean, and the 50% trimmed harmonic mean.

SOLUTION:

The mean is

$$\frac{(\frac{1}{2} + \frac{1}{2} + \frac{1}{4} + \frac{1}{8})}{4} = \frac{(\frac{4}{8} + \frac{4}{8} + \frac{2}{8} + \frac{1}{8})}{4}$$

$$= \frac{(\frac{11}{8})}{4}$$

$$= \frac{11}{32}$$

The 50% trimmed mean is

$$\frac{(\frac{1}{2} + \frac{1}{4})}{2} = \frac{(\frac{2}{4} + \frac{1}{4})}{2}$$

$$= \frac{(\frac{3}{4})}{2}$$

$$= \frac{3}{8}$$

The harmonic mean is the inverse of

$$\frac{(2 + 2 + 4 + 8)}{4} = \frac{16}{4} = 4.$$

Thus, the harmonic mean is $1/4$. The 50% trimmed harmonic mean is the inverse of

$$\frac{(2 + 4)}{2} = \frac{6}{2} = 3.$$

Thus, the 50% trimmed harmonic mean is $1/3$.

√ • **PROBLEM 1-60**

What is the harmonic mean of $\{1, \frac{1}{2}\}$.

SOLUTION:

The harmonic mean is the inverse of

$$\frac{(1+2)}{2} = \frac{3}{2},$$

which is $\frac{2}{3}$.

✳✳✳✳✳✳

REVIEW OF VENN DIAGRAMS

A Venn diagram is a pictorial means of representing the overlap among various sets. Typically, there is a rectangular region drawn to denote the universal set. Subsets of this universal set are typically drawn as circles inside the rectangle. Sets which are mutually exclusive are drawn so as not to overlap. Sets which are not mutually exclusive are drawn so that they do overlap, and this overlapping portion represents their intersection. The interpretation of any circle is that the points inside represent the set being depicted, and the points outside the circle but inside the rectangle are the complement of the set being depicted. As an example, consider the Venn diagram shown here.

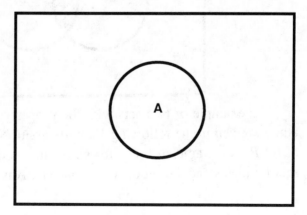

The interior of the circle is set A, and the outside of the circle is A^c. Together A and A^c form the universal set, here depicted by the entire rectangle. That is, $A \cup A^c$ is the universal set. Venn diagrams may be more complicated than the one just presented. For example, a Venn diagram may show more than one set. In the case of two sets, there are three possibilities. The sets could be mutually exclusive, they could overlap, or one could be a subset of the other. An example of mutually exclusive sets is given in the following Venn diagram. Notice that $A \cap B$ is the null set.

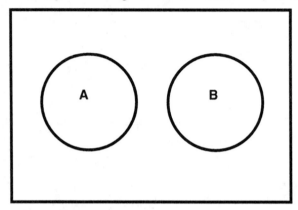

An example of overlapping sets is given in the following Venn diagram. Notice that $A \cap B$ is not the empty set, since A and B were drawn to overlap. The intersection of these sets is denoted by x. An example of sets for which this could be useful would be the set of soccer players and the set of statisticians, since these sets overlap.

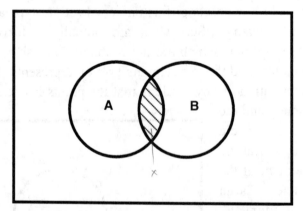

An example of two sets with the property that one is a subset of the other is given in the following Venn diagram. Notice that set A is a subset of set B. An example of sets for which this could be useful would be the set of athletes and the set of soccer players. Any soccer player is an athlete but it is not the case that any athlete is a soccer player. Thus, the set of soccer players is a proper subset of the set of athletes.

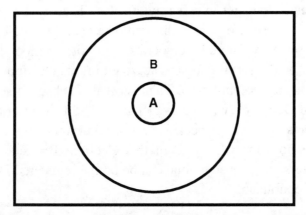

When there are more than two sets depicted in a Venn diagram, then there are many possible varieties. One such variety with three sets is given in the following Venn diagram. Notice that set A intersects set B, with $A \cap B$ denoted by v. The portion of set A which is not in set B is $A - B$, here denoted as u. The part of set B not in set A is denoted by w and x. Set B intersects set C, and the intersection is $B \cap C$, denoted by x. The part of set B not overlapping with either set A or set C is w. The part of set C not overlapping with set B is denoted by y. Notice that sets A and C do not overlap, so sets A and C are mutually exclusive. We denote by z the set of points not belonging to set A, set B, or set C. That is,

$$z = (A \cup B \cup C)^c = A^c \cap B^c \cap C^c.$$

An example of sets for which this could be useful would be the following. Let A be the set of registered Democrats, let B be the set of males, and let C be the set of registered Republicans. Clearly A and C have no overlap, so they are disjoint (mutually exclusive). But B would intersect with both A and C.

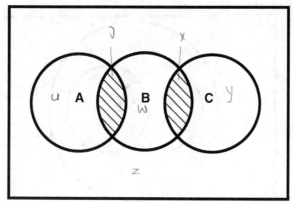

Another possibility for three sets is shown in the following Venn diagram. Notice that set A is a subset of set B, that set C intersects with set B, and that set C does not intersect with set A. That is, $A \cap C$ is the null set. An example of sets for which this could be useful would be as follows. Let A be the set of registered Democrats who vote Democrat in a certain election, let B be the set of people who voted in this election, and let C be the set of registered Republicans. Then set A is a subset of set B, because any registered Democrat who votes Democrat had to vote in this election. Set B intersects with set C because we would expect there to be some registered Republicans who vote in this election. But set A and set C should not intersect because no one can be both a registered Democrat and a registered Republican.

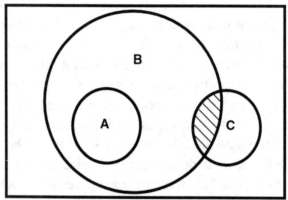

Yet another possibility with three sets is as follows. Sets A and B are both subsets of set C, and sets A and B overlap. This situation is shown in the following Venn diagram. An example of sets for which this could be useful would be as follows. Let set A be the set of soccer players, let set B be the set of football players, and let set C be the set of athletes. Then sets A and B should overlap because some people play both soccer and football. Each set will be a subset of set C because any soccer player or football player must be an athlete.

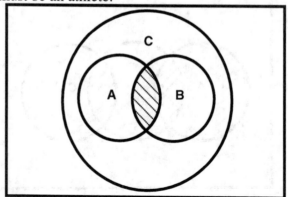

When there are more than three sets in the Venn diagram, then there are even more patterns possible. As an example with six sets consider the following Venn diagram. It would be difficult to come up with a good realistic example which would be depicted by this Venn diagram because there are mutually exclusive events, events which are subsets of other events, and events which overlap with other events in a rather complicated fashion.

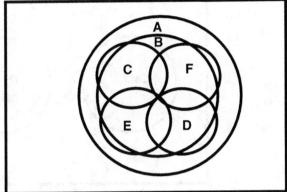

When a Venn diagram needs to show both a set and its complement, this can be accomplished in two equivalent ways. These ways may not seem to be equivalent, but in terms of set theory they are. The first is simply to draw a circle, with the interior designated to represent the set, and the exterior designated to represent the complement of the set. As an example, consider the following Venn diagram.

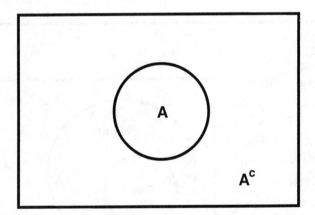

The other way is simply to draw a line, either horizontal or vertical (or even diagonal), between two sides of the border of the Venn diagram. One side of the line represents the set, and the other side of the line represents the complement of the set.

Draw a Venn diagram showing set of dogs and set of cats.

SOLUTION:

Since these two sets do not overlap, the Venn diagram should look as follows.

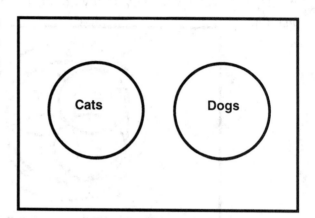

√ • **PROBLEM 1–62**

Draw a Venn diagram showing set of felines, set of cats, and set of dogs.

SOLUTION:

Since every cat is a feline but not every feline is a cat, the set of cats is a subset of the set of felines. Neither set intersects with the set of dogs, so the Venn diagram should look as follows.

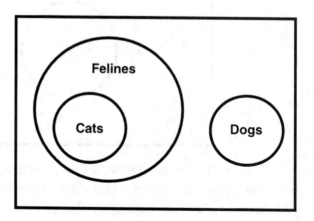

✓ • PROBLEM 1–63

Draw a Venn diagram showing the set of mammals, set of canines, set of dogs, set of felines, and set of cats.

SOLUTION:

The set of dogs is a subset of the set of canines, which in turn is a proper subset of the set of mammals. Likewise, the set of cats is a subset of the set of felines, which in turn is a subset of the set of mammals. The Venn diagram should, therefore, have one set inside another and both separated from the third set, as follows.

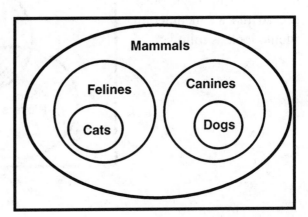

• PROBLEM 1–64

Draw a Venn diagram showing all the sets mentioned in Problem 1–63, but also including the set of animals weighing under 20 pounds.

SOLUTION:

This new set would intersect with each set mentioned in Problem 1–63, as well as with the complement of each such set. Thus, the Venn diagram should appear as follows.

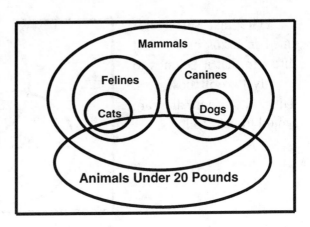

• PROBLEM 1–65

Draw a Venn diagram showing the set of probabilists, the set of soccer players, and the set of females.

SOLUTION:

In this case each set intersects with each other set, so the Venn diagram should look as follows.

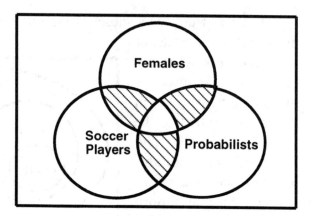

• PROBLEM 1–66

Draw a Venn diagram showing the set of tosses of three coins in which the first coin lands heads, the set of tosses of three coins in which the second coin lands heads, and the set of tosses of three coins in which the third coin lands heads. Also label the set in which exactly two coins land heads.

SOLUTION:

The last set is defined in terms of the first three, in that it belongs to exactly two of those sets. Thus, the Venn diagram would look as follows.

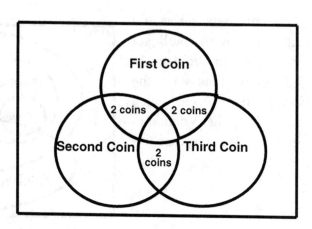

• PROBLEM 1–67

Draw a Venn diagram showing the set of males, the set of females, the set of athletes, and the set of non-athletes.

SOLUTION:

This can be accomplished in two ways, as shown below. We can use either circles or lines. If we use circles, then the Venn diagram should look as follows.

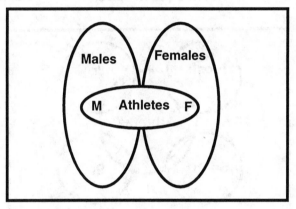

If we use lines, then the Venn diagram should look as follows.

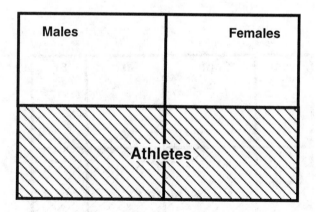

Draw a Venn diagram showing the set of freshman, the set of sopho-
mores, the set of juniors, the set of seniors, the set of athletes, and the
set of non-athletes.

SOLUTION:

This can be accomplished in two ways, as shown below. We can use
either circles or lines. If we use circles, then the Venn diagram should look
as follows:

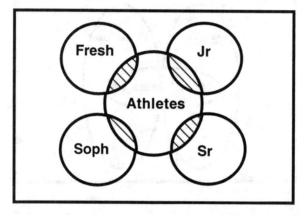

If we use lines, then the Venn diagram should look as follows:

Fresh	Soph	Jr	Sr
	Athletes		

• PROBLEM 1–69

Draw a Venn diagram showing the set of soccer players, the set of students, and the set of history majors who play soccer.

SOLUTION:

Any history major who plays soccer is a soccer player, but it is not the case that any soccer player is a history major. Thus, the set of history majors who play soccer is a proper subset of the set of soccer players. In addition, any history major who plays soccer must be a student, but it is not the case that any student is a history major who plays soccer. Thus, the set of history majors who play soccer is a subset of the set of students. The Venn diagram should look as follows.

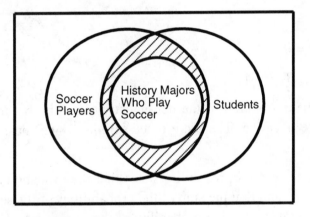

✳✳✳✳✳✳

REVIEW OF AXIOMS OF PROBABILITY

Probabilities are governed by certain rules, or axioms. Most prominent among these are the laws of non-negativity, total probability, and sub-additivity. These laws will be the focus of this section.

Probabilities are set functions in that they assign to each set a probability in such a way that consistency is maintained. If probabilities are to be interpreted as long-term frequencies of experiments in which a certain event occurs, then they must assume only the values which frequencies can assume. This restriction would limit the range of probabilities to [0, 1]. For example, suppose that we are considering the events A and B. We must then also consider the events which can be obtained from A and B by taking complements, unions, and intersections. Suppose someone proposes the following probabilities for some of these sets:

$$P\{A\} = 0.4$$

$$P\{B\} = 0.3$$

$$P\{A \cap B\} = -1$$

This would be a violation of the non-negativity axiom, because no probability can be negative. There are other axioms which must also be followed.

The axiom of total probability states that the probability of the universal set is one, and that the sum of the probabilities of the sets forming a partition of a larger set is the probability of that larger set. A class of sets, $\{A1, A2, ..., A(k)\}$, form a partition of a larger set, A, if

$$A1 \cup A2 \cup A3 \cup ... \cup A(k) = A$$

and if the intersection of any two of these sets is the empty set. As an example, we may partition the universal set as $A \cup A^c$ for any set A. Then it must be true that

$$P\{A\} + P\{A^c\} = 1.$$

If we let A be the empty set, then we see from this equation that the probability of the empty set must be zero, because the complement of the empty set is the universal set. As another example, we recognize that set A may be partitioned as $A \cap B$ and $A - B$ for any other set B, because

$$[A \cap B] \cup [A - B] = A$$

and $[A \cap B] \cap [A - B]$

is the empty set. Thus,

$$P\{A \cap B\} + P\{A - B\} = P\{A\}.$$

For a numerical example, suppose that the probability that a randomly chosen student is a freshman is 0.3, and the probability that a randomly chosen student is a freshman who is taking psychology is 0.2. Then the probability that a randomly chosen student is a freshman who is not taking psychology is $0.3 - 0.2 = 0.1$, because taking or not taking psychology is a partition of the set of freshman. Likewise, if, when randomly selecting a high school student, the probability of selecting a freshman is 0.3, the probability of selecting a sophomore is 0.3, and the probability of selecting a junior is 0.2, then we can find the probability of selecting a senior. First, we recognize that {freshman, sophomore, junior, senior} is a partition of the set of high school students, because the union of these sets is the universal set (in this case the set of high school students), and the intersection of any two of these sets is the empty set. Then we know by the law of total probability that

$P\{$freshman or sophomore or junior or senior$\}$

$= P\{$high school student$\}$

$= P\{$universal event$\}$

$= 1$

But we also know that because these sets are mutually exclusive, the probability of the union is the sum of the probabilities, so

$1 = P\{$freshman or sophomore or junior or senior$\}$

$= P\{$freshman$\} + P\{$sophomore$\} + P\{$junior$\} + P\{$senior$\}$

$= 0.3 + 0.3 + 0.2 + P\{$senior$\}$

Then $P\{$senior$\} = 1.0 - 0.3 - 0.3 - 0.2 = 0.2$.

The third axiom we will study is the axiom of sub-additivity. This refers to sets whose union is a given set but without restricting the sets to being mutually exclusive. Thus, the sets need not form a partition of the larger set.

Suppose that the probability that a coin lands heads is 0.5, and the coin is tossed twice. What is the probability that the coin lands heads at least once? We may denote the event "the coin lands heads at least once" as A, and express A as $A1 \cup A2$, where $A1$ refers to the event "the first toss resulted in heads" and $A2$ refers to the event "the second toss resulted in heads." If $A1$ and $A2$ were a partition of A, then by the law of total probability we would state that

$$P\{A\} = P\{A1\} + P\{A2\} = 0.5 + 0.5 = 1.0.$$

This would mean the event A is the universal event, and that it would be certain that at least one head would be observed. This is not the case, as seen by enumerating the possibilities and their associated probabilities. These are

$$P\{HH\} = (0.5)(0.5) = 0.25,$$

$$P\{HT\} = (0.5)(0.5) = 0.25,$$

$$P\{TH\} = (0.5)(0.5) = 0.25, \text{ and}$$

$$P\{TT\} = (0.5)(0.5) = 0.25.$$

Clearly, then,

$$P\{A\} = P\{HH\} + P\{HT\} + P\{TH\} = 0.25 + 0.25 + 0.25,$$

because $\{HH, HT, TH\}$ is a partition of A. Had we simply assumed that $A1$ and $A2$ were a partition of A, then we would have been counting the set $\{HH\}$ twice, since it is a subset of both $A1$ and $A2$. Consequently, we would over-estimate $P\{A\}$ by the amount $P\{HH\} = 0.25$.

What we can say, in general, is that whenever

$$A1 \cup A2 = A, P\{A\} \leq P\{A1\} + P\{A2\},$$

regardless of whether or not $A1$ and $A2$ form a partition of A. This is known as the sub-additivity property. It is seen by induction that this inequality holds for arbitrary numbers of events, not just two. We may replace the inequality with an equality provided that the sets involved are mutually exclusive.

√ • **PROBLEM 1–70**

Suppose, when selecting a patient at random from a hospital, that the probability of selecting a male is 0.7. What is the probability of selecting a female? Which axiom is being applied in this problem?

SOLUTION:

We use the axiom of total probability, along with the fact that selecting a male and selecting a female are complementary events. Then

$$P\{\text{female}\} = 1 - P\{\text{male}\} = 1 - 0.7 = 0.3.$$

√ • **PROBLEM 1–71**

If in a small company there are 100 employees of which 30 either smoke or drink and 20 smoke, then what can you say about the number that drink? Which axiom is being applied to answer this problem?

SOLUTION:

By the axiom of sub-additivity, we know that

$$P\{\text{smoker or drinker}\} \leq P\{\text{smoker}\} + P\{\text{drinker}\}.$$

There was no mention of probabilities, however, in the statement of the problem. Nevertheless, we may introduce the probabilities by setting up an artificial sampling scheme in which we randomly select an employee of the company. Then

$$P\{\text{smoker or drinker}\} = \frac{30}{100} = 0.3,$$

and $\quad P\{\text{smoker}\} = \dfrac{20}{100} = 0.2.$

Now $\quad P\{\text{drinker}\} + P\{\text{smoker}\} \geq P\{\text{smoker or drinker}\}$

so $\quad P\{\text{drinker}\} \geq P\{\text{smoker or drinker}\} - P\{\text{smoker}\} = 0.3 - 0.2 = 0.1.$

This means that there are at least 10 drinkers in the company.

We also know that anyone who drinks would qualify for "smokes and/or drinks," so the set of drinkers is a subset of those who either smoke or drink, and consequently the number of drinkers is limited by the number of smokers and/or drinkers, which is 30. Combining this with the previous result shows that the number of drinkers is between 10 and 30.

✓ • **PROBLEM 1-72**

At a given intersection a car may turn left, turn right, or go straight. If $P\{\text{left}\} = 0.6$ and $P\{\text{right}\} = 0.5$, then why would the axiom of non-negativity and the axiom of total probability be in conflict?

SOLUTION:

The axiom of total probability would require that

$$P\{\text{left}\} + P\{\text{right}\} + P\{\text{straight}\} = 1,$$

or $\quad 0.6 + 0.5 + P\{\text{straight}\} = 1,$

or $\quad P\{\text{straight}\} = 1 - 0.6 - 0.5 = -0.1.$

But this would be in direct conflict with the axiom of non-negativity, which requires that probabilities be non-negative.

∨• **PROBLEM 1-73**

The probability that a student receives an A in math is 0.2, and the probability that a student receives an A in English is 0.3. What can one say about the probability of a student receiving either an A in math or an A in English (or both)?

SOLUTION:

By the axiom of sub-additivity, we know that

$P\{A \text{ in math and/or } A \text{ in English}\} \leq P\{A \text{ in math}\}$

$+ P\{A \text{ in English}\} = 0.2 + 0.3 = 0.5.$

We also know that anyone who receives an A in math must receive either an A in math or an A in English (or both), so the set of students who receive an A in math is a subset of the set of students who receive either an A in math or an A in English (or both). Likewise, the set of students who receive an A in English is a subset of the set of students who receive either an A in math or an A in English (or both). Then

$P\{A \text{ in math and/or } A \text{ in English}\} \geq P\{A \text{ in math}\} = 0.2,$

and $P\{A \text{ in math and/or } A \text{ in English}\} \geq P\{A \text{ in English}\} = 0.3,$

so $0.3 \leq P\{A \text{ in math and/or } A \text{ in English}\} \leq 0.5.$

∨ • PROBLEM 1-74

There are three math teachers for a certain class in a certain school. The teachers are named Jones, Smith, and Taylor. The probability of being assigned to Jones' class is 0.4, and the probability of being assigned to Smith's class is 0.3. What is the probability of being assigned to Taylor's class? Which axiom is being applied?

SOLUTION:

By the axiom of total probability,

$P\{\text{Jones}\} + P\{\text{Smith}\} + P\{\text{Taylor}\} = 1,$

or $P\{\text{Taylor}\} = 1 - P\{\text{Jones}\} - P\{\text{Smith}\} = 1 - 0.4 - 0.3 = 0.3.$

In a survey carried out in a school snack shop, the following results were obtained. Of 100 boys questioned, 78 liked sweets, 74 liked ice cream, 53 liked cake, 57 liked both sweets and ice cream, 46 liked both sweets and cake, and only 31 boys liked all three. If all the boys interviewed liked at least one item, draw a Venn diagram to illustrate the results. How many boys like both ice cream and cake?

SOLUTION:

A Venn diagram is a pictorial representation of the relationship between sets. A set is a collection of objects. The number of objects in a particular set is the cardinality of a set.

To draw a Venn diagram we start with the following picture:

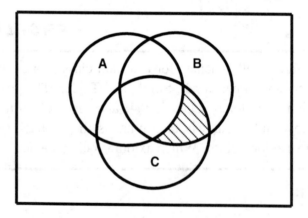

Each circle represents set *A*, *B*, or *C*, respectively. Let

  A = set of boys who liked ice cream,

  B = set of boys who liked cake, and

  C = set of boys who liked sweets.

The sections of overlap between circles represent the members of one set who are also members of another set. For example, the shaded region in the picture indicates the set of boys who are in sets *B* and *C* but not *A*. This is the set of boys who liked both cake and sweets but not ice cream. The inner section common to all three circles indicates the set of boys who belong to all three sets simultaneously.

We wish to find the number of boys who liked both ice-cream and cake. Let us label the sections of the diagram with the cardinality of these sections. The cardinality of the region common to all three sets is the number of boys who liked all three items, or 31.

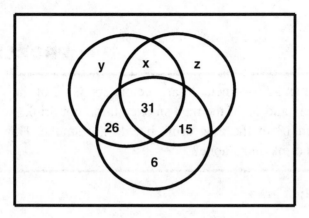

The number of boys who liked ice cream and sweets was 57. Of these 57, 31 liked all three, leaving 26 boys in set A and set C but not set B. Similarly, there are 15 boys in B and C, but not in A. There are $78 - 26 - 31 - 15 = 6$ boys in C but not in A or B.

Let x = number of boys who are in A and B but not C;

y = number of boys who are in A but not B or C; and

z = number of boys who are in B but not A or C.

We know that the sum of all the labeled areas is 100 or

$$26 + 31 + 15 + 6 + x + y + z = 100$$

$$78 + x + y + z = 100.$$

Also, there are 74 boys total in set A, or

$$x + y + 31 + 26 = 74,$$

and 53 total in set B, or

$$x + z + 46 = 53.$$

Combining: $x + y + z = 100 - 78 = 22$

$$x + y = 74 - 57 = 17$$

$$x + z = 53 - 46 = 7$$

Subtracting the second equation from the first gives $z = 5$, implying $x = 2$ and $y = 15$. Our answer is the number of boys in sets A and $B = x + 31 = 33$.

• **PROBLEM 1–76**

Of 37 men and 33 women, 36 are teetotalers. Nine of the women are non-smokers and 18 of the men smoke but do not drink. Seven of the women and 13 of the men drink but do not smoke. How many, at most, both drink and smoke?

SOLUTION:

A = set of all smokers

B = set of all drinkers

C = set of all women

D = set of all men

We construct two Venn diagrams and label them in the following way:

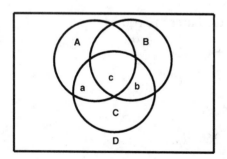
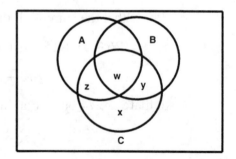

Each section on the graph indicates a subset of the group of men and women. For example, the section labeled "z" is the subset including all women who smoke but do not drink. The section labeled "b" is the subset including all men who drink but do not smoke.

In addition to being labels, these letters also will indicate the cardinality—the number of objects—in the subset. We are told there are 37 men; thus, $a + b + c + d = 37$. There are 33 women; thus, $x + y + z + w = 33$. There are 9 women non-smokers which includes $x + y$. The number of non-drinking, smoking men is $d = 18$.

Similarly, $x + z + a + d = 36$, the non-drinkers

$b = 13$, the drinking, non-smoking men

$y = 7$, the drinking, non-smoking women

Collecting all these equations, we wish to find the maximum value of $c + w$, the number of drinkers and smokers.

$$x + z + a + d = 36, \qquad a + b + c + d = 37$$

$$b = 13, d = 18, \qquad x + y + z + w = 33$$

$$y = 7, \qquad x + y = 9$$

Substituting we see that:

$$x + y - x + 7 = 9 \text{ or } x = 2.$$

From this we have

$$2 + z + a + 18 = 36 \qquad a + 13 + c + 18 = 37$$

$$a + z = 16 \qquad a + c = 6$$

$$2 + 7 + z + w = 33$$

$$z + w = 24$$

We now solve for $c + w$:

$$a = 6 - c \text{ and thus } z + 6 - c = 16 \text{ or } z - c = 10$$

$$c = z - 10 \text{ and } w = 24 - z$$

thus, $c + w = z - 10 + 24 - z = 14.$

The maximum number of drinkers and smokers is 14.

CHAPTER 2

DISCRETE RANDOM VARIABLES

Basic Attacks and Strategies for Solving Problems in this Chapter. See pages 87 to 187 for step-by-step solutions to problems.

Random variables are typically either discrete or continuous, although there are other types. For example, some random variables are mixed, with both continuous and discrete components, and others, such as random variables whose support is the Cantor set, are neither. Discrete variables are the simplest random variables to understand, so these are presented first. Instead of a probability density function, we will speak of a probability mass function, $f_X(k)$, to be interpreted as the probability that X, a discrete random variable, takes on the value k, or

$$f_X(k) = P\{X = k\}.$$

Specifying that a random variable is discrete still allows for much flexibility, and many subclasses of discrete random variables have been defined. These will be explored in the remainder of Chapter 2. As discussed earlier, a discrete random variable is supported by a finite or countably infinite set of points.

The mean of a discrete random variable is defined as

$$M_X = \Sigma_k[k][f_X(k)]$$

$$= \Sigma_k[k][P\{X = k\}],$$

where the sum extends over the values of k in the support of X. The mean, or expected value, provides a commonly used measure of central tendency of the random variable X. Notice that the expected value need not be a value assumed by X with positive probability. For example, if $P\{X = 1\} = 0.5$ and $P\{X = 2\} = 0.5$, then

$$M_X = (1)\,(0.5) + (2)\,(0.5)$$

$$= 0.5 + 1.0$$

$$= 1.5$$

But 1.5 is not in the support of X and, consequently, $P\{X = 1.5\} = 0$. What is true in general, however, is that the expected value of X is in the convex hull of the support of X (that is, it can be written as a convex combination of the elements in the support of X).

REVIEW OF UNIFORM RANDOM VARIABLES

A discrete random variable is uniform if its probability mass function is constant (i.e., does not change) over the range of its support. As an example, let X be a discrete random variable such that

$$P\{X = 1\} = 0.5$$

and $P\{X = 2\} = 0.5.$

Since $0.5 + 0.5 = 1$, all the mass has been exhausted, and we know that $\{1, 2\}$ is the entire support of X. We also know that the probability mass function assumes only the value 0.5 on the range of this support. Therefore, X is uniformly distributed. For enhanced clarity, one should specify that X is a uniformly distributed discrete random variable, because continuous random variables can also be uniformly distributed.

If we let Y be a discrete random variable such that

$$P\{Y = 1\} = 0.4$$

and $P\{Y = 5\} = 0.6,$

then Y is not uniformly distributed, because the probability mass function takes on different values (0.4 and 0.6) on the range of the support of Y.

In general, the value of the probability mass function will be the inverse of the number of points in the range of the support of a uniformly distributed random variable. For example, if X is uniformly distributed on the range $\{0, 1, 8, 9, 12\}$, then the value of the probability mass function is $1/5$, or 0.2, on all five points. The value 0.2 is required to ensure that X is, in fact, a random variable (otherwise, the probability mass function would not sum to 1). The interpretation is that X takes on the values $\{0, 1, 8, 9, 12\}$ with probability 0.2 each, so each value is equally likely, or uniformly likely.

The expected value of a uniformly distributed discrete random variable is the unweighted arithmetic average of the points in its support. This is seen by applying the general formula for the expected value of a discrete random variable to the case of a uniformly distributed discrete random variable. In particular, if we let n denote the number of points in the support of X, then

$$M_X = \Sigma_k [k][P\{X = k\}]$$

$$= \Sigma_k [k]\left[\frac{1}{n}\right],$$

which is seen to be the unweighted arithmetic mean of the points in the support of X. The expected value of X is also often denoted by $E[X]$. For example, if X is a discrete random variable which is uniformly distributed on the points $\{1, 2, 3, 4, 5\}$, then its probability mass function is $\frac{1}{5}$, or 0.2, on each of these points, and its expected value is

$$M_X = (1)\,(0.2) + (2)\,(0.2) + (3)\,(0.2) + (4)\,(0.2) + (5)\,(0.2)$$

$$= 0.2 + 0.4 + 0.6 + 0.8 + 1.0$$

$$= 3.0$$

The cumulative distribution function of a discrete uniformly distributed random variable is a step function, ranging from zero to one, which increases by $\frac{1}{n}$ at each point in the support of X, where n is the number of points in the support of X. For example, if X is a discrete random variable which is uniformly distributed on the points $\{1, 2, 3, 4, 5\}$, then its cumulative distribution function is

$$F_X(k) = 0 \text{ for } k < 1;$$

$$= 0.2 \text{ for } 1 \leq k < 2;$$

$$= 0.4 \text{ for } 2 \leq k < 3;$$

$$= 0.6 \text{ for } 3 \leq k < 4;$$

$$= 0.8 \text{ for } 4 \leq k < 5;$$

and $\qquad = 1.0 \text{ for } k \geq 5.$

Step-by-Step Solutions to Problems in this Chapter, "Discrete Random Variables"

√ • **PROBLEM 2–1**

A discrete random variable is uniformly distributed on {0, 1}. What is its probability mass function? What is its expected value? What is its cumulative distribution function?

SOLUTION:

The support of X is {0, 1}, so there are two points in the support of X, and consequently the probability mass function is $1/2$, or 0.5, on each of these two points. The expected value of X is

$$E[X] = (0)(0.5) + (1)(0.5)$$

$$= 0.0 + 0.5$$

$$= 0.5$$

Notice that this is a value not in the support of X.

The cumulative distribution function of X is

$$F_X(k) = 0 \text{ for } k < 0;$$

$$= 0.5 \text{ for } 0 \leq k < 1; \text{ and}$$

$$= 1.0 \text{ for } k \geq 1$$

The probability mass function of X is

$P\{X = 2\} = 0.3;$

$P\{X = 5\} = 0.4;$

and $P\{X = 6\} = 0.4.$

Is X a uniformly distributed discrete random variable?

SOLUTION:

Since $0.3 + 0.4 + 0.4 = 1.1 > 1.0$, X is not a random variable of any type.

The probability mass function of X is

$P\{X = 2\} = 0.3;$

$P\{X = 5\} = 0.4;$

and $P\{X = 6\} = 0.3.$

Is X a uniformly distributed discrete random variable?

SOLUTION:

Since $0.3 + 0.4 + 0.3 = 1.0$ and the probability mass function is non-negative, X is a discrete random variable. But since its probability mass function is not constant (it takes on different values at 5 and at 6, for example, both of which fall in its support), X is not uniformly distributed.

√ • **PROBLEM 2–4**

A random variable, X, is uniformly distributed on $\{5, 10, 20, 25\}$. What is its probability mass function? What is its mean? What is its median? What is its mode? What is its cumulative distribution function?

SOLUTION:

Since there are four points in the support of X on which X is uniformly distributed, its probability mass function is $^1/_4$, or 0.25, on each of these four points, and zero elsewhere. The mean of X is

$$E[X] = (5)(0.25) + (10)(0.25) + (20)(0.25) + (25)(0.25)$$

$$= 1.25 + 2.50 + 5.00 + 6.25$$

$$= 15$$

This could also have been calculated using the special formula for uniformly distributed discrete random variables

$$E[X] = (5 + 10 + 20 + 25)(0.25)$$

$$= (60)(0.25)$$

$$= 15$$

The median of X is

$$\frac{(10 + 20)}{2} = \frac{30}{2} = 15.$$

The mode of X is non-unique and, in fact, takes on the four values in the support of X, $\{5, 10, 20, 25\}$. The cumulative distribution function of X is

$$F_X(k) = 0 \text{ for } k < 5;$$

$$= 0.25 \text{ for } 5 \leq k < 10;$$

$$= 0.50 \text{ for } 10 \leq k < 20;$$

$$= 0.75 \text{ for } 20 \leq k < 25;$$

and $\qquad = 1.00 \text{ for } 25 \leq k.$

√ • **PROBLEM 2–5**

A discrete random variable is uniformly distributed on five points, four of which are {1, 2, 3, 4}. Can the fifth point be determined?

SOLUTION:

The fifth point cannot be determined. It need not fall in the succession established by the other four points. All that is known is that the probability mass function is $1/5$, or 0.2, on the fifth point, as well as on the other four points.

√ • **PROBLEM 2–6**

A coin is tossed twice. Let X denote the number of heads. The possible values of X are {0, 1, 2}. Is X a discrete random variable? Is X a uniformly distributed discrete random variable?

SOLUTION:

Since the support of X only has three points, {0, 1, 2}, X is a discrete random variable. To qualify as a uniformly distributed discrete random variable, each of these three values would need to be equally likely. If we let the probability of heads on any given toss be denoted by p, then the probability of tails on any given toss is $1 - p$. Using the methods developed in Chapter 1, it is seen that the probability mass function of X is

$$P\{X = 0\} = (1 - p)^2;$$

$$P\{X = 1\} = 2p(1 - p);$$

and $\quad P\{X = 2\} = p^2.$

If X is to be a uniformly distributed discrete random variable, then these three values would need to be equal. If

$$(1 - p)^2 = p^2,$$

then either $1 - p = p$ or $1 - p = - p$. The first case gives $2p = 1$, or $p = 1/2$, or 0.5. The second case is impossible, because adding p to both sides would lead to the false equation $1 = 0$. Now if $p = 0.5$, then

$$(1 - p)^2 = 0.5^2 = 0.25 = 0.5^2 = p^2.$$

But then

$$2p(1 - p) = 2(0.5)\,(0.5) = 0.5,$$

which is unequal to p^2. Therefore, X cannot be a uniformly distributed discrete random variable.

✓ • **PROBLEM 2–7**

Can the support of a uniformly distributed discrete random variable be countably infinite? Why or why not?

SOLUTION:

The probability mass function for a uniformly distributed discrete random variable is the inverse of the number of points in the support. If the support is countably infinite, then the probability mass function would be the inverse of infinity, or zero. But if the probability mass function is zero, then this point is not in the support of X. This contradiction shows that it would not be possible for the support of a uniformly distributed discrete random variable to be countably infinite.

✽✽✽✽✽✽

REVIEW OF BERNOULLI RANDOM VARIABLES

A discrete random variable has a Bernoulli distribution if it can take on only the values of zero and one. We let p be the probability that the Bernoulli random variable assumes the value 1, and $q = 1 - p$ is the probability that it assumes the value zero. Therefore, the probability mass function of a Bernoulli random variable is

$$P\{X = k\} = 1 - p \text{ for } k = 0;$$

$$P\{X = k\} = p \text{ for } k = 1;$$

and $\quad P\{X = k\} = 0$ for other k.

This probability mass function can be conveniently written as

$$P\{X = k\} = p^k(1 - p)^{1-k} \text{ for } k = 0, 1;$$

and $\quad P\{X = k\} = 0$ for other k.

The expected value of X, a Bernoulli random variable, is

$$E[X] = (0)\,(1 - p) + (1)\,(p)$$

$$= 0 + p$$

$$= p$$

The cumulative distribution function of X, a Bernoulli random variable, is

$$F_X(k) = 0 \text{ for } k < 0;$$

$$F_X(k) = 1 - p \text{ for } 0 \le k < 1;$$

and $\quad F_X(k) = 1$ for $1 \le k$.

Bernoulli random variables are used to model single dichotomous (having two possible outcomes) events. Regardless of the two possibilities, the Bernoulli model is applicable, as the outcomes can be coded as zero and one. For example, the single toss of a coin may be regarded as a Bernoulli random variable if we use the convention that tails corresponds to $X = 0$ and heads corresponds to $X = 1$. The only two possible outcomes are heads and tails. Likewise, randomly selecting a patient from a hospital and recording the gender of this patient would also qualify as a Bernoulli random variable if we code male to be zero and female to be one. Here, the only possible outcomes are male and female. The particular choice of codes is irrelevant. That is, the model would fit as well if we had coded male as one and female as zero.

✓ • PROBLEM 2–8

A coin is tossed twice, and X denotes the number of heads in these two tosses. Is X Bernoulli distributed?

SOLUTION:

Since there are three possible values for X, $\{0, 1, 2\}$, X is not dichotomous and, therefore, cannot be Bernoulli distributed.

✓ • PROBLEM 2–9

What is the probability of throwing a "six" with a single die?

SOLUTION:

The die may land in any of six ways:

1, 2, 3, 4, 5, or 6.

The probability of throwing a six is

$$P(6) = \frac{\text{number of ways to get a six}}{\text{number of ways the die may land}}$$

Thus, $P(6) = \dfrac{1}{6}$.

1,1	1,2	1,3	1,4	1,5	1,6
2,1	2,2	2,3	2,4	2,5	2,6
3,1	3,2	3,3	3,4	3,5	3,6
4,1	4,2	4,3	4,4	4,5	4,6
5,1	5,2	5,3	5,4	5,5	5,6
6,1	6,2	6,3	6,4	6,5	6,6

The number of possible ways that a seven will appear are circled in the figure. Let us call this set B. Thus, $B = \{ (1, 6), (2, 5), (3, 4), (4, 3), (5, 2), (6, 1) \}$.

There are six elements in B, so $P\,(7) = P\,(B) = \dfrac{6}{36} = \dfrac{1}{6}$.

In a single throw of a single die, find the probability of obtaining either a two or a five.

SOLUTION:

In a single throw, the die may land in any of six ways:

$\{1, 2, 3, 4, 5, 6\}$.

The probability of obtaining a two is

$$P(2) = \frac{\text{number of ways of obtaining a two}}{\text{number of ways the die may land}}, \quad P(2) = \frac{1}{6}.$$

Similarly, the probably of obtaining a five is

$$P(5) = \frac{\text{number of ways of obtaining a five}}{\text{number of ways the die may land}}, \quad P(5) = \frac{1}{6}.$$

As it is impossible for the single throw to result in a two and a five simultaneously, the two events are mutually exclusive. The probability that either one of two mutually exclusive events will occur is the sum of the probabilities of the separate events. Thus, the probability of obtaining either a two or a five, $P(2 \text{ or } 5)$, is

$$P(2) + P(5) = \frac{1}{6} + \frac{1}{6} = \frac{2}{6} = \frac{1}{3}.$$

If a card is drawn from a deck of playing cards, what is the probability that it will be a jack or a ten?

SOLUTION:

The probability of the union of two mutually exclusive events is $P(A \cup B) = P(A) + P(B)$. Here the symbol "$\cup$" stands for "or."

In this particular example, we only select one card at a time. Thus, we either choose a jack "or" a ten. Since no single selection can simultaneously be a jack and a ten, the two events are mutually exclusive.

$P(\text{jack or ten}) = P(\text{jack}) + P(\text{ten}).$

$$P(\text{jack}) = \frac{\text{number of ways to select a jack}}{\text{numbers of ways to choose a card}} = \frac{4}{52} = \frac{1}{13}$$

$$P(\text{ten}) = \frac{\text{number of ways to select a ten}}{\text{numbers of ways to choose a card}} = \frac{4}{52} = \frac{1}{13}.$$

$$P(\text{jack or a ten}) = P(\text{jack}) + P(\text{ten}) = \frac{1}{13} + \frac{1}{13} = \frac{2}{13}.$$

$\vee$ • PROBLEM 2-12

Suppose that we have a bag containing two red balls, three white balls, and six blue balls. What is the probability of obtaining a red or a white ball on one draw?

SOLUTION:

 Fig. A

The bag is shown in Figure A.

The probability of drawing a red ball is $2/11$, and the probability of drawing a white ball is $3/11$. Since drawing a red and drawing a white ball are mutually exclusive events, the probability of drawing a red or a white ball is the probability of drawing a red ball plus the probability of drawing a white ball, so

$$P(\text{red or white}) = \frac{2}{11} + \frac{3}{11} = \frac{5}{11}.$$

Note: In the above example the probability of drawing a blue ball would be $6/11$. Therefore, the sum of the probability of a red ball, the probability of a white ball, and the probability of a blue ball is

$$\frac{2}{11} + \frac{3}{11} + \frac{6}{11} = 1.$$

If there are no possible results that are considered favorable, then the probability $P(F)$ is obviously 0. If every result is considered favorable, then $P(F) = 1$. Hence the probability $P(F)$ of a favorable result F always satisfies the inequality

$$0 \le p(F) \le 1.$$

$\checkmark$ • **PROBLEM 2-13**

A bag contains four white balls, six black balls, three red balls, and eight green balls. If one ball is drawn from the bag, find the probability that it will be either white or green.

SOLUTION:

The probability that it will be either white or green is

$$P(\text{white or green}) = P(\text{white}) + P(\text{green}).$$

This is true because if we are given two mutually exclusive events A and B, then $P(A \text{ or } B) = P(A) + P(B)$. Note that two events, A and B, are mutually exclusive events if their intersection is the null or empty set. In this case the intersection of choosing a white ball and of choosing a green ball is the empty set. There are no elements in common. Now

$$P(\text{white}) = \frac{\text{number of ways to choose a white ball}}{\text{number of ways to select a ball}}$$

$$= \frac{4}{21},$$

and $\quad P(\text{green}) = \dfrac{\text{number of ways to choose a green ball}}{\text{number of ways to select a ball}}$

$$= \frac{8}{21}.$$

Thus, $\quad P(\text{white or green}) = \dfrac{4}{21} + \dfrac{8}{21} = \dfrac{12}{21} = \dfrac{4}{7}.$

√ • PROBLEM 2-14

Let X be the random variable denoting the result of the single toss of a fair coin. If the toss is heads, $X = 1$. If the toss results in tails, $X = 0$. What is the probability distribution of X?

SOLUTION:

The probability distribution of X is a function which assigns probabilities to the values X may assume. A proper discrete probability distribution will satisfy $\Sigma\, P(X = x) = 1$ and $P(X = x) \geq 0$ for all x. The variable X in this problem is discrete as it only takes on the values 0 and 1. To find the probability distribution of X, we must find $P(X = 0)$ and $P(X = 1)$. Let $\rho_0 = P(X = 0)$ and $\rho_1 = P(X = 1)$. If the coin is fair, the events $X = 0$ and $X = 1$ are equally likely. Thus, $\rho_0 = \rho_1 = P$. We must have $\rho_0 > 0$ and $\rho_1 > 0$. In addition, $P(X = 0) + P(X = 1) = 1$, or $\rho_0 + \rho_1 = P = P = 1$, or $2\,P = 1$, and

$$\rho_0 = \rho_1 = P = \frac{1}{2},$$

so the probability distribution of X is $f(x)$: where

$$f(0) = P(X = 0) = \frac{1}{2},$$

$$f(1) = P(X = 1) = \frac{1}{2}, \text{ and}$$

$f(k) = P(X = k) = 0$ for k other than 0 or 1. We see that this is a proper probability distribution for our variable X.

✓ • **PROBLEM 2–15**

Are there circumstances under which a discrete random variable can be both uniformly distributed and Bernoulli distributed?

SOLUTION:

If the support of the discrete uniform random variable is {0, 1}, then this random variable is also Bernoulli distributed with $p = 1 - p = 0.5$.

✓ • **PROBLEM 2–16**

A random variable X is Bernoulli distributed with $p = 0.4$. What is $E[X]$?

SOLUTION:

Since $E[X] = p$ for Bernoulli random variables, $E[X] = 0.4$.

✓ • **PROBLEM 2–17**

A Bernoulli random variable takes on the value zero with probability 0.2. If this random variable is denoted by X, then what is $E[X]$?

SOLUTION:

For a Bernoulli random variable, the probability of zero is $1 - p$. In this case, then, $1 - p = 0.2$, so $p = 1 - 0.2 = 0.8$. Therefore,

$E[X] = p = 0.8$.

✓ • **PROBLEM 2–18**

If X has a Bernoulli distribution and $E[X] = 0.9$, then what is the probability mass function of X?

SOLUTION:

For a Bernoulli distribution, $E[X] = p$. In this case, then, $p = 0.9$. The probability mass function is

$P\{X = 0\} = 0.1$;

$P\{X = 1\} = 0.9$;

and $P\{X = k\} = 0$ for other k.

This may also be written as

$P\{X = k\} = 0.9^k 0.1^{1-k}$ for $k = 0, 1$;

and $P\{X = k\} = 0$ for other k.

✓ • **PROBLEM 2–19**

Let X have a Bernoulli distribution with $p = 0.7$. What is the cumulative distribution function of X?

SOLUTION:

The cumulative distribution function of X is

$F_X(k) = 0$ for $k < 0$;

$F_X(k) = 0.3$ for $0 \leq k < 1$;

and $F_X(k) = 1$ for $1 \leq k$.

$\checkmark$ • **PROBLEM 2-20**

If X is a Bernoulli random variable and $F_X(0) = 0.4$, then what is p?

SOLUTION:

Since $F_X(0) = 1 - p$ for a Bernoulli random variable, $1 - p = 0.4$, so $p = 1 - 0.4 = 0.6$.

※※※※※※

REVIEW OF BINOMIAL RANDOM VARIABLES

The Bernoulli distribution is quite useful, but it is limited by the fact that it allows only for a single dichotomous trial. The binomial distribution is more general than the Bernoulli distribution in that an arbitrary number of dichotomous trials are allowed, as long as each trial is independent of the others and has common success probability. The three conditions that define a binomial random variable are:

1. A series of dichotomous trials occur;

2. Each trial is independent of other trials; and

3. Each trial has the same success probability.

That is, each dichotomous trial is a Bernoulli random variable, and each has the same value of p.

For example, consider tossing a coin five times, and let X record the number of heads observed. Now X may take the values $\{0, 1, 2, 3, 4, 5\}$. We may define $X1$ as

$X1 = 0$ if the first toss results in tails

and $X1 = 1$ if the first toss results in heads.

We may similarly define $X2$, $X3$, $X4$, and $X5$. Now

$$X = X1 + X2 + X3 + X4 + X5.$$

Each of the five random variables recording the outcome of a given toss is Bernoulli distributed. It is reasonable to assume independence across the different trials. Since the same coin is being used, the probability of heads is constant (the same) for each trial. Therefore, X has a binomial distribution.

The Bernoulli distribution is characterized by only one parameter, p, which is the success probability. However, the binomial distribution is characterized by two parameters: p, the common success probability for each trial, and n, the number of trials. In our example in which we tossed a coin five times, $n = 5$. These two parameters determine the probability mass function, the expected value, and the cumulative distribution function of the binomial random variable.

The probability mass function of a binomial random variable is derived by calculating the probability of each outcome (an outcome is a sequence of n successes and failures, where n is the number of trials) and grouping the outcomes by the number of successes. As a simple example, consider the case of $n = 2$. If we denote successes by S and failures by F, then the outcomes are $\{SS, SF, FS, FF\}$. We would group these as

two successes $\{SS\}$,

one success $\quad \{SF, FS\}$,

and no successes $\{FF\}$.

To find the probability of a given outcome, it is necessary to multiply the probabilities of the results of each of the n trials. For example, consider the sequence $\{SF\}$. We must multiply the probability of a success on the first trial by the probability of a failure on the second trial, or

$$P\{SF\} = P\{S1\}P\{F2\},$$

where $\{S1\}$ denotes a success on the first trial and $\{F2\}$ denotes a failure on the second trial. We will learn the rationale for this multiplication in the chapter on independence. Returning to the example,

$$P\{S1\} = p \text{ and } P\{F2\} = 1 - p.$$

Therefore, $\quad P\{SF\} = P\{S1\}P\{F2\}$

$$= p(1 - p)$$

If we list each outcome and its associated probability, we obtain

{SS}	p^2	two successes,
{SF}	$p(1-p)$	one success,
{FS}	$(1-p)p$	one success,
and {FF}	$(1-p)^2$	no successes.

Grouping again by the number of successes gives the probability mass function of the number of successes, which has a binomial distribution. We obtain

$$P\{X = 0\} = P\{FF\} = (1-p)^2;$$

$$P\{X = 1\} = P\{SF \cup FS\} = P\{SF\} + P\{FS\}$$

$$= p(1-p) + (1-p)p = 2p(1-p);$$

$$P\{X = 2\} = P\{SS\} = p^2;$$

and $P\{X = k\} = 0$ for other k.

Notice that this defines a true probability mass function, because this function is non-negative and sums to one, which is seen as follows:

$$(1-p)^2 + 2p(1-p) + p^2 = (1 - 2p + p^2) + (2p - 2p^2) + p^2$$

$$= 1 - 2p + 2p + p^2 - 2p^2 + p^2$$

$$= 1$$

The question now becomes how to find the probability mass function when $n > 2$. We may use the same approach that yielded the probability mass function for the case of $n = 2$. Specifically, we enumerate the outcomes, find the probability of each, and group them by the number of successes.

The first point to notice is that, in the case of $n = 2$, the probability of any outcome depended only on the number of successes. That is, any sequence with k successes and $n - k$ (in this case, $2 - k$) failures had probability $p^k(1-p)^{2-k}$. This will still be true for $n > 2$, with the obvious modification that the probability of any outcome with k successes and $n - k$ failures is $p^k(1-k)^{n-k}$. The order in which the successes and failures occur does not influence the probability. There are k successes, and the probability of success on any one trial is p. Therefore, we must multiply p k times, resulting in p^k. Likewise, there are $n - k$ failures, and each trial will result in failure with probability $1 - k$. Therefore, we must multiply $1 - pn - k$ times, resulting in $(1 - p)^{n-k}$. Finally, we multiply these two quantities to arrive at $p^k(1 - k)^{n-k}$, the probability of any outcome with k successes and $n - k$ failures.

The remaining task, then, is to count the number of outcomes with k successes and $n - k$ failures. This must be done for each k. This is a problem of combinations, because the problem can be formulated as finding the number of ways to find k locations among n locations in which to place the successes. This is equivalent to finding the $n - k$ locations in which to place the failures. From our earlier development, we recognize this to be

$$C(n, k) = C(n, n - k) = \frac{n!}{[(k!)\,(n - k)!]}.$$

Therefore, the probability of k successes in n trials is

$$C(n, k)p^k(1 - p)^{n-k}.$$

This is the binomial probability mass function.

The range (or support) of a binomial random variable with parameters n and p is the set of non-negative integers not exceeding n. Since n must be a non-negative integer (since n is the number of trials), n is included in the range, which is therefore $\{1, 2, 3, ..., n\}$. This obvious fact is often forgotten when the binomial is compared to the Poisson.

It is possible to derive the expected value of a binomial random variable directly from the definition of the probability mass function. However, it is both simpler and more intuitive to utilize the fact that a binomial random variable with parameters n and p may be expressed as the sum of n Bernoulli random variables, each with parameter p. By the linearity property of the expected value, then, the expected value of the binomial random variable is the sum of the expected values of the n Bernoulli random variables. We recall from the previous section that the expected value of a Bernoulli random variable with parameter p is p. If we let X have a binomial distribution with parameters n and p, denoted by (n, p), and we let $X_1, X_2, ..., X_n$ be n independent Bernoulli random variables, each with parameter p, then

$$E[X] = E[\Sigma_{i = 1 \text{ to } n} X_i]$$
$$= \Sigma_{i = 1 \text{ to } n} E[X_i]$$

$$= \Sigma_{i=1 \text{ to } n} P$$

$$E[X] = np$$

This is the expected value of a binomial random variable with parameters n and p.

The cumulative distribution function of a binomial random variable is found by summing the probability mass function over the appropriate range. For example, if we wish to find

$$F_X(k) = P\{X \leq k\},$$

then we recognize that for a binomial random variable to be less than or equal to k, it would need to be zero, one, two, or any other non-negative integer less than or equal to k. We would simply add the probability mass function over this range. Unfortunately, there is no general formula which applies to all cases. For small n, it is a simple matter to perform the addition with a calculator or a computer. For larger n, tables exist which provide the values of the cumulative distribution function for binomial random variables.

$\checkmark$ • PROBLEM 2–21

Expand $(x + 2y)^5$.

SOLUTION:

Apply the binomial theorem. If n is a positive integer, then

$$(a+b)^n = \binom{n}{0} a^n b^0 + \binom{n}{1} a^{n-1} b + \binom{n}{2} a^{n-2} b^2 + \ldots + \binom{n}{r} a^{n-r} b^r + \ldots$$

$$+ \binom{n}{n} a^0 b^n.$$

Note that $\binom{n}{r} = \dfrac{n!}{r!(n-r)!}$ and that $0! = 1$. Then we obtain

$$(x + 2y)^5 = \binom{5}{0} x^5 (2y)^0 + \binom{5}{1} x^4 (2y)^1 + \binom{5}{2} x^3 (2y)^2 + \binom{5}{3} x^2 (2y)^3 +$$

$$\binom{5}{4} x^1 (2y)^4 + \binom{5}{5} x^0 (2y)^5$$

$$= \frac{5!}{0!\,5!} x^5 + \frac{5!}{1!\,4!} x^4 (2y) + \frac{5!}{2!\,3!} x^3 (4y^2) + \frac{5!}{3!\,2!} x^2 (8y^3) +$$

$$\frac{5!}{4!\,1!} x (16y^4) + \frac{5!}{5!\,0!} 1 (32y^5)$$

$$= x^5 + \frac{5! \times 4!}{4!} x^4 (2y) + \frac{\overset{2}{5! \times 4! \times 3!}}{2! \times 1! \times 3! \underset{1}{\,} } x^3 (4y^2) + \frac{\overset{2}{5! \cdot 4! \cdot 3!}}{3! \cdot 2! \cdot 1! \underset{1}{\,}} x^2$$

$$(8y^3) + \frac{5! \times 4!}{4! \times 1!} x (16y^4) + \frac{5!}{5! \times 0!} (32y^5)$$

$$= x^5 + 10x^4 y + 40x^3 y^2 + 80x^2 y^3 + 80xy^4 + 32y^5.$$

● PROBLEM 2–22

For what values of n and p can a binomial random variable also be a uniform random variable?

SOLUTION:

Using the binomial formula,

$$P\{X = 0\} = C(n, 0)p^0(1 - p)^{n-0}$$

$$= (1)\,(1)\,(1 - p)^n$$

$$= (1 - p)^n$$

Also,

$$P\{X = n\} = C(n, n)p^n(1 - p)^{n-n}$$

$$= (1)p^n(1-p)^0$$

$$= p^n.$$

If the binomial random variable is to be a uniform random variable, then the $(n + 1)$ values in the range of the random variable, namely $\{0, 1, 2, ..., n\}$, must be equally likely. There are $(n + 1)$ points, so the probability of each must be $1/(n + 1)$. In particular, we require that

$$P\{X = 0\} = P\{X = n\}.$$

Then $(1 - p)^n = p^n$. Taking logarithms shows that

$$1 - p = p$$

$$1 = 2p$$

$$p = 0.5$$

The remaining task is to find the values of n for which the binomial random variable could also be a uniform random variable. We recall that

$$P\{X = n\} = p^n$$

$$= (0.5)^n$$

$$= \frac{1}{(n+1)}$$

If we try $n = 1$, then this equation becomes

$$(0.5)^1 = \frac{1}{(1+1)},$$

or $\qquad 0.5 = \frac{1}{2}.$

This equation is satisfied, so we may use $(n, p) = (1, 0.5)$, confirming the similar result in the section on Bernoulli random variables. Additional algebra will show that this is the only set of parameters for which this relation could hold.

Find the expansion of $(x + y)^6$.

SOLUTION:

Use the binomial theorem, which states that

$$(a + b)^n = \frac{1}{0!}a^n b^0 + \frac{n}{1!}a^{n-1}b^1 + \frac{n(n-1)}{2!}a^{n-2}b^2 + \ldots + na^1 b^{n-1} + a^0 b^n.$$

Replacing a by x and b by y gives:

$$(x + y)^6 = \frac{1}{0!}x^6 y^0 + \frac{6}{1!}x^5 y + \frac{6 \cdot 5}{2!}x^4 y^2 + \frac{6 \cdot 5 \cdot 4}{3!}x^3 y^3 + \frac{6 \cdot 5 \cdot 4 \cdot 3}{4!}x^2 y^4$$

$$+ \frac{6 \cdot 5 \cdot 4 \cdot 3 \cdot 2}{5!}x^1 y^5 + \frac{6 \cdot 5 \cdot 4 \cdot 3 \cdot 2 \cdot 1}{6!}x^0 y^6$$

$$= \frac{1}{1}x^6 + \frac{6}{1}x^5 y + \frac{6 \cdot 5}{2 \cdot 1}x^4 y^2 + \frac{6 \cdot 5 \cdot 4}{3 \cdot 2 \cdot 1}x^3 y^3 + \frac{6 \cdot 5 \cdot 4 \cdot 3}{4 \cdot 3 \cdot 2 \cdot 1}x^2 y^4$$

$$+ \frac{6 \cdot 5 \cdot 4 \cdot 3 \cdot 2}{5 \cdot 4 \cdot 3 \cdot 2 \cdot 1}xy^5 + \frac{6 \cdot 5 \cdot 4 \cdot 3 \cdot 2 \cdot 1}{6 \cdot 5 \cdot 4 \cdot 3 \cdot 2 \cdot 1}y^6$$

$$(x + y)^6 = x^6 + 6x^5 y + 15x^4 y^2 + 20x^3 y^3 + 15x^2 y^4 + 6xy^5 + y^6$$

Let X be binomially distributed with parameters 4 and 0.5. What is $E[X]$? What is the probability that X equals its expected value?

SOLUTION:

The mean of a binomial random variable is np or, in this case,

$$E[X] = (4)\,(0.5)$$

$$=$$

Now we must find

$$P\{X = E[X]\} = P\{X = 2\}.$$

Using the binomial formula shows that

$$P\{X = 2\} = C(4, 2) (0.5)^2(1 - 0.5)^{4-2}$$

$$= \frac{4!}{[(2!) (4 - 2)!] (0.25) (0.5)^2}$$

$$= \frac{24}{[(2) (2!)] (0.25) (0.25)}$$

$$= \frac{24}{[(2) (2)] (0.0625)}$$

$$= (6) (0.0625)$$

$$= 0.375$$

✓ ● PROBLEM 2–25

A basketball player shoots five free-throws in a game. His free-throw shooting percentage is 0.75. How many shots do we expect him to hit? What is the probability that he will hit two shots?

SOLUTION:

Each free-throw results in one of two outcomes. We code a basket as a success and a miss as a failure. We may assume that the five shots are independent of each other (that is, the result of one in no way influences the result of any other) and that the probability of success is constant for all shots. The constant success probability is given as 0.75. Therefore, we may use the binomial formula, which shows that

$$E[X] = np$$

$$= (5) (0.75)$$

$$= 3.75$$

Thus, we expect him to hit 3.75 of his shots. Also, the probabilility that he will hit two shots is

$$P\{X = 2\} = C(5,2)\,(0.75)^2(1 - 0.75)^{5-2}$$

$$= \frac{5!}{[(2!)\,(5 - 2)!]\,(0.5625)\,(0.25)^3}$$

$$= \frac{120}{[(2)\,(3!)]\,(0.5625)\,(0.0156)}$$

$$= \frac{120}{[(2)\,(6)]\,(0.0088)}$$

$$= (10)\,(0.0088)$$

$$= 0.088$$

✓• PROBLEM 2–26

A baseball player is a 0.300 hitter. He comes to bat three times in a game. How many hits do we expect this player to get? What is the probability that he will get exactly one hit? Assume that the player does not walk or get hit by any pitches.

SOLUTION:

Since the batter does not walk and is not hit by any pitches, each at-bat results in one of two outcomes. We code a hit as a success and an out as a failure. We may assume that the three at-bats are independent of each other (that is, the result of one in no way influences the result of any other) and that the probability of success is constant for all shots. The constant success probability is given as 0.30. Therefore, we may use the binomial formula, which shows that

$$E[X] = np$$

$$= (3)\,(0.30)$$

$$= 0.90.$$

Thus, we expect him to get 0.90 hits. Also, the probablility that he will get exactly one hit is

$$P\{X = 1\}= C(3,\ 1)\ (0.30)^1(1 - 0.30)^{3-1}$$

$$= \frac{3!}{[(1!0\ (3-1)!]\ (0.30)\ (0.70)^2}$$

$$= \frac{6}{[(1)\ (2!)]\ (0.30)\ (0.49)}$$

$$= \frac{6}{[(1)\ (2)]\ (0.147)}$$

$$= (3)\ (0.147)$$

$$= 0.441$$

✓ • **PROBLEM 2–27**

A researcher wants to estimate the proportion of females in a city. He stands on a street corner and records the gender of the first ten people who pass by. If the city is half male and half female, then how many females should the researcher expect to find? What is the probability that the researcher will find all females?

SOLUTION:

Each person passing by results in one of two outcomes. We code a female as a success and a male as a failure. We may assume that the ten people are independent of each other (that is, the result of one in no way influences the result of any other) and that the probability of success is constant for all persons. The constant success probability is given as 0.50, since the city is half male and half female. Therefore, we may use the binomial formula, which shows that

$$E[X] = np$$

$$= (10)\ (0.50)$$

$$= 5$$

Thus, the researcher should expect to find five females. Also, the probability that he will find all females is

$$P\{X = 10\} = C(10, 10) (0.50)^{10}(1 - 0.50)^{10-10}$$

$$= \frac{10!}{[(10!) (10 - 10)!] (0.50)^{10} (0.50)^{0}}$$

$$= \frac{10!}{[(10!) (0!)] (0.50)^{10} (1.00)}$$

$$= \frac{10!}{[(10!) (1)] (0.50)^{10}}$$

$$= 0.50^{10}$$

$$= 0.001$$

✓ • PROBLEM 2–28

What is the probability that the researcher from Problem 2–27 will find at least eight females? What is the probability that the researcher will find between four and six females?

SOLUTION:

Each person passing by results in one of two outcomes. We code a female as a success and a male as a failure. We may assume that the ten people are independent of each other (that is, the result of one in no way influences the result of any other) and that the probability of success is constant for all persons. The constant success probability is given as 0.50, since the city is half male and half female. Therefore, we may use the binomial formula, which shows that

$$P\{X = k\} = C(10, k) (0.50)^{k}(1 - 0.50)^{10-k}$$

$$= \frac{10!}{[(k!) (10 - k)!] (0.50)^{k} (0.50)^{10-k}}$$

$$= \frac{10!}{[(k!) (10 - k)!] (0.50)^{10}}.$$

Now the probability of finding at least eight females is

$$P\{X \geq 8\} = P\{X = 8 \text{ or } 9 \text{ or } 10\}$$

$$= P\{X = 8 \cup X = 9 \cup X = 10\}.$$

Since these three events are mutually exclusive, this probability is equal to

$$P\{X = 8\} + P\{X = 9\} + P\{X = 10\}$$

$$= \frac{10!}{[(8!)\,(10-8)!]\,(0.50)^{10}} + \frac{10!}{[(9!)\,(10-9)!]\,(0.50)} + \frac{10!}{[(10!)\,(10-10)!]\,(0.50)^{10}}$$

$$= \left\{ \frac{10!}{[(8!)\,(2!)]} + \frac{10!}{[(9!)\,(1!)]} + \frac{10!}{[(10!)\,(0!)]} \right\} (0.50)^{10}$$

$$= (45 + 10 + 1)\,(0.50)^{10}$$

$$= (56)\,(0.50)^{10}$$

$$= (56)\,(0.001)$$

$$= 0.0547$$

Likewise, the probability of finding between four and six females is

$$P\{4 \leq X \leq 6\} = P\{X = 4 \text{ or } 5 \text{ or } 6\}$$

$$= P\{X = 4 \cup X = 5 \cup X = 6\}$$

Since these three events are mutually exclusive, this probability is equal to

$$P\{X = 4\} + P\{X = 5\} + P\{X = 6\}$$

$$= \frac{10!}{[(4!)\,(10-4)!]\,(0.50)^{10}} + \frac{10!}{[(5!)\,(10-5)!]\,(0.50)} + \frac{10!}{[(6!)\,(10-6)!]\,(0.50)^{10}}$$

$$= \left\{ \frac{10!}{[(4!)\,(6!)]} + \frac{10!}{[(5!)\,(5!)]} + \frac{10!}{[(6!)\,(4!)]} \right\} (0.50)^{10}$$

$$= (210 + 252 + 210)\,(0.50)^{10}$$

$$= (672)\,(0.50)^{10}$$

$$= (672)\,(0.001)$$

$$= 0.6563.$$

 • **PROBLEM 2-29**

Is the binomial distribution appropriate to model field goals made by placekickers in football? What about extra points?

SOLUTION:

The binomial distribution is appropriate as long as there is a fixed number of trials, each trial results in either a success or failure, the probability of success is the same in each trial, and the results of the trials are independent. Excluding psychological factors that may influence the results of one field goal based on previous results, one must also consider the effect of the distance of the field goal. Since this distance will affect the probability of a success, the binomial model is not appropriate.

All extra points are taken from the same location on the field unless there is a penalty. If we incorporate the probability of a penalty into the success probability and assume that the probability of a penalty is constant for each extra point attempt, then the binomial distribution may be reasonable for multiple attempts within a given game if the game is in a dome or if the weather does not change. It would still not be reasonable for multiple attempts in different games because some stadiums have domes and some do not. Those that do have domes allow for uniformity of success probability over time within a given game and across games. Those that do not have domes will be subject to rain, snow, and wind. Thus, the success probability would change over time within a game, as well as across games.

• **PROBLEM 2-30**

Find the probability that in three rolls of a pair of dice, exactly one total of seven is rolled.

SOLUTION:

Consider each of the three rolls of the pair as a trial and of rolling a total of seven as a success. Assume that each roll is independent of the others. If X is the number of successes, then we want to find

$$P(X = 1) = \binom{3}{1} p^1 (1-p)^2,$$

where p is the probability of rolling a total of seven on a single roll. The total number of combinations is 36 and six combinations have a total equal to seven. This probability is

$$\frac{6}{36} = \frac{1}{6},$$

and hence the probability of rolling a total of seven exactly once in three rolls is

$$P(X = 1) = \binom{3}{1}\left(\frac{1}{6}\right)^1\left(\frac{5}{6}\right)^2 = 3 \times \frac{1}{6} \times \frac{25}{36} = \frac{25}{72}.$$

 ● **PROBLEM 2–31**

What is the probability of obtaining exactly four "sixes" when a die is rolled seven times?

SOLUTION:

Let X equal the number of "sixes" observed when a die is rolled seven times. If we assume that each roll is independent of each other roll and that the probability of rolling a six on one roll is $\frac{1}{6}$, then X is binomially distributed with parameters $n = 7$ and $p = \frac{1}{6}$.

Thus, $P(X = 4) = P(\text{exactly four "sixes" on seven rolls})$

$$= \binom{7}{4}\left(\frac{1}{6}\right)^4\left(\frac{5}{6}\right)^{7-4}$$

$$= \frac{7 \cdot 6 \cdot 5 \cdot 4 \cdot 3 \cdot 2 \cdot 1}{4 \cdot 3 \cdot 2 \cdot 1 \cdot 3 \cdot 2 \cdot 1}\left(\frac{1}{6}\right)^4\left(\frac{5}{6}\right)^3$$

$$= 35 \left(\frac{1}{6} \right)^4 \left(\frac{5}{6} \right)^3$$

$$P(X = 4) = 35 \left(\frac{1}{1,296} \right) \left(\frac{125}{216} \right) = \frac{4,375}{279,936} = 0. - 156.$$

√ • **PROBLEM 2-32**

A deck of cards can be dichotomized into black cards and red cards. If p is the probability of drawing a black card on a single draw and q the probability of drawing a red card, then $p = \frac{1}{2}$ and $q = \frac{1}{2}$. Six cards are sampled with replacement. What is the probability on six draws of obtaining four black and two red cards? Of obtaining all black cards?

SOLUTION:

Let X = the number of black cards observed in six draws from this deck. Then $P(X = 4)$ is the probability that four black cards and two red cards are in this sample of six. The probability of drawing a black card on a single draw is $p = \frac{1}{2}$ and since each draw is independent, X is distributed binomially with parameters of 6 and $\frac{1}{2}$. Thus,

$$P(X = 4) = \binom{6}{4} \left(\frac{1}{2} \right)^4 \left(\frac{1}{2} \right)^2 = 15 \left(\frac{1}{2} \right)^6 = \frac{15}{64}$$

and $\quad P(X = 6) = \binom{6}{6} \left(\frac{1}{2} \right)^6 \left(\frac{1}{2} \right)^0 = \left(\frac{1}{2} \right)^6 = \frac{1}{64}.$

✓ • **PROBLEM 2-33**

> Suppose that the probability of parents having a child with blond hair is $1/4$. If there are four children in the family, what is the probability that exactly half of them have blond hair?

SOLUTION:

We assume that the probability of parents having a blond child is $1/4$. In order to compute the probability that two of four children have blond hair, we must make another assumption. We must assume that the event consisting of a child being blond when it is born is independent of whether any of the other children are blond. The genetic determination of each child's hair color can be considered one of four independent trials with the probably of success, observing a blond child, equal to $1/4$.

If X is the number of children in the family with blond hair, we are interested in finding $P(X = 2)$. By our assumptions X is binomially distributed with $n = 4$ (total number of children) and $p = 1/4$.

Thus $P(X = 2) = P(\text{exactly half the children are blond})$

$$= \binom{4}{2}\left(\frac{1}{4}\right)^2\left(\frac{3}{4}\right)^2 = \frac{4!}{2!\,2!}\left(\frac{1}{4}\right)^2\left(\frac{3}{4}\right)^2$$

$$= \frac{4 \times 3}{2 \times 1}\left(\frac{1}{16}\right)\left(\frac{9}{16}\right) = \frac{27}{128} = 0.21$$

✓ • **PROBLEM 2-34**

> If a fair coin is tossed four times, what is the probability of obtaining at least two heads?

SOLUTION:

Let $X =$ the number of heads observed in four tosses of a fair coin. Then X is binomially distributed if we assume that each toss is independent. If the coin is fair, then $p = P$(a head is observed on a single toss) $= {}^1\!/_2$.

Thus, P(at least two heads in four tosses) $= P(X \geq 2)$

$$= \sum_{x=2}^{4} \binom{4}{x} \left(\frac{1}{2}\right)^x \left(\frac{1}{2}\right)^{4-x}$$

$$= \binom{4}{2}\left(\frac{1}{2}\right)^2\left(\frac{1}{2}\right)^2 + \binom{4}{3}\left(\frac{1}{2}\right)^3\left(\frac{1}{2}\right) + \binom{4}{4}\left(\frac{1}{2}\right)^4\left(\frac{1}{2}\right)^0$$

$$= \binom{4}{4}\left(\frac{1}{2}\right)^4\left(\frac{1}{2}\right)$$

✓ • **PROBLEM 2–35**

A baseball player has a 0.250 batting average (one base hit every four times, on the average). Assuming that the binomial distribution is applicable, if he is at bat four times on a particular day, what is (a) the probability that he will get exactly one hit? (b) the probability that he will get at least one hit?

SOLUTION:

Considering a hit as a success, we have P(success) $= {}^1\!/_4$,

(a) P(exactly one hit in four trials) $= \binom{4}{1}\left(\frac{1}{4}\right)^1\left(\frac{3}{4}\right)^3$

$$= 4\left(\frac{1}{4}\right)\left(\frac{27}{64}\right) = \frac{27}{64}$$

(b) P(one hit or two hits or three hits or four hits) since these are mutually exclusive events,

$$= 4\left(\frac{1}{4}\right)^1\left(\frac{3}{4}\right)^3 + \binom{4}{2}\left(\frac{1}{4}\right)^2\left(\frac{3}{4}\right)^2 + \binom{4}{3}\left(\frac{1}{4}\right)^3\left(\frac{3}{4}\right) + \binom{4}{4}\left(\frac{1}{4}\right)^4\left(\frac{3}{4}\right)^0$$

$$= \frac{27}{64} + 6 \times \frac{1}{16} \times \frac{9}{16} + 4 \times \frac{1}{16} \times \frac{3}{4} + 1 \times \frac{1}{256} \times 1$$

$$= \frac{27}{64} + \frac{27}{128} + \frac{3}{64} + \frac{1}{256} = \frac{30}{64} + \frac{27}{128} + \frac{1}{256} = \frac{175}{256}$$

There is a simpler way if we notice that the batter getting at least one hit and the batter going hitless are two mutually exclusive and exhaustive events. Because of this fact we know that

$$P(\text{one hit}) + P(\text{two hits}) + P(\text{three hits}) + P(\text{four hits}) +$$

$$P(\text{zero hits}) = 1,$$

so $\quad P(\text{at least one hit}) + P(\text{zero hits}) = 1$

or $\quad P(\text{at least one hit}) = 1 - P(\text{zero hits}).$

But $\quad P(\text{zero hits}) = \binom{4}{0}\left(\frac{1}{4}\right)^0\left(\frac{3}{4}\right)^4 = 1 \times 1 \times \frac{81}{256}$

and $\quad P(\text{at least one hit}) = 1 - \frac{81}{256} = \frac{175}{256}.$

 **• PROBLEM 2-36**

Records of an insurance company show that $\dfrac{3}{1,000}$ of the accidents reported to the company involve a fatality. Determine:

(a) the probability that no fatality is involved in 30 accidents reported.

(b) the probability that four fatal accidents are included in 20 accidents reported.

SOLUTION:

Let X be the number of fatalities involved in n accidents. Then X may be assumed to be binomially distributed with parameters n and

$$\pi = \frac{3}{1,000}.$$

This assumption will be a valid one if the number of fatalities observed can be considered the sum of the results of n independent trials. On each trial (or accident) a fatality will occur with the probability

$$\frac{3}{1,000}.$$

(a) The probability that there are no fatalities in 30 accidents is $P(X = 0)$ with $n = 30$ accidents reported and

$$\pi = \frac{3}{1,000}$$

involved a fatality. Now

$$P(X = 0) = \binom{30}{0}\left(\frac{3}{1,000}\right)^0\left(\frac{997}{1,000}\right)^{30}$$

$$= (1)\,(1)\,(0.997)^{30} = 0.9138$$

(b) The probability that there are four fatalities in 20 accidents is $P(X = 4)$ with $n = 20$.

$$P(X = 4) = \binom{20}{4}\left(\frac{3}{1,000}\right)^4\left(\frac{997}{1,000}\right)^{16}$$

$$= 0.374 \times 10^{-6}$$

√• PROBLEM 2-37

Over a long period of time a certain drug has been effective in 30 percent of the cases in which it has been prescribed. If a doctor is now administering this drug to four patients, what is the probability that it will be effective for at least three of the patients?

SOLUTION:

Let X be the number of patients on which the drug is effective. Then X is binomially distributed. There are assumed to be four independent trials, the administration of the drug to the four patients. The probability of success in a particular trial is the probability that the drug is effective on a patient and P (drug is effective on a patient) $= p = 0.30$. The probability that the drug is effective on at least three patients is the probability that X is equal to three or four. Since these two events are mutually exclusive, $P(X = 3$ or $X = 4) = P(X = 3) + P(X = 4)$ by the addition rule. Now X is distributed binomially with parameters 4 and 0.3. Thus,

$$P(X = 3) = \binom{4}{3}(0.3)^3 (0.7)^1 = 4 \ (0.027) \ (0.7) = 0.0756$$

$$P(X = 4) = \binom{4}{4}(0.3)^4 (0.7)^0 = 1 \cdot (0.0081) = 0.0081$$

and $P(X = 3$ or $X = 4) = 0.0756 + 0.0081 = 0.0837$.

This means that 8.37% of the time this drug will be effective on at least three patients.

 • **PROBLEM 2–38**

You are told that nine out of ten doctors recommend Potter's Pills. Assuming this is true, suppose you plan to choose four doctors at random. What is the probability that no more than two of these four doctors will recommend Potter's Pills?

SOLUTION:

Let X be the number of doctors among the four chosen that will recommend Potter's Pills. If each doctor is selected at random and the probability of selecting a doctor that recommends Potter's Pills is 0.9, then X is a binomially distributed random variable with parameters $n = 4$ and $p = 0.9$.

In order to make this assumption we needed to know that each trial on which a doctor was selected was independent of any other trial. This is guaranteed by our selection of doctors at random and the fact that we may treat the population as infinite for all practical purposes.

We wish to find P(no more than two of these four doctors will recommend Potter's Pills). This equals $P(X = 0, 1,$ or $2)$. Each of these outcomes is mutually exclusive, so

$$P(X = 0, 1, \text{ or } 2) = P(X = 0) + P(X = 1) + P(X = 2)$$

$$= \binom{4}{0}(0.9)^0 (0.1)^4 + \binom{4}{1}(0.9)^1 (0.1)^3 + \binom{4}{2}(0.9)^2 (0.1)^2$$

$$= (0.1)^4 + 4 (0.9) (0.1)^3 + \frac{4 \times 3 \times 2 \times 1}{2 \times 1 \times 2 \times 1}(0.9)^2 (0.1)^2$$

$$= (0.1)^4 + (3.6) (0.1)^3 + 6 (0.9)^2 (0.1)^2$$

$$= (1 \times 10^{-1})^4 + (3.6) (1 \times 10^{-1})^3 + 6 (0.81) (1 \times 10^{-1})^2$$

$$= 1 \times 10^{-4} + 36 \times 10^{-4} + 486 \times 10^{-4}$$

$$= 523 \times 10^{-4} = 0.0523$$

✓ • **PROBLEM 2-39**

The most common application of the binomial theorem in industrial work is in lot-by-lot acceptance inspection. If there are a certain number of defectives in the lot, the lot will be rejected as unsatisfactory.

It is natural to wish to find the probability that the lot is acceptable even though a certain number of defectives are observed. Let p be the fraction of defectives in the lot. Assume that the size of the sample is small compared to the lot size. This will insure that the probability of selecting a defective item remains relatively constant from trial to trial. Now choose a sample of size 18 from a lot in which 10 percent of the items are defective. What is the probability of observing zero, one, or two defectives in the sample?

SOLUTION:

Imagine that the items are drawn successively from the lot until 18 have been chosen. The probability of selecting a defective item is $p = 0.10$, the fraction of defectives in the lot. Hence, the probability of selecting a non-defective item is $1 - 0.10 = 0.90$. If X is the number of defective items observed, X is the sum of the number of defective items observed on 18 independent trials and is hence binomially distributed with parameters $n = 18$ and $p = 0.10$.

We wish to determine $P(X = 0, 1, \text{ or } 2)$. This probability is the sum of the probabilities of three mutually exclusive events. Hence $P(X = 0, 1, \text{ or } 2) = P(X = 0) + P(X = 1) + P = 2)$.

Now X is binomially distributed so

$$P(X = 0) = (0.10)^0 + (0.90)^{18} = 0.150$$

$$P(X = 1) = (0.10)^1 + (0.90)^{17} = 0.300$$

$$P(X = 2) = (0.10)^2 + (0.90)^{16} = 0.284$$

and $\quad P(X = 0, 1, \text{ or } 2) = 0.150 + 0.300 + 0.284 = 0.734$.

✓ • PROBLEM 2-40

Over a period of some years, a car manufacturing firm finds that 18 percent of their cars develop body squeaks within the guarantee period. In a randomly selected shipment, 20 cars reach the end of the guarantee period and none develop squeaks. What is the probability of this?

SOLUTION:

The car can either squeak or not squeak. The probability of a car squeaking is 18 percent or 0.18. The probability of not squeaking is $q = 1 - p = 1 - 0.18 = 0.82$. The situation we have here is a dichotomy of the type that fits the binomial distribution. There are independent trials with two possible outcomes each with a constant probability.

According to the binomial distribution,

$$P(X = k) = \binom{n}{k} p^k (1-p)^{n-k}.$$

Here, $p = 0.18$, $1 - p = 0.82$, $n = 20$, and $k = 0$. Hence,

$$P(X = 0) = (0.18)^0 (0.82)^{20} = \frac{20!}{20! \times 0!} (0.18)^0 (0.82)^{20}$$

$$= (0.82)^{20} = 0.019$$

$\sqrt{}$ • **PROBLEM 2–41**

An industrial process produces items of which 1 percent are defective. If a random sample of 100 of these are drawn from a large consignment, calculate the probability that the sample contains no defectives.

SOLUTION:

If X is the number of defectives in a sample of 100, then X is distributed binomially with parameters $n = 100$ and $p = 1\%$ or 0.01. Thus,

$$P(X = 0) = P(\text{no defectives in sample})$$

$$= \binom{100}{0} (0.01)^0 (1 - 0.01)^{100}$$

$$= (0.99)^{100} = 0.366$$

$\checkmark$ • **PROBLEM 2-42**

A proportion p of a large number of items in a batch is defective. A sample of n items is drawn and if it contains no defective items, the batch is accepted, while if it contains more than two defective items the batch is rejected. If, on the other hand, it contains one or two defectives, an independent sample of m is drawn, and if the combined number of defectives in the samples does not exceed two, the batch is accepted. Calculate the probability of accepting this batch.

SOLUTION:

The batch will be accepted only if:

(1) the first sample contains no defectives, or

(2) the first sample contains one defective and the second sample contains zero or one defective, or

(3) the first sample contains two defectives and the second sample contains zero defectives.

These three probabilities are mutually exclusive. If one occurs then none of the others can occur. Thus, if we compute the probability of each of these events, the sum of the three will be the probability of acceptance.

Let: X = the number of defectives in the first sample.

Y = the number of defectives in the second sample.

If the sampling is done with replacement, then X will be binomially distributed with the parameter n equal to the number of trials (or size of sample) and p equal to the probability of selecting a defective on one trial. Similarly, Y is binomially distributed with parameters m and p.

Again by the addition law, $P(\text{acceptance}) = P(0 \text{ defectives in first batch}) + P(\text{one in first and zero or one in second}) + P(\text{two in first and zero in second}) = P(X = 0) + P(X = 1, Y = 0 \text{ or } 1) + P(X = 2, Y = 0)$.

Now $P(X = 0) = \binom{n}{0} p^0 (1 - p)^{n - 0}$, and

$$P(X = 1, Y = 0 \text{ or } 1) = P(X = 1, Y = 0) + P(X = 1, Y = 1)$$

by the addition rule, since we are dealing with mutually exclusive events. Thus, $P(X = 1, Y = 0) = P(X = 1) \times P(Y = 0)$ by the multiplication law. Hence,

$$P(X = 1, Y = 0) = \binom{n}{1} p^1 (1 - p)^{n-1} \times \binom{m}{0} p^0 (1 - p)^m.$$

Similarly, $P(X = 1, Y = 1) = P(X = 1) \times P(Y = 1)$

$$= \binom{n}{1} p^1 (1 - p)^{n-1} \times \binom{m}{1} p^1 (1 - p)^{m-1}.$$

For similar reasons, $P(X = 2, Y = 0) = P(X = 2) P(Y = 0)$.

$$P(Y = 0) = \binom{n}{2} p^2 (1 - p)^{n-2} \times \binom{m}{0} p^0 (1 - p)^m.$$

Hence, $P(\text{acceptance})$

$$= \binom{n}{0} p^0 (1 - p)^{n-0} + \binom{n}{1} p^1 (1 - p)^{n-1} \binom{m}{0} p^0 (1 - p)^m +$$

$$\binom{n}{1} p^1 (1 - p)^{n-1} \binom{m}{1} p^1 (1 - p)^{m-1} +$$

$$\binom{n}{2} p^2 (1 - p)^{n-2} \binom{m}{0} p^0 (1 - p)^m$$

$$= (1 - p)^n + np (1 - p)^{m+n-1} + nmp^2 (1 - p)^{m+n-2}$$

$$+ \frac{1}{2} n (n - 1) p^2 (1 - p)^{m-n-2}.$$

Letting $1 - p = q$, we can write this more concisely as

$$P(\text{acceptance}) = q^n + npq^{m-1} + mnp^2 q^{m-2} + \frac{1}{2} n (n - 1) p^2 q^{m-2}.$$

The probability of hitting a target on a shot is $^2/_3$. Let X denote the number of times a person hits the target in eight shots. Find:

(a) $P(X = 3)$

(b) $P(1 < X \le 6)$

(c) $P(X > 3)$

SOLUTION:

If we assume that each shot is independent of any other shot, then X is a binomially distributed random variable with parameters $n = 8$ and $p = ^2/_3$.

Thus, $\quad P(X = 3) = \binom{8}{3}\left(\frac{2}{3}\right)^3\left(\frac{1}{3}\right)^{8-3} = \frac{8!}{3! \times 5!}\left(\frac{2}{3}\right)^3\left(\frac{1}{3}\right)^5$

$$= \frac{8 \times 7 \times 6}{3 \times 2 \times 1}\left(\frac{8}{27}\right)\left(\frac{1}{243}\right) = \frac{448}{6,561} = 0.06828, \text{ and}$$

$P(1 < X \le 6) = P(X = 2, 3, 4, 5, \text{ or } 6)$.

These events are mutually exclusive and thus

$$P(X = 2, 3, 4, 5, \text{ or } 6) = P(X = 2) + P(X = 3) + P(X = 4) + P(X = 5) + P(X = 6)$$

$$= \sum_{n=2}^{6} P(X = n)$$

$$= \sum_{n=2}^{6} \binom{8}{n}\left(\frac{2}{3}\right)^n\left(\frac{1}{3}\right)^{8-n}$$

Using tables of cumulative probabilities and the fact that

$$P(1 < X \le 6) = P(X \le 6) - P(X \le 1),$$

or calculating single probabilities and adding, we see that

$$P(1 < X \le 6) = 0.8023.$$

Finally, $P(X > 3) = P(X = 4, 5, 6, 7, \text{ or } 8)$

$$= P(X = 4) + P(X = 5) + P(X = 6) + P(X = 7) + P(X = 8)$$

$$= \sum_{n=4}^{8} P(X = n)$$

$$= \sum_{n=4}^{8} P\binom{8}{n}\left(\frac{2}{3}\right)^n \left(\frac{1}{3}\right)^{8-n}$$

Again, using a table of cumulative probabilities or calculating each single probability, we see that $P(X > 3) = 0.912$.

$$\ast\ast\ast\ast\ast\ast$$

REVIEW OF MULTINOMIAL RANDOM VARIABLES

The multinomial distribution is more general than the binomial in that it allows for more than two outcomes. This fact is evident from the prefix: "bi" indicates two, while "multi" indicates more than two. This prefix refers to the number of possible outcomes in a given trial.

An example of a trinomial distribution is the number of points awarded in a soccer game. In the first round of the 1994 World Cup, three points were awarded for a win, one point was awarded for a tie, and no points were awarded for a loss. Here, there are three possible outcomes, so the binomial model would not be appropriate.

Of course, the multinomial distribution can accommodate random variables which may take on more than three outcomes as well. To be a random variable, each possible outcome must be numerically valued. Thus, if we define a variable to take the values "win," "lose," or "tie" as the outcome of a soccer game, then this variable is not a random variable. We would first need to code these outcomes into numerical values. The number of points awarded is one such method of coding.

Other examples of multinomial random variables are the responses people make when asked their favorite color (if the outcomes are coded into numerical values), the winning candidate in an election with more than two candidates (if the outcomes are coded into numerical values), and the number facing up when a pair of dice is tossed. What makes the multinomial distribution interesting is that, like the binomial distribution, it can accommodate more than one trial. Thus, we may treat repeated tosses of pairs of dice as a multinomial random variable.

You may recall that the Bernoulli random variable was characterized by a single parameter. This was the success probability of the one trial. The binomial random variable was characterized by a pair of parameters. These were n, the number of trials, and p, the success probability on each trial. The multinomial random variable is characterized by k parameters, where k is the number of possible outcomes of any trial. These parameters are $p(i)$, the probability of the ith outcome, $i = 1, 2, ..., k - 1$, and n, the number of trials. We need not specify $p(k)$ because we know that

$$p(1) + p(2) + ... + p(k) = 1,$$

so $p(k) = 1 - p(1) - p(2) - ... - p(k - 1)$

is determined by the specification of the other probabilities.

A typical problem in the study of multinomial random variables involves calculating the probability of a given configuration. For example, suppose that a single die is tossed three times. What is the probability of obtaining one four and two threes? To solve this, we recognize that there are three tosses, and hence three trials, so $n = 3$. Each of the six outcomes in the toss of a single die is equally likely, so $p(i) = \frac{1}{6}$ for $i = 1, 2, 3, 4, 5, 6$. We have now characterized the multinomial distribution relevant to this problem. Now we proceed by enumerating all possibilities. These are too numerous to list (there are $6^3 = 216$ such possibilities), but we may speak of them by allowing the first toss to take any of the six possible values, likewise for the second, and likewise for the third. We must list all possibilities which are favorable to the event we wish to study, namely one four and two threes. These possibilities are {433, 343, 334}. There are three such possibilities, so the remaining task is to find the probability of each. Since these are mutually exclusive events, we may add these probabilities to find the probability of one four and two threes.

Notice that the 216 outcomes, in general, are not equally likely. If they were, then we would have been able to stop here and declare the probability equal to $^3/_{216}$. This will turn out to be the solution in this problem, and the 216 outcomes are equally likely in this problem, but that is only because each outcome on a given trial is equally likely.

Consider the outcome {433}. The probability of obtaining a four on the first toss is $^1/_6$. The probability of obtaining a three on the second toss is also $^1/_6$. The probability of obtaining a three on the third toss is also $^1/_6$. The three tosses are assumed to be independent, so we may multiply these probabilities. We obtain $^1/_{216}$ as the probability of {433}. We may likewise calculate the probability of {343} and {334} as $^1/_{216}$ each. Adding these probabilities gives the probability of one four and two threes as $^3/_{216}$.

Even though we did not enumerate all possible outcomes, we did enumerate those outcomes which were favorable to the event we were studying. In this example, there were only three favorable outcomes. In other problems, there may be significantly more favorable outcomes, and in these cases enumeration is quite inefficient. It will turn out that these favorable outcomes are all permutations of each other. In the previous example, the favorable outcomes were {433, 343, 334}, which are all seen to be permutations of each other. It will turn out that order does not matter, so the probability is the same for all of these permutations. What we need is a method for counting the number of such permutations and a method for finding the probability of any of them.

Having read the section on counting in Chapter 1, it should be clear that the number of outcomes which are favorable to a given event is the number of permutations of the items specified in the definition of a favorable event. In the case of the earlier example, the number of outcomes which were favorable to the event of one four and two threes was the number of permutations of one four and two threes. Since there are three locations for the four (i.e., in the first toss, the second toss, or the third toss), there are three such permutations, or three outcomes favorable to the event in question. In general, the number of permutations of n items when $n(1)$ are of a given type, $n(2)$ of another type, and so on up to $n(k)$ of the kth type is

$$\frac{n!}{[n(1)!\, n(2)!\, \ldots\, n(k)!]},$$

where $n(1) + n(2) + \ldots + n(k) = n$. To check the validity of this formula in the case we just studied, notice that $k = 2$ (we are only interested in two types of items, fours and threes), $n(1) = 1$ (one four), and $n(2) = 2$ (two threes). Also, $n = 3$ (three tosses). The formula yields

$$\frac{n!}{[n(1)!\,n(2)!]} = \frac{3!}{[(1!)\,(2!)]}$$

$$= \frac{6}{[(1)\,(2)]}$$

$$= \frac{6}{2}$$

$$= 3,$$

which agrees with our answer. Also, notice that when $k = 2$, this formula reduces to

$$\frac{n!}{[n(1)!\,n(2)!]}$$

but $\quad n(1) + n(2) = n,$

so $\quad n(2) = n - n(1).$

If we rewrite the formula, we obtain

$$\frac{n!}{\{n(1)!\,[n - n(1)!]\}} = C(n,\,n(1)),$$

which is in agreement with the binomial formula.

As a more complicated example, consider ten tosses of a pair of dice. What is the expected number of sevens? What is the probability of three fours, three sixes, three sevens, and one eight?

The probability of rolling a seven on any one toss was previously seen to be $\frac{1}{6}$. We may define a binomial random variable by declaring a seven to be a success and everything else to be a failure. If we call this binomial random variable X, then

$$E[X] = np$$

$$= (10)\left(\frac{1}{6}\right)$$

$$= \frac{10}{6}$$

$$= 1.667$$

The probability of three fours, three sixes, three sevens, and one eight is found by using the multinomial formula. There are

$$\frac{10!}{[3!\,3!\,3!\,1!]}$$

permutations with three fours, three sixes, three sevens, and one eight. The probability of each such outcome is

$$\left(\frac{1}{6}\right)^3 \left(\frac{1}{6}\right)^3 \left(\frac{1}{6}\right)^3 \left(\frac{1}{6}\right)^1 = \left(\frac{1}{6}\right)^{10}$$

Therefore, the probability of this event is given by

$$P\{\text{three fours, three sixes, three sevens, and one eight}\}$$

$$= \frac{10!}{[3!\,3!\,3!\,1!]}\left(\frac{1}{6}\right)^{10}.$$

The expected value, probability mass function, and cumulative distribution function of a multinomial random variable are not very useful concepts, because there is no one numerical outcome. The outcome consists of various counts. A binomial random variable takes on a single value (the number of successes). A multinomial random variable is technically not a random variable by the definition provided earlier, but it is a random variable if we allow for vector-valued outcomes. That is, the outcome consists of a vector of counts. In the previous example, the vector would have been

$$(0, 0, 3, 0, 3, 3, 1, 0, 0, 0, 0),$$

corresponding to no twos, no threes, three fours, etc.

A fair die is tossed five times. What is the expected number of threes? What is the probability of obtaining two twos and three threes?

SOLUTION:

We may define a binomial random variable by treating a three as a success and everything else as a failure. Then, letting this random variable be denoted by X,

$$E[X] = np$$

$$= (5) \left(\frac{1}{6} \right)$$

$$= \frac{5}{6},$$

since there are five trials (tosses) and the probability of a three on any one toss is $\frac{1}{6}$.

The probability of two twos and three threes is found by applying the multinomial formula. In particular, we would require no ones, two twos, three threes, no fours, no fives, and no sixes. The event we want can be succinctly described as the vector-valued outcome

$$(0, 2, 3, 0, 0, 0),$$

and $P\{0, 2, 3, 0, 0, 0\}$

$$= \frac{5!}{[0!\,2!\,3!\,0!\,0!\,0!]} \left(\frac{1}{6} \right)^0 \left(\frac{1}{6} \right)^2 \left(\frac{1}{6} \right)^3 \left(\frac{1}{6} \right)^0 \left(\frac{1}{6} \right)^0 \left(\frac{1}{6} \right)^0$$

$$= 10 \left(\frac{1}{6} \right)^5$$

$$= 0.0013$$

 **• PROBLEM 2-45**

A fair die is tossed four times. What is the expected number of ones? What is the probability of obtaining one one, two twos, and one six?

SOLUTION:

We may define a binomial random variable by treating a one as a success and everything else as a failure. Then, letting this random variable be denoted by X,

$$E[X] = np$$

$$= (4) \left(\frac{1}{6}\right)$$

$$= \frac{4}{6}$$

$$= \frac{2}{3},$$

since there are four trials (tosses) and the probability of a one on any one toss is $\frac{1}{6}$.

The probability of one one, two twos, and one six is found by applying the multinomial formula. In particular, we would require one one, two twos, no threes, no fours, no fives, and one six. The event we want can be succinctly described as the vector-valued outcome

$$(1, 2, 0, 0, 0, 1),$$

and $\quad P\{1, 2, 0, 0, 0, 1\}$

$$= \frac{4!}{[1! \, 2! \, 0! \, 0! \, 0! \, 1!]} \left(\frac{1}{6}\right)^1 \left(\frac{1}{6}\right)^2 \left(\frac{1}{6}\right)^0 \left(\frac{1}{6}\right)^0 \left(\frac{1}{6}\right)^0 \left(\frac{1}{6}\right)^1$$

$$= 12 \left(\frac{1}{6}\right)^4$$

$$= 0.0093$$

✓ • **PROBLEM 2–46**

An urn contains four blue balls, three red balls, two yellow balls, and one green ball. Six balls are picked without replacement. Is the multi-nomial model applicable to this situation? Why or why not?

SOLUTION:

Since the balls are being selected without replacement, the number of balls of each color will change as the experiment unfolds. For example, if a blue ball is picked first, then the second selection will have only three blue balls, and not the four that were originally in the urn. This will serve to change the probability of each outcome, in violation of the multinomial model. Thus, the multinomial model would not be applicable. *when without replacement*

✓ • **PROBLEM 2–47**

If the situation from Problem 2–46 is modified so that selection is with replacement, then is the multinomial model applicable?

SOLUTION:

Since we are now replacing the ball that was selected, each selection is made from the same configuration of balls in the urn, so the probabilities are constant across selections. Also, we may assume that each selection is independent of every other selection. Thus, the multinomial model is now applicable.

with replacement

✓ • **PROBLEM 2–48**

What are the parameters of the multinomial random variable for Problem 2–47?

SOLUTION:

There are six selections, so $n = 6$. There are ten balls in the urn, of which four are blue, so

$$p1 = \frac{4}{10} = 0.4.$$

There are three red balls, so

$$p2 = \frac{3}{10} = 0.3.$$

There are two yellow balls, so

$$p3 = \frac{2}{10} = 0.2.$$

Finally,

$$p4 = 1 - p1 - p2 - p3 = 1 - 0.4 - 0.3 - 0.2 = 0.1.$$

✓ • **PROBLEM 2-49**

Referring to Problem 2–47, what is the expected number of blue balls selected? What is the expected number of red balls selected? What is the expected number of green balls selected? What is the expected number of yellow balls selected?

SOLUTION:

We may define four binomial random variables by treating, successively, a blue ball as a success and everything else as a failure, a red ball as a success and everything else as a failure, a yellow ball as a success and everything else as a failure, and finally a green ball as a success and everything else as a failure. Letting these random variables be denoted by $X1$, $X2$, $X3$, and $X4$, respectively,

$$E[X1] = np1$$

$$= (6)\,(0.4)$$

$$= 2.4$$

$$E[X2] = np2$$

$$= (6)\,(0.3)$$

$$= 1.8$$

$$E[X3] = np3$$

$$= (6)\,(0.2)$$

$$= 1.2$$

$$E[X4] = np4$$

$$= (6)\,(0.1)$$

$$= 0.6$$

✓ • **PROBLEM 2-50**

Referring back to Problem 2–47, what is the probability of selecting two blue balls, two red balls, one yellow ball, and one green ball?

SOLUTION:

The probability of two blue balls, two red balls, one yellow ball, and one green ball is found by applying the multinomial formula. The event we want can be succinctly described as the vector-valued outcome

$$(2, 2, 1, 1),$$

and $\quad P\{2, 2, 1, 1\} = 6!/[2!2!1!1!](4/10)^2(3/10)^2(2/10)^1(1/10)^1$

$$= (6!/4)\,(4^2)\,(3^2)\,(2^1)\,(1^1)/10^{(2+2+1+1)}$$

$$= (180)\,(16)\,(9)\,(2)/10^6$$

$$= 0.05184.$$

√ • **PROBLEM 2-51**

A given intersection in a small city allows for three possibilities. Drivers may continue straight, turn left, or turn right. The probabilities of these events are 0.5, 0.2, and 0.3, respectively. A researcher observes ten drivers at this intersection. What is the expected number of drivers who turn? What is the probability of seeing five drivers continue straight, two turn left, and three turn right?

SOLUTION:

We may define a binomial random variable by treating a driver who turns as a success and a driver who continues straight as a failure. Then, letting this random variable be denoted by X,

$$E[X] = np$$

$$= (10)\,(0.2 + 0.3)$$

$$= (10)\,(0.5)$$

$$= 5$$

The probability of five drivers continuing straight, two turning left, and three turning right is found by applying the multinomial formula. The event we want can be succinctly described as the vector-valued outcome

$$(5, 2, 3),$$

and $\quad P\{5, 2, 3\} = 10!/[5!2!3!](5/10)^5(2/10)^2(3/10)^3$

$$= (2{,}520)\,(5^5)\,(2^2)\,(3^3)/10^{(5\,+\,2\,+\,3)}$$

$$= (2{,}520)\,(5^5)\,(2^2)\,(3^3)/10^{(10)}$$

$$= (2{,}520)\,(5^5)\,(2^2)\,(3^3)/[(5^{10})\,(2^{10})]$$

$$= (2{,}520)\,(3^3)/[(5^5)\,(2^8)]$$

$$= (2{,}520)\,(27)/[(3125)\,(256)]$$

$$= 68{,}040/800{,}000$$

$$= 0.0851$$

A pair of coins is tossed three times. If the probability of heads for each coin is 0.50, then what is the expected number of trials on which both coins are heads? What is the probability that one trial results in no heads, one trial in one heads, and one trial in two heads? What if the probability of heads of the two coins is each 0.70? What if the probability that one of the coins lands heads is 0.50 and the probability that the other coin lands heads is 0.70?

SOLUTION:

We may define a binomial random variable by treating a trial in which both coins land heads as a success and a trial with either one head or no heads as a failure. Then, letting this random variable be denoted by X,

$$E[X] = np.$$

We need to find p, the probability of two heads in a given trial. Using the binomial formula with $n = 2$ (two coins) and $p = 0.50$ (probability of heads for either coin),

$$P\{\text{two heads}\} = P\{HH\}$$

$$= C(2, 2) (0.5)^2(1 - 0.5)^{2-2}$$

$$= (1) (0.25) (1)$$

$$= 0.25$$

Now, $E[X] = np$

$$= (3) (0.25)$$

$$= 0.75$$

Therefore, we expect 0.75 trials out of the three to result in both coins landing heads.

To find the probability of one trial resulting in no heads, one trial resulting in one heads, and one trial resulting in two heads, we need to find the probability of each of these possible outcomes in a given trial. We already found $P\{HH\} = 0.25$. Now,

$$P\{\text{no heads}\} = P\{TT\}$$

$$= C(2, 0) (0.5)^0(1 - 0.5)^{2-0}$$

$$= (1) (1) (0.25)$$

$$= 0.25$$

and $P\{\text{one head}\} = C(2, 1) (0.5)^1 (1 - 0.5)^{2-1}$

$$= (2) (0.5) (0.5)$$

$$= 0.5$$

Then the probability of one trial resulting in no heads, one trial resulting in one heads, and one trial resulting in two heads is

$$P\{1, 1, 1\} = 3!/[1!1!1!](0.25)^1(0.50)^1(0.25)^1$$

$$= (6) (0.25) (0.50) (0.25)$$

$$= \frac{6}{32}$$

$$= \frac{3}{16}.$$

If the probability of heads for each coin is changed from 0.50 to 0.70, then using the binomial formula with $n = 2$ (two coins) and $p = 0.70$ (probability of heads for either coin),

$$P\{\text{two heads}\} = P\{HH\}$$

$$= C(2, 2) (0.7)^2(1 - 0.7)^{2-2}$$

$$= (1) (0.49) (1)$$

$$= 0.49.$$

Now, $E[X] = np$

$$= (3) (0.49)$$

$$= 1.47.$$

Therefore, we expect 1.47 trials out of the three to result in both coins landing heads.

To find the probability of one trial resulting in no heads, one trial resulting in one heads, and one trial resulting in two heads, we need to find the probability of each of these possible outcomes in a given trial. We already found $P\{HH\} = 0.49$. Now,

$$P\{\text{no heads}\} = P\{TT\}$$

$$= C(2\,,0)\,(0.7)^0(1-0.7)^{2-0}$$

$$= (1)\,(1)\,(0.09)$$

$$= 0.09$$

and $P\{\text{one head}\} = C(2,1)\,(0.7)^1\,(1-0.7)^{2-1}$

$$= (2)\,(0.7)\,(0.3)$$

$$= 0.42$$

Then the probability of one trial resulting in no heads, one trial resulting in one heads, and one trial resulting in two heads is

$$P\{1,\,1,\,1\} = 3!/[1!1!1!](0.49)^1(0.42)^1(0.09)^1$$

$$= (6)\,(0.49)\,(0.42)\,(0.09)$$

$$= 0.1111$$

If the probability of heads for one coin is 0.50 and the probability of heads for the other coin is 0.70, then the binomial formula would not apply, because the success probability (the probability of heads) would change across coins. Nevertheless, we can compute the probabilities of each outcome as

$$P\{\text{two heads}\} = P\{HH\}$$

$$= (0.5)\,(0.7)$$

$$= 0.35;$$

$$P\{\text{one head}\} = P\{HT \cup TH\}$$

$$= P\{HT\} + P\{TH\}$$

$$= (0.5)\,(1-0.7) + (1-0.5)\,(0.7)$$

$$= (0.5)\,(0.3) + (0.5)\,(0.7)$$

$$= 0.15 + 0.35$$

$$= 0.50$$

and $P\{\text{no heads}\} = P\{TT\}$

$$= (1-0.5)\,(1-0.7)$$

$$= (0.5)\,(0.3)$$

$$= 0.15$$

Now, $E[X] = np$

$$= (3) (0.35)$$

$$= 1.05.$$

Therefore, we expect 1.05 trials out of the three to result in both coins landing heads.

The probability of one trial resulting in no heads, one trial resulting in one heads, and one trial resulting in two heads is

$$P\{1, 1, 1\} = 3!/[1!1!1!](0.35)^1(0.50)^1(0.15)^1$$

$$= (6) (0.35) (0.50) (0.15)$$

$$= 0.1575$$

✓ • **PROBLEM 2–53**

Suppose a die has been loaded so that the [•] face lands uppermost three times as often as any other face while all the other faces occur equally often. What is the probability of a [••] on a single toss? What is the probability of a [•] ?

SOLUTION:

Let p equal the probability of the [•] face landing uppermost. We know that $P([•]) = 3P$(any other face). We also know that faces with j dots, $j = 2, 3, 4, 5, 6$, occur equally often. Thus,

$$\sum_{j=1}^{6} P(j \text{ dots}) = 1,$$

and $P(\text{one dot}) + \sum_{j=2}^{6} P(j \text{ dots}) = 1$

or $p + 5\left(\dfrac{1}{3}P\right) = 1.$

Thus, $p = \dfrac{3}{8}$ and p (2 dots) $= \dfrac{1}{3}$ $P = \dfrac{1}{8}$.

The probability of a $\boxed{\,\bullet\,}$ is $\dfrac{3}{8}$.

• PROBLEM 2–54

If a pair of dice is tossed twice, find the probability of obtaining a sum total of five on both tosses.

SOLUTION:

The ways to obtain five in one toss of the two dice are:

(1, 4), (4, 1), (3, 2), and (2, 3).

Hence, we can throw five in one toss in four ways. Each die has six faces and there are six ways for a die to fall. Then the pair of dice can fall in $6 \times 6 = 36$ ways. The probability of throwing five in one toss is:

$$\frac{\text{number of ways to throw a five in one toss}}{\text{number of ways that a pair of dice can fall}} = \frac{4}{36} = \frac{1}{9}.$$

Now the probability of throwing a five on both tosses is:

P(throwing five on first toss and throwing five on second toss).

"And" implies multiplication if events are independent, thus

P(throwing five on first toss and throwing five on second toss)

$= P$(throwing five on first toss) $\times P$(throwing five on second toss),

since the results of the two tosses are independent. Consequently, the probability of obtaining five on both tosses is

$$\left(\frac{1}{9}\right)\left(\frac{1}{9}\right) = \frac{1}{81}.$$

• **PROBLEM 2-55**

A bag contains three white, two black, and four red balls. Four balls are drawn at random with replacement. Calculate the probabilities that

(a) The sample contains just one white ball.

(b) The sample contains just one white ball given that it contains just one red ball.

SOLUTION:

Since there are nine balls and we are sampling with replacement and choosing the balls at random on each draw

$$P(\text{white ball}) = \frac{3}{9} = \frac{1}{3},$$

$$P(\text{black ball}) = \frac{2}{9},$$

$$P(\text{red ball}) = \frac{4}{9}.$$

(a) On each draw, $P(\text{white}) + P(\text{black or red}) = 1$. Let X be the number of white balls. Then X is distributed binomially with $n = 4$ trials and $P(\text{white ball}) = 1/3$. Thus,

$$P \text{ (just one white)} = P \, (X = 1)$$

$$= \binom{4}{1}\left(\frac{1}{3}\right)^1\left(1 - \frac{1}{3}\right)^{4-1}$$

$$= 4\left(\frac{1}{3}\right)\left(\frac{2}{3}\right)^3 = \frac{32}{81}$$

(b) $P(\text{just one white} \mid \text{just one red})$

$$= \frac{P(\text{just one white and just one red})}{P(\text{just one red})}$$

If Y is the number of red balls, then Y is distributed binomially with parameters $n = 4$ and $p = \frac{4}{9}$.

Thus, $P(\text{just one red}) = P(Y = 1)$

$$= \binom{4}{1}\left(\frac{4}{9}\right)^1\left(1 - \frac{4}{9}\right)^{4-1}$$

$$= 4\left(\frac{4}{9}\right)\left(\frac{5}{9}\right)^3, \text{ and}$$

$P(\text{just one white and just one red})$

$\quad = P(\text{one white, one red, and two blacks}).$

Any particular sequence of outcomes in which one white ball is chosen, one red ball is chosen, and two black balls are chosen has probability $\left(\frac{3}{9}\right)^1\left(\frac{2}{9}\right)^2\left(\frac{4}{9}\right)^1$. We now must find the number of such distinguishable arrangements. There are $\binom{4}{1}$ ways to select the position of the white ball. There are now three positions available to select the position of the red ball and $\binom{3}{1}$ ways to do this. The position of the black balls are now fixed. There are thus

$$\binom{4}{1}\binom{3}{1} = \frac{4!}{1! \times 3!}\frac{3!}{1! \times 2!} = \frac{4!}{1! \times 2! \times 1!}$$

distinguishable arrangements.

Thus, $P(\text{one red ball, one white ball, and two black balls})$

$$= \frac{4!}{1! \times 2! \times 1!} \times \left(\frac{3}{9}\right)\left(\frac{2}{9}\right)^2\left(\frac{4}{9}\right)^1 = \frac{4 \times 3 \times 3 \times 4 \times 4}{9^4}, \text{ so}$$

$$P(\text{just one white} \mid \text{just one red}) = \frac{\dfrac{4 \times 3 \times 3 \times 4 \times 4}{9^4}}{4\left(\dfrac{4}{9}\right)\left(\dfrac{5}{9}\right)^3}$$

$$= \frac{4 \times 3 \times 3 \times 4 \times 4}{4 \times 4 \times 5 \times 5 \times 5} = \frac{36}{125}$$

✓ • PROBLEM 2–56

Three electric motors from a factory are tested. A motor is either discarded, returned to the factory, or accepted. If the probability of acceptance is 0.7, the probability of return is 0.2, and the probability of discard is 0.1, what is the probability that of three randomly selected motors one will be returned, one will be accepted, and one will be discarded? What is the probability that two motors will be accepted, one returned, and zero discarded?

SOLUTION:

Let the probability that one is returned, one accepted, and one discarded be denoted by $P(1, 1, 1)$. Since the motors are selected at random, each selection is independent and the probability that an arrangement consisting of one returned, one accepted, and one discarded is observed is $(0.7) (0.2) (0.1) = 0.14$. We now count the number of possible arrangements in which one engine is discarded, one returned, and one accepted.

Let us count the number of arrangements in the following way. First choose the one motor from three that will be returned. There are $\binom{3}{1}$ ways to do this. Now choose one motor from the remaining two which will be accepted. There are $\binom{2}{1}$ ways to do this. Once the one motor that will be accepted is chosen from the remaining two, the motor that will be discarded is left over and hence selected automatically. Altogether there are $\binom{3}{1}$ arrangements of motors that will consist of one accepted, one returned, and one discarded.

Hence, $P(1, 1, 1) = \binom{3}{1}\binom{2}{1}(0.7)(0.2)(0.1) = \dfrac{3!}{1! \times 2!}\dfrac{2!}{1! \times 1!}(0.014)$

$$= 6(0.014) = 0.084$$

Similarly, the probability of selecting two motors that will be accepted, one returned, and zero discarded is computed in two steps. The probability of observing one particular arrangement of this form is $(0.7)^2$ $(0.2)^1 (0.1)^0$. We now count the number of arrangements which lead to this observation. There are $\binom{3}{2}$ ways to choose the two motors that will be accepted. There are $\binom{1}{1}$ ways to choose the one motor that will be returned. Multiplying from the remaining one, we see that there are

$$\binom{3}{2}\binom{1}{1} = \dfrac{3!}{2! \times 1! \times 0!}$$

possible arrangements. The probability of observing a sample in which two motors are accepted is thus

$$\dfrac{3!}{2! \times 1! \times 0!}(0.7)^2 (0.2)^1 (0.1)^0 = 3\,(0.7)^2 (0.2)^1 (0.1)^0 = 0.294.$$

The coefficient $\begin{pmatrix} n \\ k_1, k_2, \ldots, k_r \end{pmatrix}$ is called the multinomial coefficient and counts the number of ways n objects can be labeled in r ways; k_1 in the first category, k_2 in the second, up to k_r in the rth, with $k_1 + k_2 + \ldots + k_r = n$, and

$$\begin{pmatrix} n \\ k_1, k_2, \ldots, k_r \end{pmatrix} = \dfrac{n!}{k_1! \, k_2! \ldots k_r!}$$

✓ • PROBLEM 2–57

A survey was made of the number of people who read classified ads in a newspaper. Thirty people were asked to indicate which one of the following best applies to them: (1) read no ads (N); (2) read "articles for sale" ads (S); (3) read "help wanted" ads (H); (4) read all ads (A).

(a) Use the multinomial theorem for the expansion of

$$(N + S + H + A)^{30}$$

to find the coefficients of the terms involving

(1) _____ $N^{10} A^{10} H^{10}$

(2) _____ $N^5 S^{10} H^{10} A^5$

(b) Assuming the following probabilities, what is the probability that 10 read no ads, 10 read "help wanted" ads, and 10 read all ads?

$$P\{N\} = \frac{30}{100}$$

$$P\{S\} = \frac{40}{100}$$

$$P\{H\} = \frac{20}{100}$$

$$P\{A\} = \frac{10}{100}.$$

SOLUTION:

(a) We can generalize the binomial distribution to instances in which the independent, identical "trials" have more than just two possible outcomes. Recall that the binomial distribution had its origins in connection with a sequence of "Bernoulli trials," each of which had only two possibilities for an outcome. Now consider a sequence of independent trials, each trial having k possible outcomes, $O_1, O_2, O_3, \ldots, O_k$ with respective probabilities $p_1, p_2, p_3, \ldots, p_k$. There is the relation $p_1 + p_2 + p_3 + \ldots + p_k =$

1, so that any one probability can be obtained from the remaining $k - 1$. Consider the random variables $X_1, \ldots, X_k$, where X_i is the frequency of O_i among n trials. Note that $X_1 + X_2 + \ldots + X_k = n$ since all trials must have some outcome. The joint distribution of $(X_1, \ldots, X_k)$ is called multinomial. We can derive the probability function of the k-nomial distribution by a method similar to the binomial. For a particular sequence of results, $f_1 A_1$'s, $f_2 A_2$'s, etc., the probability, according to the multiplication rule, is simply the product of the corresponding probabilities:

$$p_1^{f_1} \, p_2^{f_2} \ldots p_k^{f_k}.$$

Such a sequence can come in many orders—the number of which is the number of ways of arranging n objects, f_1 of one kind, $\ldots$, and f_k of the kth kind. This is $n!$ divided by a factorial for each group of like objects. Hence, the total probability for all sequences with given frequencies is

$$P(X = f_1, \ldots \text{ and } X_k = f_k) = \frac{n!}{r_1! \, r_k!} p_1^{f_1} \, p_2^{f_2} \ldots p_k^{f_k},$$

provided $\sum_i f_i = n$. We use the term "multinomial" since (as in the particular case $k = 2$) the probabilities we have are the terms in a multinomial expansion

multinomial coefficients !

$$(p_1 + \ldots + p_k)^n = \sum \frac{n!}{f_1! \ldots f_k!} p_1^{f_1} p_2^{f_2} \ldots p_k^{f_k} = 1.$$

The sum extends to all sets of nonnegative integers that sum to n. In our problem, we have four possible outcomes N, A, S, H.

(1) We are looking for the coefficient of $p_1^{10}, p_2^{10}, p_3^{10}, p_4^{10}$. It is

$$\frac{30!}{10! \times 10! \times 10! \times 0!}$$

but since $0!$ is 1, we have

$$\frac{30!}{10! \times 10! \times 10!}.$$

(2) We are looking for the coefficient of $p_1^5, p_2^5, p_3^{10}, p_4^{10}$. By our multinomial derivation it is

$$\frac{30!}{5!\times 5!\times 10!\times 10!}.$$

(b) In part (a-1) we substitute

$$p_1 = \frac{30}{100} = 0.3, p_2 = \frac{10}{100} = 0.1, p_3 = \frac{40}{100} = 0.4, \text{ and } p_4 = \frac{20}{100}$$

$$= 0.2.$$

$$\frac{30!}{10!\times 10!\times 10!} P(N)^{10}\, P(A)^{10}\, P(H)^{10}$$

$$= \frac{30!}{10!\times 10!\times 10!}(0.3)^{10}\,(0.2)^{10}\,(0.1)^{10}.$$

✓ • **PROBLEM 2–58**

Find the coefficient of $a_1^2\, a_2\, a_3$ in the expansion of $(a_1 + a_2 + a_3)^4$.

SOLUTION:

The binomial theorem states that if n is a positive integer, then

$$(a + b)^n = a^n b^0 + na^{n-1} b^1 + \frac{n(n-1)}{1\times 2}a^{n-2} b^2 + \frac{n(n-1)(n-2)}{1\times 2\times 3}a^{n-3}$$

$$b^3 + \dots + na^1 b^{n-1} + a^0 b^n.$$

Use the binomial theorem, but for convenience, associate the terms $(a_2 + a_3)$, then expand the expression.

$$[a_1 + (a_2 + a_3)]^4 = a_1^4 + 4a_1^3\,(a_2 + a_3) + \frac{4\times 3}{1\times 2}\,a_1^2 + (a_2 + a_3)^2$$

$$+ \frac{4\times 3\times 2}{1\times 2\times 3}a_1 + (a_2 + a_3)^3 + (a_2 + a_3)^4.$$

Notice that the only term involving $a_1^2 a_2\, a_3$ is the third term with coefficient $\frac{4\times 3}{2}$ and, further, that $(a_2 + a_3)^2$ must be expanded also. This expansion is

$$(a_2 + a_3)^2 = a_2^2 + 2a_2a_3 + a_3^2.$$

Therefore, the third term becomes:

$$\frac{4 \times 3}{1 \times 2} a_1^2 (a_2 + a_3)^2 = \frac{4 \times 3}{1 \times 2} a_1^2 (a_2^2 + 2a_2a_3 + a_3^2)$$

$$= 6a_1^2 a_2^2 + 12a_1^2 a_2 a_3 + 6a_1^2 a_3^2$$

Hence, the coefficient of $a_1^2\, a_2 a_3$ is 12.

✓ • PROBLEM 2-59

A die is tossed 12 times. Let X_i denote the number of tosses in which i dots come up for i = 1, 2, 3, 4, 5, and 6. What is the probability that we obtain two of each value?

SOLUTION:

We have a series of independent successive trials with six possible outcomes each with constant probability $1/6$. The multinomial distribution,

$$P(X_1 = f_1, X_2 = f_2, \ \dots \ X_k = f_k)$$

$$= \frac{n!}{f_1!\, f_2! \dots f_k!}\, p_1^{f_1} p_2^{f_2} \dots p_k^{f_k},$$

is called for. Hence,

$$P(X_1 = 2, X_2 = 2, X_3 = 2, X_4 = 2, X_5 = 2, X_6 = 2)$$

$$= \frac{12!}{2! \times 2! \times 2! \times 2! \times 2! \times 2!} \left(\frac{1}{6}\right)^2 \left(\frac{1}{6}\right)^2 \dots \left(\frac{1}{6}\right)^2$$

$$= \frac{12!}{2^6} \left[\left(\frac{1}{6}\right)^2\right]^6 = \frac{1,925}{559,872} = 0.0034$$

✳✳✳✳✳✳

REVIEW OF GEOMETRIC RANDOM VARIABLES

Geometric random variables are similar to binomial random variables, with one important difference. A binomial random variable is the number of successes in a given number of trials. A geometric random variable is the number of trials required to observe the first success. For example, if we toss a coin until we observe a heads and then record the number of tosses required, then, under fairly reasonable assumptions, the random variable defined as the number of required tosses follows a geometric distribution. The required assumptions are that each trial must result in either a success or a failure, the probability of success is constant across trials, and the results of all trials are independent. These are the same assumptions underlying the binomial distribution.

As an example, consider a batter who hits 0.250. How many at-bats would we expect this batter to require before getting a hit? A more appropriate question might be "what is the probability that k at-bats are required prior to this player getting his first hit?" To answer this question, notice that if k at-bats are required, then the first $(k-1)$ at-bats must have resulted in outs, and then the kth at-bat must be a hit. Since the probability of a success on any given at-bat is 0.250, the probability of an out is $1 - 0.250 = 0.750$. Since the at-bats are independent, the probability of $(k-1)$ outs followed by a hit is $(0.750)^{(k-1)} (0.250)$. This is the probability of the batter requiring k at-bats to record his first hit.

The geometric distribution is characterized by a single parameter, p, which is the success probability on any given trial. With this information, we may compute $P\{X = k\}$, where X is a geometric random variable (p), as

$$P\{X = k\} = P\{(k-1) \text{ failures followed by a success}\}$$

$$= P\{\text{failure}\}^{(k-1)} P\{\text{success}\}$$

$$P\{x = k\} = (1 - p)^{(k-1)} p$$

This is the probability mass function for positive integer k. The probability mass function is zero for any other value of k, because the observed value must be a positive integer in order to be interpreted as the required number of trials to achieve a success.

Using the theory of infinite sequences, it can be shown that the expected value of a geometric random variable is $1/p$. Some textbooks state that the expected value of a geometric random variable is

$$\frac{(1-p)}{p}.$$

The apparent discrepancy is due to alternative parameterizations of the geometric distribution. If we let the random variable Y be the number of failures prior to the first success and let the random variable X be the number of trials required to achieve the first success, then $X = Y + 1$. Therefore,

$$E[X] = E[Y] + 1.$$

Some textbooks would call X a geometric random variable, while others call Y a geometric random variable. We consider X to be a geometric random variable. Now,

$$E[Y] = \frac{(1-p)}{p},$$

so $\qquad E[X] = E[Y + 1]$

$$= E[Y] + 1,$$

(handwritten annotation:)
$$E[x] = \frac{1}{p} \qquad X = Y+1$$
$$E[Y] = \frac{(1-p)}{p}$$

and $\qquad E = \left[\dfrac{(1-p)}{p}\right] + 1$

$$= \left(\frac{1}{p}\right) - \left(\frac{p}{p}\right) + \left(\frac{p}{p}\right)$$

$$= \frac{1}{p}$$

The cumulative distribution function of a geometric random variable may be easily found by noting that if X is a geometric random variable with parameter p, then

$$F_X(k) = P\{X \le k\}$$

$$= 1 - P\{X > k\}$$

But the event $\{X > k\}$ may be simplified, because X is greater than k if more than k trials are required to produce the first success. This is equivalent to specifying that the first $(k - 1)$ trials result in failures. The probability of this is $(1-p)^{k-1}$. Then,

$$P\{x > k\} = (1-p)^{k-1}$$

$$F_X(k) = P\{X \le k\}$$
$$= 1 - P\{X > k\}$$
$$= 1 - (1-p)^{k-1}$$

✓ • **PROBLEM 2–60**

Let X be a geometric random variable with parameter 0.5. What is the expected value of X?

SOLUTION:

The general formula for the expected value of a geometric random variable is

$$E[X] = \frac{1}{p}.$$

If $p = 0.5$, then

$$E[X] = \frac{1}{0.5} = 2.$$

Thus, we would expect two trials before seeing the first success.

• **PROBLEM 2–61**

An amateur basketball player shoots foul shots until he makes one. Any given shot will be successful with probability 0.4, and the success of each shot is independent of the success of any other shot. How many shots would we expect this player to take? What is the probability that this player takes exactly one shot? What is the probability that this player takes at least three shots?

SOLUTION:

The expected number of shots is

$$E[X] = \frac{1}{p}$$

$$= \frac{1}{0.4}$$

$$= 2.5$$

The player takes exactly one shot if and only if the player scores on the first shot. The probability of scoring on any shot, including the first one, is 0.4. We can also use the probability mass function for the geometric distribution to find

$$P\{X = 1\} = p(1-p)^{k-1}$$

$$= (0.4)\,(1-0.4)^{1-1}$$

$$= (0.4)\,(0.6)^0$$

$$= 0.4$$

The probability that the player shoots at least three times is the probability that the player misses the first two shots (these events are equivalent). The probability of this is

$$P\{\text{miss, miss}\} = (1-p)\,(1-p)$$

$$= (1-0.4)\,(1-0.4)$$

$$= (0.6)\,(0.6)$$

$$= 0.36$$

✓ • **PROBLEM 2-62**

A baseball player comes to bat five times in a game. This player is a 0.300 hitter, and the result of any one at-bat is independent of the result of any other at-bat. Let X be the number of the at-bat, in the sequence of his at-bats, of his first hit. Is X a geometric random variable? Why or why not?

SOLUTION:

There are only five at-bats, none of which must result in a hit. If the player gets no hits in the five at-bats, then we know that $X > 5$, but we do not observe the actual value of X. Thus, X cannot be a geometric random variable.

✓ • PROBLEM 2-63

An observer stands at an overpass of a highway and counts the cars that pass by. He stops counting when he sees a red car. Let X be the number of cars counted. If the proportion of cars which are red is 0.2, then what is the expected value of X? What is the probability that 10 cars will be observed?

SOLUTION:

Using the formulas for a geometric random variable,

$$E[X] = \frac{1}{p}$$

$$= \frac{1}{0.2}$$

$$= 5,$$

and $P\{X = 10\} = p(1-p)^{k-1}$

$$= (0.2)(1-0.2)^{10-1}$$

$$= (0.2)(0.8)^9$$

$$= (0.2)(0.1342)$$

$$= 0.02684$$

2-63= • **PROBLEM 2-64**

An observer stands at an overpass of a highway and counts the cars that pass by. He stops counting when he sees a red car. Let X be the number of cars counted. If the proportion of cars which are red is 0.2, then what is the expected value of X? What is the probability that 10 cars will be observed?

SOLUTION:

Using the formulas for a geometric random variable,

$$E[X] = \frac{1}{p}$$

$$= \frac{1}{0.2}$$

$$= 5,$$

and $P\{X = 10\} = p(1 - p)^{k-1}$

$$= (0.2)(1 - 0.2)^{10-1}$$

$$= (0.2)(0.8)^9$$

$$= (0.2)(0.1342)$$

$$= 0.02684$$

• **PROBLEM 2-65**

Someone tosses a biased coin until he observes a tails. If the probability of heads on any given trial is 0.4, then what is the expected number of tosses? What is the probability that there will be six tosses?

SOLUTION:

The question is phrased such that the stopping rule is reached when a tails is observed. Thus, a tails is a success. If the probability of a heads is

0.4, then the probability of a tails, or of a success, is $1 - 0.4 = 0.6$. Using the formulas for a geometric random variable,

$$E[X] = \frac{1}{p}$$

$$= \frac{1}{0.6}$$

$$= 1.667$$

and $\quad P\{X = 6\} = p(1 - p)^{k-1}$

$$= (0.6)(1 - 0.6)^{6-1}$$

$$= (0.6)(0.4)^5$$

$$= (0.6)(0.0102)$$

$$= 0.0061$$

• PROBLEM 2-66

Someone tosses a biased coin until he observes a tails. If the probability of heads on any given trial is 0.3, then what is the expected number of tosses? What is the probability that there will be ~~four~~ three tosses?

SOLUTION:

The question is phrased such that the stopping rule is reached when a tails is observed. Thus, a tails is a success. If the probability of a heads is 0.3, then the probability of a tails, or of a success, is $1 - 0.3 = 0.7$. Using the formulas for a geometric random variable,

$$E[X] = \frac{1}{p}$$

$$= \frac{1}{0.7}$$

$$= 1.4286,$$

and $\quad P\{X = 3\} = p(1 - p)^{k-1}$

$$= (0.7)(1 - 0.7)^{3-1}$$

$$= (0.7)(0.3)^2$$

$$= (0.7)(0.09)$$

$$= 0.063$$

√ • **PROBLEM 2-67**

An absent-minded professor has five keys. One of the keys opens the door to his apartment. One night he arrives at his building, reaches into his pocket, and selects a key at random from those on his chain. He tries it in the lock. If it doesn't work, he replaces the key and again selects at random from the five keys. He continues this process until he finally finds his key, then stops. Let X be the number of attempts the professor makes. what is the probability distribution of X?

SOLUTION:

This is a special type of binomial random variable. Each time the professor reaches into his pocket can be considered a trial. The professor always replaces the key so we assume that the trials are independent except if the correct key is chosen. There are five keys and he is selecting at random. The probability of success on a given trial is $^1/_5$ thus and the probability that he selects the wrong key is $^4/_5$. We are not sure how many attempts he will make, but we know that if he selects the correct key, he will stop the process. We compute the probability distribution of X as

$P(X = 1) =$ probability that he picks the right key on the first draw

$$= \frac{1}{5}.$$

$P(X = 2) =$ probability that he picks a wrong key first and the right key second

$$= \left(\frac{4}{5}\right)\left(\frac{1}{5}\right).$$

$P(X = 3)$ = probability that he picks two wrong keys first and the right key third

$$= \left(\frac{4}{5}\right)\left(\frac{4}{5}\right)\left(\frac{1}{5}\right).$$

In general, $P(X = k)$ = probability that $k - 1$ wrong keys are tried and the kth key selected is the correct one.

$$P(X = k) = \left(\frac{4}{5}\right)^{k-1}\left(\frac{1}{5}\right).$$

This distribution is known as the geometric distribution.

✓ • **PROBLEM 2–68**

Find the mean and variance of the geometric distribution:

$$F(x) = (1 - p)^{x-1}p; \, x = 1, 2, 3,\dots.$$

SOLUTION:

By definition

$$E(x) = \sum_x x f(x)$$

$$= \sum_{x=1}^{\infty} x (1 - p)^{x-1}p$$

$$= p \sum_{x=1}^{\infty} x (1 - p)^{x-1};$$

recall that $\dfrac{d}{dz} z^n = nz^{n-1}$; thus

$$p \sum_{x=1}^{\infty} x\,(1-p)^{x-1} = p \sum_{x=1}^{\infty} x \frac{d}{d(1-P)}(1-p)^x$$

$$= p\left[\frac{d}{d(1-p)} \left(\sum_{x=1}^{\infty}(1-p)^x \right) \right].$$

We can put back the $x = 0$ term since it is a constant and always differentiates to zero. Also note that

$$\sum_{x=1}^{\infty} (1-p)^x$$

is a geometric series and therefore sums to

$$\frac{1}{1-(1-p)} = \frac{1}{p}.$$

Hence, $E(x) = p\left(\dfrac{d}{d(1-p)} \left(\dfrac{1}{p} \right) \right).$

Let $q = 1 - p$. Then

$$E(x) = p\left(\frac{d}{dq} \left(\frac{1}{1-q} \right) \right)$$

$$= p\left(\frac{-1}{(1-q)^2}\,(-1) \right)$$

$$= p\left(\frac{-1}{p^2}\,(-1) \right) = \frac{1}{p}$$

To find the variance, we must find the $E[x\,(x-1)]$.

$$E[x(x-1)] = \sum_{x} x(x-1)\,f(x)$$

$$= \sum_{x=1}^{\infty} x\,(x-1)\,(1-p)^{x-1}p$$

$$= p(1-p) \sum_{x=1}^{\infty} x\,(x-1)\,(1-p)^{x-2}.$$

Let $q = 1 - p$. Then

$$E[x(x-1)] = pq \sum_{x=1}^{\infty} x(x-1)\, q^{x-2}$$

$$= pq \sum_{x=2}^{\infty} \frac{d^2(q^x)}{dq^2}$$

$$= pq \times \frac{d^2}{dq^2} \sum_{x=0}^{\infty} q^x$$

We can put in the $x = 0$ and $x = 1$ terms since they are constants and differentiate to zero. The sum is again geometric and sums to

$$\frac{1}{1-q}$$

for $0 < q < 1$. Thus

$$E[x(x-1)] = pq\left(\frac{d^2}{dq}\frac{1}{1-q}\right) = pq\left(\frac{+1}{(1-q)^2}\right)$$

$$= pq\left(\frac{+2}{(1-q)^3}\right) = \frac{2pq}{p^3} = \frac{2q}{p}, \text{ and}$$

$$\mathrm{Var}(x) = E[x^2] - (E[x])^2 = E[x(x-1)] + E[x] - (E[x])^2$$

$$= \frac{2q}{p^2} + \frac{1}{p} - \left(\frac{1}{p}\right)^2 = \frac{2q+p-1}{p^2}$$

$$= \frac{2(1-p)+p-1}{p^2} = \frac{2-2p+p-1}{p^2}$$

$$\mathrm{Var}(x) = \frac{1-p}{p^2} \qquad *$$

******

REVIEW OF NEGATIVE BINOMIAL RANDOM VARIABLES

The negative binomial distribution generalizes the geometric distribution, in that it allows for additional successes prior to the success at which we stop the trials. Recall that the interpretation of the geometric random variable was the number of trials required to observe the first success. However, a geometric random variable would not be appropriate if our interest was in the number of trials required to observe the second success, or the third success, or, indeed, any success other than the first one. The negative binomial distribution helps to bridge this gap.

For example, consider tossing a fair coin until the second heads is observed. In particular, let X denote the number of trials required to observe two successes. Then X has a negative binomial distribution, and X is a negative binomial random variable.

A negative binomial random variable is characterized by a pair of parameters. The first parameter is the success probability on any given trial, denoted p. The second parameter is the number of successes required, denoted n. We will derive the probability mass function in a manner similar to that used to derive the probability mass function for the geometric distribution.

We derive the probability mass function of the negative binomial distribution by finding the probability that a negative binomial random variable takes on the value k for all values k. We notice that the negative binomial random variable X takes on the value k if k trials are required to observe n successes. Clearly, then, k cannot be less than n. Also, since k is the required number of trials, k must be valued as an integer. Thus, we may restrict attention to values of k which are positive integers at least as large as n. For such k, we notice that $X = k$ if k trials are required to observe n successes; therefore, there are n successes and $k - n$ failures in the k trials. Since we did not stop prior to the kth trial, we also know that the nth success did not occur prior to the kth trial. Thus, the nth success must have occurred on the kth trial. To summarize, we have $(n - 1)$ successes and $(k - n)$ failures in the first $(k - 1)$ trials, followed by a success on the kth trial. The probability of this event is the probability that X takes on the value k, or $P\{X = k\}$.

We find the probability of this event the same way we found the probability mass function for the binomial distribution. There are many outcomes which would lead to the event $\{X = k\}$. Each of these outcomes is a permutation of the $(n - 1)$ successes and $(k - n)$ failures in the first $(k - 1)$ trials. Each of these outcomes results in n successes and $(k - n)$ failures, so the probability of any of these outcomes is $p^n(1 - p)^{k-n}$. The remaining task is to find the number of outcomes which lead to the event $\{X = k\}$. This question is tantamount to asking how many permutations there are of $(n - 1)$ successes and $(k - n)$ failures in the first $(k - 1)$ trials. The answer is

$$C(k - 1, n - 1), \text{ or } \frac{(k-1)!}{[(n-1)!\,(k-n)!]}.$$

Now,

$$P\{X = k\} = \frac{(k-1)!}{[(n-1)!\,(k-n)!]p^n(1-p)^{k-n}} \quad \text{for integer } k,\ k \geq n.$$

Just as a binomial random variable with parameters n and p can be viewed as a sum of n Bernoulli random variables, each with parameter p, likewise a negative binomial random variable with parameters n and p can be viewed as a sum of n geometric random variables, each with parameter p. Then we may find the expected value of a negative binomial random variable X, with parameters n and p, by letting $X1, X2, \ldots, Xn$ be geometric random variables, each with parameter p. Then

$$E[X] = E[\Sigma_{i=1 \text{ to } n} Xi]$$

$$= \Sigma_{i-1 \text{ to } n} E[Xi]$$

$$= \Sigma_{i=1 \text{ to } n} \frac{1}{p}$$

$$= \frac{n}{p}$$

Notice that as n becomes larger, the expected value becomes larger. This is reasonable, because we would expect more trials to be required if we require more successes. In addition, as p becomes larger, the expected value becomes smaller. If a success becomes more likely on any given trial, then fewer trials should be expected to be required to observe a given number of successes.

✓ • **PROBLEM 2-69**

Let X be a negative binomial random variable with parameters 10 and 0.5. Then what is $P\{X = 8\}$?

SOLUTION:

This probability is zero, since there is no way to observe 10 successes in only eight trials. Recall that k must be at least as large as n, and in this problem $k = 8$ and $n = 10$.

✓ • **PROBLEM 2-70**

Let X be a negative binomial random variable with parameters 2 and 0.5. Then what is $E[X]$? What is $P\{X = 8\}$?

SOLUTION:

We use the negative binomial formula with $n = 2$, $p = 0.5$, and $k = 8$ to derive

$$E[X] = \frac{n}{p}$$

$$= \frac{2}{0.5}$$

$$= 4$$

Also, $\quad P\{X = 8\} = C(k - 1, n - 1)p^n (1 - p)^{k-n}$

$$= C(7, 1) (0.5)^2 (1 - 0.5)^{8-2}$$

$$= \frac{7!}{[1! (7 - 1)!] (0.25) (0.5)^5}$$

$$= (7) (0.25) (0.0156)$$

$$= 0.0273$$

√• **PROBLEM 2-71**

Let X be a negative binomial random variable with parameters 3 and 0.6. Then what is $E[X]$? What is $P\{X = 5\}$?

SOLUTION:

We use the negative binomial formula with $n = 3$, $p = 0.6$, and $k = 5$ to derive

$$E[X] = \frac{n}{p}$$

$$= \frac{3}{0.6}$$

$$= 5$$

Also, $P\{X = 5\} = C(k - 1, n - 1)p^n(1 - p)^{k-n}$

$$= C(4, 2) (0.6)^3(1 - 0.6)^{5-3}$$

$$= \frac{4!}{[2!(4-2)!](0.216)(0.4)^2}$$

$$= \frac{4!}{[2!2!](0.216)(0.16)}$$

$$= (6)(0.216)(0.16)$$

$$= 0.2074$$

√• **PROBLEM 2-72**

A basketball player shoots free-throws until he hits four of them. His probability of scoring any one of them is 0.7, and the success of any one shot is independent of the success of any other shot. How many shots do we expect this player to shoot? What is the probability that the player requires four shots?

SOLUTION:

We apply the negative binomial formula with $n = 4$, $p = 0.7$, and $k = 4$ to derive

$$E[X] = \frac{n}{p}$$

$$= \frac{4}{0.7}$$

$$= 5.7143$$

Also, $P\{X = 4\} = C(k - 1, n - 1)p^n(1 - p)^{k-n}$

$$= C(3, 3) \, (0.7)^4(1 - 0.7)^{4-4}$$

$$= \frac{3!}{[3! \, (3 - 3)!] \, (0.2401) \, (0.3)^0}$$

$$= \frac{3!}{[3! \, 0!] \, (0.2401) \, (1)}$$

$$= (1) \, (0.2401) \, (1)$$

$$= 0.2401$$

******

REVIEW OF POISSON RANDOM VARIABLES

Poisson random variables are derived from count data under a fairly broad set of assumptions. The details of the assumptions are beyond the scope of this book, but in summary, we will treat any random variable which counts the number of some occurrence for which no upper limit may be assigned a priori as Poisson. As examples, we may consider many of the random variables discussed in the earlier section on random variables which were said to be countably infinite. This would include the number of phone calls received in a day, the number of thunderstorms in a year, the number of cars passing a given intersection in an hour, or the number of goals scored in a soccer game. At this point, it might be a good idea to review the section on random variables to better understand the concept that no upper limit exists on these random variables.

The possible values that a Poisson random variable can assume are the set of non-negative integers, or {0, 1, 2, ...}. A Poisson random variable is characterized by a single parameter, L. If X is a Poisson random variable with parameter L, then

$$E[X] = L, \quad L = \mu = np$$

so L is the mean of X. The probability mass function of a Poisson random variable is given by

$$P\{X = k\} = \frac{e^{-L}L^k}{k!} \text{ for } k = 0, 1, ... \qquad P(x=k) = \frac{\mu^x e^{-\mu}}{x!}$$

Here, let us suppose that $e = 2.71828....$

As previously mentioned, the expected value of a Poisson random variable with parameter L is L, or $E[X] = L$, if X is a Poisson random variable with parameter L. When we learn about higher moments in a later chapter, we will see that the variance of a Poisson random variable with parameter L is also L.

• PROBLEM 2–73

If X is a Poisson random variable with parameter 4, then what is $E[X]$? What is $P\{X = 0\}$? What is $P\{X = 4\}$?

SOLUTION:

Using the Poisson formula with $L = 4$, we see that

$$E[X] = L$$

$$= 4$$

Also, $P\{X = 0\} = \dfrac{e^{-L}L^k}{k!}$

$$= \dfrac{e^{-4}4^0}{0!}$$

$$= \dfrac{(e^{-4})(1)}{(1)}$$

$$= e^{-4}$$

Finally,

$$P\{X = 4\} = \dfrac{e^{-L}L^k}{k!}$$

$$= \dfrac{e^{-4}4^4}{4!}$$

$$= \dfrac{(e^{-4})(256)}{(24)}$$

$$= \dfrac{(2.71828)^{-4}(256)}{24}$$

$$= 0.1954$$

 • **PROBLEM 2-74**

If X is a Poisson random variable with parameter 2, then what is $E[X]$? What is $P\{X = 1\}$? What is $P\{X = 3\}$?

SOLUTION:

Using the Poisson formula with $L = 2$, we see that

$$E[X] = L$$

$$= 2$$

Also, $P\{X = 1\} = \dfrac{e^{-L}L^k}{k!}$

$$= \dfrac{e^{-2}2^1}{1!}$$

$$= \dfrac{(e^{-2})(2)}{(1)}$$

$$= 2e^{-2}$$

$$= (2)(2.71828)^{-2}$$

$$= (2)(0.1353)$$

$$= 0.2707$$

Finally,

$$P\{X = 3\} = \dfrac{e^{-L}L^k}{k!}$$

$$= \dfrac{e^{-2}2^3}{3!}$$

$$= \dfrac{(e^{-2})(8)}{6}$$

$$= \dfrac{(2.71828)^{-2}(8)}{6}$$

$$= \dfrac{(0.1353)(8)}{6}$$

$$= 0.1804$$

✓ • PROBLEM 2-75

Let X be the number of raindrops falling in a bucket during a five-second interval. Suppose the Poisson assumption is tenable and that the expected number of such raindrops is 20. Then what is $P\{X = 20\}$?

SOLUTION:

Using the Poisson formula with $L = 20$, we see that

$$P\{X = 20\} = \frac{e^{-L}L^k}{k!}$$

$$= \frac{e^{-20}20^{20}}{20!}$$

$$= \frac{(\frac{20}{e})^{20}}{20!}$$

$$= \frac{(\frac{20}{2.71828})^{20}}{20!}$$

$$= \frac{(7.3576)^{20}}{20!}.$$

It should be noted that sometimes it is difficult to come up with an actual numerical solution when the problem involves Poisson probabilities. This is especially true when the mean is large and/or the value the random variable takes on is large. Therefore, it should be acceptable in most cases to leave the answer in the form used to answer Problem 3. If this is not acceptable, then approximations such as Stirling's formula are available. At times, we will leave answers in this less refined form.

✓ • PROBLEM 2-76

Let X be the number of cars passing a given intersection during a five-second interval. Suppose the Poisson assumption is tenable and that the expected number of such cars is five. What is the probability that exactly four cars pass through this intersection during the allotted time interval?

SOLUTION:

Using the Poisson formula with $L = 5$, we see that

$$P\{X = 4\} = \frac{e^{-L}L^k}{k!}$$

$$= \frac{e^{-5}5^4}{4!}$$

$$= \frac{(2.71828)^{-5}\,(5^4)}{4!}$$

$$= \frac{(0.0067)\,(625)}{24}$$

$$= 0.1755$$

$\sqrt{}$ • PROBLEM 2-77

Let X be a Poisson-distributed random variable. If $P\{X = 4\} = P\{X = 5\}$, then what is $E[X]$?

SOLUTION:

We now need to take a closer look at the Poisson probability mass function. Doing so reveals that

$$1 = \frac{P\{X = 5\}}{P\{X = 4\}}$$

$$= \frac{\left[\frac{e^{-L}L^5}{5!}\right]}{\left[\frac{e^{-L}L^4}{4!}\right]}$$

$$= \frac{L^{5-4}(4!)}{(5!)}$$

$$= \frac{L^1}{5}$$

$$= \frac{L}{5}$$

Thus, $L = 5$.

• **PROBLEM 2-78**

Are there any values of L for which there exists a non-negative integer k such that $P\{X = k\} = P\{X = k + 1\}$? If so, then for which values of L?

SOLUTION:

We approach this problem in a similar manner to Problem 2–76. Then

$$1 = \frac{P\{X = k+1\}}{P\{X = k\}}$$

$$= \frac{[\frac{e^{-L}L^{k+1}}{k+1!}]}{[\frac{e^{-L}L^k}{k!}]}$$

$$= \frac{L^{(k+1)-k}(k!)}{(k+1!)}$$

$$= \frac{L^1}{(k+1)}$$

$$= \frac{L}{(k+1)}.$$

Thus, $L = k + 1$. Since k is a non-negative integer, $(k + 1)$ must be a strictly positive integer. Then L would have to be $\{1, 2, 3, ...\}$.

V • **PROBLEM 2-79**

Defects occur along the length of a cable at an average of six defects per 4,000 feet. Assume that the probability of k defects in t feet of cable is given by the probability mass function:

$$P(k \text{ defects}) = \frac{e^{-\frac{6t}{4,000}}\left(\frac{6t}{4,000}\right)^k}{k!}$$

for $k = 0, 1, 2, ...$ Find the probability that a 3,000-foot cable will have at most two defects.

SOLUTION:

The probability of exactly k defects in 3,000 feet is determined by the given discrete probability distribution as $P(k$ defects in 3,000 ft.)

$$= \frac{e^{-\frac{6(3,000)}{4,000}} \left(\frac{6(3,000)}{4,000} \right)^k}{k!}$$

$$= \frac{e^{-4.5}(4.5)^k}{k!}, k = 0, 1, 2, \ldots.$$

The probability of at most two defects is $P(\text{at most two defects}) = P(\text{zero, one, or two defects}).$

The events "zero defects," "one defect," and "two defects" are all mutually exclusive, thus,

$$P(\text{at most two defects}) = P(\text{zero defects}) + P(\text{one defect})$$

$$+ P(\text{two defects})$$

$$= \frac{e^{-4.5}(4.5)^0}{0!} + \frac{e^{-4.5}(4.5)^1}{1!} + \frac{e^{-4.5}(4.5)^2}{2!}$$

$$= e^{-4.5} \left(1 + 4.5 + \frac{(4.5)^2}{2!} \right)$$

$$= 0.1736$$

✓• PROBLEM 2–80

Suppose that flaws in plywood occur at random with an average of one flaw per 50 square feet. What is the probability that a four foot × eight foot sheet will have no flaws? At most one flaw? To get a solution: assume that the number of flaws per unit area is Poisson distributed.

SOLUTION:

A random variable X is defined to have a Poisson distribution if the density of X is given by

$$P(X = k) = \frac{e^{-\lambda}\lambda^k}{k!} \text{ for } k = 0, 1, 2, \dots,$$

where $\lambda > 0$. The Poisson distribution has the unique property that the expectation equals the variance and they equal the value of the parameter λ. For this problem, calculate the expected value and use that as λ. We expect one flaw per 50 square feet. Hence, we expect $1/50$ flaws per square foot. We have $4 \times 8 = 32$ sq. ft. We expect $\lambda = 32/50$ flaws, so $P(\text{no flaws}) =$

$$P(X = 0) = \frac{e^{\frac{32}{50}}\left(\dfrac{32}{50}\right)^0}{0!} = e^{-\frac{32}{50}} = e^{-0.64},$$

$$P(\text{at most one flaw}) = P(\text{no flaws}) + P(1 \text{ flaw})$$

$$= e^{-0.64}\left[\frac{e^{-\frac{32}{50}}\left(\dfrac{32}{50}\right)^1}{1!} + 1\right]$$

$$= e^{-0.64} + 0.64\, e^{-0.64}$$

Given that the random variable X has a Poisson distribution with mean $\mu = 2$, find the variances s^2 and compute $P(1 \le x)$.

SOLUTION:

The density function for a random variable X with Poisson distribution is

$$f(x) = \frac{e^{-\lambda}\lambda^x}{x!} \text{ when } x = 0, 1, 2, \dots, f(x) = 0 \text{ when } x \neq 0, 1, 2, \dots,$$

and λ is a constant that is specified for the particular circumstances. We are given that the mean $\mu = 2$, but we are not given s^2. But recall that a Poisson random variable has the unique property that expectation equals the variance. Hence $\lambda = s^2 = 2$. Now

$$P(1 \leq x) = 1 - P(x = 0)$$

$$= 1 - \frac{e^{-\lambda}\lambda^0}{0!} = 1 - \frac{e^{-2} \times 1}{1} = 1 - \frac{1}{e^2}$$

$$= 1 - 0.135 = 0.865$$

✓ • **PROBLEM 2-82**

Given that 4% of the items in an incoming lot are defective, what is the probability that at most one defective item will be found in a random sample of size 30? Find the Poisson approximation.

SOLUTION:

We use the binomial distribution for three reasons: (1) the selection of the 30 items can be considered a sequence of success-failure trials, because each item is either defective or non-defective; (2) the probability that an item is defective (or non-defective) does not change; and (3) the outcome of each trial is independent of the results of the other trials.

Since the events (there are no defectives in the sample of 30 items) and (there is exactly one defective in the sample) are exclusive (they cannot both occur), we can add the probabilities of their occurrence to find

$$P(d \leq 1) = P(d = 0) + P(d = 1),$$

where d is the number of defective items. Now

$$P(d \leq 1) = \sum_{d=0}^{d=1} \binom{30}{d} (0.04)^d (0.96)^{30-d}$$

$$= \binom{30}{0} (0.04)^0 (0.96)^{30-0} + \binom{30}{1} (0.04)^1 (0.96)^{29}$$

$$= \frac{30!}{30!\,0!} (1) (0.96)^{30} + 30 (0.04) (0.96)^{29}$$

$$= (0.96)^{30} + 30 \, (0.04) \, (0.96)^{29} = 0.661$$

Since $np = $ (number of trials) $\times$ (probability that an item is defective)

$$= 30 \times 0.04 = 1.2 < 5$$

and a sample of 30 items is not considered small, we can find an approximation for $P(d \leq 1)$ by using the Poisson distribution

$$f(d) = \frac{e^{-\lambda} \lambda^d}{d!}.$$

Substitute $np = 1.2$ for λ and add $P(d = 0)$ and $P(d = 1)$:

$$\sum_{d=0}^{d=1} \frac{(1.2)^d e^{-1.2}}{d!} = \frac{1}{e^{-1.2}} \left[\frac{(1.2)^0}{0!} + \frac{1.2}{1} \right]$$

$$= \frac{1}{e^{-1.2}} (1 + 1.2) = \frac{2.2}{e^{-1.2}}$$

The table shows that for one or less occurrences of a defective item, with $np = 1.2$, the probability is 0.663, which differs from the exact probability by only 0.002.

$\checkmark$ • **PROBLEM 2-83**

Consider the Poisson distribution $\dfrac{e^{-\lambda} \lambda^k}{k!}$

Prove $\dfrac{e^{-\lambda} \lambda^{K-1}}{(k-1)!} < \dfrac{e^{-\lambda} \lambda^K}{k!}$ for $k < \lambda$,

$\dfrac{e^{-\lambda} \lambda^{K-1}}{(k-1)!} > \dfrac{e^{-\lambda} \lambda^K}{k!}$ for $k > \lambda$, and

$\dfrac{e^{-\lambda} \lambda^{K-1}}{(k-1)!} = \dfrac{e^{-\lambda} \lambda^K}{k!}$ if λ is an integer and $k = \lambda$.

SOLUTION:

Consider the ratio:

$$R = \frac{\dfrac{e^{-\lambda}\lambda^{k-1}}{(k-1)!}}{\dfrac{e^{-\lambda}\lambda^{k}}{k!}}.$$

If $R > 1$, then $\dfrac{e^{-\lambda}\lambda^{k-1}}{(k-1)!} > \dfrac{e^{-\lambda}\lambda^{k}}{k!}.$

If $R < 1$, then $\dfrac{e^{-\lambda}\lambda^{k-1}}{(k-1)!} < \dfrac{e^{-\lambda}\lambda^{k}}{k!}.$

If $R = 1$, then $\dfrac{e^{-\lambda}\lambda^{k-1}}{(k-1)!} = \dfrac{e^{-\lambda}\lambda^{k}}{k!}.$ Now

$$R = \frac{\dfrac{e^{-\lambda}\lambda^{k-1}}{(k-1)!}}{\dfrac{e^{-\lambda}\lambda^{k}}{k!}} = \frac{\dfrac{\lambda^{k-1}}{(k-1)!}}{\dfrac{\lambda^{k}}{k!}} = \frac{\lambda^{k-1}}{(k-1)!}\frac{k!}{\lambda^{k}} = \frac{k}{\lambda}$$

Hence, if $k < 1$, $R < 1$; if $k > 1$, $R > 1$; and if $k = \lambda$, $R = 1$. The result follows immediately. Note that λ must be an integer for $\lambda = k$, since k is an integer.

• PROBLEM 2–84

Customers enter a department store "at random" at a rate of four per minute. Assume that the number entering the store in any given time interval has a Poisson distribution. Determine the probability that at least one customer enters the store in a given half-minute interval.

SOLUTION:

We again are discussing the specific occurrence of events in a length of time. The problem describes a Poisson process. The mean rate of occurrence is $\lambda = 4$. Hence, the probability that customers enter Macy's in an interval of time t is

$$\frac{e^{-\lambda t}(\lambda t)^k}{k!}$$

or in our case

$$\frac{e^{-4}4^k}{k!}.$$

Given $t = \frac{1}{2}$ minute,

$$P(X = k) = \frac{e^{-4\left(\frac{1}{2}\right)}\left(4\times\frac{1}{2}\right)^k}{k!} = \frac{e^{-2}2^k}{k!}.$$

We want $P(X \geq 1)$. Note that

$$P(X \geq 1) = 1 - P(X = 0) = 1 - \frac{e^{-2}2^0}{0!}$$

$$= 1 - e^{-2} = 0.865$$

• PROBLEM 2-85

Suppose X_t, the number of phone calls that arrive at an exchange during a period of time length t, has a Poisson distribution with parameter λt. The probability that an operator answers any given phone call is equal to p, $0 \leq p \leq 1$. If Y_t denotes the number of phone calls answered, find the distribution of Y_t.

SOLUTION:

We want to find $P(Y_t = k)$, $k = 0, 1, 2, \ldots$.

This is an advanced exercise in conditional probability. If we are given $X_t = r$, we have r Bernoulli trials and a success constitutes the operator answering the call. Hence, given $X_t = r$, Y_t is binomially distributed, or

$$P(Y_t = k \mid X_t = r) = \binom{r}{k}p^k(1-p)^{r-k}, k = 0, 1, 2, \ldots, r.$$

By the Law of Total Probability:

$$P(Y_t = k) = \sum_{r=k}^{\infty} P(Y_t = k \cap X_t = r)$$

$$= \sum_{r=k}^{\infty} \{P(Y_t = k \mid X_t = r)\} \{ P(X_t = r)\}$$

from the definition of conditional probability

$$= \sum_{r=k}^{\infty} \binom{r}{k} p^k (1-p)^{r-k} e^{-\lambda t} \frac{(\lambda t)^r}{r!}$$

$$= \frac{e^{-\lambda t} (\lambda t)^k p^k}{k!} \sum_{r=k}^{\infty} \frac{(1-p)^{r-k} (\lambda t)^{r-k}}{(r-k)!} .$$

Let $i = r - k$. We see that:

$$P(Y_t = k) = \frac{e^{-\lambda t} (\lambda t)^k p^k}{k!} \sum_{i=0}^{\infty} \frac{(1-p)^i (\lambda t) i}{i!}$$

$$= \frac{e^{-\lambda t} (\lambda t)^k p^k}{k!} \sum_{i=0}^{\infty} \frac{[(1-p)\lambda t]^i}{i!}$$

$$= \frac{e^{-\lambda t} (\lambda t)^k p^k}{k!} e^{(1-p)\lambda t}$$

$$= \frac{e^{-\lambda t} e^{\lambda t} e^{-\lambda p t} (\lambda p t)^k}{k!}$$

$$= \frac{e^{-\lambda p t} (\lambda p t)^k}{k!}$$

In conclusion, we see that Y_t has a Poisson distribution with parameter $p\lambda t$. This is referred to as a thinned Poisson process.

$$*\!*\!*\!*\!*\!*$$

REVIEW OF HYPERGEOMETRIC RANDOM VARIABLES

The hypergeometric distribution is used primarily for contingency tables, or cross-classified data. For example, patients in a hospital may be classified both by age (over 40 or under 40) and by gender (male or female). Thus, each patient would be cross-classified. In this example, suppose that the total numbers of males, females, patients over 40, and patients under 40 were known. All that remains to be determined is the number of males over 40. If we knew this, then by subtraction we would also know the number of males under 40, the number of females over 40, and the number of females under 40. The distribution of any one of these quantities is said to be hypergeometric.

The hypergeometric distribution is most frequently applied to the tag-recapture model for estimating the size of a biological population and to testing for defective items. As an example of the first application, let us say we want to know the number of fish in a lake. A number of fish from this lake are captured, tagged, and released back into the lake for redistribution among the population-at-large. After a given period of time, more fish are captured. The random quantity is the number of fish among the second batch to be captured who were also captured in the first batch. This number may be determined by counting the number of fish in the second batch who have tags.

The population size is fixed (but unknown to the experimenter), and the numbers of fish captured in the first batch, not captured in the first batch, captured in the second batch, and not captured in the second batch are also fixed. Thus, all margins are fixed. The number of fish who were captured in both batches follows the hypergeometric distribution. The cross-classification in this example refers to the classification as either captured or not captured in the first batch and either captured or not captured in the second batch.

In the second application of the hypergeometric distribution, testing for defective items, the typical problem involves a number of items received, of which some are defective and some are not. A sample of these items is taken, and each item in the sample is tested. The random quantity is the number of items in the sample which are defective. The cross-classification in this example refers to classifying each item as defective or not and as belonging to the sample or not. Each margin is fixed, as it is known ahead of time how many items will be sampled, and the numbers of defective items and non-defective items in the population are fixed (but not known to the experimenter).

When testing for defective items, it should be mentioned that if the sampling is with replacement, then the binomial model is the appropriate one. In the more realistic case of sampling without replacement, however, the hypergeometric model becomes the appropriate one. Therefore, we will assume throughout this section that sampling is performed without replacement, and thus that the hypergeometric model is appropriate.

The probability mass function of the hypergeometric distribution is derived by considering the probability that a hypergeometric random variable takes on any given value. To demonstrate the method of finding this probability, consider again testing for defective items. We may represent the situation with the following table:

	Sampled	Not Sampled	Total
Defective	X	$D - X$	D
Not Defective	$S - X$	$N - D - S + X$	$N - D$
Total	S	$N - S$	N

We let D be the (unknown) number of defective items, N the (known) total number of items, and S the (known) number of items sampled. Finally, X is the number of defective items in the sample. For X to take on the value k, we would require that there be k defective items in the sample and $S - X$ non-defective items in the sample. The number of ways to pick k defective items out of the D total defective items is $C(D, k)$. Likewise, the number of ways to pick $S - X$ non-defective items out of the $N - D$ total non-defective items is $C(N - D, S - k)$. Multiplying these quantities together provides the total number of ways that X could be k. All outcomes from this sampling scheme are equally likely, so to obtain the probability that X takes on the value k we must divide this number by the total number of possible outcomes (samples). We are selecting S items out of N, so there are $C(N, S)$ total outcomes possible. Thus,

$$P\{X = k\} = \frac{C(D, k)\, D(N - D, S - k)}{C(N, S)}.$$

This is the hypergeometric probability mass function. We must note that the possible values of k are such that each cell in the table is non-negative.

In addition, no cell in the table can exceed the margin. Thus, we obtain

$$0 \le k \le D,$$

$$0 \le D - k \le D,$$

$$0 \le S - k \le N - D,$$

$$0 \le N - D - S + k \le N - D,$$

$$0 \le k \le S,$$

$$0 \le D - k \le N - S,$$

$$0 \le S - k \le S,$$

and $\quad 0 \le N - D - S + k \le N - S.$

Each of these inequalities makes good intuitive sense if one considers what would happen if it did not hold. For example, if the first inequality did not hold, then either there would be a negative number of defective items in the sample or there would be more defective items in the sample than there are in the entire batch. Clearly, this is impossible.

Many of these inequalities are redundant, and we can summarize them in the following set of inequalities:

$$0 \le k,$$

$$D + S - N \le k,$$

$$k \le D,$$

and $\quad k \le S.$

This can also be written as

Possible values for the number of defective items

$$\text{MAX}(0, D + S - N) \le k \le \text{MIN}(D, S).$$

• PROBLEM 2-86

Suppose that there are four defective items in a batch of 10 items, and that five items are selected for testing. What are the possible values for the number of defective items in the sample? What is the probability that there are two defective items in the sample?

SOLUTION:

The range of possible values for the number of defective items in the sample is given by the formula $MAX(0, D + S - N) \le k \le MIN(D, S)$. In this case, $N = 10$, $D = 4$, and $S = 5$. Thus,

$$MAX(0, 4 + 5 - 10) \le k \le MIN(4, 5)$$

$$MAX(0, -1) \le k \le 4$$

$$0 \le k \le 4$$

There can be between zero and four defective items in the sample. Using the probability mass function of the hypergeometric distribution, we obtain

$$P\{X = k\} = \frac{C(D, k)\, D(N - D, S - k)}{C(N, S)}$$

for k in the range. In our case, we wish to find $P\{X = 2\}$, so $k = 2$, which is in the range of $\{0, 1, 2, 3, 4\}$. Then

$$P\{X = 2\} = \frac{C(4, 2)\, C(10 - 4, 5 - 2)}{C(10, 5)}$$

$$= \frac{(6)C(6, 3)}{252}$$

$$= \frac{(6)(20)}{252}$$

$$= \frac{120}{252}$$

$$= 0.4762.$$

✓• **PROBLEM 2–87**

Suppose that there are five defective items in a batch of 10 items, and that six items are selected for testing. What are the possible values for the number of defective items in the sample? What is the probability that there are two defective items in the sample?

SOLUTION:

The range of possible values for the number of defective items in the sample is given by the formula $MAX(0, D + S - N) \le k \le MIN(D, S)$. In this case, $N = 10$, $D = 5$, and $S = 6$. Thus,

$$MAX(0, 5 + 6 - 10) \le k \le MIN(5, 6)$$

$$MAX(0, 1) \le k \le 5$$

$$1 \le k \le 5$$

There can be between one and five defective items in the sample. Thus, there must be at least one defective item in the sample. Using the probability mass function of the hypergeometric distribution, we obtain

$$P\{X = k\} = \frac{C(D, k)\, C(N - D, S - k)}{C(N, S)}$$

for k in the range. In our case, we wish to find $P\{X = 2\}$, so $k = 2$, which is in the range of $\{1, 2, 3, 4, 5\}$. Then

$$P\{X = 2\} = \frac{C(5,2)\, C(10 - 5, 6 - 2)}{C(10,6)}$$

$$= \frac{(10)C(5,4)}{210}$$

$$= \frac{(10)\,(5)}{210}$$

$$= \frac{50}{210}$$

$$= 0.2381.$$

✓• **PROBLEM 2-88**

Suppose that there are three defective items in a batch of five items, and that two items are selected for testing. What are the possible values for the number of defective items in the sample? What is the probability that there are no defective items in the sample? What would be the range and $P\{X = 0\}$ if we were sampling with replacement?

SOLUTION:

The range of possible values for the number of defective items in the sample is given by the formula $\text{MAX}(0, D + S - N) \leq k \leq \text{MIN}(D, S)$. In this case, $N = 5$, $D = 3$, and $S = 2$. Thus,

$$\text{MAX}(0, 3 + 2 - 5) \leq k \leq \text{MIN}(3, 2)$$

$$\text{MAX}(0, 0) \leq k \leq 2$$

$$0 \leq k \leq 2$$

There can be between zero and two defective items in the sample. Using the probability mass function of the hypergeometric distribution, we obtain

$$P\{X = k\} = \frac{C(D, k)\, D(N - D, S - k)}{C(N, S)}$$

for k in the range. In our case, we wish to find $P\{X = 0\}$, so $k = 0$, which is in the range of $\{0, 1, 2\}$. Then

$$P\{X = 0\} = \frac{C(3, 0)\, C(5 - 3, 2 - 0)}{C(5, 2)}$$

$$= \frac{(1)\, C(2, 2)}{10}$$

$$= \frac{(1)\,(1)}{10}$$

$$= \frac{1}{10}$$

$$= 0.1$$

If we were sampling with replacement, then the binomial model would be appropriate. The sample still has two items in it, so $n = 2$. The entire batch has three defective items out of five, so the proportion of defective items is $3/5$, or 0.60. Since we replace the item after testing it, we are always sampling from a distribution with two non-defective items and three defective items, so the probability of encountering a defective is always 0.60. Then using the binomial probability mass function shows that

$$P\{X = 0\} = C(2, 0)\, (0.6)^0\, (1 - 0.6)^{2-0}$$

$$= (1) (1) (0.4)^2$$

$$= (1) (1) (0.16)$$

$$= 0.16$$

Notice that it is more likely to obtain no defective items when sampling with replacement than it is when sampling without replacement. This phenomenon can be understood if we consider the situation in more detail. There will be no defective items in the sample if both items selected in the sample are non-defective. Having picked the first non-defective item (which occurs with probability $^2/_5 = 0.40$), we must now select another non-defective item. If we are sampling with replacement, then we replace the non-defective item and the probability of selecting a non-defective item in the second draw is again $^2/_5 = 0.40$. However, if we had been sampling without replacement, then there would remain only four items (there were five items, but one was selected), of which only one is non-defective (there were two items, but one was selected). Thus, the probability of selecting a non-defective item on the second draw, having selected a non-defective item on the first draw, is $^1/_4 = 0.25$.

$\sqrt{}$ • **PROBLEM 2–89**

Determine the probability distribution of the number of spades in a five-card poker hand from an ordinary deck of 52 cards.

SOLUTION:

Let X = number of spades in a five-card poker hand, which can take on the values 0, 1, 2, 3, 4, or 5.

To find the probability distribution of X, we calculate

$$P(X = k) = \frac{\text{number of poker hands with } k \text{ spades}}{\text{total number of poker hands}}.$$

The total number of poker hands is the number of ways five objects may be selected from 52 objects. Thus, the total number of poker hands is

$$\binom{52}{5}.$$

To count the number of poker hands with k spades, we first count the number of ways k spades may be chosen from the 13 spades available. There are

$$\binom{13}{k}$$

ways to do this. If k of the cards in the hand are spades, $5 - k$ cards must be non-spades. The number of ways the remaining $5 - k$ cards may be selected from the available non-spades is

$$\binom{52-13}{5-k} = \binom{39}{5-k}.$$

Thus, the total number of poker hands with k spades is the product of these two expressions, or

$$\binom{13}{k}\binom{39}{5-k}.$$

Thus, $P(X = k) = \dfrac{\binom{13}{k}\binom{39}{5-k}}{\binom{52}{5}}$ for $k = 0, 1, 2, 3, 4, 5.$

CHAPTER 3

CONTINUOUS RANDOM VARIABLES

> **Basic Attacks and Strategies for Solving Problems in this Chapter. See pages 192 to 298 for step-by-step solutions to problems.**

Discrete random variables are easily understood because of the fact that the probability mass function, $f_x(k)$, can be interpreted as the probability that the discrete random variable x takes on the value k. In contrast, there is no such easily interpretted function for continuous random variables. If X is a continuous random variable, then the probability that X takes on any given value is zero. This fact is easily forgotten, but is certainly worth remembering.

A continuous random variable has no probability mass function. Instead it has a probability density function. Both discrete and continuous random variables have cumulative distribution functions, and these are interpreted the same way for each. That is, $F_x(k) = P\{X \le k\}$ whether X is a discrete random variable or a continuous random variable. Thus cumulative distribution functions are often easier to work with than probability density functions for the purpose of describing continuous random variables.

It might help, when trying to understand the nature of continuous random variables, to consider several example of continuous random variables. Suppose that you begin walking home from a friend's house. You may say that it takes 10 minutes to walk between these two homes. If you were to actually time the travel times, however, you might find that no two times were exactly the same (if you measure the time accurately enough). Of course for everyday usage it is perfectly acceptable to round off, and if the actual times were nine minutes, 54 seconds; nine minutes, 56 seconds; and 10 minutes, two seconds, then we may just call all of these "ten minutes." If we wish to be accurate, however, then we must distinguish these as different times. The actual time required to walk between the two homes is a continuous random variable.

What makes this travel time a continuous random variable is the fact that it can assume any value within an entire range of values. That is, if there is no rounding off and if times are measured exactly, then it is not the case that the travel time could only take certain values. There is no reason why it couldn't take, for example, nine minutes and 54.9683 seconds. Even though the probability of the continuous random variable taking on any given value is zero, the possibility still exists. It is worth understanding that events of zero probability do occur in everyday life.

If a football is thrown, then the distance between the location where the football lands and the location where the thrower was standing is a continuous random variable. One cannot enumerate the possible values that this random variable can take on. In fact, it can take on any value within a range. The probability that it takes on any given value is zero. Nevertheless, it will take on a value (that is, there will be some distance between where the football lands and the thrower). Thus, an event with probability zero will occur no matter what value the continuous random variable takes on.

The probability density function of a continuous random variable is the first derivative of the cumulative distribution function of the continuous random variable. That is, it measures the rate of change of the cumulative distribution function at any given point. The probability density function is useful because it, too, has an interpretation. This interpretation is as follows: The probability that a random variable falls between two values, say a and b, is the definite integral of the probability density function between these two values, a and b.

There are many classes of continuous random variables, just like there were many classes of discrete random variables. We will study some of the most useful and most frequently applied continuous random variables in this chapter. This will include uniform, exponential, normal, chi-square, t, and F random variables.

Certain properties are common to all continuous random variables. For example, to be a continuous random variable the probability density function would need to be non-negative and integrate to one when integrated over the entire range of the random variable. The cumulative distribution function would need to be a non-decreasing function which takes the value zero at negative infinity and one at positive infinity. The cumulative distribution function is also required to be right-continuous.

Functions of continuous random variables may be either continuous or discrete. Functions of discrete random variables, however, must be discrete.

The expected value of a continuous random variable is found by integrating, not summing. Integration may be viewed as a continuous analogue of summation. In particular, the expected value of a continuous random variable is the definite integral, over the entire range, of the product of k and the probability density function. This will be made clear by the examples which are given in the sections describing particular continuous distributions.

Since the probability of a continuous random variable taking on any given value is zero, the probability of falling in an interval (or indeed the probability of falling in any set) is independent of whether or not the endpoints of the interval (or set) are included. In particular, for any continuous random variable X and any real number k, $P\{X < k\} = P\{X \le k\}$, and $P\{X > k\} = P\{X \ge k\}$. We will therefore use these expressions interchangeably in the remainder of this chapter.

REVIEW OF UNIFORM RANDOM VARIABLES

Just as there was a class of discrete uniform random variables, there is also a class of continuous uniform random variables. A continuous uniform random variable is characterized by two parameters. These are the upper and lower limits of the range of the random variable. For example, if a continuous random variable is continuous on the range [0, 1], then the lower limit is zero and the upper limit is one.

What makes a continuous random variable uniform is the fact that its probability density function is uniform over its range. The range of a continuous uniform random variable is most frequently taken to be an interval on the real line. The range need not be such an interval, but for our purposes we will consider this to be the case.

Since the range of a continuous uniform random variable is an interval and the probability density function is uniform over this range, we can determine the common value of this probability density function by appealling to the fact that the probability density function must integrate to one over this range. We know from basic calculus that the integral of a constant function over any range is the value of the function times the volume of the range. Here the range is an interval, so its volume is its length, or the difference between its upper and lower limits. Then we obtain

$$1 = f(x) (b - a),$$

where $f(x)$ is the value of the probability density function on the range $[a, b]$, a is the lower limit of the range of the continuous uniform random variable, and b is the upper limit of the range of the continuous uniform random variable. Now we divide by $(b - a)$ to obtain

$$f(x) = \frac{1}{(b-a)}. \qquad \textit{Uniform density function}$$

This is the value of the probability density function of a continuous uniform random variable with parameters a and b on the range $[a, b]$. The value of the probability density function is zero everywhere else.

The expected value of a continuous uniform random variable may be found by the general method of integrating the product of k and the probability density function over the range, $[a, b]$. Since the probability density function is constant (uniform), this can be factored out of the integral. What remains is the product of this probability density function, which was previously seen to be $1/(b - a)$, and the integral from a to b of k, where k is the integration variable which indexes the range $[a, b]$. This integral is $k^2/2$, to be evaluated from a to b. The definite integral is thus $(b^2 / 2) - (a^2 / 2) = (b^2 - a^2)/2$. Recall that this is to be multiplied by $1 / (b - a)$ to obtain the expected value. But $b^2 - a^2 = (b + a) (b - a)$, so we have the equation

$$E[X] = [(b^2 - a^2) / 2] [1 / (b - a)]$$

$$= [(b + a) (b - a) / 2] / (b - a)$$

$$E[X] = \frac{b + a}{2}$$

Step-by-Step Solutions to Problems in this Chapter, "Discrete Random Variables"

$\sqrt{}$ • **PROBLEM 3–1**

The simplest continuous random variable is the one whose distribution is constant over some interval (a, b) and zero elsewhere. This is the uniform distribution.

$$f(x) = \begin{cases} \dfrac{1}{b-a}, & a \leq X \leq b \\ 0, & \text{elsewhere} \end{cases}$$

Find the mean and variance of this distribution.

SOLUTION:

By definition,

$$E(x) = \int_{-\infty}^{\infty} x\, f(x)\, dx = \int_{a}^{b} \frac{1}{b-a} x\, dx$$

$$= \frac{1}{b-a} \int_{a}^{b} x\, dx = \frac{1}{b-a} \frac{x^2}{2} \Bigg|_{a}^{b}$$

$$= \frac{b^2 - a^2}{2} \left(\frac{1}{b-a} \right) = \frac{a+b}{2}$$

For the variance we must first find $E(X^2)$. By definition,

$$E(X^2) = \int_{-\infty}^{\infty} x^2 \, f(x) \, dx$$

$$= \int_a^b x^2 \frac{1}{b-a} \, dx$$

$$= \frac{1}{b-a} \int_a^b x^2 \, dx$$

$$= \frac{1}{b-a} \frac{x^3}{3} \Bigg]_a^b$$

$$= \frac{b^3 - a^3}{3(b-a)}$$

But var $(X) = E\,[X^2] - (E\,[x])^2$

$$= \frac{b^3 - a^3}{3(b-a)} - \left(\frac{b+a}{2}\right)^2$$

$$= \frac{b^3 - a^3}{3(b-a)} - \frac{\left(a^2 + 2ab + b^2\right)}{4}$$

$$= \frac{(b^2 + ab + a^2)(b-a)}{3(b-a)} - \frac{(a^2 + 2ab + b^2)}{4}$$

$$= \frac{(b^2 + ab + a^2)}{3} - \frac{(a^2 + 2ab + b^2)}{4}$$

$$= \frac{(4b^2 + 4ab + 4a^2)}{12} - \frac{(3a^2 + 6ab + 3b^2)}{12} = \frac{(b-a)^2}{12}$$

✓ • **PROBLEM 3-2**

Let X be a continuous random variable. Find a density function such that the probability that X falls in an interval (a, b) $(0 < a < b < 1)$ is proportional to the length of the interval (a, b). Check that this is a proper probability density function.

SOLUTION:

The probabilities of a continuous random variable are computed from a continuous function called a density function in the following way. If $f(x)$ is graphed,

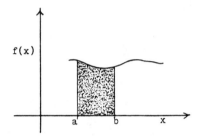

then $P\{a \leq X \leq b\}$ = the area under the curve $f(x)$ from a to b.

With this definition some conditions on $f(x)$ must be imposed. Namely, $f(x)$ must be non-negative and the total area between $f(x)$ and the x-axis must be equal to 1.

We also see that if probability is defined in terms of area under a curve, the probability that a continuous random variable is equal to a particular value, $P\{X = a\}$, is the are under $f(x)$ at the point a. The area of a line is zero, thus $P\{X = a\} = 0$. Therefore,

$$P\{a < X < b\} = P\{a \leq X \leq b\}.$$

To find a density function for $0 < X < 1$, such that $P\{a < X < b\}$ is proportional to the length of (a, b), we look for a function $f(x)$ that is positive and the area under $f(x)$ between zero and one is equal to one. It is reasonable to expect that the larger the interval the larger the probability that x is in the interval.

A density function that satisfies these criteria is

$$f(x) = \begin{cases} 1, & 0 < x < 1 \\ \\ 0 & \text{otherwise} \end{cases}.$$

A graph of this density function is

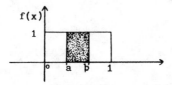

The probability that X is between a and b is the area of the shaded region. This is the area of a rectangle. The area of a rectangle is base x height. Thus,

$$P\{a \le X \le b\} = (b - a) \times 1 = b - a.$$

Similarly, $\quad P\{X \le k\} = (k - 0) \times 1 = k$ for $0 < k < 1$.

Often the density function is more complicated and integration must be used to calculate the area under the density function.

To check that this is a proper probability density function, we must check that the total area under $f(x)$ is one. The total area under this density function is $(1 - 0) \times 1 = 1$.

✓ • **PROBLEM 3-3**

Suppose X is a continuous uniform random variable with parameters 0 and 1. What is $E[X]$? What is the probability density function? What is $P\{X = 0.5\}$? What is $P\{X \le 0.5\}$?

SOLUTION:

The general formula for the expected value of a continuous uniform random variable is given by

$$E[X] = \frac{a+b}{2}.$$

Here $a = 0$ and $b = 1$. Thus,

$$E[X] = \frac{0+1}{2}$$

$$= \frac{1}{2}$$

$$= 0.5$$

The probability density function of a continuous uniform random variable is $1 / (b - a)$ on the range $[a, b]$ and 0 elsewhere. Thus, the probability density function of this particular continuous uniform random variable is

$$f_x(k) = \frac{1}{b-a}$$

$$= \frac{1}{1-0}$$

$$= \frac{1}{1}$$

$$= 1 \text{ for } 0 \leq k \leq 1$$

and $\quad f_x(k) = 0$ for $k < 0$ or $k > 1$.

Recall that for any continuous random variable, including a continuous uniform random variable, $P\{X = k\} = 0$ for any single value of k. Thus, $P\{X = 0.5\} = 0$.

Finally, $P\{X \leq 0.5\}$ can be found as the integral over the range $\{X \leq 0.5\}$ of the probability density function. This works out to be the integral over $[0, 0.5]$ of the function which is 1 on this range. Calculation shows this integral to be 0.5, so

$$P\{X \leq 0.5\} = 0.5.$$

• **PROBLEM 3-4**

Suppose X is a continuous uniform random variable with parameters -2 and 2. What is $E[X]$? What is the probability density function? What is $p\{X < -2\}$? What is $P\{X < -1\}$? What is $P\{X < 0\}$? What is $P\{X < 1\}$? What is $P\{X < 2\}$?

SOLUTION:

The general formula for the expected value of a continuous uniform random variable is given by

$$E[X] = \frac{a+b}{2}.$$

Here $a = -2$ and $b = 2$. Thus,

$$E[X] = \frac{-2+2}{2}$$

$$= \frac{0}{2}$$

$$= 0$$

The probability density function of a continuous uniform random variable is $1 / (b - a)$ on the range $[a, b]$ and 0 elsewhere. Thus, the probability density function of this particular continuous uniform random variable is

$$f_x(k) = \frac{1}{b-a}$$

$$= \frac{1}{2-(-2)}$$

$$= \frac{1}{4}$$

$$= 0.25 \text{ for } -2 \le k \le 2$$

and $\quad f_x(k) = 0$ for $k < -2$ or $k > 2$.

We can find $P\{X \le -2\}$ as the integral over the range $\{X \le -2\}$ of the probability density function. This works out to be the integral over [–2, –2] of the function which is 0.25 on this range. Calculation shows this integral to be 0 (since this is the length of the range of integration), so

$$P\{X \le -2\} = 0.$$

This could also have been found as

$$P\{X \le -2\} = (0.25) \ [(-2) - (-2)]$$

$$= (0.25) \ (0)$$

$$= 0.$$

Likewise, $P\{X \le -1\} = (0.25) \ [(-1) - (-2)]$

$$= (0.25) \ (1)$$

$$= 0.25;$$

$$P\{X \le 0\} = (0.25) \ [(0) - (-2)]$$

$$= (0.25) \ (2)$$

$$= 0.50;$$

$$P\{X \le 1\} = (0.25) \ [(1) - (-2)]$$

$$= (0.25) \ (3)$$

$$= 0.75;$$

and $\qquad P\{X \le 2\} = (0.25) \ [(2) - (-2)]$

$$= (0.25) \ (4)$$

$$= 1.0.$$

✓ • **PROBLEM 3–5**

Suppose X is a continuous uniform random variable with parameters –3 and 5. What is $E[X]$? What is the probability density function? What is $P\{X \le -5\}$? What is $P\{X < -3\}$? What is $P\{X < 0\}$? What is $P\{X \le 4\}$?

SOLUTION:

The general formula for the expected value of a continuous uniform random variable is given by

$$E[X] = \frac{a+b}{2}.$$

Here $a = -3$ and $b = 5$. Thus

$$E[X] = \frac{-3+5}{2}$$

$$= \frac{2}{2}$$

$$= 1$$

The probability density function of a continuous uniform random variable is $1 / (b - a)$ on the range $[a, b]$ and 0 elsewhere. Thus, the probability density function of this particular continuous uniform random variable is

$$f_x(k) = \frac{1}{b-a}$$

$$= \frac{1}{5-(-3)}$$

$$= \frac{1}{8}$$

$$= 0.125 \text{ for } -3 \leq k \leq 5$$

and $f_x(k) = 0$ for $k < -3$ or $k > 5$.

We can compute $P\{X \leq -5\}$ as

$$P\{X \leq -5\} = 0$$

because the probability density function is zero for $k \leq -5$. Likewise,

$$P\{X \leq -3\} = 0$$

because the probability density function is zero for $k \leq -3$. We also compute $P\{X \leq 0\}$ as

$$P\{X \le 0\} = (0.125) [(0) - (-3)]$$

$$= (0.125) (3)$$

$$= 0.375$$

and
$$P\{X \le 4\} = (0.125) [(4) - (-3)]$$

$$= (0.125) (7)$$

$$= 0.875$$

✓ • PROBLEM 3–6

Suppose X is a continuous uniform random variable with parameters 5 and 10. What is $E[X]$? What is the probability density function? What is $P\{X < 0\}$? What is $P\{X < 6\}$? What is $P\{X < 10\}$? What is $P\{X > 7\}$?

SOLUTION:

The general formula for the expected value of a continuous uniform random variable is given by

$$E[X] = \frac{a+b}{2}.$$

Here $a = 5$ and $b = 10$. Thus,

$$E[X] = \frac{5+10}{2}$$

$$= \frac{15}{2}$$

$$= 7.5$$

The probability density function of a continuous uniform random variable is $1 / (b - a)$ on the range $[a, b]$ and 0 elsewhere. Thus, the probability density function of this particular continuous uniform random variable is

$$f_x(k) = \frac{1}{b-a}$$

$$= \frac{1}{10-5}$$

$$= \frac{1}{5}$$

$$= 0.2 \text{ for } 5 \le k \le 10$$

and $\qquad f_x(k) = 0$ for $k < 5$ or $k > 10$.

We can compute $P\{X \le 0\}$ as

$$P\{X \le 0\} = 0$$

because the probability density function is zero for $k \le 0$. Likewise,

$$P\{X \le 6\} = (0.2) \, [6-5]$$

$$= (0.2) \, (1)$$

$$= 0.2$$

$$P\{X \le 10\} = (0.2) \, [10-5]$$

$$= (0.2) \, (5)$$

$$= 1$$

and $\qquad P\{X > 7\} = (0.2) \, [10-7]$

$$= (0.2) \, (3)$$

$$= 0.6$$

• PROBLEM 3-7

Suppose X is a continuous uniform random variable with parameters -10 and 10. What is $E[X]$? What is the probability density function? What is $P\{|X| < 2\}$? What is $P\{X < 6\}$? What is $P\{X < 10\}$? What is $P\{|X| > 7\}$?

SOLUTION:

The general formula for the expected value of a continuous uniform random variable is given by

$$E[X] = \frac{a+b}{2}.$$

Here $a = -10$ and $b = 10$. Thus,

$$E[X] = \frac{(-10)+(10)}{2}$$

$$= \frac{0}{2}$$

$$= 0$$

The probability density function of a continuous uniform random variable is $1 / (b - a)$ on the range $[a, b]$ and 0 elsewhere. Thus, the probability density function of this particular continuous uniform random variable is

$$f_x(k) = \frac{1}{b-a}$$

$$= \frac{1}{10-(-10)}$$

$$= \frac{1}{20}$$

$$= 0.05 \text{ for } -10 \le k \le 10$$

and $\quad f_x(k) = 0$ for $k < -10$ or $k > 10$.

We can compute $P\{|X| < 2\}$ as

$$P\{|X| < 2\} = P\{-2 < X < 2\}$$

$$= (0.05) [2 - (-2)]$$

$$= (0.05) [4]$$

$$= 0.2$$

$$P\{X < 6\} = (0.05) [6 - (-10)]$$

$$= (0.05)(16)$$

$$= 0.8$$

$$P\{X < 10\} = (0.05)[10 - (-10)]$$

$$= (0.05)(20)$$

$$= 1$$

$$P\{|X| > 7\} = 1 - P\{|X| < 7\}$$

$$= 1 - (0.05)[7 - (-7)]$$

$$= 1 - (0.05)(14)$$

$$= 1 - 0.7$$

$$= 0.3$$

✓ • **PROBLEM 3–8**

Suppose X is a continuous uniform random variable with parameters -2 and 10. What is $E[X]$? What is the probability density function? What is $P\{|X| < 1\}$? What is $P\{|X| < 4\}$? What is $P\{|X| > 3\}$?

SOLUTION:

The general formula for the expected value of a continuous uniform random variable is given by

$$E[X] = \frac{a+b}{2}.$$

Here $a = -2$ and $b = 10$. Thus,

$$E[X] = \frac{(-2) + (10)}{2}$$

$$= \frac{8}{2}$$

$$= 4$$

The probability density function of a continuous uniform random variable is $1 / (b - a)$ on the range $[a, b]$ and 0 elsewhere. Thus, the probability density function of this particular continuous uniform random variable is

$$f_x(k) = \frac{1}{b-a}$$

$$= \frac{1}{10-(-2)}$$

$$= \frac{1}{12}$$

$$= 0.0833 \text{ for } -2 \leq k \leq 10$$

and $\quad f_x(k) = 0$ for $k < -2$ or $k > 10$.

We can compute $P\{|X| < 1\}$ as

$$P\{|X| < 2\} = P\{-1 < X < 1\}$$

$$= \frac{1}{12} [1 - (-1)]$$

$$= \frac{1}{12} [2]$$

$$= \frac{2}{12}$$

$$= \frac{1}{6}$$

$$P\{|X| < 4\} = P\{-4 < X < 4\}$$

$$= P\{-4 < X < -2\} + P\{-2 < X < 4\}$$

We break up this probability because the probability density function takes on different values below -2 and above -2. Then

$$P\{-4 < X < -2\} + P\{-2 < X < 4\} = (0) [(-2) - (-4)] + \left(\frac{1}{12}\right) [4 - (-2)]$$

$$= (0) (2) + \left(\frac{1}{12}\right) (6)$$

$$= 0 + 0.5$$

$$= 0.5$$

and $\quad P\{|X| > 3\} = 1 - P\{|X| < 3\}$

$$= 1 - P\{-3 < X < 3\}$$

$$= 1 - P\{-3 < X < -2\} - P\{-2 < X < 3\}$$

$$= 1 - (0) [(-2) - (-3)] - \left(\frac{1}{12}\right) [3 - (-2)]$$

$$= 1 - (0) (1) - \left(\frac{1}{12}\right) (5)$$

$$= 1 - 0 - \frac{5}{12}$$

$$= \frac{7}{12}$$

√ • PROBLEM 3-9

Suppose X is a continuous uniform random variable with parameters a and 20. If $E[X] = 15$, then what is a?

SOLUTION:

We know that

$$15 = E[X]$$

$$= \frac{a+b}{2}$$

$$= \frac{a+20}{2}$$

Therefore, $a + 20 = 30$,

$$a = 30 - 20$$

$$= 10$$

• PROBLEM 3-10

If X is a continuous uniform random variable with parameters 0 and b, and with probability density function 1, then what is b?

SOLUTION:

We know that

$$1 = f_x(k)$$

$$= \frac{b-a}{2} \qquad = \frac{1}{b-a}$$

$$= \frac{b-0}{2} \qquad = \frac{1}{b-0}$$

$$= \frac{b}{2} \qquad = \frac{1}{b}$$

Then $\qquad b = (1)(2) \qquad b = 1$

$$= 2$$

• PROBLEM 3-11

If X is a continuous random variable with parameters $-b$ and b, then what is $E[X]$? What is b if the probability density function is $1/20$?

SOLUTION:

We compute

$$E[X] = \frac{a+b}{2}$$

$$= \frac{(-b)+b}{2}$$

$$= \frac{0}{2}$$

$$= 0$$

Also, $\qquad \dfrac{1}{20} = f_x(k)$

$$= \frac{1}{b-a}$$

$$= \frac{1}{b-(-b)}$$

$$= \frac{1}{2}b$$

Then $\qquad 2b = 20$

$$b = \frac{20}{2}$$

$$= 10$$

✓ • **PROBLEM 3-12**

Consider the hardness of steel as a random variable, X, with values between 50 and 70 on the Rockwell B scale. We can assume that the hardness has density function

$$f(x) = 0 \qquad \text{when } x < 50,$$

$$f(x) = \frac{1}{20} \qquad \text{when } 50 \le x \le 70,$$

$$f(x) = 0 \qquad \text{when } x > 70.$$

Graph this density function. Compute the probability that the hardness of a randomly selected steel specimen is less than 65.

SOLUTION:

Graph of $f(x)$.

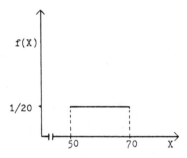

We use the cumulative distribution function $F(a) = P\{X \le a\}$ to compute $P\{X < 65\}$.

$$F(a) = \int_{-\infty}^{a} f(x)\, dx = \int_{50}^{a} \frac{1}{20}\, dx = \frac{1}{20} \times x\big]_{50}^{a} = \frac{a - 50}{20} = F(a)$$

when $50 \le x \le 70$. (When $b < 50$, $F(b) = \int_{-\infty}^{b} 0\, dx = 0$. When $b > 70$,

$$F(b) = \int_{-\infty}^{50} f(x)\, dx + \int_{50}^{70} f(x)\, dx + \int_{70}^{b} f(x)\, dx = 0 + \frac{20}{20} + 0 = 1.)$$

We find that

$$P\{X < 65\} = F(65) = \frac{65 - 50}{20} = \frac{15}{20} = \frac{3}{4}.$$

• PROBLEM 3-13

Find the probability that three random points on the circumference of a circle all lie on a semicircle.

SOLUTION:

Note that the first two points do not matter. There will always be a common semicircle for any two random points. The placement of the third point can cause trouble, as in the following diagram:

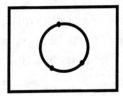

Let us examine the ways we can place the third point so as to still be in a semicircle. The angle formed by the placement of the first two points is denoted by Θ.

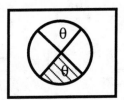

By the previous diagram, we see that if the third point is placed anywhere on the arc of the nonshaded region, then the three points will lie on a semicircle. There is an arc of angle $2\pi - \theta$ on which we can place the point. We will assume that the probability of placing the point is uniform. Hence,

$$Pr_\theta \text{(Semicircle)} = \frac{\text{Possible angle of placement}}{2\pi}$$

$$P\{\text{Semicircle} \mid \Theta = \theta\} = \frac{2\pi - \theta}{2\pi}$$

If one is bothered by the use of a "semicircle" as a random variable, the following random variable can be set up:

$$X = \begin{cases} 0 & \text{if no semicircle} \\ 1 & \text{if a semicircle exists.} \end{cases}$$

Now note the following series of equalities:

$$P\{\text{semicircle}\} = P\{X = 1\}$$

$$= \int P(X = 1 \mid \Theta = \theta) \, F(\theta) \, d\theta$$

$$= \int \frac{2\pi - \theta}{2\pi} F(\theta) \, d\theta$$

We will now assume that Θ is uniformly distributed. If the first two points are coincident, then $\Theta = 0$. The largest possible value of Θ is when the first two points are at extreme ends of a diameter. Then $\Theta = \pi$. Hence,

$$F(\theta) = \frac{1}{\pi - 0} = \frac{1}{\pi} \qquad \text{for } 0 \leq \Theta \leq \pi.$$

Finally,

$$P\{X = 1\} = \int_0^\pi \frac{2\pi - \theta}{2\pi} \left(\frac{1}{\pi} \right) d\theta$$

$$= \int_0^\pi \left(\frac{1}{\pi} - \frac{\theta}{2\pi^2} \right) d\theta = \left[\frac{\theta}{\pi} - \frac{\theta^2}{4\pi^2} \right]_0^\pi$$

$$= \frac{\pi}{\pi} - \frac{\pi^2}{4\pi^2} - 0 + 0 = 1 - \frac{1}{4} = \frac{3}{4}$$

******

REVIEW OF EXPONENTIAL RANDOM VARIABLES

Exponential random variables are said to possess a lack of memory, and they are often applied to waiting times. The lack of memory property, or memorylessness, is an easily misunderstood concept. Imagine waiting in line or being put on hold when you call a government agency. There is a distribution (unknown to you) dictating how long you will wait. Suppose that you have already waited a given length of time. There is now another distribution dictating how much longer you will wait. If these two distributions coincide, then the distribution is said to lack memory, or to be memoryless. The exponential distribution is the only continuous distribution to have this property.

Written more formally, the lack of memory property states that

$$P\{X > k + c \text{ given that } X > k\} = P\{X > c\}.$$

We cannot say much more about this until we study conditional probability in a future chapter.

There are two commonly used parameterizations, or ways of writing the probability density function, of the exponential distribution. The more common parameterization is

$$f_x(k) = Le^{-Lk} \text{ for } k > 0$$

and $\quad f_x(k) = 0$ for other k.

Using this parameterization, the expected value of an exponential random variable is

$$E[X] = \frac{1}{L}. \qquad Var[x] = \frac{1}{L^2}$$

Sometimes instead the probability density function is written as

or

$$f_x(k) = \frac{e^{-k/L}}{L} \text{ for } k > 0 \qquad \boxed{P(x < 1) = F(1)}$$

and $\quad f_x(k) = 0$ otherwise.

Using this parameterization,

$$E[X] = L. \qquad Var[x] = L^2$$

This is a more convenient parameterization if primary interest lies in the expected value. Because there are two ways to write the probability density function, it would be ambiguous to speak of the parameter characterizing the exponential distribution. To avoid this ambiguity, we will speak of the expected value of an exponential random variable. Integration shows that the cumulative distribution function for an exponential random variable with mean $1 / L$ is given by

$$F_x(k) = 1 - e^{-Lk} \text{ for } k > 0$$

and $\qquad F_x(k) = 0$ for $k \leq 0$.

✓ • **PROBLEM 3-14**

Consider the exponential distribution $f(x) = \lambda e^{-\lambda x}$ for $x > 0$. Find the moment generating function and, from it, the mean and variance of the exponential distribution.

SOLUTION:

By definition $M_x(t) = E(e^{tx})$

$$= \int_{-\infty}^{\infty} e^{tx} f(x) \, dx$$

$$= \int_{x=0}^{\infty} e^{tx} \lambda e^{-\lambda t} \, dx$$

$$= \int_0^{\infty} \lambda e^{(t-\lambda)x} \, dx = \lambda \int_0^{\infty} e^{(t-\lambda)x} \, dx$$

$$= \lambda \left[\frac{-1}{t-\lambda} e^{(t-\lambda)x} \right]_0^{\infty}$$

$$= \frac{\lambda}{\lambda-t} \left[e^{(t-\lambda)x} \right]_0^{\infty}$$

Consider $t < \lambda$. Then $\lambda - t > 0$ and $t - \lambda < 0$. Hence,

$$e^{(t-\lambda)x} = e^{-kx} \text{ and } M_x(t) = \frac{\lambda}{\lambda-t} (0 - (-1)) = \frac{\lambda}{\lambda-t} \text{ for } t < \lambda.$$

The mean is

$$E(x) = M'_x(t)|_{t=0}$$

$$M'_x(t) = \frac{d}{dt}\left(\frac{\lambda}{\lambda - t}\right) = \lambda\left(\frac{d}{dt}\frac{1}{\lambda - t}\right)$$

$$= \lambda\left(\frac{1}{(\lambda - t)^2}\right)\frac{d}{dt}(\lambda - t) = \frac{\lambda}{(\lambda - t)^2}$$

$$M'_x(0) = E(x) = \frac{\lambda}{(\lambda - 0)^2} = \frac{\lambda}{\lambda^2} = \frac{1}{\lambda}.$$

Also by the moment generating function's properties

$$E(x^2) = M''_x(t)|_{t=0}$$

We calculate

$$M''_x(t) = \frac{d}{dt}\frac{\lambda}{(\lambda - t)^2} = \lambda\frac{d}{dt}\frac{1}{(\lambda - t)^2}$$

$$= \lambda\frac{-2}{(\lambda - t)^2}\frac{d}{dt}(\lambda - t) = \frac{2\lambda}{(\lambda - t)^3}$$

Now $$M''_x(0) = E(x^2) = \frac{2\lambda}{(\lambda)^3} = \frac{2\lambda}{\lambda^2}$$

and $$\text{var}(X) = E(x^2) - (E[x])^2$$

$$= \frac{2}{\lambda^2} - \left(\frac{1}{\lambda}\right)^2 = \frac{1}{\lambda^2}$$

V • **PROBLEM 3–15**

Suppose that X is exponentially distributed with mean 1. What is $P\{X > 1\}$?

SOLUTION:

We use the formula for the cumulative distribution of an exponentially distributed random variable to find

$$P\{X > 1\} = 1 - F_x(1)$$

$$= 1 - e^{-(1)(1)}$$

$$= 1 - e^{-1}$$

$$= 1 - \frac{1}{e}$$

$$= 1 - \frac{1}{2.718}$$

$$= 1 - 0.3679$$

$$= 0.6321$$

✓ • PROBLEM 3-16

Suppose that X is exponentially distributed with mean $1/2$. What is $P\{X > 1\}$?

SOLUTION:

We use the formula for the cumulative distribution of an exponentially distributed random variable to find

$$P\{X > 1\} = 1 - F_x(1)$$

$$= 1 - e^{-(2)(1)}$$

$$= 1 - e^{-2}$$

$$= 1 - 0.1353$$

$$= 0.8647$$

• PROBLEM 3-17

Suppose that X is exponentially distributed with mean 0.2. What is $P\{X > 4\}$?

SOLUTION:

Since the mean is 0.2, or 1/5, we use the formula for the cumulative distribution of an exponentially distributed random variable with parameter $1/0.2 = 5$ to find

$$P\{X > 4\} = 1 - F_x(4)$$

$$= 1 - e^{-(5)\,(4)}$$

$$= 1 - e^{-20}$$

$$= 1 - 0.0000$$

$$= 1.0000$$

• PROBLEM 3-18

Engineers determine that the lifespans of electric light bulbs manufactured by their company have the exponential distribution,

$$f(x) = \frac{1}{1,000} e^{\frac{-x}{1,000}}$$

when $x \geq 0$ and $f(x) = 0$, $x < 0$. Compute the probability that a randomly selected light bulb has a lifespan of less than 1,000 hours. Graph the density function.

SOLUTION:

The cumulative distribution function $F(a) = P\{X \leq a\}$ is used to compute $P\{X < 1,000\}$. We find the area under the graph of $f(x)$ from 0 to a (the area from $-\infty$ to 0 is 0 because $f(x) = 0$ when $x < 0$).

$$\text{Now } P\{X \le a\} = F(a) = \int_0^a f(x)\,dx = \int_0^a \frac{1}{1,000} e^{\frac{x}{1,000}}\,dx$$

$$= \int_0^a \frac{1}{1,000} e^{-\frac{x}{1,000}}\,dx = \frac{1}{1,000}\left[-1,000 e^{-\frac{x}{1,000}}\,dx\right]_0^a$$

$$= \left[e^{-\frac{x}{1,000}}\,dx\right]_0^a = -\left[e^{-\frac{a}{1,000}} - e^0\right]$$

$$= 1 - e^{-\frac{a}{1,000}} = F(a)$$

$$P\{X \le 1,000\} = F(1,000) = 1 - e^{-\frac{1,000}{1,000}} = 1 - e^{-1}$$

$$= 1 - \frac{1}{e}$$

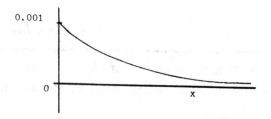

Graph of $f(x) = 0.001\, e^{-0.001x}$
When $x = 0$, $f(x) = 0.001$. As $x \to \infty$, $f(x) \to 0$.

The probability density function of the length of life of a certain component is given by

$$f(t) = ke^{-kt} \qquad (0 < t < \infty).$$

An apparatus contains three components of this type and the failure of one may be assumed independent of the failure of the others.

Find the probability that

(a) None will have failed by t_0 hours.

(b) Exactly one will fail in the first t_0 hours, another in the second t_0, and the third after more than $2t_0$ hours.

SOLUTION:

First let us find the cumulative distribution function of T. This is

$$F(t) = P\{T \le t\} = \int_{-\infty}^{t} f(x)\, dx$$

$$= \int_0^t ke^{-kx}\, dx = -e^{-kx}\Big|_0^t = 1 - e^{-kt}.$$

Note that $P\{T \ge t\} = 1 - P\{T \le t\}$

$$= 1 - (1 - e^{-kt}) = e^{-kt}.$$

(a) For none to have failed at $T = t_0$, the three must have lifetimes greater than t_0. Since the lifetimes are independent (and identically distributed), the probability of this is the product

$$P\{T_1 \ge t_0\} \times P\{T_2 \ge t_0\} \times P\{T_3 \ge t_0\}$$

$$= [P\{T_1 \ge t_0\}]^3$$

$$= (-e^{-kt})^3 = -e^{-3kt_0}.$$

(b) To solve part b, we make use of the following calculations:

$$P\{T \le t_0\} = F(t_0) = 1 - e^{-kt_0},$$

$$P\{t_0 \le T_2 \le 2t_0\} = F(2t_0) - F(t_0)$$

$$= 1 - e^{-2kt_0} - (1 - e^{-kt_0})$$

$$= e^{-kt_0} - e^{-2kt_0},$$

and $\qquad P\{T_3 \geq 2t_0\} = 1 - F(2t_0) = 1 - (1 - e^{-2kt_0})$

$$= e^{-2kt_0}.$$

If we simply multiply these three quantities, we obtain the probability that one will fail in the first t_0, another in the next t_0, and the third after $2t_0$; but in a specific order. We must also account for the fact that the bulbs burn out in $3 \times 2 \times 1 = 6$ ways. Hence the probability we want is

$$6 \times P\{T_1 \leq t_0\} \times P\{t_0 \leq T_2 \leq 2t_0\} \times P\{T_3 \leq 2t_0\}$$

$$= 6\,(1 - e^{-kt_0})\,(e^{-kt_0} - e^{-2kt_0})\,(e^{-2kt_0})$$

$$= 6\,e^{-3kt_0}\,(1 - e^{-kt_0})\,(1 - e^{-kt_0})$$

$$= 6\,e^{-3kt_0}\,(1 - 2e^{-kt_0} + e^{-2kt_0})$$

$$= 6\,e^{-3kt_0} - 12\,e^{-4kt_0} + 6\,e^{-5kt_0}.$$

✓ • PROBLEM 3-20

If the random variable X has an exponential distribution; i.e., $f(x) = \lambda e^{-\lambda x}$ for $X \geq 0$, show that for a, b positive

$$P\{X > a + b \mid X > a\} = P\{X > b\}.$$

SOLUTION:

First note that

$$P\{X > x\} = \int_x^\infty f(t)\,dt = \int_x^\infty \lambda e^{-\lambda t}\,dt$$

$$= -e^{-\lambda t}\Big|_x^\infty = 0 - (-e^{-\lambda x}) = e^{-\lambda x}$$

Now, by definition

$$P\{X > a + b \mid X > a\} = \frac{P(X > a + b \text{ and } X > a)}{P(X > a)}.$$

But if $X > a + b$, it will be greater than a also, since $b > 0$. Thus, we have

$$\frac{P(X > a + b)}{P(X > a)} = \frac{e^{-\lambda(a+b)}}{e^{-\lambda a}}$$

$$= \frac{(e^{-\lambda a})(e^{-\lambda b})}{e^{-\lambda a}} = e^{-\lambda b} = P(X > b)$$

This is referred to as the lack of memory property.

✓ • **PROBLEM 3-21**

This problem will show an analogy between the geometric and exponential distributions. Show that the result of the last problem also
holds if X is distributed geometrically.

SOLUTION:

We want to show that if X has the distribution $P\{X > x\} = (1 - p)^{x - 1}$
p, $x = 1, 2, 3,...$, then for nonnegative a and b

$$P\{X > a + b \mid X > a\} = P\{X > b\}.$$

First note that $P\{X > k\}$

$$= \sum_{x=k+1}^{\infty} P(X > x) = \sum_{x=k+1}^{\infty} (1 - p)^{x-1} p$$

$$= p \sum_{x=k+1}^{\infty} (1 - p)^{x-1} = p \sum_{x=k+1}^{\infty} (1 - p)^{x}$$

$$= p \frac{(1 - p)^k}{1 - (1 - p)}$$

$$= p \frac{(1 - p)^k}{p} = (1 - p)^k \text{ (using the theory of geometric series)}$$

By definition, $P\{X > a + b \mid X > a\}$

$$= \frac{P(X > a + b \text{ and } X > a)}{P(X > a)}.$$

Since $b \geq 0$, if $X > a + b$ then $X > a$ too. Hence we have

$$\frac{P(X > a + b)}{P(X > a)} = \frac{(1 - p)^{a+b}}{(1 - p)^a}$$

$$= \frac{(1 - p)^a (1 - p)^b}{(1 - p)^a} \quad (1 - p)^b$$

$$= P\{X > b\}$$

The last two problems may be interpreted as follows: if we have already spent some time in waiting, the distribution of further waiting time is the same as that of the initial waiting time. It is as if we waited in vain! A suggestive way of saying this is that the random variable X has no memory. This turns out to be a fundamental property of these two distributions and is basic for the theory of Markov processes. Distributions with this property are said to have the Markov property.

✳✳✳✳✳✳

REVIEW OF NORMAL RANDOM VARIABLES

The normal distribution is the most commonly used of all probabilistic distributions in all areas of statistical application. There are many reasons for this prevalence, not the least of which are closure under the process of averaging and the central limit theorem. Closure under the process of averaging ensures that the mean of a set of normal random variables is also a random variable with a normal distribution. The central limit theorem appears in many forms, so actually it is a collection of theorems, but for our purposes we will simplify this collection and consider the central limit theorem to state that whenever the sample size is large enough, say, for example, there are at least 30 observations, then the mean of these observations follows, approximately, the normal distribution. Of course if the original random variables are normally distributed, then we do not require the central limit theorem to tell us that the mean is approximately normally distributed, because we know from closure under the process of averaging that the mean is exactly normally distributed. But the central limit theorem applies even when the original random variables are not normally distributed.

The probability density function of a normal random variable is of no use to us, but it is worth noting that when plotted it gives the familiar bell-shaped curve so commonly referred to in the statistical literature. The cumulative distribution function of a normal random variable cannot be written in closed (algebraic) form. Tables are required, but fortunately these tables are fairly wide-spread. Almost every introductory statistical text has a normal table in the back of the book.

The normal distribution is characterized by two parameters. These are the mean and the variance. Each set of these parameters gives rise to a different normal distribution. The mean can be any real number, positive or negative. The variance must be non-negative, but otherwise is arbitrary. If a book were to include tables of the cumulative distribution function of each of these normal distributions, then there would not be enough paper in the world to fit all of these tables. Fortunately, this is not necessary.

Any linear function of a normally distributed random variable is also a normally distributed random variable. To illustrate, let X be a normally distributed random variable with mean M and standard deviation S. Let $Y = aX + b$ be an arbitrary linear function of X. Then Y is a normally distributed random variable with mean $aM + b$ and standard deviation aS. The importance of this fact will be seen when we discuss the standard normal distribution and its tabulated distribution.

There are two key properties of the normal distribution which allow for tabulation of the cumulative distribution function of only a single normal distribution. First, the normal probability density function is symmetric about the mean. Second, when we standardize a normal random variable by subtracting from it its mean and then dividing it by its standard deviation (to be discussed in a future chapter), the result is a normal random variable with mean zero and standard deviation one. This is known as a standard normal random variable, and this is the one which is most commonly tabulated in textbooks.

If X is distributed normally with mean two and standard deviation three, and we are asked to find the probability that $X > 4$ (for example),

(handwritten: $M = 2$, $\sigma = 3$)

then we define Z to be $(X - 2) / 3$. Now Z is also a random variable, and it turns out that Z is normally distributed with mean zero and standard deviation one. Then

$$P\{X > 4\} = P\left\{\frac{(X-2)}{3} > \frac{(4-2)}{3}\right\}$$

$$= P\left\{Z > \frac{2}{3}\right\}$$

This probability can be looked up in any normal table.

To save space, most normal tables only tabulate non-negative values. Thus, they cannot be used directly to answer questions about negative numbers. If a question involves negative numbers, such as, find $P\{X > -3\}$, then we use the fact that the normal distribution is symmetric about its mean. Mathematically, this symmetry is described by stating that if X is a normal random variable with mean M and standard deviation S, then for any value k it is true that

$$P\{X > M + k\} = P\{X < M - k\}$$

and $\qquad P\{X < M + k\} = P\{X > M - k\}.$

Returning to our example, X is a normal random variable with mean two and standard deviation three. We first must write -3 as a deviation from the mean ($-3 = 2 - 5$). Then we use the symmetry to obtain

$$P\{X > -3\} = P\{X > 2 - 5\}$$

$$= P\{X < 2 + 5\}$$

$$= P\{X < 7\}$$

$$= P\left\{\frac{(X-2)}{3} < \frac{(7-2)}{3}\right\}$$

$$= P\left\{Z < \frac{5}{3}\right\}$$

$$= P\{Z < 1.67\}$$

and this probability can again be looked up in any normal table. Typically, Z is used to denote the standard normal distribution.

The strategy for solving problems which ask for probabilities involving the normal distribution is first to write what is being asked for. Typically, this will be of the form

$$P\{X > k\}$$

or $\qquad P\{X < k\}$

for some given k, and the mean and standard deviation of X will be given as M and S. Our next step is to equate this probability to one involving X after being standardized. Of course whatever we do to one side of the inequality must also be done to the other side of the inequality. Thus, k must be "standardized" as well. Then we obtain

$$P\{X > k\} = P\left\{ \frac{(X - M)}{S} > \frac{(k - M)}{S} \right\}$$

or $\qquad P\{X < k\} = P\left\{ \frac{(X - M)}{S} < \frac{(k - M)}{S} \right\}.$

Now we replace the quantity $(X - M)/S$ with Z, since any normal random variable which is standardized has a standard normal (Z) distribution. We obtain

$$P\{X > k\} = P\{Z > (k - M)/S\}$$

or $\qquad P\{X < k\} = P\{Z < (k - M)/S\}.$

The numbers k, M, and S are all known so we can evaluate the right-hand side of the inequality in the expression. If the result is non-negative, then we look it up in the table for the standard normal distribution. If, however, it is negative, then we use the symmetry of the normal distribution about its mean and look up the absolute value of this quantity in the table of the normal distribution, being careful to change the direction of the inequality.

Different books have different types of tables for the normal cumulative distribution, but all contain equivalent information. That is, from any one such table any other such table can be derived. These tables are typically indexed by cutoffs. The tables may contain

1.　the probability of a standard normal random variable exceeding this cutoff (which is one minus the cumulative distribution function),

2.　the probability of a standard normal random variable being less than this cutoff (this would directly give the cumulative distribution function of the standard normal distribution),

3. the probability of a standard normal random variable falling between zero and the cutoff (which is the cumulative distribution function minus 0.5), or

4. the probability of a standard normal random variable falling within plus or minus the absolute value of the cutoff (which is twice what is tabulated in tables of the third type).

This book provides a table of the second type, so it provides the cumulative distribution function directly. Thus, there is no need for transformations if one wishes to evaluate the cumulative distribution function of the standard normal distribution. For example,

$$P\{Z < 0.14\} = 0.5557,$$

as seen from the table. A more realistic example may ask for $P\{X > -0.5\}$ when X is a random variable with a normal distribution with mean 0.2 and standard deviation 1.4. Then we would need to calculate

$$P\{X > -0.5\} = P\left\{\frac{(X - 0.2)}{1.4} > \frac{(-0.5 - 0.2)}{1.4}\right\}$$

$$= P\left\{Z > \frac{(-0.7)}{1.4}\right\}$$

$$= P\{Z > -0.5\}$$

$$= 1 - P\{Z < -0.5\}$$

$$= 1 - P\{Z > 0.5\}$$

$$= P\{Z < 0.5\}$$

$$= 0.6915$$

It was merely a coincidence that the problem $P\{X < -0.5\}$ converted to $P\{Z < -0.5\}$ after the standardization. Typically, the cutoff for X will not be the same as the cutoff for Z.

✓ • PROBLEM 3-22

If X is a normally distributed random variable with mean five and standard deviation one, then express $P\{X < 0\}$ as a probability involving a standard normal distribution and a non-negative number.

SOLUTION:

We write

$$P\{X < 0\} = P\left\{\frac{(X - 5)}{1} < \frac{(0 - 5)}{1}\right\}$$

$$= P\{Z < -5\}$$

$$= P\{Z > 5\}$$

✓ • PROBLEM 3-23

If X is a normally distributed random variable with mean four and standard deviation two, then express $P\{X < 1\}$ as a probability involving a standard normal distribution and a non-negative number.

SOLUTION:

We write

$$P\{X < 1\} = P\left\{\frac{(X - 4)}{2} < \frac{(1 - 4)}{2}\right\}$$

$$= P\left\{Z < -\frac{3}{2}\right\}$$

$$= P\{Z < -1.5\}$$

$$= P\{Z > 1.5\}$$

If X is a normally distributed random variable with mean zero and standard deviation five, then express $P\{X > 5\}$ as a probability involving a standard normal distribution and a non-negative number.

SOLUTION:

We write

$$P\{X > 5\} = P\left\{\frac{(X-0)}{5} > \frac{(5-0)}{5}\right\}$$

$$= P\{Z > 1\}$$

If X is a normally distributed random variable with mean M and standard deviation S, then what is $P\{X > M\}$?

SOLUTION:

We write

$$P\{X > M\} = P\{X > M + 0\}.$$

By the symmetry of the normal distribution, we know that

$$P\{X > M + 0\} = P\{X < M - 0\}$$

$$= P\{X < M\}.$$

Thus, $\quad P\{X > M\} = P\{X < M\}.$

Also, $\quad P\{X < M\} + P\{X = M\} + P\{X > M\} = 1,$

so $\quad P\{X < M\} + P\{X > M\} = 1 - P\{X = M\}.$

But a normal random variable is a continuous random variable, so

$$P\{X + M\} = 0,$$

and $\quad P\{X < M\} + P\{X > M\} = 1.$

Combining this with the earlier result that

$$P\{X < M\} = P\{X > M\}$$

implies that $P\{X > M\} + P\{X > M\} = 1$,

so $\qquad 2P\{X > M\} = 1$,

and $\qquad P\{X > M\} = \dfrac{1}{2}$

$$= 0.5.$$

√• PROBLEM 3-26

If X is a normally distributed random variable with mean three and standard deviation 0.5, then what is $P\{X > 3.5\}$?

SOLUTION:

We write

$$P\{X > 3.5\} = P\left\{\frac{(X-3)}{0.5} > \frac{(3.5-3)}{0.5}\right\}$$

$$= P\left\{Z > \frac{0.5}{0.5}\right\}$$

$$= P\{Z > 1\}$$

$$= 1 - P\{Z < 1\}$$

$$= 1 - 0.8413$$

$$= 0.1587$$

$\checkmark$ • **PROBLEM 3-27**

If X is a normally distributed random variable with mean 25 and standard deviation 5, then what is $P\{X > 22.5\}$?

SOLUTION:

We write

$$P\{X > 22.5\} = P\left\{\frac{(x - 25)}{5} > \frac{(22.5 - 25)}{5}\right\}$$

$$= P\left\{Z > \frac{(-2.5)}{5}\right\}$$

$$= P\left\{Z > -\frac{1}{2}\right\}$$

$$= P\{Z < 0.5\}$$

$$= 0.6915$$

$\checkmark$ • **PROBLEM 3-28**

If X is a normally distributed random variable with mean -2 and standard deviation 0.1, then what is $P\{X < -2.025\}$?

SOLUTION:

We write

$$P\{X < -2.025\} = P\left\{\frac{[X - (-2)]}{0.1} < \frac{[-2.025 - (-2)]}{0.1}\right\}$$

$$= P\left\{Z < \frac{(-0.025)}{0.1}\right\}$$

$$= P\{Z < -0.25\}$$

$$= P\{Z > 0.25\}$$

$$= 1 - P\{Z < 0.25\}$$

$$= 1 - 0.6 \text{ (approximately)}$$

$$= 0.4$$

 **• PROBLEM 3-29**

If X is a normally distributed random variable with mean 100 and standard deviation 500, then what is $P\{X > 100\}$?

SOLUTION:

We write

$$P\{X > 100\} = P\left\{\frac{(X - 100)}{500} > \frac{(100 - 100)}{500}\right\}$$

$$= P\{Z > 0\}$$

$$= 0.5$$

• PROBLEM 3-30

If X is a normally distributed random variable with mean -25 and standard deviation 0.15, then what is $P\{X < -25.15\}$?

SOLUTION:

We write

$$P\{X < -25.15\} = P\left\{\frac{[X - (-25)]}{0.15} < \frac{[-25.15 - (-25)]}{0.15}\right\}$$

$$= P\left\{Z < \frac{(-0.15)}{0.15}\right\}$$

$$= P\{Z < -1\}$$

$$= P\{Z > 1\}$$

$$= 1 - P\{Z < 1\}$$

$$= 1 - 0.8413$$

$$= 0.1587$$

$\checkmark$ • **PROBLEM 3-31**

If X is a normally distributed random variable with standard deviation one and $P\{X > 5\} = 0.6915$, then what is $E[X]$?

SOLUTION:

We let $M = E[X]$. Then

$$0.6915 = P\{X > 5\}$$

$$= P\left\{\frac{(X - M)}{1} > \frac{(5 - M)}{1}\right\}$$

$$= P\{Z > 5 - M\}$$

But $\quad 0.6915 = P\{Z < 0.5\}$

$$= 1 - P\{Z > 0.5\}$$

$$= P\{Z > -0.5\}$$

Then we may equate $(5 - M)$ and -0.5, resulting in the equation

$$5 - M = -0.5$$

$$M = 5.5$$

Thus, $\quad E[X] = M$

$$= 5.5$$

If X is a normally distributed random variable with standard deviation three and $P\{X < -2\} = 0.5792$, then what is $E[X]$?

SOLUTION:

We let $M = E[X]$. Then

$$0.5792 = P\{X < -2\}$$

$$= P\left\{\frac{(X-M)}{3} < \frac{[(-2)-M]}{3}\right\}$$

$$= P\left\{Z < \frac{(-2-M)}{3}\right\}$$

But $\quad 0.5792 = P\{Z < 0.20\}$.

Then we may equate $\dfrac{(-2-M)}{3}$ and 0.20, resulting in the equation

$$\frac{(-2-M)}{3} = 0.20$$

$$= \frac{1}{5}$$

so $\qquad -2 - M = \dfrac{3}{5}$

$$-M = 2 + \frac{3}{5}$$

$$-M = \frac{13}{5}$$

$$M = -\frac{13}{5}.$$

$\sqrt{\,}$ • **PROBLEM 3-33**

If Z is a standard normal variable, use the table of standard normal probabilities to find:

(a) $P\{Z<0\}$;

(b) $P\{-1<Z<1\}$; and

(c) $P\{Z>2.54\}$.

SOLUTION:

The normal distribution is the familiar "bell-shaped" curve. It is a continuous probability distribution that is widely used to describe the distribution of heights, weights, and other characteristics.

The density function of the standard normal distribution is

$$f(x) = \frac{1}{\sqrt{2\pi}}\exp\left(\frac{-x^2}{2}\right) \qquad -\infty < x < \infty .$$

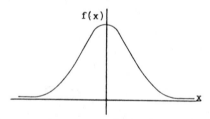

The probability of a standard normal variable being found in a particular interval can be found with the help of tables found in the backs of most statistics textbooks.

(a) To find the probability $P\{Z<0\}$, we can take advantage of the fact that the normal distribution is symmetric about its mean of zero. Thus $P\{Z>0\} = P\{Z<0\}$. We know that

$$P\{Z>0\} + P\{Z<0\} = 1$$

because $Z>0$ and $Z<0$ are essentially exhaustive events since $P\{Z=0\} = 0$. Thus,

$$2P\{Z<0\} = 1 \text{ or } P\{Z<0\} = \frac{1}{2}.$$

(b) To find $P\{-1 < Z < 1\}$ we use the tables of the standard normal distribution. We obtain

$$P\{-1 < Z < 1\} = P\{Z < 1\} - P\{Z < -1\}.$$

Reading across the row headed by 1 and down the column labeled 0.00, we see that $P\{Z < 1.0\} = 0.8413$.

$$P\{Z < -1\} = P\{Z > 1\}$$

by the symmetry of the normal distribution. We also know that

$$P\{Z > 1\} = 1 - P\{Z < 1\}.$$

Substituting, we see that

$$P\{-1 < Z < 1\} = P\{Z < 1\} - [1 - P\{Z < 1\}]$$
$$= 2P\{Z < 1\} - 1$$
$$= 2\,(0.8413) - 1$$
$$= 0.6826$$

(c) $P\{Z > 2.54\} = 1 - P\{Z < 2.54\}$ and reading across the row labeled 2.5 and down the column labeled 0.04, we see that $P\{Z < 2.54\} = 0.9945$. Substituting,

$$P\{Z > 2.54\} = 1 - 0.9945 = 0.0055.$$

✓• PROBLEM 3-34

Find $P\{-0.47 < Z < 0.94\}$.

SOLUTION:

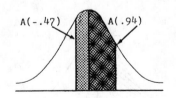

A(-.47)   A(.94)

The probability $P\{-0.47 < Z < 0.94\}$ is equal to the shaded area above. To find the value of the shaded area, we add the areas labeled $A(-0.47)$ and $A(0.94)$. That is,

$$P\{-0.47 < Z < 0.94\} = A(-0.47) + A(0.94).$$

By the symmetry of the normal distribution, $A(-0.47) = A(0.47) = 0.18082$ from the table. Also $A(0.94) = 0.32639$, so

$$P\{-0.47 < Z < 0.94\} = 0.18082 + 0.32639 = 0.50721.$$

• PROBLEM 3–35

Find $\Phi(-0.45)$.

SOLUTION:

Note that $\Phi(-0.45) = P\{Z \leq -0.45\}$, where Z is distributed normally with mean 0 and variance 1.

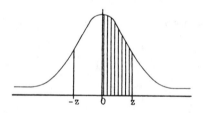

Let $A(Z)$ be the area under the curve from 0 to Z. From our table we find $A(0.45) = 0.17364$ and by the symmetry of the normal distribution,

$$A(-0.45) = A(0.45) = 0.17364.$$

We wish to find $\Phi(-0.45)$, the shaded area below.

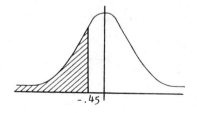

We know that $\Phi(0) = 0.5000$ and from the diagram below we know that $\Phi(0) - A(-0.45) = \Phi(-0.45)$.

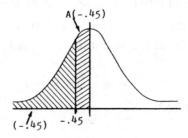

Substituting, we see that $\Phi(0) - A(-0.45) = 0.5000 - 0.17364 = \Phi(-0.45)$ and $\Phi(0.45) = 0.32636$.

• PROBLEM 3-36

Find $P\{-0.47 < Z < 0.94\}$ using $\Phi(-0.47)$ and $\Phi(0.94)$.

SOLUTION:

By definition

$$\Phi(-0.47) = 0.5000 - A(-0.47)$$

$$= 0.5000 - A(0.47)$$

and $\qquad \Phi(0.94) = 0.5000 + A(0.94).$

Hence, $P\{-0.47 < Z < 0.94\} = \Phi(0.94) - F(-0.47)$

$$= [0.5000 + A(0.94)] - [0.5000 - A(0.47)]$$

$$= 0.82539 - 0.31918 = 0.50721.$$

• PROBLEM 3-37

In a normal distribution, what is the Z-score equivalent of the median? What is the Z-score above which only 16 percent of the distribution lies? What percentage of the scores lie below a Z-score of +2.0?

SOLUTION:

The median is the number such that half of a probability distribution lies above or below it. Equivalently, the median is a number $\tilde{m}$ such that a random observation X from a distribution is equally likely to be above or below it. Thus,

$$P\{X \geq \tilde{m}\} = P\{X \leq \tilde{m}\} = \frac{1}{2}.$$

To find the Z-score equivalent of the median, we wish to find some number $\tilde{m}$ such that

$$P\{Z \geq \tilde{m}\} = P\{Z \leq \tilde{m}\} = \frac{1}{2},$$

where Z is a normally distributed random variable with mean 0 and variance 1.

From the tables or from the fact that the normal distribution is symmetric about its mean, we have

$$P\{Z \geq 0\} = P\{Z \leq 0\} = \frac{1}{2}.$$

Thus, the median is $\tilde{m} = 0$.

To find the Z-score above which 16 percent of the distribution lies, we find a constant C such that

$$P\{Z \geq C\} = 16\% = 0.160 \text{ or equivalently}$$

$$P\{Z \leq C\} = 1 - 0.160 = 0.840.$$

Searching for 0.8400 in the body of the table and then reading up the appropriate row and column, we find that

$$P\{Z < 1\} = 0.84, \text{ and thus } C = 1.$$

To find the proportion of scores that lie below a Z-score of 2, we wish to find $P\{Z < 2.00\}$. Reading across the column labeled 2.0 and then down the row headed by 0.00, we find

$$P\{Z < 2.00\} = 0.9772,$$

but 0.9772 is 97.72% of 1; thus, 97.72% of the Z-scores lie below 2.00.

✓ • **PROBLEM 3–38**

Given a random variable x with density

$$f(x) = \frac{1}{\sqrt{18\pi}} e^{-\left(\frac{x^2-10x+25}{18}\right)}, \quad -\infty < x < \infty.$$

Is this distribution normal? What is the maximum value of the density?

SOLUTION:

A normal distribution can be written in the form

$$f(x) = \frac{1}{\sigma\sqrt{2\pi}} \exp\left(-\frac{(x-\mu)^2}{2\sigma^2}\right), \quad \text{when} - \infty < x < \infty.$$

Rewrite $(x^2 - 10x + 25)$ as $(x - 5)^2$ and 18 as $2 \times 9 = 2 \times 3^2$. Also $\sqrt{18\pi} = \sqrt{9 \times 2\pi} = 3\sqrt{2\pi}$. Thus $\mu = 5$ and $\sigma = 3$. Substitution gives

$$f(x) = \frac{1}{3\sqrt{2\pi}} e^{-\left(\frac{(x-5)^2}{2\times3^2}\right)}$$

The density of a normal distribution reaches its maximum at $x = \mu$, so we substitute $x = 5$:

$$f(x) = \frac{1}{3\sqrt{2\pi}} e^{-\left(\frac{(5-5)^2}{2\times3^2}\right)} = \frac{1}{3\sqrt{2\pi}} e^0$$

$$= \frac{1}{3\sqrt{2\pi}}$$

Thus, the maximum value of $f(x)$ is $\frac{1}{3\sqrt{2\pi}}$.

√• **PROBLEM 3-39**

Given that x has a normal distribution with mean 10 and standard deviation 4, find $P\{x < 15\}$.

SOLUTION:

A graph of this density function will look like this:

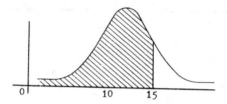

We wish to find $P\{x < 15\}$ or the area of the shaded region. It would be possible to construct tables which would supply such probabilities for many different values of the mean and standard deviation. Luckily, this is not necessary. We may shift and scale our density function in such a way so that only one table is needed.

First, the mean is subtracted from x, giving a new random variable, $x - 10$. This new random variable is still normally distributed, but $E(x - 10)$, the mean of $x - 10$, is $E(x) - 10 = 0$. We have shifted our distribution so that it is centered at 0.

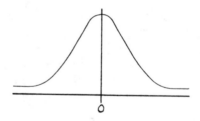

We can scale our new random variable by dividing by the standard deviation, thus creating a new random variable $z = \left(\dfrac{x - 10}{4}\right)$; the variance of Z is

$$\text{var } z = \left(\frac{x-10}{4}\right) = \frac{\text{var } x}{4^2} = \frac{(\text{standard deviation of } x)^2}{16} = 1.$$

Fortunately, our new random variable Z is still normally distributed and has mean 0 and variance 1. This new random variable is referred to as a Z-score or standard normal random variable and tables for its probabilities are widespread.

To solve our problem we first convert an x-score to a Z-score and then consult the appropriate table. We find that

$$P\{x < 15\} = P\left\{\frac{x-10}{4} < \frac{15-10}{4}\right\}$$

$$= P\left\{Z < \frac{5}{4}\right\} = F(1.25) = 0.5000 + A(1.25)$$

$$= 0.5000 + 0.39439 = 0.89439$$

 **• PROBLEM 3–40**

If a random variable X is normally distributed with a mean of 118 and a standard deviation of 11, what Z-scores correspond to raw scores of 115, 134, and 99?

SOLUTION:

To convert a raw score to a Z-score, we subtract the mean and divide by the standard deviation, or

$$\text{Z-score} = \frac{\text{raw score} - \text{mean}}{\text{standard deviation}}.$$

Thus, $\dfrac{115-118}{11} = \dfrac{-3}{11} = -0.27$;

a Z-score of –0.27 corresponds to a raw score of 115. Also,

$$Z = \frac{134-118}{11} = \frac{16}{11} = +1.45$$

or a Z-score of 1.45 corresponds to a raw score of 134. And

$$Z = \frac{99 - 118}{11} = -1.73,$$

or a Z-score of –1.73 corresponds to a raw score of 99.

✓• PROBLEM 3-41

If X has a normal distribution with mean 9 and standard deviation 3, find $P\{5 < X < 11\}$.

SOLUTION:

First we convert our X-scores to Z-scores by subtracting the mean and dividing by the standard deviation. Next, we consult tables for the standard normal distribution.

Thus $\quad P\{5 < X < 11\} = P\left\{\frac{5-9}{3} < \frac{X-9}{3} < \frac{11-9}{3}\right\}$

$$= P\left\{\frac{-4}{3} < Z < \frac{2}{3}\right\} = \Phi(0.66) - \Phi(-1.33)$$

$$= 0.74537 - 0.09176 = 0.65361$$

✓• PROBLEM 3-42

An electrical firm manufactures light bulbs that have a lifetime that is approximately normally distributed with a mean of 800 hours and a standard deviation of 40 hours. Of 100 bulbs, about how many will have lifetimes between 778 and 834 hours?

SOLUTION:

The probability that X, the lifetime of a randomly selected bulb, is between 778 and 834 hours is $P\{778 < X < 834\}$. Standardizing, we see

that $P\{778 < X < 834\}$

$$= P\left\{\frac{778 - \mu}{\sigma} \le \frac{X - \mu}{\sigma} \le \frac{834 - \mu}{\sigma}\right\}$$

$$= P\left\{\frac{778 - 800}{40} \le Z \le \frac{834 - 800}{40}\right\}$$

$$= P\left\{\frac{-22}{40} < Z < \frac{34}{40}\right\} = P\{-0.55 < Z < 0.85\}$$

$$= P\{Z < 0.85\} - P\{Z < -0.55\} = 0.802 - \{1 - 0.709\}$$

$$= 0.511$$

Thus, 51.1% of the bulbs manufactured will have lifetimes between 778 and 834 hours. On the average, 51 of 100 light bulbs will have life-times between 778 and 834 hours.

• PROBLEM 3-43

Given a normal population with $\mu = 25$ and $\sigma = 5$, find the probability that an assumed value of the variable will fall in the interval 20 to 30.

SOLUTION:

We wish to find the probability that a normally distributed random variable, X, with mean $\mu = 25$ and standard deviation $\sigma = 5$, will lie in the interval $(20, 30)$, $P\{20 < X < 30\}$. We convert X from a normally distrib-uted variable with mean 25 and standard deviation 5 to Z, a normally distributed random variable with mean 0 and standard deviation 1. The formula for conversion is $Z = \dfrac{X - \mu}{\sigma}$. Thus,

$$P\{20 < Z < 30\} = P\left\{\frac{20 - \mu}{\sigma} < \frac{X - \mu}{\sigma} < \frac{30 - \mu}{\sigma}\right\}$$

$$= P\left\{\frac{20 - 25}{5} < Z < \frac{30 - 25}{5}\right\}$$

$$= P\{-1 < Z < 1\}$$

To find this probability invovling the random variable Z, we resort to prepared tables which are usually found in statistics texts. There are a variety of such tables and we find $P\{-1 < Z < 1\}$ three different ways to illustrate the various types of tables.

(1) This type of table gives $P\{0 < Z < a\}$. To find the $P\{-1 < Z < 1\}$, we first find $P\{0 < Z < 1\}$. This is $P\{0 < Z < 1\} = 0.341$. Next use the fact that the standard normal distribution is symmetric about 0, hence, $P\{0 < Z < a\} = P\{-a < Z < 0\}$.

From this fact,

$$P\{-1 < Z < 0\} = P\{0 < Z < 1\} = 0.341$$

$$P\{-1 < Z < 1\} = P\{-1 < Z < 0\} + P\{0 < Z < 1\}$$

$$= 2(0.341) = 0.682$$

(2) Another type of table gives $P\{Z \le a\}$ for various values of a. To use this table we note that

$$P\{-1 \le Z \le 1\} = P\{Z \le 1\} - P\{Z \le -1\};$$

from the table we see that

$$P\{Z \le 1\} = 0.841 \text{ and } P\{Z \le -1\} = 0.159.$$

Thus, $P\{-1 \le Z \le 1\} = 0.841 - 0.159 = 0.682.$

(3) This type of table gives $P\{Z \ge a\}$ for certain values of a.

$$P\{-1 \le Z \le 1\} = P\{-1 \le Z\} - P\{1 \le Z\}$$

But $\qquad P\{-1 \le Z\} = P\{1 \ge Z\}$ by symmetry;

$$= 1 - P\{1 \le Z\}$$

Thus, $P\{-1 \le Z \le 1\} = [1 - P\{1 \le Z\}] - P\{1 \le Z\}$

$$= 1 - 2P\{1 \le Z\} = 1 - 2(0.1587) = 0.682$$

✓• **PROBLEM 3-44**

A television company manufactures transistors that have an average life span of 1,000 hours and a standard deviation of 100 hours. Find the probability that a transistor selected at random will have a life span between 875 hours and 1,075 hours. Assume the distribution is normal.

SOLUTION:

The probability that a transistor selected at random will have a life span between 875 hours and 1,075 hours can be expressed symbolically as $P\{875 < X < 1,075\}$. Life spans of transistors are normally distributed, but we must standardize X (the random variable which represents life span) in order to use the standard normal table. We do this by subtracting its mean and dividing the resulting difference by its standard deviation. We are given that the mean (average life span) is 1,000 hours, and that the standard deviation is 100 hours.

Letting Z denotes our standard normal random variable,

$$Z = \frac{X - \mu}{\sigma} = \frac{X - 1,000}{100}.$$

We want to find the area under the standard normal curve between the Z values for $X = 875$ and $X = 1,075$, so we compute

$$Z(875) = \frac{875 - 1,000}{100} = \frac{-125}{100} = -1.25,$$

and
$$Z(1,075) = \frac{1,075 - 1,000}{100} = \frac{75}{100} = 0.75.$$

In terms of Z,

$$P\{875 < X < 1,075\} = P\{-1.25 < Z < 0.75\}.$$

Since some tables give areas under the standard normal curve only for positive Z values, we put $P\{-1.25 < Z < 0.75\}$ in its equivalent form: $P\{0 < Z < 0.75\} + P\{0 < Z < 1.25\}$. The symmetry of the standard normal curve allows us to do this.

Reading the table we find $P\{0 < Z < 0.75\} = 0.2734$ and $P\{0 < Z <$

1.25} = 0.3944. The total area between $Z = -1.25$ and $Z = 0.75$ is $0.2734 + 0.3944 = 0.6678$, and this is the probability that a randomly selected transistor will function between 875 and 1,075 hours.

√ • **PROBLEM 3–45**

The true weights of ten-pound sacks of potatoes processed at a certain packaging house have a normal distribution with mean 10 (pounds) and variance 0.01 (square pounds). What is the probability that a sack purchased at the grocery store will weigh at least 9 lbs. 14 oz.?

SOLUTION:

Let X be the true weight of a 10-pound sack of potatoes. Our question asks what is the $P\{9$ lbs. 14 oz. $\leq X\}$?

Now 9 lbs. 14 oz. $= 9\dfrac{14}{16}$ lbs. $= 9.875$ lbs.

We will subtract the mean, 10, and divide by the standard deviation, $\sqrt{0.01} = 0.1$, to standardize and convert the X-score to a Z-score. This results in

$$P\{9.875 \text{ lbs.} < X\} = P\left\{\frac{9.875 - 10}{0.1} < \frac{X - 10}{0.1}\right\}$$

$$= P\{-1.25 < Z\} = 1 - P\{Z < -1.25\}$$

$$= 1 - \Phi(-1.25) = 1 - 0.10565 = 0.89435$$

√ • **PROBLEM 3–46**

If a distribution has a mean of 15 and a standard deviation of 2, what Z-score corresponds to a raw score of 19? What Z-score corresponds to a raw score of 14?

SOLUTION:

One interpretation of the conversion from X-scores to Z-scores is taken from the meaning of the standard deviation. If a distribution of X-scores has a certain known mean and standard deviation, the Z-score can be thought of as the number of standard deviations from the mean.

For example, in the current problem the distribution has a mean of 15 and a standard deviation of 2. To find the Z-score equivalent of 19, we can either standardize score 19 by subtracting the mean and dividing by the standard deviation or equivalently we can find how many standard deviations 19 is from 15.

The standard deviation is 2, and so 19 is a distance of 2 standard deviations from the mean, since $15 + 2(2) = 19$. The Z-score corresponding to 19 is two standard deviations from 15, thus $Z = 2$ corresponds to 19. That is,

$$P\{X = 19\} = P\left\{\frac{19 - 15}{12}\right\} = P\{Z = 2\}.$$

The Z-score that corresponds to an X-score of 14 is the number of standard deviations 14 is from 15. Since 14 is one unit below 15 and one unit is $1/2$ the standard deviation, the Z-score corresponding to 14 is –0.5.

✓ • **PROBLEM 3-47**

Given a population of values for which $\mu = 100$ and $\sigma = 15$, find the percentage of values that lie within one standard deviation of the mean. Assume a normal distribution.

SOLUTION:

The observation that will lie within one standard deviation of the mean are those values greater than $100 - 15 = 85$ and less than $100 + 15 = 115$.

$$P\{85 < X < 115\} = P\{-1 < Z < 1\}$$

because 85 is one standard deviation below the mean and 115 is one standard deviation above the mean. Now

$$P\{-1 < Z < 1\} = P\{Z < 1\} - P\{Z < -1\}$$

$$= 0.841 - 0.159 = 0.682$$

Thus, 68.2% of the values lie within one standard deviation of the mean.

✓ **• PROBLEM 3-48**

Let X be a normally distributed random variable with mean $\mu = 2$ and $\sigma^2 = 9$. Find the probability that X is less than 8 and greater than 5.

SOLUTION:

The probability of a continuous random variable is defined to be

$$P\{a < X < b\} = \int_a^b f(x)\, dx$$

where $f(x)$ is the density function of the random variable X. The density function of a normally distributed random variable with mean μ and variance σ^2 is

$$f(x) = \frac{1}{\sqrt{2\pi\sigma^2}} e^{-\frac{(x-\mu)^2}{2\sigma^2}} \qquad -\infty < x < \infty .$$

Thus, $P\{a < X < b\} = \int_a^b \frac{1}{\sqrt{2\pi\sigma^2}} e^{-\frac{(x-\mu)^2}{2\sigma^2}}\, dx$

$$= \int_a^\infty \frac{1}{\sqrt{2\pi\sigma^2}} e^{-\frac{(x-\mu)^2}{2\sigma^2}}\, dx - \int_b^\infty \frac{1}{\sqrt{2\pi\sigma^2}} e^{-\frac{(x-\mu)^2}{2\sigma^2}}\, dx$$

$$= P\{X > a\} - P\{X \geq b\}$$

These integrals are quite difficult to evaluate directly so we transform them in the following manner.

Let $Z = \dfrac{X - \mu}{\sigma}$ $\qquad dz = \dfrac{dx}{\sigma}$

and the lower limits of integration become $\dfrac{b - \mu}{\sigma}$ and $\dfrac{a - \mu}{\sigma}$. Thus,

$$P\{a < X \le b\} = \int_a^\infty \frac{1}{\sqrt{2\pi}} e^{-\frac{(x-\mu)^2}{2\sigma^2}} \frac{dx}{\sigma} - \int_b^\infty \frac{1}{\sqrt{2\pi}} e^{-\frac{(x-\mu)^2}{2\sigma^2}} \frac{dx}{\sigma}$$

$$= \int_{\frac{a-\mu}{\sigma}}^\infty \frac{1}{\sqrt{2\pi}} e^{-\frac{Z^2}{2}} dZ - \int_{\frac{b-\mu}{\sigma}}^\infty \frac{1}{\sqrt{2\pi}} e^{-\frac{Z^2}{2}} dZ$$

$$= P\left\{ Z > \frac{a - \mu}{\sigma} \right\} - P\left\{ Z > \frac{b - \mu}{\sigma} \right\}$$

If the density function of a normal random variable has a mean of 0 and a variance of 1, then the density may be written as,

$$f(Z) = \frac{1}{\sqrt{2\pi}} e^{-\frac{Z^2}{2}} \qquad -\infty < x < \infty.$$

This density function is known as the density of a standard normal random variable. The integral of this density has been computed and

$$P\{Z < a\} = \int_{-\infty}^a \frac{1}{\sqrt{2\pi}} e^{-\frac{Z^2}{2}} dZ$$

has been found for many constants a.

The procedure of transforming a random variable that is normally distributed with mean μ and variance σ^2 to a new random variable that is normally distributed with mean 0 and variance is called "standardizing" or "converting an X-score to a Z-score." Such a transformation is accomplished by subtracting μ, the mean, and dividing by σ, the standard deviation. Thus,

$$Z = \frac{X - \mu}{\sigma}.$$

To solve our problem we wish to find $P\{X < 5\}$ and $P\{X < 8\}$ when X is distributed normally with mean $\mu = 2$ and $\sigma^2 = 9$. We have seen that

$$P\{X > 5\} = P\left\{Z > \frac{5-2}{\sqrt{9}}\right\} = P\left\{Z \geq \frac{3}{3}\right\} = P\{Z \geq 1\}$$

and $\qquad P\{X < 8\} = P\left\{\frac{X-2}{3} > \frac{8-2}{3}\right\}$

$$= P\left\{Z > \frac{6}{3}\right\} = P\{Z > 2\}$$

From the table of probabilities for the normal distribution, we see that

$$P\{Z > 1\} = 0.1587 \text{ and } P\{Z > 2\} = 0.{-}228;$$

thus, $\quad P\{5 < X < 8\} = P\{1 < Z < 2\}$

$$= 0.1587 - 0.0228 = 0.1359$$

✓ **• PROBLEM 3-49**

A food processor packages instant coffee in small jars. The weights of the jars are approximately normally distributed with a standard deviation of 0.3 ounces. If 5 percent of the jars weigh more than 12.492 ounces, what is the mean weight of the jars?

SOLUTION:

Let X be the weight of a randomly selected jar. Five percent of the jars weigh more than 12.492 ounces. Thus, $P\{X > 12.492\} = 0.05$.

To find the mean of X given a standard deviation of $\sigma = 0.3$, we convert X-scores to Z-scores.

We know that

$$P\{X > 12.492\} = P\left\{\frac{X - \mu}{\sigma} > \frac{12.492 - \mu}{\sigma}\right\}$$

$$= \left\{Z > \frac{12.492 - \mu}{\sigma}\right\}$$

$$= 0.05$$

From the table of the normal distribution,

$$P\{Z > 1.64\} = 0.05.$$

Thus $\left\{Z > \dfrac{12.492 - \mu}{\sigma}\right\} = 1.64.$ Now

$$\sigma = 0.3, \text{ so } \mu = 12.492 - 1.64\,\sigma$$

$$= 12.492 - (1.64)\,(0.3) = 12.492 - 0.492$$

$$= 12 \text{ ounces}$$

✓ • **PROBLEM 3–50**

The demand for meat at a grocery store during any week is approximately normally distributed with a mean demand of 5,000 lbs and a standard deviation of 300 lbs.

(a) If the store has 5,300 lbs of meat in stock, what is the probability that it is overstocked?

(b) How much meat should the store have in stock per week so as to not run short more than 10 percent of the time?

SOLUTION:

(a) Let the random variable X denote the demand for meat. If the demand is less than the quantity of meat the store has in stock, the store will be overstocked. Thus, if $X < 5,300$, the store will be overstocked. Then $P\{X < 5,300\}$ can be found by converting the X-score to a Z-score. That is,

$$P\{X < 5,300\} = P\left\{\frac{X - \mu}{\sigma} < \frac{5,300}{\sigma}\right\}$$

$$= \left\{Z < \frac{5,300 - 5,000}{300}\right\} = P\{Z < 1\}$$

$$= 0.8413$$

Thus, if the store keeps 5,300 lbs of meat in stock, demand will be less than supply 84.13% of the time.

(b) The store will not run short if $X > q$. We wish to find the number q such that $X < 90\%$ of the time. Equivalently, we wish to find q such that

$$P\{X < q\} = 0.90$$

$$P\{X < q\} = P\left\{\frac{X - \mu}{\sigma} > \frac{q - \mu}{\sigma}\right\} = 0.90$$

$$= \left\{Z < \frac{q - 5{,}000}{300}\right\} = 0.90.$$

From the table of the standard normal distribution,

$$P\{Z < 1.282\} = 0.90. \text{ Thus, } \frac{q - 5{,}000}{300} = 1.282$$

or $q = 5{,}000 + (1.282)\ 300 = 5{,}384.6.$

If the store orders 5,384.6 pounds of meat a week, they will run short only 10 percent of the time.

✓ • **PROBLEM 3–51**

A lathe produces washers whose internal diameters are approximately normally distributed with mean equal to 0.373 inches and standard deviation of 0.002 inches. If specifications require that the internal diameters be 0.375 inches plus or minus 0.004 inches, what percentage of production will be unacceptable?

SOLUTION:

Let X be a random variable representing the internal diameter of a randomly selected washer. Now X is normally distributed with mean 0.373 inches and a standard deviation of 0.002 inches.

If X is greater than $0.375 + 0.004 = 0.379$ inches or less than $0.375 - 0.004 = 0.371$ inches, the washer will be unacceptable. Now

$$P\{X > 0.379\} + P\{X < 0.371\}$$

$$= P\left\{\frac{X-\mu}{\sigma} > \frac{0.379-\mu}{\sigma}\right\} + P\left\{\frac{X-\mu}{\sigma} < \frac{0.371-\mu}{\sigma}\right\}$$

$$= P\left\{Z > \frac{0.379-0.373}{0.002}\right\} + P\left\{Z < \frac{0.371-0.373}{0.002}\right\}$$

$$= P\left\{Z > \frac{0.006}{0.002}\right\} + P\left\{Z < \frac{-0.002}{0.002}\right\}$$

$$= P\{Z > 3\} + P\{Z < -1\}$$

$$= 0.001 + (1 - 0.841) = 0.001 + 0.159$$

$$= 0.160.$$

Thus $P\{\text{washer is unacceptable}\} = 0.160$ or 16% of the washers produced will be unacceptable.

✓• PROBLEM 3-52

The life of a machine is normally distributed with a mean of 3,000 hours. From past experience, 50 percent of these machines last less than 2,632 or more than 3,368 hours. What is the standard deviation of the lifetime of a machine?

SOLUTION:

Let X be the random variable denoting the life of this machine. We know that X is normally distributed with mean 3,000 and the probability that X is greater than 3,368 or less than 2,632 is

$$P\{X < 2,632\} + P\{X > 3,368\} = 0.5.$$

Converting X to a standard normal variable with mean 0 and standard deviation 1 we see that

$$P\{X < 2,632\} = P\left\{\frac{X-\mu}{\sigma} < \frac{2,632-\mu}{\sigma}\right\}$$

$$= P\left\{Z < \frac{2,632-\mu}{\sigma}\right\}$$

and $\quad P\{X > 3,368\} = P\left\{\dfrac{X-\mu}{\sigma} < \dfrac{3,368-\mu}{\sigma}\right\}$

$$= P\left\{Z < \dfrac{3,368-\mu}{\sigma}\right\}.$$

Substituting $\mu = 3000$ into these equations we see that

$$P\{X < 2,632\} = P\left\{Z < \dfrac{-368}{\sigma}\right\}$$

and $\quad P\{X > 3,368\} = P\left\{Z > \dfrac{368}{\sigma}\right\}.$

By the symmetry of the normal distribution we know that:

$$P\{Z < -C\} = P\{Z > C\}.$$

Thus, $P\{X < 2,632\} = P\left\{Z < \dfrac{-368}{\sigma}\right\}$

$$= P\left\{Z > \dfrac{368}{\sigma}\right\} = P\{X > 3,368\}$$

Taking advantage of this fact, we let

$$P\{X < 2,632\} = P\{X > 3,368\} = P\left\{Z > \dfrac{368}{\sigma}\right\}.$$

Thus, $\quad P\left\{Z > \dfrac{368}{\sigma}\right\} + P\left\{Z > \dfrac{368}{\sigma}\right\} = 0.5$

or $\quad P\left\{Z > \dfrac{368}{\sigma}\right\} = \dfrac{0.5}{2} = 0.25.$

Searching through the table of standardized Z-scores, we see that

$P\{Z > 0.67\} = 0.25$, very nearly.

Thus, $\dfrac{368}{\sigma} = 0.67$ or $s = \dfrac{368}{0.67} = 549$ hours.

$\sqrt{}$ • PROBLEM 3-53

The mean height of a soldier in an army regiment is 70 inches. Ten percent of the soldiers in the regiment are taller than 72 inches. Assuming that the heights of the soldiers in this regiment are approximately normally distributed, what is the standard deviation?

SOLUTION:

Let X be the height of a randomly selected soldier. We are given that X is normally distributed with mean $\mu = E(X) = 70$ inches and $P\{X > 72\} = 0.10$.

To find the standard deviation of X, we convert X from an X-score to a Z-score by subtracting the mean and dividing by the unknown standard deviation. Thus,

$$P\{X > 72\} = P\left\{\frac{X-\mu}{\sigma} > \frac{72-\mu}{\sigma}\right\} = 0.10$$

$$= P\left\{Z > \frac{72-\mu}{\sigma}\right\} = 0.10.$$

Checking the table of the standard normal distribution, we wish to find the value C such that $P\{Z > C\} = 0.10$. To do this we inspect the body of the table until the four-digit number closest to 0.10 is located. This is 0.1003. Reading across the row to the left and up the column, we see that $C = 1.28$. Thus,

$$P\{X > 1.28\} = 0.10.$$

We know that

$$P\left\{Z > \frac{72-\mu}{\sigma}\right\} = P\{X > 1.28\} = 0.10.$$

Thus, $\dfrac{72-\mu}{\sigma} = 1.28.$

We have been given that $\mu = 70$; thus, substituting for μ and solving yields

$$\frac{72-70}{\sigma} = 1.28, \qquad \sigma = \frac{72-70}{1.28} = \frac{2}{1.28} = 1.56 \text{ inches.}$$

✓• **PROBLEM 3-54**

The height of soldiers are normally distributed. If 13.57 percent of the soldiers are taller than 72.2 inches and 8.08 percent are shorter than 67.2 inches, what are the mean and the standard deviation of the heights of the soldiers?

SOLUTION:

Let X be the random variable denoting the heights of the soldiers. If 13.57 percent of the soldiers are taller than 72.2 inches, the probability that a randomly selected soldier's height is greater than 72.2 is

$$P\{X > 72.2\} = 0.1357.$$

Similarly, the probability that a randomly selected soldier's height is less than 67.2 inches is

$$P\{X < 67.2\} = 0.0808.$$

To find the mean and variance of X from this information, we convert the X-scores to Z-scores by subtracting the mean and dividing by the standard deviation.

Thus, $P\{X > 72.2\} = 0.1357$

$$P\left\{ \frac{X-\mu}{\sigma} > \frac{72.2-\mu}{\sigma} \right\} = 0.1357 \qquad P\left\{ Z > \frac{72.2-\mu}{\sigma} \right\} = 0.1357.$$

From the table of Z-scores we know that

$$P\{Z > 1.1\} = 0.1357. \text{ Thus, } \frac{72.2-\mu}{\sigma} = 1.1.$$

Similarly, $P\{X < 67.2\} = 0.0808$ implies

$$P\left\{ \frac{X-\mu}{\sigma} < \frac{67.2-\mu}{\sigma} \right\} = 0.0808 \text{ or}$$

$$P\left\{Z < \frac{67.2 - \mu}{\sigma}\right\} = 0.0808.$$

By the symmetry of the normal distribution,

$$P\{Z < -C\} = P\{Z > C\};$$

thus, $P\left\{Z < \dfrac{67.2 - \mu}{\sigma}\right\} = P\left\{Z > \dfrac{-67.2 + \mu}{\sigma}\right\}.$

From the table we see that $P\{Z > 1.4\} = 0.0808$;

thus, $\dfrac{-67.2 + \mu}{\sigma} = 1.4.$

We now have two equations involving μ and σ. These are

$$\frac{72.2 - \mu}{\sigma} = 1.1 \text{ and } -\frac{67.2 + \mu}{\sigma} = 1.4.$$

Multiplying both equations by σ and adding them together gives

$$72.2 - \mu = (1.1)\,\sigma$$

and $$-67.2 + \mu = (1.4)\,\sigma$$

$$5 = (2.5)\,\sigma$$

Thus, $\sigma = \dfrac{5}{2.5} = 2.$

Substituting 2 into either of our original equations gives

$$\mu = 72.2 - (1.1)2 = 70.$$

Thus, the mean of the distribution of heights is $\mu = 70$ and the standard deviation is $\sigma = 2$.

✓ • PROBLEM 3–55

Suppose the weights of adult males are normally distributed and that 6.68 percent are under 130 lbs in weight, and 77.45 percent are between 130 and 180 lbs. Find the parameters of the distribution.

SOLUTION:

Let the random variable X denote the weight of adult males. We are given that X is normally distributed and that $P\{X \leq 130\} = 6.68\%$ and $P\{130 \leq X \leq 180\} = 77.45\%$. Equivalently, $P\{X \leq 130\} = 0.0668$ and $P\{130 \leq X \leq 180\} = 0.7745$. We are asked to find the parameters of this distribution, μ and σ^2, the mean and variance. Now

$$\begin{aligned} P\{X \leq 130\} &+ P\{130 \leq X \leq 180\} \\ &= P\{X \leq 130\} + [P\{X \leq 180\} - P\{X \leq 130\}] \\ &= P\{X \leq 180\}. \end{aligned}$$

Thus, $P\{X \leq 180\} = 0.0668 + 0.7745 = 0.8413$.

Converting from X-scores to Z-scores, we see that

$$P\left\{\frac{X - \mu}{\sigma} \leq \frac{130 - \mu}{\sigma}\right\} = 0.0668$$

and $\quad P\left\{\frac{X - \mu}{\sigma} \leq \frac{180 - \mu}{\sigma}\right\} = 0.8413$

or $\quad P\left\{Z \leq \frac{130 - \mu}{\sigma}\right\} = 0.0668$

and $\quad P\left\{Z \leq \frac{180 - \mu}{\sigma}\right\} = 0.8413.$

From the table of the standard normal distributions, we know that

$$P\{Z < -1.5\} = 0.0668 \text{ and } P\{Z \leq 1\} = 0.8413.$$

Thus, $\quad \dfrac{130 - \mu}{\sigma} = -1.5$

and $\quad \dfrac{180 - \mu}{\sigma} = 1$

or $\quad 130 = \mu - (1.5)\sigma$

and $\quad 180 = \mu + (1)\sigma.$

Subtracting these two equations we see that

$- 50 = (-2.5)\sigma$ or $\sigma = 20$ and

$180 = \mu + 20$ or $\mu = 180 - 20 = 160$.

 **PROBLEM 3-56**

The average grade on a mathematics test is 82, with a standard deviation of 5. If the instructor assigns A's to the highest 12 percent and the grades follow approximately a normal distribution, what is the lowest grade that will be assigned A?

SOLUTION:

We relate the given information to the normal curve by thinking of the highest 12 percent of the grades as 12 percent of the area under the right side of the curve. Then the lowest grade assigned A is that point on the X-axis for which the area under the curve to its right is 12 percent of the total area.

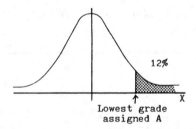

The standard normal curve is symmetric about the Y-axis; this means that if we take the additive inverse of any Z-score, its Y value will be unchanged. For example, the area to the right of $Z = 2$ is equal to the area to the left of $Z = -2$; $P\{Z \geq 2\} = P\{Z \leq -2\}$. It follows that the area under the curve to the right of $Z = 0$ is exactly half the total area under the curve. Therefore, the area between the Y-axis and the desired X-score is $50\% - 12\% = 38\%$ of the total area, which is 1.

If we can find a K for which $P\{0 < Z < K\} = 0.38$, K can be converted to an X-score which is the lowest grade assigned A.

Using the table of areas under the standard normal curve, we locate 0.380 and see that its Z-score is 1.175. This mean that $P\{0 < Z < 1.175\} =$

0.380. This is equivalent to $P\{Z > 1.175\} = 0.500 - 0.380 = 0.120$.

Now we can convert $Z = 1.175$ to an X-score by solving the equation $1.175 = \dfrac{X - \mu}{\sigma}$ for X. We are told that the average grade on the test is $82 = \mu$ (the mean) and the standard deviation is 5. Substituting we have $1.175 = \dfrac{X - 82}{5}$ and $5(1.175) = X - 82$, so that $X = 5(1.175) + 82 = 87.875$. This means that

$$P\{Z > 1.175\} = P\{X > 87.875\} = 0.120.$$

Since all grades are integers, the integer just above 87.875 is 88, which is the lowest grade assigned an A.

✓ • **PROBLEM 3-57**

A teacher decides that the top 10 percent of students should receive A's and the next 25 percent B's. If the test scores are approximately normally distributed with mean 70 and standard deviation 10, find the scores that should be assigned A's and B's.

SOLUTION:

We wish to find two numbers, a and b. If X is the random variable denoting a student's test score and X is assumed to be approximately normal, then any score such that $X > a$ will get an A. Any score such that $b < X < a$ will get a B. In addition, only 10 percent of the students should receive A's. We should choose a to reflect this fact. Thus we wish to find a such that $P\{X > a\} = 0.10$. Similiarly, if 25 percent of the students are to receive B's, b must be chosen so that $P\{b < X < a\} = 0.250$. But,

$$P\{b < X < a\} + P\{x > a\} = P\{X > b\}$$

$$= 0.250 + 0.10 = 0.350$$

Thus, our conditions on a and b become

$$P\{X > b\} = 0.350$$

and $\quad P\{X > a\} = 0.10$.

Since we know the mean and standard deviation of X to be 70 and 10, we can convert X-scores to Z-scores.

$$P\{X > b\} = P\left\{\frac{X - \mu}{\sigma} > \frac{b - \mu}{\sigma}\right\} = 0.350$$

$$= P\left\{Z > \frac{b - 70}{10}\right\} = 0.350$$

and

$$P\{X > a\} = P\left\{\frac{X - \mu}{\sigma} > \frac{a - \mu}{\sigma}\right\} = 0.10$$

$$= P\left\{Z > \frac{a - 70}{10}\right\} = 0.10.$$

From the table of the standard normal distribution

$$P\{Z > 0.385\} = 0.35$$

and

$$P\{Z > 1,282\} = 0.10.$$

Thus, $\dfrac{b - 70}{10} = 0.385$ and $\dfrac{a - 70}{10} = 1.282$

and

$$a = 70 + (1.282)10$$

$$b = 70 + (0.385)10$$

or

$$a = 82.82 \text{ and } b = 73.85.$$

Thus, if a student scores over 83 he receives an A, while a student who scores between 74 and 83 receives a B.

$\checkmark$ • **PROBLEM 3–58**

The IQs of the army recruits in a given year are approximately normally distributed with $\mu = 110$ and $s = 8$. The army wants to give special training to the 10 percent of those recruits with the highest IQ scores. What is the lowest IQ score acceptable for this special training?

SOLUTION:

Let X denote the IQ score of a randomly selected recruit. We wish to find the number such that 10 percent of the distribution of IQ scores is above this number. Thus this number K will be specified by

$$P\{X \geq K\} = 0.10.$$

Standardizing X by subtracting the mean of X, 110, and dividing by the standard deviation, 8 we obtain

$$P\{X \geq K\} = P\left\{\frac{X-110}{8} \geq \frac{K-110}{8}\right\} = 0.10.$$

But $\dfrac{X-110}{8} = Z$ is normally distributed with mean 0 and standard deviation 1. Thus, from the table of the standard normal,

$$P\{Z > 1.282\} = 0.10. \text{ Hence, } \frac{K-110}{8} = 1.282, \text{ or}$$

$$K = 110 + 8(1.282) = 120.256.$$

Thus, the lowest IQ score for this special training is 121.

All recruits with IQ scores of 121 or above will receive this training.

✓ • PROBLEM 3–59

Let X be a normally distributed random variable representing the hourly wage in a certain craft. The mean of the hourly wage is $4.25 and the standard deviation is $.75.

(a) What proportion of workers receives an hourly wage between $3.50 and $4.90?

(b) What hourly wage represents the 95th percentile?

SOLUTION:

(a) We seek

$P\{3.50 \le X \le 4.90\}.$

Converting to Z-scores we see that

$$P\{3.50 \le X \le 4.90\} = P\left\{\frac{3.50 - \mu}{\sigma} \le Z \le \frac{4.90 - \mu}{\sigma}\right\}$$

$$= P\left\{\frac{3.50 - 4.25}{0.75} \le Z \le \frac{4.90 - 4.25}{0.75}\right\}$$

$$= P\left\{\frac{-0.75}{0.75} \le Z \le \frac{0.65}{0.75}\right\}$$

$$= P\{-1 \le Z \le 0.87\}$$

$$= P\{Z \le 0.87\} - P\{Z \le -1\}$$

$$= P\{Z \le 0.87\} - [1 - P\{Z \ge -1\}]$$

$$= P\{Z \le 0.87\} - [1 - P\{Z \le -1\}]$$

$$= 0.809 - [1 - 0.841] = 0.650$$

Thus, 65 percent of the hourly wages are between $3.50 and $4.90.

(b)   The 95th percentile is that number Z_α such that

$$P\{X \le K\} = 0.95.$$

To find Z_α, we first convert to Z-scores. Thus,

$$P\{X \le Z_a\} = P\left\{\frac{X - 4.25}{0.75} \le \frac{K - 4.25}{0.75}\right\} = 0.95$$

$$= P\left\{Z \le \frac{K - 4.25}{0.75}\right\} = 0.95.$$

But $P\{Z \le 1.645\} = 0.95$ thus $\dfrac{K - 4.25}{0.75} = 1.645,$

$$K = 4.25 + (0.75)\,(1.645) = 5.48.$$

Thus, 95 percent of the craftsmen have hourly wages less than $5.48.

A soft-drink machine can be regulated to discharge an average of seven ounces per cup. If the amount of drink dispensed per cup is approximately normally distributed with a standard deviation of 0.3 ounces,

(a) what fraction of the cups will contain more than 7.1 ounces?

(b) if the cups hold exactly eight ounces, what is the probability that a cup will overflow?

(c) what should be the cup size so that the cups will overflow only 1 percent of the time?

SOLUTION:

Let Y be the amount of drink discharged into a cup. Then Y is assumed to be a normally distributed random variable with a mean of seven ounces and a standard deviation of 0.3 ounces.

(a) The fraction of cups which will contain more than 7.1 ounces is found from $P\{Y > 7.1\}$. Standardizing or converting the Y-score to a Z-score, we see that

$$P\{Y > 7.1\} = P\left\{ \frac{Y-\mu}{\sigma} > \frac{7.1-\mu}{\sigma} \right\}$$

$$= P\left\{ Z > \frac{7.1-7}{0.3} \right\} = P\left\{ Z > \frac{0.1}{0.3} \right\}$$

$$= P\{Z > 0.33\} = 0.37$$

Thus, about 37 percent of the cups will contain more than 7.1 ounces.

(b) A cup will overflow if $Y > 8$. The probability of an overflow is

$$P\{Y > 8\} = P\left\{ \frac{Y-\mu}{\sigma} > \frac{8-\mu}{\sigma} \right\} = P\left\{ Z > \frac{8-7}{0.3} \right\}$$

$$= P\{Z > 3.33\}$$

$$= 0.0004$$

(c) The problem is to find a cup size such that the cups will over-flow only 1 percent of the time. We wish to find some number, C, such that

$$P\{Y > C\} = 0.01.$$

$$P\{Z > 2.33\} = 0.01 \text{ and}$$

$$\left\{ \frac{Y - \mu}{\sigma} > \frac{C - \mu}{\sigma} \right\} = P\left\{ Z > \frac{C - 7}{0.3} \right\} = 0.01.$$

The proper cup size, C, is thus determined by

$$\frac{C - 7}{0.3} = 2.33;$$

$$C = (0.3)\,(2.33) + 7 = 7.699.$$

Thus if the cups hold 7.7 ounces, they will overflow 1 percent of the time.

✓ • **PROBLEM 3–61**

> Miniature poodles have a mean height of 12 inches and a standard deviation of 1.8 inches. If height is measured to the nearest inch, find the percentage of poodles having a height of at least 14 inches.

SOLUTION:

Let X be the height of a randomly selected poodle. Then X has mean 12 and standard deviation 1.8. Because the heights are measured to the nearest inch, any height that is greater than 13.5 and less than 14.5 is recorded as 14 inches.

To find the percentage of poodles such that height, X, is recorded as at least 14 inches, we must find the percentage of poodles whose true heights are greater than 13.5 inches.

Now $P\{X > 13.5\}$ can be found by converting X to a random variable Z that is normally distributed with meanm 0 and variance 1.

$$P\{X > 13.5\} = P\left\{\frac{X - \mu}{\sigma} > \frac{13.5 - \mu}{\sigma}\right\}$$

$$= P\left\{Z > \frac{13.5 - 12}{1.8}\right\} = P\{Z \geq 0.83\}$$

From the table this is found to be = 0.2033.

Thus, about 20 percemt of these miniature poodles have heights that are at least 14 inches.

$\sqrt{}$ • PROBLEM 3-62

A binomial random variable has a mean of 6 and a standard deviation of 1.5. What percent of the area under the probability histogram is to the left of 5; to the right of 7.0?

SOLUTION:

Let X be the binomial random variable with a mean of 6 and a standard deviation of 1.5. The percent of area under the probability histo-gram to the left of 5 is $Pr_B(X \leq 5)$, a binomial probability. This probability can be approximated by a normal probability, so

$$Pr_B(X \leq 5) \cong Pr_N(Y \leq 5.5) \text{ where } Pr_N(Y \leq 5.5)$$

is the probability that a normally distributed variable Y is less than 5.5. The addition of 0.5 is necessary because a discrete distribution is being approximated by a continuous distribution.

The new normally distributed random variable Y has the same mean and standard deviation as X. Thus, the mean of Y is 6 and the standard deviation of Y is 1.5. To find

$$P\{X \leq 5\} \approx P\{Y \leq 5.5\}$$

we standardize the variable Y by subtracting the mean and dividing by the standard deviation. Thus

$$P\{Y \leq 5.5\} = P\left\{\frac{Y - \mu}{\sigma} \leq \frac{5.5 - \mu}{\sigma}\right\}$$

$$= P\left\{Z \le \frac{5.5 - 6}{1.5}\right\}$$

where Z is distributed normally with mean zero and variance 1.

Thus, $P\left\{Z \le \frac{5.5 - 6}{1.5}\right\} = P\{Z \le -0.33\}$

and from the table of the standard normal distributions,

$P\{Z \le -0.33\} = 0.37.$

Thus, the probability that X is less than 5 is approximately $P\{X \le 5\}$ $= 0.37$. The percentage to the right of 7.0 is the $P\{X \ge 7.0\}$, where X is binomially distributed with mean 6 and standard deviation 1.5. To correct for the approximation of a discrete random variable by a continuous random variable, subtract $\frac{1}{2}$ from 7.

Thus, $\qquad P\{X \ge 7\} \cong P\left\{Y \ge 7 - \frac{1}{2}\right\}$

$$\cong P\{Y \ge 6.5\}$$

where Y is normally distributed with mean 6 and standard deviation 1.5.

Standardizing Y by subtracting the mean and dividing by the standard deviation yields

$$P\{Y \ge 6.5\} = P\left\{\frac{Y - 6}{1.5} \ge \frac{6.5 - 6}{1.5}\right\}$$

$$= P\left\{Z \ge \frac{0.5}{1.5}\right\},$$

where Z is normally distributed with mean 0 and standard deviation 1. From the table of the normal distributions

$$P\left\{Z \ge \frac{0.5}{1.5}\right\} = P\{Z \ge 0.33\} = 0.37.$$

$P\{Z \ge 7\} \cong P\{Y \ge 6.5\} = P\{Z \ge 0.33\} = 0.37.$

3-62 =   • PROBLEM 3-63

A binomial random variable has a mean of 6 and a standard deviation of 1.5. What percent of the area under the probability histogram is to the left of 5; to the right of 7.0?

SOLUTION:

Let X be the binomial random variable with a mean of 6 and a standard deviation of 1.5. The percent of area under the probability histogram to the left of 5 is $Pr_B(X \leq 5)$, a binomial probability. This probability can be approximated by a normal probability, so

$$Pr_B(X \leq 5) \cong Pr_N(Y \leq 5.5) \text{ where } Pr_N(Y \leq 5.5)$$

is the probability that a normally distributed variable Y is less than 5.5. The addition of 0.5 is necessary because a discrete distribution is being approximated by a continuous distribution.

The new normally distributed random variable Y has the same mean and standard deviation as X. Thus, the mean of Y is 6 and the standard deviation of Y is 1.5. To find

$$P\{X \leq 5\} \approx P\{Y \leq 5.5\}$$

we standardize the variable Y by subtracting the mean and dividing by the standard deviation. Thus

$$P\{Y \leq 5.5\} = P\left\{\frac{Y - \mu}{\sigma} \leq \frac{5.5 - \mu}{\sigma}\right\}$$

$$= P\left\{Z \leq \frac{5.5 - 6}{1.5}\right\}$$

where Z is distributed normally with mean zero and variance 1.

$$\text{Thus, } P\left\{Z \leq \frac{5.5 - 6}{1.5}\right\} = P\{Z \leq -0.33\}$$

and from the table of the standard normal distributions,

$$P\{Z \leq -0.33\} = 0.37.$$

Thus, the probability that X is less than 5 is approximately $P\{X \leq 5\}$ = 0.37. The percentage to the right of 7.0 is the $P\{X \geq 7.0\}$, where X is binomially distributed with mean 6 and standard deviation 1.5. To correct for the approximation of a discrete random variable by a continuous random variable, subtract $\frac{1}{2}$ from 7.

Thus, $\qquad P\{X \geq 7\} \cong P\left\{Y \geq 7 - \frac{1}{2}\right\}$

$$\cong P\{Y \geq 6.5\}$$

where Y is normally distributed with mean 6 and standard deviation 1.5.

Standardizing Y by subtracting the mean and dividing by the standard deviation yields

$$P\{Y \geq 6.5\} = P\left\{\frac{Y-6}{1.5} \geq \frac{6.5-6}{1.5}\right\}$$

$$= P\left\{Z \geq \frac{0.5}{1.5}\right\}$$

where Z is normally distributed with mean 0 and standard deviation 1. From the table of the normal distributions,

$$P\left\{Z \geq \frac{0.5}{1.5}\right\} = P\{Z \geq 0.33\} = 0.37.$$

$$P\{X \geq 7\} \cong P\{Y \geq 6.5\} = P\{Z \geq 0.33\} = 0.37.$$

✓ • PROBLEM 3–64

A multiple-choice test has 200 questions, each with four possible answers, of which only one is correct. What is the probability that sheer guesswork yields from 25 to 30 correct answers from 80 of the 200 problems about which the student has no knowledge?

SOLUTION:

Let X be the number of correct answers in the 80 questions about which the student has no knowledge. If the student is guessing, the probability of selecting the correct answer is $\frac{1}{4}$. It may also be assumed that random guesswork will imply that each question is answered independently of any other question. With these assumptions, X is binomially distributed with parameters $n = 80$ and $P = \frac{1}{4}$. Hence, $E(X) = np = 80 \times \frac{1}{4} = 20$ and

$$\sqrt{\text{Var } X} = \sqrt{np(1-p)} = \sqrt{80 \times \frac{1}{4} \times \frac{3}{4}} = \sqrt{15} = 3.87.$$

We wish to find $P\{25 \leq X \leq 30\}$. This probability is found exactly to be

$$P\{25 \leq X \leq 30\} = \sum_{j=25}^{30} \binom{80}{j}\left(\frac{1}{4}\right)^j\left(\frac{3}{4}\right)^{80-j}$$

This expression is quite tedious to calculate and we thus use the normal approximation to the binomial. Let Y be normally distributed with mean $np = 20$ and standard deviation $\sqrt{np(1-p)} = 3.87$. Then

$$P\{25 \leq X \leq 30\} \cong \left\{25 - \frac{1}{2} \leq Y \leq 30 + \frac{1}{2}\right\}$$

We add and subtract $\frac{1}{2}$ to improve the approximation of a discrete random variable by a continuous random variable. To calculate, $P\{24.5 \leq Y \leq 30.5\}$, we standardize Y by subtracting the mean and then dividing by the standard deviation. Thus,

$$P\{24.5 \leq Y \leq 30.5\}$$

$$= P\left\{\frac{24.5 - 20}{3.87} \leq \frac{Y - 20}{3.87} \leq \frac{30.5 - 20}{3.87}\right\}$$

$$= P\left\{\frac{4.5}{3.87} \leq Z \leq \frac{10.5}{3.87}\right\}$$

where Z is normally distributed with mean 0 and standard deviation 1. From the table of the standard normal distributions,

$$P\left\{\frac{4.5}{3.87} \leq Z \leq \frac{10.5}{3.87}\right\} = P\{1.163 \leq Z \leq 2.713\}$$

$$= P\{Z \leq 2.713\} - P\{Z \leq 1.163\}$$

$$= 0.9966 - 0.8776 = 0.1190$$

Thus, the approximate probability that the student correctly answers between 25 and 30 questions by sheer guesswork is 0.1190.

√ • **PROBLEM 3-65**

What is the probability that in 100 throws of an unbiased coin the number of heads obtained will be between 45 and 60, inclusive?

SOLUTION:

Let X be the number of heads obtained in $n = 100$ throws. We wish to find $P\{45 \leq X \leq 60\}$. This is a binomial probability and may be approximated by a normal probability.

If a coin is unbiased there is a probability $p = \frac{1}{2}$ of a head on any particular toss. Thus, the mean number of head is $E(X) = np = (100) \frac{1}{2} = 50$. The standard deviation is

$$\sqrt{\text{Var } X} = \sqrt{np\,(1-p)} = \sqrt{100 \times \frac{1}{2} \times \frac{1}{2}} = \sqrt{\frac{100}{4}} = \sqrt{25} = 5$$

To correct for the approximation of a discrete random variable X by a continuous random variable Y, we extend the boundaries by adding $\frac{1}{2}$ to 60 and subtracting $\frac{1}{2}$ from 45. Thus,

$$P\{45 \leq X \leq 60\} \cong P\left\{45 - \frac{1}{2} \leq Y \leq 60 + \frac{1}{2}\right\}$$

where Y is normally distributed with mean $np = 50$ and standard deviation 5. To find $P\{44.5 \leq Y \leq 60.5\}$ we standardize Y by subtracting the mean and dividing by the standard deviation. Thus,

$$P\{44.5 \leq Y \leq 60.5\}$$

$$= P\left\{\frac{44.5 - 50}{5} \leq Z \leq \frac{60.5 - 50}{5}\right\}$$

$$= P\left\{\frac{-5.5}{5} \leq Z \leq \frac{10.5}{5}\right\}$$

$$= P\{-1.1 \leq Z \leq 2.1\}$$

where Z is normally distributed with mean 0 and standard deviation 1. From the table of the standard normal,

$$P\{-1.1 \leq Z \leq 2.1\} = P\{Z \leq 2.1\} - P\{Z \leq -1.1\}$$

$$= 0.982 - (1 - P\{Z \leq -1.1\}$$

$$= 0.982 - 1 + 0.864$$

$$= 0.846$$

Thus, there is an approximate probability of 0.846 that the number of heads will be between 45 and 60.

• PROBLEM 3-66

Forty percent of all graduate students on a campus are married. If 100 graduate students are selected at random what is the probability that the proportion of married students in this particular sample will be between 32% and 47%?

SOLUTION:

Let X be the random variable denoting the number of married students in a random sample of size 100. Because 40% of the students are married, the probability of a randomly selected student being married is $p =$ 0.4. The number of married graduate students is approximately binomially distributed.

The expected number of married students in the sample of size 100 is $np = (100)\,(0.4)$ and the standard deviation of X is

$$\sqrt{np\,(1-p)} = \sqrt{100\,(0.4)\,(1-0.4)}$$

$$= \sqrt{100\left(\frac{4}{10}\right)\left(\frac{6}{10}\right)}.$$

Using the normal approximation to the binomial,

$$\frac{X - np}{\sqrt{\text{Var }X}} = \frac{X - np}{\sqrt{np(1-p)}}$$

is approximately normally distributed with mean 0 and standard deviation 1. But dividing the numerator and denominator by n,

$$\frac{X-np}{\sqrt{\text{Var }X}}=\frac{\dfrac{X}{n}-\dfrac{np}{n}}{\dfrac{1}{4}\sqrt{np(1-p)}}=\frac{\dfrac{X}{n}-p}{\sqrt{\dfrac{p(1-p)}{n}}}\cdot$$

Thus, $\dfrac{\dfrac{X}{n}-p}{\sqrt{\dfrac{p(1-p)}{n}}}$ is also approximately normally distributed with

mean zero and standard deviation 1.

The quantity $\dfrac{X}{n}$ is the proportion of married students observed in the sample of size n.

We are interested in the probability that $\dfrac{X}{n}$, the sample proportion, is between the values 0.32 and 0.47, or

$$P\left\{0.32<\frac{X}{n}<0.47\right\}.$$

Substituting $n=100$ and $P=0.40$, we standardize $\dfrac{X}{n}$ and find that

$$P\left\{\frac{0.32-p}{\sqrt{\dfrac{p(1-p)}{n}}}<\frac{\dfrac{X}{n}-p}{\sqrt{\dfrac{p(1-p)}{n}}}<\frac{0.47-p}{\sqrt{\dfrac{p(1-p)}{n}}}\right\}$$

$$=P\left\{\frac{0.32-0.04}{\sqrt{\dfrac{(0.04)(0.6)}{100}}}<\frac{\dfrac{X}{n}-p}{\sqrt{\dfrac{p(1-p)}{100}}}<\frac{0.47-0.04}{\sqrt{\dfrac{(0.04)(0.6)}{100}}}\right\}$$

But $Z=\dfrac{\dfrac{X}{n}-p}{\sqrt{\dfrac{p(1-p)}{100}}}$ is approximately a standard normal variable.

Thus,

$$P\left\{0.32 < \frac{X}{n} < 0.47\right\} = P\left\{\frac{-0.08}{0.49} < Z < \frac{0.07}{0.49}\right\}$$

where Z is standard normal.

From the table of the standard normal distribution,

$$P\left\{\frac{-0.08}{0.49} < Z < \frac{0.07}{0.49}\right\} = P(-1.63 < Z < 1.43)$$

$$= 0.8720$$

Thus, the probability that $\frac{X}{100}$, the sample proportion, is between 0.32 and 0.47 is .8720.

$\checkmark$ • **PROBLEM 3-67**

The probability that an electronic switch will operate successfully is 0.98. A randsom sample of 1000 switches were tested and 30 were found to be defective. What is the probability of finding 30 or more defective switches in the sample?

SOLUTION:

The probability that a randomly selected switch is defective is (1 – 0.98) = 0.02. Letting $n = 1,000$ and $p = 0.02$, we compute the expected number of defective switches, $np = (1,000)(0.02) = 20$ and the standard deviation is

$$\sqrt{np(1-p)} = \sqrt{1,000(0.02)(0.98)} = \sqrt{20(0.98)} = 4.43.$$

Thinking of the number of defective switches as a random variable X, we can use the standard normal curve to find an approximate value of the binomial probability, $P\{X \geq 30\}$. Because a discrete random variable is being approximated by a continuous random variable, $P\{X \geq 30\}$ is approximated by the normal probability $P\{X > 29.5\}$. We must convert 29.5 to a Z-score in order to use the table:

$$\frac{29.5 - np}{\sqrt{np\,(1-p)}} = \frac{29.5 - 20}{4.43} = \frac{9.5}{4.43} = \frac{950}{443} \cong 2.14.$$

It follows that $P\{X > 29.5\} = P\{Z > 2.14\}$

$P\{Z > 2.14\} = 1 - P\{Z > 2.14\}.$

$$= 1 - \Phi(2.14) = 1 - 0.9838 = 0.0162.$$

For tables that give probabilities from 0 to a positive K,

$P\{Z > 2.14\} = 1 - P\{Z \leq 2.14\}$

$$= 1 - \left\{ \frac{1}{2} + \Phi \times (2.14) \right\} = 1 - (0.5 + 0.4838)$$

$$= 1 - 0.9838 = 0.0162.$$

The probability that 30 or more switches will be defective is 0.0162.

• PROBLEM 3-68

In a random sample of 10,000 claims filed against an automobile insurance company, 75% exceeded $300. What is the probability that of the next 400 claims filed more than 72% will be above $300?

SOLUTION:

Let X be a random variable denoting the number of the claims exceeding $300 that are among the next 400 filed against this insurance company. We have a good idea that the probability of a claim exceeding $300 being filed is 0.75. We wish to find the probability that X is greater than 72% of 400. That is, we want the probability that of the next 400 claims, more than 72% will be above $300, or $P\{X > 72\% \text{ of } 400\}$  $P\{X > 288\}.$

Now X is a binomially distributed random variable with mean $np = (400)(0.75) = 300$ and standard deviation

$$\sqrt{np\,(1-p)} = \sqrt{400\,(0.75)\,(0.25)} = \sqrt{75} = 8.66.$$

Using the normal approximation to the binomial, the binomial probability

$P\{X > 288\}$ is closely approximated by $P\{Y > 287.5\}$ where Y is normally distributed with mean $E(Y) = np = 300$ and standard deviation,

$$\sqrt{np\,(1-p)} = 8.66.$$

Thus, we standardize Y to find its probability

$$P\{Y > 287.5\} = P\left\{\frac{Y - \mu}{\sqrt{\text{Var } Y}} > \frac{287.5 - \mu}{\sqrt{\text{Var } Y}}\right\}$$

$$= P\left\{Z > \frac{287.5 - 300}{8.66}\right\}$$

where Z is normally distributed with mean 0 and standard deviation 1.

$$P\{Z > -1.44\} = 0.9251.$$

Thus, the probability that there are more than 288 claims of $300 is 0.925.

✓ • **PROBLEM 3-69**

A new car was designed on the assumption that 60% of its sales would be to female customers. If a random sample of 500 purchasers is selected, what is the probability that at least 275 of them are female?

SOLUTION:

Let X be the number of female purchasers observed in the random sample of 500 purchasers. Now X may be assumed to be binomially distributed with parameters $n = 500$ and $p = 0.60$.

We wish to estimate the binomial probability that $X > 275$. X has mean $E(X) = np = 500\,(0.60) = 300$ and standard deviation of $\sqrt{np\,(1-p)}$ $= 10.9$. Using the normal approximation to the binomial,

$$P\{X > 275\} \cong P\left\{Y > 275 - \frac{1}{2}\right\}$$

where Y is normally distributed with mean $np = 300$ and standard deviation, $\sqrt{np\,(1-p)} = 10.9$.

The $^1/_2$ is subtracted from 275 to correct for a discrete random variable being approximated by a continuous random variable. To compute $P\{Y > 274.5\}$ we convert Y to a standard normal random variable by subtracting its mean and dividing by its standard deviation. Thus

$$P\{Y > 274.5\} = P\left\{\frac{Y-p}{\sqrt{np\,(1-p)}} > \frac{274.5-np}{\sqrt{np\,(1-p)}}\right\}$$

$$= P\left\{Z > \frac{274.5-300}{10.9}\right\}$$

where Z is normally distributed with mean 0 and standard deviation 1. Thus,

$$P\{X > 275\} \cong P\{Z > -2.34\}$$

and from the table of the standard normal,

$$P\{Z > -2.34\} = P\{Z < 2.34\}$$

$$= 0.99$$

Thus, the probability that there are more than 275 female purchasers in a random sample of 500 purchasers given $P = 0.60$ is approximately 0.99.

$\checkmark$ • **PROBLEM 3-70**

A company produces light bulbs and knows that, on the average, 10% are defective and will not pass inspection. What is the probability that at least 15% of a random sample of 100 bulbs is defective?

SOLUTION:

Let X be the number of defective bulbs in a random sample of size 100. If, on the average, 10% of the bulbs are defective, and each bulb in the sample is selected independently from the entire population of bulbs, X

may be assumed to be a binomially distributed random variable with parameters $n = 100$ and $p = 0.10$. The expected number of defective bulbs is $E(X) = np = 10$ and the standard deviation is

$$\sqrt{\text{Var } X} = \sqrt{np\,(1-p)} = \sqrt{100\,(0.1)\,(1-0.9)} = \sqrt{9} = 3.$$

We wish to find the probability that there are more than 15 defective light bulbs in the sample of size 100.

Using the normal approximation to the binomial,

$$P\{X \geq 15\} \cong P\{Y \geq 14.5\},$$

where Y is normally distributed with mean np and standard deviation $\sqrt{np\,(1-p)}$. To find $P\{Y \geq 14.5\}$ we standardize Y by subtracting the mean and dividing by the standard deviation. Thus,

$$P\{X \geq 15\} \cong P\{Y \geq 14.5\} = P\left\{Z > \frac{14.5 - 10}{3}\right\}$$

where $Z = \dfrac{Y - np}{np(1-p)}$

is normally distributed with mean 0 and variance 1. From the table of the standard normal

$$P\{Z \geq 1.5\} = 1 - P\{Z < 1.5\}$$

$$= 1 - 0.9332 = 0.0668.$$

Thus, the probability that there are at least 15 light bulbs in the sample is approximately 0.067.

✓ • **PROBLEM 3–71**

The diameters of a large shipment of ball bearings are normally distributed with a mean of 2.0 cm and a standard deviation of 0.01 cm. If three ball bearings are selected at random from the shipment, what is the probability that exactly two of the selected ball bearings will have a diameter larger than 2.02 cm?

SOLUTION:

We will solve this problem in two steps. First, using the normal distribution we will determine the probability that the diameter of any one ball bearing is greater than 2.02 cm. Second, using the binomial formula,

$$P\{X = x\} = \binom{n}{x} p^x \{1 - p\}^{n-x},$$

we determine the probability that exactly two diameters exceed 2.02 cm.

Step 1: Since X is normally distributed, we can standardize it by subtracting the mean and dividing by the standard deviation. Then

$$p = P\{X > 2.02\}$$

$$= P\left\{\frac{X - \mu}{\sigma} > \frac{2.02 - \mu}{\sigma}\right\}$$

$$= P\left\{\text{Standard Normal Quantity} > \frac{2.02 - \mu}{\sigma}\right\}$$

Substituting, $p = P\left\{\text{Standard Normal Quantity} > \frac{2.02 - \mu}{0.01}\right\}$

$$p = P\{\text{Standard Normal Quantity} > 2\}.$$

From the standard normal table, $P = 0.0228$.

Step 2: We want $P\{X = 2\} = \binom{n}{2} p^2 (1 - p)^{n-2}$,

p was found to be 0.0228 and $n = 3$. Hence,

$$P\{X = 2\} = \binom{3}{2}(0.0228)^2 (1 - 0.0228)$$

$$= \frac{3!}{2!\,1!} (0.0228)^2 (0.9772) = 3 (0.00051984) (0.9772)$$

$$= 0.00152$$

✓ • **PROBLEM 3-72**

A poultry farmer wished to make a comparison between two feed mixtures. One flock of hens was fed from mixture 1 and another flock from mixture 2. In a six-week period, the flock being fed from mixture 1 increased egg production by 25%, while those fed from mixture 2 increased egg production by 20%. Random samples of 200 and 300 hens were selected from the respective flocks. Let $\hat{p}_1$ be the proportion of the sample from the first flock with increased egg production, and let $\hat{p}_2$ be the proportion of the sample from the second flock. Find

(a) the expected difference between the two proportions,

(b) the standard error of this difference, and

(c) the probability that hens fed from mixture 1 increased their egg production more than those fed from mixture 2.

SOLUTION:

Let p_1 and p_2 denote the population proportions representing the percentage increase in egg production of hens who were fed mixtures 1 and 2, respectively. We are given that $p_1 = 0.25$ and $p_1 = 0.20$.

After the random samples of size 200 and 300 have been selected, $\hat{p}_1$ and $\hat{p}_2$ will denote the proportions representing the percentage increase in egg production observed in the two samples. Now

$$\hat{p}_1 = \frac{Y_1}{200} \text{ will be the observed increase in egg production } (Y_1)$$

divided by the size of the first sample population.

$$\hat{p}_2 = \frac{Y_2}{300} \text{ will be the observed increase in egg production } (Y_2)$$

divided by the size of the second sample population.

(a) The expected difference between $\hat{p}_1$ and $\hat{p}_2$ is

$$E(\hat{p}_1 \text{ and } \hat{p}_2) = E(\hat{p}_1) - E(\hat{p}_2)$$

by the properties of expectation. To find we need to know that Y_1 and Y_2 may be assumed to be binomially distributed with parameters $n_1 = 200$ and $p_1 = 0.25$ and $n_2 = 300$ and $p_2 = 0.20$, respectively. Thus,

$$E(Y_1) = n_1 p_1 = (200)(0.25) = 50 \text{ and}$$

$$E(Y_2) = n_2 p_2 = (300)(0.20) = 60.$$

$$\text{Var } Y_1 = n_1 p_1 \{1 - p_1\} = 37.5 \text{ and}$$

$$\text{Var } Y_2 = n_2 p_2 \{1 - p_2\} = 48.$$

Substituting, we find the expected value of

$$\hat{p}_1 - \hat{p}_2 = \frac{Y_1}{n_1} - \frac{Y_2}{n_2} ;$$

$$E(\hat{p}_1 - \hat{p}_2) = E(\hat{p}_1) - E(\hat{p}_2)$$

$$= E\left(\frac{Y_1}{200}\right) - E\left(\frac{Y_2}{300}\right) = \frac{E(Y_1)}{200} - \frac{E(Y_2)}{300}$$

$$= \frac{50}{200} - \frac{60}{300} = 0.25 - 0.20 = 0.05$$

(b) To find the standard error or standard deviation of this difference, we first find Var $(\hat{p}_1 - \hat{p}_2)$. Using the properties of variance, we see that Var $(ax + by) = a^2 \text{ Var } X + b^2 \text{ var } Y$ when X and Y are independent. Therefore, var $(\hat{p}_1 - \hat{p}_2) = \text{Var } \hat{p}_1 + (-1)^2 \text{ Var } \hat{p}_2$

$$= \text{Var } \frac{Y_1}{n_1} + \text{Var } \frac{Y_2}{n_2} = \frac{1}{n_1^2} \text{Var } Y_1 + \frac{1}{n_2^2} \text{Var } Y_2$$

$$= \frac{p_1(1 - p_1)}{n_1} + \frac{p_2(1 - p_2)}{n_2} = \frac{(0.25)(0.75)}{200} + \frac{(0.20)(0.80)}{300}$$

$$= 0.0009375 + 0.000533 = 0.00147$$

The standard error of $\hat{p}_1 - \hat{p}_2$ is

$$\sqrt{\text{Var }(\hat{p}_1 - \hat{p}_2)} = \sqrt{0.00147} = 0.038.$$

(c) The probability that the sample of hens fed from mixture 1 increased their egg production more than the sample fed from mixture 2 is $p\{\hat{p}_1 > \hat{p}_2\}$ or

$$P\{\hat{p}_1 - \hat{p}_2 > 0\}.$$

To compute this probability, we use the normal approximation to the binomial. Thus,

$$P\{\hat{p}_1 - \hat{p}_2 > 0\} \cong P\{Y > 0\}$$

where Y is distributed normally with mean $E(\hat{p}_1 - \hat{p}_2) = 0.05$ and standard deviation 0.038.

Standardizing, we see that

$$P\{Y > 0\} \cong P\left\{\frac{Y - 0.05}{.038} > \frac{0 - 0.05}{0.038}\right\}$$

$$= P\left\{Z > \frac{0 - 0.05}{0.038}\right\} = P\{Z \geq -1.31\}$$

$$= 1 - P\{Z > 1.31\} = 0.9049$$

Thus, the probability is 0.9049 as the sample of hens fed from mixture 1 increased their egg production more than the sample fed from mixture 2.

✓ • PROBLEM 3-73

The receiving department of a television manufacturer uses the following rule in deciding whether to accept or reject a shipment of 100,000 small parts shipped every week by a supplier: select a sample of 400 parts from each lot received. If 3% or more of the selected parts are defective, reject the lot; if the proportion of defectives is less than 3%, accept that lot. What is the probability of rejecting a lot that actually contains 2% defectives?

SOLUTION:

Let X be the number of defective parts in a sample of 400. If the probability of selecting a defective item is 0.02, we want to find the probability that 3% or more of the sample is defective. Equivalently, we wish to find the probability that $X \geq 3\%$ of 400 or $X \geq (0.03)(400) = 12$.

The expected number of defectives is $E(X) = (0.02)\ 400 = 8$ and the standard deviation of the number of defectives is

$$\sqrt{\text{Var } X} = \sqrt{np\ (1-p)} = \sqrt{400\ (0.2)\ (0.98)} = 2.8$$

since X is distributed binomially with parameters $n = 400$ and $p = 0.02$.

We now employ the normal approximation to the binomial to find the probability that $X \geq 12$. We obtain

$$P\{X \geq 12\} \cong P\{Y \geq 11.5\},$$

where Y is normally distributed with mean $np = 8$ and standard deviation 2.8. We standardize Y by subtracting the mean and dividing by the standard deviation. Thus,

$$P\{X \geq 12\} \cong P\{Y \geq 11.5\}$$

$$\cong P\left\{\frac{Y - np}{\sqrt{np\ (1-p)}} \geq \frac{11.5 - np}{\sqrt{np\ (1-p)}}\right\}$$

where $Z = \dfrac{Y - np}{\sqrt{np\ (1-p)}}$ is normally distributed with mean 0 and standard deviation 1. From the table of the standard normal,

$$P\{Y \geq 11.5\} = P\left\{Z \geq \frac{11.5 - 8}{2.8}\right\}$$

$$= P\{Z \geq 1.25\} = 1 - 0.8944 = 0.1056.$$

Thus, given that 2% of the population of light bulbs is defective, there is a probability of approximately 0.1056 of observing 3% defective in the sample of size 400.

• **PROBLEM 3-74**

Show by integration that

$$f(x) = \frac{1}{\sigma\sqrt{2\pi}} \exp\left(-\frac{1}{2}\left(\frac{x-\mu}{\sigma}\right)^2\right),$$

the normal distribution, is an actual probability density function.

SOLUTION:

We must show that

$$\int_{-\infty}^{\infty} \frac{1}{\sigma\sqrt{2\pi}} e^{-\frac{1}{2}\left(\frac{x-\mu}{\sigma}\right)^2} dx = 1.$$

Let $t = \frac{x-\mu}{\sigma}$. Then $x = \sigma t + \mu$ and $dx = \sigma dt$.

Our integral becomes

$$I = \int_{-\infty}^{\infty} \frac{1}{\sigma\sqrt{2\pi}} e^{-\frac{t^2}{2}} \sigma dt = \int_{-\infty}^{\infty} \frac{1}{\sqrt{2\pi}} e^{-\frac{t^2}{2}} dt.$$

We want to show $I = 1$. Since we are taking the integral of a positive function, I must be at least 0. Hence, all we need to do to show $I = 1$ is to show $I^2 = 1$. Now

$$I^2 = \left(\frac{1}{\sqrt{2\pi}} \int_{-\infty}^{\infty} e^{-\frac{t^2}{2}} dt\right)\left(\frac{1}{\sqrt{2\pi}} \int_{-\infty}^{\infty} e^{-\frac{w^2}{2}} dw\right).$$

Each of the two integrals is a constant, independent of any variables; hence, we can take one inside the integral sign of the other, so

$$I^2 = \frac{1}{\sqrt{2\pi}} \int_{-\infty}^{\infty} \left(\int_{-\infty}^{\infty} \frac{1}{\sqrt{2\pi}} e^{-\frac{t^2}{2}} dt\right) e^{-\frac{w^2}{2}} dw.$$

We now write the iterated integrals as one double integral, or

$$I^2 = \frac{1}{\sqrt{2\pi}} \int_{-\infty}^{\infty} \int_{-\infty}^{\infty} e^{-\frac{1}{2}(t^2+w^2)} dt\, dw.$$

We now transform to polar coordinates by the substitutions $t = r \sin q$ and $w = r \cos q$. Now $t^2 + w^2 = r^2 \sin^2 q + r^2 \cos^2 q = r^2 (\sin^2 q + \cos^2 q) = r^2 \times 1 = r^2$. By the change of variables formula

$$dtdw = \left| \det \begin{pmatrix} \dfrac{\partial t}{\partial r} & \dfrac{\partial t}{\partial \theta} \\ \dfrac{wt}{\partial r} & \dfrac{\partial w}{\partial \theta} \end{pmatrix} \right| drd\theta$$

$$= \left| \det \begin{pmatrix} \sin \theta & r \cos \theta \\ \cos \theta & -r \sin \theta \end{pmatrix} \right| drd\theta$$

$$= \left| -r \sin^2 \theta - r \cos^2 \theta \right| drd\theta$$

$$= \left| -r \left(\sin^2 \theta - r \cos^2 \theta \right) \right| drd\theta$$

$$= \left| -r \right| drd\theta = rdrd\theta$$

Substituting our derived quantities,

$$I^2 = \frac{1}{\sqrt{2\pi}} \int_{\theta=0}^{2\pi} \int_{r=0}^{\infty} e^{-\frac{1}{2}r^2} rd \, rd \, \theta.$$

There might be some confusion about the limits. In the original coordinates, $\{-\infty < t < \infty, -\infty < w < \infty\}$ covers the entire Euclidean plane.

Now $r = \sqrt{x^2 + y^2}$, the distance of a point from the origin. To cover the entire plane we must include the points at all distances from $(0, 0)$. Hence, $0 \le r < \infty$. The angle, q, can be shown to equal $\arctan \left(\dfrac{t}{w} \right)$, or the angle between the line connecting the origin with the point and the positive x-axis. To cover the entire plane q must be allowed to include any value $0 \le q < 2p$. Now

$$I^2 = \frac{1}{2\pi} \int_{\theta=0}^{2\pi} \left(\int_{r=0}^{\infty} re^{-\frac{1}{2}r^2} \, dr \right) d\theta.$$

We must evaluate $\displaystyle\int_{r=0}^{\infty} re^{-\frac{1}{2}r^2}\,dr$.

Let $u = -\dfrac{1}{2}r^2$; then $du = -rdr$ and

$$\int_{r=0}^{\infty} re^{-r^2}\,dr = -\int_0^{-\infty} e^u\,du = -e^u\Big]_0^{-\infty} = -\left[e^{-\infty} - e^0\right] \to -[0-1] = 1.$$

Now

$$I^2 = \frac{1}{2\pi}\int_{\theta=0}^{2\pi} 1 \times d\theta = \frac{1}{2\pi}\int_{\theta=0}^{2\pi} d\theta$$

$$= \frac{1}{2\pi}[\theta]_0^{2\pi} = \frac{1}{27}(2\pi - 0) = 1$$

as was to be shown.

• PROBLEM 3-75

Find the expected value of a normally distributed random variable with parameters μ and σ^2.

SOLUTION:

A random variable X with probability density function:

$$f(x) = \frac{1}{\sqrt{2\pi\sigma^2}}e^{-\frac{(x-\mu)^2}{2\sigma^2}} \quad \text{for } -\infty < X < \infty$$

is normally distributed with parameters μ and σ^2.

Thus $E(X) = \displaystyle\int_{-\infty}^{\infty} \frac{X}{\sqrt{2\pi\sigma^2}}e^{-\frac{(x-\mu)^2}{2\sigma^2}}\,dx$.

Let $u = \dfrac{x - \mu}{\sigma}$ and $du = \dfrac{dx}{\sigma}$.

Substituting we see that

$$E(X) = \int_{-\infty}^{\infty} \frac{(\mu + \sigma u)}{\sqrt{2\pi}} e^{-u^2} du$$

$$= \int_{-\infty}^{\infty} \frac{\mu}{\sqrt{2\pi}} e^{-\frac{u^2}{2}} du + \int_{-\infty}^{\infty} \frac{\sigma u}{\sqrt{2\pi}} e^{-\frac{u^2}{2}} du$$

$$= \mu \int_{-\infty}^{\infty} \frac{1}{\sqrt{2\pi}} e^{-\frac{u^2}{2}} du + \frac{\sigma}{\sqrt{2\pi}} \int_{-\infty}^{\infty} u e^{-\frac{u^2}{2}} du;$$

but $\quad \dfrac{1}{\sqrt{2\pi}} e^{-\frac{u^2}{2}} = f(u) \ -\infty < X < \infty$

is the probability density function of a normal distribution with parameters $\mu = 0$ and $\sigma^2 = 1$. Thus, by the definition of a probability mass function,

$$\int_{-\infty}^{\infty} f(u) = 1.$$

Hence, $\qquad E(X) = \mu + \dfrac{\sigma}{\sqrt{2\pi}} \int_{-\infty}^{\infty} u e^{-\frac{u^2}{2}} du$

but $\qquad \displaystyle\int_{-\infty}^{\infty} u e^{-\frac{u^2}{2}} du = -\int_{-\infty}^{\infty} u e^{-\frac{u^2}{2}} [-(u)] du$

$$= -e^{-\frac{u^2}{2}} \Bigg]_{-\infty}^{\infty} = -\lim_{u \to \infty} e^{-\frac{u^2}{2}} + \lim_{u \to -\infty} e^{-\frac{u^2}{2}}$$

$$= -0 + 0 = 0$$

Thus, $\qquad E(X) = \mu + 0 = \mu.$

✳✳✳✳✳✳

REVIEW OF CHI-SQUARE RANDOM VARIABLES

The chi-square distribution is derived from the normal distribution, as are the *t*-distribution and the *F*-distribution. These three distributions are different from the other distributions we have studied previously by virtue of the fact that they arise as the distributions of certain functions of sets of normal variables. They are not often used to directly model any real-world random phenomena.

If X has a normal distribution with mean zero and standard deviation one (i.e., the standard normal distribution), then X^2 has a chi-square distribution with one degree of freedom. The chi-square distribution is characterized by a single parameter, the degrees of freedom. If $X1$ and $X2$ both have standard normal distributions, and if they are statistically independent (a concept we will study in a later chapter), then $X1^2 + X2^2$ has a chi-square distribution with two degrees of freedom. Likewise, the sum of the squares of k independent standard normal random variables will be a random variable with k degrees of freedom.

Like the normal distribution, the chi-square distribution also has a cumulative distribution which cannot be written in closed form. Thus, there are tables listing the values of the cumulative distribution function of the chi-square distribution. These tables are typically indexed by the degrees of freedom.

PERCENTAGE POINTS OF THE x^2 – DISTRIBUTION–VALUES
x^2 IN TERMS OF Q AND v

v/Q	0.1	0.05	.025	0.01	0.005	0.001	0.0005	0.0001
1	2.70554	3.84146	5.02389	6.63490	7.87944	10.828	12.116	15.137
2	4.60517	5.99147	7.37776	9.21034	10.5966	13.816	15.202	18.421
3	6.25139	7.81473	9.34840	11.3449	12.8381	16.266	17.730	21.108
4	7.77944	9.48773	11.1433	13.2767	14.8602	18.467	19.997	23.513
5	9.23635	11.0705	12.8325	15.0863	16.7496	20.515	22.105	25.745
6	10.6446	12.5916	14.4494	16.8119	18.5476	22.458	24.103	27.856
7	12.0170	14.0671	16.0128	18.4753	20.2777	24.322	26.018	29.877
8	13.3616	15.5073	17.5346	20.0902	21.9550	26.125	27.868	31.828
9	14.6837	16.9190	19.0228	21.6660	23.5893	27.877	29.666	33.720
10	15.9871	18.3070	20.4831	23.2093	25.1882	29.588	31.420	35.564
11	17.2750	19.6751	21.9200	24.7250	26.7569	31.264	33.137	37.367
12	18.5494	21.0261	23.3367	26.2170	28.2995	32.909	34.821	39.134
13	19.8119	22.3621	24.7356	27.6883	29.8194	34.528	36.478	40.871
14	21.0642	23.6848	26.1190	29.1413	31.3193	36.123	38.109	42.579
15	22.3072	24.9958	27.4884	30.5779	32.8013	37.697	39.719	44.263
16	23.5418	26.2962	28.8454	31.9999	34.2672	39.252	41.308	45.925
17	24.7690	27.5871	30.1910	33.4087	35.7185	40.790	42.879	47.566
18	25.9894	28.8693	31.5264	34.8053	37.1564	42.312	44.434	49.189
19	27.2036	30.1435	32.8523	36.1908	38.5822	43.820	45.973	50.796
20	28.4120	31.4104	34.1696	37.5662	39.9968	45.315	47.498	52.386
21	29.6151	32.6705	35.4789	38.9321	41.4010	46.797	49.011	53.962
22	30.8133	33.9244	36.7807	40.2894	42.7956	48.268	50.511	55.525
23	32.0069	35.1725	38.0757	41.6384	44.1813	49.728	52.000	57.075
24	33.1963	36.4151	39.3641	42.9798	45.5585	51.179	53.479	58.613
25	34.3816	37.6525	40.6465	44.3141	46.9278	52.620	54.947	60.140
26	35.5631	38.8852	41.9232	45.6417	48.2899	54.052	56.407	61.657
27	36.7412	40.1133	43.1944	46.9630	49.6449	55.476	57.858	63.164
28	37.9159	41.3372	44.4607	48.2782	50.9933	56.892	59.300	64.662
29	39.0875	42.5569	45.7222	49.5879	52.3356	58.302	60.735	66.152
30	40.2560	43.7729	46.9792	50.8922	53.6720	59.703	62.162	67.633
40	51.8050	55.7585	59.3417	63.6907	66.7659	73.402	76.095	82.062
50	63.1671	67.5048	71.4202	76.1539	79.4900	86.661	89.560	95.969
60	74.3970	79.0819	83.2976	88.3794	91.9517	99.607	102.695	109.503
70	85.5271	90.5312	95.0231	100.425	104.215	112.317	115.578	122.755
80	96.5782	101.879	106.629	112.329	116.321	124.839	128.261	135.783
90	107.565	113.145	118.136	124.116	128.299	137.208	140.782	148.627
00	118.498	124.342	129.561	135.807	140.169	149.449	153.167	161.319
X	1.2816	1.6449	1.9600	2.3263	2.5758	3.0902	3.2905	3.7190

$$Q(x^2|v) = \left[2^{\frac{v}{2}} \Gamma\left(\frac{v}{2}\right) \right]^{-1} \int_{x^2}^{\infty} e^{-\frac{t}{2}} t^{\frac{v}{2}-1} dt$$

THE *t*-DISTRIBUTION

Like the chi-square distribution, the *t*-distribution is also derived from the normal distribution and arises as the distribution of certain functions of sets of normal variables. They are not often used to directly model any real-world random phenomena but are used to test the popular *t*-test. Like the chi-square distribution, the *t*-distribution has a cumulative distribution function which is not available in closed form. The cumulative distribution function must, therefore, be tabulated.

If X has a normal distribution with mean M and standard deviation S, then $(X - M) / S$ also has a normal distribution, but with mean zero and standard deviation one. In most cases in practice, however, one would not know the true value of S. This value can be estimated from the data, and we may refer to the estimate as s. The actual formula for computing s is not important right now. What is important is to recognize that s, unlike S, is a random variable complete with a distribution. This is in contrast to S, which is just a number. Now $(X - M) / S$ and X / S are normally distributed by virtue of being linear functions of normal random variables. But $(X - M) / s$ and X / s are not normally distributed. They are not linear functions of normal random variables, since they also depend on s, a random variable itself. But the distribution of $(X - M) / s$ is known and tabulated. This distribution is referred to as the *t*-distribution.

The *t*-distribution is characterized by a single parameter, the degrees of freedom. The degrees of freedom is a reflection of the amount of data used to estimate S by s. As we will see when we study the laws of large numbers, as the sample size becomes infinite our estimate becomes perfect. That is, with an infinite amount of data s tends to S. Then $(X - M) / s$ will also tend to $(X - M) / S$. Thus, it seems reasonable that as the number of degrees of freedom increases the *t*-distribution becomes closer and closer to the normal distribution. This is, in fact, the case.

The *t*-distribution is bell-shaped, like the normal distribution. In fact, upon visual inspection of the *t*-distribution and the normal distribution one will find them to be indistinguishable from each other. Nevertheless, they are different and one must keep in mind the situation at hand when deciding upon which one to use.

The *t*-table in this book is indexed along the left margin by the degrees of freedom, and across the top by the cutoff. For example, if X has a *t*-distribution with five degrees of freedom, then $P\{X < 1.476\} = 0.8$ and

$P\{X < 4.773\} = 0.995$. This is found from reading the fifth row of the *t*-table, corresponding to five degrees of freedom, and looking at the columns which correspond, respectively, to 0.8 and 0.995. Notice that if we wish to find that value k for which $P\{X < k\} = 0.97$, then we would need to interpolate. What we do know, however, is that $P\{X < 2.571\} = 0.95 < 0.97$ and $P\{X < 3.365\} = 0.98 > 0.97$. Therefore, k would need to satisfy

$$2.571 < k < 3.365.$$

When a question asks for a value which is not explicitly provided in the table, an answer in the form of a range, as given here, should usually be acceptable, provided that it is the smallest range possible given the table.

PERCENTAGE POINTS OF THE *t*-DISTRIBUTION— VALUES OF *t* IN TERMS OF *A* AND *υ*

v/*A*	0.2	0.5	.08	0.9	0.95	0.98	0.99	0.995	0.998	0.999	0.9999
1	0.325	1.000	3.078	6.314	12.706	31.821	63.657	127.321	318.309	636.619	6366.198
2	0.289	0.816	1.886	2.920	4.303	6.965	9.925	14.089	22.327	31.598	99.992
3	0.277	0.765	1.638	2.353	3.182	4.541	5.841	7.453	10.214	12.924	28.000
4	0.271	0.741	1.533	2.132	2.776	3.747	4.604	5.598	7.173	8.610	15.544
5	0.267	0.727	1.476	2.015	2.571	3.365	4.032	4.773	5.893	6.869	11.178
6	0.265	0.718	1.440	1.943	2.447	3.143	3.707	4.317	5.208	5.959	9.082
7	0.263	0.711	1.415	1.895	2.365	2.998	3.499	4.029	4.785	5.408	7.885
8	0.262	0.706	1.397	1.860	2.306	2.896	3.355	3.833	4.501	5.041	7.120
9	0.261	0.703	1.383	1.833	2.262	2.821	3.250	3.690	4.297	4.781	6.594
10	0.260	0.700	1.372	1.812	2.228	2.764	3.169	3.581	4.144	4.587	6.211
11	0.260	0.697	1.363	1.796	2.201	2.718	3.106	3.497	4.025	4.437	5.921
12	0.259	0.695	1.356	1.782	2.179	2.681	3.055	3.428	3.930	4.318	5.694
13	0.259	0.694	1.350	1.771	2.160	2.650	3.012	3.372	3.852	4.221	5.513
14	0.258	0.692	1.345	1.761	2.145	2.624	2.977	3.326	3.787	4.140	5.363
15	0.258	0.691	1.341	1.753	2.131	2.602	2.947	3.286	3.733	4.073	5.239
16	0.258	0.690	1.337	1.746	2.120	2.583	2.921	3.252	3.686	4.015	5.134
17	0.257	0.689	1.333	1.740	2.110	2.567	2.898	3.223	3.646	3.965	5.044
18	0.257	0.688	1.330	1.734	2.101	2.552	2.878	3.197	3.610	3.922	4.966
19	0.257	0.688	1.328	1.729	2.093	2.539	2.861	3.174	3.579	3.883	4.897
20	0.257	0.687	1.325	1.725	2.086	2.528	2.845	3.153	3.552	3.850	4.837
21	0.257	0.686	1.323	1.721	2.080	2.518	2.831	3.135	3.527	3.819	4.784
22	0.256	0.686	1.321	1.717	2.074	2.508	2.819	3.119	3.505	3.792	4.736
23	0.256	0.685	1.319	1.714	2.069	2.500	2.807	3.104	3.485	3.768	4.693
24	0.256	0.685	1.318	1.711	2.064	2.492	2.797	3.090	3.467	3.745	4.654
25	0.256	0.684	1.316	1.708	2.060	2.485	2.787	3.078	3.450	3.725	4.619
26	0.256	0.684	1.315	1.706	2.056	2.479	2.779	3.067	3.435	3.707	4.587
27	0.256	0.684	1.314	1.703	2.052	2.473	2.771	3.057	3.421	3.690	4.558
28	0.256	0.683	1.313	1.701	2.048	2.467	2.763	3.047	3.408	3.674	4.530
29	0.256	0.683	1.311	1.699	2.045	2.462	2.756	3.038	3.396	3.659	4.506
30	0.256	0.683	1.310	1.697	2.042	2.457	2.750	3.030	3.385	3.646	4.482
40	0.255	0.681	1.303	1.684	2.021	2.423	2.704	2.971	3.307	3.551	4.321
60	0.254	0.679	1.296	1.671	2.000	2.390	2.660	2.915	3.232	3.460	4.169
120	0.254	0.677	1.289	1.658	1.980	2.358	2.617	2.860	3.160	3.373	4.025
∞	0.253	0.674	1.282	1.645	1.960	2.326	2.576	2.807	3.090	3.291	3.891

$$A = A(t|v) = \left[\sqrt{v}\,B\left(\tfrac{1}{2},\tfrac{v}{2}\right)\right]^{-1} \int_{-t}^{t} \left(1 + \tfrac{x^2}{v}\right)^{-\left(\frac{v+1}{2}\right)} dx$$

Suppose that X is a random variable with the t-distribution with three degrees of freedom. Then what is $P\{X > 0.765\}$?

SOLUTION:

We look across the row of the table of the t-distribution which corresponds to three degrees of freedom. Doing so reveals that

$$P\{X > 0.765\} = 1 - P\{X < 0.765\}$$

$$= 1 - 0.5$$

$$= 0.5$$

$\sqrt{}$ • **PROBLEM 3-77**

Suppose that X is a random variable which follows a t-distribution with 20 degrees of freedom. Then what is $P\{X < 4.837\}$?

SOLUTION:

We look across the row of the table of the t-distribution which corresponds to 20 degrees of freedom. Doing so reveals that

$$P\{X < 4.837\} = 0.9999.$$

$\sqrt{}$ • **PROBLEM 3-78**

Suppose that X is a random variable which follows a t-distribution with 15 degrees of freedom. Then what is $P\{1.753 < X < 2.131\}$?

SOLUTION:

We look across the row of the table of the t-distribution which corresponds to 15 degrees of freedom. Doing so reveals that

$$P\{X < 1.753\} = 0.9$$

and $$P\{X < 2.131\} = 0.95.$$

Now $$0.95 = P\{X < 2.131\}$$

$$= P\{X < 1.753 \cup 1.753 < X < 2.131\}$$

by mutual exclusivity $$= P\{X < 1.753\} + P\{1.753 < X < 2.131\}$$

$$= 0.90 + P\{1.753 < X < 2.131\}.$$

Finally,

$$P\{1.753 < X < 2.131\} = 0.95 - 0.90$$

$$= 0.05$$

✓ • PROBLEM 3-79

Suppose that X is a random variable which follows a *t*-distribution with 40 degrees of freedom. Then what is $P\{2.971 < X < 3.307\}$?

SOLUTION:

We look across the row of the table of the *t*-distribution which corresponds to 40 degrees of freedom. Doing so reveals that

$$P\{X < 2.971\} = 0.995$$

and $$P\{X < 3.307\} = 0.998.$$

Now $$0.998 = P\{X < 3.307\}$$

$$= P\{X < 2.971 \cup 2.971 < X < 3.307\}$$

by mutual exclusivity $$= P\{X < 2.971\} + P\{2.971 < X < 3.307\}$$

$$= 0.995 + P\{2.971 < X < 3.307\}.$$

Finally,

$$P\{2.971 < X < 3.307\} = 0.998 - 0.995$$

$$= 0.003$$

• PROBLEM 3-80

Suppose that X is a random variable which follows a t-distribution and $P\{X < 3.252\} = 0.995$. Then how many degrees of freedom does this distribution have?

SOLUTION:

We look down the column of the t-table which corresponds to 0.995. Doing so reveals that

$$P\{X < 3.252\} = 0.995$$

if X is a random variable with a t-distribution with 16 degrees of freedom.

✓ • PROBLEM 3-81

Suppose that X is a random variable which follows a t-distribution and $P\{X < 3.527\} = 0.998$. Then how many degrees of freedom does this distribution have?

SOLUTION:

We look down the column of the t-table which corresponds to 0.998. Doing so reveals that

$$P\{X < 3.527\} = 0.998$$

if X is a random variable with a t-distribution with 21 degrees of freedom.

✓ • PROBLEM 3-82

Suppose that X is a random variable which follows a t-distribution with 11 degrees of freedom. What is the value, k, such that $P\{X < k\} = 0.2$?

SOLUTION:

We look across the row of the *t*-table which corresponds to 11 degrees of freedom and down the column corresponding to 0.2. Doing so reveals that

$$P\{X < 0.260\} = 0.2$$

if X is a random variable with a *t*-distribution with 11 degrees of freedom.

 • **PROBLEM 3-83**

Suppose that X is a random variable which follows a *t*-distribution with 23 degrees of freedom. What is the value, k, such that $P\{X < k\} = 0.8$?

SOLUTION:

We look across the row of the *t*-table which corresponds to 23 degrees of freedom and down the column corresponding to 0.8. Doing so reveals that

$$P\{X < 1.319\} = 0.8$$

if X is a random variable with a *t*-distribution with 23 degrees of freedom.

******

REVIEW OF THE *F*-DISTRIBUTION

Like the chi-square distribution and the *t*-distribution, the *F*-distribution is also derived from the normal distribution and arises as the distribution of certain functions of sets of normal variables. They are not often used to directly model any real-world random phenomena, but are the distribution used to test the popular analysis of variance model in applied statistics.

The *F*-distribution is also known as the variance-ratio distribution, and as this name would suggest, it is used to test for differences in variances between two independent populations. The *F*-distribution was named after R. A. Fisher, one of the most prominent statisticians of the twentieth century. The cumulative distribution function of the *F*-distribution is not available in closed form, and hence must be tabulated.

If $X1$ has a chi-square distribution with $df1$ degrees of freedom, $X2$ has a chi-square distribution with $df2$ degrees of freedom, and $X1$ and $X2$ are independent, then $(X1 / df1) / (X2 / df2)$ has an *F*-distribution with numerator degrees of freedom $df1$ and denominator degrees of freedom $df2$. The *F*-distribution is characterized by two parameters. These are, as alluded to, the numerator degrees of freedom and the denominator degrees of freedom. It turns out that there is a connection between the *t*-distribution and the *F*-distribution. In particular, if X has a *t*-distribution with df degrees of freedom, then X^2 has an *F*-distribution with one degree of freedom in the numerator and df degrees of freedom in the denominator. But if X has a *t*-distribution with infinite degrees of freedom, then X has a normal distribution with mean zero and standard deviation one. Thus, X^2 has both an *F*-distribution with one numerator degree of freedom and infinite denominator degrees of freedom (by virtue of being the square of a random variable with a *t*-distribution with infinite degrees of freedom) and also a chi-square distribution with one degree of freedom (by virtue of being the square of a random variable with a normal distribution with mean zero and standard deviation one). Thus, we have established that the *F*-distribution with one degree of freedom in the numerator and infinite degrees of freedom in the denominator is also the chi-square distribution with one degree of freedom.

The table of the *F*-distribution which is provided here only tabulates the cutoffs corresponding to 0.5 and 0.25. That is, given the numerator degrees of freedom and the denominator degrees of freedom, we can find

k such that

$$P\{X > k\} = p$$

provided that $p = 0.5$ or $p = 0.25$. For example, if X has an F-distribution with 15 degrees of freedom in the numerator and six degrees of freedom in the denominator, then the table reveals that

$$P\{X > 1.07\} = 0.5.$$

Likewise, $P\{X > 1.76\} = 0.25$.

PERCENTAGE POINTS OF THE F-DISTRIBUTION–VALUES OF F IN TERMS OF Q, v_1, v_2

$$Q(F|v_1, v_2) = 0.5$$

v_1/v_2	1	2	3	4	5	6	8	12	15	20	30	60	∞
1	1.00	1.50	1.71	1.82	1.89	1.94	2.00	2.07	2.09	2.12	2.15	2.17	2.20
2	0.667	1.00	1.13	1.21	1.25	1.28	1.32	1.36	1.38	1.39	1.41	1.43	1.44
3	0.585	0.881	1.00	1.06	1.10	1.13	1.16	1.20	1.21	1.23	1.24	1.25	1.27
4	0.549	0.828	0.941	1.00	1.04	1.06	1.09	1.13	1.14	1.15	1.16	1.18	1.19
5	0.528	0.799	0.907	0.965	1.00	1.02	1.05	1.09	1.10	1.11	1.12	1.14	1.15
6	0.515	0.780	0.886	0.942	0.977	1.00	1.03	1.06	1.07	1.08	1.10	1.11	1.12
7	0.506	0.767	0.871	0.926	0.960	0.983	1.01	1.04	1.05	1.07	1.08	1.09	1.10
8	0.499	0.757	0.860	0.915	0.948	0.971	1.00	1.03	1.04	1.05	1.07	1.08	1.09
9	0.494	0.749	0.852	0.906	0.939	0.962	0.990	1.02	1.03	1.04	1.05	1.07	1.08
10	0.490	0.743	0.845	0.899	0.932	0.954	0.983	1.01	1.02	1.03	1.05	1.06	1.07
11	0.486	0.739	0.840	0.893	0.926	0.948	0.977	1.01	1.02	1.03	1.04	1.05	1.06
12	0.484	0.735	0.835	0.888	0.921	0.943	0.972	1.00	1.01	1.02	1.03	1.05	1.06
13	0.481	0.731	0.832	0.885	0.917	0.939	0.967	0.996	1.01	1.02	1.03	1.04	1.05
14	0.479	0.729	0.828	0.881	0.914	0.936	0.964	0.992	1.00	1.01	1.03	1.04	1.05
15	0.478	0.726	0.826	0.878	0.911	0.933	0.960	0.989	1.00	1.01	1.02	1.03	1.05
16	0.476	0.724	0.823	0.876	0.908	0.930	0.958	0.986	0.997	1.01	1.02	1.03	1.04
17	0.475	0.722	0.821	0.874	0.906	0.928	0.955	0.983	0.995	1.01	1.02	1.03	1.04
18	0.474	0.721	0.819	0.872	0.904	0.926	0.953	0.981	0.992	1.00	1.02	1.03	1.04
19	0.473	0.719	0.818	0.870	0.902	0.924	0.951	0.979	0.990	1.00	1.01	1.02	1.04
20	0.472	0.718	0.816	0.868	0.900	0.922	0.950	0.977	0.989	1.00	1.01	1.02	1.03
21	0.471	0.716	0.815	0.867	0.899	0.921	0.948	0.976	0.987	0.998	1.01	1.02	1.03
22	0.470	0.715	0.814	0.866	0.898	0.919	0.947	0.974	0.986	0.997	1.01	1.02	1.03
23	0.470	0.714	0.813	0.864	0.896	0.918	0.945	0.973	0.984	0.996	1.01	1.02	1.03
24	0.469	0.714	0.812	0.863	0.895	0.917	0.944	0.972	0.983	0.994	1.01	1.02	1.03
25	0.468	0.713	0.811	0.862	0.894	0.916	0.943	0.971	0.982	0.993	1.00	1.02	1.03
26	0.468	0.712	0.810	0.861	0.893	0.915	0.942	0.970	0.981	0.992	1.00	1.01	1.03
27	0.467	0.711	0.809	0.861	0.892	0.914	0.941	0.969	0.980	0.991	1.00	1.01	1.03
28	0.467	0.711	0.808	0.860	0.892	0.913	0.940	0.968	0.979	0.990	1.00	1.01	1.02
29	0.466	0.710	0.808	0.859	0.891	0.912	0.940	0.967	0.978	0.990	1.00	1.01	1.02
30	0.466	0.709	0.807	0.858	0.890	0.912	0.939	0.966	0.978	0.989	1.00	1.01	1.02
40	0.463	0.705	0.802	0.854	0.885	0.907	0.934	0.961	0.972	0.983	0.994	1.01	1.02
60	0.461	0.701	0.798	0.849	0.880	0.901	0.928	0.956	0.967	0.978	0.989	1.00	1.01
120	0.458	0.697	0.793	0.844	0.875	0.896	0.923	0.950	0.961	0.972	0.983	0.994	1.01
∞	0.455	0.693	0.789	0.839	0.870	0.891	0.918	0.945	0.956	0.967	0.978	0.989	1.00

if $X \sim T(df) \Rightarrow X^2 \sim F(1, df)$

✓ • **PROBLEM 3-84**

Suppose that X is a random variable with an F-distribution with five degrees of freedom in the numerator and five degrees of freedom in the denominator. Then what is $P\{X > 1.00\}$? What is $P\{X > 1.89\}$?

SOLUTION:

We look up five degrees of freedom in the numerator and five degrees of freedom in the denominator in each of the two tables provided under the F-distribution (i.e., corresponding to 0.5 and to 0.25). Doing so reveals that

$$P\{X > 1.00\} = 0.50,$$

and $\quad P\{X > 1.89\} = 0.25.$

✓ • **PROBLEM 3-85**

Suppose that X is a random variable with an F-distribution with eight degrees of freedom in the numerator and five degrees of freedom in the denominator. Then what is $P\{X > 1.05\}$? What is $P\{X > 1.89\}$?

SOLUTION:

We look up eight degrees of freedom in the numerator and five degrees of freedom in the denominator in each of the two tables provided under the F-distribution (i.e., corresponding to 0.5 and to 0.25). Doing so reveals that

$$P\{X > 1.05\} = 0.50,$$

and $\quad P\{X > 1.89\} = 0.25.$

• PROBLEM 3–86

Suppose that X is a random variable with an F-distribution with 16 degrees of freedom in the numerator and 20 degrees of freedom in the denominator. Then what is $P\{X < 1.01\}$? What is $P\{X < 1.40\}$?

SOLUTION:

We look up 16 degrees of freedom in the numerator and 20 degrees of freedom in the denominator in each of the two tables provided under the F-distribution (i.e., corresponding to 0.5 and to 0.25). Doing so reveals that

$$P\{X < 1.01\} = 1 - P\{X > 1.01\}$$

$$= 1 - 0.50$$

$$= 0.50,$$

and $\quad P\{X < 1.40\} = 1 - P\{X > 1.40\}$

$$= 1 - 0.25$$

$$= 0.75$$

• PROBLEM 3–87

Suppose that X is a random variable with an F-distribution with 21 degrees of freedom in the numerator and four degrees of freedom in the denominator. Then what is $P\{X < 0.867\}$? What is $P\{X < 1.46\}$?

SOLUTION:

We look up 21 degrees of freedom in the numerator and 4 degrees of freedom in the denominator in each of the two tables provided under the F-distribution (i.e., corresponding to 0.5 and to 0.25). Doing so reveals that

$$P\{X < 0.867\} = 1 - P\{X > 0.867\}$$

$$= 1 - 0.50$$

$$= 0.50,$$

and
$$P\{X < 1.46\} = 1 - P\{X > 1.46\}$$

$$= 1 - 0.25$$

$$= 0.75.$$

• PROBLEM 3–88

Find the tenth quantile point of an F–distribution with 15 and seven degrees of freedom.

SOLUTION:

We know that if the pth quantile ξ_p is given for an F-distribution with m and n degrees of freedom, then the quantile ξ'_{1p} for an F-distribution with n and m degrees of freedom is given by $\dfrac{1}{\xi_p}$.

Following this, we see

$$\xi_{0.10} (15, 7) = \frac{1}{\xi_{0.90} (7, 15)} = \frac{1}{2.16} = 0.463.$$

CHAPTER 4

MOMENTS

> **Basic Attacks and Strategies for Solving Problems in this Chapter. See pages 303 to 393 for step-by-step solutions to problems.**

The moments of a statistical distribution are characteristics which, to a certain extent, define the distribution. We must distinguish moments from central moments, which can also, to a certain extent, define the distribution. For $r > 0$ and integer-valued, we define the rth moment of a random variable X as

$$E[X^r],$$

or the expected value of the rth power of X.

We define the rth central moment of a random variable, X, as

$$E[(X - M)]^r],$$

where $M = E[X]$

is the first moment of X. Thus, the first moment of any random variable is its mean, or expected value. The first central moment of any random variable is

$$E[(X - M)] = E[X] - M$$

$$= M - M$$

$$= 0.$$

The central moments other than the first central moment are independent of the first central moment, because the first central moment (the mean) is subtracted away from the random variable in the formula.

The second central moment of any random variable is known as its variance. The variance is a measure of how spread-out the distribution is, in contrast to the mean, which is a measure of the location of the random variable. Not surprisingly, then, the mean is known as a location parameter, and the variance is known as a scale parameter.

The square root of the second central moment, or the square root of the variance, is the standard deviation. The first and second moments are the most frequently referred-to moments. As will be seen, however, other moments are quite useful as well. When we study moment-generating functions in a latter section, we will see how the entire set of moments can determine the distribution of a random variable under certain conditions. However, it is not true that the set of moments always determines the distribution. One condition under which it does is the existence of the moment-generating function.

The first subsection will treat the first moment in more detail, including the common problem of finding the mean of a linear function of a random variable. The second subsection will present an alternative formula for computing the mean when the random variable is non-negative and integer-valued. The third subsection will treat the second moment. The fourth subsection will treat higher moments. The fifth subsection will consider how the set of all moments can be generated by moment-generating functions (under certain conditions, such as the existence of the moment-generating function). The final subsection will treat the Chebyshev Inequality.

REVIEW OF EXPECTED VALUE

The expected value, or mean, of a random variable is the most frequently used moment. As previously mentioned, this is the first moment of a random variable X and is denoted by

$$E[X].$$

If X is a discrete random variable, then $E[X]$ can be found as an appropriate sum, or

$$E[X] = \Sigma_k k f_x(k)$$

$$= \Sigma_k k P\{X = k\}.$$

If X is a continuous random variable, then $E[X]$ cannot be found as a sum, but it can be found as an appropriate integral. In fact, it would be written exactly as the sum which was used for the expected value of a discrete random variable, except that the summation notation is replaced with an integral sign. That is,

$$E[X] = \int x f_x(x)dx,$$

where I denotes the integral sign.

Technically, the expected value is only defined if $I|x|f_x(x)dx$ is finite. There is a well-known continuous random variable, known as the Cauchy distribution, for which this integral is not finite. Thus, the Cauchy distribution has no mean.

The expected value satisfies certain properties which make it a useful summary measure. First and foremost, the expected value is a linear operator. This means that for any numbers a, b, and c, and for any random variables X and Y, it is true that

$$E[a + bX + cY] = a + bE[X] + cE[Y].$$

Thus, if $f(X)$ is a linear function of a random variable X, then $f(X)$ is also a random variable and, moreover,

$$E[f(X)] = f(E[X]).$$

This relationship would not hold in general if f is not a linear function. In fact, Jensen's inequality states that

$$E[f(X)] \geq f(E[X])$$

if f is a convex function, with strict inequality if f is a strictly convex function. A function is convex if its second derivative is non-negative everywhere. In fact, some functions are convex even though they do not have second derivatives, but this definition will suffice for our purposes.

When we are dealing with a discrete uniform random variable, we can say more about the expected value. In this case, the expected value is simply the unweighted mean of the possible values of the random variable. In this case, the expected value is symmetric in its arguments, in that the expected value is invariant to arbitrary permutations. That is, if we switch the order in which the possible values of the random variable appear, the expected value remains unchanged. This is certainly an appealing property.

When considering a discrete uniform random variable, the expected value is also a monotonically increasing function of each of its arguments. That is, if we were to hold all the possible values of the random variable constant except for one possible value, then increasing the numerical value of this one possible value would result in an increase of the expected value, and decreasing the numerical value of this one possible value would result in a decrease of the expected value. In particular, increasing the numerical value of one possible value by k, while holding all other possible values constant, would increase the expected value by k/n, where n is the number of possible values.

A typical problem dealing with the expectation of a random variable might ask one to find the expected value of a linear function of a random variable whose expected value is known. For example, suppose that X is a normally distributed random variable with mean four and standard deviation two. Let $Y = 2X + 1$. Then find $E[Y]$.

The first step in solving this problem is to recognize the information which is provided yet which serves no purpose toward solving this problem. The two critical pieces of useless information are:

1.   the fact that X has a normal distribution;

and

2.   the fact that the standard deviation of X is two.

Thus, we may restate the problem, using only the relevant information, as "Suppose that $E[X] = 4$. Then what is $E[2X + 1]$?" Now we utilize the fact that the expected value is a linear operator, so

$$E[f(X)] = f(E[X]),$$

since f is a linear function. Now define

$$f(X) = 2X + 1.$$

Then $$Y = f(X)$$

$$= 2X + 1,$$

and we wish to find $E[Y]$. We write

$$E[Y] = E[2X + 1]$$

$$= E[f(X)]$$

$$= f(E[X])$$

$$= 2E[X] + 1$$

$$= (2)(2) + 1$$

$$= 4 + 1$$

$$= 5.$$

Notice that the expected value of a degenerate random variable is the same as the constant to which this random variable is always equal. That is, if X is a degenerate random variable, then there exists a constant k such that

$$P\{X = k\} = 1.$$

In this case, $E[X] = k$.

The expected value, or mean, is often confused with the median. Both are referred to as averages when speaking informally. Each is a "balance point" of the distribution. The median is the point such that half of the mass is to the right of the median and half of the mass is to the left of the median. The mean is the balance point in the sense that if the entire distribution were to be balanced on a single point, then this point would need to be placed at the mean. When the distribution is symmetric, the mean and the median coincide.

Step-by-Step Solutions to Problems in this Chapter, "Moments."

✓ • **PROBLEM 4–1**

Let X be a random variable whose value is determined by the flip of a fair coin. If the coin lands heads up $X = 1$, if tails then $X = 0$. Find the expected value of X.

SOLUTION:

The expected value of X, written $E(X)$, is the theoretical average of X. If the coin were flipped many, many times and the random variable X was observed each time, the average of X would be considered the expected value. The expected value of a discrete variable such as X is defined as

$$E(X) = x_1 P(X = x_1) + x_2 P(X = x_2) + \ldots + x_n P(X = x_n)$$

where $x_1, x_2, x_3, \ldots, x_n$ are the values X may take on and $P(X = x_j)$ is the probability that X actually equals the value x_j.

For our problem, the random variable X takes on only two values, 0 and 1. X assumes these values with

$$P(X = 1) = P(X = 0) = \frac{1}{2}.$$

Thus, according to our definition,

$$E(X) = 0 \times P(X = 0) + 1 \times P(X = 1)$$

$$= 0 \times \frac{1}{2} + 1 \times \frac{1}{2} = 0 + \frac{1}{2} = \frac{1}{2}.$$

• PROBLEM 4-2

Let X be the random variable defined as the number of dots observed on the upturned face of a fair die after a single toss. Find the expected value of X.

SOLUTION:

The random variable X can take on the values 1, 2, 3, 4, 5, or 6. Since the die is fair we assume that each value is observed with equal probability. Thus, $P(X = 1) = P(X = 2) = \ldots = P(X = 6)$

$$= \frac{1}{6}.$$

The expected value of X is

$$E(X) = \sum x P(X = x).$$

Hence $E(X) = 1 \times \frac{1}{6} + 2 \times \frac{1}{6} + 3 \times \frac{1}{6} + 4 \times \frac{1}{6} + 5 \times \frac{1}{6} + 6 \times \frac{1}{6}$

$$= \frac{1}{6}(1 + 2 + 3 + 4 + 5 + 6)$$

$$= \frac{21}{6} = 3\frac{1}{2}.$$

$\checkmark$ **• PROBLEM 4–3**

Suppose that X has a uniform continuous distribution with parameters zero and one, and that $Y = 3X + 2$. What is $E[Y]$?

SOLUTION:

Recall that the expected value of a uniform continuous random variable is the mean of the two parameters, or $\dfrac{a+b}{2}$. In this case,

$$E[X] = \frac{a+b}{2}$$

$$= \frac{0+1}{2}$$

$$= \frac{1}{2}$$

$$= 0.5.$$

Now let $Y = f(X) = 3X + 2$. Then, because $f(X)$ is a linear function,

$$E[Y] = E[3X + 2]$$

$$= E[f(X)]$$

$$= f(E[X])$$

$$= f(0.5)$$

$$= (3)\,(0.5) + 2$$

$$= 1.5 + 2$$

$$= 3.5.$$

$\checkmark$ **• PROBLEM 4–4**

Suppose that X is a random variable whose expected value is five. If $Y = 4X - 2$, then what is $E[Y]$?

SOLUTION:

Let $Y = f(X) = 4X - 2$. Then, because $f(X)$ is a linear function,

$$E[Y] = E[4X - 2]$$
$$= E[f(X)]$$
$$= f(E[X])$$
$$= f(5)$$
$$= (4)(5) - 2$$
$$= 20 - 2$$
$$= 18.$$

✓ • PROBLEM 4-5

Suppose that X is a random variable whose expected value is seven. If $Y = 4X - 8$, then what is $E[Y]$?

SOLUTION:

Let $Y = f(X) = 4X - 8$. Then, because $f(X)$ is a linear function,

$$E[Y] = E[4X - 8]$$
$$= E[f(X)]$$
$$= f(E[X])$$
$$= f(7)$$
$$= (4)(7) - 8$$
$$= 28 - 8$$
$$= 20.$$

Suppose that X is a discrete random variable such that

$$f_x(0) = 0.5;$$

$$f_x(1) = 0.4;$$

and $\quad f_x(4) = 0.1.$

What is $E[X]$? If $Y = 4X - 8$, then what is $E[Y]$?

SOLUTION:

We recall that the expected value of a discrete random variable is given by

$$E[X] = \Sigma_k k f_x(k)$$

$$= \Sigma_k k P\{X = k\}.$$

In this case,

$$E[X] = (0)\,(0.5) + (1)\,(0.4) + (4)\,(0.1)$$

$$= 0 + 0.4 + 0.4$$

$$= 0.8.$$

Let $Y = f(X) = 4X - 8$. Then, because $f(X)$ is a linear function,

$$E[Y] = E[4X - 8]$$

$$= E[f(X)]$$

$$= f(E[X])$$

$$= f(0.8)$$

$$= (4)\,(0.8) - 8$$

$$= 3.2 - 8$$

$$= -4.8.$$

Notice that we could have found $E[Y]$ directly by first finding the probability mass function of Y. This could have been accomplished by computing

$$P\{Y = -8\} = P\{4X - 8 = -8\}$$

$$= P\{4X = 8 - 8\}$$

$$= P\{4X = 0\}$$
$$= P\{X = 0\}$$
$$= 0.5;$$
$$P\{Y = -4\} = P\{4X - 8 = -4\}$$
$$= P\{4X = 8 - 4\}$$
$$= P\{4X = 4\}$$
$$= P\{X = 1\}$$
$$= 0.4;$$

and $P\{Y = 8\} = P\{4X - 8 = 8\}$
$$= P\{4X = 8 + 8\}$$
$$= P\{4X = 16\}$$
$$= P\{X = 4\}$$
$$= 0.1.$$

Then $f_y(-8) = 0.5;$
$$f_y(-4) = 0.4;$$
and $\qquad f_y(8) = 0.1.$

Finally, $E[Y] = (-8)\,(0.5) + (-4)\,(0.4) + (8)\,(0.1)$
$$= (-4) + (-1.6) + (0.8)$$
$$= -4.8.$$

This agrees with the previous answer.

• PROBLEM 4–7

Suppose that X is a discrete random variable such that

$$f_x(10) = 0.3;$$

$$f_x(12) = 0.4;$$

and $f_x(18) = 0.3$.

What is $E[X]$? If $Y = 3X - 12$, then what is $E[Y]$?

SOLUTION:

We recall that the expected value of a discrete random variable is given by

$$E[X] = \Sigma_k k f_x(k)$$

$$= \Sigma_k k P\{X = k\}.$$

In this case,

$$E[X] = (10)\,(0.3) + (12)\,(0.4) + (18)\,(0.3)$$

$$= 3.0 + 4.8 + 5.4$$

$$= 13.2.$$

Let $Y = f(X) = 3X - 12$. Then, because $f(X)$ is a linear function,

$$E[Y] = E[3X - 12]$$

$$= E[f(X)]$$

$$= f(E[X])$$

$$= f(13.2)$$

$$= (3)\,(13.2) - 12$$

$$= 39.6 - 12$$

$$= 27.6.$$

Notice that we could have found $E[Y]$ directly by first finding the probability mass function of Y. This could have been accomplished by computing

$$P\{Y = 18\} = P\{3X - 12 = 18\}$$

$$= P\{3X = 12 + 18\}$$

$$= P\{3X = 30\}$$
$$= P\{X = 10\}$$
$$= 0.3;$$

$$P\{Y = 24\} = P\{3X - 12 = 24\}$$
$$= P\{3X = 12 + 24\}$$
$$= P\{3X = 36\}$$
$$= P\{X = 12\}$$
$$= 0.4;$$

and $P\{Y = 42\} = P\{3X - 12 = 42\}$
$$= P\{3X = 12 + 42\}$$
$$= P\{3X = 54\}$$
$$= P\{X = 18\}$$
$$= 0.3.$$

Then $f_Y(18) = 0.3;$

$f_Y(24) = 0.4;$

and $f_Y(42) = 0.3.$

Finally, $E[Y] = (18)\,(0.3) + (24)\,(0.4) + (42)\,(0.3)$
$$= (5.4) + (9.6) + (12.6)$$
$$= 27.6.$$

This agrees with the previous answer.

✓ • **PROBLEM 4-8**

What is the expected value of a binomial random variable with parameters n and p?

SOLUTION:

Let X be a binomial random variable with parameters n and p. Then X can be expressed as the number of successes in n independent Bernoulli trials, each of which has success probability p.

Let X_i be a Bernoulli random variable such that

$$X_i = 1 \text{ if the } i^{th} \text{ trial is a success}$$

and $\qquad X_i = 0$ if the ith trial is a failure.

Then $\qquad X = \Sigma_{i = 1 \text{ to } x} X_i.$

Because the expected value is a linear operator,

$$E[X] = E[\Sigma_{i = 1 \text{ to } n} X_i]$$

$$= \Sigma_{i = 1 \text{ to } n} E[X_i]$$

$$= \Sigma_{i = 1 \text{ to } n} p$$

$$= p\Sigma_{i = 1 \text{ to } n} 1$$

$$= pn$$

$$= np.$$

✓ • PROBLEM 4-9

Suppose that two basketball players shoot foul shots. One player is particularly good, and scores 90% of his foul shots. The other player is not so good, and scores only 50% of his foul shots. If the good player takes 10 shots and the bad player takes 20 shots, then whom would you expect to score more?

SOLUTION:

By Problem 4–8 we know that for a binomial random variable X with parameters n and p,

$$E[X] = np.$$

Therefore, we expect the good player to score on

$$(10)\,(0.9) = 9$$

shots, while the bad player would be expected to score on

$$(20) (0.5) = 10$$

shots. Therefore, the bad player should score more.

✓• **PROBLEM 4–10**

Let X be a Bernoulli random variable with parameter p. Let $Y = f(X)$, where $f(x) = x^2$. What is $E[Y]$?

SOLUTION:

We know that

$$P\{X = 0\} = 1 - p$$

and

$$P\{X = 1\} = p.$$

Then

$$P\{Y = 0\} = P\{X^2 = 0\}$$

$$= P\{X = 0\} = 1 - p,$$

and

$$P\{Y = 1\} = P\{X^2 = 1\}$$

$$= P\{X = -1 \cup X = 1\}$$

$$= P\{X = -1\} + P\{X = 1\}$$

$$= 0 + p$$

$$= p.$$

Thus, Y has the same distribution as X. Then

$$E[Y] = E[X]$$

$$= (0) (1 - p) + (1) (p)$$

$$= 0 + p$$

$$= p.$$

Notice that we can find $E[Y]$ for $Y = f(X)$ even though in this case $f(X)$ is not a linear function.

$\sqrt{}$ • PROBLEM 4-11

Let X be a Bernoulli random variable with parameter p. Let $Y = f(X)$, where $f(x) = x^{200}$. What is $E[Y]$?

SOLUTION:

We know that

$$P\{X = 0\} = 1 - p$$

and $\qquad P\{X = 1\} = p.$

Then $\qquad P\{Y = 0\} = P\{X^{200} = 0\}$

$$= P\{X = 0\} = 1 - p,$$

and $\qquad P\{Y = 1\} = P\{X^{200} = 1\}$

$$= P\{X = -1 \cup X = 1\}$$

$$= P\{X = -1\} + P\{X = 1\}$$

$$= 0 + p$$

$$= p,$$

where we ignore complex solutions to the equation

$$X^{200} = 1.$$

Thus, Y has the same distribution as X. Then
$$E[Y] = E[X]$$

$$= (0)(1 - p) + (1)(p)$$

$$= 0 + p$$

$$= p.$$

Notice that we can find $E[Y]$ for $Y = f(X)$ even though in this case $f(X)$ is not a linear function.

Let X be a discrete random variable such that

$$P\{X = -1\} = 0.8,$$

$$P\{X = 1\} = 0.2,$$

and $\qquad P\{X = x\} = 0$ otherwise.

Let $Y = f(X)$, where $f(x) = x^{201}$. What is $E[Y]$?

SOLUTION:

We know that

$$P\{Y = -1\} = P\{X^{201} = -1\}$$

$$= P\{X = -1\} = 0.8,$$

and $\qquad P\{Y = 1\} = P\{X^{201} = 1\}$

$$= P\{X = 1\}$$

$$= 0.2,$$

where we ignore complex solutions to the equations

$$X^{201} = -1$$

and $\qquad X^{201} = 1.$

Thus, Y has the same distribution as X. Then

$$E[Y] = E[X]$$

$$= (-1)\,(0.8) + (1)\,(0.2)$$

$$= -0.8 + 0.2$$

$$= -0.6.$$

Notice that we can find $E[Y]$ for $Y = f(X)$ even though in this case $f(X)$ is not a linear function.

Let X be a discrete random variable such that

$$P\{X = -1\} = 0.8,$$

$$P\{X = 1\} = 0.2,$$

and $\qquad P\{X = x\} = 0$ otherwise.

Let $Y = f(X)$, where $f(x) = x^{202}$. What is $E[Y]$?

SOLUTION:

We know that

$$P\{Y = 1\} = P\{X^{202} = 1\}$$

$$= P\{X = -1 \cup X = 1\}$$

$$= P\{X = -1\} + P\{X = 1\}$$

$$= 0.8 + 0.2$$

$$= 1,$$

where we ignore complex solutions to the equation

$$X^{202} = 1.$$

Thus, Y has a degenerate distribution, because

$$P\{Y = 1\} = 1$$

and $\qquad P\{Y = k\} = 0$ otherwise.

Then $\qquad E[Y] = (1)\,(1)$

$$= 1.$$

Notice that we can find $E[Y]$ for $Y = f(X)$ even though in this case $f(X)$ is not a linear function.

If

$$P\{X = -1\} = p,$$

$$P\{X = 0\} = q,$$

and $\quad P\{X = 1\} = r,$

with $\quad p + q + r = 1$

(that is, $P\{X = k\} = 0$ for k other than -1, 0, or 1), then find $E[Y]$, where $Y = X^n$ for positive integer n.

SOLUTION:

The last several problems provide partial solutions to this problem, but we must find the pattern that will allow us to generalize to the case of arbitrary exponent n, such that n is a positive integer. We break this problem into two parts.

First, let n be an even positive integer. Then

$$X^n = 1 \text{ if } X = -1,$$

$$X^n = 0 \text{ if } X = 0,$$

and $\qquad X^n = 1 \text{ if } X = 1.$

That is, $\quad P\{X^n = 0\} = P\{X = 0\}$

$$= q,$$

and $\qquad P\{X^n = 1\} = P\{X = -1 \cup X = 1\}$

$$= P\{X = -1\} + P\{X = 1\}$$

$$= p + r.$$

Now $E[X^n] = (0)\,(q) + (1)\,(p + r)$

$$= 0 + (p + r)$$

$$= p + r.$$

On the other hand, if n is an odd positive integer, then

$$X^n = -1 \text{ if } X = -1,$$

$$X^n = 0 \text{ if } X = 0,$$

and $\qquad X^n = 1 \text{ if } X = 1.$

That is, $P\{X^n = -1\} = P\{X = -1\}$

$$= p,$$

$$P\{X^n = 0\} = P\{X = 0\}$$

$$= q,$$

and $P\{X^n = 1\} = P\{X = 1\}$

$$= r.$$

Now X^n has the same distribution as X, so

$$E[X^n] = E[X]$$

$$= (-1)(p) + (0)(q) + (1)(r)$$

$$= (-p) + (0) + (r)$$

$$= r - p.$$

• PROBLEM 4–15

What is the nth moment of a Bernoulli random variable with parameter r?

SOLUTION:

Consider Problem 4–14, with $p = 0$. Then what results is a random variable X, such that

$$P\{X = 0\} = q$$

and $P\{X = 1\} = r,$

with $q + r = 1.$

That is, X is Bernoulli with parameter r. Now the nth moment is

$$E[X^n],$$

which, by Problem 4–14, is $r + p$ if n is even, and $r - p$ if n is odd. But here $p = 0$, so either way,

$$E[X^n] = r,$$

the parameter of the Bernoulli. Thus, all moments of a Bernoulli random variable with parameter r are r.

• PROBLEM 4-16

Let X be any random variable, and let Y be a Bernoulli random variable with parameter $p = 0.5$. Let X and Y be independent, and define Z as

$$Z = X \text{ if } Y = 0$$

and $Z = -X \text{ if } Y = 1.$

Find $E[Z]$.

SOLUTION:

It is clear that Z has a symmetric distribution, since

$$P\{Z = k\} = P\{X = k, Y = 0 \cup X = -k, Y = 1\}$$
$$= P\{X = k, Y = 0\} + P\{X = -k, Y = 1\}$$
$$= P\{X = k\}P\{Y = 0\} + P\{X = -k\}P\{Y = 1\}$$
$$= P\{X = k\} (1 - p) + P\{X = -k\} (p)$$
$$= P\{X = k\} (1 - 0.5) + P\{X = -k\} (0.5)$$
$$= P\{X = k\} (0.5) + P\{X = -k\} (0.5)$$
$$= (0.5) [P\{X = k\} + P\{X = -k\}],$$

and $\quad P\{Z = -k\} = P\{X = -k, Y = 0 \cup X = k, Y = 1\}$
$$= P\{X = -k, Y = 0\} + P\{X = k, Y = 1\}$$
$$= P\{X = -k\}P\{Y = 0\} + P\{X = k\}P\{Y = 1\}$$
$$= P\{X = -k\} (1 - p) + P\{X = k\} (p)$$
$$= P\{X = -k\} (1 - 0.5) + P\{X = k\} (0.5)$$
$$= P\{X = -k\} (0.5) + P\{X = k\} (0.5)$$
$$= (0.5) [P\{X = -k\} + P\{X = k\}]$$
$$= (0.5) [P\{X = k\} + P\{X = -k\}]$$
$$= P\{X = k\}.$$

In particular, Z has a distribution which is symmetric about zero. Then both the mean and the median are equal to the point about which the distribution of Z is symmetric. Since the distribution of Z is symmetric about zero,

$$E[Z] = 0.$$

✓ • PROBLEM 4–17

Suppose the earnings of a laborer denoted by X are given by the following probability function.

X	0	8	12	16
$P(X = x)$	0.3	0.2	0.3	0.2

Find the laborer's expected earnings.

SOLUTION:

The laborer's expected earnings are denoted by $E(X)$, the expected value of the random variable X.

The expected value of X is defined to be

$E(X) = (0) \, P(X) = 0) + (8) \, P(X = 8) + (12) \, P(X = 12) + (16) \, P(X = 16)$

$= (0) \, (0.3) + (8) \, (0.2) + (12) \, (0.3) + (16) \, (0.2)$

$= 0 + 1.6 + 3.6 + 3.2$

$= 8.4.$

Thus the expected earnings are 8.4.

✓ • PROBLEM 4–18

A brush salesman sells door-to-door. His products are short and long brushes. The profit on the long brush is $0.30 and on the short one it is $0.10. The chances of selling a long brush are one out of ten calls, and the chances of selling a short one are two out of ten calls. The chances of no sales are seven out of ten calls. Find the expected profit per call.

SOLUTION:

Let P be a random variable representing the profit per call. We wish to find $E(P)$. The probability distribution of P, given in the problem, is summarized in the table below;

P		$P(P = p)$
long brush	0.30	0.1
short brush	0.10	0.2
no sale	0.00	0.7

Thus

$$E(P) = (0.30)\ P(P = 0.30) + (0.10)\ P(P = 0.10) + (0.0)\ P(P = 0.0)$$

$$= (0.30)\ (0.1) + (0.10)\ (0.2) + (0)\ (0.7)$$

$$= 0.03 + 0.02 + 0.00 = 0.05$$

The expected profit per call is $0.05 or 5 cents.

✓ • **PROBLEM 4–19**

The State of New Hampshire conducts an annual lottery to raise funds for the school districts in the state. Assume a million tickets are sold. One ticket is the winning ticket and the winner receives $10,000. If each ticket costs $0.25, find the expected value of a randomly purchased ticket and the revenue that the lottery generates for the school districts in the state.

SOLUTION:

Let X be the value of a randomly purchased lottery ticket. Then

$$X = -\$0.25 \text{ with probability } \frac{999,999}{1,000,000}.$$

This is because 999,999 of 1,000,000 lottery tickets have no value and the buyers of these tickets lost the $0.25 price.

However,

$$X = \$10,000 - \$0.25 \text{ with probability } \frac{1}{1,000,000}.$$

This reflects the fact that one of the million tickets wins \$10,000 minus the purchase price of the ticket, thus the winner receives \$10,000 − \$0.25.

The expected value of the random variable X is the expected value of a randomly-purchased lottery ticket. By definition of expected value,

$$E(X) = \$[10,000 - 0.25] \times \frac{1}{1,000,000} + [-\$0.25] \times \frac{999,999}{1,000,000}.$$

Rearranging terms we see that

$$E(X) = \$10,000 \times \left[\frac{1}{1,000,000}\right] + \left[\frac{-\$0.25 - (\$0.25)(999,999)}{1,000,000}\right]$$

$$= \$10,000 \left[\frac{1}{1,000,000}\right] - \$0.25\left[\frac{1,000,000}{1,000,000}\right]$$

$$= \$\frac{1}{100} - \$0.25$$

$$= \$0.01 - \$0.25 = -\$0.24.$$

Thus, the expected value of an average lottery ticket is −0.24. Each buyer loses an average of 24 cents on a lottery ticket.

The total revenue is the number of tickets sold times the price of each ticket or $\$(0.25)(1,000,000) = \$250,000$. The net revenue, after the prize is paid is

$$\$250,000 - \$10,000 = \$240,000.$$

Thus the school districts receive \$240,000.

Suppose a shipping company buys a new trailer truck for $10,000. If the truck is lost either through accident or theft, it is regarded as a complete loss. The chance of loss is 0.001; hence, the chance of no loss is 0.999. Find the expected loss.

SOLUTION:

Let L be the random variable representing the loss that the shipping company takes in the course of a year, taking on the values 0 and 10,000. The probability distribution of L is $P(L = 0) = 0.999$ and $P(L = 10,000) = 0.001$. This information is summarized in the following table,

	l	$P(L = l)$
No loss	0	0.999
loss	10,000	0.001

To find the expected loss, we calculate the expected value of the random variable L. This is,

$$E(L) = l_1\, P(L = l_1) + l_2\, P(L = l_2)$$

$$= 0\, P(L = 0) + 10,000\, P(L = 10,000)$$

$$= 0\, (0.999) + (10,000)\, (0.001)$$

$$= 10.$$

Thus the expected loss is 10 dollars.

In the previous problem, suppose 1,000 shipping companies, each having a truck worth $10,000, form an industry association to protect themselves against the loss of a new truck. How much should the firms pay in total to the association to insure their trucks?

SOLUTION:

The expected loss for all the companies combined is

$$L_T = L_1 + L_2 + L_3 + \ldots + L_{1,000}$$

where L_i represents the loss of the ith company. The expected loss of all 1,000 companies is $E(L_T)$.

By the properties of expectation,

$$E(L_T) = E(L_1 + L_2 + \ldots + L_{1,000})$$

$$= E(L_1) + E(L_2) + \ldots + E(L_{1,000}).$$

The expected loss of each company has been found to be $E(L_i) = \$10$. Thus

$$E(L_T) = \underbrace{10 + 10 + \ldots + 10}_{1,000 \text{ terms}}$$

$$= (1000) \, 10 = 10,000.$$

On the average, there will be a loss of 10,000 a year among the 1,000 companies. Some years the loss will be greater than $10,000, some years the loss will be less than $10,000, but on the average the loss will be $10,000 a year. Dividing this loss equally among all 1,000 companies gives the annual premium each company should pay. Thus,

$$\text{premium} = \frac{10,000}{1,000} = 10 \text{ dollars.}$$

Here X is an example of a binomially-distributed random variable. We note that for a binomial random variable

$$E(X) \text{ also equals } 4 \times \frac{1}{2} = n \times p = 2.$$

This formula $E(X) = np$ is true for all binomial random variables.

✓ • PROBLEM 4–22

Find the expected number of boys on a committee of three selected at random from four boys and three girls.

SOLUTION:

Let X represent the number of boys on the committee, which can be equal to 0, 1, 2, or 3. The probability that there are zero boys on the committee is

$$P(X = 0) = \frac{\text{number of ways zero boys can be picked}}{\text{number of ways a committee of three can be chosen}}.$$

The number of ways a committee of three can be chosen from the four boys and three girls is the number of ways three can be selected from seven or $\binom{7}{3}$.

The number of ways a committee of three can be chosen that contains zero boys is $\binom{4}{0} \times \binom{3}{3}$, the number of ways zero boys are chosen from four multiplied by the number of ways three girls are chosen from the three available. Thus

$$P(X = 0) = \frac{\binom{4}{0} \times \binom{3}{3}}{\binom{7}{3}}.$$

Similarly,

$$P(X = 1) = \frac{\binom{4}{1} \times \binom{3}{2}}{\binom{7}{3}},$$

$$P(X = 2) = \frac{\binom{4}{2} \times \binom{3}{1}}{\binom{7}{3}}$$

and
$$P(X = 3) = \frac{\binom{4}{3} \times \binom{3}{0}}{\binom{7}{3}} .$$

By definition, the expected number of boys is

$$E(X) = (0)\, P(X = 0) + (1)\, P(X = 1) + (2)\, P(X = 2) + (3)\, P(X = 3)$$

$$= (0)\frac{\binom{4}{0} \times \binom{3}{3}}{\binom{7}{3}} + (1)\frac{\binom{4}{1} \times \binom{3}{2}}{\binom{7}{3}} + (2)\frac{\binom{4}{2} \times \binom{3}{1}}{\binom{7}{3}} + (3)\frac{\binom{4}{3} \times \binom{3}{0}}{\binom{7}{3}}$$

$$= (1)\frac{\dfrac{4!}{3!\,1!} \times \dfrac{3!}{2!\,1!}}{\binom{7}{3}} + (2)\frac{\dfrac{4!}{2!\,2!} \times \dfrac{3!}{2!\,1!}}{\binom{7}{3}} + (3)\frac{\dfrac{4!}{3!3!} \times \dfrac{3!}{0!3!}}{\binom{7}{3}}$$

$$= \frac{1}{\binom{7}{3}} [(4)\,(3) + (2)\,(6)\,(3) + (3)\,(4)\,(1)]$$

$$= \frac{12 + 36 + 12}{\binom{7}{3}} = \frac{60}{\dfrac{7!}{3!\,4!}} \qquad = \frac{60}{35} = 1.7$$

$$= \frac{52}{\dfrac{7 \times 6 \times 5}{3 \times 2 \times 1}} = \frac{52}{35} = 1.5.$$

Thus, if a committee of three is selected at random repeatedly it would contain on the average 1.5 boys.

$\checkmark$ • **PROBLEM 4-23**

Let the random variable X represent the number of defective radios in a shipment of four radios to a local appliance store. Assume that each radio is equally likely to be defective or non-defective, hence the probably that a radio is defective is $p = \frac{1}{2}$. Also assume that each radio is defective or non-defective independently of the other radios. Find the expected number of defective radios.

SOLUTION:

First we find the probability distribution of X, the number of defective radios in the shipment of four. This can assume the values 0, 1, 2, 3, or 4.

If X is 0, then zero radios are defective. This can only take place if each is non-defective. By the independence assumption

$$P(X = 0) = \left(\frac{1}{2}\right)\left(\frac{1}{2}\right)\left(\frac{1}{2}\right)\left(\frac{1}{2}\right)$$

$$= \frac{1}{2^4} = \frac{1}{16}.$$

Similarly, $P(X = 1) = P$(one radio is defective, three are not)

$$= \frac{\text{number of favorable outcomes}}{\text{number of possible outcomes}}$$

$$= \frac{4}{2^4} = \frac{4}{16} = \frac{1}{4} \text{ Now}$$

$P(X = 2) = P$(two radios are defective)

$$= \frac{\text{number of ways two can be chosen for four}}{\text{number of ways to choose four radios}}$$

$$= \binom{4}{2}\left(\frac{1}{2}\right)^2 = \frac{6}{16}.$$

By symmetry,

$$P(X = 1) = P(X = 3) = \frac{4}{16} = \frac{1}{4}$$

and $\qquad P(X = 0) = P(X = 4) = \frac{1}{16}.$

The expected number of defective radios is

$$E(X) = 0 \times \frac{1}{16} + 1 \times \frac{4}{16} + 2 \times \frac{6}{16} + 3 \times \frac{4}{16} + 4 \times \frac{1}{16}$$

$$= \frac{4}{16} + \frac{12}{16} + \frac{12}{16} + \frac{4}{16} = \frac{32}{16} = 2.$$

✓• PROBLEM 4-24

Let Y be the Rockwell hardness of a particular alloy of steel. Assume that Y is a continuous uniformly distributed random variable that can take on any value between 50 and 70. Find the expected Rockwell hardness.

SOLUTION:

The random variable Y has a density function that is sketched below.

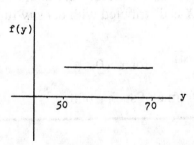

In order for Y to have a proper probability density function, the area under the density function must be 1. The area under the density function of Y is in the shape of a rectangle with length 20. Thus the height of the rectangle, $f(y)$, must satisfy

$$f(y) (20) = 1 \quad 50 < y < 70,$$

where the probability density function $f(y)$ represents the width of this rectangle. Solving for $f(y)$, we find the probability density function to be

$$f(y) = \frac{1}{20} \qquad\qquad 50 < y < 70.$$

To find the expected value of a continuous random variable we use the technique of integration. Thus

$$E(Y) = \int_{50}^{70} y f(y)\, dy$$

$$E(Y) = \int_{50}^{70} y \frac{1}{20}\, dy = \frac{1}{20}\left(\frac{y^2}{2}\right)\Bigg|_{50}^{70}$$

$$= \frac{1}{20}\left(\frac{70^2 - 50^2}{2}\right) = \frac{(70+50)\,(70-50)}{40}$$

$$= \frac{70+50}{2} = \frac{120}{2} = 60.$$

Thus, the expected Rockwell hardness of this alloy is 60.

• PROBLEM 4–25

Let X be a random variable denoting the hours of life in an electric light bulb. Suppose X is distributed with density function

$$f(x) = \frac{1}{1,000}\, e^{-\frac{x}{1,000}} \qquad \text{for } x > 0$$

Find the expected lifetime of such a bulb.

SOLUTION:

The expected value of a random variable is the "sum" of all the values of the random variable multiplied by their probabilities. In the continuous case, this "summing" necessitates integration. Thus,

$$E(X) = \int_{\text{all } x} x\, f(x)\, dx.$$

In our problem, x can take all positive values; thus

$E(X) = \int_0^\infty x\,f(x)\,dx.$

$= \int_0^\infty \dfrac{x}{1{,}000} e^{-\frac{x}{1{,}000}}\,dx.$

Integrating by parts, let $u = x$ and

$dv = \dfrac{1}{1{,}000} e^{-\frac{x}{1{,}000}}\,dx;$ then $du = dx$ and $v = -e^{-\frac{x}{1{,}000}}.$

Thus

$E(X) = uv\Big|_0^\infty - \int_0^\infty v\,du$

$E(X) = -xe^{-\frac{x}{1{,}000}}\Big|_0^\infty - \int_0^\infty -e^{-\frac{x}{1{,}000}}\,dx$

$= -1{,}000 \int_0^\infty -e^{-\frac{x}{1{,}000}}\,dx$

$= -1{,}000 \times e^{-\frac{x}{1{,}000}}\Big|_0^\infty$

$= -1{,}000\,[0 - 1] = 1{,}000.$

Thus, the expected lifetime of the bulb is 1,000 hours.

Find $E(X)$ for the continuous random variables with probability density functions;

a) $f(x) = 2x,$ $\qquad\qquad 0 < x < 1.$

b) $f(x) = \dfrac{1}{2\sqrt{x}},$ $\qquad\qquad 0 < x < 1.$

c) $f(x) = 6x(1 - x),$ $\qquad 0 < x < 1.$

d) $f(x) = \dfrac{1}{2}x^2 e^{-x},$ $\qquad 0 < x < \infty.$

e) $f(x) = \dfrac{1}{x^2},$ $\qquad\qquad 0 < x < \infty.$

f) $f(x) = 1 - |1 - x|,$ $\quad 0 \le x \le 2.$

SOLUTION:

For a continuous random variable, X,

$$E(X) = \int_{-\infty}^{\infty} x\, f(x)\, dx.$$

It is possible that $f(x) = 0$ for large portions of the real line reducing $E(X)$ to a proper integral.

√ (a) $E(X) = \int_0^1 x \times 2x\, dx = \int_0^1 2x^2\, dx = \left.\dfrac{2}{3}x^3\right|_0^\infty$

$$= \dfrac{2}{3}[1 - 0] = \dfrac{2}{3}.$$

√ (b) $E(X) = \int_0^1 x\, \dfrac{1}{2\sqrt{x}}\, dx = \dfrac{1}{2}\int_0^1 \sqrt{x}\, dx$

$$= \dfrac{1}{2} \times \left.\dfrac{x^{\frac{1}{2}+1}}{1 + \dfrac{1}{2}}\right|_0^1 = \left.\dfrac{1}{2} \times \dfrac{2}{3}x^{\frac{3}{2}}\right|_0^1 = \dfrac{1}{3}.$$

√(c) $E(X) = \int_0^1 x[6x(1-x)]\,dx = 6\int_0^1 (x^2 - x^3)\,dx$

$$= 6\left[\frac{x^3}{3} - \frac{x^4}{4}\right]_0^1 = 6\left(\frac{1}{3} - \frac{1}{4}\right) = \frac{6}{12} = \frac{1}{2}.$$

(d) $E(X) = \int_0^\infty x \times f(x)\,dx = \int_0^\infty \frac{1}{2}x^3 e^{-x}\,dx.$

Using integration by parts,

let $u = x^3$ thus $du = 3x^2\,dx$

$dv = e^{-x}\,dx \; v = -e^{-x}$

and we see that

$$E(X) = \frac{1}{2}\left[-x^3 e^{-x}\Big|_0^\infty - \int_0^\infty -e^{-x}3x^2\,dx\right]$$

$$= \frac{1}{2}\left[0 + 0 + 3\int_0^\infty x^2 e^{-x}\,dx\right]$$

$$= \frac{3}{2}\int_0^\infty x^2 e^{-x}\,dx = 3\int_0^\infty \frac{1}{2}x^2 e^{-x}\,dx.$$

But the integrand is $f(x) = \frac{1}{2}x^2 e^{-x}$, our original density function, and, by definition, a density function is a positive-vaulted function $f(x)$ such that

$\int_0^\infty f(x)\,dx = 1$; thus

$E(X) = 3\int_0^\infty f(x)\,dx = 3.$

(e) $E(X) = \int_0^\infty x \times \frac{1}{x^2}\,dx = \int_0^\infty \frac{1}{x}\,dx = \lim_{b\to\infty}\int_1^b \frac{dx}{x}$

$$= \lim_{b\to\infty}\left[\log b - \log 1\right]$$

$$= \lim_{b\to\infty}\log b = \infty;$$

thus the expected value of x does not exist.

(f) $E(X) = \int_0^2 x f(x)\, dx$

$\quad = \int_0^2 x(1 - |\,1 - x\,|)\, dx$

$\quad = \int_0^2 [x - x\,|\,1 - x\,|]\, dx$

$\quad = \dfrac{1}{2} x^2 \Big]_0^2 - \int_0^2 x\,|\,1 - x\,|\, dx$

$\quad = 2 - \int_0^2 x\,|\,1 - x\,|\, dx$

but $x\,|\,1 - x\,| = \begin{cases} x\,(1 - x) & \text{for } 0 \le x \le 1 \\ x\,(x - 1) & \text{for } 1 \le x \le 2 \end{cases}$

Thus, $E(X) = 2 - \left[\int_0^1 x\,(1 - x)\, dx + \int_1^2 x\,(x - 1)\, dx \right]$

$\quad = 2 - \int_0^1 x\, dx + \int_0^1 x^2\, dx - \int_1^2 x^2 + \int_1^2 x\, dx$

$\quad = 2 - \dfrac{1}{2} x^2 \Big]_0^1 + \dfrac{1}{3} x^3 \Big]_0^1 - \dfrac{1}{3} x^3 \Big]_1^2 + \dfrac{1}{2} x^2 \Big]_1^2$

$\quad = 2 - \dfrac{1}{2} + \dfrac{1}{3} - \dfrac{8}{3} + \dfrac{1}{3} + \dfrac{4}{2} - \dfrac{1}{2}$

$\quad = 1.$

• PROBLEM 4-27

The lifetime x (in hours) of electronic tubes mass-produced by a standard process is a random variable with a probability distribution having the density function

$\qquad axe^{-\alpha x}$

for $x \ge 0$. Prove that the expected lifetime of the tubes is $\dfrac{2}{\alpha}$. Also, show that the probability that a randomly-selected tube will have a lifetime $\ge m$ is

$(1 + \alpha m)e^{-\alpha m}$.

A research engineer suggests certain modifications in the production process which would alter the lifetime distribution by increasing the expected lifetime to $\dfrac{2}{\beta}$ ($\beta < \alpha$). But because of the cost of introducing the change, the manufacturer does not consider it worthwhile unless the modified process also ensures that the probability of the lifetime of a randomly-selected tube being $\geq m$ is increased by a fraction λ (> 0). Prove that the manufacturer's condition for introducing the new process is satisfied if

$$\beta < \alpha - \frac{1}{m}\, \log_e (1 + \lambda).$$

SOLUTION:

The expected lifetime of the electronic tubes, X, will be

$$E(X) = \int_0^\infty x\, f(x)\, dx = \int_0^\infty x\, \alpha^2 x e^{-\alpha x}\, dx$$

$$= \int_0^\infty \alpha^2\, x^2 e^{-\alpha x}\, dx$$

Integrating by parts: $\int u\, dv = uv - \int v\, du$.

Let $\quad u = x^2$ then $\quad du = 2x\, dx$

$$dv = e^{-\alpha x}\, dx \quad v = \frac{-e^{-\alpha x}}{\alpha}$$

and $\quad E(X) = \alpha^2 \left[\frac{-x^2 e^{-\alpha x}}{\alpha} \Bigg|_0^\infty - \int_0^\infty \frac{-e^{-\alpha x}}{\alpha} \times 2x\, dx \right]$

$$= \alpha^2 \left[0 + 0 + \frac{2}{\alpha} \int_0^\infty x e^{-\alpha x}\, dx \right]$$

$$= 2\alpha \int_0^\infty x e^{-\alpha x}\, dx.$$

Integrate by parts again, letting

$u = x$ then $du = dx$

$$dv = e^{-\alpha x}\, dx \qquad v = \frac{-e^{-\alpha x}}{\alpha}$$

and

$$E(X) = 2\alpha \left[\frac{-x^2 e^{-\alpha x}}{\alpha} \Bigg|_0^\infty - \int_0^\infty \frac{-e^{-\alpha x}}{\alpha}\, dx \right]$$

$$= 2\alpha \left[0 + \frac{1}{\alpha} \int_0^\infty e^{-\alpha x}\, dx \right] = 2 \int_0^\infty e^{-\alpha x}\, dx = \frac{-2}{\alpha} \int_0^\infty e^{-\alpha x} \Bigg]_0^\infty$$

$$= \frac{-2}{\alpha}[0-1] = \frac{2}{\alpha}.$$

Now $P(p \geq m) = \int_m^\infty f(x)\, dx = \int_m^\infty \alpha^2\, x e^{-\alpha x}\, dx.$

Integrating by parts, let

$$u = x \text{ and } du = dx$$

$$dv = e^{-\alpha x}\, dx \qquad v = \frac{-e^{-\alpha x}}{\alpha}.$$

Thus $P(X \geq m) = \alpha^2 \left[\frac{-x^2 e^{-\alpha x}}{\alpha} \Bigg|_m^\infty - \int_m^\infty \frac{-e^{-\alpha x}}{\alpha}\, dx \right]$

$$= \alpha^2 \left[0 + \left(\frac{-m e^{-\alpha m}}{\alpha} \right) + \frac{1}{\alpha} \int_m^\infty \frac{-e^{-\alpha x}}{\alpha}\, dx \right]$$

$$= \alpha m e^{-\alpha m} + \alpha \int_m^\infty - e^{-\alpha x}\, dx$$

$$= \alpha m e^{-\alpha m} + \alpha \left(\frac{-e^{-\alpha x}}{\alpha} \Bigg|_m^\infty \right)$$

$$= \alpha m e^{-\alpha m} + \alpha \left[-\left(\frac{-e^{-\alpha x}}{\alpha} \right) \right].$$

Now $P(X \geq m) = \alpha m e^{-\alpha m} + e^{-\alpha m} = e^{-\alpha m}(1 + \alpha m).$

If the expected lifetime of the tube is increased to $\dfrac{2}{\beta}$ ($\beta < \alpha$), this is,

in effect, a change in the probability density function. The density function has been transformed to

$$f(x) = \beta^2\, xe^{-x\beta}.$$

Thus $\quad P(X \geq m) = (1 + m\beta)\, e^{-m\beta}$

using the same calculations as before except that α is replaced by β.

The plant manager demands that $P(X \geq m)$ be increased by a fraction λ. This means that $P(X \geq m,$ before the change) $+ \lambda\, P(X \geq m,$ before the change) $\leq P(X \geq m,$ after the change).

This condition can be rewritten as

$$(1 + \alpha m)e^{-\alpha m} + \lambda(1 + \alpha m)e^{-\alpha m} \leq (1 + \beta m)e^{-\beta m}$$

or $\quad (1 + \lambda)\,(1 + \alpha m)e^{-\alpha m} \leq (1 + \beta m)e^{-\beta m}$

$$(1 + \lambda)\left(\frac{1 + \alpha m}{1 + \beta m}\right)e^{-\alpha m} \leq e^{-\beta m}.$$

Any value of β that satisfies this inequality will also satisfy the inequality $(1 + \lambda)\, e^{-m\beta}$. This is because $(1 + \lambda)e^{-\alpha m} < e^{-\beta m}$ implies that

$$\left(\frac{1 + \alpha m}{1 + \beta m}\right) > 1,\ \text{so}$$

$$(1 + \lambda)e^{-\alpha m} < (1 + \lambda)\left(\frac{1 + \alpha m}{1 + \beta m}\right)e^{-\alpha m} \leq e^{-\beta m}.$$

Now $(1 + \lambda)e^{-\alpha m} < e^{-\beta m}$ implies

$$\log_e (1 + \lambda) - \alpha m < -\beta m$$

$$\beta m < \alpha m - \log_e (1 + \lambda)$$

or $\quad \beta < \alpha - \dfrac{1}{m}\log_e (1 + \lambda).$

• PROBLEM 4–28

Find the expected value of the random variable X if X is distributed with probability density function

$f(x) = \lambda e^{-\lambda x}$ for $0 < X < \infty$.

SOLUTION:

To find this expected value we will compute the expected value from $F(x) = P(X \le x)$. For our random variable,

$$P(X \le x) = \int_0^x f(t)\, dt = \int_0^x \lambda e^{-\lambda t}\, dt$$

$$= \int_0^x (-\lambda) e^{-\lambda x}$$

$$= -e^{-\lambda t}\Big|_0^x - e^{-\lambda t} - (-e^{-\lambda \times 0})$$

$$= 1 - e^{-\lambda x}.$$

Since $E(X) = \int_0^x x\, f(x)\, dx = \int_0^x x\, \lambda e^{-\lambda x}\, dx$; and $x = \int_0^x dt$,

$$E(X) = \int_0^x f(x) \left[\int_0^x dt \right] dx.$$

This is an iterated integration over the shaded region,

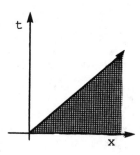

Reversing the order of integration, we integrate with respect to x first. The variable x is integrated from t to ∞ and t is integrated from 0 to ∞:

$$\int_0^\infty f(x) \left[\int_0^x dt \right] dx = \int_0^\infty \left[\int_t^\infty f(x)\, dx \right] dt.$$

But $\int_t^\infty f(x)\, dx = P(X \geq t) = 1 - P(X < t) = 1 - F(t)$

or $E(X) = \int_0^\infty [1 - F(t)]\, dt.$

Thus, $E(X) = \int_0^\infty \left[1 - \left(1 - e^{-\lambda t}\right)\right] dt$

$$= \int_0^\infty e^{-\lambda t}\, dt = -\frac{1}{\lambda} e^{-\lambda t} \Big|_0^\infty$$

$$= -\frac{1}{\lambda}[0 - 1] = \frac{1}{\lambda}$$

• PROBLEM 4-29

A platoon of soldiers is controlling a small cannon. They know that the muzzle velocity of their cannon is v_0. Unfortunately, the cannon's support apparatus does not allow them to measure precisely the angle the cannon makes with the horizontal plane. They assume that this angle is a continuous random variable, uniformly distributed between the values $\frac{\pi}{4}$ and $\frac{\pi}{2}$. Find the expected horizontal distance which the shell travels.

SOLUTION:

This problem requires an elementary knowledge of two-dimensional kinematics. Let θ = the random variable representing the angle the cannon makes with the horizontal. The horizontal distance the shell travels can be computed to be $X = (v_0 \cos \theta)t$, where t is the time the projectile is in the air. The time the projectile is in the air is

$$t = \frac{2 v_0 \sin \theta}{g},$$

where g is the acceleration due to gravity.

Now $X = (v_0 \cos \theta)\, \dfrac{2 v_0 \sin \theta}{g} = 2 v_0^2 \, \dfrac{\cos \theta \sin \theta}{g}.$

The density function of θ is

$$g(\theta) = \frac{1}{\dfrac{\pi}{2} - \dfrac{\pi}{4}}, \quad \frac{\pi}{4} \leq \theta \leq \frac{\pi}{2}$$

or $\qquad g(\theta) = \dfrac{4}{\pi}, \quad \dfrac{\pi}{4} \leq \theta \leq \dfrac{\pi}{2}.$

Thus the expected value of X is

$$E(X) = E\left[\frac{2 v_0^2 \sin\theta \cos\theta}{g}\right] = \int_\theta f(\theta)\, g(\theta)\, d\theta,$$

where $\qquad x = f(\theta) = \dfrac{2 v_0^2 \sin\theta \cos\theta}{g}.$

Thus, $\quad E(X) \displaystyle\int_{\frac{\pi}{4}}^{\frac{\pi}{2}} \frac{2 v_0^2 \sin\theta \cos\theta}{g} \times \frac{4}{\pi}\, d\theta$

$$= \frac{8 v_0^2}{\pi g} \int_{\frac{\pi}{4}}^{\frac{\pi}{2}} \sin\theta \cos\theta\, d\theta.$$

Let $u = \sin\theta$ then $du = \cos\theta\, d\theta$ and

$$E(X) = \frac{8 v_0^2}{\pi g} \int_{\frac{\sqrt{2}}{2}}^{1} u\, du = \frac{8 v_0^2}{\pi g} \times \frac{1}{2} u^2 \Big|_{\frac{\sqrt{2}}{2}}^{1}$$

$$= \frac{8 v_0^2}{\pi g} \times \frac{1}{2}\left[2\left(\frac{\sqrt{2}}{2}\right)^2\right]$$

$$= \frac{8 v_0^2}{\pi g} \times \frac{1}{2}\left[1 - \frac{1}{2}\right]$$

$$= \frac{2 v_0^2}{\pi g}.$$

Thus, if the soldiers fire their cannon many times they can expect the shell to fall a horizontal distance of $\dfrac{2 v_0^2}{\pi g}$ units away on average.

• PROBLEM 4–30

A factory has to decide the amount of y of lengths of a certain cloth to produce. The demand X for lengths is uniformly distributed over the interval (a, b). For each length sold a profit of m dollars is made, while for each length not sold a loss of n dollars is incurred. Find the expected profit and maximize this with respect to y.

SOLUTION:

The form of the profit is related to the value of y, the amount of lengths of cloth produced. If the demand is greater than the amount produced we will sell everything made and $P(X) = my$ is the profit when demand is X.

If we make too many lengths and the demand is less than y, then we will still sell X, for a profit of mX, but we will lose n dollars on each of the extra $y - X$ lengths for a total loss of $n(y - X)$. The net profit will be $mX - n(y - X)$.

More succinctly,

if $X \geq y$ then $P(X) = my$, and

if $X <$ then $P(X) = mX - n(y - X)$.

The expected profit is $E[P(X)] = \int_a^b P(X) f(x)\, dx$, where $f(x)$ is the p.d.f. of X.

Now X is uniformly distributed over (a, b), so

$$f(x) = \frac{1}{b-a}, \qquad a \leq x \leq b$$

$$= 0 \text{ otherwise.}$$

Hence $E[P(X)] = \frac{1}{b-a} \int_a^b P(X)] = P(X)\, dx.$

If $y \leq a$ then always $X \geq a \geq y$ and

$$E[P(X)] = \frac{1}{b-a} \int_a^b my\, dx = \frac{my}{b-a} x \Big|_a^b = my,$$

which will increase until $y = a$.

If $y \geq b$ then always $X \leq b \leq y$ and

$$E[P(X)] = \frac{1}{b-a} \int_a^b \left[mx - n(y-x) \right] dx$$

$$= \frac{1}{b-a} \int_a^b \left[(m+n)x - ny \right] dx$$

$$= \frac{m+n}{2(b-a)} x^2 \Big|_a^b - \frac{ny}{b-a} x \Big|_a^b$$

$$= \frac{m+n}{2(b-a)} \left[b^2 - a^2 \right] - ny$$

$$= \frac{m+n}{2(b-a)} (b-a)(b+a) - ny$$

$$= \frac{m+n}{2} (b+a) - ny$$

which is strictly decreasing from $y = b$.

A graph of our $E[P(X)]$ with respect to y so far is

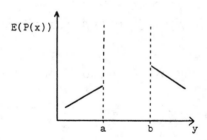

When $a \leq y \leq b$

$$E[P(X)] = \frac{1}{b-a} \left[\int_a^b P(x) \, dx \right]$$

$$= \frac{1}{b-a} \left[\int_a^y P(x) \, dx + \int_y^b P(x) \, dx \right]$$

$$= \frac{1}{b-a} \left[\int_a^y [mx - n(y-x)] \, dx + \int_y^b my \, dx \right]$$

$$= \frac{1}{b-a}\left[\int_a^y [(m+n)x - ny]\,dx\Big|_y^b\right]$$

$$= \frac{1}{b-a}\left[\frac{m+n}{2}x^2\Big|_a^y - nyx\Big|_a^y + my(b-y)\right]$$

$$= \frac{1}{b-a}\left[\frac{m+n}{2}\left(y^2 - a^2\right) - ny(y-a) + myb - my^2\right]$$

$$E[P(X)] = \frac{1}{b-a}\left[\frac{-(m+n)}{2}y^2 + (na + mb)y + \frac{m+n}{2}a^2\right]$$

We see that the expected profit is a polynomial in y.

To maximize $E[P(X)]$ we differentiate and then solve for y when $\dfrac{dE[P(X)]}{dy} = 0$. Now

$$\frac{dE[P(X)]}{dy} = \frac{1}{b-a}\left[-(m+n)\,y + (na + mb)\right] = 0$$

implies that $y = \dfrac{na + mb}{m+n}$ is the amount of cloth lengths that will maximize the expected profit.

Another Formula for the Mean

Suppose that X is a non-negative discrete random variable which only takes on integer-valued numbers as its possible values. Then there is another formula for computing the mean of X. We write

$$E[X] = \Sigma_{x = 0 \text{ to } \infty}\, xP\{X = x\}$$

$$= \Sigma_{x = 0 \text{ to } \infty}\, x[F_x(x) - F_x(x - 1)],$$

because $\quad F_x(x) - F_x(x - 1) = P\{X \le x\} - P\{X \le x - 1\}$

$$= (P\{X < x\} + P\{X = x\}) - P\{X \le x - 1\}.$$

But X only takes on integer values, so

$$P\{X < x\} = P\{X \le x - 1\},$$

and $\quad F_x(x) - F_x(x - 1) = (P\{X < x\} + P\{X = x\}) - P\{X \le x - 1\}$

$$= (P\{X \le x - 1\} + P\{X = x\}) - P\{X \le x - 1\}$$

$$= P\{X = x\}.$$

Thus,
$$E[X] = \Sigma_{x=0 \text{ to } \infty} \, x[F_x(x) - F_x(x-1)],$$

$$= \Sigma_{x=0 \text{ to } \infty} \, x\{[1-F_x(x-1)] - [1 - F_x(x)]\}$$

$$= \Sigma_{x=0 \text{ to } \infty} \, x[1 - F_x(x-1)] - \Sigma_{x=0 \text{ to } \infty} \, x[1 - F_x(x)].$$

Notice that this sum cannot be split without first subtracting the cumulative distribution functions from one, because otherwise these sums are each infinite, and the difference is therefore undefined. Proceeding,

$$E[X] = \Sigma_{x=0 \text{ to } \infty} x[1 - F_x(x-1)] - \Sigma_{x=0 \text{ to } \infty} x[1 - F_x(x)]$$

$$= \Sigma_{x=1 \text{ to } \infty} \, x[1 - F_x(x-1)] - \Sigma_{x=1 \text{ to } \infty} \, x[1 - F_x(x)],$$

because when $x = 0$, each sum is zero. Now, letting

$$y = x - 1,$$

we have
$$x = y + 1,$$

so
$$E[X] = \Sigma_{x=1 \text{ to } \infty} x[1 - F_x(x-1)] - \Sigma_{x=1 \text{ to } \infty} x[1 - F_x(x)]$$

$$= \Sigma_{y=0 \text{ to } \infty} \, (y + 1)[1 - F_x(y)] - \Sigma_{x=1 \text{ to } \infty} \, x[1 - F_x(x)]$$

$$= \Sigma_{y=0 \text{ to } \infty} \, y[1 - F_x(y)] + \Sigma_{y=0 \text{ to } \infty} \, [1 - F_x(y)]$$
$$- \Sigma_{x=1 \text{ to } \infty} \, x[1 - F_x(x)]$$

$$= \Sigma_{y=1 \text{ to } \infty} \, y[1 - F_x(y)] + \Sigma_{y=0 \text{ to } \infty} [1 - F_x(y)]$$
$$- \Sigma_{x=1 \text{ to } \infty} x[1 - F_x(x)]$$

$$E[x] = \Sigma_{y=0 \text{ to } \infty} \, [1 - F_x(y)]. \qquad y = x - 1$$

This is a useful formula for calculating the expected value of X when the cumulative distribution function of X is given.

• **PROBLEM 4–31**

Illustrate the alternate formula for the expected value for a Bernoulli random variable.

SOLUTION:

There are only two possible values for a Bernoulli random variable: zero and one. Each of these values is non-negative and integer-valued, so the above result applies.

Let p be the parameter of the Bernoulli random variable. Then

$$P\{X = 0\} = 1 - p$$

and $\quad P\{X = 1\} = p.$

The standard formula would give

$$E[X] = (0)\, P\{X = 0\} + (1)\, P\{X = 1\}$$

$$= (0)\,(1 - p) + (1)\,(p)$$

$$= 0 + p$$

$$= p.$$

The alternate formula gives

$$E[X] = \Sigma_{x = 0 \text{ to } \infty}\, [1 - F_x(x)]$$

$$= [1 - F_x(0)] + [1 - F_x(1)] + \Sigma_{x = 2 \text{ to } \infty}\, [1 - F_x(x)]$$

$$= [1 - P\{X \le 0\}] + [1 - P\{X \le 1\}] + \Sigma_{x = 2 \text{ to } \infty}\, [1 - P\{X \le x\}]$$

$$= [1 - P\{X = 0\}] + [1 - P\{X = 0 \cup X = 1\}]$$
$$\quad + \Sigma_{x = 2 \text{ to } \infty}\, [1 - P\{X < x + 1\}]$$

$$= [1 - (1 - p)] + [1 - (P\{X = 0\} + P\{X = 1\})]$$
$$\quad + \Sigma_{x = 3 \text{ to } \infty}\, [1 - P\{X < x\}]$$

$$= [p] + [1 - (1 - p + p)] + \Sigma_{x = 3 \text{ to } \infty}\, [1 - 1]$$

$$= p + [1 - (1)] + \Sigma_{x = 3 \text{ to } \infty}\, [0]$$

$$= p + [1 - 1] + 0$$

$$= p + [0]$$

$$= p.$$

The two formulas agree.

Illustrate the alternate formula for the expected value for a multinomial random variable which can only take the values zero, one, and two.

SOLUTION:

For such a multinomial random variable, there are only three possible values: zero, one, and two. Each of these values is non-negative and integer-valued, so the above result applies.

Let

$$P\{X = 0\} = p0,$$

$$P\{X = 1\} = p1,$$

and $$P\{X = 2\} = p2.$$

Clearly, $p0 + p1 + p2 = 1$.

The standard formula would give

$$E[X] = (0)\,(p0) + (1)\,(p1) + (2)\,(p2)$$

$$= p1 + 2p2.$$

The alternate formula gives

$$E[X] = \Sigma_{x = 0 \text{ to } \infty}\,[1 - F_x(x)]$$

$$= [1 - F_x(0)] + [1 - F_x(1)] + [1 - F_x(2)] + \Sigma_{x = 3 \text{ to } \infty}\,[1 - F_x(x)]$$

$$= [1 - P\{X \le 0\}] + [1 - P\{X \le 1\}] + [1 - P\{X \le 2\}] + \Sigma_{x = 3 \text{ to } \infty}\,[1 - P\{X \le x\}]$$

$$= [1 - P\{X = 0\}] + [1 - P\{X = 0 \cup X = 1\}] + [1 - P\{X = 0 \cup X = 1 \cup X = 2\}] + \Sigma_{x = 3 \text{ to } \infty}\,[1 - P\{X < x + 1\}]$$

$$= [1 - p0] + [1 - p0 - p1] + [1 - p0 - p1 - p2] + \Sigma_{x = 3 \text{ to } \infty}\,[1 - P\{X < x\}]$$

$$= [p1 + p2] + [p2] + [0] + \Sigma_{x = 4 \text{ to } \infty}\,[1 - 1]$$

$$= p1 + 2p2 + \Sigma_{x = 4 \text{ to } \infty}\,[0]$$

$$= p1 + 2p2 + 0$$

$$= p1 + 2p2.$$

The two formulas agree. The standard formula calculates the expected value of X by summing these quantities horizontally (that is, $p1$ plus $2p2$), while the alternate formula calculates the expected value of X by summing these quantities vertically (that is, $1 - p0$ plus $1 - p1$).

• PROBLEM 4-33

Illustrate the alternate formula for the expected value for a multinomial random variable which can only take the values zero, one, two, and three.

SOLUTION:

For such a multinomial random variable, there are only four possible values: zero, one, two, and three. Each of these values is non-negative and integer-valued, so the above result applies.

Let

$$P\{X = 0\} = p0,$$

$$P\{X = 1\} = p1,$$

$$P\{X = 2\} = p2,$$

and $\qquad p\{X = 3\} = p3.$

Clearly, $p0 + p1 + p2 + p3 = 1$.

The standard formula would give

$$E[X] = (0)\,(p0) + (1)\,(p1) + (2)\,(p2) + (3)\,(p3)$$

$$= p1 + 2p2 + 3p3.$$

The alternate formula gives

$$E[X] = \Sigma_{x = 0 \text{ to } \infty} [1 - F_x(x)]$$

$$= [1 - F_x(0)] + [1 - F_x(1)] + [1 - F_x(2)] + [1 - F_x(3)]$$
$$+ \Sigma_{x = 4 \text{ to } \infty} [1 - F_x(x)]$$

$$= [1 - P\{X \le 0\}] + [1 - P\{X \le 1\}] + [1 - P\{X \le 2\}]$$
$$+ [1 - P\{X \le 3\}] + \Sigma_{x = 4 \text{ to } \infty} [1 - P\{X \le x\}]$$

$$= [1 - P\{X = 0\}] + [1 - P\{X = 0 \cup X = 1\}]$$

$$+ [1 - P\{X = 0 \cup X = 1 \cup X = 2\}]$$
$$+ [1 - P\{X = 0 \cup X = 1 \cup X = 2 \cup X = 3\}]$$
$$+ \Sigma_{x = 4 \text{ to } \infty} [1 - P\{X < x + 1\}]$$

$$= [1 - p0] + [1 - p0 - p1] + [1 - p0 - p1 - p2]$$
$$+ [1 - p0 - p1 - p2 - p3]$$
$$+ \Sigma_{x = 5 \text{ to } \infty} [1 - P\{X < x\}]$$

$$= [p1 + p2 + p3] + [p2 + p3] + [p3] + [0]$$
$$+ \Sigma_{x = 5 \text{ to } \infty} [1 - 1]$$

$$= p1 + 2p2 + 3p3 + \Sigma_{x = 4 \text{ to } \infty} [0]$$

$$= p1 + 2p2 + 3p3 + 0$$

$$= p1 + 2p2 + 3p3.$$

The two formulas agree. Then the standard formula calculates the expected value of X by summing these quantities horizontally (that is, $p1$ plus $2p2$ plus $3p3$), while the alternate formula calculates the expected value of X by summing these quantities vertically (that is, $1 - p0$ plus $1 - [p0 + p1]$ plus $1 - [p0 + p1 + p2]$).

✓ • **PROBLEM 4-34**

Let X be a discrete uniform random variable which takes on the values $\{1, 2, 3, 4, 5, 6, 7, 8, 9, 10\}$ each with probability $1/10$. Notice that X is also a multinomial random variable. Find the expected value of X in two different ways.

SOLUTION:

The standard formula gives

$$E[X] = \Sigma_{x = 1 \text{ to } 10} x P\{X = x\}$$

$$= \Sigma_{x = 1 \text{ to } 10} x \left(\frac{1}{10} \right)$$
$$= \left(\frac{1}{10} \right) [\Sigma_{x = 1 \text{ to } 10} x].$$

There is a well–known formula in mathematics which states that

$$\Sigma_{x=1 \text{ to n}} x = n\ \frac{n+1}{2}.$$

Thus, $E[X] = \left(\dfrac{1}{10}\right) [\Sigma_{x=1 \text{ to } 10} x]$

$$= \left(\frac{1}{10}\right) [(10)\ (10+1)/2]$$

$$= \left(\frac{1}{10}\right) [(10)\ (11)/2]$$

$$= \left(\frac{1}{10}\right) [(110)/2]$$

$$= \left(\frac{1}{10}\right) [55]$$

$$= 5.5.$$

The alternate formula gives

$$E[X] = \Sigma_{x=0 \text{ to } \infty} [1 - F_x(x)].$$

Now $F_x(x) = 0$ for $x < 1$,

$$F_x(x) = \frac{1}{10} \text{ for } 1 \le x < 2,$$

$$F_x(x) = \frac{2}{10} \text{ for } 2 \le x < 3,$$

$$F_x(x) = \frac{3}{10} \text{ for } 3 \le x < 4,$$

$$F_x(x) = \frac{4}{10} \text{ for } 4 \le x < 5,$$

$$F_x(x) = \frac{5}{10} \text{ for } 5 \le x < 6,$$

$$F_x(x) = \frac{6}{10} \text{ for } 6 \le x < 7,$$

$$F_x(x) = \frac{7}{10} \text{ for } 7 \le x < 8,$$

$$F_x(x) = \frac{8}{10} \text{ for } 8 \le x < 9,$$

$$F_x(x) = \frac{9}{10} \text{ for } 9 \le x < 10,$$

and $F_x(x) = 1$ for $10 \le x$.

Therefore,

$$1 - F_x(x) = 1 - 0$$

$$= 1 \text{ for } x < 1,$$

$$1 - F_x(x) = 1 - \frac{1}{10}$$

$$= \frac{9}{10} \text{ for } 1 \le x < 2,$$

$$1 - F_x(x) = 1 - \frac{2}{10}$$

$$= \frac{8}{10} \text{ for } 2 \le x < 3,$$

$$1 - F_x(x) = 1 - \frac{3}{10}$$

$$= \frac{7}{10} \text{ for } 3 \le x < 4,$$

$$1 - F_x(x) = 1 - \frac{4}{10}$$

$$= \frac{6}{10} \text{ for } 4 \le x < 5,$$

$$1 - F_x(x) = 1 - \frac{5}{10}$$

$$= \frac{5}{10} \text{ for } 5 \le x < 6,$$

$$1 - F_x(x) = 1 - \frac{6}{10}$$

$$= \frac{4}{10} \text{ for } 6 \leq x < 7,$$

$$1 - F_x(x) = 1 - \frac{7}{10}$$

$$= \frac{3}{10} \text{ for } 7 \leq x < 8,$$

$$1 - F_x(x) = 1 - \frac{8}{10}$$

$$= \frac{2}{10} \text{ for } 8 \leq x < 9,$$

$$1 - F_x(x) = 1 - \frac{9}{10}$$

$$= \frac{1}{10} \text{ for } 9 \leq x < 10,$$

and $\quad 1 - F_x(x) = 1 - 1$

$$= 0 \text{ for } 10 \leq x.$$

Finally, then,

$$E[X] = \Sigma_{x = 0 \text{ to } \infty} [1 - F_x(x)]$$

$$= \Sigma_{x = 0 \text{ to } 9} [1 - F_x(x)] + \Sigma_{x = 10 \text{ to } \infty} [1 - F_x(x)]$$

$$= \Sigma_{x = 0 \text{ to } 9} [1 - F_x(x)] + \Sigma_{x = 10 \text{ to } \infty} [0]$$

$$= \Sigma_{x = 0 \text{ to } 9} [1 - F_x(x)] + (0) \Sigma_{x = 10 \text{ to } \infty} 1$$

$$= \Sigma_{x = 0 \text{ to } 9} [1 - F_x(x)] + (0)$$

$$= \Sigma_{x = 0 \text{ to } 9} [1 - F_x(x)]$$

$$= [1 - F_x(0)] + [1 - F_x(1)] + [1 - F_x(2)] + [1 - F_x(3)]$$

$$+ [1 - F_x(4)] + [1 - F_x(5)] + [1 - F_x(6)] + [1 - F_x(7)]$$

$$+ [1 - F_x(8)] + [1 - F_x(9)]$$

$$= 1 + \frac{9}{10} + \frac{8}{10} + \frac{7}{10} + \frac{6}{10} + \frac{5}{10} + \frac{4}{10} + \frac{3}{10} + \frac{2}{10} + \frac{1}{10}$$

$$= \left(\frac{1}{10}\right) (10 + 9 + 8 + 7 + 6 + 5 + 4 + 3 + 2 + 1).$$

There is a well-known formula in mathematics which states that

$$\Sigma_{x = 1 \text{ to } n} x = (n)(n + 1)/2.$$

Thus

$$E[X] = \left(\frac{1}{10}\right)[\Sigma_{x = 1 \text{ to } 10} x]$$

$$= \left(\frac{1}{10}\right) [(10) \frac{10 + 1}{2}]$$

$$= \left(\frac{1}{10}\right) [(10) \frac{11}{2}]$$

$$= \left(\frac{1}{10}\right) [\frac{110}{2}]$$

$$= \left(\frac{1}{10}\right) [55]$$

$$= 5.5.$$

Again, both formulas give the same answer of 5.5, as expected.

• PROBLEM 4-35

Does this alternate formula for the mean apply only to non-negative, integer-valued random variables?

SOLUTION:

Generalizations do exist, but the random variable cannot be unbounded on both the positive and negative sides. The simplest extension is to the case when the random variable is positive and discrete, but not necessarily integer-valued.

✳✳✳✳✳✳

REVIEW OF VARIANCE AND STANDARD DEVIATION

As mentioned earlier in the chapter, the second central moment is known as the variance, and is denoted, for a random variable X, as $V(X)$. That is,

$$V(X) = E[(X - E[X])^2].$$

Any quantity that is squared is necessarily non-negative, and is zero only if the quantity being squared is uniformly zero. The expected value of a non-negative quantity is also non-negative; consequently, the variance is always non-negative and is zero only when $X = E[X]$ for all values of X. This is possible only for degenerate random variables which satisfy the equation

$$P\{X = k\} = 1$$

for some value of k. As random variables go, the degenerate ones are not particularly interesting. The point of this discussion was to point out that if a variance is computed and turns out to be negative, then there is an error in the calculations. If it turns out to be zero, then the random variable would have to be degenerate. These rules provide useful checks of calculations of variances. If we open the square in the formula for the variance, then we obtain the alternate formula

$$V(X) = E[(X - E[X])^2]$$
$$= E\{X^2 + (E[X])^2 - 2XE[X]\}$$
$$= E[X^2] + (E[X])^2 - 2E[X]E[X]$$
$$= E[X^2] + (E[X])^2 - 2(E[X])^2$$
$$= E[X^2] - (E[X])^2.$$

This formula relates the first moment and the second moment to the second central moment (the variance).

As an example of a problem which could be asked about variances, consider a random variable X, such that $E[X] = 2$ and $E[X^2] = 4$. Then you may be asked to find the variance of X, or $V(X)$. The formula just presented yields

$$V(X) = E[X^2] - (E[X])^2$$
$$= 4 * 2^2 \qquad 4 - 4 = 0$$
$$= 4 * 4$$
$$= 8.$$

The variance satisfies certain properties which make its calculation more convenient. For example, if X and Y are independent random variables, then

$$V(X + Y) = V(X) + V(Y).$$

If X and Y are not independent, then there is another formula involving the covariance between X and Y (which would be zero if the two random variables were independent); however, we will defer discussion of this topic until later in the book. Adding a constant to a random variable does not affect its variance. That is,

$$V(X + k) = V(X)$$

for all random variables X and constants k. Now recall that as a constant, k is a degenerate random variable, meaning that $V(k) = 0$. Thus, the first equation may be applied, replacing Y by k (as will be seen later, any random variable and any constant are statistically independent random variables), and we would obtain

$$9V(X + k) = V(X) + V(k)$$

$$= V(X) + 0$$

$$= V(X)$$

If a random variable is multiplied by a constant, then the variance is multiplied by the square of this constant. That is,

$$V(kX) = k^2 V(X)$$

for all random variables X and constants k. This can be seen by considering the definition of the variance,

$$V(X) = E[X^2] - (E[X])^2,$$

and applying this to the random variable kX. We obtain

$$V(kX) = E[(kX)^2] - (E[kX])^2$$

$$= E[k^2X^2] - (kE[X])^2$$

$$= k^2E[X^2] - k^2(E[X])^2$$

$$= k^2\{E[X^2] - (E[X])^2\}$$

$$= k^2 V(X).$$

Combining the formula for the variance of a product of a constant and a random variable with the formula for the variance of a sum of a constant and a random variable yields the useful property of the variance of a linear combination. Namely,

$$V(aX + b) = V(aX) + V(b)$$
$$= a^2V(X) + 0$$
$$= a^2V(X)$$

for any random variable X and any constants a and b.

If X is a random variable with a Bernoulli distribution with parameter p, then $V(X) = p(1 - p)$. If X is a binomial random variable with parameters n and p, then X can be written as the sum of n independent Bernoulli random variables, each with parameter p. The formula for the variance of a sum then shows that $V(X) = np(1 - p)$. If X is a normally distributed random variable with mean M and standard deviation S, then $V(X) = S^2$.

• **PROBLEM 4–36** omit

Suppose that X is a random variable such that $E[X] = 5$ and $E[X^2] = 10$. Then find the variance of X.

SOLUTION: $E[x^2] \geq E^2[x]$

Using the formula for the variance of a random variable, we obtain

$$V(X) = E[X^2] - (E[X])^2$$
$$= 10 \mp 5^2$$
$$= 10 \mp 25$$
$$= 35.$$
$$-15$$

• **PROBLEM 4–37** OMIT

Suppose that X is a random variable such that $E[X] = -2$ and $E[X^2] = 6$. Find the variance of X.

SOLUTION:

Using the formula for the variance of a random variable, we obtain

$$V(X) = E[X^2] - (E[X])^2$$
$$= 6 + (-2)^2$$
$$= 6 + 4$$
$$= 10.$$

✓ • **PROBLEM 4–38**

Suppose that X is a random variable such that $E[X] = 0$ and $V[X] = 1$. Find $E[X^2]$.

SOLUTION:

Using the formula for the variance of a random variable, we obtain

$$V(X) = E[X^2] - (E[X])^2,$$

so $E[X^2] = V(X) + (E[X])^2$

$$= 1 + 0^2$$
$$= 1 + 0$$
$$= 1.$$

✓ • **PROBLEM 4–39**

If $V(X) = 4$, then what is $V(2X + 1)$?

SOLUTION:

Using the formula for the variance of a linear function of a random variable (since $f(X) = 2X + 1$ is a linear function), we see that

$$V(2X + 1) = 2^2 V(X) + V(1)$$
$$= 4V(X) + 0$$

$$= (4)\,(4)$$

$$= 16.$$

• PROBLEM 4-40

If $V(X) = 3$, then what is $V(4X + 2)$?

SOLUTION:

Using the formula for the variance of a linear function of a random variable (since $f(X) = 4X + 2$ is a linear function), we see that

$$V(4X + 2) = 4^2 V(X) + V(2)$$

$$= 16 V(X) + 0$$

$$= (16)\,(3)$$

$$= 48.$$

• PROBLEM 4-41

If $E[X] = 1$ and $V(X) = 4$, then what is $E[2X^2 + 3X + 2]$?

SOLUTION:

We compute

$$E[2X^2 + 3X + 2] = 2E[X^2] + 3E[X] + 2$$

$$= 2\{V(X) + (E[X])^2\} + (3)\,(1) + 2$$

$$= 2\{4 + 1^2\} + 3 + 2$$

$$= 2(4 + 1) + 3 + 2$$

$$= (2)\,(5) + 5$$

$$= 10 + 5$$

$$= 15.$$

✓ • **PROBLEM 4–42**

If $E[X] = 2$ and $V(X) = 3$, then what is $E[3X^2 + X + 14]$?

SOLUTION:

We compute

$$E[3X^2 + X + 14] = 3E[X^2] + E[X] + 14$$
$$= 3\{V(X) + (E[X])^2\} + 2 + 14$$
$$= 3\{3 + 2^2\} + 16$$
$$= 3(3 + 4) + 16$$
$$= (3)\,(7) + 16$$
$$= 21 + 16$$
$$= 37.$$

✓ • **PROBLEM 4–43**

If X is a Bernoulli random variable with parameter 0.5, then what is $V(X)$?

SOLUTION:

As seen earlier, for Bernoulli random variables,

$$V(X) = p(1 - p).$$

In this case,

$$V(X) = p(1 - p)$$
$$= (0.5)\,(1 - 0.5)$$
$$= (0.5)\,(0.5)$$
$$= 0.25.$$

✓• **PROBLEM 4–44**

If X is a Bernoulli random variable with parameter 0.3, then what is $V(X)$?

SOLUTION:

As seen earlier, for Bernoulli random variables,

$$V(X) = p(1 - p).$$

In this case,

$$V(X) = p(1 - p)$$
$$= (0.3) (1 - 0.3)$$
$$= (0.3) (0.7)$$
$$= 0.21.$$

✓• **PROBLEM 4–45**

Let X is a Bernoulli random variable with parameter p. For what value of p will $V(X)$ be maximized?

SOLUTION:

Since

$$V(X) = p(1 - p)$$
$$= p - p^2,$$

we simply need to use the basics of calculus to solve this problem. If we differentiate the function $f(p) = p(1 - p)$, then we obtain

$$f'(p) = 1 - 2p.$$

Equating this to zero yields

$$1 - 2p = 0$$

so $2p = 1,$

or $p = 0.5.$

Since $f''(p) = -2 < 0$, this is a local maximum. Examination of the monotonicity of the function as p approaches 0.5 from either side shows this to be a global maximum.

$\sqrt{}$ • PROBLEM 4–46

A basketball player shoots free throw shots. The probability of success is 0.8 on each shot. The player decides to record the result of his 11th shot by defining X to be one if the shot is successful, and zero otherwise. Then what is the variance of X? What is the standard deviation of X?

SOLUTION:

Clearly, by the way it is defined, X is a Bernoulli random variable with parameter 0.8. Then the variance of X can be found as

$$V(X) = p(1-p)$$
$$= (0.8)\,(1 - 0.8)$$
$$= (0.8)\,(0.2)$$
$$= 0.16.$$

The standard deviation is found as the square root of the variance. In this case,

$$S = V^{0.5}$$
$$= 0.16^{0.5}$$
$$= 0.4.$$

$\sqrt{}$ • PROBLEM 4–47

If X is a binomial random variable with parameters 10 and 0.4, then what is $V(X)$? What is the standard deviation of X?

SOLUTION:

The variance of a binomial random variable with parameters n and p is

$$V(X) = np(1 - p).$$

In this case, we have

$$V(X) = np(1 - p)$$

$$= (10)\,(0.4)\,(1 - 0.4)$$

$$= (10)\,(0.4)\,(0.6)$$

$$= 2.4.$$

The standard deviation of X is found as the square root of the variance of X. In this case,

$$S = V^{0.5}$$

$$= 2.4^{0.5}$$

$$= 1.5492.$$

✓ • PROBLEM 4-48

If X is the number of heads obtained when tossing 20 fair coins, then what is $V(X)$? What is the standard deviation of X?

SOLUTION:

By construction, X is a binomial random variable with parameters 20 and 0.5. The variance is then

$$V(X) = np(1 - p)$$

$$= (20)\,(0.5)\,(1 - 0.5)$$

$$= (20)\,(0.5)\,(0.5)$$

$$= 5.$$

The standard deviation of X is found as the square root of the variance of X. In this case,

$$S = V^{0.5}$$

$$= 5^{0.5}$$

$$= 2.2361.$$

√ • **PROBLEM 4-49**

If X is a normally distributed random variable with mean four and standard deviation two, then what is the variance of X? What is the variance of $4X - 1$? What is the standard deviation of $4X - 1$?

SOLUTION:

The variance of a normal random variable is the square of the standard deviation. In this case, then,

$$V(X) = S^2$$

$$= 2^2$$

$$= 4.$$

Also, $V(4X - 1) = 4^2 V(X) + V(-1)$

$$= (16)\,(4) + 0$$

$$= 64 + 0$$

$$= 64.$$

The standard deviation of X is found as the square root of the variance of X. In this case, the standard deviation of $4X - 1$ is the square root of the variance of $4X - 1$, or

$$S = V^{0.5}$$

$$= 64^{0.5}$$

$$= 8.$$

√ • **PROBLEM 4-50**

Is the variance always larger than the standard deviation?

SOLUTION:

Since the variance is the square of the standard deviation, the variance will be larger than the standard deviation whenever one of these quantities is larger than one in absolute value. Since neither can be negative, this would be whenever either one of these quantities is larger than one, in which case the other must also exceed one. But when one is less than one (and consequently both are less than one), the standard deviation is larger than the variance, since for X in the range $(0,1)$ it is true that

$$X > X^2. \qquad \text{when} \quad 0 < x < 1$$

• PROBLEM 4-51

Let X be a trichotomous random variable such that

$$P\{X = -1\} = p,$$

$$P\{X = 0\} = q,$$

$$P\{X = 1\} = r,$$

and $P\{X = k\} = 0$ for other values of k.

That is, $p + q + r = 1$.

Then find $V(Y)$, where $Y = X^n$ for n, a positive even integer.

SOLUTION:

Note that

$$X^n = 1 \text{ if } X = -1,$$

$$X^n = 0 \text{ if } X = 0,$$

and $$X^n = 1 \text{ if } X = 1.$$

That is, $\quad P\{X^n = 0\} = P\{X = 0\}$

$$= q,$$

and $\quad P\{X^n = 1\} = P\{X = -1 \cup X = 1\}$

$$= P\{X = -1\} + P\{X = 1\}$$

$$= p + r.$$

Now $\quad E[Y] = E[X^n]$

$$= (0)\,(q) + (1)\,(p + r)$$

$$= 0 + (p + r)$$

$$= p + r.$$

Also,

$$E[Y^2] = E[(X^n)^2]$$
$$= E[X^{2n}].$$

But if n is a positive even integer, then $2n$ must also be a positive even integer. Therefore,

$$E[X^{2n}] = E[X^n]$$
$$= p + r.$$

Now $V(Y) = E[Y^2] - (E[Y])^2$

$$= (p + r) - (p + r)^2$$
$$= (p + r)[1 - (p + r)].$$

• PROBLEM 4-52

Suppose that the height of a certain population follows a normal distribution with mean height 70 inches and standard deviation six inches. Let X be the random variable measuring height. What is the variance of the height in terms of feet?

SOLUTION:

The variance is given by

$$V(X) = SD^2$$
$$= (6 \text{ inches})^2$$
$$= 6^2 \text{ inches}^2$$
$$= 36 \text{ inches}^2.$$

It may not be possible to convert the unit, inches^2, to an equivalent measure involving units in terms of feet. But consider $Y = X/12$, which is the height in terms of feet. Then

$$V(Y) = V(X/12)$$
$$= V(X)/12^2$$
$$= V(X)/144$$

$= [SD(X)]^2/144$

$= (6)^2/144$

$= (36)/144$

$= 1/4.$

This allows the desired conversion of units from inches to feet.

$\sqrt{}$ • **PROBLEM 4-53**

Given the probability distribution of the random variable X in the table below, compute $E[X]$ and var (X).

x_i	$P(X = x_i)$
0	$\dfrac{8}{27}$
1	$\dfrac{12}{27}$
2	$\dfrac{6}{27}$
3	$\dfrac{1}{27}$

SOLUTION:

First $E[X] = \sum\limits_i x_i P(X = x_i)$ and var $(X) = E[(X - E[X])^2]$.

Thus,

$E[X] = (0) P(X = 0) + (1) P(X = 1) + (2) P(X = 2) + (3) P(X = 3)$

$= (0)\dfrac{8}{27} + (1)\dfrac{12}{27} + (2)\dfrac{6}{27} + (3)\dfrac{1}{27}$

$= 0 + \dfrac{12}{27} + \dfrac{12}{27} + \dfrac{3}{27} = \dfrac{27}{27} = 1.$ Also,

$$\text{var }(X) = (0 - 1)^2\, P(X = 0) + (1 - 1)^2\, P(X = 1)$$
$$+ (2 - 1)^2\, P(X = 2) + (3 - 1)^2\, P(X = 3)$$

$$= (1^2)\frac{8}{27} + (0^2)\frac{12}{27} + (1^2)\frac{6}{27} + (2^2)\frac{1}{27}$$

$$= \frac{8}{27} + \frac{6}{27} + \frac{4}{27} = \frac{18}{27} = \frac{2}{3}.$$

$\checkmark$ • **PROBLEM 4–54**

Given the following table of probabilities for values x_i of the random variable X, which represents the number of defective radios in a shipment of four, find the variance and standard deviation of X.

x_i	$P(X = x_i)$
0	$\dfrac{1}{16}$
1	$\dfrac{4}{16}$
2	$\dfrac{6}{16}$
3	$\dfrac{4}{16}$
4	$\dfrac{1}{16}$

SOLUTION:

The variance of a random variable X is defined to be

$$E[X - E(X)]^2 = \sigma^2.$$

Since we have a discrete set of data, the most efficient method of finding the variance is to construct a table which will extend the given one. First compute the expected number of defective radios:

$$E[X] = \sum_{i=0}^{4} x_i \, P(X = x_i)$$

$$= 0 \times \left(\frac{1}{16}\right) + 1 \times \left(\frac{4}{16}\right) + 2 \times \left(\frac{6}{16}\right) + 3 \times \left(\frac{4}{16}\right) + 4 \times \left(\frac{1}{16}\right)$$

$$= \left(\frac{4}{16}\right) + \left(\frac{12}{16}\right) + \left(\frac{12}{16}\right) + \left(\frac{4}{16}\right) = \left(\frac{32}{16}\right) = = 2.$$

x_i	$P(X = x_i)$	$E(X) = (x_i - 2)$	$(x_i - 2)^2$	$(x_i - 2)^2 \, P(X = x_i)$
0	$\frac{1}{16}$	-2	4	$\frac{4}{16}$
1	$\frac{4}{16}$	-1	1	$\frac{4}{16}$
2	$\frac{6}{16}$	0	0	0
3	$\frac{4}{16}$	1	1	$\frac{4}{16}$
4	$\frac{1}{16}$	2	4	$\frac{4}{16}$

The variance of a discrete random variable X is defined to be

$$\sigma^2 = \sum_{i=1}^{n} (x_i - E[X])^2 \, P(X = x_i).$$

Observe that in this problem σ^2 is the sum of the entries in the last column of the table, so

$$\sigma^2 = \frac{4}{16} + \frac{4}{16} + 0 + \frac{4}{16} + \frac{4}{16} = \frac{16}{16} = 1.$$

The standard deviation of s of X is

$$\sigma = \sqrt{\sigma^2} = \sqrt{1} = 1.$$

Use the properties of expectation to find the variance of the sum of two independent random variables.

SOLUTION:

The variance of the sum of two independent random variables is defined to be

$$\text{var } (X + Y) = E[(X + Y - E[X + Y])^2];$$

squaring inside the square brackets:

$$\text{var } (X + Y) = E[(X + Y)^2 - 2(X + Y) E[X + Y] - (E[X + Y])^2].$$

Squaring again yields:

$$\text{var } (X + Y) = E[X^2 + 2XY + Y^2 - 2(X + Y) E[X + Y] - (E[X + Y])^2].$$

But $(E[X + Y])^2 = (E[X] + E[Y])^2$

$$= [E[X]]^2 + 2E[X] \, E[Y] + [E[Y]]^2.$$

Substituting we see that:

$$\text{var } (X + Y) = E[X^2 + 2XY + Y^2 - 2(X + Y) E[X + Y] + (E[X])^2$$
$$+ 2E(X) \, E(Y) + [E(Y)]^2;$$

but $E[X + Y]$, $E[X^2]$, $E[X] \, E[Y]$, and $E[Y]^2$ are constants, and the expected value of a constant equals that constant, thus

$$\text{var } (X + Y) = E[X^2 + 2XY + Y^2] - 2E[X + Y] \, E[X + Y] + [E[X + Y]]^2$$
$$= E[X^2 + 2XY + Y^2] - 2 \, E[X + Y]]^2 + [E[X + Y]]^2$$
$$= E[X^2 + 2XY + Y^2] - [E[X + Y]]^2$$
$$= E[X^2] + 2E[XY] + E[Y^2] - [E[X] + Y]]^2$$

But since X and Y are independent,

$$E[XY] = E[X] \, E[Y].$$

Thus,

$$\text{var } (X + Y) = E[X^2] + 2E[X] \, E[Y] + [E[Y^2] - [E[X]]^2$$
$$- 2E[X] \, E[Y] - [E[Y]]^2$$
$$= E \, [X^2] - (E \, [X])^2 + E \, [Y^2] - ([Y])^2$$
$$= \text{var } X + \text{var } Y.$$

• PROBLEM 4-56

Find the variance of the random variable $X + b$ where X has variance var X and b is a constant.

SOLUTION:

$$\text{var } (X + b) = E([X + b]^2) - (E[X + b])^2$$

$$= E[X^2 + 2bX + b^2] - [E[X] + b]^2$$

$$= E[X^2] + 2bE[X] + b^2 - (E[X])^2 - (E[X])^2 - 2E[X]b - b^2,$$

thus   var $(X + b) = E[X^2] - (E[X])^2 = $ var (X).

• PROBLEM 4-57

Find the variance of the random variable $Y = aX$ where a is a constant and X has variance var $X = \sigma^2$.

SOLUTION:

We wish to find var $(Y) = $ var (aX). We know that var $Y = E[Y]^2 - (E[Y])^2$. But $Y^2 = a^2X^2$ and $E[Y] = E[aX] = aE[X]$.

Now

$$\text{var } (aX) = E[a^2X^2] - (aE[X])^2 = a^2E[X^2] - a^2 (E[X])^2$$

$$= a^2 (E[X^2] - E[X^2] - E[X]^2 = a^2 \text{ var } [X].$$

✓ • PROBLEM 4-58

A population consists of the measurements 2, 3, 3, 4, 4, 4, 5, 5, 5, 6, 6, 7. Compute: (a) μ, (b) σ^2.

SOLUTION:

Because the entire population is known, we may calculate μ and σ^2 directly. This is only possible when the entire population is known. If we have a sample form the entire population, we can only calculate estimates of μ and σ^2.

To find μ, we multiply each value in the population by its frequency of occurrence. Thus,

$$E[X] = \mu = 2\frac{1}{12} + 3\frac{2}{12} + 4\frac{3}{12} + 5\frac{3}{12} + 6\frac{2}{12} + 7\frac{1}{12}$$

$$\mu = \frac{2+6+12+15+12+7}{12} = \frac{54}{12} = 4.5.$$

We also could have found μ by adding the population values and dividing by the number of values in the population.

By definition

$$E[X - \mu]^2 = \sum_i (X_i - \mu)^2 \, P(X_i)$$

$$= \sum_i (X_i - \mu)^2 \, \frac{1}{n}$$

$$= \frac{1}{n} \sum_i (X_i - \mu)^2,$$

the average squared deviation from the mean μ.

Now

$$\sigma^2 = \frac{\displaystyle\sum_{i=1}^n (X_i - \mu)^2}{n}$$

$$= \frac{(2-4.5)^2 + 2(3-4.5)^2 + 3(4-4.5)^2 + 3(5-5.45)^2}{12}$$
$$\quad \frac{+2(6-4.5)^2 + (7-4.5)^2}{12}$$

$$= \frac{(-2.5)^2 + 2(-1.5)^2 + 3(-0.5)^2 + 3(0.5)^2 + 2(1.5)^2 + (2.5)^2}{12}$$

$$= \frac{2(2.5)^2 + 4(1.5)^2 + 6(0.5)^2}{12}$$

$$= \frac{12.5 + 4(2.25) + 1.5}{12}$$

$$= \frac{12.5 + 10.5}{12} = \frac{23}{12} = 1.9.$$

√• PROBLEM 4-59

If X and Y are independent random variables with variances $\sigma_x^2 = 1$ and $\sigma_y^2 = 2$, find the variance of the random variable $Z = 3X - 2Y + 5$.

SOLUTION:

Using the rules of variance,

$$\text{var}(Z) = \text{var}(3X - 2Y + 5) = \text{var}(3X) + \text{var}(-2Y) + \text{var}(5)$$

(because X and Y are independent)

$$= 3^2 \text{ var}(X) + (-2)^2 \text{ var}(Y) + 0$$

because var $(aX) = a^2$ var (X) and the variance of a constant is zero. Now

$$\text{var}(Z) = 9 \text{ var}(X) + 4 \text{ var}(Y).$$

Since   var $(X) = 1$ and var $(Y) = 2$,

$$\text{var}(Z) = 9 \times 1 + 4 \times 2 = 9 + 8 = 17.$$

√• PROBLEM 4-60

Find the variance of a random variable X that is uniformly distributed over the interval $[0, 3]$.

SOLUTION:

The variance of X is, by definition,

$$E([X - E[X]]^2) = E[X^2] - (E[X])^2.$$

The density function of X is $f(x) = \begin{cases} \dfrac{1}{3} & 0 < x \le 3. \\ 0 \end{cases}$

Thus, $E[X] = \int\limits_0^3 x f(x)\, dx = \int\limits_0^3 \frac{x}{3}\, dx = \frac{x^2}{6}\Big|_0^3 = \frac{9}{6} = \frac{3}{2}$.

$E[X^2] = \int\limits_0^3 x^2 f(x)\, dx = \int\limits_0^3 \frac{x^2}{3}\, dx = \frac{x^2}{3}\Big|_0^3 = \frac{27}{9} = 3.$

Then the variance of X is

$$\text{var }(X) = 3 - \left(\frac{3}{2}\right)^2$$

$$= 3 - \frac{9}{4} = \frac{12-9}{4} = \frac{3}{4}.$$

✓ • **PROBLEM 4–61**

Given that the random variable X has density function

$$f(x) = \frac{1}{2}(x+1) \text{ when } -1 < x < 1$$

and $f(x) = 0$ elsewhere;

calculate the expected value and variance of X.

SOLUTION:

Recall that when X is a discrete random variable, its mean value is

$$\mu = E[X] = \Sigma x\, f(x), \text{ where } f(x) = P(X = x).$$

This sum of products is a weighted average of the values of X.

In this problem X is a continuous random variable. Therefore, we must integrate $x\, f(x)$ from -1 to 1, since $f(x) = 0$ when $x \le -1$ or $x \ge 1$. Then

$$\mu = \int\limits_{-\infty}^{\infty} x f(x)\, dx = \int\limits_{-1}^{1} x \frac{x+1}{2}\, dx$$

(we have substituted $\dfrac{x+1}{2}$ for $f(x)$)

$$= \int_{-\infty}^{\infty} \left(\frac{x^2}{2} + \frac{x}{2} \right) dx = \frac{1}{2} \int_{-1}^{1} x^2 \, dx + \frac{1}{2} \int_{-1}^{1} x \, dx$$

$$= \frac{1}{2} \frac{x^3}{3} \bigg]_{-1}^{1} + \frac{1}{2} \frac{x^2}{2} \bigg]_{-1}^{1}$$

$$= \frac{1}{2}\left(\frac{1}{3} + \frac{1}{3} \right) + \frac{1}{2}\left(\frac{1}{2} - \frac{1}{2} \right) = \frac{1}{2}\left(\frac{2}{3} \right) = \frac{1}{3} \, .$$

The variance of X is defined to be

$$\sigma^2 = E[(X - \mu)^2].$$

Since

$$(X - \mu)^2 = (X - \mu)\,(X - \mu) = X^2 - 2\mu X + \mu^2,$$

we can write

$$\sigma^2 = E[X - \mu)^2] = E[X^2 - 2\,\mu X + \mu^2]$$

$$= \int_{-1}^{1} (X^2 - 2\mu X + \mu^2)\, f(x)\, dx$$

$$= \int_{-1}^{1} X^2 f(x)\, dx - 2\mu \int_{-1}^{1} x f(x)\, dx + \mu^2 \int_{-1}^{1} 1 f(x)\, dx$$

$$= E[X^2] - 2\mu\, E[X] + \mu^2\, E[1]$$

$$= E[X^2] - 2\mu^2 + \mu^2\, E[1] = 1$$

(because $f(x)$ is a density function and must satisfy the condition that $\int_{\infty}^{\infty}$

$f(x)\, dx = 1$). Now,

$$E[X^2] - 2\mu^2 + \mu^2 = E[X^2]\, \mu^2$$

$$= \int_{-\infty}^{\infty} X^2 f(x)\, dx - \left(\frac{1}{3} \right)^2$$

$$= \int_{-1}^{1} X^2 \left(\frac{x^2 - 1}{2} \right) dx - \frac{1}{9}$$

$$= \int_{-1}^{1} \frac{x^3}{2} dx + \int_{-1}^{1} \frac{x^2}{2} dx - \frac{1}{9}$$

$$= \frac{x^4}{8} \Big|_{-1}^{1} + \frac{x^3}{6} \Big|_{-1}^{1} - \frac{1}{9}$$

$$= \left(\frac{1}{8} - \frac{1}{8} \right) + \frac{1}{6} - \left(\frac{-1}{6} \right) - \frac{1}{9}$$

$$= \frac{1}{3} - \frac{1}{9} = \frac{2}{9}.$$

• PROBLEM 4-62

Let X be a random variable with probability density given by

$$f(x) = \lambda e^{-\lambda x} \quad 0 < x < \infty.$$

Find var $[X]$.

SOLUTION:

The variance of X is, by definition,

$$\text{var }(X) = E(X - E[X])^2 = E[X^2] - (E[X])^2.$$

We have found $E[X]$ to be $\frac{1}{\lambda}$ in previous problems, thus

$$\text{var }(X) = E[X^2] - \frac{1}{\lambda^2}.$$

We now find $E[X^2] = \int_0^\infty x^2 f(x)\, dx = \int_0^\infty x^2 \lambda e^{-\lambda x}\, dx;$

let $u = x^2$, $dv = \lambda e^{-\lambda x} dx$, then $du = 2x\, dx$ and $v = -e^{-\lambda x}$.

Thus, $\int_0^\infty x^2 \lambda e^{-\lambda x}\, dx = -x^2 e^{-\lambda x} \Big]_0^\infty - \int_0^\infty -e^{-\lambda x}\, 2x\, dx$

$$= 0 + 2 \int_0^\infty x e^{-\lambda x}\, dx$$

$$= \frac{2}{\lambda} \times \int_0^\infty \lambda x e^{-\lambda x} dx;$$

but $\int_0^\infty \lambda x e^{-\lambda x} dx = E[X] = \frac{1}{\lambda}$. Thus, $E[X^2] = \frac{2}{\lambda^2}$.

Therefore, var $(X) = E[X^2] - (E[X])^2 = \frac{2}{\lambda^2} - \frac{1}{\lambda^2} = \frac{1}{\lambda^2}$.

• PROBLEM 4-63

Let Y be distributed with a Pareto distribution with parameters X_0 and θ. The density function of such a random variable is:

$$f(y) = \begin{cases} \dfrac{\theta X_0^\theta}{y^{\theta+1}} & y > X_0 \text{ with } X_0, \theta > 0 \text{ otherwise.} \end{cases}$$

What is the variance of Y?

SOLUTION:

We first find $E[Y]$, the expected value of Y. By definition,

$$E[Y] = \int_{-\infty}^\infty y f(y) \, dy = \int_{X_0}^\infty \frac{y \theta X_0^\theta}{y^{\theta+1}} \int_{X_0}^\infty \frac{y \theta X_0^\theta}{y^{\theta+1}} \, dy$$

$$= \int_0^\infty \frac{\theta X_0^\theta}{y^\theta} \, dy = \theta X_0^\theta \int_0^\infty \frac{dy}{y^\theta}$$

$$= \theta X_0^\theta \left[\frac{y^{-\theta+1}}{-\theta+1} \right]_{X_0}^\infty = \theta X_0^\theta \int_0^\infty \frac{X_0^{-\theta+1}}{-\theta+1}$$

$$= \frac{\theta X_0}{-\theta+1} \text{ for } \theta > 1.$$

Similarly, $E[Y^2] = \int_{X_0}^\infty y^2 \frac{\theta X_0^\theta}{y^{\theta+1}} \, dy = \int_{X_0}^\infty \frac{\theta X_0^\theta}{y^{\theta-1}} \, dy$

$$= \theta X_0{}^\theta \int_{X_0}^{\infty} y^{-\theta+1}\, dy = \theta\, X_0{}^\theta \left[\frac{y^{-\theta+2}}{-\theta+2} \right]_{X_0}^{\infty}$$

$$= \frac{\theta X_0^\theta X_0{}^{-\theta+2}}{\theta-2}$$

$$= \frac{\theta X_0^2}{-\theta+1} \quad \text{for } \theta > 2.$$

By definition, the variance of Y is

$$\text{var}\,(Y) = E[Y^2] - (E[Y])^2$$

$$= \frac{\theta X_0^2}{\theta-2} - \frac{\theta^2 X_0^2}{(\theta+1)^2}$$

$$= \frac{(\theta-1)^2(\theta X_0^2) - \theta^2 X_0^2(\theta-2)}{(\theta-2)\,(\theta-1)^2}$$

$$= \frac{(\theta^2-2\theta+1)\,(\theta X_0^2) - \theta^3 X_0^2 + \theta^2 X_0^2}{(\theta-2)\,(\theta-1)^2}$$

$$= \frac{\theta^3 X_0^2 - 2\theta^2 X_0^2 + \theta X_0^2 - \theta^3 X_0^2 - 2\theta^2 X_0^2}{(\theta-2)\,(\theta-1)^2}$$

$$= \frac{\theta X_0^2}{(\theta-2)\,(\theta-1)} \quad \text{for } \theta > 2.$$

✱✱✱✱✱✱

REVIEW OF HIGHER MOMENTS

As one might expect, the most common moments, besides the first and second, are the third and fourth. In fact, the frequency with which moments are referred to declines as the order of the moment increases.

There are special names given to the third and fourth moments. Just because there are no common names given to the moments beyond the fourth should not be taken to mean that these moments have no importance. All the moments will be seen to play a prominent role, since the set of moments determines the entire distribution when the moment-generating function, to be discussed in the next section, exists.

The third central moment is known as the skewness, and is here denoted by $M3$. That is,

$$M3 = E[(X - M)^3].$$

The skewness provides little information regarding the shape of the distribution. It is known that a continuous random variable whose probability density function is symmetric or a discrete random variable whose probability mass function is symmetric has a skewness of zero. This would apply to a normal random variable with any parameters (mean and standard deviation), a t-distributed random variable with any number of degrees of freedom, a Bernoulli random variable with parameter 0.5, a binomial random variable with arbitrary first parameter n and $p = 0.5$, and a continuous uniform random variable with arbitrary parameters.

If the left tail of the probability mass function or probability density function is longer than the right tail of the probability mass function or probability density function, then the random variable and its associated distribution are said to be skewed to the left. For such random variables, the skewness is negative. Alternatively, if the right tail of the probability mass function or probability density function is longer than the left tail of the probability mass function or probability density function, then the random variable and its associated distribution are said to be skewed to the right. For such random variables, the skewness is positive. The exponential distribution with any parameter is one example of a random variable with positive skewness.

Of course, it is possible that one tail is longer than the other in different regions of the probability density function or the probability mass function, in which case there is an offsetting, and the skewness could be either positive or negative. If the skewness is zero, this does not imply that the probability density function or the probability mass function is symmetric, even though the converse of this statement is true.

Another measure of skewness is the ratio of the difference between the mean and the median and the standard deviation, or

$$\frac{\text{mean} - \text{median}}{\text{standard deviation}}.$$

Long right tails will enlarge the mean, while long left tails will make the mean smaller. Changes to the tails will not affect the median. Therefore, it should be clear from the formula that random variables with probability mass functions or probability density functions with longer right tails than left tails will have means which exceed the median, and, therefore, this alternative measure of skewness will be positive. Alternatively, random variables with probability mass functions or probability density functions with longer left tails than right tails will have medians which exceed the mean, and, therefore, this alternative measure of skewness will be negative. The standard deviation appears in the denominator to standardize this quantity. The range of this quantity is limited to the range $(-1, 1)$.

The fourth central moment is known as the kurtosis. The kurtosis is a measure of how flat the graph of the probability density function is around its center. The quantity considered is actually a function of the kurtosis, and not the kurtosis itself. This function is defined as

$$(K/V^2) - 3,$$

where K is the kurtosis, V is the variance, and three is used so that the kurtosis of the normal distribution is zero. Positive values of this quantity indicate that the probability density function is more sharply peaked around its center than the normal distribution, while negative values of this quantity indicate that the probability density function is less sharply peaked, or flatter, around its center than the normal distribution.

 **• PROBLEM 4-64**

If X is a Bernoulli random variable with parameter 0.4, then what is its skewness? What is its kurtosis?

SOLUTION:

We compute each using the definitions. Then the skewness is

$$E[(X - M)^3].$$

But for a Bernoulli random variable, $M = p$, which in this case is 0.4. Now X takes on the value zero with probability $1 - 0.4 = 0.6$, and takes on the value one with probability 0.4. Thus,

$$E[(X - M)^3] = E[(X - 0.4)^3]$$
$$= (0 - 0.4)^3 (0.6) + (1 - 0.4)^3 (0.4)$$
$$= (-0.064) (0.6) + (0.6)^3 (0.4)$$
$$= -0.0384 + (0.216) (0.4)$$
$$= 0.0864 - 0.0384$$
$$= 0.048.$$

Since the skewness is positive, the right tail is longer than the left tail.

The kurtosis is

$$(E[(X - p)^4]/V^2) - 3.$$

Now $E[(X - p)^4] = (0 - 0.4)^4 (0.6) + (1 - 0.4)^4 (0.4)$
$$= (0.0256) (0.6) + (0.6)^4 (0.4)$$
$$= 0.0154 + (0.1296) (0.4)$$
$$= 0.0154 + 0.0518$$
$$= 0.0672.$$

We know that

$$V(X) = p(1 - p)$$

for a Bernoulli random variable, so

$$V(X) = (0.4) (1 - 0.4)$$
$$= (0.4) (0.6)$$
$$= 0.24,$$

and $V(X)^2 = 0.24^2$
$$= 0.0576.$$

Then $(E[(X - p)^4]/V^2) - 3 = (0.0672/0.0576) - 3$
$$= 1.1667 - 3$$
$$= -1.8333.$$

• **PROBLEM 4-65**

If X is a continuous uniformly distributed random variable with parameters zero and one, then what are its mean, variance, skewness, and kurtosis?

SOLUTION:

We already know that the mean is the unweighted average of the parameters, or

$$M = \frac{L+U}{2}$$

$$= \frac{0+1}{2}$$

$$= \frac{1}{2}$$

$$= 0.5,$$

where L is the lower limit parameter and U is the upper limit parameter of the continuous uniform random variable. But we can also derive this directly by integrating, from zero to one, the product of the function whose expectation we want (X) and the probability density function ($1/[1 - 0] = 1/1 = 1$). Therefore, we integrate the function X as X ranges from zero to one, and we obtain $X^2/2$ from $X = 0$ to $X = 1$, giving

$$M = \frac{1^2}{2} - \frac{0^2}{2}$$

$$= \frac{1}{2} - \frac{0}{2}$$

$$= 0.5.$$

The variance of X, $V(X)$, can be found similarly by integrating, from zero to one, the product of the function whose expectation we want, $(X - M)^2$, or $(X - 0.5)^2$, and the probability density function, which is one. Therefore, we integrate the function $(X - 0.5)^2$ as X ranges from zero to one, and we obtain $(X - 0.5)^3/3$ from $X = 0$ to $X = 1$, giving

$$V(X) = \left[\frac{(1-0.5)^3}{3}\right] - \left[\frac{(0-0.5)^3}{3}\right]$$

$$= \left[\frac{(0.5)^3}{3}\right] - \left[\frac{(-0.5)^3}{3}\right]$$

$$= \frac{1}{24} - \left(-\frac{1}{24}\right)$$

$$= \frac{1}{24} + \frac{1}{24}$$

$$= \frac{2}{24}$$

$$= \frac{1}{12}.$$

The skewness of X can be found by integrating, from zero to one, the product of the function whose expectation we want, $(X - M)^3$, or $(X - 0.5)^3$, and the probability density function, which is one. Therefore, we integrate the function $(X - 0.5)^3$ as X ranges from zero to one, and we obtain $(X - 0.5)^4/4$ from $X = 0$ to $X = 1$, giving

$$\text{skewness} = \left[\frac{(1-0.5)^4}{4}\right] - \left[\frac{(0-0.5)^4}{4}\right]$$

$$= \left[\frac{(0.5)^4}{4}\right] - \left[\frac{(-0.5)^4}{4}\right]$$

$$= \frac{1}{64} - \left(\frac{1}{64}\right)$$

$$= 0.$$

This result could have been predicted from the fact that a continuous uniform random variable has a probability density function which is symmetric about its mean, and thus its skewness must be zero.

The kurtosis of X can be found by first finding $E[(X - M)^4]$. This intermediate step can be accomplished by integrating, from zero to one, the product of the function whose expectation we want, $(X - M)^4$, or $(X - 0.5)^4$, and the probability density function, which is one. Therefore, we integrate the function $(X - 0.5)^4$ as X ranges from zero to one, and we obtain $(X - 0.5)^5/5$ from $X = 0$ to $X = 1$, giving

$$E[(X - M)^4] = \left[\frac{(1 - 0.5)^5}{5}\right] - \left[\frac{(0 - 0.5)^5}{5}\right]$$

$$= \left[\frac{(0.5)^5}{5}\right] - \left[\frac{(-0.5)^5}{5}\right]$$

$$= \frac{1}{160} - \left(-\frac{1}{160}\right)$$

$$= \frac{1}{160} + \frac{1}{160}$$

$$= \frac{2}{160}$$

$$= \frac{1}{80}.$$

Now the kurtosis is found by computing

$$\text{kurtosis} = \left\{\frac{E[(X - M)^4]}{V(X)}\right\} - 3$$

$$= \left[\frac{\frac{1}{80}}{\frac{1}{12}}\right] - 3$$

$$= \frac{12}{80} - 3$$

$$= \frac{3}{20} - \frac{60}{20}$$

$$= -\frac{57}{20}.$$

The fact that the kurtosis is negative indicates that the graph of the probability density function of a continuous uniform random variable is flatter than that of a normal random variable. Of course we already knew this, because the graph of the probability density function of a continuous uniform random variable is completely flat (this is, in fact, the defining characteristic of a continuous uniform random variable).

✳✳✳✳✳✳

REVIEW OF MOMENT-GENERATING FUNCTIONS

There are many generating functions. For example, in a more advanced text one can find mention of the moment-generating function, the factorial moment-generating function, the cumulant-generating function, and the characteristic function. We will focus our attention on the moment-generating function, which is the most basic of these generating functions.

The moment-generating function of a random variable X is defined to be $E[e^{tX}]$, where e is a numerical constant. In particular,

$$e = 2.718.$$

The moment-generating function is a function of t, as well as of the random variable X. The moment-generating function is said to exist if this expectation exists for all t in an open interval around $t = 0$ (that is, for all t satisfying $|t| < k$, for some positive k). As in the previous subsection, the moment-generating function can be computed by either summing or integrating the product of the probability density function (or the probability mass function, for a discrete random variable) and the function e^{tX}.

The usefulness of the moment-generating function stems from the fact that when it exists, it is also differentiable in a neighborhood of the origin. This means that the derivative may be computed, as may higher derivatives. If we take the rth derivative and then take the limit as t approaches zero, then we obtain $E[X^r]$, or the rth moment.

Conversely, the existence of the moment-generating function guarantees that the set of moments determines the entire distribution. That is, knowledge of the distribution function is adequate to determine the moment-generating function, and the moment-generating function can generate all moments which, by virtue of the existence of the moment-generating function, can determine the distribution. In this sense, the moment-generating function, when it exists, contains the same information as the cumulative distribution function and the probability mass function (for a discrete random variable) or the probability density function (for a continuous random variable).

√ • **PROBLEM 4–66**

What is the moment-generating function of the discrete uniform distribution?

SOLUTION:

We need to find $E[e^{tX}]$ when X assumes n values, say $k(1)$, $k(2)$,..., and $k(n)$, each with probability $1/n$. This expected value may be found as

$$E[e^{tX}] = \Sigma_{j = 1 \text{ to } n} \, e^{tk(n)}/n.$$

This expression cannot be simplified without making further assumptions about the values of $k(1)$, $k(2)$,..., $k(n)$.

• **PROBLEM 4–67**

Use the moment-generating function to find the expected value of a discrete uniform random variable.

SOLUTION:

The expected value can be obtained by differentiating the moment-generating function once, with respect to t, and then taking the limit as t tends to zero. Doing so yields

$$E[X] = d/dt \, E[e^{tX}] \text{ when } t = 0$$

$$= d/dt \, \Sigma_{j = 1 \text{ to } n} \, e^{tk(n)}/n \text{ when } t = 0$$

$$= \Sigma_{j = 1 \text{ to } n} \, d/dt \, e^{tk(n)}/n \text{ when } t = 0$$

$$= \Sigma_{j = 1 \text{ to } n} \, [k(n)] \, [e^{tk(n)}]/n \text{ when } t = 0$$

$$= \Sigma_{j = 1 \text{ to } n} \, [k(n)][e^0]/n$$

$$= \Sigma_{j = 1 \text{ to } n} \, [k(n)] \, [1]/n$$

$$= \Sigma_{j = 1 \text{ to } n} \, k(n)/n,$$

or the unweighted average of the n possible values that X can assume.

• PROBLEM 4–68

What is the moment-generating function of a continuous uniform random variable?

SOLUTION:

We need to find $E[e^{tX}]$ when X is a continuous uniform random variable with lower parameter L and upper parameter U. This expected value may be found as the integral, from L to U, of the product of the probability density function, $1/(U - L)$, and e^{tX}. This integral becomes $[t/(U - L)]e^{tX}$, evaluated between $X = L$ and $X = U$. This becomes

$$[t/(U - L)]\ [e^{tU} - e^{tL}].$$

This expression cannot be simplified.

• PROBLEM 4–69

What is the moment–generating function of a Bernoulli random variable?

SOLUTION:

We need to find $E[e^{tX}]$ when X is a Bernoulli random variable with parameter p. This expected value may be found as the sum, from zero to one, of the product of the probability mass function and e^{tX}. This sum becomes

$$E[e^{tX}] = (e^{t0})\ P\{X = 0\} + (e^{t1})\ P\{X = 1\}$$
$$= (e^{0})\ (1 - p) + (e^{t})\ (p)$$
$$= (1)\ (1 - p) + pe^{t}$$
$$= 1 - p + pe^{t}.$$

This expression cannot be simplified.

• PROBLEM 4–70

Use the moment-generating function to find the expected value of a Bernoulli random variable?

SOLUTION:

The expected value can be obtained by differentiating the moment-generating function once, with respect to t, and then taking the limit as t tends to zero. Doing so yields

$$E[X] = d/dt \; E[e^{tX}] \text{ when } t = 0$$

$$= d/dt \; 1 - p + pe^t \text{ when } t = 0$$

$$= pe^t \text{ when } t = 0$$

$$= pe^0$$

$$= (p)\,(1)$$

$$= p.$$

✳✳✳✳✳✳

REVIEW OF THE CHEBYSHEV INEQUALITY

The Chebyshev inequality is a general inequality which holds true for all non-negative random variables. Its proof is straightforward, but will not be given here. A special case of this inequality places an upper bound on the probability of a random variable assuming a value far from its mean, where distance is defined partially in terms of the variance of the random variable. The most general form of the inequality places an upper bound on the probability of a random variable exceeding a given cutoff in terms of the expected value of the random variable. Of course, these inequalities can be reversed, resulting in lower bounds on the probability of a random variable being close to its mean, or to a random variable taking on a value smaller than some cutoff, respectively. It is required that the random variable take on only non-negative values.

Let X be any random variable, and let g be a non-negative function, so that $g(X)$ is a non-negative random variable. Then

$$P\{g(X) \geq k\} \leq E[g(X)]/k$$

and $\quad P\{g(X) \leq k\} \geq 1 - \{E[g(X)]/k\}$

for all positive k. We include the equality in the inequalities to allow for the possibility that X or $g(X)$ is discrete. If $g(X)$ is continuous, then X is also continuous, and the "$\geq$" can be replaced by "$>$", while the "$\leq$" can be replaced by "$<$."

The most common choice of $g(X)$ is

$$g(X) = (X - M)^2,$$

where $\quad M = E[X]$.

Now $g(X) \geq 0$, since the square of any quantity is necessarily non-negative. Using this value for $g(X)$ results in the following inequalities:

$$P\{(X - M)^2 \geq k\} \leq E[(X - M)^2]/k = V(X)/k,$$

and $\quad P\{(X - M)^2 \leq k\} \geq 1 - \{E[(X - M)^2]/k\} = 1 - \{V(X)/k\},$

where $V(X)$ is the variance of X and k is any non-negative number. These inequalities may be expressed equivalently as

$$P\{|X - M| > k\} \leq V(X)/k^2$$

and $\quad P\{|X - M| < k\} \geq 1 - \{V(X)/k^2\}.$

If we let $g(X) = (X - M)^2/V(X)$, then we obtain

$$P\{(X - M)^2/V(X) \geq k\} \leq E[(X - M)^2/V(X)]/k$$

$$= \{V(X)/V(X)\}/k$$

$$= 1/k.$$

This can be rewritten as

$$P\{(X - M)^2 \geq kV(X)\} \leq 1/k$$

and $\quad P\{(X - M)^2 \leq kV(X)\} \geq 1 - (1/k).$

$P(|x - \mu| \geq k\sigma) \leq \frac{1}{k^2}$

$P(u(x) \geq c) \leq \frac{E(u(x))}{c}$

Let X be a non-negative continuous random variable with an arbitrary continuous distribution. Suppose that

$$E[X] = 4$$

and $V(X) = 9.$

Then what can we say about $P\{X > 13\}$?

SOLUTION:

Since X is continuous,

$$P\{X > 13\} = P\{X \geq 13\}.$$

Since X is non-negative we may use Chebyshev's inequality to say the following:

$$P\{X > 13\} \leq \frac{E[X]}{13} = \frac{4}{13}$$

$$= 0.3077.$$

The variance is irrelevant to this calculation.

Let X be a continuous random variable with an arbitrary continuous distribution. Suppose that

$$E[X] = 0$$

and $V(X) = 1.$

Then what can we say about $P\{|X| > 2\}$?

SOLUTION:

Since X is continuous,

$$P\{|X| > 2\} = P\{|X| \geq 2\}.$$

Since $|X|$ is non-negative, we may use Chebyshev's inequality to say the following:

$$P\{|X| > 2\} \le E[|X|]/2.$$

But we do not know E[|X|]. However, we may proceed by writing

$$P\{|X| > 2\} = P\{X^2 > 4\} \le E[X^2]/4$$

$$= \{V(X) + E[X]^2\}/4$$

$$= \{1 + 0^2\}/4$$

$$= \{1 + 0\}/4$$

$$= 1/4$$

$$= 0.25.$$

√ • PROBLEM 4-73

Suppose that one wishes to toss a fair coin until there is a high probability that the proportion of heads is close to the proportion of tails. In particular, how many tosses of this coin are required to guarantee (via the Chebyshev Inequality) that the probability that the proportion of heads differs from 0.5 by no more than 0.2 is at least 75%?

SOLUTION:

We want to find n such that

$$P\{0.5 - 0.2 < X^* < 0.5 + 0.2\} \ge 0.75.$$

But $P\{0.5 - 0.2 < X^* < 0.5 + 0.2\} = P\{|X^* - 0.5| < 0.2\}$

$$\ge 1 - V(X^*)/k^2,$$

by Chebyshev's Inequality,

where $k = 0.2$.

Therefore, we want to find n such that

$$1 - V(X^*)/k^2 = 1 - V(X^*)/(0.2)^2$$

$$= 1 - V(X^*)/0.04$$

$$= 0.75.$$

Then $\qquad V(X^*) / 0.04 = 1 - 0.75$

$$= 0.25,$$

and $\qquad V(X^*) = (0.04)\,(0.25)$

$$= 0.01.$$

But $\qquad V(X^*) = V(X)/n$

$$= (0.5)\,(1 - 0.5)/n$$

$$= (0.5)\,(0.5)/n$$

$$= 0.25/n$$

$$= 1/(4n).$$

Therefore, $\qquad V(X^*) = 0.01$

$$= 1/(4n),$$

so $\qquad 1/(4n) = 1/100,$

$$4n = 100,$$

and $\qquad n = 25.$

√ • PROBLEM 4-74

Suppose that one wishes to toss a fair coin until there is a high probability that the proportion of heads is close to the proportion of tails. In particular, how many tosses of this coin are required to guarantee (via the Chebyshev Inequality) that the probability that the proportion of heads differs from 0.5 by no more than 0.1 is at least 75%?

SOLUTION:

We want to find n such that

$$P\{0.5 - 0.1 < X^* < 0.5 + 0.1\} \geq 0.75.$$

But $\quad P\{0.5 - 0.1 < X^* < 0.5 + 0.1\} = P\{|X^* - 0.5| < 0.1\}$

$$\geq 1 - V(X^*)/k^2,$$

by Chebyshev's Inequality,

where $k = 0.1$.

Therefore, we want to find n such that

$$1 - V(X^*)/k^2 = -V(X^*) / (0.1)^2$$

$$= 1 - V(X^*) / 0.01$$

$$= 0.75.$$

Then $V(X^*) / 0.01 = 1 - 0.75$

$$= 0.25$$

and $$V(X^*) = (0.01)(0.25)$$

$$= 0.0025.$$

But $$V(X^*) = V(X)/n$$

$$= (0.5)(1 - 0.5)/n$$

$$= (0.5)(0.5)/n$$

$$= 0.25/n$$

$$= 1/(4n).$$

Therefore,

$$V(X^*) = 0.0025$$

$$= 1/(4n),$$

so $1/(4n) = 1/400,$

$$4n = 400,$$

and $n = 100.$

• PROBLEM 4–75

When is the Chebyshev Inequality of no use? That is, when is the bound provided by the Chebyshev Inequality available more directly?

SOLUTION:

Consider the probability

$$P\{(X - M)^2 < k^2\}.$$

By Chebyshev's Inequality, we know that

$$P\{(X - M)^2 < k^2\} \geq 1 - V(X)/k^2.$$

But if $k^2 = V(X)$, then we know that

$$P\{(X - M)^2 < k^2\} \geq 1 - V(X)/k^2$$

$$= 1 - V(X)/V(X)$$

$$= 1 - 1$$

$$= 0.$$

But we already know that

$$P\{(X - M)^2 < k^2\} \geq 0,$$

by virtue of its being a probability.

The situation is even worse if $k^2 < V(X)$ because, in this case,

$$P\{(X - M)^2 < k^2\} \geq 1 - V(X)/k^2$$

$$< 1 - V(X)/V(X)$$

$$= 1 - 1$$

$$= 0.$$

That is, the Chebyshev bound for a probability is actually negative. Of course, we already know that this probability is at least as large as a negative number, because it is a probability; therefore, it must be non-negative.

• PROBLEM 4–76

Can you find a random variable for which the bound given in Problem 4–75 cannot be improved upon?

SOLUTION:

Consider a dichotomous random variable, X, such that

$$P\{X = r\} = 0.5,$$

$$P\{X = -r\} = 0.5,$$

and $P\{X = k\} = 0$ for k other than k or $-k$.

Now $E[X] = (r)\,(0.5) + (-r)\,(0.5)$

$$= 0,$$

and $V(X) = E[X^2] - (E[X])^2$

$$= E[X^2] - (0)^2$$

$$= E[X^2] - 0$$

$$= E[X^2]$$

$$= (r^2)\,(0.5) + (-r)^2(0.5)$$

$$= r^2/2 + r^2/2$$

$$= 2r^2/2$$

$$= r^2.$$

Then by Chebyshev's Inequality,

$$P\{(X - M)^2 < k^2\} \geq 1 - V(X)/k^2,$$

so $P\{(X - 0)^2 < k^2\} \geq 1 - r^2/k^2,$

or $P\{X^2 < k^2\} \geq 1 - r^2/k^2.$

This is only the lower bound on this probability which is offered by the Chebyshev Inequality. It is not necessarily the exact probability. Recall that this lower bound is valid for all random variables, regardless of the distribution. Of course, random variables with different distributions should be expected to have different values of this probability. For the random variable we are presently considering,

$$P\{X^2 < k^2\} = 0 \text{ if } k^2 < r^2$$

and $P\{X^2 < k^2\} = 1$ if $k^2 > r^2,$

since $P\{X^2 = r^2\} = 1.$

But for $k^2 < r^2$, the lower bound on the probability, as given by Chebyshev's Inequality, is

$$P\{X^2 < k^2\} \geq 1 - r^2/k^2,$$

which is less than zero. Thus, zero becomes the lower bound, and for the particular random variable we are considering, zero is also the exact probability.

√ • **PROBLEM 4-77**

Given that the discrete random variable X has density function $f(x)$ given by

$$f(-1) = \frac{1}{8}, f(0) = \frac{6}{8}, f(1) = \frac{1}{8}, \text{ use Chebyshev's inequality,}$$

$$P(|X - \mu| \geq k\sigma) \leq \frac{1}{k^2},$$

to find the upper bound when $k = 2$. What does this tell us about the possibility of improving the inequality to make the upper bound closer to the exact probability?

SOLUTION:

In order to use the inequality, we need to know the mean and variance of X. We compute

$$\mu = E[x] = \sum_x x f(x) = (-1)\left(\frac{1}{8}\right) + \left(0 \times \frac{6}{8}\right) + \left(1 \times \frac{1}{8}\right)$$

$$= \frac{1}{8} - \frac{1}{8} = 0, \text{ and}$$

$$\sigma^2 = E[(X - \mu)^2] = E[(X - 0)^2] = E[X]^2$$

$$= \sum_x x^2 f(x) = (-1)^2 \left(\frac{1}{8}\right) + 0 + (1)^2 \left(\frac{1}{8}\right) = \frac{1}{8} + \frac{1}{8} = \frac{1}{4}.$$

When $k = 2$, $P(|X - \mu| \geq k\sigma)$

$$= P\left(|X| \geq 2\sqrt{\frac{1}{4}}\right) = P(|X| > 1) \leq \frac{1}{2^2} = \frac{1}{4}.$$

The exact probability is $P(|X| \geq 1) = P(X \leq -1 \text{ or } X \geq 1)$, with $P(X < 1) = 0 = P(X > 1)$ because the sum of the probabilities for $x = -1$, $x = 0$, and $x = 1$ is

$$\frac{1}{8} + \frac{6}{8} + \frac{1}{8} = \frac{8}{8} = 1.$$

Therefore, we need to consider only

$$P(X = -1) = \frac{1}{8} \text{ and } P(X = 1) = \frac{1}{8}.$$

Since $x = -1$ and $x = 1$ are mutually exclusive events, we can add their probabilities:

$$\frac{1}{8} + \frac{1}{8} = \frac{2}{8} = \frac{1}{4}.$$

Therefore, the exact probability is $P(|X| \geq 1) = \frac{1}{4}$, which equals the upper bound given by Chebyshev's inequality, so that we cannot improve the inequality for the random variable in this example.

CHAPTER 5

JOINT DISTRIBUTIONS

Basic Attacks and Strategies for Solving Problems in this Chapter. See pages 401 to 463 for step-by-step solutions to problems.

Up to this point, we have confined our discussion to one random variable at a time. Often, however, greater insight may be obtained by studying the relationships between two variables or among several variables. Regression analysis, the analysis of variance (ANOVA), the analysis of covariance (ANCOVA), other univariate linear models, the multivariate analysis of variance (MANOVA), and other multivariate analyses all depend, to some extent, on how different variables covary. This topic will be taken up in this chapter.

To distinguish the case of several random variables from the case of a single random variable, the word "joint" is added to denote the former. For example, a pair of discrete random variables has a joint probability mass function, while a pair of continuous random variables has a joint probability density function. As in the univariate (single random variable) case, the intuition is more natural in the discrete case. In fact, the simplest case is the one in which each variable is dichotomous (Bernoulli, for example).

Suppose, then, that X and Y are Bernoulli random variables. Each may result in a one (success) or a zero (failure). Therefore, there are four possible outcomes:

$$(X, Y) = (0, 0),$$

$$(X, Y) = (0, 1),$$

$$(X, Y) = (1, 0),$$

and $(X, Y) = (1, 1).$

Each of these four outcomes has a probability, and the sum of these four

probabilities must be one. The joint distribution of X and Y is characterized by specifying its range and the probability of each outcome in the
range. We have already considered the range. The probabilities of the four
outcomes are arbitrary, as long as each probability is non-negative and the
sum of the four probabilities is one. For example, we may have

$$P\{0, 0\} = 0.1,$$

$$P\{0, 1\} = 0.2,$$

$$P\{1, 0\} = 0.3,$$

and $P\{1, 1\} = 0.4.$

Clearly, each of these probabilities is non-negative, and the sum of the
four probabilities is $0.1 + 0.2 + 0.3 + 0.4 = 1$. This is a legitimate joint
probability mass function.

One may ask what we know about X and Y when we know their joint
distribution. It turns out that we know the entire distribution of both X and
Y if we know the joint distribution between them. This knowledge permits
calculation of all of the moments of both X and Y, including their means
and variances.

First, we will find the probability mass function of X. We know that,
by virtue of being a Bernoulli random variable, the range of X is $\{0, 1\}$.
This information is also available from the joint probability mass function
of X and Y, since each outcome in the range has X as being either zero or
one. The task remains to find the probabilities $P\{X = 0\}$ and $P\{X = 1\}$.
This can be accomplished by summing the appropriate outcomes of the
range of the joint probability mass function. Recall that

$$P\{0, 0\} = 0.1,$$

$$P\{0, 1\} = 0.2,$$

$$P\{1, 0\} = 0.3,$$

and $P\{1, 1\} = 0.4.$

Now we must find those outcomes for which $X = 0$, and those outcomes
for which $X = 1$. Clearly, the first two, (0, 0) and (0, 1), specify that $X = 0$,
while the last two, (1, 0) and (1, 1), specify that $X = 1$. Then

$$P\{X = 0\} = P\{X = 0, (Y = 0 \text{ or } Y = 1)\}$$

$$= P\{X = 0, Y = 0 \cup X = 0, Y = 1\}$$

$$= P\{X = 0, Y = 0\} + P\{X = 0, Y = 1\},$$

because these two outcomes are mutually exclusive. Now

$$P\{X = 0\} = P\{X = 0, \, Y = 0\} + P\{X = 0, \, Y = 1\}$$
$$= P\{0, 0\} + P\{0, 1\}$$
$$= 0.1 + 0.2$$
$$= 0.3$$

Likewise,

$$P\{X = 1\} = P\{X = 1, \, (Y = 0 \text{ or } Y = 1)\}$$
$$= P\{X = 1, \, Y = 0 \cup X = 1, \, Y = 1\}$$
$$= P\{X = 1, \, Y = 0\} + P\{X = 1, \, Y = 1\},$$

because these two outcomes are mutually exclusive. Now

$$P\{X = 1\} = P\{X = 1, \, Y = 0\} + P\{X = 0, \, Y = 1\}$$
$$= P\{1, 0\} + P\{1, 1\}$$
$$= 0.3 + 0.4$$
$$= 0.7$$

Thus, we have found the marginal probability mass function of X to be

$$P\{X = 0\} = 0.3$$

and $P\{X = 1\} = 0.7$.

We can proceed similarly to find the marginal probability mass function of Y. This results in the following set of calculations:

$$P\{Y = 0\} = P\{(X = 0 \text{ or } X = 1), \, Y = 0\}$$
$$= P\{X = 0, \, Y = 0 \cup X = 1, \, Y = 0\}$$
$$= P\{X = 0, \, Y = 0\} + P\{X = 1, \, Y = 0\},$$

because these two outcomes are mutually exclusive. Now

$$P\{Y = 0\} = P\{X = 0, \, Y = 0\} + P\{X = 1, \, Y = 0\}$$
$$= P\{0, 0\} + P\{1, 0\}$$
$$= 0.1 + 0.3$$
$$= 0.4$$

Likewise,

$$P\{Y = 1\} = P\{(X = 0 \text{ or } X = 1), \, Y = 1\}$$

$$= P\{X = 0, Y = 1 \cup X = 1, Y = 1\}$$

$$= P\{X = 0, Y = 1\} + P\{X = 1, Y = 1\},$$

because these two outcomes are mutually exclusive. Now

$$P\{Y = 1\} = P\{X = 0, Y = 1\} + P\{X = 1, Y = 1\}$$

$$= P\{0, 1\} + P\{1, 1\}$$

$$= 0.2 + 0.4$$

$$= 0.6$$

Thus, we have found the marginal probability mass function of Y to be

$$P\{Y = 0\} = 0.4$$

and $P\{Y = 1\} = 0.6.$

So it is seen that, in general, it is possible to calculate the marginal probability mass functions (that is, the probability mass functions of each individual random variable) by summing, in an appropriate manner, the joint probability mass function. However, it is not true that one can determine the joint probability mass function merely from knowledge of the marginal probability mass functions.

✳✳✳✳✳✳

REVIEW OF DISCRETE RANDOM VARIABLES

As illustrated above, knowledge of the joint probability mass function is adequate to determine the marginal probability mass functions. When dealing with discrete random variables, this can be accomplished by summing the cell probabilities. A cell is a particular combination of values of each discrete random variable involved. This term is not used when any of the random variables are continuous. For example, if X and Y are both Bernoulli random variables, then there are four cells, namely

$$(X, Y) = (0, 0),$$

$$(X, Y) = (0, 1),$$

$$(X, Y) = (1, 0),$$

and $(X, Y) = (1, 1).$

In this section, we will study more general discrete random variables, and we will not limit ourselves to merely two such random variables. Suppose, then, that we are dealing with k discrete random variables, where k can be any arbitrary positive integer (including two). We make no assumptions on these random variables except that they are all discrete. In general, it is still true that the marginal probability mass functions can be found by summing the joint probability mass function.

Let us denote the k discrete random variables by $X1$, $X2$,..., Xk. Suppose that

$$P\{Xi = Aij\} = Pij$$

for $i = 1, 2, ..., k$

and $j = 1, 2, ..., Ni.$

Here, Ni is the number of possible outcomes for Xi. That is, there are Ni different values that the discrete random variable Xi can assume. Now any set of Aij, one for each value of i between 1 and k (that is, one for each random variable), is a cell. The joint probability mass function assigns a non-negative probability to each cell in such a way that the probabilities sum to one when they are summed across all cells.

Suppose that we sum the probabilities not across all cells, but instead only across those cells for which $X1 = A11$, for example. Then we obtain $P\{X1 = A11\}$, or $P11$. The same holds true for $X1 = A12$, or any other value that $X1$ can take on. The same is also true for any of the other $(k - 1)$ random variables. For example, if we want to find the probability that $X4 = A42$, then we sum the probabilities across all cells for which $X4 = A42$. This will yield the desired probability.

For example, suppose that $X1$, $X2$, and $X3$ are all multinomial random variables, and that $N1 = 3$, $N2 = 4$, and $N3 = 5$. Then we would have

$$N1 \times N2 \times N3 = 3 \times 4 \times 5$$

$$= 60 \text{ cells.}$$

Suppose that each of these cells has probability $1/60$, and that the values which these random variables assume are

$$X1 = \{1, 2, 3\},$$

$$X2 = \{1, 2, 3, 4\},$$

and $X3 = \{1, 2, 3, 4, 5\}$.

To find $P\{X3 = 5\}$, for example, we would sum the probabilities for all cells for which $X3 = 5$. We must figure out which cells have $X3 = 5$. In this case, there would be 12 such cells. This is readily seen by observing that each such cell restricts $X3$ to being 5, but $X1$ and $X2$ are free to vary within their respective ranges. Since $X1$ can take on three distinct values and $X2$ can take on four distinct values, the total number of combinations is

$$N1 \times N2 = 3 \times 4$$
$$= 12$$

These 12 cells are

1	$\{1, 1, 5\}$,
2	$\{1, 2, 5\}$,
3	$\{1, 3, 5\}$,
4	$\{1, 4, 5\}$,
5	$\{2, 1, 5\}$,
6	$\{2, 2, 5\}$,
7	$\{2, 3, 5\}$,
8	$\{2, 4, 5\}$,
9	$\{3, 1, 5\}$,
10	$\{3, 2, 5\}$,
11	$\{3, 3, 5\}$,

and   12 $\{3, 4, 5\}$.

Now each of these 12 cells has probability $1/60$. Therefore, when we sum the probabilities across these cells, we obtain

$$P\{X3 = 5\} = (12) \left(\frac{1}{60} \right)$$
$$= \frac{12}{60}$$
$$= \frac{1}{5}$$
$$= 0.2$$

It turns out that

$$P\{X3 = 1\} = 0.2,$$
$$P\{X3 = 2\} = 0.2,$$
$$P\{X3 = 3\} = 0.2,$$
$$P\{X3 = 4\} = 0.2,$$

and $P\{X3 = 5\} = 0.2$.

Therefore, $X3$ is a uniformly distributed discrete multinomial random variable with range $\{1, 2, 3, 4, 5\}$. It can also be verified that $X1$ and $X2$ are uniformly distributed discrete random variables with ranges $\{1, 2, 3\}$ and $\{1, 2, 3, 4\}$, respectively.

One may ask if we can find other joint probabilities from the joint probability mass function. For example, suppose that $X1$, $X2$, and $X3$ are all Bernoulli random variables. Then there are $2 \times 2 \times 2 = 8$ cells, and we would be given the probability of each of these eight cells. But suppose that we wanted to find a probability concerning only two of these three random variables. For example, suppose we wanted to find $P\{X1 = 0, X2 = 1\}$. This can be accomplished in the same way as was used to find probabilities concerning only a single random variable. In particular, if we sum the probabilities across all cells for which $X1 = 0$ and $X2 = 1$, then we will obtain $P\{X1 = 0, X2 = 1\}$. The eight cells are

$$\{X1, X2, X3\} = \{0, 0, 0\},$$
$$\{X1, X2, X3\} = \{0, 0, 1\},$$
$$\{X1, X2, X3\} = \{0, 1, 0\},$$
$$\{X1, X2, X3\} = \{0, 1, 1\},$$
$$\{X1, X2, X3\} = \{1, 0, 0\},$$
$$\{X1, X2, X3\} = \{1, 0, 1\},$$
$$\{X1, X2, X3\} = \{1, 1, 0\},$$

and $\{X1, X2, X3\} = \{1, 1, 1\}$.

Now it is clear that $X1 = 0$ and $X2 = 1$ for the third and fourth cells. That is, $X1 = 0$ and $X2 = 1$ for $(0, 1, 0)$ and for $(0, 1, 1)$. Thus,

$$P\{X1 = 0, X2 = 1\} = P\{(0, 1, 0) \cup (0, 1, 1)\}$$
$$= P\{(0, 1, 0)\} + P\{(0, 1, 1)\}$$

This is the sum of the probabilities for the cells for which $X1 = 0$ and $X2 = 1$, as stated. This method works with any number of discrete random variables, even if they are not Bernoulli random variables.

Step-by-Step Solutions to Problems in this Chapter, "Joint Distribution."

✓ • PROBLEM 5–1

If there are four Bernoulli random variables, then how many cells are there?

SOLUTION:

Each of these Bernoulli random variables has two possible values. Therefore, there are $2 \times 2 \times 2 \times 2 = 2^4 = 16$ possible combinations of these four random variables, or 16 cells.

✓ • PROBLEM 5–2

If there are three discrete random variables, each with three levels, then how many cells are there?

SOLUTION:

Each of these discrete random variables has three possible values. Therefore, there are $3 \times 3 \times 3 = 3^3 = 27$ possible combinations of these three random variables, or 27 cells.

✓ • PROBLEM 5–3

If there is a binomial random variable with parameters 5 and 0.5, and a discrete uniform random variable with support {2, 4, 6, 8}, then how many cells are there?

SOLUTION:

The binomial random variable can take on any of six values (0, 1, 2, 3, 4, or 5), while the discrete uniform random variable can take on any one of four values (2, 4, 6, or 8). Thus, there are $6 \times 4 = 24$ possible combinations of these random variables, or 24 cells.

✓• PROBLEM 5-4

Let X be a Bernoulli random variable and let Y be a discrete uniform random variable with support $\{1, 2, 3, 4\}$. How many cells are there?

SOLUTION:

The Bernoulli random variable can take on either of two values (0, 1), and the discrete uniform random variable can take on any one of four values (1, 2, 3, 4). Therefore, there are $2 \times 4 = 8$ cells.

✓ • PROBLEM 5-5

If the cell probabilities from Problem 5–4 are

$P\{(X, Y) = (0, 1)\} = 0.2,$

$P\{(X, Y) = (0, 2)\} = 0.2,$

$P\{(X, Y) = (0, 3)\} = 0.2,$

$P\{(X, Y) = (0, 4)\} = 0.2,$

$P\{(X, Y) = (1, 1)\} = 0.05,$

$P\{(X, Y) = (1, 2)\} = 0.05,$

$P\{(X, Y) = (1, 3)\} = 0.05,$

and $P\{(X, Y) = (1, 4)\} = 0.05,$

then what is the parameter of the Bernoulli random variable?

SOLUTION:

For a Bernoulli random variable, the parameter p is the expected value, and

$$p = P\{X = 1\}.$$

We can find $P\{X = 1\}$ by summing the probabilities of the cells for which $X = 1$. In this case, there are four such cells, namely $(1, 1)$, $(1, 2)$, $(1, 3)$, and $(1, 4)$. Each of these four cells has probability 0.05. Therefore,

$$p = P\{X = 1\}$$

$$= P\{(1, 1) \cup (1, 2) \cup (1, 3) \cup (1, 4)\}$$

$$= P\{(1, 1)\} + P\{(1, 2)\} + P\{(1, 3)\} + P\{(1, 4)\}$$

$$= 0.05 + 0.05 + 0.05 + 0.05$$

$$= 0.2$$

 • **PROBLEM 5–6**

Let W, X, Y, and Z be discrete random variables. Their joint probability mass function is given by

$$P\{(W, X, Y, Z) = (0, 0, 0, 0)\} = 0.2,$$

$$P\{(W, X, Y, Z) = (0, 0, 1, 0)\} = 0.1,$$

$$P\{(W, X, Y, Z) = (0, 0, 2, 0)\} = 0.1,$$

$$P\{(W, X, Y, Z) = (0, 1, 0, 0)\} = 0.1,$$

$$P\{(W, X, Y, Z) = (0, 1, 1, 0)\} = 0.1,$$

$$P\{(W, X, Y, Z) = (0, 1, 2, 0)\} = 0.1,$$

$$P\{(W, X, Y, Z) = (1, 0, 0, 0)\} = 0.05,$$

$$P\{(W, X, Y, Z) = (1, 0, 1, 0)\} = 0.05,$$

$$P\{(W, X, Y, Z) = (1, 0, 2, 0)\} = 0.05,$$

$$P\{(W, X, Y, Z) = (1, 1, 0, 0)\} = 0.05,$$

$$P\{(W, X, Y, Z) = (1, 1, 1, 0)\} = 0.05,$$

and $P\{(W, X, Y, Z) = (1, 1, 2, 0)\} = 0.05.$

What is the joint probability mass function of W, X, and Y?

SOLUTION:

We seek the joint probability mass function for all random variables except for Z. But Z is a constant random variable. That is, $P\{Z = 0\} = 1$. Therefore, the joint probability mass function for the remaining three variables is

$$P\{(W, X, Y) = (0, 0, 0)\} = 0.2,$$

$$P\{(W, X, Y) = (0, 0, 1)\} = 0.1,$$

$$P\{(W, X, Y) = (0, 0, 2)\} = 0.1,$$

$$P\{(W, X, Y) = (0, 1, 0)\} = 0.1,$$

$$P\{(W, X, Y) = (0, 1, 1)\} = 0.1,$$

$$P\{(W, X, Y) = (0, 1, 2)\} = 0.1,$$

$$P\{(W, X, Y) = (1, 0, 0)\} = 0.05,$$

$$P\{(W, X, Y) = (1, 0, 1)\} = 0.05,$$

$$P\{(W, X, Y) = (1, 0, 2)\} = 0.05,$$

$$P\{(W, X, Y) = (1, 1, 0)\} = 0.05,$$

$$P\{(W, X, Y) = (1, 1, 1)\} = 0.05,$$

and $P\{(W, X, Y) = (1, 1, 2)\} = 0.05.$

• PROBLEM 5-7

For the variables in Problem 5–6, find the joint probability mass function of W and X.

SOLUTION:

The joint probability mass function of W and X is derived by summing the probabilities from the appropriate cells. For example,

$$P\{(W, X) = (0, 0)\} = P\{(0, 0, 0, 0) \cup (0, 0, 1, 0) \cup (0, 0, 2, 0)\}$$

$$= P\{(0, 0, 0, 0)\} + P\{(0, 0, 1, 0)\} + P\{(0, 0, 2, 0)\}$$

$$= 0.2 + 0.1 + 0.1$$

$$= 0.4$$

Likewise,

$$P\{(W, X) = (0, 1)\} = P\{(0, 1, 0, 0) \cup (0, 1, 1, 0) \cup (0, 1, 2, 0)\}$$

$$= P\{(0, 1, 0, 0)\} + P\{(0, 1, 1, 0)\} + P\{(0, 1, 2, 0)\}$$

$$= 0.1 + 0.1 + 0.1$$

$$= 0.3,$$

$$P\{(W, X) = (1, 0)\} = P\{(1, 0, 0, 0) \cup (1, 0, 1, 0) \, u \, (1, 0, 2, 0)\}$$

$$= P\{(1, 0, 0, 0)\} + P\{(1, 0, 1, 0)\} + P\{(1, 0, 2, 0)\}$$

$$= 0.05 + 0.05 + 0.05$$

$$= 0.15,$$

and $\quad P\{(W, X) = (1, 1)\} = P\{(1, 1, 0, 0) \cup (1, 1, 1, 0) \, u \, (1, 1, 2, 0)\}$

$$= P\{(1, 1, 0, 0)\} + P\{(1, 1, 1, 0)\} + P\{(1, 1, 2, 0)\}$$

$$= 0.05 + 0.05 + 0.05$$

$$= 0.15$$

Therefore, the joint probability mass function of W and X is

$$P\{(W, X) = (0, 0)\} = 0.40,$$

$$P\{(W, X) = (0, 1)\} = 0.30,$$

$$P\{(W, X) = (1, 0)\} = 0.15,$$

and $\quad P\{(W, X) = (1, 1)\} = 0.15.$

✓ • **PROBLEM 5–8**

For the variables in Problem 5–6, find the joint probability mass function of W and Y.

SOLUTION:

The joint probability mass function of W and Y is also derived by summing probabilities from appropriate cells. In particular,

$$P\{(W, Y) = (0, 0)\} = P\{(0, 0, 0, 0) \cup (0, 1, 0, 0)\}$$

$$= P\{(0, 0, 0, 0)\} + P\{(0, 1, 0, 0)\}$$

$$= 0.2 + 0.1$$
$$= 0.3,$$
$$P\{(W, Y) = (0, 1)\} = P\{(0, 0, 1, 0) \cup (0, 1, 1, 0)\}$$
$$= P\{(0, 0, 1, 0)\} + P\{(0, 1, 1, 0)\}$$
$$= 0.1 + 0.1$$
$$= 0.2,$$
$$P\{(W, Y) = (0, 2)\} = P\{(0, 0, 2, 0) \cup (0, 1, 2, 0)\}$$
$$= P\{(0, 0, 2, 0)\} + P\{(0, 1, 2, 0)\}$$
$$= 0.1 + 0.1$$
$$= 0.2,$$
$$P\{(W, Y) = (1, 0)\} = P\{(1, 0, 0, 0) \cup (1, 1, 0, 0)\}$$
$$= P\{(1, 0, 0, 0)\} + P\{(1, 1, 0, 0)\}$$
$$= 0.05 + 0.05$$
$$= 0.1,$$
$$P\{(W, Y) = (1, 1)\} = P\{(1, 0, 1, 0) \cup (1, 1, 1, 0)\}$$
$$= P\{(1, 0, 1, 0)\} + P\{(1, 1, 1, 0)\}$$
$$= 0.05 + 0.05$$
$$= 0.1,$$

and
$$P\{(W, Y) = (1, 2)\} = P\{(1, 0, 2, 0) \cup (1, 1, 2, 0)\}$$
$$= P\{(1, 0, 2, 0)\} + P\{(1, 1, 2, 0)\}$$
$$= 0.05 + 0.05$$
$$= 0.1$$

Thus, the joint probability mass function of W and Y is

$$P\{(W, Y) = (0, 0)\} = 0.3,$$
$$P\{(W, Y) = (0, 1)\} = 0.2,$$
$$P\{(W, Y) = (0, 2)\} = 0.2,$$
$$P\{(W, Y) = (1, 0)\} = 0.1,$$
$$P\{(W, Y) = (1, 1)\} = 0.1,$$

and $P\{(W, Y) = (1, 2)\} = 0.1.$

✓ • **PROBLEM 5-9**

For the variables in Problem 5–6, find the joint probability mass function of W and Z.

SOLUTION:

The joint probability mass function of W and Z is derived by summing probabilities from appropriate cells. In particular,

$$P\{(W, Z) = (0, 0)\} = P\{(0, 0, 0, 0) \cup (0, 0, 1, 0) \cup (0, 0, 2, 0)$$

$$\cup (0, 1, 0, 0) \cup (0, 1, 1, 0) \, u \, (0, 1, 2, 0)\}$$

$$= P\{(0, 0, 0, 0)\} + P\{(0, 0, 1, 0)\}$$

$$+ P\{(0, 0, 2, 0)\} + P\{(0, 1, 0, 0)\}$$

$$+ P\{(0, 1, 1, 0)\} + P\{(0, 1, 2, 0)\}$$

$$= 0.2 + 0.1 + 0.1 + 0.1 + 0.1 + 0.1$$

$$= 0.7,$$

and $\quad P\{(W, Z) = (1, 0)\} = P\{(1, 0, 0, 0) \cup (1, 0, 1, 0)$

$$\cup (1, 0, 2, 0) \cup (1, 1, 0, 0) \cup (1, 1, 1, 0)$$

$$\cup (1, 1, 2, 0)\}$$

$$= P\{(1, 0, 0, 0)\} + P\{(1, 0, 1, 0)\}$$

$$+ P\{(1, 0, 2, 0)\} + P\{(1, 1, 0, 0)\}$$

$$+ P\{(1, 1, 1, 0)\} + P\{(1, 1, 2, 0)\}$$

$$= 0.05 + 0.05 + 0.05 + 0.05 + 0.05 + 0.05$$

$$= 0.3$$

Thus, the joint probability mass function of W and Z is

$$P\{(W, Z) = (0, 0)\} = 0.7,$$

and $\quad P\{(W, Z) = (1, 0)\} = 0.3.$

Consider a bag containing two white and four black balls. If two balls are drawn at random without replacement from the bag, let X and Y be random variables representing the results of these two drawings. Let 0 correspond to drawing a black ball and 1 correspondS to drawing a white ball. Find the joint, marginal, and conditional distributions of X and Y.

SOLUTION:

We compute

$$P(X = 0) = P(\text{a black ball is drawn first})$$

$$= \frac{\text{number of black balls}}{\text{total number of balls}} = \frac{4}{6} = \frac{2}{3}, \text{ and}$$

$$P(X = 1) = P(\text{a white ball is drawn first})$$

$$= \frac{\text{number of white balls}}{\text{total number of balls}} = \frac{2}{6} = \frac{1}{3}.$$

We may use the notion of conditional probability to find the probability of a particular event on the second draw given a particular event on the first. We may talk about conditional distribution for the variable Y given X. A conditional distribution is defined in terms of conditional probability.

Now $P(Y = y \mid X = x) = f(y \mid x)$ is the conditional distribution of Y given X, $f(x, y) = P(X = x, Y = y)$ is the joint distribution of X and Y, and $f(x) = P(X = x)$ is the marginal distribution of X.

The conditional probabilities may be calculated directly from the problem. We then use the conditional probabilities and marginal distribution of X to find the joint distribution of X and Y.

Now $P(Y = 0 \mid X = 0) = P$ (black ball is second | black ball first)

$$= \frac{\text{number of black balls} - 1}{\text{total number of balls } - 1} = \frac{4 - 1}{6 - 1} = \frac{3}{5},$$

$$P(Y = 1 \mid X = 0) = P(\text{white second | black first})$$

$$= \frac{\text{number of white balls}}{\text{total number of balls} - 1} = \frac{2}{6 - 1} = \frac{2}{5},$$

$P(Y = 0 \mid X = 1) = P$ (black ball second | white ball first)

$$= \frac{\text{number of black balls}}{\text{total number of balls} - 1} = \frac{4}{6-1} = \frac{4}{5}, \text{ and}$$

$P(Y = 1 \mid X = 1) = P(\text{white ball second white first})$

$$= \frac{\text{number of white balls} - 1}{\text{total number of balls} - 1} = \frac{2-1}{6-1} = \frac{1}{5}.$$

We now calculate the joint probabilities of X and Y as

$$\frac{P(X = 0, Y = 0)}{P(X = 0)} = P(Y = 0 \mid X = 0), \text{ or}$$

$$P(X = 0 \mid Y = 0) = P(X = 0) \, P(Y = 0 \mid X = 0) = \frac{2}{3} \times \frac{3}{5} = \frac{6}{15}.$$

Similarly,

$$P(X = 1 \mid Y = 0) = P(Y = 0 \mid X = 1) \, P(X = 1) = \frac{4}{5} \times \frac{1}{3} = \frac{4}{15},$$

$$P(X = 0 \mid Y = 1) = P(Y = 1 \mid X = 0) \, P(X = 0) = \frac{2}{5} \times \frac{2}{3} = \frac{4}{15}, \text{ and}$$

$$P(X = 1 \mid Y = 1) = P(Y = 1 \mid X = 1) \, P(X = 1) = \frac{1}{5} \times \frac{1}{3} = \frac{1}{15}.$$

Summarizing these results in the following table, we see:

	0	1	$P(Y = y)$
0	$\frac{6}{15}$	$\frac{4}{15}$	$\frac{10}{15}$
1	$\frac{4}{15}$	$\frac{1}{15}$	$\frac{5}{15}$
$P(X = x)$	$\frac{10}{15}$	$\frac{5}{15}$	

This is the joint distribution of X and Y, with the marginal distribution indicated. The conditional distribution of Y given X is

$$P(Y = y \mid X = x) = \frac{P(Y = y, X = x)}{P(X = x)} \begin{cases} \dfrac{6/15}{10/15} = \dfrac{3}{5} & x = y = 0 \\[2mm] \dfrac{4/15}{5/15} = \dfrac{4}{5} & x = 1; y = 0 \\[2mm] \dfrac{4/15}{10/15} = \dfrac{2}{5} & x = 0; y = 1 \\[2mm] \dfrac{1/15}{5/15} = \dfrac{1}{5} & x = y = 1 \end{cases}$$

For any fixed value of X, we see that $f(y \mid x) = P(Y = y \mid X = x)$ is a proper probability distribution for Y since

$$\sum_{y=0}^{1} P(Y = y \mid X = 0) = P(Y = 0 \mid X = 0) + P(Y = 1 \mid X = 0)$$

$$= \frac{3}{5} + \frac{2}{5} = 1$$

and $\quad \displaystyle\sum_{y=0}^{1} P(Y = y \mid X = 1) = P(Y = 0 \mid X = 1) + P(Y = 1 \mid X = 1)$

$$= \frac{1}{5} + \frac{4}{5} = 1.$$

✓ • **PROBLEM 5–11**

Consider the joint distribution of X and Y given in the form of a table below. The cell (i, j) corresponds to the joint probability that $X = i$, $Y = j$, for $i = 1, 2, 3, j = 1, 2, 3$.

	1	2	3
1	0	$\dfrac{1}{6}$	$\dfrac{1}{6}$
2	$\dfrac{1}{6}$	0	$\dfrac{1}{6}$
3	$\dfrac{1}{6}$	$\dfrac{1}{6}$	0

Check that this is a proper probability distribution. What are the marginal distributions of X and Y?

SOLUTION:

A joint probability mass function gives the probabilities of events. These events are composed of the results of two (or more) experiments. An example might be the toss of two dice. In this case, each event of outcome has two numbers associated with it. The numbers are the outcomes from the toss of each die. The probability distribution of the pair (X, Y) is

$$P(X = i, y = j) = \frac{1}{36} \quad i = 1, 2, 3, 4, 5, 6 \quad j = 1, 2, 3, 4, 5, 6.$$

Another example is the toss of two dice where $X =$ number observed on first die; $Y =$ the larger of the two numbers.

In order for $f(x, y) = P(X = x, Y = y)$ to be a proper joint probability, the sum of $P(X = x, Y = y)$ over all points in the sample space must equal 1. Also, each probability must be non-negative.

In the case of the pair of tossed dice,

$$\sum_x \sum_y P(X = x, Y = y) = \sum_{i=1}^{6} \sum_{j=1}^{6} \frac{1}{36} = \frac{6}{36} = \frac{6 \times 6}{36} = 1.$$

Thus, this is a proper probability distribution. In our original example, it is clear that each probability is nonnegative. Also,

$$\sum_{i=1}^{3} \sum_{j=1}^{3} P(X = i, Y = j)$$

$$= \sum_{i=1}^{3} [P(X = i, Y = 1) + P(X = i, Y = 2) + P(X = i, Y = 3)]$$

$$= \sum_{i=1}^{3} P(X = i, Y = 1) + \sum_{i=1}^{3} P(X = i, Y = 2) = \sum_{i=1}^{3} P(X = 1, Y = 3)$$

$$= \left(0 + \frac{1}{6} + \frac{1}{6}\right) + \left(\frac{1}{6} + 0 + \frac{1}{6}\right) + \left(\frac{1}{6} + \frac{1}{6} + 0\right)$$

$$= \frac{1}{3} + \frac{1}{3} + \frac{1}{3} = 1$$

Thus, the probability distribution specified in the table is a proper distribution. We can compute the individual probability distributions of X

and Y. These are called the marginal distributions of X and Y and are calculated in the following way.

We wish to find the probability that $X = 1, 2, 3$. For example,

$$P(X = 1) = P(X = 1, Y = 1, 2, \text{ or } 3).$$

Because the events "$X = 1, Y = 1$," "$X = 1, Y = 2$," "$X = 1, Y = 3$" are mutually exclusive,

$$P(X = 1) = P(X = 1, Y = 1) + P(X = 1, Y = 2) + P(X = 1, Y = 3)$$

$$= \sum_{i=1}^{3} P(X = 1, Y = i)$$

Thus, $P(X = 1) = 0 + \dfrac{1}{6} + \dfrac{1}{6} = \dfrac{1}{3}$.

Similarly,

$$P(X = 2) = \sum_{i=1}^{3} P(X = 2, Y = i) = \frac{1}{6} + 0 + \frac{1}{6} = \frac{1}{3},$$

and $\quad P(X = 3) = \sum_{i=1}^{3} P(X = 3, Y = i) = \dfrac{1}{6} + \dfrac{1}{6} + 0 = \dfrac{1}{3}.$

We similarly compute the marginal probabilities of Y as

$$P(Y = 1) = P(X = 1, Y = 1) + P(X = 2, Y = 1) + P(X = 3, Y = 1)$$

$$= 0 + \frac{1}{6} + \frac{1}{6} = \frac{2}{6} = \frac{1}{3},$$

$$P(Y = 2) = \sum_{j=1}^{3} P(X = j, Y = 2) = \frac{1}{6} + 0 + \frac{1}{6} = \frac{1}{3}, \text{ and}$$

$$P(Y = 3) = \sum_{j=1}^{3} P(X = j, Y = 3) = \frac{1}{6} + \frac{1}{6} + 0 = \frac{1}{3}.$$

To see why these are called marginal probabilities we examine the way they were computed. The marginal probabilities of X were found by summing along the rows of the table of the joint distribution. The marginal probabilities of Y were found by summing along the columns of the table of the joint distribution. The probabilities resulting from these summations are often placed in the margins as in the table below, hence the name marginal probabilities.

• PROBLEM 5-12

Consider the table representing the joint distribution between X' and Y'.

	1	2	3
1	$\dfrac{1}{9}$	$\dfrac{1}{9}$	$\dfrac{1}{9}$
2	$\dfrac{1}{9}$	$\dfrac{1}{9}$	$\dfrac{1}{9}$
3	$\dfrac{1}{9}$	$\dfrac{1}{9}$	$\dfrac{1}{9}$

Find the marginal distributions of X' and Y'. Are X' and Y' independent? In the previous problem, were X and Y independent?

SOLUTION:

The marginal distributions of X' and Y' are found by summing across the rows and columns of the table above. That is,

$$P(X' = 1) = \sum_{i=1}^{3} P(X' = 1, Y' = i) = \frac{1}{9} + \frac{1}{9} + \frac{1}{9} = \frac{1}{3},$$

$$P(X' = 2) = \sum_{i=1}^{3} P(X' = 2, Y' = i) = \frac{1}{9} + \frac{1}{9} + \frac{1}{9} = \frac{1}{3},$$

and $\quad P(X' = 3) = \sum_{i=1}^{3} P(X' = 3, Y' = i) = \frac{1}{9} + \frac{1}{9} + \frac{1}{9} = \frac{1}{3}.$

Similarly,

$$P(X' = 2) = \sum_{j=1}^{3} P(X' = j, Y' = i) = \frac{1}{9} + \frac{1}{9} + \frac{1}{9} = \frac{1}{3},$$

$$P(X' = 2) = \sum_{j=1}^{3} P(X' = j, Y' = 2) = \frac{1}{9} + \frac{1}{9} + \frac{1}{9} = \frac{1}{3},$$

and $\quad P(X' = 3) = \sum_{j=1}^{3} P(X' = j, Y' = 3) = \frac{1}{9} + \frac{1}{9} + \frac{1}{9} = \frac{1}{3}.$

The marginal distributions are hence

$$P(X' = x) = \begin{cases} \dfrac{1}{3} & x = 1, 2, 3 \\ 0 & \text{otherwise} \end{cases}$$

and $\quad P(Y' = y) = \begin{cases} \dfrac{1}{3} & y = 1, 2, 3 \\ 0 & \text{otherwise} \end{cases}$

Two random variables, X and Y, will be independent if and only if

$P(X = x, Y = y) = P(X = x) P(Y = y)$, for all x and y.

Checking X' and Y' we see that for all x and y,

$$P(X' = x, Y' = y) = \frac{1}{9} = P(X' = x) P(Y' = y) = \frac{1}{3} \times \frac{1}{3} = \frac{1}{9}.$$

In the previous problem, consider $P(X = i, Y = i)$ for $i = 1, 2, 3$. Now

$$P(X = i) P(Y = i) = \frac{1}{3} \times \frac{1}{3} = \frac{1}{9}$$

for $i = 1, 2$, and 3, but the joint probability function specivied that

$P(X = i, Y = i) = 0$ for $i = 1, 2$, and 3.

Thus, $\quad P(X = i) P(Y = i) \neq P(X = i, Y = i)$

and X and Y are not independent.

• PROBLEM 5–13

Consider the experiment of tossing two tetrahedra (regular four-sided polyhedron) each with sides labeled 1 to 4.

Let X denote the number on the downturned face of the first tetrahedron and Y the larger of the two downturned numbers. Find the joint density of X and Y.

SOLUTION:

The values that a pair (X, Y) may assume are:

$$(1, 1) \quad (1, 2) \quad (1, 3) \quad (1, 4)$$

$$(2, 2) \quad (2, 3) \quad (2, 4)$$

$$(3, 3) \quad (3, 4)$$

$$(4, 4)$$

The probability that two numbers are observed as the downturned faces of the tetrahedra is

$$P(X_1 = x, X_2 = t) \text{ for } \quad x = 1, 2, 3, 4$$

$$t = 1, 2, 3, 4.$$

Let $X_1 =$ the result of the toss of the first tetrahedron,

$X_2 =$ the result of the toss of the second tetrahedron,

If all outcomes of X_1 and X_2 are equally likely, then

$$P(X_1 = x, X_2 = t) = \frac{1}{16} \text{ for } \quad x = 1, 2, 3, 4$$

$$t = 1, 2, 3, 4.$$

We calculate the probabilities of X and Y in terms of the probabilities for X_1 and X_2 as

$$P(X = 1, Y = 1) = P(X_1 = 1, X_2 = 1) = \frac{1}{16}$$

and $P(X = 1, Y = 2) = P(1 \text{ die is } 1 \text{ and } Y = \max \{X_1, X_2\} = 2)$

$$= P(X_1 = 1, X_2 = 2) = \frac{1}{16}.$$

Similarly,

$$P(X = 1, Y = 3) = P(1 \text{ die is } 1 \text{ and } Y = \max \{X_1, X_2\} = 3)$$

$$= P(X_1 = 1, X_2 = 3) = \frac{1}{16}$$

and $P(X = 1, Y = 4) = P(1 \text{ die is } 1 \text{ and } Y = \max \{X_1, X_2] = 4)$

$$= P(X_1 = 1, X_2 = 4) = \frac{1}{16}.$$

But $P(X = 2, Y = 1) = 0$; it is impossible for 1 toss to be 2 and the larger of the two tosses to be 1.

For the same reasons

$$P(X = 3, Y = 1) = 0 \text{ and } P(X = 4, Y = 1) = 0.$$

Also $P(X = 3, Y = 2) = P(X = 4, Y = 3) = P(X = 4, Y = 2) = 0.$

Continuing,

$$P(X = 2, Y = 2) = P(X_1 = 2, \max\{X_1, X_2\} = 2)$$

$$= P(X_1 = 2, X_2 = 1 \text{ or } 2) = P(X_1 = 2, X_2 = 1)$$

$$+ P(X_1 = 2, X_2 = 2)\frac{1}{16} + \frac{1}{16} = \frac{1}{8},$$

$$P(X = 2, Y = 3) = P(X_1 = 2, \max\{X_1, X_2\} = 3)$$

$$= P(X_1 = 2, X_2 = 3) = \frac{1}{16},$$

$$P(X = 2, Y = 4) = P(X_1 = 2, \max\{X_1, X_2\} = 4)$$

$$= P(X_1 = 2, X_2 = 4) = \frac{1}{16},$$

$$P(X = 3, Y = 3) = P(X_1 = 3, \max\{X_1, X_2\} = 3)$$

$$= P(X_1 = 3, X_2 = 1, 2, \text{ or } 3) = P(X_1 = 3, X_2 = 1)$$

$$+ P(X_1 = 3, X_2 = 2) + P(X_1 = 3, X_2 = 3)$$

$$= \frac{1}{16} + \frac{1}{16} + \frac{1}{16} = \frac{3}{16},$$

$$P(X_1 = 3, Y = 4) = P(X_1 = 3, \max\{X_1, X_2\} = 4)$$

$$= P(X_1 = 3, X_2 = 4) = \frac{1}{16}, \text{ and}$$

$$P(X = 4, Y = 4) = P(X_1 = 4, \max\{X_1, X_2\} = 4)$$

$$= P(X_1 = 4, X_2 = 1, 2, 3, \text{ or } 4) = \frac{4}{16} = \frac{1}{4},$$

$$P(X_1 = 4, X_2 = 1) + P(X_1 = 4, X_2 = 2)$$

$$+ P(X_1 = 4, X_2 = 3 + P(x_1 = 4, X_2 = 4)$$

Thus the distribution for X and Y is:

	1	2	3	4	$P(Y = y)$
1	$\dfrac{1}{16}$	0	0	0	$\dfrac{1}{16}$
2	$\dfrac{1}{16}$	$\dfrac{2}{16}$	0	0	$\dfrac{3}{16}$
3	$\dfrac{1}{16}$	$\dfrac{1}{16}$	$\dfrac{3}{16}$	0	$\dfrac{5}{16}$
4	$\dfrac{1}{16}$	$\dfrac{1}{16}$	$\dfrac{1}{16}$	$\dfrac{4}{16}$	$\dfrac{7}{16}$
$P(X = x)$	$\dfrac{4}{16}$	$\dfrac{4}{16}$	$\dfrac{4}{16}$	$\dfrac{4}{16}$	

The marginal probabilities of X and Y are given and we see that they are dependent random variables because

$$P(X = x,\ Y = y) \neq P(X = x)\,P(Y = y).$$

• PROBLEM 5–14

Show, by altering the joint density of X and Y in the previous problem, that it is not always possible to construct a unique joint distribution from a pair of given marginal distributions.

SOLUTION:

The joint density of X and Y with its marginal distributions is given by the table below:

	1	2	3	4
1	$\dfrac{1}{16}$	0	0	0
2	$\dfrac{1}{16}$	$\dfrac{2}{16}$	0	0
3	$\dfrac{1}{16}$	$\dfrac{1}{16}$	$\dfrac{3}{16}$	0
4	$\dfrac{1}{16}$	$\dfrac{1}{16}$	$\dfrac{1}{16}$	$\dfrac{4}{16}$
$P(X = x)$	$\dfrac{4}{16}$	$\dfrac{4}{16}$	$\dfrac{4}{16}$	$\dfrac{4}{16}$

Imagine that we are given the marginal distributions of X and Y above and asked to construct the joint distribution of X and Y. There are an infinite number of possibilities for this distribution, as seen by the table below. For any ε, $0 < \varepsilon < \dfrac{1}{16}$, this joint distribution will yield the given marginal distributions. Thus, these marginal distributions do not specify a unique joint distribution.

	1	2
1	$\dfrac{1}{16} + \varepsilon$	ε
2	$\dfrac{1}{16} + \varepsilon$	$\dfrac{2}{16} + \varepsilon$

• PROBLEM 5-15

A loom stops from time to time and the number X of stops in unit running time is assumed to have a Poisson distribution with parameter μ. For each stop, there is a probability θ that a fault will be produced in the fabric being woven. Occurrences associated with different stops may be assumed independent. Let Y be the number of fabric faults so produced in unit running time. What is the distribution of Y?

SOLUTION:

For any K, $P(Y = k) = \sum_{x=0}^{\infty} P(Y = k \mid X = x) \, P(X = x)$

$$= \sum_{x=0}^{\infty} P(Y = k \mid X = x) \, \frac{(\mu t)^x e^{-\mu t}}{x!},$$

because X is a distributed Poisson with parameter μ.

Each time there is a stop, $P(\text{fault in the cloth}) = \theta$. In the interval $[0, t]$ if there are x stops, the probability that k of these stops result in faults is

$$\binom{x}{k} \theta^k (1-\theta)^{x-k}.$$

Hence for $k = 0, 1, 2,\dots$

$P(Y = k) =$

$$\sum_{x=k}^{\infty} \binom{x}{k} \theta^k (1-\theta)^{x-k} \frac{(\mu t)^x e^{-\mu t}}{x!} = \sum_{x-k=0}^{\infty} \frac{x! \, \theta^k (1-\theta)^{x-k}}{(x-k)! \, k!} \frac{(\mu t)^x e^{-\mu t}}{x!}$$

$$= \frac{\theta^k e^{-\mu t} (\mu t)^k}{k!} \sum_{x-k=0}^{\infty} \frac{[(1-\theta)\mu t]^{x-k}}{(x-k)!}$$

$$= \frac{(\theta \mu t)^k e^{-\mu t}}{k!} e^{(1-\theta)\mu t} = \frac{(\theta \mu t)^k e^{-\theta \mu t}}{k!}$$

Thus, Y, the number of fabric faults produced in time t is a distributed Poisson with parameter $\theta \mu$.

✳✳✳✳✳✳

REVIEW OF CONTINUOUS RANDOM VARIABLES

Continuous random variables may be treated the same way as discrete random variables, except that when one wishes to find a probability density function of one random variable when what is known is a joint probability density function of this and other random variables, then the summation, which was required for discrete random variables, is replaced by integration. The simplest examples of joint probability density functions for continuous random variables are those derived from continuous uniform random variables.

As an example, let X be a continuous uniform random variable on the interval $[0, 1]$, and let Y be a continuous uniform random variable on the interval $[2, 4]$. Then we may speak of probabilities such as $P\{X < 0.5, Y > 3\}$. We cannot find this probability given only the information we have at hand (the marginal probability density functions). However, the joint probability function would suffice to find this probability, as well as any other dealing with X, Y, or X and Y.

Suppose that (X, Y) has a joint probability density function which specifies that it is uniformly distributed over the two-dimensional region $[0, 1] \times [0, 1]$. A set of continuous random variables has a uniform joint probability density function if this joint probability density function is constant over its entire range. By integration, it is seen that both X and Y are continuous uniformly distributed random variables with range $[0, 1]$. In general, it is not true that if a joint distribution is uniformly distributed, then each individual variable is also uniformly distributed. For example, suppose that (X, Y) has a joint distribution which is uniformly distributed over the region $[0, 1] \times [0, 1] \cup [1, 3] \times [1, 3]$. The area of this region can be found by finding the area of each component region. Now the area of $[0, 1] \times [0, 1]$ is

$$(1 - 0) \times (1 - 0) = 1 \times 1$$

$$= 1,$$

while the area of the other component region is

$$(3 - 1) \times (3 - 1) = 2 \times 2$$

$$= 4.$$

Thus, the entire region has area $4 + 1 = 5$, so the joint probability density function is $1/5$ over this entire region and 0 everywhere else. Clearly, the range of X (and of Y) is $[0, 3]$. If X were a continuous uniform random variable on this range, then for any k such that $0 < k < 3$, it would be true that $P\{X < k\} = k/3$. But in fact, $P\{X < 1\} = \frac{1}{5}$, which is not $\frac{1}{3}$. There-fore, X is not a continuous uniform random variable, even though it is a component of a joint continuous uniform set of random variables.

In contrast, if a set of continuous random variables jointly has a multivariate normal distribution (which has roughly the same properties as a univariate normal distribution, except that matrices replace numbers), then each component random variable must also be normally distributed. However, this does not imply that any set of normally distributed random variables has a multivariate normal distribution. In fact, this is not true, but an example of random variables for which this fails is beyond the scope of this book.

It is not common to speak of joint continuous probability distribu-tions for particular distributions other than the normal or uniform distribu-tions.

When given a joint probability density function, integration of this joint probability density function with respect to certain variables will leave the joint probability density function of the remaining variables. If there is only one remaining variable (if the integration is with respect to all but one variable), then what remains is the marginal probability density function of this random variable.

A joint cumulative distribution function for random variables $X1$, $X2$, ..., Xn is a generalization of the cumulative distribution function for a single random variable. In particular, it is defined as

$$F_{X1, X2, \ldots, Xn}(k1, k2, \ldots, kn) = P\{X1 \le k1, X2 \le k2, \ldots, Xn \le kn\}.$$

This joint cumulative distribution function is non-decreasing in each argu-ment (that is, when holding constant all others). As all values tend to negative infinity, this function tends to zero. As all values tend to positive infinity, this function tends to one. Its range is between zero and one.

✓ • PROBLEM 5–16

Let (X, Y) be uniformly distributed over the region $[1, 4] \times [2, 3]$. What is the joint probability density function?

SOLUTION:

The joint probability density function is uniform, hence, constant over this range. This joint probability density function must integrate to one when integrated over its entire range and, therefore, the value of the joint probability density function is the multiplicative inverse of the area of the region. The area of this region is

$$A = (4 - 1) \times (3 - 2)$$

$$= 3 \times 1$$

$$= 3$$

Therefore, the joint probability density function is

$$f(X, Y) = \frac{1}{3} \text{ on } [1, 4] \times [2, 3]$$

and $f(X, Y) = 0$ otherwise.

√ • **PROBLEM 5–17**

Let (X, Y) have a joint probability density function of $f(X, Y) = 4xye^{-x-y}$ for positive x and y. What is the marginal probability density function of X?

SOLUTION:

The marginal probability density function of X is found by integrating the joint probability density function with respect to y. Doing so leaves $f(X) = 2xe^{-x}$ for positive X. Thus, the marginal probability density function of X is

$$f(X) = 2xe^{-x} \text{ for } x > 0$$

and $f(X) = 0$ otherwise.

√ • **PROBLEM 5–18**

Let $F(X)$ be a cumulative distribution function. Is $F(X, Y) = F(X) + F(Y)$ a joint cumulative distribution function?

SOLUTION:

As X tends to positive infinity, $F(X)$ tends to one. As Y tends to positive infinity, $F(Y)$ also tends to one. Thus, as both random variables tend to positive infinity, $F(X, Y)$ tends to $1 + 1 = 2$. This is not one, so $F(X, Y)$ cannot be a proper joint cumulative distribution function.

• PROBLEM 5–19

Use $f(x, y) = \begin{cases} e^{-x}e^{-y} & x > 0, \ y > 0 \\ 0 & \text{otherwise} \end{cases}$

to find the probability that $\{1 < X < 2 \text{ and } 0 < Y < 2\}$.

SOLUTION:

We solve this problem by recognizing that $P(1 < X < 2 \text{ and } 0 < Y < 2)$ is the volume over the shaded rectangle:

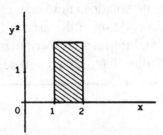

This volume over the rectangle and under $f(x, y)$ is pictured below:

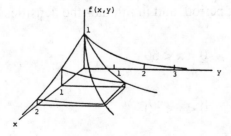

To find this volume we integrate X from 1 to 2 and Y from 0 to 2. Thus,

$$P(1 < X < 2 \text{ and } 0 < Y < 2)$$

$$= \int_0^2 \int_1^2 f(x, y)\, dx\, dy$$

$$= \int_0^2 e^{-y} \left(\int_1^2 e^{-x}\, dx \right) dy$$

$$= \int_0^2 e^{-y}\, dy \left[e^{-x} \big|_1^2 \right] = \int_0^2 e^{-y}\, dy (e^{-1} - e^{-2})$$

$$= e^{-y} \big|_0^2 (e^{-1} - e^{-2})$$

$$= (e^0 - e^{-2})(e^{-1} - e^{-2}) = (1 - e^{-2})(e^{-1} - e^{-2})$$

$$= (0.865)(0.233) = 0.20$$

• PROBLEM 5–20

Two individuals agree to meet at a certain spot sometime between 5:00 and 6:00 P.M. They will each wait 10 minutes starting from when they arrive. If the other person does not show up during that 10-minute interval, they will leave. Assume the arrival times of the two individuals are independent and uniformly distributed over the hour-long interval. Find the probability that the two will actually meet.

SOLUTION:

Let X be the arrival time of the first individual and Y be the arrival time of the second individual. Then X and Y have uniform distributions over any hour-long period, and in minutes the densities are:

$$f(x) = \frac{1}{60} \qquad 0 < x < 60$$

$$g(y) = \frac{1}{60} \qquad 0 < y < 60$$

Furthermore, X and Y are independent. Thus, the joint density of X and Y will be the product of the individual density functions.

$$h(x, y) = f(x)\, g(y) = \begin{cases} \dfrac{1}{60} \times \dfrac{1}{60} & 0 < x < 60 \text{ and } 0 < y < 60 \\ 0 & \text{otherwise} \end{cases}$$

We now try to formulate the event "a meeting takes place" in terms of X and Y.

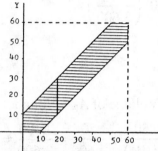

Consider the shaded region above. If the point (x, y) lies within this shaded region, a meeting will take place. To see that this is true, we arbitrarily test the point $X = 20$. If $X = 20$, the first individual arrives at 5:20. If the second individual arrived at any time between 5:10 and 5:30, there will be a meeting. Thus, Y may take on a value between 10 and 30. This region is described mathematically by $|X - Y| < 10$. The absolute value signs reflect the fact that the order of arrival is unimportant in assuring a meeting — only the proximity or closeness of the arrival times is important. Thus, $P(\text{a meeting}) = P(|X - Y| < 10)$ equals the volume over the shaded region in the $x - y$ plane under $f(x, y)$.

This volume can be divided into three regions, A_1, A_2, A_3.

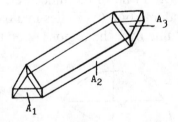

The volume of A_2 is the volume of a rectangular parallelapiped (box-shaped region), and A_1 and A_3 are right prisms of equal volume.

The volume of A_2 is length $\times$ width $\times$ height

$$= \left(10\sqrt{2}\right)\left(50\sqrt{2}\right)\left(\frac{1}{3,600}\right)$$

$$= 2\,(500)\left(\frac{1}{3,600}\right).$$

And the volume of A_3 and A_1 each is (Area of base) $\times$ height

$$= \frac{1}{2}\,(10)\,(10)\left(\frac{1}{3,600}\right)$$

$$= \frac{50}{3,600}.$$

Thus, $P(|X - Y| < 10) = $ Volume of A_2 + Volume of A_1 + Volume of A_3

$$= \frac{1,000}{3,600} + \frac{50}{3,600} + \frac{50}{3,600} = \frac{1,100}{3,600} = \frac{11}{36}.$$

• PROBLEM 5-21

Suppose (X, Y) has a distribution which is uniform over a unit circle centered at $(0, 0)$. Find the joint density of (X, Y) and the marginal densities of X and Y. Are X and Y independent?

SOLUTION:

The pairs of points (X, Y) lie in the unit circle with center at $(0, 0)$. The probability that a random point (X, Y) lies in a particular region of this circle is given by the volume over the region, A, and under a joint density function $f(x, y)$.

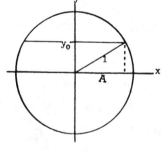

In the case of the uniform joint density function, the density function is a constant such that the total volume over some area in the (x, y) plane and under $f(x, y) = c > 0$ is 1.

The total area of the unit circle is πr^2 where $r = 1$. Thus, the area is π. In order for the total volume to equal 1,

$$c\pi = 1 \text{ or } c = \frac{1}{\pi}.$$

Thus, $f(x, y) = \begin{cases} \dfrac{1}{\pi} & \text{for } x^2 + y^2 < 1 \\ 0 & \text{otherwise} \end{cases}$.

The marginal distributions are found by "summing" over all values of the other variable after one variable is fixed. Because the variables are continuous, the "summing" must be performed by integration. Thus, the marginal distributions of X and Y are respectively:

$$g(x) = \int_{\text{all } y} f(x, y)\, dy \qquad\qquad x^2 + y^2 < 1$$

and

$$h(y) = \int_{\text{all } x} f(x, y)\, dx \qquad\qquad x^2 + y^2 < 1$$

In our problem let x be fixed, $x = x_0$, then $y^2 < 1 - x_0^2$ or

$$|y| < \sqrt{1 - x_0^2} \text{ or } y < \sqrt{1 - x_0^2} \text{ and } -y > \sqrt{1 - x_0^2}. \text{ Thus,}$$

$$g(x_0) = \int_{-\sqrt{1-x_0^2}}^{\sqrt{1-x_0^2}} f(x, y)\, dy = \int_{-\sqrt{1-x_0^2}}^{\sqrt{1-x_0^2}} \frac{1}{\pi}\, dy$$

$$= \frac{2\sqrt{1 - x_0^2}}{\pi}, \qquad\qquad 1 < x_0 < -1.$$

Similarly, for fixed $y = y_0$, $-\sqrt{1 - y_0^2} < x < \sqrt{1 - y_0^2}$

$$h(y_0) = \int_{-\sqrt{1-y_0^2}}^{\sqrt{1-y_0^2}} f(x, y)\, dx = \int_{-\sqrt{1-y_0^2}}^{\sqrt{1-y_0^2}} \frac{1}{\pi}\, dx = \frac{x}{\pi}\Bigg]_{-\sqrt{1-y_0^2}}^{\sqrt{1-y_0^2}}$$

$$= \frac{2\sqrt{1 - y_0^2}}{\pi}, \qquad\qquad -1 < y < 1.$$

Now X and Y will be independent if and only if the joint density is the product of the marginal densities or $f(x, y) = g(x) h(y)$ for each (x, y) pair. In this problem we see that

$$g(x_0) h(y_0) = \frac{2\sqrt{1 - x_0^2}}{\pi} \times \frac{2\sqrt{1 - y_0^2}}{\pi}$$

$$= \frac{4}{\pi^2} \sqrt{1 - x_0^2} \, 2\sqrt{1 - y_0^2}$$

which is not equal to $\dfrac{1}{\pi} = f(x, y)$ uniformly in (x, y). Thus, X and Y are dependent (that is, not independent).

$\checkmark$ • **PROBLEM 5–22**

Given that the joint density function of X and Y is

$$f(x, y) = 6x^2y \text{ where } \begin{cases} 0 < x < 1 \text{ and} \\ 0 < y < 1, \end{cases}$$

$$= 0 \text{ elsewhere,}$$

find $P\left(0 < x < \dfrac{3}{4}, \dfrac{1}{3} < y < 2\right)$.

SOLUTION:

The joint density function of two random variables represents a surface over the region on which it is defined. The volume under the surface is always 1. We need to find the volume over the region bounded by the given limits. We construct a double integral:

$$\int_{y=\frac{1}{3}}^{y=2} \int_{x=0}^{x=\frac{3}{4}} f(x, y) \, dx \, dy = \int_{y=\frac{1}{3}}^{y=1} \int_{x=0}^{x=\frac{3}{4}} 6x^2y \, dx \, dy \int_{y=1}^{y=2} \int_{x=0}^{x=\frac{3}{4}} 0 \, dx \, dy; \, ;$$

because $f(x, y) = 0$ where $y \geq 1$. This becomes

$$\int_{y=\frac{1}{3}}^{y=2} \int_{x=0}^{x=\frac{3}{4}} f(x, y)\, dx\, dy = 6 \int_{y=\frac{1}{3}}^{y=1} \frac{x^3}{3} y \bigg]_0^{\frac{3}{4}} dy = 6 \int_{y=\frac{1}{3}}^{y=1} \frac{9}{64} y\, dy$$

$$= \frac{54}{64} \frac{y^2}{2} \bigg]_{\frac{1}{3}}^1 = \frac{27}{32}\left(\frac{1}{2} - \frac{1}{18}\right)$$

$$= \frac{27}{32}\left(\frac{8}{18}\right) = \frac{27}{32}\left(\frac{4}{9}\right)$$

$$= \frac{3}{8} = P(0 < x < \frac{3}{4}, \frac{1}{3} < y < 2)$$

✓• PROBLEM 5-23

Find the marginal density of X and the conditional density of Y given X, given that

$$f(x, y) = \begin{cases} 2 & x + y < 1, \ x \geq 0, \ y > 0 \\ 0 & \text{otherwise} \end{cases}$$

SOLUTION:

The marginal density of X is the area under the cross-section at $X = x$ as a function of x:

$$f(x) = \int_{-\infty}^{\infty} f(x, y)\, dy = \int_0^{1-x} 2\, dy = 2\,(1 - x)$$

for $0 \leq x \leq 1$.

The conditional distribution of Y given $X = x$ is

$$f(y \mid x) = \frac{f(x, y)}{f(x)} = \frac{2}{2(1 - x)} \quad \text{for } x + y < 1, \quad 1 > x \geq 0, \qquad y > 0$$

or for fixed x, $0 < x < 1$,

$$f(y \mid x) = \begin{cases} \dfrac{1}{1-x} & 0 < y < 1 - x \\ 0 & \text{otherwise} \end{cases}.$$

Note that for some fixed x such that $0 < x < 1$, $f(y \mid x)$ is a constant density for $0 < y < 1 - x$.

✓ • PROBLEM 5-24

Let

$$f(x, y) = = \begin{cases} 2 - x - y & 0 < x < 1, \quad 0 < y < 1 \\ 0 & \text{otherwise} \end{cases}$$

Find the conditional distribution of Y given X.

SOLUTION:

The conditional distribution of Y given $X = x$ is defined to be

$$f(y \mid X = x) = \frac{f(x, y)}{f(x)},$$

where $g(x)$ is the marginal distribution of X and $f(x, y)$ is the joint distribution of X and Y.

The marginal distribution of X is

$$g(x) = \int_{-\infty}^{\infty} f(x, y)\, dy = \int_{0}^{1} (2 - x - y)\, dy$$

$$= (2 - x)y - \frac{y^2}{2} \Big]_{0}^{1} = 2 - x - \frac{1}{2} = \frac{3}{2} - x \text{ for } 0 < x < 1.$$

Thus the conditional density is

$$f(y \mid x) = \frac{2 - y - x}{\dfrac{3}{2} - x}, \quad 0 < y < 1 \text{ and } x \text{ fixed.}$$

✓• PROBLEM 5-25

Conditional probabilities can often be used to calculate unconditional probabilities. Show that the marginal distribution of X can be calculated from the conditional distribution of X given Y and the marginal distribution of Y.

SOLUTION:

Let $h(y)$ be the marginal density of Y and let $f(X \mid Y)$ be the conditional density of X given Y. Also let $f(x, y)$ be the joint density of X and Y. Now

$$f(x \mid y) = \frac{f(x, y)}{h(y)}$$

by definition, or

$$f(x, y) = f(x \mid y) \, h(y).$$

But the marginal density of X is $g(x) = \int_{-\infty}^{\infty} f(x, y) \, dy$.

Substituting for $f(x, y)$, we see that $g(x) = \int_{-\infty}^{\infty} f(x \mid y) \, h(y) \, dy$.

• PROBLEM 5-26

Let a random variable Y represent the diameter of a shaft and a random variable X represent the inside diameter of the housing that is intended to support the shaft. By design the shaft is to have diameter 99.5 units and the housing inside diameter 100 units. If the manufacturing process of each of the items is imperfect, so that in fact Y is uniformly distributed over the interval (98.5, 100.5) and X is uniformly distributed over (99, 101), what is the probability that a particular shaft can be successfully paired with a particular housing, when "successfully paired" is taken to mean that $X - h < Y < X$ for some small positive quantity h? Assume that X and Y are independent.

SOLUTION:

We wish to find $P(X - h < Y < X)$ where X is distributed with density $f(x) = \frac{1}{2}$, $99 < x < 101$, and Y is distributed with density $f(y) = \frac{1}{2}$, $98.5 < y < 100.5$.

To find the probability that $X - h < Y < X$, we condition on the value of X. Thus,

$$P(X - h < Y < X) = \int_{-\infty}^{\infty} P(X - h < Y < X \mid X = x) f(x)\, dx$$

$$= \int_{99}^{101} P(X - h < Y < X)\, \frac{1}{2}\, dx.$$

Let $h = \frac{1}{2}$, then since $\frac{1}{2}$ is 25% of the interval $(99, 101)$,

$$P\left(X - \frac{1}{2} < Y < X\right) = \text{for } 99 < x < 100.5.$$

Also for $x > 100.5$, then values close to X are not in the range of Y. We can only consider the interval from $X - \frac{1}{2}$ to 100.5. Hence,

$$P(X - ZZ < Y < X) = [100.5 - (x - .5)]\frac{1}{2} \quad < X < 101.$$

Thus, $\int_{99}^{101} P(X - h < Y < X)\, \frac{1}{2}\, dx = \int_{99}^{100.5} \frac{1}{2} \times \frac{1}{4} + \int_{100.5}^{101} \frac{100.5 - (x - 5)}{2}\, dx$

$$= \frac{1}{8} x \Big]_{99}^{100.5} + \int_{100.5}^{101} \frac{101 - x}{2}\, dx$$

$$= \frac{1}{8} \times (100.5 - 99) + \frac{101x}{2} - \frac{x^2}{4} \Big]_{100.5}^{101}$$

$$= \frac{1.5}{8} + \left(\frac{10{,}201}{2} - \frac{10{,}201}{4}\right) - \left(\frac{10{,}150.5}{2} - \frac{10{,}100.25}{4}\right)$$

$$= 0.1875 + \frac{10,201}{4} - \frac{10,200.75}{4}$$

$$= 0.1875 + 0.625 = 0.25$$

• PROBLEM 5-27

Show by the convolution technique that $Z = X + Y$, where X and Y are two independent standard normal random variables, is normally distributed with mean zero and variance two.

SOLUTION:

If X and Y are two independent standard normal random variables, then each has respective density

$$f(x) = \frac{1}{\sqrt{2\pi}} e^{\frac{-x^2}{2}} \qquad -\infty < x < \infty$$

and

$$g(y) = \frac{1}{\sqrt{2\pi}} e^{\frac{-y^2}{2}} \qquad -\infty < y < \infty.$$

The joint density of X and Y is $f(x)\, g(y)$. Thus, the density function of $Z = X + Y$ is

$$h(z) = \int_{-\infty}^{\infty} f(x)\, g(z-x)\, dx$$

$$= \int_{-\infty}^{\infty} \frac{1}{\sqrt{2\pi}} e^{\frac{-x^2}{2}} \frac{1}{\sqrt{2\pi}} e^{\frac{-(z-x)^2}{2}}\, dx$$

$$= \int_{-\infty}^{\infty} \frac{1}{\sqrt{2\pi}} e^{\frac{-(z-x)^2}{2} - \frac{x^2}{2}}\, dx$$

$$= \int_{-\infty}^{\infty} \frac{1}{2\pi} e^{\frac{-(z^2 - 2zx + x^2)}{2} - \frac{x^2}{2}/2}\, dx$$

But the exponent is $\dfrac{-z^2 + 2zx - x^2 - x^2}{2}$

$$= -\frac{z^2}{2} - (x^2 - zx)$$

$$= -\frac{z^2}{2} - \left(x^2 - zx + \frac{z^2}{4} \right) + \frac{z^2}{4}$$

$$= -\frac{z^2}{4} - \left(x - \frac{z}{2} \right)^2$$

Thus,

$$h(z) = \frac{1}{\sqrt{2\pi}} e^{-\frac{z^2}{4}} \int_{-\infty}^{\infty} \frac{1}{\sqrt{2\pi}} e^{\left(\frac{x-z}{2}\right)^2} \, dx$$

$$= \frac{1}{\sqrt{2\pi}} e^{-\frac{z^2}{4}} \times \frac{\sqrt{\frac{1}{2}}}{\sqrt{\frac{1}{2}}} \int_{-\infty}^{\infty} \frac{1}{\sqrt{2\pi}} e^{-\left(\frac{x-z}{2}\right)^2} \, dx$$

$$= \frac{1}{\sqrt{2}\sqrt{2\pi}} e^{-\frac{z^2}{4}} \int_{-\infty}^{\infty} \frac{1}{\sqrt{\frac{1}{2}}\sqrt{2\pi}} e^{-\left(\frac{x-z}{2}\right)^2} \, dx$$

● PROBLEM 5–28

If X_1 and X_2 are two independent standard normal random variables and $Y_1 = X_1 + X_2$, $Y_2 = \dfrac{X_1}{X_2}$, find the density function of Y_2.

SOLUTION:

We will first find the joint density of Y_1, Y_2 and then integrate with respect to Y_1 to find the marginal density of Y_2. Even though we are only interested in the distribution of Y_2, we must define the other transformation, Y_1, in order to utilize this approach. This is because we require a one-to-one transformation, which requires an equal number of output variables (i.e., Y_1 and Y_2) as input variables (i.e., X_1 and X_2). Also, a determinant is only defined for a square matrix.

The density functions of x_1 and x_2 are:

$$f_1(x_1) = \frac{1}{\sqrt{2\pi}} e^{\frac{-x_1^2}{2}} \qquad -\infty < x_1 < \infty$$

and $\quad f_2(x_2) = \frac{1}{\sqrt{2\pi}} e^{\frac{-x_2^2}{2}} \qquad -\infty < x_2 < \infty.$

By the independence of X_1 and X_2, the joint density of X_1 and X_2 is the product of the individual densities or

$$f(x_1, x_2) = f_1(x_1) f_2(x_2) = \frac{1}{2\pi} e^{\frac{-\left(x_1^2 + x_2^2\right)}{2}} \qquad -\infty < x_1, x_2 < \infty.$$

The transformation mapping (X_1, X_2) to (Y_1, Y_2) is one-to-one, hence invertible. We may solve for (X_1, X_2) in terms of (Y_1, Y_2). Writing $X_1 = X_2 Y_2$ and

$$Y_1 = X_1 + X_2, \text{ thus } Y_1 = X_2 Y_2 + X_2 \text{ or } X_2 = \frac{Y_1}{Y_2 + 1}.$$

Similarly, $X_2 = \dfrac{X_1}{Y_2}$ and thus $Y_1 = X_1 + \dfrac{X_1}{Y_2}$ or

$$X_1 = \frac{Y_1}{1 + 1/Y_2} = \frac{Y_1 Y_2}{1 + Y_2}.$$

Let $w_1(y_1, y_2) = \dfrac{y_1 y_2}{1 + y_2} = x_1$ and $w_2(y_1, y_2) = \dfrac{y_1}{1 + y_2} = x_2.$

The Jacobian matrix of this transformation is

$$J = \begin{vmatrix} \dfrac{\partial w_1}{\partial y_1} & \dfrac{\partial w_1}{\partial y_2} \\ \dfrac{\partial w_2}{\partial y_1} & \dfrac{\partial w_2}{\partial y_2} \end{vmatrix}.$$

In this case,

$$\frac{\partial w_1}{\partial y_1} = \frac{y_2}{1+y_2},$$

$$\frac{\partial w_1}{\partial y_2} = \frac{y_1}{(1+y_2)^2},$$

$$\frac{\partial w_2}{\partial y_1} = \frac{1}{1+y_2},$$

$$\frac{\partial w_2}{\partial y_2} = \frac{-y_1}{(1+y_2)^2},$$

and

$$|\det J| = \left| \left(\frac{y_2}{1+y_2}\right)\left(\frac{-y_1}{(1+y_2)^2}\right) - \left(\frac{y_1}{(1+y_2)^2}\right)\left(\frac{1}{1+y_2}\right) \right|$$

$$= \left| \frac{-y_1 y_2 - y_1}{(1+y_2)^3} \right| = \left| \frac{-y_1(1+y_2)}{(1+y_2)^3} \right| = \frac{|y_1|}{(1+y_2)^2}.$$

The joint density of Y_1 and Y_2 is

$$g(y_1, y_2) = f[w_1(y_1, y_2), w_2(y_1, y_2)] \, |J|$$

$$= f_1[w_1(y_1, y_2) f_2(w_2(y_1, y_2)] \, |J|$$

$$= \frac{1}{\sqrt{2\pi}} e^{-\frac{1}{2}\left(\frac{y_1 y_2}{1+y_2}\right)} \times \frac{1}{\sqrt{2\pi}} e^{-\frac{1}{2}\left(\frac{y_1}{1+y_2}\right)^2} \times \frac{|y_1|}{(1+y_2)^2}$$

$$= \frac{1}{2\pi} \times \frac{|y_1|}{(1+y_2)^2} \times e^{-\frac{1}{2}\left[\frac{(y_1 y_2)^2 + y_1^2}{(1+y_2)^2}\right]}$$

$$= \frac{|y_1|}{2\pi(1+y_2)^2} \times e^{-\frac{1}{2}\left[\frac{(1+y_2^2)y_1^2}{(1+y_2)^2}\right]}$$

for $-\infty < y_1, y_2 < \infty$.

We wish to find the marginal distribution of Y_2; we have

$$g_2(y_2) = \int_{-\infty}^{\infty} g(y_1, y_2) \, dy_1$$

$$= \int_{-\infty}^{\infty} \frac{|y_1|}{2\pi(1+y_2)^2} \exp\left\{-\frac{1}{2}\left[\frac{(1+y_2^2)y_1^2}{(1+y_2)^2}\right]\right\} dy_1.$$

Let $\quad u = \frac{1}{2}\left[\frac{(1+y_2^2)y_1^2}{(1+y_2)^2}\right]$

then $\quad du = \frac{(1+y_2^2)}{(1+y_2)^2} y_1 \, dy_1$

and $\quad \int_0^{\infty} \frac{y_1}{2\pi(1+y_2)^2} \exp\left\{-\frac{1}{2}\frac{(1+y_2^2)y_1^2}{(1+y_2)^2}\right\} dy_1$

$$= \int_0^{\infty} \frac{y_1}{2\pi(1+y_2)^2} \exp\left\{-\frac{1}{2}\left[\frac{(1+y_2^2)y_1^2}{(1+y_2)^2}\right]\right\} dy_1$$

$$= \frac{1}{2\pi(1+y_2^2)} \int_0^{\infty} \frac{(1+y_2^2)y_1}{(1+y_2)^2} \exp\{-u\} \, dy_1$$

$$= \frac{1}{2\pi(1+y_2^2)} \int_0^{\infty} e^{-u} \, du .$$

If $y_1 < 0$, $|y_1| = -y$; let $u = -\frac{1}{2}\frac{(1+y_2^2)y_1^2}{(1+y_2)^2}$.

Then $\quad du = \frac{-y_1(1+y_2^2)}{(1+y_2)^2} dy_1$

and $\quad = \int_{-\infty}^{0} \frac{-y_1}{2\pi(1+y_2)^2} \exp\left\{-\frac{1}{2}\frac{(1+y_2^2)y_1^2}{(1+y_2)^2}\right\} dy_1$

$$= \frac{1}{2\pi(1+y_2^2)} \int_{-\infty}^{0} e^u \, du .$$

Thus, $g_2(y_2) = \frac{1}{2\pi(1+y_2^2)}\left[\int_{-\infty}^{0} e^{-u} \, du + \int_{-\infty}^{0} e^u \, du\right]$

$$= \frac{1}{2\pi(1+y_2^2)}\left[-e^{-u}\Big|_0^{\infty} + e^u\Big|_{-\infty}^{0}\right]$$

$$= \frac{1}{2\pi(1+y_2{}^2)}[1+1]$$

$$= \frac{1}{\pi(1+y_2{}^2)} \qquad -\infty < y_2 < \infty.$$

• PROBLEM 5-29

Consider a probability distribution for random orientations in which the probability of an observation in a region on the surface of the unit hemisphere is proportional to the area of that region. Two angles, u and v, will determine the position of an observation. It can be shown that the position of an observation is jointly distributed with density function

$$f(u, v) = \frac{\sin u}{2\pi} \qquad 0 < v < 2\pi, \qquad 0 < u < \frac{\pi}{2}.$$

Two new variables, X and Y, are defined, where

$$X = \sin u \cos v$$

$$Y = \sin u \sin v.$$

Find the joint density function of X and Y.

SOLUTION:

In the region $0 < u < \dfrac{\pi}{2}$ and $0 < v < 2\pi$, this transformation is one-to-one and the mapping is pictured below.

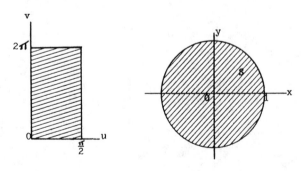

We now find u and v in terms of x and y. Let

$$x^2 = \sin^2 u \cos^2 v$$

$$y^2 = \sin^2 u \sin^2 v;$$

adding we see that

$$x^2 + y^2 = \sin^2 u \, (\cos^2 v + \sin^2 v)$$

$$= \sin^2 u.$$

Thus, $\sin u = \sqrt{x^2 + y^2}$ and $u = \sin^{-1} \sqrt{x^2 + y^2}$

Also, $\dfrac{y}{x} = \dfrac{\sin u \sin v}{\sin u \cos v} = \dfrac{\sin v}{\cos v} = \tan v.$

Hence, $v = \tan^{-1} \dfrac{y}{x}.$

The Jacobian of the original transformation is

$$\frac{\partial (u, v)}{\partial (x, y)} = \frac{1}{\dfrac{\partial (x, y)}{\partial (u, v)}}.$$

Thus, we find

$$\frac{\partial (x, y)}{\partial (u, v)} = \begin{bmatrix} \dfrac{\partial x}{\partial u} & \dfrac{\partial x}{\partial v} \\ \dfrac{\partial y}{\partial u} & \dfrac{\partial y}{\partial v} \end{bmatrix}$$

$$= \left| \det \begin{pmatrix} \cos u \cos v & -\sin u \sin v \\ \sin v \cos u & \cos v \sin u \end{pmatrix} \right|$$

$$= |\cos^2 v (\cos u) (\sin u) + \sin^2 v (\cos u) (\sin u) |$$

$$= |(\cos u) (\sin u) |$$

Thus, $\dfrac{\partial (u, v)}{\partial (x, y)} = [(\cos u) (\sin u)]^{-1}.$

The joint density of X and Y is

$$g(x, y) = f\left(\sin^{-1}\left(\sqrt{x^2 + y^2}\right), \tan^{-1}\frac{y}{x}\right) \times \frac{\partial (u, v)}{\partial (x, y)}$$

$$= \frac{\sin\left(\sin^{-1}\sqrt{x^2 + y^2}\right)}{2\pi} \times \frac{1}{\cos u \sin u}$$

$$= \frac{\sqrt{x^2 + y^2}}{2\pi} \times \frac{1}{\cos u \sin u}$$

But $\quad \sin^2 u = X^2 + Y^2$;

thus $\quad 1 - \cos^2 u = X^2 + Y^2$

or $\quad \cos u = \sqrt{1 - (X^2 + Y^2)}$

and $\quad \sin u = \sqrt{X^2 + Y^2}$.

$$******$$

MIXED RANDOM VARIABLES

The term "mixed random variables" means different things to different statisticians. To some, this term indicates a random variable with both continuous and discrete components. To others, it indicates joint probability density functions in which some of the component random variables are continuous and others are discrete. We will be using the latter definition when considering joint distributions, but the former definition when considering a single random variable.

The most common example of a joint distribution in which some random variables are continuous and others are discrete is the analysis of variance (ANOVA). The simplest ANOVA model is the one-way ANOVA. This model specifies that for each level of the discrete random variable, the continuous random variable has a normal distribution. The variance of this normal distribution does not depend on the level of the discrete random variable, but the mean of the normal distribution does.

Consider taking a sample of college students from a given university and recording the gender and height of each student. The gender could be coded as

male $= 0$

and female $= 1$,

while the height could be measured in inches. It is not unreasonable to model the heights of the males as following a normal distribution and, likewise, it is not unreasonable to model the heights of the females as following a normal distribution. However, it would be unreasonable to model all heights as following a normal distribution. This is because studies of height have shown it to follow a bimodal distribution (its probability density function has two peaks). As one might expect, this is due to different mean heights among males and females. If a distribution is bimodal, then it cannot be unimodal and, therefore, cannot be normally distributed. Thus, it is imperative to allow for different mean heights across genders. The ANOVA is one way to accomplish this.

As a more concrete example, suppose that in a population there are as many males as females and that the heights of males are normally distributed with mean 70 inches and standard deviation two inches, while the heights of females are normally distributed with mean 64 inches and standard deviation two inches. This completely specifies a joint distribution between a Bernoulli (discrete) random variable (gender) and a normal (continuous) random variable (height). One could ask questions such as:

1. What is the probability that a randomly selected female has a height of at least 58 inches?

2. What is the probability that a randomly selected male has a height of no more than 75 inches?

3. What is the probability that a randomly selected person has a height of between 59 inches and 65 inches?

4. What is the probability that a person is a male given that this person has a height of at least 60 inches?

5. What is the 90th percentile of heights among males (that is, for what value k is it true that $P\{X > k\} = 0.10$, where X is the height of a randomly selected male)?

6. What is the probability that a person is a female given that this person has a height of at least 70 inches?

Of these six questions, only the third can be answered by using only a marginal distribution. Of course, this marginal distribution is the distribution of heights for all people, and not just for males or just for females. Therefore, some work would be required to find this marginal distribution from the joint distribution.

We solve the first problem as follows. Let X be a random variable denoting the height of a randomly selected female. Then

$$P\{X \geq 58\} = P\{X > 58\}$$

$$= P\{(X - 64)/2 > (58 - 64)/2\}$$

$$= P\{Z > -6/2\}$$

$$= P\{Z > -3\}$$

$$= 0.9987,$$

as found from the normal table.

We solve the second problem as follows. Let X be a random variable denoting the height of a randomly selected male. Then

$$P\{X \leq 75\} = P\{X < 75\}$$

$$= P\{(X - 70)/2 < (75 - 70)/2\}$$

$$= P\{Z < 5/2\}$$

$$= P\{Z < 2.5\}$$

$$= 0.9938,$$

as found from the normal table.

We solve the third problem as follows. Let X be a random variable denoting the height of a randomly selected person, which could be either a male or a female. Because we have assumed that there are as many males as females in this population, the randomly selected person has an equal chance of being a male as being a female. Then

$$P\{59 \leq X \leq 65\} = P\{59 < X < 65\}$$

$$= P\{59 < X < 65 \cap \text{the entire sample space}\},$$

since the set $\{59 < X < 65\}$ is a subset of the entire sample space and, in general, an intersection of two sets, one of which is a subset of the other, is the smaller set, or the set which is the subset of the other. Now

$$P\{59 < X < 65 \cap \text{the entire sample space}\}$$

$$= P\{59 < X < 65 \cap (\text{male} \cup \text{female})\},$$

since $\{(\text{male} \cup \text{female})\} = $ the entire sample space. That is, (male, female) is a partition of the entire sample space, because each person must be one or the other, and no person can be both. Therefore, we continue

$$P\{59 < X < 65 \cap (\text{male} \cup \text{female})\}$$

$$= P\{(59 < X < 65 \cap \text{male}) \cup (59 < X < 65 \cap \text{female})\}$$

$$= P\{59 < X < 65 \cap \text{male}\} + P\{59 < X < 65 \cap \text{female}\}$$

$$= P\{\text{male}\} \, P\{59 < X < 65 \text{ for a male}\}$$

$$+ \, P\{\text{female}\} \, P\{59 < X < 65 \text{ for a female}\}$$

$$= (0.5) \, P\{(59 - 70)/2 < (X - 70)/2 < (65 - 70)/2 \text{ for a male}\}$$

$$+ \, (0.5) \, P\{(59 - 64)/2 < (X - 64)/2 < (65 - 64)/2 \text{ for a female}\}$$

$$= (0.5) \, P\{-11/2 < Z < -5/2\} + (0.5) \, P\{-5/2 < Z < 1/2\}$$

$$= (0.5) \, P\{-5.5 < Z < -2.5\} + (0.5) \, P\{-2.5 < Z < 0.5\}$$

$$= (0.5) \, (0.0062 - 0.0000) + (0.5) \, (0.6915 - 0.0062)$$

$$= (0.5) \, (0.6915)$$

$$= 0.3458$$

We solve the fourth problem as follows. Let X be a random variable denoting the height of a randomly selected male. Then

$$P\{X \geq 60\} = P\{X > 60\}$$

$$= P\{(X - 70)/2 > (60 - 70)/2\}$$

$$= P\{Z > -10/2\}$$

$$= P\{Z > -5\}$$

$$= 1,$$

as found from the normal table.

We solve the fifth problem as follows. Let X be a random variable denoting the height of a randomly selected male. Then

$$P\{0.10\} = \{X \geq k\}$$

$$= P\{X > k\}$$

$$= P\{(X - 70)/2 > (k - 70)/2\}$$

$$= P\{Z > (k-70)/2\}$$

But the normal table reveals that

$$P\{Z > 1.28\} = 0.10.$$

Therefore, we may equate $(k-70)/2$ and 1.28. We obtain

$$(k-70)/2 = 1.28$$

$$k - 70 = (2)(1.28)$$

$$k - 70 = 2.56$$

$$k = 70 + 2.56$$

$$k = 72.56$$

Thus, 72.56 is the 90th percentile of heights for males.

We cannot solve the sixth problem until we study conditional probability, particularly Bayes theorem.

• PROBLEM 5–30

Suppose that defensive football players are classified as defensive linemen, linebackers, and defensive secondary players. Suppose further that the distribution of the amount of weight that each type can bench press is as follows:

the amount that linemen can bench is normally distributed with mean 500 pounds and standard deviation 50 pounds,

the amount that linebackers can bench is normally distributed with mean 400 pounds and standard deviation 50 pounds, and

the amount that secondary players can bench is normally distributed with mean 300 pounds and standard deviation 50 pounds.

A large group of players try out for a team. The ratios of these players are such that there are as many secondary players as there are linemen, but there are only three-quarters of this number of linebackers. What is the probability that a randomly selected player is a linebacker?

SOLUTION:

Suppose that there are X players, of which Y are linemen. Then there are also Y defensive secondary players, as we are given that there are an equal number of linemen and defensive secondary players. We also know that there are $3Y/4$ linebackers, because there are three-quarters of this number of linebackers. The probability of selecting a linebacker is the number of linebackers divided by the number of players, or $(3Y/4)/X$. But we also know that there are $Y + Y + (3/4)Y$ players, so

$$X = Y + Y + (3/4)Y$$

$$= 2.75Y$$

Now the probability of selecting a linebacker is

$$(3/4)Y/2.75Y = 0.75Y/2.75Y$$

$$= 0.75/2.75$$

$$= 1.5/5.5$$

$$= 3/11$$

√ • PROBLEM 5–31

Referring to Problem 5–30, given that a linebacker is selected, what is the probability that he can bench press at least 350 pounds?

SOLUTION:

Let X be a random variable with the distribution of the amount of weight a randomly selected linebacker can bench press. Then X is distributed normally with mean 400 pounds and standard deviation 50 pounds. Therefore,

$$P\{X \geq 350\} = P\{X > 350\}$$

$$= P\{(X - 400)/50 > (350 - 400)/50\}$$

$$= P\{Z > -50/50\}$$

$$= P\{Z > -1\}$$

$$= 0.8413,$$

from the normal table.

$\sqrt{\bullet}$ **PROBLEM 5-32**

Referring to Problem 5–30, given that a lineman is selected, what is the probability that he can bench press at least 350 pounds?

SOLUTION:

Let X be a random variable with the distribution of the amount of weight a randomly selected lineman can bench press. Then X is distributed normally with mean 500 pounds and standard deviation 50 pounds. Therefore,

$$P\{X \geq 350\} = P\{X > 350\}$$

$$= P\{(X - 500)/50 > (350 - 500)/50\}$$

$$= P\{Z > -150/50\}$$

$$= P\{Z > -3\}$$

$$= 0.9987,$$

from the normal table.

$\sqrt{\bullet}$ **PROBLEM 5-33**

Referring again to Problem 5–30, given that the selected player plays defensive secondary, what is the probability that he can bench press at least 350 pounds?

SOLUTION:

Let X be a random variable with the distribution of the amount of weight a randomly selected defensive secondary player can bench press. Then X is distributed normally with mean 300 pounds and standard deviation 50 pounds. Therefore,

$$P\{X \geq 350\} = P\{X > 350\}$$

$$= P\{(X - 300)/50 > (350 - 300)/50\}$$

$$= P\{Z > 50/50\}$$

$$= P\{Z > 1\}$$

$$= 0.1587,$$

from the normal table.

• PROBLEM 5–34

Referring again to Problem 5–30, what is the probability that he can bench press at least 350 pounds and that he is a lineman?

SOLUTION:

This problem is different from the previous ones in that it is not given that the player chosen is a lineman, but rather the question involves the probability of a lineman being chosen. Then

$P\{X \geq 350 \cap \text{lineman}\}$

$= P\{X > 350 \cap \text{lineman}\}$

$= P\{\text{lineman}\}\, P\{X > 350 \text{ for a lineman}\}$

$= (4/11)\,(0.9987)$

$= 0.3632,$

from the normal table.

• PROBLEM 5–35

Referring again to Problem 5–30, what is the probability that he can bench press at least 350 pounds and that he is a linebacker?

SOLUTION:

Like the previous problem,

$P\{X \geq 350 \cap \text{linebacker}\}$

$= P\{X > 350 \cap \text{linebacker}\}$

$= P\{\text{linebacker}\}\, P\{X > 350 \text{ for a linebacker}\}$

$$= (3/11) (0.8413)$$

$$= 0.2294,$$

from the normal table.

 **• PROBLEM 5–36**

Referring to Problem 5–30, what is the probability that he can bench press at least 350 pounds and that he is a defensive secondary player?

SOLUTION:

Like the previous problem,

$$P\{X \geq 350 \cap \text{secondary}\}$$

$$= P\{X > 350 \cap \text{secondary}\}$$

$$= P\{\text{secondary}\}\, P\{X > 350 \text{ for a secondary}\}$$

$$= (4/11) (0.1587)$$

$$= 0.0577,$$

from the normal table.

 **• PROBLEM 5–37**

Referring to Problem 5–30, what is the probability that he can bench press at least 350 pounds?

SOLUTION:

This problem is yet again of a different type. We proceed as follows:

$$P\{X \geq 350\}$$

$$= P\{X > 350\}$$

$$= P\{X > 350 \cap \text{the entire sample space}\}$$

$$= P\{X > 350 \cap (\text{secondary} \cup \text{linebacker} \cup \text{lineman})\}$$

$$= P\{(X > 350 \cap \text{secondary}) \cup (X > 350 \cap \text{linebacker})$$

$$\cup (X > 350 \cap \text{lineman})\}$$

$$= P\{\text{secondary}\}\{X > 350 \text{ for a secondary player}\}$$

$$+ P\{\text{linebacker}\}\{X > 350 \text{ for a linebacker}\}$$

$$+ P\{\text{lineman}\}\{X > 350 \text{ for a lineman}\}$$

$$= (4/11)(0.1587) + (3/11)(0.8413) + (4/11)(0.9987)$$

$$= 0.0577 + 0.2294 + 0.3632$$

$$= 0.6503$$

✱✱✱✱✱✱

REVIEW OF JOINT CUMULATIVE DISTRIBUTION FUNCTIONS

The joint cumulative distribution function of a set of random variables is a multivariate function. That is, this is a function of more than one variable (or this function is said to take more than one argument). In particular, for a set of random variables, say $X1$, $X2$, ..., Xn, the joint cumulative distribution function is defined as

$$F_{X1, X2, \ldots, Xn}(k1, k2, \ldots, kn) = P\{X1 \leq k1, X2 \leq k2, \ldots, Xn \leq kn\}.$$

If this joint cumulative distribution is continuous over its entire range, then each random variable considered is continuous. This joint cumulative distribution function cannot be computed based only on the marginal probability density functions of the individual random variables. The joint probability density function is required. In fact, knowledge of the joint probability density function is enough to compute the joint cumulative distribution function (by summing and/or integrating), and also knowledge of the joint cumulative distribution function is enough to compute the joint probability density function (by differencing and/or differentiating). Let us consider an example.

Suppose that a joint cumulative distribution function is given by

$$F_{X, Y}(k1, k2) = (k1)(k2) \text{ for } 0 < k1 < 1 \text{ and } 0 < k2 < 1.$$

Then it is seen that both X and Y are continuous random variables (because the joint cumulative distribution function is continuous over its entire range). Therefore, the joint probability mass function can be found by differentiating the joint cumulative distribution function. That is,

$$f_{X, Y}(k1, k2) = d^2/(dk1 \; dk2) \, F_{X, Y}(k1, k2).$$

The order in which we perform this differentiation is immaterial to the final result. Now

$$f_{X, Y}(k1, k2)$$

$$= d^2/(dk1 \; dk2) \, F_{X, Y}(k1, k2)$$

$$= d^2/(dk1 \; dk2) \, (k1)(k2) \text{ for } 0 < k1 < 1 \text{ and } 0 < k2 < 1$$

$$= d/dk1 \; k1 \text{ for } 0 < k1 < 1 \text{ and } 0 < k2 < 1$$

$$= 1 \text{ for } 0 < k1 < 1 \text{ and } 0 < k2 < 1$$

Since this joint probability density function is constant over its range, we are considering a continuous uniform distribution. We must check first that this is actually a joint probability density function. Since it is non-negative, the only task that remains is to check that it integrates to one. The integral of the function which is uniformly one is equal to the area over which this function is to be integrated. In this case, this is the area of the rectangle formed by the boundaries of the region

$$0 < k1 < 1$$

and $\quad 0 < k2 < 1.$

These boundaries are $k1 = 0$, $k1 = 1$, $k2 = 0$, and $k2 = 1$. The area of this region is

$$\text{Area} = (1 - 0) \times (1 - 0)$$

$$= 1 \times 1$$

$$= 1$$

Thus, this is a proper joint probability density function, and we found it by differentiating the joint cumulative distribution function.

Suppose that, instead, we had been given that the joint probability density function was given by

$f_{X,Y}(k1, k2) = 1$ for $0 < k1 < 1$ and $0 < k2 < 1$,

and we were asked to find the joint cumulative distribution function. We would then need to integrate, which would reveal that

$F_{X,Y}(k1, k2) =$ the integral over $0 < k1 < 1$ and $0 < k2 < 1$

of the joint probability density function

$\quad = $ the integral over $0 < k1 < 1$ and $0 < k2 < 1$ of 1

$\quad = (k1)(k2)$ for $0 < k1 < 1$ and $0 < k2 < 1$

$\quad = $ the joint cumulative distribution function

This simple example shows that differentiating, with respect to each variable, the joint cumulative distribution function of several continuous random variables yields the joint probability density function. Likewise, integrating the joint probability density function of several continuous random variables yields the joint cumulative distribution function. One may wonder if this is also true for discrete random variables.

Consider a joint probability mass function given by

$f_{X,Y}(k1, k2) = 0.28$ for $(X, Y) = (0, 0)$,

$f_{X,Y}(k1, k2) = 0.12$ for $(X, Y) = (0, 1)$,

$f_{X,Y}(k1, k2) = 0.42$ for $(X, Y) = (1, 0)$,

and $\quad f_{X,Y}(k1, k2) = 0.18$ for $(X, Y) = (1, 1)$.

Then the joint cumulative distribution function can be found as

$F_{X,Y}(k1, k2) = P\{X1 \leq k1 \cap X2 \leq k2\}$,

which, as expected, depends on the values of $k1$ and $k2$. There are actually nine cases to consider, as follows:

$F_{X,Y}(k1, k2) = P\{X1 \leq k1 \cap X2 \leq k2\}$

$\quad = 0.00$ if $k1 < 0$ and $k2 < 0$,

$F_{X,Y}(k1, k2) = P\{X1 \leq k1 \cap X2 \leq k2\}$

$\quad = 0.00$ if $0 \leq k1 < 1$ and $k2 < 0$,

$F_{X,Y}(k1, k2) = P\{X1 \leq k1 \cap X2 \leq k2\}$

$\quad = 0.00$ if $1 \leq k1$ and $k2 < 0$,

$F_{X,Y}(k1, k2) = P\{X1 \leq k1 \cap X2 \leq k2\}$

$$= 0.00 \text{ if } k1 < 0 \text{ and } 0 \le k2 < 1,$$

$$F_{X, Y}(k1, k2) = P\{X1 \le k1 \cap X2 \le k2\}$$

$$= 0.00 \text{ if } k1 < 0 \text{ and } 1 \le k2,$$

$$F_{X, Y}(k1, k2) = P\{X1 \le k1 \cap X2 \le k2\}$$

$$= 0.28 \text{ if } 0 \le k1 < 1 \text{ and } 0 \le k2 < 1,$$

$$F_{X, Y}(k1, k2) = P\{X1 \le k1 \cap X2 \le k2\}$$

$$= 0.70 \text{ if } 1 \le k1 \text{ and } 0 \le k2 < 1,$$

$$F_{X, Y}(k1, k2) = P\{X1 \le k1 \cap X2 \le k2\}$$

$$= 0.40 \text{ if } 0 \le k1 < 1 \text{ and } 1 \le k2,$$

and $\quad F_{X, Y}(k1, k2) = P\{X1 \le k1 \cap X2 \le k2\}$

$$= 1.00 \text{ if } 1 \le k1 \text{ and } 1 \le k2.$$

Each of these values of $F_{X, Y}(k1, k2)$ can be found by considering those points for which $X1 \le k1$ and $X2 \le k2$, and by summing the probabilities of these points. For example, if $0 \le k1 < 1$ and $1 \le k2$, then the only points that would satisfy $X1 \le k1$ and $X2 \le k2$ would be $(X1, X2) = (0, 0)$ and $(X1, X2) = (0, 1)$. The probabilities of these points are 0.28 and 0.12, respectively. Adding these two probabilities results in $P\{X1 \le k1 \cap X2 \le k2\}$, or $F_{X, Y}(k1, k2)$, which is seen to be $0.28 + 0.12 = 0.40$.

When given the joint cumulative distribution function, it is possible to find the marginal cumulative distribution functions by evaluating the joint cumulative distribution function at infinity for all variables other than the one for which the marginal cumulative distribution function is desired. For example, suppose that the joint cumulative distribution function of three variables is given by

$$F_{X, Y, Z}(k1, k2, k3)$$

$$= (k1)(k2)(k3) \text{ for } 0 < k1 < 1, 0 < k2 < 1, \text{ and } 0 < k3 < 1,$$

$$F_{X, Y, Z}(k1, k2, k3)$$

$$= 0 \text{ for } k1 \le 0,$$

$$F_{X, Y, Z}(k1, k2, k3)$$

$$= 0 \text{ for } k2 \le 0,$$

$$F_{X, Y, Z}(k1, k2, k3)$$

$$= 0 \text{ for } k3 \le 0,$$

$F_{X, Y, Z}(k1, k2, k3)$

$= (k1)(k2)$ for $k3 \geq 1, 0 < k1 < 1,$ and $0 < k2 < 1,$

$F_{X, Y, Z}(k1, k2, k3)$

$= (k1)(k3)$ for $k2 \geq 1, 0 < k1 < 1,$ and $0 < k3 < 1,$

$F_{X, Y, Z}(k1, k2, k3)$

$= (k2)(k3)$ for $k1 \geq 1, 0 < k2 < 1,$ and $0 < k3 < 1,$

$F_{X, Y, Z}(k1, k2, k3)$

$= k1$ for $0 < k1 < 1, k2 \geq 1,$ and $k3 \geq 1,$

$F_{X, Y, Z}(k1, k2, k3)$

$= k2$ for $0 < k2 < 1, k1 \geq 1,$ and $k3 \geq 1,$

$F_{X, Y, Z}(k1, k2, k3)$

$= k3$ for $0 < k3 < 1, k1 \geq 1,$ and $k2 \geq 1,$

and $\quad F_{X, Y, Z}(k1, k2, k3)$

$= 1$ for $k1 \geq 1, k2 \geq 1,$ and $k3 \geq 1.$

Then the marginal cumulative distribution function of X is given by

$F_X(k) = F_{X, Y, Z}(k, \text{infinity}, \text{infinity}),$

$F_X(k) = F_{X, Y, Z}(k, 1, 1)$

$= k$ for $0 < k < 1,$

$F_X(k) = 0$ for $k \leq 0,$

and $\quad F_X(k) = 1$ for $k \geq 1.$

Likewise, the joint cumulative probability of X and Y can be found by substituting infinity (or, in this case, the upper limit of one) for Z, resulting in

$F_{X, Y}(k1, k2) = F_{X, Y, Z}(k1, k2, \infty)$

$= F_{X, Y, Z}(k1, k2, 1)$

$= (k1)(k2)$ for $0 \leq k1 < 1$ and $0 \leq k2 < 1,$

$= k1$ for $0 \leq k1 < 1$ and $k2 \geq 1,$

$= k2$ for $0 \leq k2 < 1$ and $k1 \geq 1,$

$= 1$ for $k1 \geq 1$ and $k2 \geq 1,$

and $\quad = 0$ for $k1 < 0$ or $k2 < 0.$

• PROBLEM 5-38

Let

$$f_{X,Y}(k1, k2) = c(k1)(k2) \text{ for } 0 < k1 < 1, 0 < k2 < 1.$$

For how many values of c will this be a joint probability density function? For which value(s) of c will this be a joint probability density function?

SOLUTION:

To be a joint probability density function, this function needs to be non-negative, and it needs to integrate to one. The first requirement shows

that $c\,(k1)\,(k2) \geq 0,$

so $c \geq 0/(k1)\,(k2) = 0.$

Thus, c must be non-negative. Let I denote the integral sign. The second requirement shows that

$$1 = I_{0 \text{ to } 1}\, I_{0 \text{ to } 1}\, cxy\, dx\, dy$$

$$= cI_{0 \text{ to } 1}\, y[I_{0 \text{ to } 1}\, x\, dx]\, dy$$

$$= cI_{0 \text{ to } 1}\, y[x^2/2]_{0 \text{ to } 1}\, dy$$

$$= cI_{0 \text{ to } 1}\, y[(1^2/2) - (0^2/2)]\, dy$$

$$= cI_{0 \text{ to } 1}\, y(1/2 - 0/2)\, dy$$

$$= cI_{0 \text{ to } 1}\, y(1/2 - 0)\, dy$$

$$= cI_{0 \text{ to } 1}\, y1/2\, dy$$

$$= (c/2)I_{0 \text{ to } 1}\, y\, dy$$

$$= (c/2)[y^2/2]_{0 \text{ to } 1}$$

$$= (c/2)[(1^2/2) - (0^2/2)]$$

$$= (c/2)[1/2 - 0/2]$$

$$= (c/2)[1/2 - 0]$$

$$= (c/2)[1/2]$$

$$= c/4$$

Thus, $c/4 = 1,$

so $\quad c = (4)\,(1)$

$\quad\quad = 4.$

This is the only value of c for which $c(k1)\,(k2)$ is a joint probability density function over the range specified.

• PROBLEM 5–39

For the joint probability density function given in Problem 5–38, what is the joint cumulative distribution function?

SOLUTION:

We write

$$F_{X,\,Y}(k1, k2) = P\{X \le k1, Y \le k2\}$$

$$= I_{0 \text{ to } k2}\, I_{0 \text{ to } k1}\, 4xy\, dx\, dy$$

$$= 4I_{0 \text{ to } k2}\, y[I_{0 \text{ to } k1}\, xdx]\, dy$$

$$= 4I_{0 \text{ to } k2}\, y[x^2/2]_{0 \text{ to } k1}\, dy$$

$$= 4I_{0 \text{ to } k2}\, y[(k1^2/2) - (0^2/2)]\, dy$$

$$= 4I_{0 \text{ to } k2}\, y(k1^2/2 - 0/2)\, dy$$

$$= 4I_{0 \text{ to } k2}\, y(k1^2/2 - 0)\, dy$$

$$= 4I_{0 \text{ to } k2}\, yk1^2/2\, dy$$

$$= (4k1^2/2)I_{0 \text{ to } k2}\, y\, dy$$

$$= (2k1^2)[y^2/2]_{0 \text{ to } k2}$$

$$= (2k1^2)\,[(k2^2/2) - (0^2/2)]$$

$$= (2k1^2)[k2^2/2 - 0/2]$$

$$= (2k1^2)[k2^2/2 - 0]$$

$$= (2k1^2)[k2^2/2]$$

$$= (k1)^2(k2)^2 \text{ for } 0 < k1 < 1 \text{ and } 0 < k2 < 1$$

Therefore, the joint cumulative distribution function is

$$F_{X,\,Y}(k1, k2) = P\{X \le k1, Y \le k2\}$$

$$= (k1)^2(k2)^2 \text{ for } 0 < k1 < 1 \text{ and } 0 < k2 < 1,$$

$$= 0 \text{ for } k1 \leq 0,$$

$$= 0 \text{ for } k2 \leq 0,$$

$$= (k1)^2 \text{ for } 0 < k1 < 1 \text{ and } k2 \geq 1,$$

$$= (k2)^2 \text{ for } 0 < k2 < 1 \text{ and } k1 \geq 1,$$

and $$= 1 \text{ for } k1 \geq 1 \text{ and } k2 \geq 1.$$

• PROBLEM 5–40

What is the marginal cumulative distribution of X for the joint distribution given in Problems 5–38 and 5–39?

SOLUTION:

The marginal cumulative distribution of X is

$$F_X(k) = F_{X,Y}(k, \text{infinity})$$

$$= F_{X,Y}(k, 1)$$

$$= (k)^2 (1)^2$$

$$= (k)^2(1)$$

$$= k^2 \text{ for } 0 \leq k < 1,$$

$$F_X(k) = 0 \text{ for } k < 0,$$

and $$F_X(k) = 1 \text{ for } k \geq 1.$$

• PROBLEM 5–41

Let

$$F_{X,Y}(k1, k2) = c(k1)^3(k2)^3 \text{ for } 0 < k1 < 1, 0 < k2 < 1.$$

For how many values of c will this be a joint cumulative distribution function? For which value(s) of c will this be a joint cumulative distribution function?

SOLUTION:

To be a joint cumulative distribution, $F_{X, Y}(k1, k2) = c(k1)^3(k2)^3$ needs to be right-continuous and non-decreasing for $0 < k1 < 1, 0 < k2 < 1$. We would also need $F_{X, Y}(1, 1) = 1$ and $F_{X, Y}(0, 0) = 0$, since the upper limit of each variable is 1 and the lower limit of each random variable is 0. This function is continuous, hence right-continuous, for any value of c. This function is non-decreasing for any non-negative value of c. Thus, c must be non-negative. For any value of c, it is true that $F_{X, Y}(0, 0) = 0$. This just leaves the final requirement,

$$1 = F_{X, Y}(1, 1)$$

$$= c(k1)^3(k2)^3$$

$$= c(1)^3(1)^3$$

$$= c(1)(1)$$

$$= c$$

Thus, $c = 1$ is the only value of c that makes this function a joint cumulative distribution function.

• PROBLEM 5–42

For the joint cumulative distribution function given in Problem 5–41, what is the joint probability density function?

SOLUTION:

We must differentiate the joint cumulative distribution function with respect to both $k1$ and $k2$. Doing so shows that

$$f_{X, Y}(k1, k2) = d^2/(d\,k1)(d\,k2)\, F_{X, Y}(k1, k2)$$

$$= d^2/(d\,k1)(d\,k2)\,(c)(k1)^3\,(k2)^3$$

$$= d^2/(d\,k1)(d\,k2)\,(1)\,(k1)^3(k2)^3$$

$$= d^2/(d\,k1)(d\,k2)\,(k1)^3(k2)^3$$

$$= d/(d\,k2)\,3(k1)^2(k2)^3$$

$$= 3(k1)^2\,d/(d\,k2)\,(k2)^3$$

$$= 3(k1)^2 \, 3(k2)^2$$

$$= 9(k1)^2(k2)^2$$

Then $f_{X, Y}(k1, k2) = 9(k1)^2(k2)^2$ for $0 < k1 < 1$ and $0 < k2 < 1$,

$f_{X, Y}(k1, k2) = 0$ for $k1 \leq 0$,

$f_{X, Y}(k1, k2) = 0$ for $k2 \leq 0$,

$f_{X, Y}(k1, k2) = 0$ for $k1 \geq 1$,

and $f_{X, Y}(k1, k2) = 0$ for $k2 \geq 1$.

• PROBLEM 5-43

Let

$f_{X, Y}(k1, k2) = 0.00$ for $(k1, k2) = (3, 2)$,

$f_{X, Y}(k1, k2) = 0.15$ for $(k1, k2) = (4, 2)$,

$f_{X, Y}(k1, k2) = 0.10$ for $(k1, k2) = (3, 4)$,

$f_{X, Y}(k1, k2) = 0.20$ for $(k1, k2) = (4, 4)$,

$f_{X, Y}(k1, k2) = 0.25$ for $(k1, k2) = (3, 6)$,

and $f_{X, Y}(k1, k2) = 0.30$ for $(k1, k2) = (4, 6)$.

Then what is the joint cumulative distribution function of X and Y?

SOLUTION:

The joint probability mass function can be conveniently displayed in a table, as illustrated below.

	X		
Y	$X = 3$	$X = 4$	Total
$Y = 2$	0.00	0.15	0.15
$Y = 4$	0.10	0.20	0.30
$Y = 6$	0.25	0.30	0.55
Total	0.35	0.65	1.00

The joint cumulative distribution function may be found by summing the probabilities in appropriate cells. This joint cumulative distribution function may also be displayed in a table, such as the one below.

	X	
Y	X = 3	X = 4
Y = 2	0.00	0.15
Y = 4	0.10	0.45
Y = 6	0.35	1.00

For example,

$$F_{X, Y}(4, 4) = P\{X \le 4, Y \le 4\}$$

$$= P\{(3, 2) \cup (4, 2) \cup (3, 4)\ u\ (4, 4)\}$$

$$= P\{(3, 2)\} + P\{4, 2)\} + P\{(3, 4)\} + P\{(4, 4)\}$$

$$= 0.00 + 0.15 + 0.10 + 0.20$$

$$= 0.45,$$

as shown in the table.

✓ • PROBLEM 5-44

For the joint distribution shown in Problem 5–43, what are the marginal probability mass functions and the marginal cumulative distribution functions of X?

SOLUTION:

By summing the probabilities of the appropriate cells, we see that

$$P\{X = 3\} = P\{(3, 2) \cup (3, 4) \cup (3, 6)\}$$

$$= P\{(3, 2)\} + P\{(3, 4)\} + P\{(3, 6)\}$$

$$= 0.00 + 0.10 + 0.25$$

$$= 0.35,$$

as shown in the total row of the first table under the column headed by $X = 3$. Thus, we see that

$$P\{X = 3\} = 0.35$$

and $\quad P\{X = 4\} = 0.65.$

Likewise,

$$P\{Y = 2\} = 0.15,$$

$$P\{Y = 4\} = 0.30,$$

and $\quad P\{Y = 6\} = 0.55.$

Recall that the marginal cumulative distribution function of either X or Y may be found by substituting, in the joint cumulative distribution function, the upper limit of the "other" variable. That is, if we want to find the marginal cumulative distribution function of Y, then we substitute $X = 4$ (since 4 is the upper limit of X) in the joint cumulative distribution function. Looking at the column headed by $X = 4$ in the second table reveals that

$$P\{Y \leq 2\} = 0.15,$$

$$P\{Y \leq 4\} = 0.45,$$

and $\quad P\{Y \leq 6\} = 1.00.$

Likewise,

$$P\{X \leq 3\} = 0.35$$

and $\quad P\{X \leq 4\} = 1.00.$

• PROBLEM 5-45

Given that the joint density function of the random variables X, Y, and Z is $f(x, y, z) = e^{-(x + y + z)}$ when $0 < x < \infty$, $0 < y < \infty$, $0 < z < \infty$, find the cumulative distribution function $F(x, y, z)$ of X, Y, and Z.

SOLUTION:

The cumulative distribution function of one variable gives the area under the density curve to the left of the particular value of x. The distribution function of the two variables gives the volume under the surface represented by the bivariate density function over the region bounded by the specified values of x and y. This is obtained by integration with respect to each variable. The number given by a distribution function of three variables can be interpreted as a four-dimensional volume. It is obtained by constructing an iterated triple integral and integrating with respect to each variable. We compute

$$F(x, y, z) = \int_0^z \int_0^y \int_0^x e^{-u-v-w} \, du \, dv \, dw$$

$$= \int_0^z \int_0^y \int_0^x (e^{-u}) (e^{-v-w}) \, du \, dv \, dw$$

$$= \int_0^z \int_0^y (e^{-v-w}) (1 - e^{-x}) \, dv \, dw$$

$$= (1 - e^{-x}) \int_0^z e^{-w} e^{-v} \, dv \, dw$$

$$= (1 - e^{-x}) \int_0^z e^{-w} (1 - e^{-y}) \, dw$$

$$= (1 - e^{-x}) (1 - e^{-y}) (1 - e^{-z})$$

for $x, y, z > 0$.

• PROBLEM 5-46

Let X and Y be jointly distributed with density function

$$f(x, y) = \begin{cases} \dfrac{1}{1-x} & 0 < x < 1, \ 0 < y < 1 \\ 0 & \text{otherwise} \end{cases}.$$

Find $F(\lambda \mid X > Y) = P(X \le \lambda \mid X > Y)$.

SOLUTION:

By the definition of conditional probability,

$$P(A \mid B) = \frac{P(A \text{ and } B)}{P(B)}.$$

Thus, $F(\lambda \mid X > Y) = P(X \le \lambda \mid X > Y)$

$$= \frac{P(X \leq \lambda \text{ and } X > Y)}{P(X > Y)}.$$

The shaded region represents the area where $X \leq \lambda$ and $X > Y$. Thus, $P(X \leq \lambda \text{ and } X > Y)$ is the volume over the shaded region under the curve

$$f(x, y) = \frac{1}{1-x}.$$

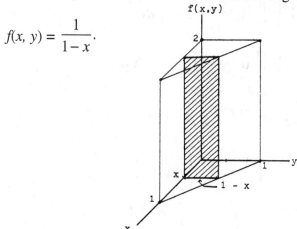

This volume is that of a right prism. Thus, $P(X \leq \lambda \text{ and } X > Y) =$ volume of right prism whose base is the shaded region in the figure and whose height is 1.

Thus,

$$P(X \leq 1 \text{ and } X > Y) = (\text{Area of base}) \times \text{height} = \frac{1}{2} \lambda \times \lambda \times 1 = ZZ,$$

and $P(X > Y)$ equals the volume over the triangle with vertices $(0, 0)$, $(1, 1)$, and $(1, 0)$ and under $f(x, y) = 1$.

This is in the shape of a right prism with a base of area $\frac{1}{2}$ and a height of 1. The volume of this region is thus

$$\frac{1}{2} \yen \frac{1}{2} \text{ and } P(X > Y) = \frac{1}{2}.$$

Thus,

$$\frac{P(X \leq \lambda \mid X > Y)}{P(X > Y)} = \frac{\dfrac{\lambda^2}{2}}{\dfrac{1}{2}} = \lambda^2.$$

The conditional CDF for x given $x > y$ is therefore

$$P(X \leq \lambda \mid X > Y) = \begin{cases} \lambda^2 & 0 < \lambda < 1 \\ 0 & \lambda < 0 \\ 1 & \lambda > 1 \end{cases}$$

NORMAL PROBABILITY FUNCTIONS AND DERIVATIVES

x	$P(x)$	$Z(x)$	$Z^{(1)}(x)$
0.00	0.50000 00000 00000	0.39894 22804 01433	0.00000 00000 00000
0.02	0.50797 83137 16902	0.39886 24999 23666	-0.00797 72499 98473
0.04	0.51595 34368 52831	0.39862 32542 04605	-0.01594 49301 68184
0.06	0.52392 21826 54107	0.39822 48301 95607	-0.02389 34898 11736
0.08	0.53188 13720 13988	0.39766 77055 11609	-0.03181 34164 40929
0.10	0.53982 78372 77029	0.39695 25474 77012	-0.03969 52547 47701
0.12	0.54775 84260 20584	0.39608 02117 93656	-0.04752 96254 15239
0.14	0.55567 00048 05907	0.39505 17408 34611	-0.05530 72437 16846
0.16	0.56355 94628 91433	0.39386 83615 68541	-0.06301 89378 50967
0.18	0.57142 37159 00901	0.39253 14831 20429	-0.07065 56669 61677
0.20	0.57925 97094 39103	0.39104 26939 75456	-0.07820 85387 95091
0.22	0.58706 44226 48215	0.38940 37588 33790	-0.08566 88269 43434
0.24	0.59483 48716 97796	0.38761 66151 25014	-0.09302 79876 30003
0.26	0.60256 81132 01761	0.38568 33691 91816	-0.10027 76759 89872
0.28	0.61026 12475 55797	0.38360 62921 53479	-0.10740 97618 02974
0.30	0.61791 14221 88953	0.38138 78154 60524	-0.11441 63446 38157
0.32	0.62551 58347 23320	0.37903 05261 52702	-0.12128 97683 68865
0.34	0.63307 17360 36028	0.37653 71618 33254	-0.12802 26350 23306
0.36	0.64057 64332 17991	0.37391 06053 73128	-0.13460 78179 34326
0.38	0.64802 72924 24163	0.37115 38793 59466	-0.14103 84741 56597
0.40	0.65542 17416 10324	0.36827 01403 03323	-0.14730 80561 21329
0.42	0.66275 72731 51751	0.36526 26726 22154	-0.15341 03225 01305
0.44	0.67003 14463 39407	0.36213 48824 13092	-0.15933 93482 61761
0.46	0.67724 18897 49653	0.35889 02910 33545	-0.16508 95338 75431
0.48	0.68438 63034 83778	0.35553 25285 05997	-0.17065 56136 82879
0.50	0.69146 24612 74013	0.35206 53267 64299	-0.17603 26633 82150
0.52	0.69846 82124 53034	0.34849 25127 58974	-0.18121 61066 34667
0.54	0.70540 14837 84302	0.34481 80014 39333	-0.18620 17207 77240
0.56	0.71226 02811 50973	0.34104 57886 30353	-0.19098 56416 32997
0.58	0.71904 26911 01436	0.33717 99438 22381	-0.19556 43674 16981
0.60	0.72574 68822 49927	0.33322 46028 91800	-0.19993 47617 35080
0.62	0.73237 11065 31017	0.32918 39607 70765	-0.20409 40556 77874
0.64	0.73891 37003 07139	0.32506 22640 84082	-0.20803 98490 13813
0.66	0.74537 30853 28664	0.32086 38037 71172	-0.21177 01104 88974
0.68	0.75174 77695 46430	0.31659 29077 10893	-0.21528 31772 43407
0.70	0.75803 63477 76927	0.31225 39333 66761	-0.21857 77533 56733
0.72	0.76423 75022 20749	0.30785 12604 69853	-0.22165 29075 38294
0.74	0.77035 00028 35210	0.30338 92837 56300	-0.22450 80699 79662
0.76	0.77637 27075 62401	0.29887 24057 75953	-0.22714 30283 89724
0.78	0.78230 45624 14267	0.29430 50297 88325	-0.22955 79232 34894
0.80	0.78814 46014 16604	0.28969 15527 61483	-0.23175 32422 09186
0.82	0.79389 19464 14187	0.28503 63584 89007	-0.23372 98139 60986
0.84	0.79954 58067 39551	0.28034 38108 39621	-0.23548 88011 05281
0.86	0.80510 54787 48192	0.27561 32471 53457	-0.23703 16925 51973
0.88	0.81057 03452 23288	0.27086 39717 98338	-0.23836 02951 82537
0.90	0.81593 98746 53241	0.26608 52498 98755	-0.23947 67249 08879
0.92	0.82121 36203 85629	0.26128 63012 49553	-0.24038 33971 49589
0.94	0.82639 12196 61376	0.25647 12944 25620	-0.24108 30167 60083
0.96	0.83147 23925 33162	0.25164 43410 96117	-0.24157 85674 54192
0.98	0.83645 69406 72308	0.24680 94905 67043	-0.24187 33007 55702
1.00	0.84134 47460 68543	0.24197 07245 19143	-0.24197 07245 19143
	$\left[\dfrac{(-5)1}{10}\right]$	$\left[\dfrac{(-5)2}{10}\right]$	$\left[\dfrac{(-5)3}{10}\right]$

$$Z(x) = \frac{1}{\sqrt{2\pi}} e - \frac{1}{2}s^2 \quad P(x) = \int_{-\infty}^{x} Z(t)\,dt \quad Z^{(n)}(x) = \frac{d^n}{dx^n} Z(x) \quad He_n(x) = (-1)^n Z^{(n)}(x) / Z(x)$$

NORMAL PROBABILITY FUNCTIONS AND DERIVATIVES

x	$Z^{(2)}(x)$	$Z^{(3)}(x)$	$Z^{(4)}(x)$	$Z^{(5)}(x)$	$Z^{(6)}(x)$
0.00	−0.39894 22804	0.00000 000	1.19682 684	0.00000 000	−5.98413 421
0.02	−0.39870 29549	0.02392 856	1.19563 029	−0.11962 684	−5.97575 893
0.04	−0.39798 54570	0.04780 928	1.19204 400	−0.23891 887	−5.95066 325
0.06	−0.39679 12208	0.07159 445	1.18607 800	−0.35754 249	−5.90893 742
0.08	−0.39512 26322	0.09523 664	1.17774 897	−0.47516 649	−5.85073 151
0.10	−0.39298 30220	0.11868 881	1.16708 019	−0.59146 327	−5.77625 460
0.12	−0.39037 66567	0.14190 445	1.15410 144	−0.70610 997	−5.68577 399
0.14	−0.38730 87267	0.16483 771	1.13884 890	−0.81878 968	−5.57961 395
0.16	−0.38378 53315	0.18744 353	1.12136 503	−0.92919 252	−5.45815 435
0.18	−0.37981 34631	0.20967 776	1.10169 839	−1.03701 674	−5.32182 895
0.20	−0.37540 09862	0.23149 727	1.07990 350	−1.14196 980	−5.17112 356
0.22	−0.37055 66169	0.25286 011	1.05604 063	−1.24376 938	−5.00657 387
0.24	−0.36528 98981	0.27372 555	1.03017 556	−1.34214 434	−4.82876 317
0.26	−0.35961 11734	0.29405 426	1.00237 941	−1.43683 568	−4.63831 979
0.28	−0.35353 15588	0.31380 836	0.97272 834	−1.52759 737	−4.43591 441
0.30	−0.34706 29121	0.33295 156	0.94130 327	−1.61419 723	−4.22225 716
0.32	−0.34021 78003	0.35144 923	0.90818 965	−1.69641 762	−3.99809 459
0.34	−0.33300 94659	0.36926 849	0.87347 711	−1.77405 617	−3.76420 646
0.36	−0.32545 17909	0.38637 828	0.83725 919	−1.84692 643	−3.52140 244
0.38	−0.31755 92592	0.40274 947	0.79963 298	−1.91485 840	−3.27051 871
0.40	−0.30934 69179	0.41835 488	0.76069 880	−1.97769 904	−3.01241 439
0.42	−0.30083 03372	0.43316 939	0.72055 987	−2.03531 269	−2.74796 802
0.44	−0.29202 55692	0.44716 995	0.67932 193	−2.08758 144	−2.47807 382
0.46	−0.28294 91055	0.46033 566	0.63709 291	−2.13440 537	−2.20363 810
0.48	−0.27361 78339	0.47264 779	0.59398 256	−2.17570 278	−1.92557 548
0.50	−0.26404 89951	0.48408 982	0.55010 207	−2.21141 033	−1.64480 520
0.52	−0.25426 01373	0.49464 748	0.50556 372	−2.24148 307	−1.36224 740
0.54	−0.24426 90722	0.50430 874	0.46048 050	−2.26589 443	−1.07881 949
0.56	−0.23409 38293	0.51306 383	0.41496 574	−2.28463 613	−0.79543 249
0.58	−0.22375 26107	0.52090 525	0.36913 279	−2.29771 801	−0.51298 749
0.60	−0.21326 37459	0.52782 777	0.32309 457	−2.30516 783	−0.23237 218
0.62	−0.20264 56463	0.53382 841	0.27696 332	−2.30703 091	+0.04554 255
0.64	−0.19191 67607	0.53890 643	0.23085 017	−2.30336 981	0.31990 583
0.66	−0.18109 55308	0.54306 327	0.18486 483	−2.29426 388	0.58988 999
0.68	−0.17020 03472	0.54630 259	0.13911 528	−2.27980 875	0.85469 355
0.70	−0.15924 95060	0.54863 016	0.09370 741	−2.26011 583	1.11354 405
0.72	−0.14826 11670	0.55005 386	0.04874 473	−2.23531 162	1.36570 074
0.74	−0.13725 33120	0.55058 359	+0.00432 808	−2.20553 714	1.61045 709
0.76	−0.12624 37042	0.55023 127	−0.03944 465	−2.17094 715	1.84714 311
0.78	−0.11524 98497	0.54901 073	−0.08247 882	−2.13170 944	2.07512 746
0.80	−0.10428 89590	0.54693 765	−0.12468 324	−2.08800 401	2.29381 943
0.82	−0.09337 79110	0.54402 952	−0.16597 047	−2.04002 228	2.50267 061
0.84	−0.08253 32179	0.54030 551	−0.20625 697	−1.98796 617	2.70117 643
0.86	−0.07177 09916	0.53578 644	−0.24546 336	−1.93204 726	2.88887 745
0.88	−0.06110 69120	0.53049 467	−0.28351 458	−1.87248 587	3.06536 044
0.90	−0.05055 61975	0.52445 403	−0.32034 003	−1.80951 008	3.23025 923
0.92	−0.04013 35759	0.51768 968	−0.35587 378	−1.74335 486	3.38325 538
0.94	−0.02985 32587	0.51022 810	−0.39005 463	−1.67426 103	3.52407 854
0.96	−0.01972 89163	0.50209 689	−0.42282 627	−1.60247 436	3.65250 673
0.98	−0.00977 36558	0.49332 478	−0.45413 732	−1.52824 456	3.76836 628
1.00	0.00000 00000	0.48394 145	−0.48394 145	−1.45182 435	3.87153 159
	$\begin{bmatrix} (-5)6 \\ 6 \end{bmatrix}$	$\begin{bmatrix} (-4)1 \\ 6 \end{bmatrix}$	$\begin{bmatrix} (-4)3 \\ 6 \end{bmatrix}$	$\begin{bmatrix} (-4)7 \\ 6 \end{bmatrix}$	$\begin{bmatrix} (-3)2 \\ 7 \end{bmatrix}$

$$P(-x) = 1 - P(x) \qquad Z(-x) = Z(x) \qquad Z^{(n)}(-x) = (-1)^n Z^{(n)}(x)$$

CHAPTER 6

CONDITIONAL PROBABILITY

> **Basic Attacks and Strategies for Solving Problems in this Chapter. See pages 474 to 541 for step-by-step solutions to problems.**

Conditional probability is similar to what we previously referred to as probability, in that both share the same properties. For clarification, we will use the term "unconditional probability" to distinguish one from the other.

Conditional probability is the probability of an event given that another event has occurred. If we wish to know the probability of event A given that event B has occurred, then we denote this quantity by $P\{A \mid B\}$. To see why this is different from $P\{A\}$, or the unconditional probability of A, consider the following Venn diagram:

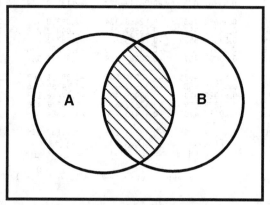

The unconditional probability of A, or $P\{A\}$, is the proportion of the entire Venn diagram which comprises the circle representing event A. If we agree that the area of the entire Venn diagram is one, then the unconditional probability of A, $P\{A\}$, is the area of the circle representing event A.

But what exactly is the conditional probability of A given B, $P\{A \mid B\}$? Since we already know that event B has occurred, we restrict our attention to the circle representing B. In essence, this circle becomes the new entire Venn diagram. Now the probability of A must be referred to this new Venn diagram. Therefore, the new probability of A is the proportion of the new Venn diagram (the circle representing event B) which comprises the circle representing event A.

If one considers the event that is defined as that part of A which is in the new Venn diagram (the circle representing event B), then it will be seen that this event is the event in which both A and B occur. This is precisely $A \cap B$. Now we see that the conditional probability of event A given that event B has occurred is

$$P\{A \mid B\} = (\text{area of event } A \text{ within event } B) / (\text{area of event } B)$$

$$= (\text{area of event } A \cap B) / (\text{area of event } B)$$

$$= P\{A \cap B\} / P\{B\},$$

as long as $P\{B\} > 0$. This is the definition of conditional probability.

As an example, consider the following table, in which each person is cross-classified by gender and by political affiliation.

		Political Affiliation		
		Democrat	Republican	Total
Gender	Male	20	25	45
	Female	35	20	55
	Total	55	45	100

The cell counts and margin totals determine the numbers of people with each set of characteristics. For example, there are 35 Democratic females and 20 Republican females, for a total of $35 + 20 = 55$ females. There are 100 total people.

From this table we can answer a great many questions. For example, we can answer questions such as:

1. What is the probability of selecting a male?

2. What is the probability of selecting a female?

3. What is the probability of selecting a Democrat?

4. What is the probability of selecting a Republican?

5. What is the probability of selecting a Democratic male?

6. What is the probability of selecting a Democratic female?

7. What is the probability of selecting a Republican male?

8. What is the probability of selecting a Republican female?

Each of these questions can be answered by simply dividing the number of people with the desired characteristics by the total number of people. Thus, the solutions to these eight questions are:

1.
$$P\{\text{male}\} = \frac{\text{number of males}}{\text{number of people}}$$

$$= \frac{45}{100}$$

$$= 0.45$$

2.
$$P\{\text{female}\} = \frac{\text{number of females}}{\text{number of people}}$$

$$= \frac{55}{100}$$

$$= 0.55$$

3.
$$P\{\text{Democrat}\} = \frac{\text{number of Democrats}}{\text{number of people}}$$

$$= \frac{55}{100}$$

$$= 0.55$$

4.
$$P\{\text{Republican}\} = \frac{\text{number of Republicans}}{\text{number of people}}$$

$$= \frac{45}{100}$$

$$= 0.45$$

5. $$P\{\text{Democratic male}\} = \frac{\text{number of Democratic males}}{\text{number of people}}$$

$$= \frac{20}{100}$$

$$= 0.20$$

6. $P\{\text{Democratic female}\} = \dfrac{\text{number of Democratic females}}{\text{number of people}}$

$$= \frac{35}{100}$$

$$= 0.35$$

7. $P\{\text{Republican male}\} = \dfrac{\text{number of Republican males}}{\text{number of people}}$

$$= \frac{25}{100}$$

$$= 0.25$$

8. $P\{\text{Republican female}\} = \dfrac{\text{number of Republican females}}{\text{number of people}}$

$$= \frac{20}{100}$$

$$= 0.20$$

These eight questions all involve unconditional probabilities. Notice that for each of the calculations involved in these questions the denominator was 100, or the total number of people. But the table also allows us to answer other questions, such as:

9. What is the probability that a male is a Democrat?

10. What is the probability that a male is a Republican?

11. What is the probability that a female is a Democrat?

12. What is the probability that a female is a Republican?

13. What is the probability that a Democrat is a male?

14. What is the probability that a Democrat is a female?

15. What is the probability that a Republican is a male?

16. What is the probability that a Republican is a female?

For simplicity, we abbreviate so that

M = male,

F = female,

D = Democrat,

and R = Republican.

Also, we use the notation #, where, for example, #(M) is the number of males, and #(M, D) is the number of male Democrats.

These questions all involve conditional probabilities. For example, question 9 asks for the probability that a male is a Democrat. This is the same as asking for the probability that a randomly selected person is a Democrat given that this person is a male. To answer this question, we consider only males, or the first row of the table. The second row becomes irrelevant. In particular, these next eight questions can be answered using conditional probabilities as follows:

9. $P\{D \mid M\} = \dfrac{P\{D, M\}}{P\{M\}}$

$= \dfrac{\#(D, M)}{\#(M)}$

$= \dfrac{20}{45}$

$= \dfrac{4}{9}$

$= 0.4444$

10. $P\{R \mid M\} = \dfrac{P\{R, M\}}{P\{M\}}$

$= \dfrac{\#(R, M)}{\#(M)}$

$= \dfrac{25}{45}$

$= \dfrac{5}{9}$

$= 0.5555$

11. $P\{D \mid F\} = \dfrac{P\{D, F\}}{P\{F\}}$

$= \dfrac{\#(D, F)}{\#(F)}$

$= \dfrac{35}{55}$

$= \dfrac{7}{11}$

$= 0.6364$

12. $P\{R \mid F\} = \dfrac{P\{R, F\}}{P\{F\}}$

$= \dfrac{\#(R, F)}{\#(F)}$

$= \dfrac{20}{55}$

$= \dfrac{4}{11}$

$= 0.3636$

13. $P\{M \mid D\} = \dfrac{P\{M, D\}}{P\{D\}}$

$= \dfrac{\#(M, D)}{\#(D)}$

$= \dfrac{20}{55}$

$= \dfrac{4}{11}$

$= 0.3636$

14. $P\{F \mid D\} = \dfrac{P\{F, D\}}{P\{F\}}$

          $= \dfrac{\#(F, D)}{\#(D)}$

          $= \dfrac{35}{55}$

          $= \dfrac{7}{11}$

          $= 0.6364$

15. $P\{M \mid R\} = \dfrac{P\{M, R\}}{P\{R\}}$

          $= \dfrac{\#(M, R)}{\#(R)}$

          $= \dfrac{25}{45}$

          $= \dfrac{5}{9}$

          $= 0.5555$

16. $P\{F \mid R\} = \dfrac{P\{F, R\}}{P\{R\}}$

          $= \dfrac{\#(F, R)}{\#(R)}$

          $= \dfrac{20}{45}$

          $= \dfrac{4}{9}$

          $= 0.4444$

     As is typically the case, conditional probability is simpler in the discrete case than in the continuous case. In the continuous case, there is the issue of potentially conditioning on events of probability zero. This does not arise in the discrete case.

Consider the following example. An urn contains two black balls and two white balls. Two balls are selected at random without replacement. What is the probability that the second ball drawn is black? What is the probability that the second ball drawn is black given that the first ball drawn was black? What is the probability that the second ball drawn is black given that the first ball drawn was white? What if the drawing is done with replacement?

The second ball drawn may be either black or white. Since there are two black balls and two white balls, there are $2 + 2 = 4$ balls total. Since any one of these four balls will be selected with equal probability,

$$P\{B2\} = P\{\text{black on the second draw}\}$$

$$= \frac{2}{2+2}$$

$$= \frac{2}{4}$$

$$= 0.5$$

If the first ball selected was black, however, then we have more information, which we need to use prudently. There were two black balls in the urn to start, but having picked one of these black balls on the first draw, there now remains only one black ball. However, there are still two white balls. Thus,

$$P\{B2 \mid B1\} = P\{\text{second ball drawn is black given}$$

$$\text{that the first ball drawn was black}\}$$

$$= \frac{1}{3}$$

$$= 0.3333$$

Notice that picking a black ball on the first draw has reduced the probability of drawing a black ball on the second draw from 0.5 to 0.3333. The conditional probability is smaller than the unconditional probability.

If the first ball selected was white, then we again have more information, which we need to use prudently. There were two white balls in the urn to start, but having picked one of these white balls on the first draw, there now remains only one white ball. However, there are still two black balls. Thus,

$$P\{B2 \mid W1\} = P\{\text{second ball drawn is black given}$$

$$\text{that the first ball drawn was white}\}$$

$$= \frac{2}{3}$$

$$= 0.6667$$

Notice that picking a white ball on the first draw has increased the probability of drawing a black ball on the second draw from 0.5 to 0.6667. The conditional probability is larger than the unconditional probability.

If the drawing is done with replacement, then no matter what color the chosen ball is on the first draw, it will be replaced, so there will always be two white balls and two black balls in the urn. All four balls will be equally likely to be chosen, so the probability of picking a black ball will always be 0.5. That is, the conditional probabilities will be the same as the unconditional probabilities.

As a general rule, once we condition on certain events, the probabilities of other events may change. They need not always change, but it cannot be assumed that they will not change. Thus, we must compute the conditional probabilities even if we already know the unconditional probability.

Step-by-Step Solutions to
Problems in this Chapter,
"Conditional Probability."

√ • **PROBLEM 6–1**

Consider drawing two cards from a standard deck of cards. What is the probability of drawing a king on the second draw?

SOLUTION:

There are four kings and 52 cards. Thus,

$$P\{K2\} = \frac{\#(K)}{\#(\text{cards})}$$

$$= \frac{4}{52}$$

$$= \frac{1}{13}$$

$$= 0.0769$$

√ • **PROBLEM 6–2**

Consider drawing, without replacement, two cards from a standard deck of cards. What is the probability of drawing a king on the second draw given that a king was drawn on the first draw?

SOLUTION:

There are four kings and 52 cards. Having picked a king on the first draw, there are now three kings left and 51 cards left. Thus,

$$P\{K2 \mid K1\} = \frac{\#(K \text{ left})}{\#(\text{cards left})}$$

$$= \frac{3}{51}$$

$$= \frac{1}{17}$$

$$= 0.0588$$

√ • **PROBLEM 6–3**

Consider drawing, without replacement, two cards from a standard deck of cards. What is the probability of drawing a king on the second draw given that a king was not drawn on the first draw?

SOLUTION:

There are four kings and 52 cards. Having picked a card other than a king on the first draw, there are now four kings left and 51 cards left. Thus,

$$P\{K2 \mid \text{not } K1\} = \frac{\#(K \text{ left})}{\#(\text{cards left})}$$

$$= \frac{4}{51}$$

$$= 0.0784$$

✓ • PROBLEM 6-4

Consider drawing, without replacement, two cards from a standard deck of cards. What is the probability of drawing two kings?

SOLUTION:

To pick two kings requires that a king be picked first and second. That is, we must draw one of the four kings, and then one of the three remaining kings. Thus,

$$P\{K1, K2\} = P\{K1\} \, P\{K2 \mid K1\}$$

$$= \frac{\#(K)}{\#(\text{cards})} \frac{\#(K \text{ left})}{\#(\text{cards left})}$$

$$= \frac{4}{52} \frac{3}{51}$$

$$= \frac{1}{13} \frac{1}{17}$$

$$= (0.0769)\,(0.0588)$$

$$= 0.0045$$

✓ • **PROBLEM 6-5**

A fair coin is tossed twice, and the result is one heads and one tails. What is the probability that the first toss resulted in heads?

SOLUTION:

Before we condition on the fact that there was one heads and one tails, the sample space would have been

{HH, HT, TH, and TT}.

Each of these four possibilities would have probability 1/4, or 0.25. Thus,

$P\{HT\} = 0.25$.

But once we condition on the one heads and one tails, we find that

$P\{HT \mid \text{one heads and one tails}\}$

$= P\{HT \mid HT \text{ or } TH\}$

$= P\{HT \text{ and } (HT \text{ or } TH)\} / P\{HT \text{ or } TH\}$,

since this is the definition of conditional probability. But

$\{HT \text{ and } (HT \text{ or } TH)\} = \{HT\}$.

Thus,

$P\{HT \text{ and } (HT \text{ or } TH)\} \setminus P\{HT \text{ or } TH\}$

$$= \frac{P\{HT\}}{P\{HT \text{ or } TH\}}$$

$$= \frac{0.25}{(0.25 + 0.25)}$$

$$= \frac{1}{2}$$

$= 0.5$

A fair coin is tossed twice, and the first toss results in heads. What is the probability that both tosses result in heads?

SOLUTION:

Before we condition on the fact that the first toss resulted in heads, the sample space would have been

{*HH, HT, TH,* and *TT*}.

Each of these four possibilities would have probability $1/4$, or 0.25. Thus,

$P\{HH\} = 0.25.$

But once we condition on the fact that the first toss resulted in heads,

$P\{HH \mid \text{heads on the first toss}\} = P\{HH \mid HH \text{ or } HT\}$

$= P\{HH \text{ and } (HH \text{ or } HT)\} / P\{HH \text{ or } HT\},$

since this is the definition of conditional probability. But

$\{HH \text{ and } (HH \text{ or } HT)\} = \{HH\}.$

Thus,

$$\frac{P\{HH \text{ and } (HH \text{ or } HT)\}}{P\{HH \text{ or } HT\}} = \frac{P\{HH\}}{P\{HH \text{ or } HT\}}$$

$$= \frac{0.25}{0.25 + 0.25}$$

$$= \frac{1}{2}$$

$$= 0.5$$

A fair coin is tossed twice, and at least one toss results in heads. What is the probability that both tosses result in heads?

SOLUTION:

Before we condition on the fact that at least one toss resulted in heads, the sample space would have been

$\{HH, HT, TH, \text{and } TT\}$.

Each of these four possibilities would have probability $1/4$, or 0.25. Thus,

$P\{HH\} = 0.25$.

But once we condition on the fact that at least one toss resulted in heads, we find that

$P\{HH \mid \text{at least one heads}\} = P\{HH \mid HH \text{ or } HT \text{ or } TH\}$

$$= \frac{P\{HH \text{ and } (HH \text{ or } HT \text{ or } TH)\}}{P\{HH \text{ or } HT \text{ or } TH\}},$$

since this is the definition of conditional probability. But

$\{HH \text{ and } (HH \text{ or } HT \text{ or } TH)\} = \{HH\}$.

Thus,

$$\frac{P\{HH \text{ and } (HH \text{ or } HT \text{ or } TH)\}}{P\{HH \text{ or } HT \text{ or } TH\}} = \frac{P\{HH\}}{P\{HH \text{ or } HT \text{ or } TH\}}$$

$$= \frac{0.25}{0.25 + 0.25 + 0.25}$$

$$= \frac{1}{3}$$

$$= 0.3333$$

• PROBLEM 6–8

Explain the discrepancy between the answers to Problems 6–6 and 6–7.

SOLUTION:

While it is true that $P\{HH \mid H1\} = P\{HH \mid H2\} = 0.5$, neither of these is the same as $P\{HH \mid$ at least one heads$\}$. The difference is in what is being conditioned on. As a general rule, the more likely the event on which we condition, the less different the conditional and the unconditional probabilities will be. Now $P\{HH\} = 0.25$ is the unconditional probability. Also, $P\{$at least one heads$\} = 0.75$ and $P\{H1\} = 0.5$, so it is not surprising that when we condition on the event $\{$at least one heads$\}$, the conditional probability is closer to the unconditional one than when we condition on the event $\{$heads on the first toss$\}$. In particular,

$$P\{HH \mid \text{at least one heads}\} = 0.3333,$$

which is closer to

$$P\{HH\} = 0.25$$

than is

$$P\{HH \mid H1\} = 0.5.$$

✓ • **PROBLEM 6-9**

Consider playing five-card poker. You draw a total of five cards. Having seen that your first four cards are hearts, what is the probability that the fifth card will also be a heart, giving you a flush?

SOLUTION:

There are 52 cards total and 13 hearts total. Having received four hearts already, there remain $13 - 4 = 9$ hearts and $52 - 4 = 48$ cards. Thus,

$$P\{H5 \mid H1, H2, H3, H4\} = \frac{\#\,\text{hearts left}}{\#\,\text{cards left}}$$

$$= \frac{13 - 4}{52 - 4}$$

$$= \frac{9}{48}$$

$$= 0.1875$$

• PROBLEM 6-10

Consider playing five-card poker. You draw a total of five cards. Having seen that four of your cards are hearts and one is not, you try for a flush by discarding the card that is not a heart and asking for one additional card. What is the probability that the card you are dealt next is a heart?

SOLUTION:

There are 52 cards total and 13 hearts total. Having received four hearts already, there remain $13 - 4 = 9$ hearts. But you were also dealt a card that was not a heart. This card was discarded, and consequently it is not one of the cards which you can be dealt next. Thus, there are $52 - 4 - 1 = 47$ cards remaining. Thus,

$$P\{H \mid \text{four hearts and a non-heart}\} = \frac{\#\text{hearts left}}{\#\text{cards left}}$$

$$= \frac{13 - 4}{52 - 5}$$

$$= \frac{9}{47}$$

$$= 0.1915$$

Your chances are slightly better than they were in Problem 6–9.

• PROBLEM 6-11

What is the probability of being dealt all four aces in the first four cards you are dealt?

SOLUTION:

This probability is

$$P\{A1, A2, A3, A4\}$$

$$= P\{A1\}P\{A2 \mid A1\}P\{A3 \mid A1, A2\}P\{A4 \mid A1, A2, A3\}$$

$$= \left(\frac{4}{52}\right)\left(\frac{3}{51}\right)\left(\frac{2}{50}\right)\left(\frac{1}{49}\right)$$

$$= 0.0000036938$$

An urn contains one black ball, one white ball, and one red ball. If the black ball is drawn, then it is replaced along with one other black ball. If the white ball is drawn, then it is replaced along with two other white balls. If the red ball is drawn, then it is discarded. What is the probability of drawing a red ball on the second draw?

SOLUTION:

We need to address this problem conditional of the color of the ball drawn first. Thus, we write

$$P\{R2\} = P\{R2 \cap (\text{the universal set})\},$$

since any set, when intersected with the universal set, will be the original set. Now

$$P\{R2 \cap (\text{the universal set})\} = P\{R2 \cap (B1 \cup W1 \cup R1)\},$$

since $\{(B1 \cup W1 \cup R1)\}$ is the universal set. That is, the color of the first ball drawn must be red, white, or black, so $\{B1, R1, W1\}$ is a partition of the universal set, and the union of these sets is the universal set. Now

$$P\{R2 \cap (B1 \cup W1 \cup R1)\}$$
$$= P\{(R2 \cap B1) \cup (R2 \cap W1) \cup (R2 \cap R1)\}$$
$$= P\{(B1 \cap R2) \cup (W1 \cap R2) \cup (R1 \cap R2)\}$$
$$= P\{(B1 \cap R2)\} + P\{(W1 \cap R2)\} + P\{(R1 \cap R2)\}$$
$$= P\{B1\}P\{R2 \mid B1\} + P\{W1\}P\{R2 \mid W1\} + P\{R1\}P\{R2 \mid R1\}$$

$$= \left(\frac{1}{3}\right)\left(\frac{1}{4}\right) + \left(\frac{1}{3}\right)\left(\frac{1}{5}\right) + \left(\frac{1}{3}\right)\left(\frac{0}{2}\right)$$

$$= \left(\frac{1}{12}\right) + \left(\frac{1}{15}\right) + 0$$

$$= \left(\frac{5}{60}\right) + \left(\frac{4}{60}\right) + \left(\frac{0}{60}\right)$$

$$= \frac{4+5+0}{60}$$

$$= \frac{9}{60}$$

$$= \frac{3}{20}$$

$$= 0.15$$

For example, notice that $P\{R2 \mid W1\} = \frac{1}{5}$, because if the white ball was picked first, then it is returned along with two other white balls. Thus, there would be one red ball, one black ball, and three white balls, for a total of five balls.

✓ • **PROBLEM 6-13**

Find the probability that a face card is drawn on the first draw and an ace on the second in two consecutive draws, without replacement, from a standard deck of cards.

SOLUTION:

This problem illustrates the notion of conditional probability. The conditional probability of an event, say event B, given the occurrence of a previous event, say event A, is written $P(B \mid A)$. This is the conditional probability of B given A, and is defined to be $\frac{P(AB)}{P(A)}$, where

$P(AB)$ = Probability of the joint occurrence of events A and B.

Let A = event that a face card is drawn on the first draw.

B = event that an ace is drawn on the second draw.

We wish to find the probability of the joint occurrence of these events, $P(AB)$, which is equal to $P(A)\, P(B \mid A)$.

The probability that a face card is drawn on the first draw is

$$\frac{12}{52} = \frac{3}{13}.$$

The probability that an ace is drawn on the second draw given that a face card is drawn on the first is the number of ways an ace can be drawn on the second draw given a face card is drawn on the first divided by the total number of possible outcomes of the second draw, or

$$\frac{4}{51};$$

since there will be only 51 cards left in the deck after the face card is drawn. Thus,

$$P(AB) = \frac{3}{13} \times \frac{4}{51} = \frac{4}{13 \times 17} = \frac{4}{221}.$$

√• PROBLEM 6–14

A survey was made of 100 customers in a department store. Sixty of the 100 indicated that they visited the store because of a newspaper advertisement. The remainder had not seen the ad. A total of 40 customers made purchases; of these customers, 30 had seen the ad. What is the probability that a person who did not see the ad made a purchase? What is the probability that a person who saw the ad made a purchase?

SOLUTION:

In the problem, we are told that only 40 customers made purchases. Of these 40, only 30 had seen the ad. Thus, 10 of 100 customers made purchases without seeing the ad. The probability of selecting such a customer at random is

$$\frac{10}{100} = \frac{1}{10}.$$

Let A represent the event of "a purchase," B the event of "having seen the ad," and $\bar{B}$ the event of "not having seen the ad."

Symbolically, $P(A \cap \overline{B}) = {}^1/_{10}$. We are told that 40 of the customers did not see the ad. Thus,

$$P(\overline{B}) = \frac{40}{100} = \frac{4}{10}.$$

Dividing, we obtain

$$\frac{1/10}{4/10} = \frac{1}{4},$$

and, by definition of conditional probability, $P(A \mid \overline{B}) = {}^1/_4$. Thus, the probability that a customer made a purchase given that they did not see the ad is ${}^1/_4$.

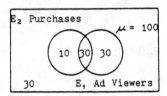

To solve the second problem, note that 30 purchasers saw the ad. The probability that a randomly-selected customer saw the ad *and* made a purchase is

$$\frac{30}{100} = \frac{3}{10}.$$

Since 60 of the 100 customers saw the ad, the probability that a randomly-picked customer saw the ad is

$$\frac{60}{100} = \frac{6}{10}.$$

Dividing, we obtain

$$P(A \mid B) = \frac{P(A \cap B)}{P(B)} = \frac{3/10}{6/10} = \frac{3}{6} = \frac{1}{2}.$$

A coin is tossed three times, and two heads and one tail fall. What is the probability that the first toss was heads?

SOLUTION:

This problem is one of conditional probability. Given two events, p_1 and p_2, the probability that event p_2 will occur on the condition that we have event p_1 is

$$P\left(\frac{P_1}{P_2}\right) = \frac{P(p_1 \text{ and } p_2)}{P(p_1)} = \frac{P(p_1 p_2)}{P(p_1)}.$$

Define

p_1: two heads and one tail fall,

p_2: the first toss is heads.

Then $\quad P(p_1) = \dfrac{\text{number of ways to obtain two heads and one tail}}{\text{number of possibilities resulting from three tosses}}$

$$= \frac{\{H, H, T\}, \{H, T, H\}, \{T, H, H\}}{\{H, H, H\}, \{H, H, T\}, \{H, T, H\}, \{T, T, H\},}$$
$$\{T, H, T\}, \{T, H, H\}, \{T, T, T\}, \{H, T, T\}$$

$$= \frac{3}{8}$$

Also $P(p_1 p_2) = P(\text{two heads and one tail and the first toss is heads})$

$$= \frac{\text{number of ways to obtain } p_1 \text{ and } p_2}{\text{number of possibilities resulting from three tosses}}$$

$$= \frac{\{H, H, T\}, \{H, T, H\}}{8} = \frac{2}{8} = \frac{1}{4},$$

$$P\left(\frac{p_1}{p_2}\right) = \frac{P(p_1 p_2)}{P(p_1)} = \frac{1/4}{3/8} = \frac{2}{3}.$$

✓ • **PROBLEM 6–16**

A coin is tossed three times. Find the probability that all three are heads if it is known that

   (a) the first is heads.

   (b) the first two are heads.

   (c) two of them are heads.

SOLUTION:

This problem is one of conditional probability. If we have two events, A and B, the probability of event A given that event B has occurred is

$$P\left(\frac{A}{B}\right) = \frac{P(AB)}{P(B)}.$$

(a)   We are asked to find the probability that all three tosses are heads given that the first toss is heads. The first event is A and the second is B. Then

$P(AB)$ = probability that all three tosses are heads given that the first toss is heads

$P(AB) = \dfrac{\text{the number of ways that all three tosses are heads}}{\text{given that the first toss is a head}}{\text{the number of possibilities resulting}}{\text{from three tosses}}$

$$= \frac{\{H, H, T\},\{H, T, H\},\{T, H, H\}}{\substack{\{H, H, H\},\{H, H, T\},\{H, T, H\},\{T, T, H\}, \\ \{T, H, T\},\{T, H, H\},\{T, T, T\}}}$$

$$= \frac{1}{8}.$$

$P(B) = P(\text{first toss is a head})$

$$= \frac{\substack{\text{the number of ways to obtain a head} \\ \text{on the first toss}}}{\substack{\text{the number of ways to obtain a head} \\ \text{or a tail on the first of three tosses}}}$$

$$= \frac{\{H, H, H\}, \{H, H, T\}, \{H, T, H\}, \{H, T, T\}}{8}$$

$$= \frac{4}{8} = \frac{1}{2}.$$

$$P\left(\frac{A}{B}\right) = \frac{P(AB)}{P(B)} = \frac{1/8}{1/2} = \frac{1}{8} \times \frac{1}{2} = \frac{1}{4}.$$

To see what happens, in detail, we note that if the first toss is head, the logical possibilities are *HHH, HHT, HTH, HTT*. There is only one of these for which the second and third are heads. Hence,

$$P\left(\frac{A}{B}\right) = \frac{1}{4}.$$

(b) The problem here is to find the probability that all three tosses are heads given that the first two tosses are heads. Then

$P(AB) =$ the probability that all three tosses are heads given that the first two are heads

$$= \frac{\text{the number of ways to obtain three heads given that the first two tosses are heads}}{\text{the number of possibilities resulting from three tosses}}$$

$$= \frac{1}{8}.$$

Now $P(B) =$ the probability that the first two are heads

$$= \frac{\text{the number of ways to obtain heads on the first two tosses}}{\text{the number of possibilities resulting from three tosses}}$$

$$= \frac{\{H, H, H\}, \{H, H, T\}}{8} = \frac{2}{8} = \frac{1}{4}.$$

Finally, $P\left(\frac{A}{B}\right) = \frac{P(AB)}{P(B)} = \frac{1/8}{1/4} = \frac{4}{8} = \frac{1}{2}.$

(c) In this last part, we are asked to find the probability that all three are heads on the condition that any two of them are heads.

Define:

A = the event that all three are heads

B = the event that two of them are heads

$P(AB)$ = the probability that all three tosses are heads knowing that two of them are heads

$$= \frac{1}{8}.$$

Now $P(B)$ = the probability that two tosses are heads

$$= \frac{\text{the number of ways to obtain at least two heads out of three tosses}}{\text{the number of possibilities resulting from three tosses}}$$

$$= \frac{\{H, H, H\}, \{H, H, T\}, \{H, T, H\}, \{T, H, H\}}{8}$$

$$= \frac{4}{8} = \frac{1}{2}.$$

So $\quad P\left(\dfrac{A}{B}\right) = \dfrac{P(AB)}{P(B)} = \dfrac{1/8}{1/2} = \dfrac{2}{8} = \dfrac{1}{4}.$

● PROBLEM 6-17

A committee is composed of six Democrats and five Republicans. Three Democrats are men, and three Republicans are men. If a man is chosen for chairman, what is the probability that he is a Republican?

SOLUTION:

Let E_1 be the event that a man is chosen, and E_2 the event that the man is a Republican.

We are looking for $P(E_2 \mid E_1)$. From the definition of conditional probability

$$P(E_2 \mid E_1) = \frac{P(E_1 \cap E_2)}{P(E_1)}.$$

Of the 11 committee members, three are both male and Republican, hence

$$P(E_1 \cap E_2) = \frac{\text{number of male Republicans}}{\text{number of committee members}} = \frac{3}{11}.$$

Of all the members, six are men; three Democrats and three Republicans, therefore,

$$P(E_1) = \frac{6}{11}.$$

Furthermore,

$$P(E_2 \mid E_1) = \frac{P(E_1 \cap E_2)}{P(E_1)} = \frac{3/11}{6/11} = \frac{3}{6} = \frac{1}{2}.$$

• PROBLEM 6-18

A hand of five cards is to be dealt at random and without replacement from an ordinary deck of 52 playing cards. Find the conditional probability of an all-spade hand given that there will be at least four spades in the hand.

SOLUTION:

Let C_1 be the event that there are at least four spades in the hand and C_2 that there are five. We want $P(C_2 \mid C_1)$.

Now, $C_1 \cap C_2$ is the intersection of the events. Since C_2 is contained in C_1, $C_1 \cap C_2 = C_2$. Therefore,

$$P(C_2 \mid C_1) = \frac{P(C_1 \cap C_2)}{P(C_1)} = \frac{P(C_2)}{P(C_1)};$$

$$P(C_2) = P(\text{five spades}) = \frac{\text{number of possible five spade hands}}{\text{number of total hands}}.$$

The denominator is $\binom{52}{5}$ since we can choose any five out of 52 cards. For the numerator we can have only spades, of which there are 13. We must choose five; hence, we have $\binom{13}{5}$ and

$$P(C_2) = \binom{13}{5} \div \binom{52}{5}.$$

$P(C_1) = P(\text{four or five spades})$

$$= \frac{\text{number of possible four or five spades}}{\text{number of total hands}}.$$

The denominator is still $\binom{52}{5}$. The numerator is $\binom{13}{5}$ + (number of four spade hands). To obtain a hand with four spades, we can choose any four of the 13, $\binom{13}{4}$. We must also choose one of the 39 other cards, $\binom{39}{1}$. By the Fundamental Principle of Counting, the number of four spade hands is $\binom{13}{4}\binom{39}{1}$. Hence, the numerator is $\binom{13}{5} + \binom{13}{4}\binom{39}{1}$ and

$$P(C_1) = \frac{\binom{13}{5} + \binom{13}{4}\binom{39}{1}}{\binom{52}{5}}.$$

Thus,

$$P(C_2 \mid C_1) = \frac{P(C_2)}{P(C_1)} = \frac{\dfrac{\binom{13}{5}}{\binom{52}{5}}}{\dfrac{\binom{13}{5} + \binom{13}{4}\binom{39}{1}}{\binom{52}{5}}}$$

$$= \frac{\binom{13}{5}}{\binom{13}{5} + \binom{13}{4}\binom{39}{1}} = 0.0444.$$

Find the probability of drawing a spade on a draw from a deck of cards and rolling a seven on a roll of a pair of dice.

SOLUTION:

$$\text{Now } P(\text{spade}) = \frac{13}{52}, \text{ and } P(\text{rolling } 7) = \frac{1}{6}.$$

We must now somehow combine these two probabilities to compute the joint probability of the two events. To do this we assume independence. Because drawing a spade is physically unconnected to rolling a seven, the probabilities of these two events should be unrelated. This is reflected in the statement that $P(A \mid B) = P(A)$. By our rule for conditional probability, this implies that $P(AB) = P(B) P(A \mid B) = P(B) \times P(A)$.

Two events with this property are called independent, and in general the probability of the joint occurrence of independent events is equal to the product of the probability that the events occur in isolation.

In our example,

$$P(AB) = P(A) P(B)$$

$$= \frac{13}{52} \times \frac{1}{6}$$

$$= \frac{1}{4} \times \frac{1}{6} = \frac{1}{24}$$

A bowl contains eight chips. Three of the chips are red and the remaining five are blue. If two chips are drawn successively, at random and without replacement, what is the probability that the first chip drawn is red and the second drawn is blue?

SOLUTION:

The probability that the first chip drawn is red is denoted $P(R_1)$. Since sampling is performed at random and without replacement, the classical probability model is applicable. Thus,

$$P(R_1) = \frac{\text{number of red chips}}{\text{total number of chips}}$$

$$= \frac{3}{8}.$$

We now wish to calculate the conditional probability that a blue chip is drawn on the second draw given a red chip was drawn on the first. Denote this by $P(B_2 \mid R_1)$. The second chip is sampled without replacement. Thus,

$$P(B_2 \mid R_1) = \frac{\text{number of blue chips}}{\text{total of chips after one red chip is drawn}}$$

$$= \frac{5}{8-1} = \frac{5}{7}$$

The probability we wish to find is $P(R_1 \text{ and } B_2)$. By the multiplication rule,

$$P(R_1 \text{ and } B_2) = P(R_1)\, P(B_2 \mid R_1)$$

$$= \left(\frac{3}{8}\right)\left(\frac{5}{7}\right) = \frac{15}{56}.$$

Thus the probability that a red chip and then a blue chip are respectively drawn is $^{15}/_{56}$.

$\sqrt{\bullet}$ **PROBLEM 6–21**

Find the probability that three face cards are drawn in three succes-sive draws (without replacement) from a deck of cards.

SOLUTION:

Define Events A, B, and C as follows:

Event A: a face card is drawn on the first draw

Event B: a face card is drawn on the second draw

Event C: a face card is drawn on the third draw

Let ABC = the event that three successive face cards are drawn on three successive draws.

Let $D = AB$ = the event that two successive face cards are drawn on the first two draws. Then $P(ABC) = P(DC) = P(D) \, P(C \mid D)$ by the properties of conditional probability. But

$$P(D) = P(AB) = P(A) \, P(B \mid A).$$

We have shown that $P(ABC) = P(A) \, P(B \mid A) \, P(C \mid AB)$. Now

$$P(A) = \frac{\text{number of face cards}}{\text{total number of cards}} = \frac{12}{52}.$$

$$P(B \mid A) = \frac{\text{number of face cards} - 1}{\text{total number of cards in the deck} - 1} = \frac{11}{51},$$

$$P(C \mid AB) = \frac{12 - 2}{52 - 2} = \frac{10}{50},$$

and $\quad P(ABC) = \dfrac{12}{52} \times \dfrac{11}{51} \times \dfrac{10}{50} = \dfrac{11}{1,105} = 0.010.$

The above is an example of sampling without replacement.

✓ • **PROBLEM 6–22**

> If four cards are drawn at random and without replacement from a deck of 52 playing cards, what is the probability of drawing all four aces?

SOLUTION:

We will do this problem in two ways. First we will use the classical model of probability, which tells us

$$\text{Probability} = \frac{\text{number of favorable outcomes}}{\text{all possible outcomes}},$$

assuming all outcomes are equally likely.

There is one of four aces we can draw first. Once that is done any one of three can be taken second. We have two choices for third and only one for fourth. Using the Fundamental Principle of Counting, we see that there are $4 \times 3 \times 2 \times 1$ possible favorable outcomes. Also, we can choose any one of 52 cards first. There are 51 possibilities for second, etc. The Fundamental Principle of Counting tells us that there are $52 \times 51 \times 50 \times 49$ possible outcomes in the drawing of four cards. Thus,

$$\text{Probability} = \frac{4 \times 3 \times 2 \times 1}{52 \times 51 \times 50 \times 49} = \frac{1}{270,725} = 0.0000037.$$

Our second method of solution involves the multiplication rule and shows some insights into its origin and its relation to conditional probability. The formula for conditional probability

$$P(A \mid B) = \frac{P(A \cap B)}{P(B)}$$

can be extended as follows:

$$P(A \mid B \cap C \cap D) = \frac{P(A \cap B \cap C \cap D)}{P(B \cap C \cap D)};$$

thus $\quad P(A \cap B \cap C \cap D) = P(A \mid B \cap C \cap D) \, P(B \cap C \cap D)$

but $\quad P(B \cap C \cap D) = P(B \mid C \cap D) \, P(C \cap D)$

therefore

$$P(A \cap B \cap C \cap D) = P(A \mid B \cap C \cap D) \, P(B \mid C \cap D) \, P(C \cap D)$$

but $\quad P(C \cap D) = P(C \mid D) \, P(D)$

hence $\quad P(A \cap B \cap C \cap D)$

$$= P(A \mid B \cap C \cap D) \, P(B \mid C \cap D) \, P(C \mid D) \, P(D).$$

Let

$D =$ drawing an ace on the first card

$C =$ drawing an ace on the second card

$B =$ drawing an ace on the third card

$A =$ drawing an ace on the fourth card.

Our conditional probability extension becomes $P(\text{four aces}) = P(\text{on fourth} \mid \text{first three}) \times P(\text{third} \mid \text{first two}) \times P(\text{second} \mid \text{on first}) \times P(\text{on first})$.

Assuming all outcomes are equally likely, $P(\text{on first draw}) = {}^4/_{52}$. There are four ways of success in 52 possibilities. Once we pick an ace there are 51 remaining cards, three of which are aces. This leaves a probability of ${}^3/_{51}$ for picking a second ace once we have chosen the first. Once we have two aces there are 50 remaining cards, two of which are aces; thus, $P(\text{on third} \mid \text{first two}) = {}^2/_{50}$. Similarly, $P(\text{fourth ace} \mid \text{first three}) = {}^1/_{49}$. According to our formula above

$$P(\text{four aces}) = \frac{1}{49} \times \frac{2}{50} \times \frac{3}{51} \times \frac{4}{52} = 0.0000037.$$

 **• PROBLEM 6–23**

Four cards are to be dealt successively, without replacement, from an ordinary deck of playing cards. Find the probability of receiving a spade, a heart, a diamond, and a club, in that order.

SOLUTION:

Let the events of drawing a spade, heart, diamond, or club be denoted by S, H, D, or C. We wish to find $P(S, H, D, C)$, where the order of the symbols indicates the order in which the cards are drawn. This can be rewritten as

$$P(S, H, D, C) = P(S, H, D) \, P(C \mid S, H, D)$$

by the multiplication rule.

Continuing to apply the multiplication rule yields

$$P(S, H, D, C) = P(S) \, P(H \mid S) \, P(D \mid S, H) \, P(C \mid S, H, D).$$

The product of these conditional probabilities will yield the joint probability. Because each card is drawn at random, the classical model is an apt one. Now,

P(drawing a spade on the first draw)

$$= \frac{\text{number of spades}}{\text{number of cards in the deck}}.$$

$$P(S) = \frac{13}{52}.$$

$$P(H \mid S) = \frac{\text{number of hearts}}{\text{number of cards after a spade is drawn}}$$

$$= \frac{13}{52 - 1} = \frac{13}{51}.$$

$$P(D \mid S, H) = \frac{\text{number of diamonds}}{\text{number of cards after a heart and spade are drawn}}$$

$$= \frac{13}{52 - 2} = \frac{13}{50}.$$

$$P(C \mid S, H, D) = \frac{\text{number of clubs}}{\text{number of cards after a heart, spade and diamond are drawn}}$$

$$= \frac{13}{52 - 3} = \frac{13}{49}.$$

Thus, $$P(S, H, D, C) = \frac{13}{52} \times \frac{13}{51} \times \frac{13}{50} \times \frac{13}{49}.$$

An electronic device contains two easily removed subassemblies, *A* and *B*. If the device fails, the probability that it will be necessary to replace *A* is 0.50. Some failures of *A* will damage *B*. If *A* must be replaced, the probability that *B* will also have to be replaced is 0.70. If it is not necessary to replace *A*, the probability that *B* will have to be replaced is only 0.10. In what percentage of all failures will you be required to replace both *A* and *B*?

SOLUTION:

This situation may be pictured by the following tree diagram. Each "branch" of the tree denotes a possible event which might occur if device *A* fails.

If device *A* fails, *A* will be replaced or not replaced. These first two outcomes are represented by the first two branches of the tree diagram. The branches are labeled with their respective probabilities.

Given that *A* is replaced, the behavior of *B* is described by the two secondary branches emanating from the primary branch denoting replacement of *A*.

If *A* is not replaced, *B*'s possible behavior is described by the secondary branches, emanating from the branch denoting non-replacement of *A*. The tree diagram, each branch labeled by its respective probability, is thus:

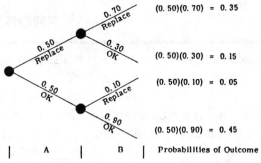

		Probabilities of Outcome

$(0.50)(0.70) = 0.35$

$(0.50)(0.30) = 0.15$

$(0.50)(0.10) = 0.05$

$(0.50)(0.90) = 0.45$

| | A | | B | | Probabilities of Outcome |

The Probability that both A and B must be replaced is 0.35.

The conditional probabilities that B is not replaced given A is replaced, and that B is not replaced given A is not replaced can also be found by $P(B'\,|\,A)$ and $P(B'\,|\,A')$, respectively. Also let

$P(B\,|\,A)$ = probability B is replaced given A is replaced and

$P(B\,|\,A')$ = probability B is replaced given A is not replaced.

If A is replaced, then B can be replaced or not replaced. These events are mutually exclusive and exhaustive; thus

$P(B'\,|\,A) + P(B\,|\,A) = 1$

$P(B\,|\,A) = 0.7$

thus $P(B'\,|\,A) = 1 - P(B\,|\,A) = 1 - 0.7 = 0.3.$

Similarly, if A is not replaced, B may be replaced or not replaced. Given that A is not replaced, these events are mutually exclusive and exhaustive,

thus $P(B'\,|\,A') + P(B\,|\,A') = 1.$

But $P(B\,|\,A') = 0.1;$

thus $P(B'\,|\,A') = 1 - 0.1 = 0.9.$

The problem asks for the probability that both A and B are replaced. Using the multiplication rule,

$P(A$ and B are replaced)

$= P(A$ is replaced$)\, P(B$ is replaced $|\, A$ is replaced$)$

$P(A$ is replaced$)\, P(B\,|\,A)$

$= (0.5)\,(0.7) = 0.35.$

The probability that both A and B are replaced is 0.35.

A bag contains one white ball and two red balls. A ball is drawn at random. If the ball is white then it is put back in the bag along with another white ball. If the ball is red then it is put back in the bag with two extra red balls. Find the probability that the second ball drawn is red. If the second ball drawn is red, what is the probability that the first ball drawn was red?

SOLUTION:

Let W_i or R_i be the event that the ball chosen on the ith draw is white or red, respectively. Assuming that each ball is chosen at random, a tree diagram of this problem can be drawn showing the possible outcomes.

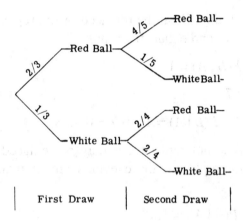

The probabilities of different outcomes are labeled on the "branches" of this tree. These probabilities depend on the number of balls of each color in the bag at the time of the draw. For example, before the first draw there are two red balls and one white ball. Thus, two of three balls on the average will result in a red ball being chosen or $P(R_i) = \frac{2}{3}$.

If a red ball is chosen on the first draw then two more red balls are added to the bag. There are now four red balls and one white ball in the bag, so on the average four of five balls chosen will result in a red ball. Thus, $P(R_2$ given a red ball on the first draw$) = P(R_2 \mid R_1) = \frac{4}{5}$. The other probabilities are computed in a similar fashion.

We wish to compute $P(R_2)$, the probability that the second ball drawn is red. As we see from the tree diagram there are two ways this can happen; thus, $P(R_2) = P(R_1$ and R_2 or W_1 and $R_2)$. The events R_1 and R_2 and W_1 and R_2 are mutually exclusive.

Thus $P(R_2) = P(R_1$ and $R_2) + P(W_1$ and $R_2)$.

But $P(R_1$ and $R_2) = P(R_2 \mid R_1) \times P(R_1)$

and $P(W_1$ and $R_2) = P(R_2 \mid W_1) \times P(W_1)$

by the definition of conditional probability.

From our diagram,

$$P(R_2 \mid R_1) = \frac{4}{5} \text{ and } P(R_2 \mid W_1) = \frac{2}{4}$$

also $P(R_1) = \frac{2}{3}$ and $P(W_1) = \frac{1}{3}$.

Thus, $P(R_2) = P(R_2 \mid R_1) P(R_1) + P(R_2 \mid W_1) P(W_1)$

$$= \frac{4}{5} \times \frac{2}{3} + \frac{2}{4} \times \frac{1}{3}$$

$$= \frac{8}{15} + \frac{1}{6} = \frac{16+5}{30} = \frac{21}{30} = \frac{7}{10}.$$

Now we wish to find $P(R_1 \mid R_2)$.

From the definition of conditional probability

$$P(R_1 \mid R_2) = \frac{P(R_1 \text{ and } R_2)}{P(R_2)}.$$

We also know that $P(R_2) = P(R_2 \mid R_1) P(R_1) + P(R_2 \mid W_1) P(W_1)$ by the previous problem.

We also know that

$$P(R_1 \text{ and } R_2) = P(R_2 \mid R_1) \times P(R_1)$$

Putting these together we see that

$$P(R_1 \mid R_2) = \frac{P(R_1 \mid R_2) P(R_1)}{P(R_1 \mid R_2) P(R_1) + P(R_2 \mid W_1) P(W_1)}$$

$$= \frac{\dfrac{4}{5} \times \dfrac{2}{3}}{\dfrac{4}{5} \times \dfrac{2}{3} + \dfrac{2}{4} \times \dfrac{1}{3}}$$

$$= \frac{\dfrac{8}{15}}{\dfrac{7}{10}} = \frac{10 \times 8}{7 \times 15} = \frac{16}{21}$$

Note that in order to compute these probabilities, we needed to know the number of red and white balls in the bag at the beginning.

✳✳✳✳✳✳

REVIEW OF SIMPSON'S PARADOX

Perhaps the best way to introduce Simpson's paradox is to present an example and solve it. Therefore, we will present an example with three discrete random variables. The joint probability mass function will be provided in the following tables.

Table 1

Hospital 1		Disease		
		Cancer	Cold	Total
	Die	64	4	68
Outcome	Live	16	16	32
	Total	80	20	100

Table 2

Hospital 2	Disease			
		Cancer	Cold	Total
	Die	18	24	42
Outcome	Live	2	56	58
	Total	20	80	100

Table 3

	Hospital			
		Hospital 1	Hospital 2	Total
	Cancer	80	20	100
Disease	Cold	20	80	100
	Total	100	100	200

Table 4

	Hospital			
		Hospital 1	Hospital 2	Total
	Die	68	42	110
Outcome	Live	32	58	90
	Total	100	100	200

Table 5

	Disease			
		Cancer	Cold	Total
	Die	82	28	110
Outcome	Live	18	72	90
	Total	100	100	200

Table 6

Cancer	Hospital		
		Hospital 1	Hospital 2	Total
	Die	64	18	82
Outcome	Live	16	2	18
	Total	80	20	100

Table 7

Cold	Hospital		
		Hospital 1	Hospital 2	Total
	Die	4	24	28
Outcome	Live	16	56	72
	Total	20	80	100

Table 8

Die	Hospital		
		Hospital 1	Hospital 2	Total
	Cancer	64	18	82
Disease	Cold	4	24	28
	Total	68	42	110

Table 9

Live	Hospital		
		Hospital 1	Hospital 2	Total
	Cancer	16	2	18
Disease	Cold	16	56	72
	Total	32	58	90

The nine tables (one table for each of the three pairs of variables, plus six tables to separate the counts based on the levels of the third variable) are an example of Simpson's paradox. To understand this paradox, study the nine tables, and then decide to which of the two hospitals you would prefer to go.

Notice that there is much redundant information provided in these nine tables. For example, the information in Table 1 and Table 2 is equivalent to the information in Table 6 and Table 7, which is also equivalent to the information in Table 8 and Table 9. The information in any of these pairs of tables would be enough to construct Table 3, Table 4, and Table 5 (but the converse of this statement is not true).

If you look closely at Table 4, then you may get the mistaken impression that Hospital 2 is better, because 58 patients out of 100 live in Hospital 2, while only 32 patients out of 100 live in Hospital 1. Certainly a 58% chance of surviving a hospital stay is to be preferred over a 32% chance of surviving a hospital stay!

But now consider the condition for which you went in. The tables indicate that the two hospitals treat both cancer and the common cold (and nothing else, for simplification). In particular, look carefully at Table 6 and Table 7.

Table 6 indicates that of those patients who wish to have their cancer treated, 16 of 80 (20%) survive at Hospital 1, whereas only 2 of 20 (10%) survive at Hospital 2. Clearly, then, there is some indication that Hospital 1 is better than Hospital 2 for treating cancer.

Table 7 indicates that of those patients who wish to have their cold treated, 16 of 20 (80%) survive at Hospital 1, whereas only 56 of 80 (70%) survive at Hospital 2. Clearly, then, there is also some indication that Hospital 1 is better than Hospital 2 for treating the common cold.

It would seem that Hospital 2 is better than Hospital 1 in general, but if you have a cold or cancer then you would do better in Hospital 1. However, these are the only two conditions treated in either hospital! How can this be?

The solution is that Hospital 1 is the better hospital, and this fact is clouded when the tables are aggregated (that is, there is one table that combines data for both cancer patients and patients with the common cold). Much better insight is offered when a separate table is presented for each disease. But why is this material presented in a chapter on conditional probability, in a section on discrete random variables?

We have implicitly defined one hospital to be better than another if it has a higher survival rate. In particular, we compare

$$p_1 = P\{\text{survive at Hospital 1}\}$$

to $\qquad p_2 = P\{\text{survive at Hospital 2}\}.$

We may evaluate these quantities as

$$p_1 = P\{\text{survive at Hospital 1}\}$$

$$= \frac{32}{100}$$

$$= 0.32,$$

since 32 patients survived at Hospital 1 (of the 100 patients treated there), and

$$p_2 = P\{\text{survive at Hospital 2}\}$$

$$= \frac{58}{100}$$

$$= 0.58,$$

since 58 patients survived at Hospital 2 (of the 100 patients treated there).

But now we recognize that neither p_1 nor p_2 is indicative of reality, because we must consider the conditions being treated. Both Hospital 1 and Hospital 2 do better with the common cold than they do with cancer, but for either condition, Hospital 1 does better. Hospital 2 only appears better because it treats proportionally more patients with the common cold, while Hospital 1 treats proportionally more patients with cancer. To reflect this, we must modify our definition of superiority of a hospital.

Let us then refrain from assigning any overall definition of superiority of one hospital over another, but rather let us consider superiority with respect to treating cancer patients and superiority with respect to treating patients with the common cold. Of course, if either hospital is superior for both, then we will declare this to be the overall superior hospital.

What we need now are conditional probabilities, or

$$p_{11} = P\{\text{survive at Hospital 1 given that the patient has cancer}\},$$

$$p_{12} = P\{\text{survive at Hospital 1 given that the patient has a cold}\},$$

$$p_{21} = P\{\text{survive at Hospital 2 given that the patient has cancer}\},$$

and $\quad p_{22} = P\{\text{survive at Hospital 2 given that the patient has a cold}\}.$

With these definitions, Hospital 1 is the better cancer hospital if $p_{11} > p_{21}$, while Hospital 2 is the better cancer hospital if $p_{11} < p_{21}$. They are equivalent cancer hospitals if $p_{11} = p_{21}$.

Likewise, Hospital 1 is the better hospital for treating the common cold if $p_{12} > p_{22}$, while Hospital 2 is the better hospital for treating the common cold if $p_{12} < p_{22}$. They are equivalent hospitals for treating the common cold if $p_{11} = p_{22}$.

The probabilities p_{11}, p_{12}, p_{21}, and p_{22} are all conditional probabilities. For example, p_{11} is the conditional probability of survival given that the patient has cancer. This may be evaluated as

$p_{11} = P\{\text{survive at Hospital 1 given the patient has cancer}\}$

$= P\{\text{survive at Hospital 1} \mid \text{cancer}\}$

$= P\{\text{survive at Hospital 1, cancer}\}/P\{\text{cancer at Hospital 1}\}$

$= \#\{\text{survive at Hospital 1, cancer}\}/\#\{\text{cancer at Hospital 1}\}$

$= \dfrac{16}{80}$

$= \dfrac{1}{5}$

$= 0.20$, or 20%.

✓• PROBLEM 6–26

Evaluate p_{12}, p_{21}, and p_{22} for the example given in the previous section (the hospitals).

SOLUTION:

We reason similarly to the way in which we evaluated p_{11}, and find

$p_{12} = P\{\text{survive at Hospital 1 given the patient has a cold}\}$

$= P\{\text{survive at Hospital 1} \mid \text{cold}\}$

$= P\{\text{survive at Hospital 1, cold}\}/P\{\text{cold at Hospital 1}\}$

$= \#\{\text{survive at Hospital 1, cold}\}/\#\{\text{cold at Hospital 1}\}$

$$= \frac{16}{20}$$

$$= \frac{4}{5}$$

$$= 0.80, \text{ or } 80\%$$

$p_{21} = P\{\text{survive at Hospital 2 given the patient has cancer}\}$

$\quad = P\{\text{survive at Hospital 2 | cancer}\}$

$\quad = P\{\text{survive at Hospital 2, cancer}\}/P\{\text{cancer at Hospital 2}\}$

$\quad = \#\{\text{survive at Hospital 2, cancer}\}/\#\{\text{cancer at Hospital 2}\}$

$$= \frac{2}{20}$$

$$= \frac{1}{10}$$

$$= 0.10, \text{ or } 10\%$$

and $\quad p_{22} = P\{\text{survive at Hospital 2 given the patient has a cold}\}$

$\quad = P\{\text{survive at Hospital 2 | cold}\}$

$\quad = P\{\text{survive at Hospital 2, cold}\}/P\{\text{cold at Hospital 2}\}$

$\quad = \#\{\text{survive at Hospital 2, cold}\}/\#\{\text{cold at Hospital 2}\}$

$$= \frac{56}{80}$$

$$= \frac{7}{10}$$

$$= 0.70, \text{ or } 70\%$$

● PROBLEM 6–27

Could Simpson's paradox occur if there are any zero cell counts?

SOLUTION:

Consider the following example:

Table 1

Hospital 1		Disease		
		Cancer	Cold	Total
	Die	55	0	55
Outcome	Live	10	10	20
	Total	65	10	75

Table 2

Hospital 2		Disease		
		Cancer	Cold	Total
	Die	10	35	45
Outcome	Live	0	55	55
	Total	10	90	100

Table 3

		Hospital		
		Hospital 1	Hospital 2	Total
	Cancer	65	10	75
Disease	Cold	10	90	100
	Total	75	100	175

Table 4

		Hospital		
		Hospital 1	Hospital 2	Total
	Die	55	45	100
Outcome	Live	20	55	75
	Total	75	100	175

Table 5

		Disease		
		Cancer	Cold	Total
	Die	65	35	100
Outcome	Live	10	65	75
	Total	75	100	175

Table 6

Cancer		Hospital		
		Hospital 1	Hospital 2	Total
	Die	55	10	65
Outcome	Live	10	0	10
	Total	65	10	75

Table 7

Cold		Hospital		
		Hospital 1	Hospital 2	Total
	Die	0	35	35
Outcome	Live	10	55	65
	Total	10	90	100

Table 8

Die		Hospital		
		Hospital 1	Hospital 2	Total
	Cancer	55	10	65
Disease	Cold	0	35	35
	Total	55	45	100

Table 9

Live	Hospital			
		Hospital 1	Hospital 2	Total
	Cancer	10	0	10
Disease	Cold	10	55	65
	Total	20	55	75

For the data presented in these nine tables, we may compare the surviving proportions among hospitals to find that

$$P\{\text{survive at Hospital 1}\} = \frac{20}{75}$$

$$= \frac{4}{15}$$

$$= 0.2667,$$

and $P\{\text{survive at Hospital 2}\} = \frac{55}{100}$

$$= 0.55,$$

so it would seem that Hospital 2 is the better hospital. But considering only the cancer patients, we find that

$$P\{\text{survive at Hospital 1 given cancer}\}$$

$$= P\{\text{survive at Hospital 1} \mid \text{cancer}\}$$

$$= \frac{10}{65}$$

$$= \frac{2}{13}$$

$$= 0.1538,$$

while $P\{\text{survive at Hospital 2 given cancer}\}$

$$= P\{\text{survive at Hospital 2} \mid \text{cancer}\}$$

$$= \frac{0}{10}$$

$$= 0.0000,$$

so Hospital 1 is better for treating cancer. Likewise, when considering only patients with the common cold, we find that

$P\{$survive at Hospital 1 given cold$\}$

$= P\{$survive at Hospital 1 | cold$\}$

$$= \frac{10}{10}$$

$$= 1.0000,$$

while $P\{$survive at Hospital 2 given cold$\}$

$= P\{$survive at Hospital 2 | cold$\}$

$$= \frac{55}{90}$$

$$= \frac{11}{18}$$

$$= 0.61111,$$

so it is seen that Hospital 1 is also better for treating the common cold. Thus, we have an example of Simpson's paradox with zero cell counts. Of course, this is not the only such example. In fact, there are infinitely many such examples.

• PROBLEM 6–28

Could Simpson's paradox occur if there are any zero margin totals?

SOLUTION:

We will again use the hospital example to answer this question. To have Simpson's paradox occur with zero margin totals would require that

$P\{$survive at Hospital 1$\} < P\{$survive at Hospital 2$\}$,

$P\{$survive at Hospital 1 | cancer$\} > P\{$survive at Hospital 2 | cancer$\}$,

and $P\{$survive at Hospital 1 | cold$\} > P\{$survive at Hospital 2 | cold$\}$.

There are three possibilities to consider, corresponding to the three types of margin totals. There is one type for each pair of variables (and there are three such pairs).

Suppose that there is a zero margin for disease by hospital. Then there would be four possibilities. These are:

1. Nobody at Hospital 1 has cancer.

2. Nobody at Hospital 1 has a cold.

3. Nobody at Hospital 2 has cancer.

4. Nobody at Hospital 2 has a cold.

Under any of these conditions, at least one of the probabilities required for Simpson's paradox could not be calculated. For example, if nobody at Hospital 1 has cancer, then it is impossible to assess the survival probability of cancer patients at Hospital 1, and, consequently, it is impossible to determine if this probability is higher or lower than the corresponding probability for Hospital 2. Then Simpson's paradox cannot occur.

Suppose that there is a zero margin for disease by outcome. Then there would be four possibilities. These are:

1. Nobody with cancer dies.

2. Nobody with cancer lives.

3. Nobody with a cold dies.

4. Nobody with a cold lives.

Under any of these conditions, at least one of the probabilities required for Simpson's paradox would be zero. For example, if nobody with cancer lives, then this would necessarily be true at both Hospital 1 and at Hospital 2, so the survival probability of cancer patients would be equal at the two hospitals and, therefore, Simpson's paradox could not occur.

Finally, suppose that there is a zero margin for hospital by outcome. Then there would be four possibilities. These are:

1. Nobody at Hospital 1 dies.

2. Nobody at Hospital 1 lives.

3. Nobody at Hospital 2 dies.

4. Nobody at Hospital 2 lives.

Under any of these conditions, at least one of the probabilities required for Simpson's paradox would be zero. For example, if nobody at Hospital 1 dies, then this would necessarily be true for both cancer patients and patients with the common cold. In this case, Hospital 1 would necessarily have a higher survival probability than Hospital 2, both overall and for cancer patients and patients with the common cold. Again, Simpson's paradox could not occur. Thus, Simpson's paradox cannot occur with zero margins.

• PROBLEM 6-29

Suppose that X, the height of the mother, has a continuous uniform distribution with range [59, 71] inches and Y, the height of the father, has a continuous uniform distribution with range [65, 77] inches. Let $M = (X + Y)/2$ be the mean height of the parents. Conditional on X and Y, Z, the height of a child, has a continuous uniform distribution with range [$M - 6$, $M + 6$] inches. What is the conditional cumulative distribution function of Z conditional on X and Y?

SOLUTION:

We need to find $P\{Z < k \mid X, Y\}$. Now the range of Z is given to be [$M - 6$, $M + 6$] inches, so we know that

$$P\{Z < k \mid X, Y\} = 0 \text{ for } k \leq M - 6,$$

and $\quad P\{Z < k \mid X, Y\} = 1 \text{ for } k \geq M + 6.$

For $M - 6 < k < M + 6$, we compute

$$P\{Z < k \mid X, Y\} = [k - (M - 6)] / [(M + 6) - (M - 6)]$$

$$= (k + 6 - M) / [6 + 6]$$

$$= (k + 6 - M) / [12],$$

by virtue of the formula for the cumulative distribution function of the continuous uniform random variable.

• PROBLEM 6-30

Let X and Y be independent and identically distributed, each with a continuous uniform distribution and range [0, 1]. Let $Z = XY$. What is the range of Z? What is the cumulative distribution function of Z?

SOLUTION:

Since Z is a monotonically increasing function of X when Y is held constant, and Z is a monotonically increasing function of Y when X is held constant, Z will take on its maximum value when both X and Y take on their maximum values. Likewise, Z will take on its minimum value when X and Y take on their minimum values. Therefore, the lower limit of the range of Z is $(0) (0) = 0$, and the upper limit of the range of Z is $(1) (1) = 1$. The range of Z is [0, 1].

Because the range of Z is [0, 1], we know that

$$P\{Z < k\} = 0 \text{ for } k < 0,$$

and $P\{Z < k\} = 1 \text{ for } k > 1.$

Now for k in the range [0, 1], we compute

$$P\{Z < k\} = P\{XY < k\}.$$

A graph facilitates the solution to this problem. Draw the coordinate axes, and label them X and Y. The range of the joint probability density function of X and Y is the unit square (that is, X between 0 and 1 and Y between 0 and 1). The task remains to draw the area corresponding to $XY < k$.

Plot the curve $Y = k / X$. This curve will cut through the unit square, creating a wedge in the upper right-hand corner. We observe that $XY < k$ under and left of this curve. We need the area of the region under and left of this curve.

It may seem that

$$P\{XY < k\} = I_{X = 0 \text{ to } 1} I_{Y = 0 \text{ to } k/X} 1 \, dy \, dx,$$

since this is the region whose area we want and the joint probability density function is one divided by the area, or just one. But performing this integration will result in an infinite probability. The problem is that the range of Y is not from zero to k / X, but rather from zero to the minimum of k / X and one. That is, for small X (for $X < k$), k / X is greater than one, but Y is still bounded by one. Thus,

$$P\{XY < k\} = I_{X=0 \text{ to } k} I_{Y=0 \text{ to } 1} \, 1 \, dy \, dx + I_{x=k \text{ to } 1} I_{Y=0 \text{ to } k/X} \, 1 \, dy \, dx$$

$$= I_{x=0 \text{ to } k} [Y]_{0 \text{ to } 1} \, dx + I_{x=k \text{ to } 1} [Y]_{0 \text{ to } k/X} \, dx$$

$$= I_{X=0 \text{ to } k} [1 - 0] \, dx + I_{X=k \text{ to } 1} [k/X - 0] \, dx$$

$$= I_{x=0 \text{ to } k} [1] \, dx + I_{x=k \text{ to } 1} [k/X] \, dx$$

$$= [X]_{0 \text{ to } k} + (k)I_{X=k \text{ to } 1} [1/X] \, dx$$

$$= [k - 0] + (k)[\ln(X)]_{k \text{ to } 1}$$

$$= k + (k)[\ln(1) - \ln(k)]$$

$$= k + (k)[0 - \ln(k)]$$

$$= k - (k)\ln(k)$$

• PROBLEM 6–31

Let X, Y, and Z be as in Problem 6–30. What is the probability density function of Z?

SOLUTION:

Because the range of Z is $[0, 1]$, we know that

$$f_Z(k) = 0 \text{ for } k < 0,$$

and $\quad f_Z(k) = 0 \text{ for } k > 1.$

Now for k in the range $[0, 1]$, we compute

$$f_Z(k) = d/dk \, P\{Z < k\}$$

$$= d/dk \, [k - (k)\ln(k)]$$

$$= 1 - [(k/k) + \ln(k)]$$

$$= - \ln(k)$$

$$= \ln(1/k)$$

This is the probability density function of Z. It is non-negative on the range zero to one, and if this function is integrated from zero to one, then the integral will be one, showing this to be a proper probability density function.

• **PROBLEM 6–32**

Suppose the random vector (X, Y) is distributed with probability density

$$f(x, y) = \begin{cases} & 0 < x < 1 \\ x + y & 0 < y < 1 \\ 0 & \text{otherwise} \end{cases}.$$

Find $E[XY]$, $E[X + Y]$, and $E[X]$.

SOLUTION:

By definition,

$$E[g(x, y) = \iint_{(x,y)} g(x, y) f(x, y) \, dx \, dy.$$

Thus, if $g(x, y) = xy$, we have:

$$E[xy] = \int_0^1 \int_0^1 xy(x + y) \, dx \, dy$$

$$= \int_0^1 \left[\int_0^1 (x^2 y + xy^2) \, dx \right] dy$$

$$= \int_0^1 \left[\frac{x^3 y}{3} + \frac{x^2 y^2}{2} \right]_0^1 dy$$

$$= \int_0^1 \left(\frac{y}{3} + \frac{y^2}{2} \right) dy = \left[\frac{y^2}{6} + \frac{y^3}{6} \right]_0^1 = \frac{2}{6} = \frac{1}{3}$$

Also,

$$E[X + Y] = \int_0^1 \int_0^1 (x + y)^2 \, dx \, dy$$

$$= \int_0^1 \int_0^1 (x^2 + 2x + y)^2 \, dx \, dy$$

$$= \int_0^1 \left[\frac{x^3}{3} + \frac{2x^2 y}{2} + y^2 x \right]_0^1 dy$$

$$= \int_0^1 \left(\frac{1}{3} + y + y^2 \right) dy$$

$$= \left[\frac{y}{3} + \frac{y^2}{2} + \frac{y^3}{3} \right]_0^1 = \frac{1}{3} + \frac{1}{2} + \frac{1}{3} = \frac{7}{6},$$

$$E[X] = \int_0^1 \int_0^1 x(x+y) \, dx \, dy$$

$$= \int_0^1 \left[\frac{x^3}{3} + \frac{x^2 y}{2} \right]_0^1 dy$$

$$= \int_0^1 \left(\frac{1}{3} + \frac{y}{2} \right) dy = \left[\frac{y}{3} + \frac{y^2}{3} \right]_0^1$$

$$= \frac{1}{3} + \frac{1}{4} = \frac{7}{12}$$

• PROBLEM 6-33

Let the three-dimensional random variable (X_1, X_2, X_3) have the density function $f(x_1, x_2, x_3) = 8(x_1 x_2 x_3)$ for $0 < x_1 < 1, 0 < x_2 < 1, 0 < x_3 < 1$.

Find $E[3X_1 + 2X_2 + 6X_3]$, $E[X_1 X_2 X_3]$, and $E[X_1 X_2]$.

SOLUTION:

We know that $E[g(x_1, x_2, x_3)] =$

$$\iiint_{\text{all } x_i} [g(x_1, x_2, x_3) f(x_1, x_2, x_3)] \, dx_1 \, dx_2 \, dx_3.$$

Thus when

$$g(x_1, x_2, x_3) = 3x_1 + 2x_2 + 6x_3, \quad E[3x_1 + 2x_2 + 6x_3]$$

$$= \int_0^1 \int_0^1 \int_0^1 (3x_1 + 2x_2 + 6x_3) \, 8x_1 x_2 x_3 \, dx_1 \, dx_2 \, dx_3$$

$$= 8 \int_0^1 \int_0^1 x_2 x_3 \left[\int_0^1 (3x_1^2 + 2x_1 x_2 + 6x_1 x_3 \, dx_1 \right] dx_2 \, dx_3$$

$$= 8 \int_0^1 \int_0^1 x_2 x_3 \left[\frac{3x_1^3}{3} + \frac{2x_1^2 x_2}{2} + \frac{6x_1^2 x_3}{2} \right] dx_2 \, dx_3$$

$$= 8 \int_0^1 \int_0^1 x_2 x_3 \left[1 + x_2 + 3x_3 \right] dx_2 \, dx_3$$

$$= 8 \int_0^1 x_3 \left[\int_0^1 (1 + x_2 + 3x_3) \, x_2 \, dx_2 \right] dx_3$$

$$= \int_0^1 x \left| \frac{x_2^2}{2} + \frac{x_2^3}{3} + \frac{3x_2^2 x_3}{2} \right|_0^1 dx$$

$$= \int_0^1 x \left[\frac{1}{2} + \frac{1}{3} + \frac{3x_3}{2} \right] dx$$

$$= \int_0^1 \left[\frac{5}{6} + \frac{3x_3}{2} \right] x_3 \, dx_3 = 8 \left[\frac{5}{12} x_3^3 + \frac{x_3^3}{2} \right]_0^1$$

$$= 8 \left(\frac{5}{12} + \frac{1}{2} \right) = 8 \left(\frac{11}{12} \right) = 2 \left(\frac{11}{3} \right)$$

$$= \frac{22}{3}.$$

Also, $E[X_1 X_2 X_3] = \int_0^1 \int_0^1 \int_0^1 (x_1 x_2 x_3) \, 8x_1 x_2 x_3 \, [dx_1 \, dx_2 \, dx_3]$

$$= 8 \int_0^1 \int_0^1 \int_0^1 x_1^2 x_2^2 x_3^2 \, dx_1 \, dx_2 \, dx_3$$

$$= 8 \int_0^1 \int_0^1 x_2^2 x_3^2 \left[\int_0^1 x_1^2 \, dx_1 \right] dx_2 \, dx_3$$

$$= 8 \int_0^1 \int_0^1 x_2^2 x_3^2 \left[\frac{x_1^3}{2} \right]_0^1 dx_2 \, dx_3$$

$$= \frac{8}{3} \int_0^1 \int_0^1 x_2^2 x_3^2 \, dx_2 \, dx_3 = \frac{8}{3} \int_0^1 x_3^2 \left[\frac{x_2^2}{3} \right]_0^1 dx_3$$

$$= \frac{8}{9} \int_0^1 x_3^2 \, dx_3 = \frac{8}{27},$$

and $\qquad E[X_1 X_2] = \int_0^1 \int_0^1 \int_0^1 x_1 x_2 \, 8x_1 x_2 x_3 \, dx_1 \, dx_2 \, dx_3$

$$= 8 \int_0^1 \int_0^1 x_2^2 \, x_3 \left[\int_0^1 x_1^2 \, dx_1 \right] dx_2 \, dx_3$$

$$= \frac{8}{3} \int_0^1 x_3 \left[\int_0^1 x_1{}^2 \, dx_2 \right] dx_3$$

$$= \frac{8}{9} \int_0^1 x_3 \, dx_3 = \frac{8}{9} \left[\frac{x_3{}^2}{2} \right]_0^1$$

$$= \frac{8}{9} \times \frac{1}{2} = \frac{4}{9}$$

• **PROBLEM 6-34**

Compute the conditional distribution of Y given X if X and Y are jointly distributed with density

$$f(x, y) = \begin{cases} x + y & 0 < x < 1 \\ & 0 < y < 1 \\ 0 & \text{otherwise} \end{cases}.$$

What is the conditional expectation of Y?

SOLUTION:

The conditional distribution of Y given X is defined by analogy with conditional probability to be:

$$f(y \mid x) = \frac{f(x, y)}{f(x)},$$

where $f(x, y)$ is the joint density of x and y and $f(x)$ is the marginal distribution of x.

In our example,

$$f(x) = \int_0^1 f(x, y) \, dy$$

$$= \int_0^1 (x + y) \, dy = \left[xy + \frac{y^2}{2} \right]_0^1$$

$$= x + \frac{1}{2}, \ 0 < x < 1.$$

Thus $f(y \mid x) = \dfrac{f(x, y)}{f(x)} = \dfrac{x + y}{x + \dfrac{1}{2}} \quad \begin{matrix} 0 < y < 1 \\ 0 < x < 1 \end{matrix}$.

To see that $f(y \mid x)$ is a proper density function,

$$\int_0^1 f(x, y) \, dy = \int_0^1 \frac{x + y}{x + \dfrac{1}{2}} \, dy = \left(\frac{1}{x + \dfrac{1}{2}} \right) \int_0^1 (x + y) \, dy$$

$$= \left(\frac{1}{x + \dfrac{1}{2}} \right) \left[xy + \frac{y^2}{2} \right]_0^1 = \frac{x + \dfrac{1}{2}}{x + \dfrac{1}{2}} = 1$$

The conditional expectation of Y given X is the expectation of y against the conditional density $f(y \mid x)$. Thus,

$$E(Y \mid X = x) = \int_{\text{all } y} y \, f(y \mid X) \, dy$$

For our example,

$$E(Y \mid X = x) = \int_0^1 y \left(\frac{x + y}{x + \dfrac{1}{2}} \right) dy = \left(\frac{1}{x + \dfrac{1}{2}} \right) \int_0^1 (xy + y^2) \, dy$$

$$= \frac{1}{x + \dfrac{1}{2}} \left[\frac{xy^2}{2} + \frac{y^3}{3} \right]_0^1 = \frac{\dfrac{x}{2} + \dfrac{1}{3}}{x + \dfrac{1}{2}}$$

$$= \frac{3x + 2}{3(2x + 1)}, \quad 0 < x < 1$$

• **PROBLEM 6-35**

Conditional expectations may be used to find unconditional expectations. Show that

$$E\{E[Y \mid X = x]\} = E[Y].$$

SOLUTION:

Let $f(x)$, $f(y)$, and $f(x, y)$ be the marginal distribution of X, the marginal distribution of Y, and the joint density of X and Y, respectively. Since $E(Y \mid X = x)$ is in general a function of x, say $E(Y \mid X = x) = h(x)$, then $E(Y \mid X = x) = E[h(x)]$. But the expected value of any function of a random variable is that function integrated against the density of X. Thus,

$$E(Y \mid X = x) = E[h(x)] = \int_{-\infty}^{\infty} h(x) f(x) \, dx,$$

but $\quad E(Y \mid X = x) = h(x) = \int_{-\infty}^{\infty} y f(y \mid x) \, dy.$

Thus,

$$E(Y \mid X = x) = \int_{-\infty}^{\infty} \left[\int_{-\infty}^{\infty} y f(y \mid x) \, dy \right] f(x) \, dx$$

$$= \int_{-\infty}^{\infty} \int_{-\infty}^{\infty} y f(y \mid x) f(x) \, dy \, dx.$$

Letting $\quad f(y \mid x) = \dfrac{f(x, y)}{f(x)},$

$$E(Y \mid X = x) = f(x) \, dy \, dx$$

$$= \int_{-\infty}^{\infty} \int_{-\infty}^{\infty} y f(x, y) \, dy \, dx$$

$$= \int_{-\infty}^{\infty} y \left[\int_{-\infty}^{\infty} yf(x, y) \, dx \right] dy,$$

and $\quad \int_{-\infty}^{\infty} f(x, y) \, dx = f(y).$

Thus,

$$E[Y \mid X = x)] = \int_{-\infty}^{\infty} y f(y) \, dy = E[Y].$$

******

REVIEW OF MIXED RANDOM VARIABLES

Mixed random variables have a discrete component and a continuous component. Examples of mixed random variables include survival times with fixed right-censoring time, tumor weight when it is possible that there are no tumors (and consequently the weight would be zero), and incomes, when some people are out of work.

Sometimes mixed random variables refer to a set of random variables, some of which are continuous and some of which are discrete. For example, consider again heights of children as in Problem 6–31. These heights should be affected not only by the heights of the parents (which are continuous random variables), but also by the gender of the child (which is a discrete random variable).

Suppose that X is a mother's height, Y is a father's height, Z is a child's ultimate height (as an adult), and W is defined as

$W = 1$ if the child is a boy

and $\quad W = -1$ if the child is a girl.

Let $M = (X + Y)/2$. Suppose that, conditional on known values of W, X, and Y, Z has a continuous uniform distribution with range $[M - 6 + 3W, M + 6 + 3W]$. That is, for boys, the range is

$$[M - 6 + 3, M + 6 + 3] = [M - 3, M + 9],$$

and for girls, the range is

$$[M - 6 - 3, M + 6 - 3] = [M - 9, M + 3].$$

This is a conditional distribution, and we are conditioning on both continuous random variables (the heights of the parents) and a discrete random variable (the gender of the child). This allows for several different questions to be asked and answered.

For example, what is the probability that a male grows to be taller than his mother given that his father is a foot taller than his mother?

Let the mother's height be X. Since the father is a foot (12 inches) taller than the mother, the father's height is $X + 12$. Then

$$M = \frac{X + X + 12}{2}$$

$$= \frac{2X + 12}{2}$$

$$= X + 6$$

We know that the child has a height which has a continuous uniform distribution with range

$$[M - 3, M + 9],$$

or $$[(X + 6) - 3, (X + 6) + 9],$$

which is

$$[X + 3, X + 15],$$

because the child is a boy. Then the probability that the boy has a height which is larger than the height of his mother is

$$P\{Z > X\},$$

where Z has a continuous uniform random variable on the range $[X + 3, X + 15]$. The entire range is larger than X, so $P\{Z > X\} = 1$.

$\sqrt{}$ • **PROBLEM 6-36**

Suppose that X is a mother's height, Y is a father's height, Z is a child's ultimate height (as an adult), and W is defined as

$W = 1$ if the child is a boy

and $W = -1$ if the child is a girl.

Let $M = (X + Y)/2$. Suppose that, conditional on known values of W, X, and Y, Z has a continuous uniform distribution with range $[M - 6 + 3W, M + 6 + 3W]$. That is, for boys the range is

$$[M - 6 + 3, M + 6 + 3] = [M - 3, M + 9],$$

and for girls, the range is

$$[M - 6 - 3, M + 6 - 3] = [M - 9, M + 3].$$

What is the probability that a girl will be taller than either of her parents if the two parents are the same height?

SOLUTION:

Here $X = Y$, and we wish to find $P\{Z > X\}$. Now

$$M = \frac{X+Y}{2}$$

$$= \frac{X+X}{2}$$

$$= \frac{2X}{2}$$

$$= X,$$

and the height of the child follows a continuous uniform distribution with range $[M-9, M+3]$, because the child is a girl. Since $M = X$, this range is

$$[X-9, X+3].$$

Now

$$P\{Z > X\} = \frac{(X+3)-X}{(X+3)-(X-9)}$$

$$= \frac{3}{9+3}$$

$$= \frac{3}{12}$$

$$= \frac{1}{4}$$

$$= 0.25$$

• **PROBLEM 6–37**

Let X, Y, Z, and W be as in Problem 6–36. Suppose also that a boy is as likely as a girl. What is the probability that a child will be taller than either parent if the father is six inches taller than the mother?

SOLUTION:

Here $Y = X + 6$, and we wish to find $P\{Z > Y \mid Y = X + 6\}$. Now

$$M = \frac{X+Y}{2}$$

$$= \frac{X+(X+6)}{2}$$

$$= \frac{2X+6}{2}$$

$$= X + 3$$

With probability 0.5, the child will be a boy and the height of the child will follow a continuous uniform distribution with range

$$[M - 3, M + 9],$$

or $\quad [(X + 3) - 3, (X + 3) + 9],$

or $\quad [X, X + 12].$

With probability 0.5, the child will be a girl and the height of the child will follow a continuous uniform distribution with range

$$[M - 9, M + 3],$$

or $\quad [(X + 3) - 9, (X + 3) + 3],$

or $\quad [X - 6, X + 6].$

Then

$$P\{Z > Y \mid Y = X + 6\} = E[P\{Z > Y \mid Y = X + 6\} \mid W]$$

$$= P\{W = 1\} \, P\{Z > Y \mid Y = X + 6, \, W = 1\}$$

$$+ P\{W = -1\} \, P\{Z > Y \mid Y = X + 6, \, W = -1\}$$

$$= (0.5) \, P\{Z > Y \mid Z \text{ is uniform on } [X, X + 12]\}$$

$$+ (0.5) \, P\{Z > Y \mid Z \text{ is uniform on } [X - 6, X + 6]\}$$

$$= (0.5) \, P\{Z > Y \mid Z \text{ is uniform on } [Y - 6, Y + 6]\}$$

$$+ (0.5) \, P\{Z > Y \mid Z \text{ is uniform on } [Y - 12, Y]\}$$

$$= (0.5) \, [(Y + 6) - Y]/[(Y + 6) - (Y - 6)]$$

$$+ (0.5) \, [Y - Y]/[Y - (Y - 12)]$$

$$= (0.5) \, [6]/[12] + (0.5) \, [0]/[12]$$

$$= (0.5) \, (0.5) + (0.5) \, (0)$$

$$= (0.25) + (0)$$

$$= 0.25$$

Let X, Y, Z, and W be as in Problem 6–36. Suppose also that a girl is three times as likely as a boy. What is the probability that a child will be taller than the mother if the father is four inches taller than the mother?

SOLUTION:

Here $Y = X + 4$, and we wish to find $P\{Z > X \mid Y = X + 4\}$. Now

$$M = \frac{X + Y}{2}$$

$$= \frac{X + (X + 4)}{2}$$

$$= \frac{2X + 4}{2}$$

$$= X + 2$$

Since a girl is three times as likely as a boy, we solve for the probability of each by letting p be the probability of a boy. Then the probability of a girl is $3p$, and by the law of total probability,

$$p + 3p = 1,$$

or $$4p = 1,$$

so $$p = \frac{1}{4}$$

$$= 0.25.$$

Thus, the probability of a boy is $p = 0.25$, and the probability of a girl is $3p = (3)(0.25) = 0.75$. With probability 0.25, the child is a boy and the height of this child will follow a continuous uniform distribution with range

[$M - 3, M + 9$],

or   [$(X + 2) - 3, (X + 2) + 9$],

or   [$X - 1, X + 11$].

   With probability 0.75, the child will be a girl and the height of the child will follow a continuous uniform distribution with range

[$M - 9, M + 3$],

or   [$(X + 2) - 9, (X + 2) + 3$],

or   [$X - 7, X + 5$].

   Then

$$P\{Z > X \mid Y = X + 4\} = E[P\{Z > X \mid Y = X + 4\} \mid W]$$

$$= P\{W = 1\} \, P\{Z > X \mid Y = X + 4, \, W = 1\}$$

$$+ P\{W = -1\} \, P\{Z > X \mid Y = X + 4, \, W = -1\}$$

$$= (0.25) \, P\{Z > X \mid Z \text{ is uniform on } [X - 1, X + 11]\}$$

$$+ (0.75) \, P\{Z > X \mid Z \text{ is uniform on } [X - 7, X + 5]\}$$

$$= (0.25) \, [(X + 11) - X]/[(X + 11) - (X - 1)]$$

$$+ (0.75) \, [(X + 5) - X]/[(X + 5) - (X - 7)]$$

$$= (0.25) \, [11]/[12] + (0.75) \, [5]/[12]$$

$$= \left(\frac{1}{4}\right)\left(\frac{11}{12}\right) + \left(\frac{3}{4}\right)\left(\frac{5}{12}\right)$$

$$= \left(\frac{11}{48}\right) + \left(\frac{15}{48}\right)$$

$$= \frac{26}{48}$$

$$= \frac{13}{24}$$

$$= 0.5417$$

   Sometimes there are special difficulties presented by conditional probabilities when the random variables involved are continuous. If you will recall the definition of conditional probability, then you will find a ratio whose denominator is also a probability. That is,

$P\{A \mid B\} = P\{AB\}/P\{B\}.$

If X and Y are continuous random variables and A is an event of the type

$A = \{Y > k\}$

and B is an event of the type

$B = \{X = c\},$

then we find that when we use this definition, we run into trouble. That is,

$$P\{A \mid B\} = P\{Y > k \mid X = c\}$$

$$= \frac{P\{Y > k, X = c\}}{P\{X = c\}}$$

$$= \frac{0}{0}$$

This, of course, is undefined. It would appear that we cannot condition on events of probability zero. Yet this is exactly what is done in the standard linear regression analysis. In particular, it is postulated that the distribution of Y conditional on $X = x$ has a normal distribution with mean $a + bx$ and variance S^2. Typically, the goal is to infer some properties of a and b given some sample data pairs (X, Y).

The trick is to replace the probability with the value of the probability density function. In the case of X and Y, each with continuous distributions, it is true that $P\{X = c\} = 0$, because the line corresponding to $X = c$ in the X - Y plane has zero area. But if we restrict attention to this line, then the reduced sample space has only one dimension, instead of the two dimensions of the original sample space, and consequently we may speak of lengths rather than areas.

As a more concrete example, suppose that X and Y have a joint probability density function which is uniform over the unit square. That is, X and Y are independent and identically distributed as continuous uniform random variables each with range $[0, 1]$.

Now consider $P\{Y > 0.5 \mid X = 0.2\}$. The standard definition would be

$$P\{Y > 0.5 \mid X = 0.2\} = P\{Y > 0.5, X = 0.2\}/P\{X = 0.2\}$$

$$= \frac{0}{0},$$

which is undefined. But the density may be used. In this case, the joint density is one everywhere, as is the marginal density of both X and Y. In essence, the one cancels out, and we are left with

$$P\{Y>0.5 \mid X=0.2\} = P\{Y>0.5\}$$

$$= \frac{1-0.5}{1-0}$$

$$= \frac{0.5}{1}$$

$$= 0.5$$

Another way of looking at this is to consider only the line $X = 0.2$ as the reduced sample space. Now what proportion of this line is the segment $Y > 0.5$? Since this segment is half the length of the entire segment $X = 0.2$ for $0 < Y < 1$, and since the joint probability density function is constant on this line, it is clear that $P\{Y>0.5 \mid X=0.2\} = 0.5$.

● **PROBLEM 6–39**

Suppose X has a continuous uniform distribution with range [0, 1] and that, conditional on $X = x$, Y has a continuous uniform distribution with range [0, x]. What is $P\{Y<0.4 \mid X=0.3\}$?

SOLUTION:

The standard definition would again lead to the indeterminate form 0/0, but we know that Y has a continuous uniform distribution with range [0, x] or, in this case, [0, 0.3]. Therefore, we may evaluate $P\{Y<0.4 \mid X = 0.3\}$ as

$$P\{Y<0.4 \mid X=0.3\} = 1.$$

● **PROBLEM 6–40**

Suppose X has a continuous uniform distribution with range [0, 1] and that, conditional on $X = x$, Y has a continuous uniform distribution with range [0, x]. What is $P\{Y<0.3 \mid X=0.4\}$?

SOLUTION:

The standard definition would again lead to the indeterminate form 0/0, but we know that Y has a continuous uniform distribution with range $[0, x]$ or, in this case, $[0, 0.4]$. Therefore, we may evaluate $P\{Y < 0.3 \mid X = 0.4\}$ as

$$P\{Y < 0.3 \mid X = 0.4\} = \frac{0.3 - 0}{0.4 - 0}$$

$$= \frac{0.3}{0.4}$$

$$= \frac{3}{4}$$

$$= 0.75$$

• PROBLEM 6–41

Suppose X has a continuous uniform distribution with range $[0, 1]$ and that, conditional on $X = x$, Y has a continuous uniform distribution with range $[0, x]$. What is $P\{Y < 0.3 \mid X = 0.6\}$?

SOLUTION:

The standard definition would again lead to the indeterminate form 0/0, but we know that Y has a continuous uniform distribution with range $[0, x]$ or, in this case, $[0, 0.6]$. Therefore, we may evaluate $P\{Y < 0.3 \mid X = 0.6\}$ as

$$P\{Y < 0.3 \mid X = 0.6\} = \frac{0.3 - 0}{0.6 - 0}$$

$$= \frac{0.3}{0.6}$$

$$= \frac{3}{6}$$

$$= 0.5$$

Bayes theorem is one of the most useful theorems both for probability and for statistics. This theorem allows for the calculation of $P\{B \mid A\}$ given $P\{A \mid B\}$, $P\{A\}$, and $P\{B\}$. In particular, consider the formula for conditional probability. We know that

$$P\{A \mid B\} = \frac{P\{AB\}}{P\{B\}},$$

and $$P\{B \mid A\} = \frac{P\{BA\}}{P\{A\}}$$

$$= \frac{P\{AB\}}{P\{A\}}.$$

We may also write, then,

$$P\{AB\} = P\{A\}P\{B \mid A\}$$

and $$P\{AB\} = P\{B\}P\{A \mid B\}.$$

If we equate these two, we obtain

$$P\{A\}P\{B \mid A\} = P\{B\}P\{A \mid B\},$$

or $$P\{B \mid A\} = P\{B\}P\{A \mid B\}/P\{A\}.$$

An example should help to clarify the usefulness of this theorem. Suppose that 400 people are surveyed and classified by both gender (M or F) and blood type (A, B, AB, or O). Suppose further that

$$P\{M\} = 0.5,$$
$$P\{F\} = 0.5,$$
$$P\{A\} = 0.25,$$
$$P\{B\} = 0.25,$$
$$P\{AB\} = 0.25,$$
$$P\{O\} = 0.25,$$
$$P\{A \mid M\} = 0.30,$$
$$P\{B \mid M\} = 0.20,$$
$$P\{AB \mid M\} = 0.40,$$

and $$P\{O \mid M\} = 0.10.$$

Now some blood is tested and found to be of Type AB. It is not known from whom this blood was drawn, but the question is how likely it is that this unknown person is a male. We may use Bayes theorem to solve this problem. The first step is to create a table.

		Gender		
		F	M	Total
	A	40	60	100
	B	60	40	100
Blood Type	AB	20	80	100
	O	80	20	100
	Total	200	200	400

The table can be filled in from the information provided. For example, we know that males and females occur in equal proportions, so half are males and half are females. Thus, of the 400 total people, there must be 200 males and 200 females. Likewise, the four blood types occur in equal proportions, so of the 400 people, there must be 100 with each of the four blood types. Now 30% of the males have A blood type. This is 30% of 200, or 60 males with Type A blood. Since there are 100 total people with Type A blood, there must be 100 − 60 = 40 females with Type A blood. Also, 20% of the males have Type B blood, so this means that there are 20% of 200 or 40 males with Type B blood, leaving 100 − 40 = 60 females with Type B blood; 40% of the males have Type AB blood, making 40% of 200 or 80 males with Type AB blood, leaving 100 − 80 = 20 females with Type AB blood; and 10% of the males have Type O blood, so there are 10% of 200 or 20 males with Type O blood, leaving 100 − 20 = 80 females with Type O blood.

The problem is to find $P\{M \mid AB\}$. This is quite simple when we look at the table, because we see that

$$P\{M \mid AB\} = \frac{P\{M, AB\}}{P\{AB\}}$$

$$= \frac{\#(M, AB)}{\#(AB)}$$

$$= \frac{80}{100}$$

$$= 0.80$$

This calculation was so simple that it almost seems automatic, with no need for a formula. But closer inspection reveals that

$$P\{M \mid AB\} = \frac{P\{M, AB\}}{P\{AB\}}$$

$$= \frac{P\{M\}P\{AB \mid M\}}{P\{AB\}}$$

$$= \frac{(0.50)(0.40)}{0.25}$$

$$= \frac{0.20}{0.25}$$

$$= 0.80$$

This is Bayes theorem.

• PROBLEM 6–42

Suppose that of 100 high school students, 90 like soccer and 10 do not. Also suppose that 60 like chess and 40 do not. Finally, 60% of the soccer players like chess. If you walk into a room with four chess games going on and ask, "Soccer anyone?", then how many positive responses would you expect to find?

SOLUTION:

We first need to create the appropriate table.

		Like Soccer		
		Yes	No	Total
	Yes	54	6	60
Like Chess	No	36	4	40
	Total	90	10	100

Now we are looking for $E[X]$, where $X = Y1 + Y2 + Y3 + Y4 + Y5 + Y6 + Y7 + Y8$. That is, there are eight chess players (two players per game times four games in progress), and the random variables $Y1$ through $Y8$ are one if the chess player likes soccer and zero otherwise. Even though the random variables $Y1$ through $Y8$ are not independent (as defined later in this book), it is still true that

$$E[X] = E[Y1 + Y2 + Y3 + Y4 + Y5 + Y6 + Y7 + Y8]$$

$$= E[Y1] + E[Y2] + E[Y3] + E[Y4] + E[Y5]$$

$$+ E[Y6] + E[Y7] + E[Y8]$$

But each of these random variables has a Bernoulli distribution, so the expected value is the parameter p. The task remains to find p for each of these eight Bernoulli random variables. In fact, it turns out that p is common to all eight of these Bernoulli random variables. In particular, we see that

$$p1 = P\{Y1 = 1\}$$

$$= P\{\text{chess player likes soccer}\}$$

$$= P\{\text{likes soccer} \mid \text{likes chess}\}$$

$$= \frac{P\{\text{likes soccer and likes chess}\}}{P\{\text{likes chess}\}}$$

$$= \frac{54}{60}$$

$$= \frac{9}{10}$$

$$= 0.90$$

It is seen that $p1 = p2 = p3 = p4 = p5 = p6 = p7 = p8 = 0.90$. Thus, $E[X] = (8)(0.90) = 7.2$. We would expect, on average, about 7.2 players per trial if we repeat this experiment many times.

✓ • **PROBLEM 6–43**

Suppose that of 200 baseball players, 160 are good hitters and 40 are not. Also, suppose that 80 are good fielders and 120 are not. Finally, 30% of the good hitters are also good fielders. What proportion of bad fielders are also bad hitters?

SOLUTION:

We again need to create the appropriate table, showing the cross-classification of each player by hitting ability and fielding ability, with the appropriate cell counts.

		Good Hitter		
		Yes	No	Total
Good Fielder	Yes	48	32	80
	No	112	8	120
	Total	160	40	200

We wish to find

$= P\{\text{bad hitter} \mid \text{bad fielder}\}$

$= \dfrac{P\{\text{bad hitter and bad fielder}\}}{P\{\text{bad fielder}\}}$

$= \dfrac{8}{120}$

$= \dfrac{1}{15}$

$= 0.0666$

• PROBLEM 6-44

Suppose that of 50 college students, 30 major in statistics and 20 major in chemistry. Also suppose that 40 are males and 10 are females. Finally, 20 males major in statistics. How many females major in chemistry?

SOLUTION:

We again need to create the appropriate table, showing the cross-classification of each student by gender and major, with the appropriate cell counts.

		Gender		
		Male	Female	Total
	Chemistry	20	0	20
Major	Statistics	20	10	30
	Total	40	10	50

We wish to find the number of females who major in chemistry. The table clearly shows that there are no females who major in chemistry. Had the question been phrased as one of probabilities, then we would have had to divide by the appropriate denominator, in this case the number of females, or 10.

Several years ago, there was much attention generated by a very simple question, but one that perplexed some of the best mathematicians, statisticians, and probabilists in the nation. This problem is naturally stated in terms of conditional probability, so it is treated here.

Suppose that you are on a game show, and on this game show you are presented with three doors. One of these doors has a prize behind it, and two do not. You must guess which door has the prize (of course, the doors are closed and it is not revealed to you which door actually contains the prize). For argument's sake, let us suppose that you select door #1. Now you are told that door #3 does not contain the prize. Finally, you are asked if you would like to change your selection to door #2 or stick with your original choice of door #1. What do you do?

There are several ways to model this experiment, and this may have contributed to the controversy surrounding whether there is a benefit in switching doors. If you would have been told what is behind door #3 regardless of whether it was the winner, then it makes no difference if you change doors or not. Here it is possible that you would be told that door #3 is the winner, in which case you lose whether you switch or not.

However, it is not likely that a game show would tell you that you have already lost. The objective of the game show is to attract viewers, and this is best accomplished by maximizing suspense. Therefore, let us assume that the experiment is run as follows. A random device is used to determine which door contains the prize, and each door has an equal chance. You also employ a random device to select your choice of doors, such that each door has an equal chance of being selected. Your selection is independent of the selection made by the game show.

Having made your selection, either it is correct or it is not correct. If it is not correct, then of the other two doors, one contains the prize and one does not. You will be told which door does not contain the prize, and that it is a loser. If you pick the correct door, then each of the other two doors is a loser. The game show host will randomly pick one of these and tell you that this one is a loser.

• PROBLEM 6–45

What is the probability that your original selection is the right one?

SOLUTION:

There are three doors, and thus three ways to win. These are:

1. You pick door #1 and door #1 is the winner.

2. You pick door #2 and door #2 is the winner.

3. You pick door #3 and door #3 is the winner.

Now

$$P\{\text{win}\} = P\{\text{win} \cap \text{universal set}\}$$

$$= P\{\text{win} \cap (\text{door \#1 is the winner} \cup \text{door \#2 is the winner}$$

$$\cup \text{door \#3 is the winner})\}$$

$$= P\{(\text{win} \cap \text{door \#1}) \cup (\text{win} \cap \text{door \#2}) \cup (\text{win} \cap \text{door \#3})\}$$

$$= P\{(\text{win} \cap \text{door \#1}) + (\text{win} \cap \text{door \#2}) + (\text{win} \cap \text{door \#3})\}$$

$$= P\{\text{door \#1}\}P\{\text{win} \mid \text{door \#1}\} + P\{\text{door \#2}\}P\{\text{win} \mid \text{door \#2}\}$$

$$+ P\{\text{door \#3}\}P\{\text{win} \mid \text{door \#3}\}$$

$$= \left(\frac{1}{3}\right)\left(\frac{1}{3}\right) + \left(\frac{1}{3}\right)\left(\frac{1}{3}\right) + \left(\frac{1}{3}\right)\left(\frac{1}{3}\right)$$

$$= \left(\frac{1}{9}\right) + \left(\frac{1}{9}\right) + \left(\frac{1}{9}\right)$$

$$= \frac{3}{9}$$

$$= \frac{1}{3}$$

$$= 0.3333$$

• PROBLEM 6–46

What is the probability of winning if you do not change your choice of door after being given the new information?

SOLUTION:

Having been told that a loser is a loser, you are no more or less likely to win than you were prior to being told. Had you guessed correctly originally and kept your selection, then you will still win. Had you guessed incorrectly originally and kept your selection, then you will still lose. Thus, the probability of winning if you do not change your choice of door after being given the new information is still $1/3 = 0.3333$.

• PROBLEM 6–47

What is your probability of winning if you change your choice of door after being given the new information?

SOLUTION:

To answer this question, we need a table.

		Your Choice			
		1	2	3	Total
	1	lose	win	win	$2/3$
Winner	2	win	lose	win	$2/3$
	3	win	win	lose	$2/3$
	Total	$2/3$	$2/3$	$2/3$	$2/3$

To see how the entries are derived, consider, for example, the situation in which you select door #1 and the winner is door #2. Of the two doors you did not select, door #2 and door #3, only door #3 is a loser. Thus, you will be told that door #3 is a loser. Now you will switch to the remaining door, door #2. Therefore, you will win.

On the other hand, if you select door #1 and door #1 is the winner, then you will either be told that door #2 is a loser or that door #3 is a loser. Either way, you will switch to the other, and away from the winner. Thus, you will lose.

No matter which door you pick originally, and no matter which door is the winner, your chances of winning are now $2/3$. This makes sense, because you must either switch or stay. Therefore,

$$P\{\text{win} \mid \text{switch}\} + P\{\text{win} \mid \text{stay}\} = 1.$$

This is confirmed, because

$$P\{\text{win} \mid \text{switch}\} + P\{\text{win} \mid \text{stay}\} = \frac{2}{3} + \frac{1}{3}$$

$$= 1$$

The bottom line is that you should switch.

What makes some children taller than others? To some extent, this question can be answered by considering the height of the parents. But even siblings are found with vastly different heights. Thus, there is still some degree of variability even after considering the parents. Nevertheless, the variability of height among children with common parents may be less than the variability of height among children with different parents. This can be modeled with conditional probability. This section will consider only the heights of all children aggregated, instead of breaking them down by gender. This will be done in the next section, which treats mixed random variables.

For the moment, suppose that only the height of the father affects the height of the child. We will later address the more realistic situation in which the heights of both parents affect the height of the child.

As a model, suppose that the height (meaning the tallest height ever achieved, and not the height at birth or during childhood) of a child has a uniform distribution on the range $[F - 6$ inches, $F + 6$ inches], where F is the father's height. If a man has a height of 70 inches, then what is the range of the heights of his grandchildren?

The children of this man have heights which could range between $70 - 6 = 64$ inches and $70 + 6 = 76$ inches. Therefore, the grandchildren of this man could be as short as $64 - 6 = 58$ inches and as tall as $76 + 6 = 82$ inches.

What is the range of the heights of the grandchildren if the height of a child is given to be 74 inches?

Conditional on this new information, the heights of the grandchildren now must fall within the range of $74 - 6 = 68$ inches to $74 + 6 = 80$ inches. The conditional range is different from the unconditional range, and, therefore, the conditional probability mass function must also be different from the unconditional probability mass function.

CHAPTER 7

INDEPENDENCE

Basic Attacks and Strategies for Solving Problems in this Chapter. See pages 548 to 602 for step-by-step solutions to problems.

The technical meaning of the word "independence," or of the terms "statistical independence" and "stochastic independence," is derived from the everyday meaning of the word. Independence is the lack of dependence. Statistically, this means that one random variable does not depend on another random variable, or that one event does not depend on another event. Independence is one of the most important concepts in statistics and probability. Notice that independence can refer either to events or to random variables.

Think about two events, and try to quantify the degree to which one depends on the other. The concept of dependence is distinct from the concept of causality, in that causality treats the two events differently. That is, one causes the other, while the other is caused by the first (but certainly does not cause the first).

Dependence is a property of two (or more) events without any need to distinguish any as being any different from any others. Either the set of events is dependent or it is independent. For simplicity, consider the case of two sets. Certainly, if one causes the other, then we should agree that there is dependence, or lack of independence. For example, the events defined by

$$A = \{\text{I walk in the rain without an umbrella}\}$$

and $B = \{\text{I get wet}\}$

follow a causality pattern in that A causes B.

Even without causality, however, there still may be obvious dependence. For example, being female does not cause pregnancy (although it may be said to facilitate), and pregnancy certainly does not cause a person who otherwise would have been a male to become a female. Yet we would agree that the events

$$C = \{\text{female}\}$$

and $D = \{\text{pregnant}\}$

are not independent. If we know that event D has occurred, then we also know that event C has occurred. But suppose that instead of such certainty we consider tendencies. That is, we may replace strict implication with increased probability. This is in line with statistical and probabilistic thinking.

Consider the events

$$E = \{\text{male}\}$$

and $F = \{\text{football player}\}.$

It is not true that event E causes event F. That is, being a male does not cause one to like football. Nor does event F cause event E. Liking football does not cause one to become a male. In fact, neither event implies the other. Not all football players are males, and not all males are football players. Can we conclude from this that these two events are independent? It is likely that F becomes more likely when E occurs and less likely when E does not occur.

To quantify this, we would need to estimate the following:

    1.   the proportion of people who like football,

    2.   the proportion of males who like football,

and   3.   the proportion of females who like football.

Independence would mandate that these three quantities be equal. The fact that all three quantities are not equal is testimony to the dependence of these two events. It is likely that the proportion of males who like football is larger than the proportion of people who like football, which in turn is larger than the proportion of females who like football. Hopefully you will recognize these quantities as conditional and unconditional probabilities. That is,

    1. $P\{F\}$ = the proportion of people who like football,

    2. $P\{F|E\}$ = the proportion of males who like football,

and   3. $P\{F|E^c\}$ = the proportion of females who like football.

This should serve to motivate the definition of independent events as events whose unconditional probabilities are equal to their conditional probabilities when conditioned on the other event. That is, events A and B are independent if

$$P\{A\} = P\{A|B\}$$

and $P\{B\} = P\{B|A\}.$

    We do not need to specify both conditions, because if

$$P\{A\} = P\{A|B\},$$

then $P\{B|A\} = P\{AB\}/P\{A\}$

$$= P\{BA\}/P\{A|B\}$$

$$= P\{B\}P\{A|B\}/P\{A|B\}$$

$$= P\{B\},$$

assuming that $P\{A\} > 0.$

    This development leads to an alternate definition of independent events. That is, if A and B are independent events, then

$$P\{AB\} = P\{A\}P\{B|A\}$$

$$= P\{A\}P\{B\}.$$

That is, the probability of the intersection of A and B is the product of the probabilities of A and B. This is the more well-known definition of independence.

    More will be said about independent events in the next section. The second section will discuss independent discrete random variables. The third will discuss independent continuous random variables. The fourth will explore the relationship between independence and mutual exclusivity of events. These concepts are often confused by beginning students, but those who can grasp the difference will have a solid understanding of much of what is required for the study of probability and statistics. The fifth section introduces correlation and covariance. The sixth section discusses conditional independence. The final section discusses higher order independence, or dependence among more than two events or random variables.

    As mentioned in the introduction, two events, A and B, are independent if

$$P\{A\} = P\{A|B\},$$

which is equivalent to

$$P\{B\} = P\{B|A\},$$

which is equivalent to

$$P\{AB\} = P\{A\}P\{B\}.$$

As an example, consider two Bernoulli random variables, X and Y, with joint probability mass function as given in the following table.

		X		Total	Total
		0	D	Total	
	0	0.04	0.16	0.20	
Y	1	0.16	0.64	0.80	
	Total	0.20	0.80	1.00	

Now consider the events

$$A = \{X = 0\},$$

$$B = \{X = 1\},$$

$$C = \{Y = 0\},$$

and $$D = \{Y = 1\}.$$

Six pairs can be formed from these four events:

    1. A, B,

    2. A, C,

    3. A, D,

    4. B, C,

    5. B, D,

and   6. C, D.

Which of these six pairs of events are independent?

The answer is that A and B are dependent, and C and D are dependent. All other pairs of events are independent. To see this, we will consider each of the six pairs in turn. First, we write

$$P\{AB\} = P\{X = 0, X = 1\}$$
$$= 0$$

is not equal to 0.16

$$= (0.2)(0.8)$$
$$= P\{X = 0\}P\{X = 1\}$$
$$= P\{A\}P\{B\}.$$

Thus, A and B cannot be independent.

Next,

$$P\{AC\} = P\{X = 0, Y = 0\}$$
$$= 0.04$$
$$= (0.2)(0.2)$$
$$= P\{X = 0\}P\{Y = 0\}$$
$$= P\{A\}P\{C\}.$$

Thus, A and C are independent.

Next,

$$P\{AD\} = P\{X = 0, Y = 1\}$$
$$= 0.16$$
$$= (0.2)(0.8)$$
$$= P\{X = 0\}P\{Y = 1\}$$
$$= P\{A\}P\{D\}.$$

Thus, A and D are independent.

Next,

$$P\{BC\} = P\{X = 1, Y = 0\}$$
$$= 0.16$$
$$= (0.8)(0.2)$$
$$= P\{X = 1\}P\{Y = 0\}$$
$$= P\{B\}P\{C\}.$$

Thus, B and C are independent.

Next,

$$P\{BD\} = P\{X = 1, Y = 1\}$$

$$= 0.64$$

$$= (0.8)\,(0.8)$$

$$= P\{X = 1\}P\{Y = 1\}$$

$$= P\{B\}P\{D\}.$$

Thus, B and D are independent.

Finally,

$$P\{CD\} = P\{Y = 0, Y = 1\}$$

$$= 0$$

is not equal to 0.16

$$= (0.2)\,(0.8)$$

$$= P\{Y = 0\}P\{Y = 1\}$$

$$= P\{C\}P\{D\}.$$

Thus, C and D are not independent.

To summarize, the following table describes the pattern of independence.

<table>
<tr><td colspan="2"></td><td colspan="5">Event</td></tr>
<tr><td colspan="2"></td><td>A</td><td>B</td><td>C</td><td>D</td><td>Total</td></tr>
<tr><td rowspan="4">Event</td><td>A</td><td>?</td><td>no</td><td>yes</td><td>yes</td><td>2</td></tr>
<tr><td>B</td><td>no</td><td>?</td><td>yes</td><td>yes</td><td>2</td></tr>
<tr><td>C</td><td>yes</td><td>yes</td><td>?</td><td>no</td><td>2</td></tr>
<tr><td>D</td><td>yes</td><td>yes</td><td>no</td><td>?</td><td>2</td></tr>
<tr><td>Total</td><td>2</td><td>2</td><td>2</td><td>2</td><td>8</td></tr>
</table>

Notice that each event is independent of exactly two other events. A definite pattern has developed. Events A and B are events that involve X, and events C and D are events that involve Y. Any event that involves X is independent of any event that involves Y, and vice versa. But two events that involve X (A and B) are not independent. Also, two events that involve Y (C and D) are not independent.

This makes intuitive sense, because knowledge of the occurrence of A provides information about X. In particular, we would then know that $X = 0$. This would imply that X could not be one. Hence, event B cannot occur. That is, the occurrence of A has precluded the occurrence of B, so these two events cannot be independent. Likewise, the occurrence of C has precluded the occurrence of D, so these two events cannot be independent either. As we will see in a later section, X and Y are independent random variables. Thus, any event involving one of them will be independent of any event involving the other.

We have not addressed the issue of whether an event is independent of itself. Notice the question marks in the diagonal entries of the table. This issue will be addressed in problems that follow.

Step-by-Step Solutions to Problems in this Chapter, "Independence."

• PROBLEM 7–1

Can an event be independent of itself?

SOLUTION:

The question sounds preposterous! How could knowledge of the occurrence of an event offer no information as to the occurrence of the same event? It seems that this notion can be dismissed as nonsense. However, to reinforce the meaning of independence, we should try to show this more formally.

For an event to be independent of itself, we would require

$$P\{AA\} = P\{A\}P\{A\}.$$

But $\quad P\{AA\} = P\{A\},$

because $A \cap A = A.$

That is, A occurs whenever $A \cap A$ occurs, and $A \cap A$ occurs whenever A occurs. Also,

$$P\{A\}P\{A\} = [P\{A\}]^2,$$

so for A to be independent of itself, then we would require

$$P\{A\} = P\{AA\}$$
$$= P\{A\}P\{A\}$$
$$= [P\{A\}]^2.$$

The only two real numbers which are equal to their own squares are zero, since

$$0^2 = 0,$$

and one, since

$$1^2 = 1.$$

Each of these numbers is a legitimate value for a probability, or for the probability of A, $P\{A\}$. That is, if

$$P\{A\} = 0,$$

then A is independent of itself. Also, if

$$P\{A\} = 1,$$

then A is independent of itself. Notice that had we followed our intuition and not checked more formally, then we would have been wrong!

How do we explain such "nonsense"? If $P\{A\} = 0$, then we know that A cannot occur (this is not strictly true, but for our purposes, it will suffice to assume that it is). Being given the extra information that A has not occurred (which is the only information we could get, because A cannot occur) only means that A will not occur. But we already knew that. We do not change our probability of A occurring given that it already has not occurred.

Likewise, if $P\{A\} = 1$, then A is certain to occur. Knowing that A has occurred again does not change this fact, because it was already a certain event. Thus, A is again independent of itself.

Consider two Bernoulli random variables, X and Y, with joint probability mass function as given in the following table.

		X			
		0	0	1 Total	Total
Y	0	0	0.05	0.15	0.20
	1	1	0.15	0.65	0.80
	Total		0.20	0.80	1.00

Now consider the events

$A = \{X = 0\}$,

$B = \{X = 1\}$,

$C = \{Y = 0\}$,

and $D = \{Y = 1\}$.

Six pairs can be formed from these four events:

1. A,B,

2. A,C,

3. A,D,

4. B,C,

5. B,D,

and 6. C,D.

Which of these six pairs of events are independent?

SOLUTION:

We will examine each pair in turn. First,

$P\{AB\} = P\{X = 0, X = 1\}$

$= 0$

is not equal to 0.16

$$= (0.2)(0.8)$$
$$= P\{X = 0\}P\{X = 1\}$$
$$= P\{A\}P\{B\}.$$

Thus, A and B cannot be independent.

Next,

$$P\{AC\} = P\{X = 0, Y = 0\}$$
$$= 0.05$$

is not equal to 0.04

$$= (0.2)(0.2)$$
$$= P\{X = 0\}P\{Y = 0\}$$
$$= P\{A\}P\{C\}.$$

Thus, A and C are not independent.

Next,

$$P\{AD\} = P\{X = 0, Y = 1\}$$
$$= 0.15$$

is not equal to 0.16

$$= (0.2)(0.8)$$
$$= P\{X = 0\}P\{Y = 1\}$$
$$= P\{A\}P\{D\}.$$

Thus, A and D are not independent.

Next,

$$P\{BC\} = P\{X = 1, Y = 0\}$$
$$= 0.15$$

is not equal to 0.16

$$= (0.8)(0.2)$$
$$= P\{X = 1\}P\{Y = 0\}$$
$$= P\{B\}P\{C\}.$$

Thus, B and C are not independent.

Next,

$$P\{BD\} = P\{X = 1, Y = 1\}$$

$$= 0.65$$

is not equal to 0.64

$$= (0.8)(0.8)$$

$$= P\{X = 1\}P\{Y = 1\}$$

$$= P\{B\}P\{D\}.$$

Thus, B and D are not independent.

Finally,

$$P\{CD\} = P\{Y = 0, Y = 1\}$$

$$= 0$$

is not equal to 0.16

$$= (0.2)(0.8)$$

$$= P\{Y = 0\}P\{Y = 1\}$$

$$= P\{C\}P\{D\}.$$

Thus, C and D are not independent.

Therefore, none of these pairs of events are independent.

✓● **PROBLEM 7-3**

Consider two Bernoulli random variables, X and Y, with joint probability mass function as given in the following table.

		X			
		0	0	1 ~~Total~~	Total
Y	0	0.85	0.00	0.85
	1	0.15	0.00	0.15
	Total	1.00	0.00	1.00

Now consider the events

$A = \{X = 0\}$,

$B = \{X = 1\}$,

$C = \{Y = 0\}$,

and $D = \{Y = 1\}$.

Six pairs can be formed from these four events:

1. A,B,

2. A,C,

3. A,D,

4. B,C,

5. B,D,

and 6. C,D.

Which of these six pairs of events are independent?

SOLUTION:

We will examine each pair in turn. First,

$P\{AB\} = P\{X = 0, X = 1\}$

$= 0$

$= (1.00) (0.00)$

$$= P\{X = 0\}P\{X = 1\}$$
$$= P\{A\}P\{B\}.$$

Thus, A and B are independent.

Next,

$$P\{AC\} = P\{X = 0, Y = 0\}$$
$$= 0.85$$
$$= (1.00)\,(0.85)$$
$$= P\{X = 0\}P\{Y = 0\}$$
$$= P\{A\}P\{C\}.$$

Thus, A and C are independent.

Next,

$$P\{AD\} = P\{X = 0, Y = 1\}$$
$$= 0.15$$
$$= (1.00)\,(0.15)$$
$$= P\{X = 0\}P\{Y = 1\}$$
$$= P\{A\}P\{D\}.$$

Thus, A and D are independent.

Next,

$$P\{BC\} = P\{X = 1, Y = 0\}$$
$$= 0.00$$
$$= (0.00)\,(0.85)$$
$$= P\{X = 1\}P\{Y = 0\}$$
$$= P\{B\}P\{C\}.$$

Thus, B and C are independent.

Next,

$$P\{BD\} = P\{X = 1, Y = 1\}$$
$$= 0.00$$
$$= (0.00)\,(0.15)$$

$$= P\{X = 1\}P\{Y = 1\}$$

$$= P\{B\}P\{D\}.$$

Thus, B and D are independent.

Finally,

$$P\{CD\} = P\{Y = 0, Y = 1\}$$

$$= 0$$

is not equal to 0.1275

$$= (0.85)(0.15)$$

$$= P\{Y = 0\}P\{Y = 1\}$$

$$= P\{C\}P\{D\}.$$

Thus, C and D are not independent.

Notice again that every event defined in terms of X is independent of every event defined in terms of Y. But in this case, it is also true that the two events defined in terms of X are independent of each other, because one of them has probability zero and the other has probability one.

$\checkmark$ • **PROBLEM 7-4**

If A and B are independent events, then prove that their complements, A^C and B^C, are also independent events.

SOLUTION:

We write

$$P\{A^C B^C\} = P\{A^C\} - P\{A^C B\}$$

$$= P\{A^C\} - [P\{B\} - P\{AB\}]$$

$$= P\{A^C\} - [P\{B\} - P\{A\}P\{B\}]$$

$$= P\{A^C\} - P\{B\}[1 - P\{A\}]$$

$$= P\{A^C\} - P\{B\}[P\{A^C\}]$$

$$= P\{A^C\}[1 - P\{B\}]$$

$$= P\{A^C\}[P\{B^C\}]$$
$$= P\{A^C\}P\{B^C\}.$$

✓• PROBLEM 7-5

Suppose that a basketball player takes three shots during a five-minute stretch of a game. These shots are from different locations on the court, so they have different probabilities of being successful. However, they are all independent of each other. If the first shot scores with probability 0.7, the second with probability 0.8, and the third with probability 0.9, then what is the probability that this player makes at least one shot?

SOLUTION:

This question is most easily answered by considering the complement of the event whose probability we want. The complement of the event that at least one shot is made is that none of the shots are made. Thus,

$P\{\text{make at least one shot}\}$

$= 1 - P\{\text{make no shots}\}$

$= 1 - P\{\text{miss 1}\}P\{\text{miss 2} \mid \text{miss 1}\}P\{\text{miss 3} \mid \text{miss 1, miss 2}\}$

$= 1 - P\{\text{miss 1}\}P\{\text{miss 2}\}P\{\text{miss 3}\}$

$= 1 - [1\text{-}P\{\text{score 1}\}][1 - P\{\text{score 2}\}][1 - P\{\text{score 3}\}]$

$= 1 - [1 - 0.7][1 - 0.8][1 - 0.9]$

$= 1 - [0.3][0.2][0.1]$

$= 1 - 0.006$

$= 0.994.$

Thus, it is quite likely that at least one shot will score.

As we alluded to in the previous section, discrete random variables, say X and Y, are independent if every event defined in terms of X is independent of every event defined in terms of Y. But the events defined in terms of X are generated by the simplest such events, which are the outcomes of X and their associated probabilities. This is the marginal probability mass function of X. For example,

$$P\{X \text{ in } A\} = \Sigma_{k \text{ in } A}P\{X = k\},$$

where A is some set which defines an event in terms of X. Likewise, the events defined in terms of Y are generated by the simplest such events, which are the outcomes of Y and their associated probabilities. This is the marginal probability mass function of Y.

This development lends credence to the proposed definition of independence of two discrete random variables. We require that for any set A (for which X in A is an event defined in terms of X) and any set B (for which Y in B is an event defined in terms of Y), these two events are independent, so

$$P\{X \text{ in } A, Y \text{ in } B\} = P\{X \text{ in } A\}P\{Y \text{ in } B\}.$$

If we consider the outcomes of X and Y, then this becomes

$$P\{X = k1, Y = k2\} = P\{X = k1\}P\{Y = k2\}$$

for all values of $k1$ and $k2$. This equation expresses the equality between the joint probability mass function of X and Y and the product of the marginal probability mass functions of X and Y. Thus, two discrete random variables are independent if and only if their joint probability mass function can be factored as a product of the individual marginal probability mass functions. Likewise, more than two discrete random variables are independent if their joint probability mass function can be factored into a product of the individual marginal probability mass functions. As will be seen later, this is not the same condition as each pair of random variables being independent.

Let us now return to an earlier example:

		X		
	0	0	1 Total	Total
Y	0	0.04	0.16	0.20
	1	0.16	0.64	0.80
	Total	0.20	0.80	1.00

Are X and Y independent? It was seen in the first section of this chapter that each event defined in terms of X is independent of each event defined in terms of Y. Therefore, X and Y are independent. But had we not already known this, we would need to check the following four conditions:

$$P\{X = 0, Y = 0\} = P\{X = 0\}P\{Y = 0\},$$
$$P\{X = 0, Y = 1\} = P\{X = 0\}P\{Y = 1\},$$
$$P\{X = 1, Y = 0\} = P\{X = 1\}P\{Y = 0\},$$
and $\quad P\{X = 1, Y = 1\} = P\{X = 1\}P\{Y = 1\}.$

It is not enough that one, or even some, of these conditions be true. For independence between X and Y, all four of these conditions must be true. To verify these four conditions, we see that

$$P\{X = 0, Y = 0\} = 0.04$$
$$= (0.2)(0.2)$$
$$= P\{X = 0\}P\{Y = 0\},$$

$$P\{X = 0, Y = 1\} = 0.16$$
$$= (0.2)(0.8)$$
$$= P\{X = 0\}P\{Y = 1\},$$

$$P\{X = 1, Y = 0\} = 0.16$$
$$= (0.8)(0.2)$$
$$= P\{X = 1\}P\{Y = 0\},$$

and $\quad P\{X = 1, Y = 1\} = 0.64$
$$= (0.8)(0.8)$$
$$= P\{X = 1\}P\{Y = 1\}.$$

Thus, X and Y are independent. We now consider another example.

		X		
		0	1	Total
	0	0.05	0.15	0.20
	1	0.10	0.20	0.30
Y	2	0.10	0.10	0.20
	3	0.05	0.10	0.15
	4	0.10	0.05	0.15
	Total	0.40	0.60	1.00

Are X and Y independent? We now need to check more than four conditions. In fact, the number of conditions that need to be checked is the number of points in the support (range) of the joint probability mass function. In the previous example, each random variable was Bernoulli, so each random variable had two levels. Thus, there were $(2)(2) = 4$ conditions to check. Now there are $(2)(5) = 10$ conditions to check. These are

$$P\{X = 0, Y = 0\} = P\{X = 0\}P\{Y = 0\},$$

$$P\{X = 0, Y = 1\} = P\{X = 0\}P\{Y = 1\},$$

$$P\{X = 0, Y = 2\} = P\{X = 0\}P\{Y = 2\},$$

$$P\{X = 0, Y = 3\} = P\{X = 0\}P\{Y = 3\},$$

$$P\{X = 0, Y = 4\} = P\{X = 0\}P\{Y = 4\},$$

$$P\{X = 1, Y = 0\} = P\{X = 1\}P\{Y = 0\},$$

$$P\{X = 1, Y = 1\} = P\{X = 1\}P\{Y = 1\},$$

$$P\{X = 1, Y = 2\} = P\{X = 1\}P\{Y = 2\},$$

$$P\{X = 1, Y = 3\} = P\{X = 1\}P\{Y = 3\},$$

and $\quad P\{X = 1, Y = 4\} = P\{X = 1\}P\{Y = 4\}.$

Again, it is not enough that one, or even some, of these conditions be true. For independence between X and Y, all ten of these conditions must be true. To verify these ten conditions, we see that

$$P\{X = 0, Y = 0\} = 0.05$$

is not equal to 0.08

$$= (0.40)(0.20)$$

$$= P\{X = 0\}P\{Y = 0\},$$

$$P\{X = 0, Y = 1\} = 0.10$$

is not equal to 0.12

$$= (0.40)(0.30)$$

$$= P\{X = 0\}P\{Y = 1\},$$

$$P\{X = 0, Y = 2\} = 0.10$$

is not equal to 0.08

$$= (0.40)(0.20)$$

$$= P\{X = 0\}P\{Y = 2\},$$

$$P\{X = 0, Y = 3\} = 0.05$$

is not equal to 0.06

$$= (0.40)\,(0.15)$$
$$= P\{X = 0\}P\{Y = 3\},$$

$$P\{X = 0, Y = 4\} = 0.10$$

is not equal to 0.06

$$= (0.40)\,(0.15)$$
$$= P\{X = 0\}P\{Y = 4\},$$

$$P\{X = 1, Y = 0\} = 0.15$$

is not equal to 0.12

$$= (0.60)\,(0.20)$$
$$= P\{X = 1\}P\{Y = 0\},$$

$$P\{X = 1, Y = 1\} = 0.20$$

is not equal to 0.18

$$= (0.60)\,(0.30)$$
$$= P\{X = 1\}P\{Y = 1\},$$

$$P\{X = 1, Y = 2\} = 0.10$$

is not equal to 0.12

$$= (0.60)\,(0.20)$$
$$= P\{X = 1\}P\{Y = 2\},$$

$$P\{X = 1, Y = 3\} = 0.10$$

is not equal to 0.09

$$= (0.60)\,(0.15)$$
$$= P\{X = 1\}P\{Y = 3\},$$

and $P\{X = 1, Y = 4\} = 0.05$

is not equal to 0.09

$$= (0.60)\,(0.15)$$
$$= P\{X = 1\}P\{Y = 4\}.$$

Thus, this joint probability mass function is not independent, since not one of its probabilities can be expressed as the appropriate product.

• PROBLEM 7-6

Consider the following joint probability mass function.

		X		
		0	1	Total
	0	0.08	0.12	0.20
	1	0.12	0.18	0.30
Y	2	0.08	0.12	0.20
	3	0.06	0.09	0.15
	4	0.06	0.09	0.15
	Total	0.40	0.60	1.00

Are X and Y independent?

SOLUTION:

We need to check $(5)(2) = 10$ conditions. These are:

$$P\{X = 0, Y = 0\} = P\{X = 0\}P\{Y = 0\},$$

$$P\{X = 0, Y = 1\} = P\{X = 0\}P\{Y = 1\},$$

$$P\{X = 0, Y = 2\} = P\{X = 0\}P\{Y = 2\},$$

$$P\{X = 0, Y = 3\} = P\{X = 0\}P\{Y = 3\},$$

$$P\{X = 0, Y = 4\} = P\{X = 0\}P\{Y = 4\},$$

$$P\{X = 1, Y = 0\} = P\{X = 1\}P\{Y = 0\},$$

$$P\{X = 1, Y = 1\} = P\{X = 1\}P\{Y = 1\},$$

$$P\{X = 1, Y = 2\} = P\{X = 1\}P\{Y = 2\},$$

$$P\{X = 1, Y = 3\} = P\{X = 1\}P\{Y = 3\},$$

and $\quad P\{X = 1, Y = 4\} = P\{X = 1\}P\{Y = 4\}$.

Again, it is not enough that one, or even some, of these conditions be true. For independence between X and Y, all ten of these conditions must be true. To verify these ten conditions, we see that

$$P\{X = 0, Y = 0\} = 0.08$$
$$= (0.40)\,(0.20)$$
$$= P\{X = 0\}P\{Y = 0\},$$
$$P\{X = 0, Y = 1\} = 0.12$$
$$= (0.40)\,(0.30)$$
$$= P\{X = 0\}P\{Y = 1\},$$
$$P\{X = 0, Y = 2\} = 0.08$$
$$= (0.40)\,(0.20)$$
$$= P\{X = 0\}P\{Y = 2\},$$
$$P\{X = 0, Y = 3\} = 0.06$$
$$= (0.40)\,(0.15)$$
$$= P\{X = 0\}P\{Y = 3\},$$
$$P\{X = 0, Y = 4\} = 0.06$$
$$= (0.40)\,(0.15)$$
$$= P\{X = 0\}P\{Y = 4\},$$
$$P\{X = 1, Y = 0\} = 0.12$$
$$= (0.60)\,(0.20)$$
$$= P\{X = 1\}P\{Y = 0\},$$
$$P\{X = 1, Y = 1\} = 0.18$$
$$= (0.60)\,(0.30)$$
$$= P\{X = 1\}P\{Y = 1\},$$
$$P\{X = 1, Y = 2\} = 0.12$$
$$= (0.60)\,(0.20)$$
$$= P\{X = 1\}P\{Y = 2\},$$
$$P\{X = 1, Y = 3\} = 0.09$$

$$= (0.60)(0.15)$$
$$= P\{X = 1\}P\{Y = 3\},$$

and $\quad P\{X = 1, Y = 4\} = 0.09$

$$= (0.60)(0.15)$$
$$= P\{X = 1\}P\{Y = 4\}.$$

Thus, X and Y are independent.

● PROBLEM 7-7

Consider the following joint probability mass function.

		X			
		2	4	6	Total
	3	0.08	0.08	0.04	0.20
	5	0.12	0.12	0.06	0.30
Y	6	0.08	0.08	0.04	0.20
	7	0.06	0.06	0.03	0.15
	8	0.06	0.06	0.03	0.15
	Total	0.40	0.40	0.20	1.00

Are X and Y independent?

SOLUTION:

We need to check (5)(3) = 15 conditions. These are:

$$P\{X = 2, Y = 3\} = P\{X = 2\}P\{Y = 3\},$$
$$P\{X = 2, Y = 5\} = P\{X = 2\}P\{Y = 5\},$$
$$P\{X = 2, Y = 6\} = P\{X = 2\}P\{Y = 6\},$$
$$P\{X = 2, Y = 7\} = P\{X = 2\}P\{Y = 7\},$$

$$P\{X = 2, Y = 8\} = P\{X = 2\}P\{Y = 8\},$$

$$P\{X = 4, Y = 3\} = P\{X = 4\}P\{Y = 3\},$$

$$P\{X = 4, Y = 5\} = P\{X = 4\}P\{Y = 5\},$$

$$P\{X = 4, Y = 6\} = P\{X = 4\}P\{Y = 6\},$$

$$P\{X = 4, Y = 7\} = P\{X = 4\}P\{Y = 7\},$$

$$P\{X = 4, Y = 8\} = P\{X = 4\}P\{Y = 8\},$$

$$P\{X = 6, Y = 3\} = P\{X = 6\}P\{Y = 3\},$$

$$P\{X = 6, Y = 5\} = P\{X = 6\}P\{Y = 5\},$$

$$P\{X = 6, Y = 6\} = P\{X = 6\}P\{Y = 6\},$$

$$P\{X = 6, Y = 7\} = P\{X = 6\}P\{Y = 7\},$$

and $\quad P\{X = 6, Y = 8\} = P\{X = 6\}P\{Y = 8\}.$

Again, it is not enough that one, or even some, of these conditions be true. For independence between X and Y, all 15 of these conditions must be true. To verify these 15 conditions, we see that

$$P\{X = 2, Y = 3\} = 0.08$$

$$= (0.40)\,(0.20)$$

$$= P\{X = 2\}P\{Y = 3\},$$

$$P\{X = 2, Y = 5\} = 0.12$$

$$= (0.40)\,(0.30)$$

$$= P\{X = 2\}P\{Y = 5\},$$

$$P\{X = 2, Y = 6\} = 0.08$$

$$= (0.40)\,(0.20)$$

$$= P\{X = 2\}P\{Y = 6\},$$

$$P\{X = 2, Y = 7\} = 0.06$$

$$= (0.40)\,(0.15)$$

$$= P\{X = 2\}P\{Y = 7\},$$

$$P\{X = 2, Y = 8\} = 0.06$$

$$= (0.40)\,(0.15)$$

$$= P\{X = 2\}P\{Y = 8\},$$

$$P\{X = 4, Y = 3\} = 0.08$$
$$= (0.40)\,(0.20)$$
$$= P\{X = 4\}P\{Y = 3\},$$

$$P\{X = 4, Y = 5\} = 0.12$$
$$= (0.40)\,(0.30)$$
$$= P\{X = 4\}P\{Y = 5\},$$

$$P\{X = 4, Y = 6\} = 0.08$$
$$= (0.40)\,(0.20)$$
$$= P\{X = 4\}P\{Y = 6\},$$

$$P\{X = 4, Y = 7\} = 0.06$$
$$= (0.40)\,(0.15)$$
$$= P\{X = 4\}P\{Y = 7\},$$

$$P\{X = 4, Y = 8\} = 0.06$$
$$= (0.40)\,(0.15)$$
$$= P\{X = 4\}P\{Y = 8\},$$

$$P\{X = 6, Y = 3\} = 0.04$$
$$= (0.20)\,(0.20)$$
$$= P\{X = 6\}P\{Y = 3\},$$

$$P\{X = 6, Y = 5\} = 0.06$$
$$= (0.20)\,(0.30)$$
$$= P\{X = 6\}P\{Y = 5\},$$

$$P\{X = 6, Y = 6\} = 0.04$$
$$= (0.20)\,(0.20)$$
$$= P\{X = 6\}P\{Y = 6\},$$

$$P\{X = 6, Y = 7\} = 0.03$$
$$= (0.20)\,(0.15)$$
$$= P\{X = 6\}P\{Y = 7\},$$

and $\quad P\{X = 6, Y = 8\} = 0.03$

$$= (0.20)(0.15)$$

$$= P\{X = 6\}P\{Y = 8\}.$$

Thus, X and Y are independent.

✓ • **PROBLEM 7-8**

Consider the following joint probability mass function.

		X			
		2	4	6	Total
	3	0.10	0.08	0.02	0.20
	5	0.12	0.12	0.06	0.30
Y	6	0.08	0.08	0.04	0.20
	7	0.06	0.06	0.03	0.15
	8	0.04	0.06	0.05	0.15
	Total	0.40	0.40	0.20	1.00

Are X and Y independent?

SOLUTION:

We need to check $(5)(3) = 15$ conditions. These are:

$$P\{X = 2, Y = 3\} = P\{X = 2\}P\{Y = 3\},$$

$$P\{X = 2, Y = 5\} = P\{X = 2\}P\{Y = 5\},$$

$$P\{X = 2, Y = 6\} = P\{X = 2\}P\{Y = 6\},$$

$$P\{X = 2, Y = 7\} = P\{X = 2\}P\{Y = 7\},$$

$$P\{X = 2, Y = 8\} = P\{X = 2\}P\{Y = 8\},$$

$$P\{X = 4, Y = 3\} = P\{X = 4\}P\{Y = 3\},$$

$$P\{X = 4, Y = 5\} = P\{X = 4\}P\{Y = 5\},$$

$$P\{X = 4, Y = 6\} = P\{X = 4\}P\{Y = 6\},$$

$$P\{X = 4, Y = 7\} = P\{X = 4\}P\{Y = 7\},$$

$$P\{X = 4, Y = 8\} = P\{X = 4\}P\{Y = 8\},$$

$$P\{X = 6, Y = 3\} = P\{X = 6\}P\{Y = 3\},$$

$$P\{X = 6, Y = 5\} = P\{X = 6\}P\{Y = 5\},$$

$$P\{X = 6, Y = 6\} = P\{X = 6\}P\{Y = 6\},$$

$$P\{X = 6, Y = 7\} = P\{X = 6\}P\{Y = 7\},$$

and $\quad P\{X = 6, Y = 8\} = P\{X = 6\}P\{Y = 8\}.$

Again, it is not enough that one, or even some, of these conditions be true. For independence between X and Y, all 15 of these conditions must be true. To verify these 15 conditions, we see that

$$P\{X = 2, Y = 3\} = 0.10$$

is not equal to 0.08

$$= (0.40)(0.20)$$
$$= P\{X = 2\}P\{Y = 3\},$$
$$P\{X = 2, Y = 5\} = 0.12$$
$$= (0.40)(0.30)$$
$$= P\{X = 2\}P\{Y = 5\},$$
$$P\{X = 2, Y = 6\} = 0.08$$
$$= (0.40)(0.20)$$
$$= P\{X = 2\}P\{Y = 6\},$$
$$P\{X = 2, Y = 7\} = 0.06$$
$$= (0.40)(0.15)$$
$$= P\{X = 2\}P\{Y = 7\},$$
$$P\{X = 2, Y = 8\} = 0.04$$

is not equal to 0.06

$$= (0.40)(0.15)$$
$$= P\{X = 2\}P\{Y = 8\},$$
$$P\{X = 4, Y = 3\} = 0.08$$

$$= (0.40)\,(0.20)$$
$$= P\{X = 4\}P\{Y = 3\},$$

$$P\{X = 4,\ Y = 5\} = 0.12$$

$$= (0.40)\,(0.30)$$
$$= P\{X = 4\}P\{Y = 5\},$$

$$P\{X = 4,\ Y = 6\} = 0.08$$

$$= (0.40)\,(0.20)$$
$$= P\{X = 4\}P\{Y = 6\},$$

$$P\{X = 4,\ Y = 7\} = 0.06$$

$$= (0.40)\,(0.15)$$
$$= P\{X = 4\}P\{Y = 7\},$$

$$P\{X = 4,\ Y = 8\} = 0.06$$

$$= (0.40)\,(0.15)$$
$$= P\{X = 4\}P\{Y = 8\},$$

$$P\{X = 6,\ Y = 3\} = 0.02$$

is not equal to 0.04

$$= (0.20)\,(0.20)$$
$$= P\{X = 6\}P\{Y = 3\},$$

$$P\{X = 6,\ Y = 5\} = 0.06$$

$$= (0.20)\,(0.30)$$
$$= P\{X = 6\}P\{Y = 5\},$$

$$P\{X = 6,\ Y = 6\} = 0.04$$

$$= (0.20)\,(0.20)$$
$$= P\{X = 6\}P\{Y = 6\},$$

$$P\{X = 6,\ Y = 7\} = 0.03$$

$$= (0.20)\,(0.15)$$
$$= P\{X = 6\}P\{Y = 7\},$$

and $\quad P\{X = 6,\ Y = 8\} = 0.05$

is not equal to 0.03

$$= (0.20)(0.15)$$

$$= P\{X = 6\}P\{Y = 8\}.$$

Thus, X and Y are not independent.

✓ • **PROBLEM 7–9**

Consider the following joint probability mass function.

			X		
		2	4	6	Total
	3	0.10	0.10	0.15	0.35
	5	0.05	0.05	0.10	0.20
Y	6	0.05	0.05	0.00	0.10
	7	0.00	0.10	0.05	0.15
	8	0.05	0.10	0.05	0.20
	Total	0.25	0.40	0.35	1.00

Are X and Y independent?

SOLUTION:

We need to check (5) (3) = 15 conditions. These are:

$P\{X = 2, Y = 3\} = P\{X = 2\}P\{Y = 3\}$,

$P\{X = 2, Y = 5\} = P\{X = 2\}P\{Y = 5\}$,

$P\{X = 2, Y = 6\} = P\{X = 2\}P\{Y = 6\}$,

$P\{X = 2, Y = 7\} = P\{X = 2\}P\{Y = 7\}$,

$P\{X = 2, Y = 8\} = P\{X = 2\}P\{Y = 8\}$,

$P\{X = 4, Y = 3\} = P\{X = 4\}P\{Y = 3\}$,

$P\{X = 4, Y = 5\} = P\{X = 4\}P\{Y = 5\}$,

$$P\{X = 4, Y = 6\} = P\{X = 4\}P\{Y = 6\},$$

$$P\{X = 4, Y = 7\} = P\{X = 4\}P\{Y = 7\},$$

$$P\{X = 4, Y = 8\} = P\{X = 4\}P\{Y = 8\},$$

$$P\{X = 6, Y = 3\} = P\{X = 6\}P\{Y = 3\},$$

$$P\{X = 6, Y = 5\} = P\{X = 6\}P\{Y = 5\},$$

$$P\{X = 6, Y = 6\} = P\{X = 6\}P\{Y = 6\},$$

$$P\{X = 6, Y = 7\} = P\{X = 6\}P\{Y = 7\},$$

and $\quad P\{X = 6, Y = 8\} = P\{X = 6\}P\{Y = 8\}.$

Again, it is not enough that one, or even some, of these conditions be true. For independence between X and Y, all 15 of these conditions must be true. To verify these 15 conditions, we see that

$$P\{X = 2, Y = 3\} = 0.10$$

is not equal to 0.0875

$$= (0.25)(0.35)$$
$$= P\{X = 2\}P\{Y = 3\},$$

$$P\{X = 2, Y = 5\} = 0.05$$

$$= (0.25)(0.20)$$
$$= P\{X = 2\}P\{Y = 5\},$$

$$P\{X = 2, Y = 6\} = 0.05$$

is not equal to 0.025

$$= (0.25)(0.10)$$
$$= P\{X = 2\}P\{Y = 6\},$$

$$P\{X = 2, Y = 7\} = 0.00$$

is not equal to 0.0375

$$= (0.25)(0.15)$$
$$= P\{X = 2\}P\{Y = 7\},$$

$$P\{X = 2, Y = 8\} = 0.05$$

$$= (0.25)(0.20)$$
$$= P\{X = 2\}P\{Y = 8\},$$

$$P\{X = 4, Y = 3\} = 0.10$$

is not equal to 0.14

$$= (0.40)(0.35)$$
$$= P\{X = 4\}P\{Y = 3\},$$

$$P\{X = 4, Y = 5\} = 0.05$$

is not equal to 0.08

$$= (0.40)(0.20)$$
$$= P\{X = 4\}P\{Y = 5\},$$

$$P\{X = 4, Y = 6\} = 0.05$$

is not equal to 0.04

$$= (0.40)(0.10)$$
$$= P\{X = 4\}P\{Y = 6\},$$

$$P\{X = 4, Y = 7\} = 0.10$$

is not equal to 0.06

$$= (0.40)(0.15)$$
$$= P\{X = 4\}P\{Y = 7\},$$

$$P\{X = 4, Y = 8\} = 0.10$$

is not equal to 0.08

$$= (0.40)(0.20)$$
$$= P\{X = 4\}P\{Y = 8\},$$

$$P\{X = 6, Y = 3\} = 0.15$$

is not equal to 0.1225

$$= (0.35)(0.35)$$
$$= P\{X = 6\}P\{Y = 3\},$$

$$P\{X = 6, Y = 5\} = 0.10$$

is not equal to 0.07

$$= (0.35)(0.20)$$
$$= P\{X = 6\}P\{Y = 5\},$$

$$P\{X = 6, Y = 6\} = 0.00$$

is not equal to 0.035

$$= (0.35)\,(0.10)$$
$$= P\{X = 6\}P\{Y = 6\},$$

$$P\{X = 6, Y = 7\} = 0.05$$

is not equal to 0.0525

$$= (0.35)\,(0.15)$$
$$= P\{X = 6\}P\{Y = 7\},$$

and $P\{X = 6, Y = 8\} = 0.05$

is not equal to 0.07

$$= (0.35)\,(0.20)$$
$$= P\{X = 6\}P\{Y = 8\}.$$

Thus, X and Y are not independent.

• PROBLEM 7–10

Find random variables W and Z which have the same marginal probability mass functions as X and Y, respectively, but are independent. Write the joint probability mass function for W and Z.

SOLUTION:

We retain the marginal probability mass functions of X and Y, and multiply these, per independence, to arrive at the joint probability mass function. This results in the following table.

		W			
		2	4	6	Total
	3	0.0875	0.1400	0.1225	0.35
	5	0.0500	0.0800	0.0700	0.20
Z	6	0.0250	0.0400	0.0350	0.10
	7	0.0375	0.0600	0.0525	0.15
	8	0.0500	0.0800	0.0700	0.20
	Total	0.25	0.40	0.35	1.00

• PROBLEM 7–11

Suppose that

$$f_{X,Y}(x,y) = e^{-(L1+L2)}(L1)^x(L2)^y/[x\ !\ y\ !]\ \text{for}\ x = 0,1,...;\ y = 0,1,....$$

Are X and Y independent?

SOLUTION:

We may factor the joint probability mass function as

$$f_{X,Y}(x,y) = e^{-(L1+L2)}(L1)^x(L2)^y/[x\ !\ y\ !]$$

$$= \{e^{-L1}(L1)^x/x\ !\}\{e^{-L2}(L2)_y\ !\ y\ !\}$$

$$= f_X(x)f_X(y),$$

where $f_X(x) = e^{-L1}(L1)^x/x\ !\ \text{for}\ x = 0,1,...$

and $f_Y(y) = e^{-L2}(L2)^y/y\ !\ \text{for}\ y = 0,1,...$

Then $P\{X = x,\ Y = y\} = f_{X,Y}(x,y)$

$$= f_X(x)f_Y(y)$$

$$= P\{X = x\}P\{Y = y\},$$

so X and Y are independent. They each have Poisson distributions.

******

REVIEW OF INDEPENDENT CONTINUOUS RANDOM VARIABLES

As discussed in the previous section, discrete random variables, say X and Y, are independent if

$$P\{X \text{ in } A, Y \text{ in } B\} = P\{X \text{ in } A\}P\{Y \text{ in } B\}.$$

We were able to restrict attention to the outcomes of X and Y, and thus the formula for independent discrete random variables became

$$P\{X = k1, Y = k2\} = P\{X = k1\}P\{Y = k2\}$$

for all values of $k1$ and $k2$. Thus, two discrete random variables are independent if and only if their joint probability mass function can be factored as a product of the individual marginal probability mass functions. The analogous statement is true for continuous random variables. Namely, two continuous random variables are independent if and only if their joint probability density function can be factored as a product of the individual marginal probability density functions. This should not be surprising.

Notice also that since the joint probability density function factors as

$$f_{X,Y}(k1, k2) = f_X(k1)f_Y(k2)$$

for independent events, the conditional density of Y given X is

$$f_{Y/X}(k) = f_{X,Y}(k, k2)/f_X(k2)$$

$$= f_X(k2)f_Y(k)/f_X(k2)$$

$$= f_Y(k)$$

if X and Y are independent. Thus, the conditional probability density function of Y given X is the same as the unconditional probability density function of Y. This implies, in particular, that the range of Y cannot depend on X. Thus, the range of the joint probability density function must have a rectangular shape, since otherwise the range of Y would depend on the value of X and then X and Y could not be independent.

As an example, suppose that (X, Y) has a joint distribution which is continuously uniform over the unit circle. That is,

$$f_{X,Y}(k1, k2) = c \text{ if } (k1)^2 + (k2)^2 < 1,$$

and $f_{X,Y}(k1, k2) = \text{ if } (k1)^2 + (k2)^2 \geq 1.$

To find the value of c, notice that the area of the support of this joint distribution is the area of a circle,

$$A = \pi r^2,$$

with radius one, or

$$A = \pi(1)^2$$

$$= \pi(1)$$

$$= \pi.$$

Then to be a proper joint probability density, we require

$$I_{\text{unit circle}} c = 1.$$

But $\quad I_{\text{unit circle}} c = (c) I_{\text{unit circle}}$

$$= (c) \text{ (area of unit circle)}$$

$$= (c) (\pi)$$

$$= c\pi$$

$$= 1.$$

Thus, $c = 1/\pi$. Now returning to independence, notice that the range of Y depends on the value of X. The range is determined by the formula

$$X^2 + Y^2 < 1,$$

or $\quad Y^2 < 1 - X^2,$

or $\quad -(1 - X^2)^{0.5} < Y < (1 - X^2)^{0.5}.$

As an example, if $X = 0$, then

$$-(1 - 0^2)^{0.5} < Y < (1 - 0^2)^{0.5},$$

$$-(1 - 0)^{0.5} < Y < (1 - 0)^{0.5},$$

$$-(1)^{0.5} < Y < (1)^{0.5},$$

$$-1 < Y < 1.$$

But if $X = 1$, then

$$-(1 - 1^2)^{0.5} < Y < (1 - 1^2)^{0.5},$$

$$-(1 - 1)^{0.5} < Y < (1 - 1)^{0.5},$$

$$-(0)^{0.5} < Y < (0)^{0.5},$$

$$0 < Y < 0,$$

$$Y = 0.$$

Because the range of Y depends on the value of X, X and Y cannot be independent.

• PROBLEM 7-12

Suppose that (X, Y) has a joint distribution which is continuously uniform over the range $0 < X < 1$, $3 < Y < 5$. Are X and Y independent?

SOLUTION:

The joint probability density function is

$$f_{X,Y}(k1, k2) = \frac{1}{[\text{the area of the range}]}$$

$$= \frac{1}{[(1-0)(5-3)]}$$

$$= \frac{1}{[(1)(2)]}$$

$$= \frac{1}{2}$$

$$= 0.5 \text{ when } 0 < k1 < 1 \text{ and } 3 < k2 < 5,$$

and $f_{X,Y}(k1, k2) = 0$ otherwise.

Now we may factor this joint probability density function as

$$f_{X,Y}(k1, k2) = 0.5$$

$$= (1)(0.5)$$

$$= f_X(k1)f_Y(k2).$$

Notice that these are the marginal probability density functions of X and Y. Because the joint probability density function can be so factored, X and Y are independent.

• PROBLEM 7–13

Suppose that (X, Y) has a joint distribution which is continuously uniform over the range $-1 < X + Y < 1$, $-1 < X - Y < 1$. Are X and Y independent?

SOLUTION:

Consider the shape of this region. The region defined by

$$-1 < X + Y < 1, -1 < X - Y < 1$$

is a square and, consequently, a rectangle. However, the orientation of this square is such that it does not align itself with the coordinate axes. Consider the range of Y when $X = 0$. Clearly, when $X = 0$,

$$-1 < 0 + Y < 1, -1 < 0 - Y < 1,$$

$$-1 < Y < 1, -1 < -Y < 1,$$

or $\quad -1 < Y < 1$.

But when $X = 0.5$,

$$-1 < 0.5 + Y < 1, -1 < 0.5 - Y < 1,$$

$$-1.5 < Y < 0.5, -1.5 < -Y < 0.5,$$

$$-1.5 < Y < 0.5, -0.5 < Y < 1.5,$$

or $\quad -0.5 < Y < 0.5$.

Therefore, the range of Y depends on X, so X and Y cannot be independent, even though the support of the joint distribution is technically a rectangle.

• PROBLEM 7–14

Suppose that X and Y have joint probability density function

$$f_{X,Y}(x, y) = (L1)(L2)e^{-[(L1)x + (L2)y]}$$

for $x > 0$ and $y > 0$, and

$$f_{X,Y}(x, y) = 0 \text{ otherwise.}$$

Are X and Y independent?

SOLUTION:

We may factor the joint probability density function as

$$f_{X,Y}(x, y) = (L1)(L2)e^{-[(L1)x + (L2)y]}$$

$$= (L1)e^{-(L1)x}(L2)e^{(L2)y}$$

$$= f_X(x)f_Y(y) \text{ for } x > 0, y > 0,$$

where $\qquad f_X(x) = (L1)e^{-(L1)x}$ for $x > 0$

and $\qquad f_Y(y) = (L2)e^{-(L2)y}$ for $y > 0$.

Thus, X and Y are independent. They each have exponential distributions.

 **• PROBLEM 7-15**

Suppose that X and Y have joint probability density function

$$f_{X,Y}(x, y) = x^2 + y^2 \text{ for } 0 < x < k \text{ and } 0 < y < k,$$

and $\quad f_{X,Y}(x, y) = 0$ otherwise.

What is the value of k?

SOLUTION:

We must integrate the joint probability density function over the appropriate range to ensure that it integrates to one. This, along with the fact that the joint probability density function is non-negative, would make it a proper joint probability density function. Thus,

$$1 = I_{x = 0 \text{ to } k} I_{y = \text{ to } k}(x^2 + y^2)dy \, dx$$

$$= I_{x = 0 \text{ to } k}[yx^2 + y^3/3]_{y = 0 \text{ to } k}dx$$

$$= I_{x = 0 \text{ to } k}[(kx^2 + k^3/3) - (0x^2 + 0^3/3)]dx$$

$$= I_{x = 0 \text{ to } k}[(kx^2 + k^3/3) - (0 + 0/3)]dx$$

$$= I_{x = 0 \text{ to } k}[(kx^2 + k^3/3) - (0 + 0)]dx$$

$$= I_{x = 0 \text{ to } k}[(kx^2 + k^3/3) - (0)]dx$$

$$= I_{x = 0 \text{ to } k}[kx^2 + k^3/3]dx$$

$$= [kx^3/3 + xk^3/3]_{x = 0 \text{ to } k}$$

$$= [(k)(k^3/3) + (k)(k^3/3)] - [(k)(0^3/3) + (0)(k^3/3)]$$

$$= [k^4/3 + k^4/3] - [(k)(0/3) + 0]$$

$$= [2k^4/3] - [(k)(0) + 0]$$

$$= [2k^4/3] - [0 + 0]$$

$$= [2k^4/3] - 0$$

$$= [2k^4/3].$$

Now

$$k^4 = 3/2,$$

so $\quad k = (3/2)^{0.25.}$

✓ • PROBLEM 7–16

Suppose that X and Y have the joint probability density function given in Problem 7–15, with the value of k as indicated. Does the range of Y depend on the value of X? Does the range of X depend on the value of Y?

SOLUTION:

Since both X and Y range from zero to k, neither range depends on the value of the other random variable. Thus, we cannot conclude that they are not independent at this stage.

✓ • PROBLEM 7–17

Suppose that X and Y have the joint probability density function given in Problem 7–15, with the value of k as indicated. Are X and Y independent?

SOLUTION:

It is seen that the joint probability density function cannot be factored into one component involving only X and another component involving only Y. The term $(x^2 + y^2)$ can be factored if we are willing to consider complex variable theory, but even so, the terms into which this factors would each involve both x and y. Thus, X and Y cannot be independent.

• PROBLEM 7–18

Can there be three continuous random variables, say X, Y, and Z, such that X and Z are dependent, Y and Z are dependent, but X and Y are independent? Either give an example or prove that no such example exists.

SOLUTION:

Let X and Y be any independent continuous random variables, say normal with mean zero and variance one, and let

$$Z = X + Y.$$

Clearly, X and Y are independent, but X and Z are dependent, and Y and Z are also dependent.

✓• PROBLEM 7–19

Given that the continuous random variables X and Y have joint probability density function $f(x, y) = x + y$ when $0 < x < 1$ and $0 < y < 1$, and $f(x, y) = 0$ otherwise, use the marginal probability functions to decide whether or not X and Y are stochastically independent.

SOLUTION:

The marginal probability density function of X is found by integrating the joint density function, over the entire domain of Y, with respect to y. This produces a function of x:

$$f_x(x) = \int_{-\infty}^{\infty} f(x, y) \, dy = \int_0^1 (x + y) \, dy = \int_0^1 x \, dy + \int_0^1 y \, dy$$

$$= x(y)]_0^1 + \frac{y^2}{2} \Big]_0^1 = x(1 - 0) + \left(\frac{1}{2} - 0\right) = \begin{cases} x + \dfrac{1}{2} & 0 < x < 1 \\ 0 & \text{elsewhere} \end{cases}.$$

Similarly,

$$f_y(y) = \int_{-\infty}^{\infty} f(x, y) \, dx = \int_0^1 (x + y) \, dx = \int_0^1 x \, dx + \int_0^1 y \, dx$$

$$= y(x)]_0^1 + \frac{x^2}{2} \Big]_0^1 = y(1 - 0) + \left(\frac{1}{2} - 0\right) = \begin{cases} y + \dfrac{1}{2} & 0 < y < 1 \\ 0 & \text{elsewhere} \end{cases}.$$

By definition, X and Y are stochastically independent if and only if $f(x, y) = f(x) \times f(y)$. If for some pair (x, y) $f(x, y) \neq f_x(x) \times f_y(y)$, then X and Y are said to be stochastically dependent. We calculate

$$f_x(x) \times f_y(y) = \left(x + \frac{1}{2}\right)\left(y + \frac{1}{2}\right)$$

$$= xy + \frac{1}{2}y + \frac{1}{2}x + \frac{1}{4} \neq x + y = f(x, y).$$

Therefore, X and Y are stochastically depedent.

$$\ast\ast\ast\ast\ast\ast$$

REVIEW OF RELATION BETWEEN INDEPENDENCE AND MUTUAL EXCLUSIVITY

Many people confuse independence and mutual exclusivity, even those who feel that they are clear on the distinction. Just as a review, the two definitions will be presented here. Two events, A and B, are mutually exclusive if

$$P\{A \cap B\} = 0.$$

Two events, A and B, are independent if

$$P\{A \cap B\} = P\{A\}P\{B\}.$$

Mutually exclusive events cannot both occur (or at least the probability of both occurring is zero). Independent events can both occur, but the occurrence of one in no way affects the probability of occurrence of the other. In most cases, this cannot be said for mutually exclusive events. If A and B are mutually exclusive, and if A occurs, then we know that B cannot also occur (or at least its probability is zero).

✓• PROBLEM 7–20

Can two events, A and B, be both mutually exclusive and independent?

SOLUTION:

By the formulas, we would require both

$$P\{AB\} = 0$$

and $P\{AB\} = P\{A\}P\{B\}.$

If we equate these, then we see that

$$P\{A\}P\{B\} = 0.$$

Thus, we would need at least one of these events to have probability zero.

• PROBLEM 7-21

If the probability of A is zero, then is A independent of all other events? Is A mutually exclusive of all other events?

SOLUTION:

If $P\{A\} = 0$, then

$$0 \leq P\{AB\}$$

$$\leq P\{A\} = 0,$$

so $P\{AB\} = 0,$

and A is mutually exclusive of all other events. Also,

$$P\{AB\} = 0$$

$$= P\{A\}$$

$$= P\{A\}P\{B\},$$

so A is also independent of all other events.

• PROBLEM 7-22

If the probability of A is one, then is A independent of all other events? Is A mutually exclusive of all other events?

SOLUTION:

If $P\{A\} = 1$, then

$$P\{AB\} = P\{B\},$$

which need not be zero, so A need not be mutually exclusive of all other events. Also,

$$P\{AB\} = P\{B\}$$

$$= (1)P\{B\},$$

$$= P\{A\}P\{B\},$$

so A is also independent of all other events.

＊＊＊＊＊＊

REVIEW OF RELATION AMONG INDEPENDENCE, CORRELATION, AND COVARIANCE

Many people believe that independence is synonymous with lack of correlation, which in turn is synonymous with lack of covariance. This is only partially true, as we will see.

The covariance of two random variables, X and Y, is

$$C(X, Y) = E[(X - E[X])(Y - E[Y])]$$

$$= E\{XY - YE[X] - XE[Y] + E[X]E[Y]\}$$

$$= E[XY] - E[X]E[Y] - E[Y]E[X] + E[X]E[Y]$$

$$= E[XY] - E[X]E[Y] - E[X]E[Y] + E[X]E[Y]$$

$$= E[XY] - E[X]E[Y].$$

The correlation of two random variables, say X and Y, is

$$p(X, Y) = C(X, Y)/[V(X)V(Y)]^{0.5}.$$

That is, the correlation is the covariance divided by the standard deviations.

As it turns out, independence always implies a lack of correlation (a correlation of zero), which in turn always implies a lack of covariance (a covariance of zero). Conversely, a lack of covariance always implies a lack of correlation. However, it is not the case that a lack of correlation always implies independence; this is only true for the normal distribution and the Bernoulli distribution. Basically, the reason for this is that correlation and covariance only measure linear association. For example, consider, the following table.

		X		
		0	1	Total
	−1	0.0	0.4	0.4
Y	0	0.2	0.0	0.2
	1	0.0	0.4	0.4
	Total	0.2	0.8	1.0

Clearly, X and Y are not independent. To see this, notice that

$$P\{X = 0, Y = 1\} = 0.0$$

is not equal to 0.08

$$= (0.2)\,(0.4)$$

$$= P\{X = 0\}P\{Y = 1\}.$$

In fact, these two random variables follow a functional relationship; namely, $X = Y^2$. But this is not a linear relationship. The linear association between X and Y is measured by the covariance, and is seen to be

$$C(X, Y) = E[XY] - E[X]E[Y]$$

$$= (-1 \times 1)\,(0.4) + (0 \times 0)\,(0.2) + (1 \times 1)\,(0.4)$$

$$= (-1)\,(0.4) + (0)\,(0.2) + (1)\,(0.4)$$

$$= -0.4 + 0 + 0.4$$

$$= 0.$$

Thus, X and Y are uncorrelated, despite not being independent.

• PROBLEM 7–23

Give an example of Bernoulli random variables which are correlated.

SOLUTION:

Consider the following table.

			X	
		0	1	Total
Y	0	0.4	0.3	0.7
	1	0.3	0.0	0.0
	Total	0.7	0.3	1.0

Now

$$C(X, Y) = E[XY] - E[X]E[Y]$$

$$= P\{X = 1, Y = 1\} - P\{X = 1\}P\{Y = 1\}$$

$$= 0.0 - (0.7)(0.7)$$

$$= 0.0 - 0.49$$

$$= - 0.49.$$

• PROBLEM 7-24

Prove that uncorrelated Bernoulli random variables are independent.

SOLUTION:

Suppose that X and Y are Bernoulli random variables and that

$$p(X, Y) = 0.$$

Then $C(X, Y) = 0$,

so $E[XY] - E[X]E[Y] = 0$

and $E[XY] = E[X]E[Y]$.

That is, $P\{X = 1, Y = 1\} = P\{X = 1\}P\{Y = 1\}$.

Now $P\{X = 0, Y = 1\} = P\{Y = 1\} - P\{X = 1, Y = 1\}$

$$= P\{Y = 1\} - P\{X = 1\}P\{Y = 1\}$$

$$= P\{Y = 1\}(1 - P\{X = 1\})$$

$$= P\{Y = 1\}P\{X = 0\},$$

$P\{X = 0, Y = 0\} = P\{X = 0\} - P\{X = 0, Y = 1\}$

$$= P\{X = 0\} - P\{X = 0\}P\{Y = 1\}$$

$$= P\{X = 0\}(1 - P\{Y = 1\})$$

$$= P\{X = 0\}P\{Y = 1\},$$

and $P\{X = 1, Y = 0\} = P\{Y = 0\} - P\{X = 0, Y = 0\}$

$$= P\{Y = 0\} - P\{X = 0\}P\{Y = 0\}$$

$$= P\{Y = 0\}(1 - P\{X = 0\})$$

$$= P\{Y = 0\}P\{X = 1\}.$$

Thus, all events involving X are independent of all events involving Y, so X and Y are independent. This is intuitive, because Bernoulli random variables only assume the values zero and one. These values remain intact when raised to any power. Thus, any type of higher order polynomial association would also be a linear association.

$\checkmark$ • **PROBLEM 7-25**

Find the variance of the random variable $Z = X + Y$ in terms of the variance of X and of Y if X and Y are not independent.

SOLUTION:

$$\text{var}(Z) = \text{var}(X + Y) = E[((X + Y) - E[X + Y])^2]$$

$$= E[X - E[X] + Y - E[Y])^2]$$

(because $E[X + Y] = E[X] + E[Y]$),

$$= E[(X - E[X])^2 + 2 (X - E[X]) (Y - E[Y]) + (Y - E[Y])^2],$$

and by the properties of expectation,

$$= E[(X - E[X])^2] + 2 E[(X - E[X] (Y - E[Y])] + E[Y - E[Y])^2].$$

Thus $\text{var}(Z) = \text{var}(X) + \text{var}(Y) + 2 E[(X - E[X] (Y - E[Y])].$

If X and Y are independent, $E[(X - E[X]) (Y - E[Y])] = 0$, but since X and Y are not independent, we may not assume that this cross-product is zero. The term

$$E[(X - E[X] (Y - E[Y])]$$

is called the covariance of X and Y and is a measure of the linear relation between X and Y. It is such a measure in the sense that if X is greater than $E[X]$ at the same time that Y is greater than $E[Y]$ with high probability, then the covariance of X and Y will be positive. If X is below $E[X]$ at the same time Y is above $E[Y]$ with high probability, the covariance of X and Y will be negative.

Related to the covariance is the correlation coefficient defined as:

$$\rho = \frac{\text{cov}(X, Y)}{\sqrt{\text{var} X}\sqrt{\text{var} Y}}.$$

The correlation coefficient gives a clearer picture of the linear relation between X and Y because it takes into account the variation in the individual variables X and Y.

Also, cov$(X, Y) = 0$ if X and Y are independent. The converse is not true. Further, cov$(X, Y) = $ cov(Y, X).

• PROBLEM 7–26

Find a formula for the covariance of

$$Y = \sum_{i=1}^{m} a_i Y_i \text{ and } X = \sum_{j=1}^{n} b_j X_j$$

if Y_i and X_j are random variables and a_i and b_j are constants.

SOLUTION:

Write cov$(X, Y) = $ cov$\left(\sum_{j=1}^{n} b_j X_j, \sum_{i=1}^{m} a_i Y_i \right)$

$$= E[(X - E[X])]](Y - E[Y]),$$

but $\quad E[X] = E\left[\sum_{j=1}^{n} b_j X_j \right] = \sum_{j=1}^{n} b_j E[X_j]$

and $\quad E[Y] = \sum_{i=1}^{m} a_i E[Y_i]$

by the linearity properties of expectation. Thus,

$$X - E[X] = \sum_{j=1}^{n} b_j X_j - \sum_{j=1}^{n} b_j E[X_j] = \sum_{j=1}^{n} b_j (X_j - E[X_j]),$$

and similarly,

$$Y - E[Y] = \sum_{i=1}^{m} a_i Y_i - \sum_{i=1}^{m} a_i E[Y_i] = \sum_{i=1}^{m} a_i (Y_i - E[Y_i]).$$

Thus,

$$\text{cov}(X, Y)$$

$$= E\left[\left(\sum_{j=1}^{n} b_j(X_j - E[X_j])\right) \times \left(\sum_{i=1}^{m} a_i(Y_i - E[Y_i])\right)\right]$$

$$= E\left[\left(\sum_{j=1}^{n} b_j(X_j - E[X_j])\right)\left[a_1(Y_1 - E[Y_1]) + \dots a_m(Y_m - E[Y_m])\right]\right]$$

$$= \sum_{j=1}^{n} a_1 b_j (X_j - E[X_j])(Y_1 - E[Y_1]) +$$

$$\sum_{j=1}^{n} a_2 b_j (X_j - E[X_j])(Y_2 - E[Y_2]) + \dots +$$

$$\sum_{j=1}^{n} a_n b_j (X_j - E[X_j])(Y_n - E[Y_n])]$$

$$= E\left[\sum_{j=1}^{n}\sum_{i=1}^{m} a_i b_j (X_j - E[X_j])(Y_i - E[Y_i])\right]$$

$$= \sum_{j=1}^{n}\sum_{i=1}^{m} a_i b_j E[(X_j - E[X_j])(Y_i - E[Y_i])]$$

$$= \sum_{j=1}^{n}\sum_{i=1}^{m} a_i b_j \text{cov}(X_j, Y_i).$$

✓ ● **PROBLEM 7–27**

Find ρ for X and Y if

$$f(x, y) = x + y \qquad \text{for} \qquad 0 < x < 1$$
$$0 < y < 1$$

is the joint density of X and Y.

SOLUTION:

The correlation coefficient, ρ, is defined to be

$$\rho = \frac{\text{cov}(X, Y)}{\sqrt{\text{var } X}\sqrt{\text{var } Y}}.$$

where $\text{cov}(X, Y) = E[(X - E[X]) (Y - E[Y])]$,

$\quad\quad$ var $X = E[X]^2 - [E[X]]^2$,

and $\quad$ var $Y = E[Y]^2 - [E[Y]]^2$.

Then $\quad$ $\text{cov}(X, Y) = E[X - E[X] (Y - E[Y])]$

$$= E[XY - E[X] Y - E[Y] X + E[X] E[Y]]$$

$$= E[XY] - E[X] E[Y] - E[Y] E[X] + E[X] E[Y]$$

by the properties of expectation. Thus,

$$\text{cov}(X, Y) = E[XY] - E[X] E[Y].$$

In our problem,

$$E[X] = \iint_R x f(x, y) \, dx \, dy$$

$$= \int_0^1 \int_0^1 x(x + y) \, dx \, dy = \int_0^1 \left[\frac{x^3}{3} + \frac{x^2 y}{2} \right] dy$$

$$= \int_0^1 \left[\frac{1}{3} + \frac{y}{2} \right] dy = \frac{y}{3} + \frac{y^2}{4} \Big|_0^1$$

$$= \frac{1}{3} + \frac{1}{4} = \frac{7}{12}$$

Also, $E[X^2] = \int_0^1 \int_0^1 x^2 (x + y) \, dx \, dy = \int_0^1 \int_0^1 (x^3 + x^2 y) \, dx \, dy$

$$= \int_0^1 \left[\frac{x^4}{4} + \frac{x^3 y}{3} \right]_0^1 dy = \int_0^1 \left[\frac{1}{4} + \frac{y}{3} \right] dy = \left[\frac{y}{4} + \frac{y^2}{6} \right]_0^1$$

$$= \frac{1}{4} + \frac{1}{6} = \frac{10}{24} = \frac{5}{12}$$

✳✳✳✳✳✳

REVIEW OF CONDITIONAL INDEPENDENCE

A number of years ago, a study was undertaken in which various attributes of elementary school children were recorded. After the study was completed, a preliminary analysis of the data was performed. This preliminary analysis revealed a striking and startling trend. Children with larger feet seemed to be more intelligent than children with smaller feet. The trend was clear, yet previously unseen. Nobody involved in this study could explain this phenomenon, so a statistician was called in. This statistician quickly found the source of confusion. Before we go on, can you find the source of confusion?

Shoe size was compared to the score received on a standardized exam. All students took the same exam. Those students who did well on the exam were, to a large extent, the same students who had a larger shoe size.

It occurred to nobody but the statistician that older children should tend to have both larger feet than younger children and more education than younger children. The more relevant comparison would have been of shoe sizes and test scores only for children in the same grade (or of the same age).

Thus, the proper question would have been whether shoe size and education are related within a given age group. When this question was asked, a new analysis of the data was performed. As expected, this analysis revealed no relation between shoe size and intelligence among students in the same grade.

What we see here is conditional independence of shoe size and intelligence when conditioning on age. Unconditionally, however, there is little doubt that shoe size and intelligence (at least as measured for the purposes of this study) are related.

In a certain sense, conditional independence is similar to Simpson's paradox. In Simpson's paradox, we encountered a situation in which one event had higher unconditional probability yet lower conditional probability than the other. Independence of discrete random variables is, in certain respects, nothing more than a statement concerning the fact that the probabilities of events concerning one of these discrete random variables are no more or less likely to occur for one value of the other discrete random variable than they are for any other value of the other discrete random variable. If we view the different values of the second discrete random variable as different events, then we are merely saying that different events have the same unconditional probabilities. For example, consider two Bernoulli random variables, as in the following table (this example was considered previously).

| | | X | | |
		0	1	Total
Y	0	0.4	0.3	0.7
	1	0.3	0.0	0.3
	Total	0.7	0.3	1.0

As we saw before, X and Y are not independent. This can be stated in terms of probabilities as follows. Let Y_0 be the distribution of Y when $X = 0$, and let Y_1 be the distribution of Y when $X = 1$. Then independence of X and Y would mean that for any value of k,

$$P\{Y0 = k\} = P\{Y1 = k\}.$$

Lack of independence is simply the corresponding inequality. In this case,

$$P\{Y0 = 0\} = \frac{0.4}{0.7}$$

$$= \frac{4}{7},$$

$$P\{Y0 = 1\} = \frac{0.3}{0.7}$$

$$= \frac{3}{7},$$

$$P\{Y1 = 0\} = \frac{0.3}{0.3}$$

$$= 1.0,$$

and $$P\{Y1 = 1\} = \frac{0.0}{0.3}$$

$$= 0.0.$$

Clearly, then, X and Y are not independent.

Conditional independence is defined in the same manner, except that the unconditional probabilities concerning Y_0 and Y_1 are replaced with conditional probabilities, where the conditioning is performed with respect to a third random variable (not X).

Returning to the example with shoe sizes, test scores, and grades, suppose that the data were as given in the next nine tables (for simplicity, we will only consider two grades, high and low, and we will similarly dichotomize test scores and shoe sizes into high and low).

Table 1

Small Shoe		Age		
		Young	Old	Total
Test Score	High	16	4	20
	Low	64	16	80
	Total	80	20	100

Table 2

Large Shoe		Age		
		Young	Old	Total
Test Score	High	16	64	80
	Low	4	16	20
	Total	20	80	100

Table 3

		Shoe Size		
		Small	Large	Total
Age	Young	80	20	100
	Old	20	80	100
	Total	100	100	200

Table 4

		Shoe Size		
		Small	Large	Total
Test Score	High	20	80	100
	Low	80	20	100
	Total	100	100	200

Table 5

		Age		
		Young	Old	Total
Test Score	High	32	68	100
	Low	68	32	100
	Total	100	100	200

Table 6

Young		Shoe Size		
		Small	Large	Total
Test Score	High	16	4	20
	Low	64	16	80
	Total	80	20	100

Table 7

Old	Shoe Size		
		Small	Large	Total
Test Score	High	16	64	80
	Low	4	16	20
	Total	20	80	100

Table 8

High Test Score	Shoe Size		
		Small	Large	Total
Age	Young	16	4	20
	Old	64	16	80
	Total	80	20	100

Table 9

Low Test Score	Shoe Size		
	Small	Large	Total	
Age	Young	64	16	80
	Old	16	4	20
	Total	80	20	100

The nine tables (one table for each of the three pairs of variables, plus six tables to separate the counts based on the levels of the third variable) present some interesting facts. There is independence in Table 1, Table 2, Table 6, Table 7, Table 8, and Table 9. These are the six tables which separate counts based on the levels of the third variable. Thus, there is conditional independence for all pairs of random variables conditional on the third random variable. However, there is no independence in Table 3, Table 4, or Table 5. These are the three tables for each pair of random variables without consideration of the third random variable. Thus, there is no unconditional independence.

Just like unconditional independence, conditional independence is not limited to discrete random variables. It may be applied to events or random variables, and these random variables may be either discrete or continuous.

It is possible for independent events not to be conditionally independent. It is also possible for dependent events to be conditionally independent.

• PROBLEM 7–28

Consider tossing a fair die. Let X denote the number facing up on this die. Now toss a biased coin twice, with probability of heads

$$P\{H\} = \frac{X}{6}$$

and probability of tails

$$P\{T\} = 1 - P\{H\}$$

$$= 1 - \frac{X}{6}.$$

Let Y_1 be defined as $Y_1 = 0$ if the first toss is tails

and $Y_1 = 1$ if the first toss is heads.

Let Y_2 be defined as $Y_2 = 0$ if the second toss is tails

and $Y_2 = 1$ if the second toss is heads.

Are Y_1 and Y_2 independent? Are Y_1 and Y_2 conditionally independent given X?

SOLUTION:

A set of tables will again help to clarify the situation. The first table, Table 1, presents the joint probability mass function of Y_1 and Y_2 when $X = 1$. Tables 2 through 6 provide the joint probability mass function of Y_1 and Y_2 when $X = 2$ through 6, respectively. Table 7 presents the joint probability mass function of Y_1 and Y_2 not conditioned on the value of X.

Table 1

$X = 1$	Y_1		
		0	1	Total
Y_2	0	1/36	5/36	6/36
	1	5/36	25/36	30/36
	Total	6/36	30/36	36/36

Table 2

$X = 2$	Y_1		
		0	1	Total
Y_2	0	4/36	8/36	12/36
	1	8/36	16/36	24/36
	Total	12/36	24/36	36/36

Table 3

$X = 3$	Y_1		
		0	1	Total
Y_2	0	9/36	9/36	18/36
	1	9/36	9/36	18/36
	Total	18/36	18/36	36/36

Table 4

X = 4		Y_1		
		0	1	Total
Y_2	0	16/36	8/36	24/36
	1	8/36	4/36	12/36
	Total	24/36	12/36	36/36

Table 5

X = 5		Y_1		
		0	1	Total
Y_2	0	25/36	5/36	30/36
	1	5/36	1/36	6/36
	Total	30/36	6/36	36/36

Table 6

X = 6		Y_1		
		0	1	Total
Y_2	0	36/36	0/36	36/36
	1	0/36	0/36	0/36
	Total	36/36	0/36	36/36

Table 7

		Y_1		
		0	1	Total
Y_2	0	91/216	35/216	126/216
	1	35/216	55/216	90/216
	Total	126/216	90/216	216/216

Inspection of each of the first six tables will reveal that Y_1 and Y_2 are conditionally independent for each value of X. That is, for any value of X ($x = 1, 2, 3, 4, 5$, or 6), and for $k_1 = 0$ or $k_1 = 1$, and for $k_2 = 0$ or $k_2 = 1$,

$$P\{Y_1 = k_1, Y_2 = k_2 \mid X = x\}$$
$$= P\{Y_1 = k_1 \mid X = x\} P\{Y_2 = k_2 \mid X = x\}.$$

But now consider Table 7. Here,

$$P\{Y_1 = 0, Y_2 = 0\} = 91/216$$

is not equal to (126/216) (126/216)

$$= P\{Y_1 = 0\} P\{Y_2 = 0\}.$$

Thus, Y_1 and Y_2 are not conditionally independent. This is not surprising, since for large values of X, both Y_1 and Y_2 tend to have a larger probability of being zero, while for smaller values of X, both Y_1 and Y_2 tend to have a smaller probability of being zero.

$$\ast\ast\ast\ast\ast\ast$$

REVIEW OF HIGHER ORDER INDEPENDENCE

A common misconception is that if a set of variables is pairwise independent, then the variables are independent. That is, if each pair of two such variables is independent, then it is often mistakenly assumed that the entire set of variables is independent. This is not the case.

• PROBLEM 7–29

Find an example of three events such that each pair of these events is independent, yet the set of three events is not independent.

SOLUTION:

Toss three fair coins and define event A to be

$$A = \{THT, HTH\},$$

define event B to be

$$B = \{HHH, HHT, HTH, HTT\},$$

and define event C to be

$$C = \{HHH, HTH, THH, TTH\}.$$

That is, event A specifies that there is an alternating pattern, event B specifies that the first coin landed heads, and event C specifies that the third coin landed heads.

Now

$$P\{AB\} = P\{HTH\}$$

since HTH is the only outcome which is favorable to both event A and event B. Thus,

$$P\{AB\} = P\{HTH\}$$

$$= (0.5)\,(0.5)\,(0.5)$$

$$= 0.125.$$

But $\quad P\{A\} = P\{THT \cup HTH\}$

$$= P\{THT\} + P\{HTH\}$$

$$= (0.5)\,(0.5)\,(0.5) + (0.5)\,(0.5)\,(0.5)$$

$$= 0.125 + 0.125$$

$$= 0.25,$$

and $\quad P\{B\} = P\{\text{the first coin lands heads}\}$

$$= 0.5.$$

Thus, $P\{AB\} = 0.125$

$$= (0.25)(0.5)$$

$$= P\{A\}P\{B\},$$

so events A and B are independent.

Also, $P\{AC\} = P\{HTH\}$

$$= 0.125,$$

again because HTH is the only outcome which is favorable to both event A and event C. Now we see that

$$P\{C\} = P\{\text{third coin lands heads}\}$$

$$= 0.5,$$

so $\quad P\{AC\} = 0.125$

$$= (0.25)(0.5)$$

$$= P\{A\}P\{C\},$$

so events A and C are independent.

Also, $P\{BC\} = P\{HHH \cup HTH\}$

$$= P\{HHH\} + P\{HTH\}$$

$$= (0.5)(0.5)(0.5) + (0.5)(0.5)(0.5)$$

$$= 0.125 + 0.125$$

$$= 0.25$$

$$= (0.5)(0.5)$$

$$P\{B\}P\{C\},$$

so events B and C are also independent. That is, each pair of these events is independent. But

$$P\{ABC\} = P\{HTH\},$$

because HTH is the only outcome which is favorable to event A, event B, and event C. Then

$$P\{ABC\} = P\{HTH\}$$
$$= 0.125$$

is not equal to 0.0625

$$= (0.25)\,(0.5)\,(0.5)$$
$$= P\{A\}P\{B\}P\{C\}.$$

Thus, the three events are not independent.

CHAPTER 8

Random Samples

Basic Attacks and Strategies for Solving Problems in this Chapter. See pages 609 to 669 for step-by-step solutions to problems.

Sampling is the bridge between probability theory and statistics. Probability theory allows one to predict the occurrence of random events based on assumptions about the parameters of the process generating these random events. Statistics allows one to infer likely values of the parameters of the process generating these random events given that certain events were observed and others were not. That is, data, or a sample, is gathered and analyzed to try to understand the underlying probabilistic process.

As an example, suppose that X is a Bernoulli random variable with parameter 0.5. Then $P\{X = 0\} = 0.5$ and $P\{X = 1\} = 0.5$. But suppose that Y is a Bernoulli random variable and that we do not know the value of its parameter. What we have is a sample. We may have tossed a coin 10 times, without assuming the coin to be fair, to try to estimate the probability that this coin lands heads.

If the coin lands heads seven times out of the 10 tosses, then it is reasonable to estimate the probability that the coin lands heads to be 7/10 = 0.7. Of course, we cannot be sure that this estimate is correct. If we toss the same coin 10 more times, then we may see six or eight heads this time. Thus, our estimate of the probability of heads would change.

What underlies the ability to estimate any parameter at all is knowledge of the sampling scheme. For example, suppose that a scheme other than random sampling were used. You may have asked me to tell you the results of 10 tosses of this coin. You may have assumed that I would toss the coin 10 times and tell you the results of these 10 tosses, namely seven heads and three tails.

But perhaps I like to be as positive as I can, and I really want to give you a large number. So when I toss the coin 10 times and observe no heads, I am not satisfied. I toss the coin 90 more times for a total of 100, and in these 100 tosses I observe seven heads. I feel confident that if I just keep on tossing I can get all 10 heads, but unfortunately a prior engagement pulls me away, and I must report to you the seven heads. Of course, you don't ask and I don't volunteer to you the method I used. So you believe that I observed seven heads out of 10 tosses, and you estimate the probability of heads to be 7/10 = 0.7. Had you known the truth, however, you would have estimated this probability to be 7/100 = 0.07.

The point is that one cannot just blindly take an average or compute a proportion and expect it to reflect in any meaningful way the true value of a parameter of interest. It is important to consider carefully the sampling scheme which generated the data at hand.

The most well-known sampling scheme is random sampling. Random sampling is defined by assigning equal probabilities to each possible sample. For example, suppose that a population has four elements, and each of these elements has a numerical value. Suppose that these values are {1, 2, 3, and 4}, and that sampling is performed without replacement, and that the sample will contain two of these elements. There are

$$C(4, 2) = 4!/[(2!) (4 - 2)!]$$

$$= 24/[(2) (2!)]$$

$$= 24/[(2) (2)]$$

$$= 24/4$$

$$= 6$$

possible samples. The possible samples are

{1, 2},

{1, 3},

{1, 4},

{2, 3},

{2, 4},

and   {3, 4}.

Simple random sampling, which we will hereafter refer to as random sampling, would assign each of these six pairs the same probability. Therefore, this probability would need to be 1/6. Clearly, there are other forms of sampling.

Stratified sampling forms strata, or groups of elements. For illustration, let us suppose that the first stratum is {1, 2}, and the second stratum is {3, 4}. Then stratified random sampling would require that at least one element per stratum be selected.

Cluster sampling forms clusters, which are also groups of elements. For illustration, let us suppose again that the first cluster is {1, 2}, and the second cluster is {3, 4}. Then cluster sampling would require that one cluster be chosen, and that each cluster be selected with equal probability. In this case, the probability is $1/2 = 0.5$.

The table that follows highlights the differences between random sampling, stratified random sampling, and cluster sampling.

Sample	Random Sampling Probability	Stratified Random Sampling Probability	Cluster Sampling Probability
{1, 2}	1/6	0/4	1/2
{1, 3}	1/6	1/4	0/2
{1, 4}	1/6	1/4	0/2
{2, 3}	1/6	1/4	0/2
{2, 4}	1/6	1/4	0/2
{3, 4}	1/6	0/4	1/2
Total	6/6 = 1	4/4 = 1	2/2 = 1

Notice that the stratified random sampling scheme forces the selection of at least one element from the first stratum (either 1 or 2) and at least one element from the second stratum (either 3 or 4). Thus, {1, 2} cannot be selected, and {3, 4} cannot be selected. On the contrary, cluster sampling will only take one cluster, so either {1, 2} will be selected or {3, 4} will be selected. Notice also that under all three sampling schemes, each element has the same chance of being included in the sample. This is shown in the next table.

Element	Random Sampling Probability	Stratified Random Sampling Probability	Cluster Sampling Probability
1	3/6	2/4	1/2
2	3/6	2/4	1/2
3	3/6	2/4	1/2
4	3/6	2/4	1/2

That is, each element appears in three of the six samples, each of which has probability 1/6 under simple random sampling, so each element has probability 3/6 = 1/2 of being included in the sample. Likewise, each element appears in two of the four samples, each of which has probability 1/4 under stratified random sampling, so each element has probability 2/4 = 1/2 of being included in the sample. Finally, each element appears in one of the two samples, each of which has probability 1/2 under cluster sampling, so each element has probability 1/2 of being included in the sample.

A sampling distribution is basically a fancy term for a probability mass function or a probability density function. As an example of a sampling distribution, consider again the example in which the population was finite, sampling was performed without replacement, and the sample size was two. Consider, in particular, the sample mean. This is presented as an extension of an earlier table.

Sample	Random Sampling Probability	Stratified Random Sampling Probability	Cluster Sampling Probability	Mean
{1, 2}	1/6	0/4	1/2	1.5
{1 ,3}	1/6	1/4	0/2	2.0
{1, 4}	1/6	1/4	0/2	2.5
{2, 3}	1/6	1/4	0/2	2.5
{2, 4}	1/6	1/4	0/2	3.0
{3, 4}	1/6	0/4	1/2	3.5
Total	6/6 = 1	4/4 = 1	2/2 = 1	

For example, if the sample selected is $\{1, 2\}$, then the sample mean is $(1 + 2)/2 = 1.5$. Now we can construct the sampling distribution of the mean for this distribution when the sample has two observations under each of the three sampling schemes considered. This is presented in the next table.

Mean	Random Sampling Probability	Stratified Random Sampling Probability	Cluster Sampling Probability
1.5	1/6	0/4	1/2
2.0	1/6	1/4	0/2
2.5	2/6	2/4	0/2
3.0	1/6	1/4	0/2
3.5	1/6	0/4	1/2
Total	6/6 = 1	4/4 = 1	2/2 = 1

We may compute the expected value of the sample mean under each of these three sampling schemes. For simple random sampling, it is

$$(1.5) \, (1/6) + (2.0) \, (1/6) + (2.5) \, (2/6) + (3.0) \, (1/6) + (3.5) \, (1/6)$$
$$= (1/6)[(1.5) \, (1) + (2.0) \, (1) + (2.5) \, (2) + (3.0) \, (1) + (3.5) \, (1)]$$
$$= (1/6)[1.5 + 2.0 + 5.0 + 3.0 + 3.5]$$
$$= (1/6)[15.0]$$
$$= 15/6$$
$$= 5/2$$
$$= 2.5$$

Under stratified random sampling, the expected value of the sample mean is

$$(1.5) \, (0/4) + (2.0) \, (1/4) + (2.5) \, (2/4) + (3.0) \, (1/4) + (3.5) \, (0/4)$$
$$= (1/4)[(1.5) \, (0) + (2.0) \, (1) + (2.5) \, (2) + (3.0) \, (1) + (3.5) \, (0)]$$
$$= (1/4)[0 + 2 + 5 + 3 + 0]$$
$$= (1/4)[10]$$
$$= 10/4$$
$$= 2.5$$

This is the same mean as under simple random sampling.

Under cluster sampling, the expected value of the sample mean is

$$(1.5) \, (1/2) + (2.0) \, (0/2) + (2.5) \, (0/2) + (3.0) \, (0/2) + (3.5) \, (1/2)$$
$$= (1/2)[(1.5) \, (1) + (2.0) \, (0) + (2.5) \, (0) + (3.0) \, (0) + (3.5) \, (1)]$$
$$= (1/2)[1.5 + 0.0 + 0.0 + 0.0 + 3.5]$$
$$= (1/2)[5.0]$$
$$= 5/2$$
$$= 2.5$$

Thus, the expected value of the sample mean is the same under simple random sampling, stratified random sampling, and cluster sampling. This is despite the fact that the distribution of the sample mean is different under each of these three sampling schemes.

Notice that the expected value of a single observation is

$$E[X] = (1) \, (1/4) + (2) \, (1/4) + (3) \, (1/4) + (4) \, (1/4)$$

$$= (1/4)(1 + 2 + 3 + 4)$$

$$= (1/4)\,(10)$$

$$= 10/4$$

$$= 2.5$$

It turns out that the sampling distribution of the sample mean has the same expected value as the individual observations, as seen in the previous example. This is true for sampling schemes besides simple random sampling, and it is true whether sampling with replacement or sampling without replacement. It is also true for either a finite population or an infinite population. However, the variability of the sample mean is not the same as the variability of an individual observation. In fact, when sampling with replacement (or with an infinite sample size), the variance of the sample mean is

$$V(\text{mean}) = V(X)/n,$$

where $V(X)$ is the variance of an individual observation and n is the number of individuals selected in the sample. Therefore, the standard deviation of the sample mean (referred to as the standard error of the mean) is

$$SD(\text{mean}) = SD(X)/n^{0.5},$$

where $SD(X)$ is the standard deviation of an individual observation and n is the number of individuals selected in the sample.

Step-by-Step Solutions to Problems in this Chapter, "Random Samples."

 • PROBLEM 8–1

Let X have a binomial distribution with parameters $n = 4$ and $p = 0.5$. What is the expected value of X? What is the expected value of the sample mean of two such binomial random variables?

SOLUTION:

We know that the expected value of a binomial random variable is given by

$$E[X] = np.$$

In this case,

$$E[X] = np$$
$$= (4)\,(0.5)$$
$$= 2$$

We also know that the expected value of the sample mean is equal to the expected value of an individual. In this case,

$$E[\text{mean}] = E[X]$$
$$= 2$$

• PROBLEM 8–2

Let X have a binomial distribution with parameters $n = 4$ and $p = 0.5$. What are the possible values that X assumes? Let X_2 be the sample mean of two such binomial random variables. What are the possible values that X_2 assumes?

SOLUTION:

The possible values that X can take on are (0, 1, 2, 3, 4). To find the possible values that X_2 can take on, consider the following tables.

		The First Observation				
		0	1	2	3	4
The Second Observation	0	(0, 0)	(0, 1)	(0, 2)	(0, 3)	(0, 4)
	1	(1, 0)	(1, 1)	(1, 2)	(1, 3)	(1, 4)
	2	(2, 0)	(2, 1)	(2, 2)	(2, 3)	(2, 4)
	3	(3, 0)	(3, 1)	(3, 2)	(3, 3)	(3, 4)
	4	(4, 0)	(4, 1)	(4, 2)	(4, 3)	(4, 4)

		\multicolumn{5}{c}{The First Observation}				
		0	1	2	3	4
	0	0.0	0.5	1.0	1.5	2.0
The Second	1	0.5	1.0	1.5	2.0	2.5
Observation	2	1.0	1.5	2.0	2.5	3.0
	3	1.5	2.0	2.5	3.0	3.5
	4	2.0	2.5	3.0	3.5	4.0

The entry in a given cell of the first table is the sample observed. The entry in a given cell of the second table is the numerical average of the number heading its column and the number heading its row. That is, this table lists the sample means for all possible samples of size two (two observations). Thus, it is seen that the possible values of X_2 are (0.0, 0.5, 1.0, 1.5, 2.0, 2.5, 3.0, 3.5, 4.0).

• PROBLEM 8–3

Let X have a binomial distribution with parameters $n = 4$ and $p = 0.5$. What is the variance of X? What is the variance of the sample mean of two such binomial random variables? What is the variance of the sample mean of four such binomial random variables? What is the variance of the sample mean of eight such binomial random variables?

SOLUTION:

We know that the variance of a binomial random variable is

$$V(X) = np(1 - p).$$

In this case,

$$V(X) = np(1 - p)$$
$$= (4)\,(0.5)\,(1 - 0.5)$$
$$= (4)\,(0.5)\,(0.5)$$
$$= 1$$

As was discussed in this section, the variance of a sample mean with a given number of observations is the variance of an individual observation divided by this number of observations. This number of observations, which is typically denoted by n, is not the same as what we have been calling n in this problem. What we have been calling n in this problem is four, because this is the parameter of the binomial distribution. The sample size is the number of such binomial random variables (each of which has parameter $n = 4$).

Let X_2 be the sample mean of two binomial random variables, each with parameters $n = 4$ and $p = 0.5$. Then

$$V(X_2) = V(X)/2$$

$$= 1/2$$

$$= 0.5$$

Let X_4 be the sample mean of four binomial random variables, each with parameters $n = 4$ and $p = 0.5$. Then

$$V(X_4) = V(X)/4$$

$$= 1/4$$

$$= 0.25$$

Let X_8 be the sample mean of eight binomial random variables, each with parameters $n = 4$ and $p = 0.5$. Then

$$V(X_8) = V(X)/8$$

$$= 1/8$$

$$= 0.125$$

Notice that the variance of the sample mean decreases as the sample size increases.

• PROBLEM 8-4

Let X have a binomial distribution with parameters $n = 4$ and $p = 0.5$. What happens to the variance of the sample mean of a number of such binomial random variables when this number increases to infinity?

SOLUTION:

We know that the variance of a binomial random variable is

$$V(X) = np(1 - p).$$

In this case,

$$V(X) = np(1 - p)$$
$$= (4)\,(0.5)\,(1 - 0.5)$$
$$= (4)\,(0.5)\,(0.5)$$
$$= 1$$

As was discussed in this section, the variance of a sample mean with a given number of observations is the variance of an individual observation divided by this number of observations. Thus,

$$V(\text{sample mean}) = V(X)/(\text{number of observations})$$
$$= 1/(\text{number of observations}),$$

which tends to zero as the number of observations increases without bound.

• PROBLEM 8–5

Let X be uniformly distributed on $\{0, 1, 2, 3\}$. What are the possible samples of size two if sampling is performed with replacement? What are the values of the minimum for each of these samples? What are the possible samples if sampling is performed without replacement? What are the values of the minimum for each of these samples?

SOLUTION:

The possible samples and minimums are enumerated in the following tables.

		The First Observation			
		0	1	2	3
The Second Observation	0	(0, 0)	(0, 1)	(0, 2)	(0, 3)
	1	(1, 0)	(1, 1)	(1, 2)	(1, 3)
	2	(2, 0)	(2, 1)	(2, 2)	(2, 3)
	3	(3, 0)	(3, 1)	(3, 2)	(3, 3)

		The First Observation			
		0	1	2	3
The Second Observation	0	0	0	0	0
	1	0	1	1	1
	2	0	1	2	2
	3	0	1	2	3

The entry in a given cell of the first table is the sample observed. The entry in a given cell of the second table is the minimum of the number heading its column and the number heading its row. That is, this table lists the sample minimums for all possible samples of size two (two observations). Thus, it is seen that the possible values of this minimum are (0, 1, 2, 3) when sampling is performed with replacement.

		The First Observation			
		0	1	2	3
The Second Observation	0	impossible	(0, 1)	(0, 2)	(0, 3)
	1	(1, 0)	impossible	(1, 2)	(1, 3)
	2	(2, 0)	(2, 1)	impossible	(2, 3)
	3	(3, 0)	(3, 1)	(3, 2)	impossible

		The First Observation			
		0	1	2	3
The Second Observation	0	impossible	0	0	0
	1	0	impossible	1	1
	2	0	1	impossible	2
	3	0	1	2	impossible

The entry in a given cell of the first table is the sample observed. Notice that the cells on the main diagonal are impossible, because we are now sampling without replacement and, consequently, once a given number appears in the sample, it cannot appear in the sample again.

The entry in a given cell of the second table is the minimum of the number heading its column and the number heading its row. That is, this table lists the sample minimums for all possible samples of size two (two observations). Thus, it is seen that the possible values of this minimum are (0, 1, 2) when sampling is performed without replacement. This is a different range from when sampling was performed with replacement, because when sampling is performed with replacement three is a possible value for the sample minimum. When sampling is performed without replacement, then three is no longer a possible value for the sample minimum. The reason for this should be clear. Three is the largest value that X can assume. When sampling with replacement, both observations can be three, so three would be the minimum value of this sample. But when sampling without replacement, three can only appear in the sample at most one time. Thus, at least one observation is less than three, so the sample minimum must be less than three.

• PROBLEM 8-6

Let X be uniformly distributed on {0, 1, 2, 3}. Let X^* be the sample minimum of two such discrete uniform random variables. What is the sampling distribution of X^* if the selection is with replacement?

SOLUTION:

We know from Problem 8–5 that when sampling with replacement, X^* can only assume the values $\{0, 1, 2, 3\}$. It remains to find the probability of each of these values. That is, we wish to find the probability mass function (another term for the sampling distribution when the random variable is discrete) of X^*. Let us reconsider the table of sample minimums presented in Problem 8–5. Let us add another table which provides the probability of each sample. We will then group samples by their value of the sample minimum, and accumulate the probabilities of all samples with a given value of the sample minimum. This will give the desired probability mass function.

		The First Observation			
		0	1	2	3
The Second Observation	0	0	0	0	0
	1	0	1	1	1
	2	0	1	2	2
	3	0	1	2	3

		The First Observation			
		0	1	2	3
The Second Observation	0	1/16	1/16	1/16	1/16
	1	1/16	1/16	1/16	1/16
	2	1/16	1/16	1/16	1/16
	3	1/16	1/16	1/16	1/16

These probabilities are all 1/16 because each random variable is uniform on $\{0, 1, 2, 3\}$. Thus, the probability that either random variable assumes any given value is 1/4 (there are four equally likely values which the random variables can assume). By simple random sampling, we have independence of the two random variables. Therefore, all joint probabilities may be expressed as products of marginal probabilities. Since all marginal probabilities of individual outcomes are 1/4, all joint probabilities of individual joint outcomes are

$$f_{X,Y}(x,y) = P\{X = x, Y = y\}$$
$$= P\{X = x\}P\{Y = y \mid X = x\}$$
$$= P\{X = x\}P\{Y = y\}$$
$$= (1/4)(1/4)$$
$$= 1/16$$

Now there are seven samples which have a sample minimum of zero, five samples which have a sample minimum of one, three samples which have a sample minimum of two, and one sample which has a sample minimum of three. Thus, the sampling distribution of the sample minimum when sampling with replacement from the specified discrete uniform distribution is

$$f_{X*}(k) = 1/16 \text{ for } k = 3,$$
$$f_{X*}(k) = 3/16 \text{ for } k = 2,$$
$$f_{X*}(k) = 5/16 \text{ for } k = 1,$$
$$f_{X*}(k) = 7/16 \text{ for } k = 0,$$

and $\quad f_{X*}(k) = 0/16 \text{ otherwise.}$

• PROBLEM 8–7

Let X be uniformly distributed on $\{0, 1, 2, 3\}$. Let $X*$ be the sample minimum of two such discrete uniform random variables. What is the sampling distribution of $X*$ if the selection is without replacement?

SOLUTION:

We know from Problem 8–5 that when sampling without replacement, $X*$ assumes the values $\{0, 1, 2\}$. The task remains to find the probability of each of these values. That is, we wish to find the probability mass function (another term for the sampling distribution when the random variable is discrete) of $X*$. Let us reconsider the table of sample minimums presented in Problem 8–5.

		The First Observation			
		0	1	2	3
The Second Observation	0	impossible	0	0	0
	1	0	impossible	1	1
	2	0	1	impossible	2
	3	0	1	2	impossible

Let us add another table which provides the probability of each sample.

		The First Observation			
		0	1	2	3
The Second Observation	0	0/12	1/12	1/12	1/12
	1	1/12	0/12	1/12	1/12
	2	1/12	1/12	0/12	1/12
	3	1/12	1/12	1/12	0/12

The probabilities of the impossible samples are, of course, 0, or 0/12. Now we no longer have independence between the two random variables (there is never independence when sampling without replacement). Nevertheless, the 12 possible samples are all equally likely, so each has probability 1/12, because each joint probability is

$$f_{X,Y}(x,y) = P\{X = x, Y = y\}$$
$$= P\{X = x\}P\{Y = y \mid X = x\}$$
$$= (1/4)(1/3)$$
$$= 1/12$$

Now there are six samples which have a sample minimum of zero, four samples which have a sample minimum of one, and two samples which have a sample minimum of two. Thus, the sampling distribution of the sample minimum when sampling without replacement from the specified discrete uniform distribution is

$$f_{X*}(k) = 2/12 \text{ for } k = 2,$$
$$f_{X*}(k) = 4/12 \text{ for } k = 1,$$

$f_{X*}(k) = 4/12 \text{ for } k = 1,$ ~~strikethrough~~

$f_{X*}(k) = 6/12$ for $k = 0,$

and $\quad f_{X*}(k) = 0/12$ otherwise.

Extreme values are minimums and maximums, either of the sample or of the population. The study of extreme values of the sample is facilitated by consideration of the cumulative distribution function. In fact, when the observations are independent (as they are under simple random sampling), there is often a closed-form solution for the cumulative distribution function of the maximum and of the minimum. This is important when interest centers around extreme observations instead of the mean. For example, when considering how long to build a runway for an airplane, the concern is with the worst-case scenario, in which case a longer runway is required, rather than with the mean distance required.

Suppose that X is a random variable with cumulative distribution function $F_X(x)$. Suppose that we have a simple random sample of size n with the same distribution as X, and let M be the largest of these values. Also let m be the smallest of these values. Then for a given k, what is the probability that $M < k$? What is the probability that $m < k$? We write

$$P\{M < k\} = P\{\text{largest value is less than } k\}$$

$$= P\{\text{every one of the } n \text{ values is less than } k\}$$

$$= P\{X_1 < k, X_2 < k, \ldots, X_n < k\}$$

$$= P\{X_1 < k\}P\{X_2 < k\}\ldots P\{Xn < k\}$$

$$= F_X(k)F_X(k)\ldots F_X(k)$$

$$= [F_X(k)]_n$$

This expression can be evaluated with knowledge of $F_X(k)$. Notice that we require simple random sampling so that we have independence, allowing us to factor the probability of the compound event into the product of probabilities of simple events. Likewise,

$$P\{m < k\} = 1 - P\{m > k\}$$

$$= 1 - P\{\text{the smallest of the } n \text{ observations exceeds } k\}$$

$$= 1 - P\{\text{each of the } n \text{ observations exceeds } k\}$$

$$= 1 - P\{X_1 > k, X_2 > k, \ldots, X_n > k\}$$

$$= 1 - P\{X_1 > k\}P\{X_2 > k\}\ldots P\{X_n > k\}$$

$$= 1 - [1 - F_X(k)][1 - F_X(k)]...[1 - F_X(k)]$$

$$= 1 - [1 - F_X(k)]_n$$

Again, this expression can be evaluated explicitly if we know $F_X(k)$. For example, what is the probability that the largest of five independent random variables, each with continuous uniform distribution on $[0,1]$, is greater than 0.5? Let $X*$ be the largest of these five independent continuous uniform random variables. We write

$P\{X* > 0.5\}$

$= P\{$the largest of these five independent continuous uniform random variables $> 0.5\}$

$= 1 - P\{$the largest of these five independent continuous uniform random variables $< 0.5\}$

$= 1 - P\{$each of these five independent continuous uniform random variables $< 0.5\}$

$= 1 - P\{X_1 < 0.5, X_2 < 0.5, X_3 < 0.5, X_4 < 0.5, X_5 < 0.5\}$

$= 1 - P\{X_1 < 0.5\}P\{X_2 < 0.5\}P\{X_3 < 0.5\}P\{X_4 < 0.5\}$
$P\{X_5 < 0.5\}$

$= 1 - F_{X1}(0.5)F_{X2}(0.5)F_{X3}(0.5)F_{X4}(0.5)F_{X5}(0.5)$

$= 1 - (0.5)\,(0.5)\,(0.5)\,(0.5)\,(0.5)$

$= 1 - (0.5)^5$

$= 1 - 0.03125$

$= 0.96875$

Notice that the probability that any one of these random variables exceeds 0.5 is 0.5, but the probability that the maximum exceeds 0.5, which is the same as the probability that at least one of these random variables exceeds 0.5, is 0.96875. As expected, this is a much larger probability.

For another example, what is the probability that the larger of two independent random variables, each of which has a standard normal distribution, is larger that 1.96?

Let $X*$ be the maximum of X_1 and X_2, where X_1 and X_2 are independent random variables, each of which has a standard normal distribution. We write

$$P\{X^* > 1.96\} = P\{\text{the larger of } X_1 \text{ and } X_2 > 1.96\}$$
$$= 1 - P\{\text{the larger of } X_1 \text{ and } X_2 < 1.96\}$$
$$= 1 - P\{\text{both } X_1 \text{ and } X_2 < 1.96\}$$
$$= 1 - P\{X_1 < 1.96, X_2 < 1.96\}$$
$$= 1 - P\{X_1 < 1.96\}P\{X_2 < 1.96\}$$
$$= 1 - F_{X1}(1.96)F_{X2}(1.96)$$
$$= 1 - (0.9750)\,(0.9750)$$
$$= 1 - 0.950625$$
$$= 0.049375$$

Notice that

$$P\{X_1 > 1.96\} = 0.0250,$$

and $\qquad\qquad P\{X_2 > 1.96\} = 0.0250,$

but $\quad$ $P\{\text{either } X_1 > 1.96 \text{ or } X_2 > 1.96\} = 0.049375.$

Of course, it is not surprising that this is a larger probability.

• PROBLEM 8–8

Let X_1 and X_2 both be Poisson random variables with parameter one. Also let X_1 and X_2 be independent. Let X^* be the smaller of X_1 and X_2. What is the probability that X^* is zero?

SOLUTION:

We write

$$P\{X^* = 0\} = P\{\text{smaller of } X_1 \text{ and } X_2 \text{ is zero}\}$$
$$= 1 - P\{\text{smaller of } X_1 \text{ and } X_2 \text{ exceeds zero}\}$$
$$= 1 - P\{\text{both } X_1 \text{ and } X_2 \text{ exceed zero}\}$$
$$= 1 - P\{X_1 > 0\}\{X_2 > 0\}$$
$$= 1 - [1 - P\{X_1 = 0\}][1 - P\{X_2 = 0\}]$$
$$= 1 - [1 - e^{-1}1^0/0!][1 - e^{-1}1^0/0!]$$

$$= 1 - [1 - (1/e)][1 - (1/e)]$$

$$= 1 - [(e-1)/e][(e-1)/e]$$

$$= [e^2 - (e-1)2]/e^2$$

$$= [2.71828^2 - 1.71828^2]/2.71828^2$$

$$= [7.389056099 - 2.952492442]/7.389056099$$

$$= 4.436563657/7.389056099$$

$$= 0.6004$$

✓ **• PROBLEM 8-9**

A basketball player shoots three free throws. Let X_1, X_2, and X_3 be the indicators of success for each of the three shots. That is,

$X_1 = 0$ if the first shot misses,

$X_1 = 1$ if the first shot is successful,

$X_2 = 0$ if the second shot misses,

$X_2 = 1$ if the second shot is successful,

$X_3 = 0$ if the third shot misses,

and $X_3 = 1$ if the third shot is successful.

If all the shots are independent, and each has success probability 0.8, then what is the probability that at least one shot is successful?

SOLUTION:

This problem can be formulated as one of a binomial random variable with parameters $n = 3$ and $p = 0.8$. However, we will solve it by making use of the theory of extreme values.

Notice that

{at least one shot is successful} = {max(X_1, X_2, X_3) = 1},

in the sense of set equality. That is, each set is a subset of the other, so each of these events would imply the other. Then

$P\{$at least one shot is successful$\}$

$\quad = P\{\max(X_1, X_2, X_3) = 1\}$

$\quad = 1 - P\{\max(X_1, X_2, X_3) < 1\}$

$\quad = 1 - P\{X_1 < 1, X_2 < 1, X_3 < 1\}$

$\quad = 1 - P\{X_1 < 1\}P\{X_2 < 1\}P\{X_3 < 1\}$

$\quad = 1 - P\{X_1 = 0\}P\{X_2 = 0\}P\{X_3 = 0\}$

$\quad = 1 - (0.2)\,(0.2)\,(0.2)$

$\quad = 1 - 0.008$

$\quad = 0.992$

It is highly likely that at least one of the shots will be made.

✓• PROBLEM 8–10

Suppose that a basketball player takes three shots in a game. The first shot is a layup and is successful with probability 0.9. The second shot is a free throw and is successful with probability 0.8. The third shot is a three-point shot and is successful with probability 0.5. What is the probability that all three shots are made if they are all independent of each other?

SOLUTION:

Let

$\quad X_1 = 0$ if the first shot misses,

$\quad X_1 = 1$ if the first shot is successful,

$\quad X_2 = 0$ if the second shot misses,

$\quad X_2 = 1$ if the second shot is successful,

$\quad X_3 = 0$ if the third shot misses,

and $\quad X_3 = 1$ if the third shot is successful.

This problem can be formulated in such a way that it is quite easy to solve. Namely,

$P\{$all three shots are successful$\}$

$= P\{X_1 = 1, X_2 = 1, X_3 = 1\}$

$= P\{X_1 = 1\}P\{X_2 = 1\}P\{X_3 = 1\}$

$= (0.9)\,(0.8)\,(0.5)$

$= 0.36$

However, we will solve it by making use of the theory of extreme values. Then

$P\{$all three shots are successful$\}$

$= P\{\min(X_1, X_2, X_3) = 1\}$

$= P\{X_1 = 1, X_2 = 1, X_3 = 1\}$

$= P\{X_1 = 1\}P\{X_2 = 1\}P\{X_3 = 1\}$

$= (0.9)\,(0.8)\,(0.5)$

$= 0.36$

● PROBLEM 8–11

Suppose that a basketball player plays in four games after recovering from an injury. As this player recovers, his shooting becomes more accurate. Therefore, he chooses to shoot more as his healing progresses. In the first game back, he takes four shots, each of which has a 0.4 probability of being successful. In the second game, he takes five shots, each of which has a 0.5 probability of being successful. In the third game, he takes six shots, each of which has a 0.6 probability of being successful. In the fourth game, he takes seven shots, each of which has a 0.7 probability of being successful. All shots are independent of each other. What is the probability that at least four baskets are made in each of these four games?

SOLUTION:

Let

X_1 be the number of shots made in the first game,

X_2 be the number of shots made in the second game,

*X*3 be the number of shots made in the third game,

and X_4 be the number of shots made in the fourth game.

Also let $X^* = \min(X_1, X_2, X3, X_4)$.

Then $P\{$at least four shots are made in each of the four games$\}$

$$= P\{X^* \geq 4\}$$

$$= P\{X_1 \geq 4, X_2 \geq 4, X3 \geq 4, X4 \geq 4\}$$

$$= P\{X_1 \geq 4\}P\{X_2 \geq 4\}P\{X3 \geq 4\}P\{X_4 \geq 4\}$$

$$= P\{X_1 = 4\}P\{X_2 = 4 \cup X_2 = 5\}P\{X3 = 4 \cup$$

$$X3 = 5 \cup X3 = 6\}P\{X_4 = 4 \cup X_4 = 5 \cup X_4 = 6 \cup X_4 = 7\}$$

$$= [P\{X_1 = 4\}][P\{X_2 = 4\} + P\{X_2 = 5\}]$$

$$\times [P\{X3 = 4\} + P\{X3 = 5\} + P\{X3 = 6\}][P\{X_4 = 4\}$$

$$+ P\{X_4 = 5\} + P\{X_4 = 6\} + P\{X_4 = 7\}]$$

$$= [0.026][0.156 + 0.031][0.311 + 0.187 + 0.047]$$

$$[0.227 + 0.318 + 0.247 + 0.082]$$

$$= [0.026][0.187][0.545][0.874]$$

$$= 0.00232$$

It is highly unlikely that this injured player will score at least four times in each of his first four games back after his injury.

• PROBLEM 8-12

Let X_1, X_2, X_3, and X_4 be independent standard normal random variables. What is the probability that the largest of these will exceed 1.28?

SOLUTION:

Let $X^* = \max(X_1, X_2, X_3, X_4)$. We write

$$P\{X^* > 1.28\}$$

$$= P\{$at least one of X_1, X_2, X_3, X_4 exceeds 1.28$\}$$

$$= 1 - P\{\text{all of } X_1, X_2, X_3, X_4 \text{ less than } 1.28\}$$

$$= 1 - P\{X_1 < 1.28, X_2 < 1.28, X_3 < 1.28, X_4 < 1.28\}$$

$$= 1 - P\{X_1 < 1.28\}P\{X_2 < 1.28\}P\{X_3 < 1.28\}P\{X_4 < 1.28\}$$

$$= 1 - (0.90)\,(0.90)\,(0.90)\,(0.90)$$

$$= 1 - 0.6561$$

$$= 0.3439$$

There is only a 0.10 probability that any particular one of these four random variables will exceed 1.28, but there is a much larger probability, 0.3439, that at least one of these four random variables will exceed 1.28.

● PROBLEM 8–13

Suppose that the heights of females follow a normal distribution with mean 65 inches and variance four inches, and that the heights of males follow a normal distribution with mean 70 inches and variance four inches. If the heights of married couples are assumed indepen- dent (a questionable assumption), then what is the probability that at least one member of a married couple is at least six feet tall?

SOLUTION:

Let X be the height of the female in inches, let Y be the height of the male in inches, and let

$$W = \max(X, Y).$$

Then

$P\{\text{at least one member of a married couple is at least six feet tall}\}$

$$= P\{W > 72\}$$

$$= 1 - P\{W < 72\}$$

$$= 1 - P\{X < 72, Y < 72\}$$

$$= 1 - P\{X < 72\}P\{Y < 72\}$$

$$= 1 - P\{(X - 65)/4^{0.5} < (72 - 65)/4^{0.5}\}P\{(Y - 70)/4^{0.5}$$

$$< (72 - 70)/4^{0.5}\}$$

$$= 1 - P\{Z < 7/2\}P\{Z < 2/2\}$$

$$= 1 - P\{Z < 3.5\}P\{Z < 1.0\}$$

$$= 1 - (0.9998)(0.8413)$$

$$= 1 - 0.8411$$

$$= 0.1589.$$

√ • **PROBLEM 8-14**

Suppose that one home receives an average of two phone calls per hour, and another home receives an average of three phone calls per hour. Suppose that the distributions of numbers of phone calls received in the two homes are both Poisson and independent. What is the probability that neither home receives a call in a given hour?

SOLUTION:

Let

X_1 be the number of phone calls received in the first home

and X_2 be the number of phone calls received in the second home.

Also let $X^* = \max(X_1, X_2)$.

Then $P\{\text{no calls in either home in a given hour}\}$

$$= P\{X^* = 0\}$$

$$= P\{X_1 = 0, X_2 = 0\}$$

$$= P\{X_1 = 0\}P\{X_2 = 0\}$$

$$= (e^{-2}2^0/0!)(e^{-3}3^0/0!)$$

$$= (e^{-2}1/1)(e^{-3}1/1)$$

$$= (e^{-2})(e^{-3})$$

$$= e^{-(2+3)}$$

$$= e^{-5}$$

$$= 0.0067$$

It is highly unlikely that there will be no phone calls in either home.

• **PROBLEM 8–15**

Let X_1 have a continuous uniform distribution with range $[-1, 1]$, and let X_2 have a continuous uniform distribution with range $[-2, 2]$. Assume also that X_1 and X_2 are independent. What is the probability that the smaller of X_1 and X_2 is positive?

SOLUTION:

Let

$$X^* = \min(X_1, X_2).$$

Then $P\{$the smaller of X_1 and X_2 is positive$\}$

$$= P\{X^* > 0\}$$

$$= P\{X_1 > 0, X_2 > 0\}$$

$$= P\{X_1 > 0\}P\{X_2 > 0\}$$

$$= \{[1 - 0]/[1 - (-1)]\}\{[2 - 0]/[2 - (-2)]\}$$

$$= \{1/2\}\{2/4\}$$

$$= \{1/2\}\{1/2\}$$

$$= 1/4$$

$$= 0.25$$

Notice that the probability that either continuous uniform random variable is positive is 0.5, but the probability that both are positive is only 0.25.

✳✳✳✳✳✳

REVIEW OF FINITE POPULATIONS

When sampling with replacement, it makes no difference if the population is finite or infinite. However, when sampling without replacement, this is an important consideration. In this section, we will consider sampling distributions when sampling is performed without replacement from finite populations.

When sampling with replacement or from an infinite population, the sampling distribution of the sample mean has two key properties. First, as discussed previously, its expected value is the same as the expected value of any one of the individual observations. Second, its variance is the variance of any one individual observation divided by n, where n is the sample size. To summarize, let X^* be the sample mean computed based on a sample of size n. That is,

$$X^* = \Sigma_{i=1\ to\ n} X_i/n.$$

Then $E[X^*] = E[X]$

and $V(X^*) = V(X)/n.$

These formulas are well-known even by many non-statisticians. These formulas, however, are not always applicable. In particular, the second formula is not applicable when the sampling is performed without replacement from a finite population.

Suppose that the population under study consists of N_p individuals. For an infinite population, N_p is infinite. If X^* is the sample mean computed based on n observations, with $N_p \geq n$, then

$$E[X^*] = E[X]$$

and $V(X^*) = [V(X)/n][(N_p - n)/(N_p - 1)].$

Notice that if $n = N_p$, then the sample size is equal to the population size. Since sampling is without replacement, this would mean that each element was included in the sample. Now the sample is the entire population, so we can compute the population mean exactly. There is no variability (each sample of size $n = N_p$ will give the same sample mean, namely the population mean, because there is only one such sample), so the variance should be zero. Let us see if the formula produces the desired zero. We write

$$V(X^*) = [V(X)/n][(N_p - n)/(N_p - 1)]$$

$$= [V(X)/N_p][(N_p - N_p)/(N_p - 1)]$$

$$= [V(X)/N_p][0/(N_p - 1)]$$

$$= [V(X)/N_p][0]$$

$$= 0$$

Thus, this formula is appropriate for the case of $n = N_p$. If n is close to N_p, then the variance will be small, and it will become zero as soon as n becomes equal to N_p.

Another check on this formula would be to see if it provides the correct variance as N_p gets larger. We write

$$V(X^*) = [V(X)/n][(N_p - n)/(N_p - 1)],$$

which as N_p gets large tends to

$$V(X^*) = [V(X)/n][N_p/N_p]$$

$$= [V(X)/n][1]$$

$$= V(X)/n.$$

Again, the formula proves appropriate.

✓ • **PROBLEM 8-16**

If a population consists of 10 individuals and has variance 12, then what is the sampling variance of a sample mean computed based on a sample of size four if the sampling is performed without replacement?

SOLUTION:

We use the formula

$$V(X^*) = [V(X)/n][(N_p - n)/(N_p - 1)].$$

In this case,

$$V(X) = 12,$$

$$n = 4,$$

and $\quad N_p = 10,$

so $\quad V(X^*) = [V(X)/n][(N_p - n)/(N_p - 1)]$

$$= [12/4][(10 - 4)/(10 - 1)]$$

$$= [3][(6)/(9)]$$

$$= (3)\,(2/3)$$

$$= 6/3$$

$$= 2$$

The variance has been cut from 12 to two by taking four observations rather than only one observation. Had the population been infinite, the reduction of variance would have been less pronounced, dropping from 12 to three.

 **● PROBLEM 8-17**

If a population consists of 100 individuals and has variance 24, then what is the sampling variance of a sample mean computed based on a sample of size 12 if the sampling is performed without replacement?

SOLUTION:

We use the formula

$$V(X^*) = [V(X)/n][(N_p - n)/(N_p - 1)].$$

In this case,

$$V(X) = 24,$$

$$n = 12,$$

and $\quad N_p = 100,$

so $\quad V(X^*) = [V(X)/n][(N_p - n)/(N_p - 1)]$

$$= [24/12][(100 - 12)/(100 - 1)]$$

$$= [2][(88)/(99)]$$

$$= (2)\,(8/9)$$

$$= 16/9$$

$$= 1.778$$

The variance has been cut from 24 to 1.778 by taking 12 observations rather than only one observation. Had the population been infinite, the reduction of variance would have been less pronounced, dropping from 24 to two. The amount by which the variance under sampling with replacement differs from the variance from sampling without replacement is small because the population size (100) is large, and the larger this population size, the closer it becomes to infinity. If the population were infinite, then it would make no difference in terms of the variance if the sampling were performed with or without replacement.

• PROBLEM 8–18

If a population consists of 50 individuals and has variance 10, then what is the sampling variance of a sample mean computed based on a sample of size five if the sampling is performed without replacement?

SOLUTION:

We use the formula

$$V(X^*) = [V(X)/n][(N_p - n)/(N_p - 1)].$$

In this case,

$$V(X) = 10,$$

$$n = 5,$$

and $N_p = 50,$

so $V(X^*) = [V(X)/n][(N_p - n)/(N_p - 1)]$

$$= [10/5][(50\text{-}5)/(50 - 1)]$$

$$= [2][(45)/(49)]$$

$$= 1.8367$$

The variance has been cut from 10 to 1.8367 by taking five observations rather than only one observation. Had the population been infinite, the reduction of variance would have been less pronounced, dropping from 10 to two. The amount by which the variance under sampling with replacement differs from the variance from sampling without replacement is small because the population size (50) is large, and the larger this population size, the closer it becomes to infinity. If the population were infinite, then it would make no difference in terms of the variance if the sampling were performed with or without replacement.

If a population consists of 10 individuals and has variance two, then what is the sampling variance of a sample mean computed based on a sample of size one if the sampling is performed without replacement?

SOLUTION:

We use the formula

$$V(X^*) = [V(X)/n][(N_p - n)/(N_p - 1)].$$

In this case,

$$V(X) = 2,$$

$$n = 1,$$

and $\quad N_p = 10,$

so $\quad V(X^*) = [V(X)/n][(N_p - n)/(N_p - 1)]$

$$= [2/1][(10 - 1)/(10 - 1)]$$

$$= [2/1][(9)/(9)]$$

$$= [2/1][1]$$

$$= 2/1$$

$$= 2$$

If a population consists of 10 individuals and has variance two, then what is the sampling variance of a sample mean computed based on a sample of size five if the sampling is performed without replacement?

SOLUTION:

We use the formula

$$V(X^*) = [V(X)/n][(N_p - n)/(N_p - 1)].$$

In this case,

$$V(X) = 2,$$

$$n = 5,$$

and $\quad N_p = 10,$

so $\quad V(X^*) = [V(X)/n][(N_p - n)/(N_p - 1)]$

$$= [2/5][(10 - 5)/(10 - 1)]$$

$$= [2/5][(5)/(9)]$$

$$= [2/5][5/9]$$

$$= 2/9$$

$$= 0.2222$$

The variance has been cut from two to 0.2222 by taking five observations rather than only one observation. Had the population been infinite, the reduction of variance would have been less pronounced, dropping from two to 0.4. The amount by which the variance under sampling with replacement differs from the variance from sampling without replacement is small because the population size (50) is large, and the larger this population size, the closer it becomes to infinity. If the population were infinite, then it would make no difference in terms of the variance if the sampling were performed with or without replacement.

✓ • **PROBLEM 8–21**

If a population consists of 10 individuals and has variance two, then what is the sampling variance of a sample mean computed based on a sample of size 10 if the sampling is performed without replacement?

SOLUTION:

We use the formula

$$V(X^*) = [V(X)/n][(N_p - n)/(N_p - 1)].$$

In this case,

$$V(X) = 2,$$

$$n = 10,$$

and $\qquad N_p = 10,$

so $\qquad V(X^*) = [V(X)/n][(N_p - n)/(N_p - 1)]$

$\qquad\qquad = [2/10][(10 - 10)/(10 - 1)]$

$\qquad\qquad = [2/10][(0)/(9)]$

$\qquad\qquad = [2/10][0]$

$\qquad\qquad = 0$

The variance has been reduced to zero because the population consists of only 10 individuals, and all 10 are included in the sample. Since there are no individuals in the population which are not in the sample, the entire population is known and there can be no uncertainty.

• PROBLEM 8–22

If a population consists of 10 individuals and has variance two, then what is the sampling variance as a function of the sample size, given that sampling is without replacement?

SOLUTION:

The first task is to find the range of the sample size. Since sampling is without replacement, no individual can be selected more than once. Consequently, the largest possible sample size is $n = 10$. The smallest possible sample size would be $n = 0$. Of course, the sample size must be an integer value, so the range of the sample size is

$\qquad \{0, 1, 2, 3, 4, 5, 6, 7, 8, 9, 10\}.$

We again use the formula

$\qquad V(X^*) = [V(X)/n][(N_p - n)/(N_p - 1)].$

In this case,

$\qquad V(X) = 2$

and $\qquad N_p = 10,$

so $\qquad V(X^*) = [V(X)/n][(N_p - n)/(N_p - 1)]$

$\qquad\qquad = [2/n][(10 - n)/(10 - 1)]$

$$= [2/n][(10 - n)/(9)]$$

We will evaluate this variance for each sample size in the range. Notice that the last three problems have already given us some of these variances.

When $n = 0$,

$$V(X^*) = [V(X)/n][(N_p - n)/(N_p - 1)]$$
$$= [2/n][(10 - n)/(10 - 1)]$$
$$= [2/n][(10 - n)/(9)]$$
$$= [2/0][(10 - 0)/(9)],$$

which is infinite. This is not surprising, since the sample is empty.

When $n = 1$,

$$V(X^*) = [V(X)/n][(N_p - n)/(N_p - 1)]$$
$$= [2/n][(10 - n)/(10 - 1)]$$
$$= [2/n][(10 - n)/(9)]$$
$$= [2/1][(10 - 1)/(9)]$$
$$= [2][9/9]$$
$$= [2][1]$$
$$= 2$$

as seen in Problem 8–19.

When $n = 2$,

$$V(X^*) = [V(X)/n][(N_p - n)/(N_p - 1)]$$
$$= [2/n][(10 - n)/(10 - 1)]$$
$$= [2/n][(10 - n)/(9)]$$
$$= [2/2][(10 - 2)/(9)]$$
$$= [1][8/9]$$
$$= 8/9$$
$$= 0.8889$$

When $n = 3$,

$$V(X^*) = [V(X)/n][(N_p - n)/(N_p - 1)]$$

$$= [2/n][(10 - n)/(10 - 1)]$$

$$= [2/n][(10 - n)/(9)]$$

$$= [2/3][(10 - 3)/(9)]$$

$$= [2/3][7/9]$$

$$= 14/27$$

$$= 0.5185$$

When $n = 4$,

$$V(X^*) = [V(X)/n][(N_p - n)/(N_p - 1)]$$

$$= [2/n][(10 - n)/(10 - 1)]$$

$$= [2/n][(10 - n)/(9)]$$

$$= [2/4][(10 - 4)/(9)]$$

$$= [2/4][6/9]$$

$$= [1/2][2/3]$$

$$= 1/3$$

$$= 0.3333$$

When $n = 5$,

$$V(X^*) = [V(X)/n][(N_p - n)/(N_p - 1)]$$

$$= [2/n][(10 - n)/(10 - 1)]$$

$$= [2/n][(10 - n)/(9)]$$

$$= [2/5][(10 - 5)/(9)]$$

$$= [2/5][5/9]$$

$$= [2/9]$$

$$= 0.2222$$

as seen in Problem 8–20.

When $n = 6$,

$$V(X^*) = [V(X)/n][(N_p - n)/(N_p - 1)]$$

$$= [2/n][(10 - n)/(10 - 1)]$$

$$= [2/n][(10 - n)/(9)]$$

$$= [2/6][(10 - 6)/(9)]$$

$$= [1/3][4/9]$$

$$= [4/27]$$

$$= 0.1481$$

When $n = 7$,

$$V(X^*) = [V(X)/n][(N_p - n)/(N_p - 1)]$$

$$= [2/n][(10 - n)/(10 - 1)]$$

$$= [2/n][(10 - n)/(9)]$$

$$= [2/7][(10 - 7)/(9)]$$

$$= [2/7][3/9]$$

$$= [2/7][1/3]$$

$$= 2/21$$

$$= 0.0952$$

When $n = 8$,

$$V(X^*) = [V(X)/n][(N_p - n)/(N_p - 1)]$$

$$= [2/n][(10 - n)/(10 - 1)]$$

$$= [2/n][(10 - n)/(9)]$$

$$= [2/8][(10 - 8)/(9)]$$

$$= [1/4][2/9]$$

$$= [2/36]$$

$$= 1/18$$

$$= 0.0556$$

When $n = 9$,

$$V(X^*) = [V(X)/n][(N_p - n)/(N_p - 1)]$$

$$= [2/n][(10 - n)/(10 - 1)]$$

$$= [2/n][(10 - n)/(9)]$$

$$= [2/9][(10 - 9)/(9)]$$

$$= [2/9][1/9]$$

$$= [2/81]$$

$$= 0.0247$$

When $n = 10$,

$$V(X^*) = [V(X)/n][(N_p - n)/(N_p - 1)]$$

$$= [2/n][(10 - n)/(10 - 1)]$$

$$= [2/n][(10 - n)/(9)]$$

$$= [2/10][(10 - 10)/(9)]$$

$$= [1/5][0/9]$$

$$= 0,$$

as shown in Problem 8–21.

We may combine this information into a table.

Variance of the Sample Mean Sampling Without Replacement Finite Population of Size 10 Variance of Individuals of Two	
Sample Size	Variance
0	infinite
1	2.0000
2	0.8889
3	0.5185
4	0.3333
5	0.2222
6	0.1481
7	0.0952
8	0.0556
9	0.0247
10	0.0000

Notice that the variance reduces monotonically as the sample size increases, the variance is infinite when the sample is empty, and the variance is zero when the sample is the entire population. This will be the case regardless of the particular number of individuals in the population, or the variance of each individual observation. However, the variances for the intermediate sample sizes do reflect the particular choices of a population size of 10 and a variance of two.

● PROBLEM 8–23

Suppose that a population consists of 100 individuals, and that this population has an individual variance of 10. Assuming sampling without replacement, how large a sample must be taken in order that the variance of the sample mean be no larger than one? What if sampling is with replacement?

SOLUTION:

As in Problem 8–22, the first task is to find the range of sample sizes. Since the population size is 100, the sample size can range from zero to 100, and must assume an integer value. This means that there may be no sample size for which the variance of the sample mean is exactly one, and this is why the problem was formulated as asking for a sample size such that the variance of the sample mean is no larger than one, instead of being exactly equal to one.

We know, from Problem 8–22, that if the sample size is zero, then the variance of the sample mean is infinite, which is certainly more than one. We also know that if the sample size is 100, then the variance of the sample mean is zero, which is less than one. Finally, we know that the variance of the sample mean decreases as the sample size increases. Therefore, there must be some number k such that

$$V(X^*) > 1 \text{ when } n = k$$

and $V(X^*) \leq 1$ when $n = k + 1$.

We know that $k \geq 0$ and that $k < 100$.

Now

$$V(X^*) = [V(X)/n][(N_p - n)/(N_p - 1)]$$
$$= [10/n][(100 - n)/(100 - 1)]$$

$$= [10/n][(100 - n)/99].$$

So we need

$$[10/n][(100 - n)/99] \leq 1,$$

or $99n \geq (10)(100 - n) = 1,000 - 10n.$

Then $109n \geq 1,000,$

or $n \geq 1,000/109 = 9.1743.$

Therefore, we require 10 observations in the sample. To verify this solution, consider $n = 9$ and $n = 10$.

If $n = 9$, then

$$V(X^*) = [V(X)/n][(N_p - n)/(N_p - 1)]$$
$$= [10/9][(100 - 9)/(100 - 1)]$$
$$= [10/9][(91)/(99)]$$
$$= 910/891$$
$$= 1.0213$$
$$> 1.$$

If $n = 10$, then

$$V(X^*) = [V(X)/n][(N_p - n)/(N_p - 1)]$$
$$= [10/10][(100 - 10)/(100 - 1)]$$
$$= [1][(90)/(99)]$$
$$= 90/99$$
$$= 10/11$$
$$= 0.9091$$
$$< 1.$$

Thus, 10 observations are required.

If we had been sampling with replacement, then

$$V(X^*) = V(X)/n$$
$$= 10/n,$$

so $n = 10$

would give

$$V(X^*) = V(X)/n$$

$$= 10/10$$

$$= 1$$

would suffice.

● PROBLEM 8–24

Suppose that a population consists of 1,000 individuals, and that this population has an individual variance of 10. Assuming sampling without replacement, how large a sample must be taken in order that the variance of the sample mean be no larger than one? What if sampling is with replacement?

SOLUTION:

As in Problem 8–22 and Problem 8–23, the first task is to find the range of sample sizes. Since the population size is 1,000, the sample size can range from zero to 1,000, and must assume an integer value. This means that there may be no sample size for which the variance of the sample mean is exactly one, and this is why the problem was formulated as asking for a sample size such that the variance of the sample mean is no larger than one, instead of being exactly equal to one.

We know, from Problem 8–22 and Problem 8–23, that if the sample size is zero, then the variance of the sample mean is infinite, which is certainly more than one. We also know that if the sample size is 1,000, then the variance of the sample mean is zero, which is less than one. Finally, we know that the variance of the sample mean decreases as the sample size increases. Therefore, there must be some number k such that

$$V(X^*) > 1 \text{ when } n = k$$

and $V(X^*) \le 1$ when $n = k + 1$.

We know that $k \ge 0$ and that $k < 1,000$.

Now

$$V(X^*) = [V(X)/n][(N_p - n)/(N_p - 1)]$$

$$= [10/n][(1{,}000 - n)/(1{,}000 - 1)]$$

$$= [10/n][(1{,}000 - n)/999].$$

So we need

$$[10/n][(1{,}000 - n)/999] \le 1,$$

or $999n \ge (10)(1{,}000 - n) = 10000 - 10n.$

Then $1{,}009n \ge 10{,}000,$

or $n \ge 10{,}000/1{,}009 = 9.9108.$

Therefore, we require 10 observations in the sample. To verify this solution, consider $n = 9$ and $n = 10$.

If $n = 9$, then

$$V(X^*) = [V(X)/n][(N_p - n)/(N_p - 1)]$$

$$= [10/9][(1{,}000 - 9)/(1{,}000 - 1)]$$

$$= [10/9][(991)/(999)]$$

$$= 9{,}910/8{,}991$$

$$= 1.1022$$

$$> 1$$

If $n = 10$, then

$$V(X^*) = [V(X)/n][(N_p - n)/(N_p - 1)]$$

$$= [10/10][(1{,}000 - 10)/(1{,}000 - 1)]$$

$$= [1][(990)/(999)]$$

$$= 990/999$$

$$= 10/11$$

$$= 0.9091$$

$$< 1$$

Thus, 10 observations are required.

If we had been sampling with replacement, then

$$V(X^*) = V(X)/n$$

$$= 10/n,$$

so $\qquad$ $n = 10$

would give

$$V(X^*) = V(X)/n$$

$$= 10/10$$

$$= 1$$

would suffice.

Notice that the solutions are the same in Problem 8–23 and Problem 8–24. The portions of these problems which consider sampling with replacement indicate that the results would remain the same not only if the population size increased from 100 (Problem 8–23) to 1,000 (Problem 8–24), but also if the population size increased to infinity (sampling with replacement). It can be shown that, when holding constant the individual variability, the required sample size required to produce a variance of the sample mean no larger than a specified cutoff (in this case, one) increases as the population size increases. Therefore, we may infer that a sample of size 10 would be required to produce a variance of the sample mean of no larger than one for any population of size at least 100.

 • **PROBLEM 8–25**

What is the largest sample size such that a sample of size smaller than 10 would produce a variance of the sample mean of no greater than one? Assume sampling without replacement and an individual variance of 10, as in Problem 8–23 and Problem 8–24.

SOLUTION:

The simplest way to solve this problem is to recognize that if a sample of size smaller than 10 will produce a variance of the sample mean of no greater than one, then certainly a sample of size nine will produce a variance of the sample mean of no greater than one. This may be shown to be true by the following logic.

We know that there is some sample size under 10 which will produce a variance of the sample mean of no greater than one. Let us call this sample size k. Since $k < 10$ and k must be an integer, we know that

$$k \leq 9.$$

Therefore, we know that the variance of the sample mean will be no larger if the sample size is nine than it will be if the sample size is k. Thus,

$$V(X^*)_{n=9} \le V(X^*)_{n=k} \le 1.$$

Now

$$V(X^*) = [V(X)/n][(N_p - n)/(N_p - 1)]$$
$$= [10/9][(N_p - 9)/(N_p - 1)]$$
$$\le 1.$$

Then $\quad 9(N_p - 1) \ge 10(N_p - 9),$

so $\qquad 9N_P - 9 \ge 10N_p - 90$

or $\qquad (90 - 9) \ge 10N_p - 9N_p$

or $\qquad 81 \ge N_p.$

So we would allow only populations of size 81 at most. To verify, consider $N_p = 80$ and $N_p = 81$. We see that if $N_p = 80$, then

$$V(X^*) = [V(X)/n][(N_p - n)/(N_p - 1)]$$
$$= [10/9][(80 - 9)/(80 - 1)]$$
$$= [10/9][71/79]$$
$$= 710/711$$
$$= 0.9986$$
$$< 1$$

If $N_p = 81$, then

$$V(X^*) = [V(X)/n][(N_p - n)/(N_p - 1)]$$
$$= [10/9][(81 - 9)/(81 - 1)]$$
$$= [10/9][72/80]$$
$$= 720/720$$
$$= 1$$

If $N_p = 82$, then

$$V(X^*) = [V(X)/n][(N_p - n)/(N_p - 1)]$$
$$= [10/9][(82 - 9)/(82 - 1)]$$
$$= [10/9][73/81]$$
$$= 730/729$$
$$= 1.0014$$
$$> 1$$

• PROBLEM 8–26

> If four different balls are placed at random in three different cells, find the probability that no cell is empty. Assume that there is ample room in each cell for all four balls.

SOLUTION:

There are three ways to place each of the four balls into a cell. Thus, there are $3 \times 3 \times 3 \times 3 = 3^4$ ways to put the four balls into three cells. If each arrangement is equally likely, then any one arrangement will occur with the probability

$$\frac{1}{3^4} = \frac{1}{81}$$

We now must count the number of ways the balls can be placed in the cells so that none of the cells are empty.

First we know that one cell will have two balls in it.

Choose these two balls from the four; there are

$$\binom{4}{2}$$

ways to do this. Now place these two balls in a cell; there are three ways to do this. There are two ways and one way respectively to place the two remaining balls in the two remaining cells to insure that all the cells are filled. Together, by the Fundamental Counting Principle, there are

$$\binom{4}{2} \times 3 \times 2 \times 1 \text{ or } 36$$

arrangements. Thus, the probability of observing an arrangement with no cells empty if the balls are dropped in at random is

$$\frac{36}{81} = \frac{4}{9}.$$

• PROBLEM 8–27

A box contains four black marbles, three red marbles, and two white marbles. What is the probability that a black marble, then a red marble, then a white marble is drawn without replacement?

SOLUTION:

Here we have three dependent events. There is a total of nine marbles from which to draw. We assume on the first draw we will get a black marble. The probability of drawing a black marble is

$$\frac{\text{number of ways of drawing a black marble}}{\text{number of ways of drawing one out of } (4+3+2) \text{ marbles}},$$

so $\qquad P(A) = \dfrac{4}{4+3+2} = \dfrac{4}{9}.$

There are now eight marbles left in the box.

On the second draw we get a red marble. The probability of drawing a red marble is

$$\frac{\text{number of ways of drawing a red marble}}{\text{number of ways of drawing one out of the 8 remaining marbles}},$$

so $\qquad P(B) = \dfrac{3}{8}.$

There are now seven marbles remaining in the box.

On the last draw we get a white marble. The probability of drawing a white marble is

$$\frac{\text{number of ways of drawing a white marble}}{\text{number of ways of drawing one out of the 7 remaining marbles}},$$

so $\qquad P(C) = \dfrac{2}{7}.$

When dealing with two or more dependent events, if P_1 is the probability of a first event, P_2 the probability that, after the first has happened, the second will occur, P_3 the probability that, after the first and second have happened, the third will occur, etc., then the probability that all events will happen in the given order is the product $P_1 \times P_2 \times P_3 \ldots$

Thus,

$$P(A \cap B \cap C) = P(A) \times P(B) \times P(C)$$

$$= \frac{4}{9} \times \frac{3}{8} \times \frac{2}{7} = \frac{1}{21}$$

 **• PROBLEM 8-28**

There is a box containing five white balls, four black balls, and seven red balls. If two balls are drawn one at a time from the box and neither is replaced, find the probability that

(a) both balls will be white.

(b) the first ball will be white and the second red.

(c) three balls will be drawn in the order white, black, red if a third ball is drawn.

SOLUTION:

(a)   To find the probability that both balls will be white, we express it symbolically.

P(both balls will be white)

$= P$(first ball will be white and the second ball will be white)

$= P$(first ball will be white $\times P$(second ball will be white given that the first one was)

$$= \frac{\text{number of ways to choose a white ball}}{\text{number of ways to choose a ball}}$$

$$\times \frac{\text{number of ways to choose a second white ball}}{\text{after removal of the first white ball}}{\text{number of ways to choose a ball after removal of the first ball}}$$

$$= \frac{5}{16} \times \frac{4}{15} = \frac{1}{12}.$$

(b)   P(first ball will be white and the second ball will be red)

   = P(first ball will be white) × P(the second ball will be red given the first was white)

   $= \dfrac{\text{number of ways to choose a white ball}}{\text{number of ways to choose a ball}}$

   $\times \dfrac{\text{number of ways to choose a red ball}}{\text{number of ways to choose a ball after removal of the first ball}}$

   $= \dfrac{5}{16} \times \dfrac{7}{15} = \dfrac{7}{48}.$

(c)   P(three balls drawn in the order white, black, red)

   = P(first ball is white) P(second ball is black given the first was white) P(third ball is red given the first was white and the second was black)

   $= \dfrac{\text{number of ways to choose that the first ball is white}}{\text{number of ways to choose the first ball}}$

   $\times \dfrac{\text{number of ways to choose that the second one is black}}{\text{number of ways to choose the second one}}$

   $\times \dfrac{\text{number of ways to choose that the third one is red}}{\text{number of ways to choose the third one}}$

   $= \dfrac{5}{16} \times \dfrac{4}{15} \times \dfrac{7}{14} = \dfrac{1}{24}.$

✳✳✳✳✳✳

REVIEW OF LAWS OF LARGE NUMBERS

There are two Laws of Large Numbers: the Weak Law of Large Numbers and the Strong Law of Large Numbers. In combination, these are known as the Laws of Large Numbers and will be our focus in this section.

We will see that both the Strong Law of Large Numbers and the Weak Law of Large Numbers can be stated in terms of types of convergence. One may also recognize a similarity between the Weak Law of Large Numbers and Chebyshev's inequality. In fact, Chebyshev's inequality is often used to prove the Weak Law of Large Numbers, and Chebyshev was the first to prove the Weak Law of Large Numbers.

Let M be the population mean of X, or

$$E[X] = M.$$

Suppose that a simple random sample of size n is taken, each with the distribution of X. Let $X^*(n)$ be the sample mean, or

$$X^*(n) = \Sigma_{i=1 \text{ to } n} X_i/n.$$

The Weak Law of Large Numbers states that as n increases, $X^*(n)$ will tend to become closer and closer to M. In particular,

$$\lim_{n \text{ to infinity}} P\{|X^*(n) - M| > k\} = 0 \text{ for all positive } k,$$

or, alternatively,

$$\lim_{n \text{ to infinity}} P\{|X^*(n) - M| < k\} = 1 \text{ for all positive } k.$$

This says that with high probability, in fact probability tending to one, the sample mean and the population mean will be within k of each other, for any value of k. This is equivalently stated as with low probability, in fact probability tending to zero, the sample mean differs from the population mean by more than k.

The Weak Law of Large Numbers does not apply only to simple random samples (that is, independent sampling from the same population). We will confine our attention to independent random variables, but we will allow them to have different distributions. In fact, our only interest in the distributions of these random variables will be in their first two moments (i.e., their means and variances).

Let $X^*(n)$ be the sample mean of the n independent random variables, even if they have different distributions. That is,

$$X^*(n) = \Sigma_{i=1 \text{ to } n} X_i/n.$$

Let $M(n) = E[X^*(n)]$

$$= E[\Sigma_{i = 1 \text{ to } n}X_i/n]$$

$$= \Sigma_{i = 1 \text{ to } n}E[X_i]/n.$$

Let $V(X_i)$ be the variance of the random variable X_i. If $V[X^*(n)]$ tends to zero as n tends to infinity, then the Weak Law of Large Numbers holds, or

$$\lim_{n \text{ to infinity}}P\{\mid X^*(n) - M(n) \mid > k\} = 0 \text{ for all positive } k,$$

or, alternatively,

$$\lim_{n \text{ to infinity}}P\{\mid X^*(n) - M(n) \mid < k\} = 1 \text{ for all positive } k,$$

even if the component random variables have different distributions.

Notice that

$$V[X^*(n)] = V[\Sigma_{i = 1 \text{ to } n}X_i/n]$$

$$= (1/n^2)V[\Sigma_{i = 1 \text{ to } n}X_i]$$

$$= (1/n^2)\Sigma_{i = 1 \text{ to } n}V(X_i),$$

so this is the quantity which must tend to zero in the limit as n tends to infinity.

The Strong Law of Large Numbers states that, under certain conditions, almost all sequences of $X^*(n)$, considered as a sequence, will converge to M, assuming that a simple random sample was employed. Of course, if the different component random variables are allowed to have different distributions, then M may depend upon the sample size n. The formal statement is

$$P\{X^*(n) \text{ tends to } M\} = 1.$$

The Strong Law of Large Numbers implies the Weak Law of Large Numbers, but the reverse implication does not hold.

• PROBLEM 8–29

Prove that the Weak Law of Large Numbers applies to estimating the parameter p from a binomial distribution with X/n, where X is the number of successes.

SOLUTION:

We may consider the binomial as a sum of independent Bernoulli random variables, each with parameter p. We need to establish that

$$\lim_{n \text{ to infinity}}(1/n^2)\Sigma_{t=1 \text{ to } n} V(X_i) = 0,$$

where X_i is the ith Bernoulli random variable. Now, since the variance of a Bernoulli random variable is $p(1-p)$,

$$\lim_{n \text{ to infinity}}(1/n^2)\Sigma_{i=1 \text{ to } n}V(X_i)$$

$$= \lim_{n \text{ to infinity}}(1/n^2)\Sigma_{t=1 \text{ to } n} P(1-p)$$

$$= \lim_{n \text{ to infinity}}[p(1-p)/n^2]\Sigma_{i=1 \text{ to } n}1$$

$$= \lim_{n \text{ to infinity}}[p(1-p)/n^2][n]$$

$$= \lim_{n \text{ to infinity}}[np(1-p)/n^2]$$

$$= \lim_{n \text{ to infinity}}[p(1-p)/n]$$

$$= 0$$

Thus, the Weak Law of Large Numbers applies.

• PROBLEM 8–30

Prove that the Weak Law of Large Numbers applies to estimating the mean of a normal distribution with the sample mean from a simple random sample. Assume that the variance of each observation is one.

SOLUTION:

We need to establish that

$$\lim_{n \text{ to infinity}}(1/n^2)\Sigma_{t=1 \text{ to } n}V(X_i) = 0,$$

where X_i is the ith normal random variable. Now, since the variance of each observation is given to be one,

$$\lim_{n \text{ to infinity}} (1/n^2)\Sigma_{t=1 \text{ to } n}V(X_i)$$

$$= \lim_{n \text{ to infinity}}(1/n^2)\Sigma_{t=1 \text{ to } n}1$$

$$= \lim_{n \text{ to infinity}}[1/n^2][n]$$

$$= \lim_{n \text{ to infinity}}[n/n^2]$$

$$= \lim_{n \text{ to infinity}} [1/n]$$

$$= 0$$

Thus, the Weak Law of Large Numbers applies.

• PROBLEM 8-31

Suppose that two soccer teams play an infinitely long series of games, in which they alternate sites (that is, each team hosts every other game). Does the Weak Law of Large Numbers apply to this alternating binomial sequence? If so, what converges to what?

SOLUTION:

We have already seen from Problem 8–29 that the proportion of wins among the home games will converge to the probability of winning at home, while the proportion of wins among the away games will converge to the probability of winning on the road.

Now consider the overall proportion of wins. Let X_i be the indicator of a victory in the ith game, or

$$X_i = 0 \text{ if lose the } i\text{th game}$$

and $X_i = 1$ if win the ith game.

Now let $p(H)$ be the probability of winning a game at home and let $p(A)$ be the probability of winning a game away. The variance of a home game result is $p(H)[1 - p(H)]$ and the variance of the result of an away game is $p(A)[1 - p(A)]$. If we consider only even n (that is, an equal number of home games and away games), then

$$\lim_{n \text{ to infinity}} (1/n^2) \Sigma_{i=1 \text{ to } n} V(X_i)$$

$$= \lim_{n \text{ to infinity}} (1/n^2) \Sigma_{i=1 \text{ to } n/2} [V(X_{2i-1}) + V(X_{2i})]$$

$$= \lim_{n \text{ to infinity}} (1/n^2) \Sigma_{i=1 \text{ to } n/2} \{p(H)[1 - p(H)] + p(A)[1 - p(A)]\}$$

$$= \lim_{n \text{ to infinity}} (\{p(H)[1 - p(H)] + p(A)[1 - p(A)]\}/n^2) \Sigma_{i=1 \text{ to } n/2} 1$$

$$= \lim_{n \text{ to infinity}} ((n/2)\{p(H)[1 - p(H)] + p(A)[1 - p(A)]\}/n^2)$$

$$= \lim_{n \text{ to infinity}} (\{p(H)[1 - p(H)] + p(A)[1 - p(A)]\}/2n)$$

$$= 0.$$

Thus, the Weak Law of Large Numbers applies, and the proportion of wins will tend, in the limit as the number of games gets large, to

$$E[X^*(n)] = E[\Sigma_{i = 1 \text{ to } n} X_i]/n$$

$$= E[\Sigma_{i = 1 \text{ to } n/2}(X_{2i-1} + X_{2i})]/n$$

$$= \Sigma_{i = 1 \text{ to } n/2} E[X_{2i-1} + X_{2i}]/n$$

$$= \Sigma_{i = \text{ to } n/2}(E[X_{2i-1}] + E[X_{2i}])/n$$

$$= \Sigma_{i = \text{ to } n/2}(p(H) + p(A))/n$$

$$= [(p(H) + p(A))/n]\Sigma_{i = 1 \text{ to } n/2} 1$$

$$= [(p(H) + p(A))/n][n/2]$$

$$= [(p(H) + p(A))][1/2]$$

$$= [(p(H) + p(A))]/2.$$

This is the probability of winning a game if the location has a 50% chance of being home and a 50% chance of being away.

• PROBLEM 8-32

Suppose that the random variables are no longer independent. In particular, let X have a normal distribution with mean

$$E[X] = M$$

and variance one, and let $X_1 = X_2 = \ldots = X$. That is, each random variable in the sequence is equal to this random variable X. Does the Weak Law of Large Numbers apply?

SOLUTION:

We need to establish that

$$\lim_{n \text{ to infinity}} V[X^*(n)] = 0,$$

but now it no longer suffices to show that

$$\lim_{n \text{ to infinity}}(1/n^2)\Sigma_{i = 1 \text{ to } n} V(X_i) = 0,$$

because the left-hand side is only the variance of $X^*(n)$ when the random variables are independent. Since they are not, we need to go back to

$V[X^*(n)]$. Now

$$V[X^*(n)] = V[\Sigma_{i = 1 \text{ to } n} X_i/n]$$

$$= V[\Sigma_{i = 1 \text{ to } n} X/n]$$

$$= (1/n^2)V[nX]$$

$$= (n^2/n^2)V[X]$$

$$= V(X)$$

$$= 1,$$

which is not zero, even in the limit as n goes to infinity. Thus, the Weak Law of Large Numbers does not apply.

• PROBLEM 8-33

Consider a series of Poisson random variables, X_i, with parameter i. Does the Weak Law of Large Numbers apply?

SOLUTION:

The variance of a Poisson random variable is its parameter, so

$$V(X_i) = i.$$

Then $\quad V[X^*(n)] = V[\Sigma_{i = 1 \text{ to } n} X_i/n]$

$$= (1/x^2)V[\Sigma_{i = 1 \text{ to } n} X_i]$$

$$= (1/n^2)\Sigma_{i = 1 \text{ to } n} V(X_i)$$

$$= (1/n^2)\Sigma_{i = 1 \text{ to } n} i$$

$$= (1/n^2)[n(n + 1)/2]$$

$$= (1/2n^2)[n^2 + n]$$

$$= [n^2 + n]/2n^2$$

$$= (n + 1)/2n,$$

which converges to 0.5, and not to zero. Thus, the Weak Law of Large Numbers does not apply in this case.

******

REVIEW OF TYPES OF CONVERGENCE

Convergence of a sequence of numbers to a numeric limit should be a familiar concept to most readers. The formal definition of such convergence is that X_n converges to X if, for all positive numbers k, there exists a number $N(k)$ such that whenever $n > N(k)$, it is true that

$$|X_n - X| < k.$$

This definition becomes problematic when the numbers X_n are replaced by functions or, in our case, random variables (which can be treated as functions by considering one of the functions that determines the distribution of the random variable, such as the probability mass function, probability density function, cumulative distribution function, moment-generating function, or characteristic function). Many definitions are possible for describing the convergence of a sequence of random variables to a limiting random variable. We will consider the four most common definitions.

A sequence of random variables, X_i, is said to converge almost everywhere to the limit random variable X if there exists a set A such that

$$P\{A\} = 0$$

and X_i converges to X for any sequence not in A.

Notice that for any given sequence of observed random variables, both X_i and X are simply numbers, since the random variables can be replaced with their observed values. This type of convergence is also called "convergence with probability one," for obvious reasons. Notice that X can be a number. Numbers are known as degenerate random variables, because they take on only a single value with probability one.

A sequence of random variables, X_i, is said to converge in probability to the limit random variable X if

$$\lim_{n \text{ to infinity}} P\{ |X_n - X| > k\} = 0$$

for all $k > 0$.

It turns out that convergence almost everywhere implies convergence in probability, but the reverse implication is not true. Again, X may be a degenerate random variable.

A sequence of random variables, X_i, is said to converge in L^p to the limit random variable X if

$$E[\,|X_i^p|\,] \text{ is finite,}$$

$$E[\,|X^p|\,] \text{ is finite,}$$

and $\lim_{n \text{ to infinity}} E[|X_n - X|^p] = 0.$

It turns out that for any positive, finite p, convergence in L^p implies convergence in probability, but the reverse implication is not true. Once again, X may be a degenerate random variable, taking on only one value.

A sequence of random variables, X_i, is said to converge in distribution to the limit random variable X if

$\lim_{n \text{ to infinity}} F_n(k) = F(k)$

for all k such that F is continuous at k, where

$F_n(k)$ is the cumulative distribution function of X_n evaluated at k

and $F(k)$ is the cumulative distribution function of X evaluated at k.

It should be mentioned that this "limiting random variable," X, need not actually be a random variable. As k approaches infinity, $F(k) \leq 1$, but this inequality may be strict, in which case $F(\text{infinity}) < 1$ and X is not a random variable.

It turns out that convergence in probability implies convergence in distribution, but the reverse implication is not true.

There is a fifth type of convergence which is referred to less frequently than the other four. A sequence of random variables, X_i, is said to converge weakly to the limit random variable X if

$\lim_{n \text{ to infinity}} E[X_n Y] = E[XY]$

for all bounded random variables Y.

It turns out that for any positive, finite p, convergence in L^p implies weak convergence.

• PROBLEM 8–34

Does convergence in L^p imply convergence almost everywhere?

SOLUTION:

Let U have a uniform distribution on the range $[0, 1]$, and for $i \leq j$, let Y_{ij} be defined as

$Y_{ij} = 1$ if U falls in the range $[(i-1)/j, i/j]$,

and $Y_{ij} = 0$ otherwise.

Now let X_n be the nth such random variable, ordering by increasing values of j and breaking ties by increasing values of i. That is,

$$X_1 = Y_{1,1},$$

$$X_2 = Y_{1,2},$$

$$X_3 = Y_{2,2},$$

$$X_4 = Y_{1,3},$$

and so on.

Let X be the degenerate random variable which takes on the value zero with probability one. Then

$$E[\ |X_n - X\ |^p] = E[\ |X_n - 0\ |^p]$$

$$= E[\ |X_n|^p]$$

$$= P\{X_n = 1\},$$

which tends to zero as n tends to infinity. Thus, X_n converges to $X = 0$ in L^p.

But now consider the set on which X_n converges. In fact, because the unit interval is traced out over and over again but in progressively smaller increments, the sequence will assume the value one infinitely often and will also assume the value zero infinitely often. Thus, for no observed sample sequence will the X_n converge to any limit, let alone to zero. Thus, the sequence X_n does not converge almost everywhere. This example shows that convergence in L^p does not imply convergence almost everywhere.

• PROBLEM 8–35

Does convergence in probability imply convergence in L^p?

SOLUTION:

Consider U and $Y_{i,j}$ from Problem 8–34. Now define $X_{i,j}$ to be

$$X_1 = 1^{(1/p)} Y_{1,1},$$

$$X_2 = 2^{(1/p)}Y_{1,2},$$

$$X_3 = 2^{(1/p)}Y_{2,2},$$

$$X_4 = 3^{(1/p)}Y_{1,3},$$

$$X_5 = 3^{(1/p)}Y_{2,3},$$

$$X_6 = 3^{(1/p)}Y_{3,3},$$

$$X_7 = 4^{(1/p)}Y_{1,4},$$

and so on. The coefficient of Y is the $(1/p)^{\text{th}}$ power of the second subscript of Y.

Now let X be the degenerate random variable which assumes the value zero with probability one. Then

$$P\{\,|\,X_n - X\,| > k\} = P\{\,|\,X_n - 0\,| > k\}$$

$$= P\{\,|\,X_n| > k\},$$

which tends to zero as n tends to infinity. Thus, X_n converges in probability to zero.

On the other hand,

$$E[\,|\,X_n - X\,|^p] = E[\,|\,X_n - 0\,|^p]$$

$$= E[\,|\,X_n\,|^p]$$

$$= [j(n)^{(1/p)}]^p P\{X_n = j(n)^{1/p}\} + (0)P\{X_n = 0\}$$

$$= [j(n)][1/j(n)] + (0)$$

$$= 1$$

$$> 0,$$

so X_n does not converge to zero in L^p. This example shows that convergence in probability does not imply convergence in L^p.

• PROBLEM 8–36

Does convergence almost everywhere imply convergence in L^p?

SOLUTION:

Consider a sequence of random variables defined as follows. Let U be uniformly distributed with range [0, 1]. Now let

$$X_n = n \text{ if } nU < 1$$

and $X_n = 0$ otherwise.

Let $X = 0$ (X is a degenerate random variable). Now if $U > 0$, which occurs with probability one, then for large enough n we see that $nU > 1$, so for large enough n we see that $X_n = 0$. Therefore,

$$P\{X_n \text{ converges to } X\} = 1,$$

and X_n converges almost everywhere to X.

On the other hand,

$$E[\,|\,X_n - X\,|^p\,] = E[\,|\,X_n - 0\,|^p\,]$$

$$= E[\,|\,X_n\,|^p\,]$$

$$= (n)P\{X_n = n\} + (0)P\{X_n = 0\}$$

$$= (n)\,(1/n) + 0$$

$$= 1$$

$$> 0,$$

so X_n does not converge in L^p to X.

● **PROBLEM 8-37**

What type of convergence is employed by the Weak Law of Large Numbers?

SOLUTION:

The Weak Law of Large Numbers roughly states that, under certain conditions, the sample mean converges in probability to the population mean.

• PROBLEM 8-38

What type of convergence is employed by the Strong Law of Large Numbers?

SOLUTION:

The Strong Law of Large Numbers roughly states that, under certain conditions, the sample mean converges almost everywhere to the population mean.

✱✱✱✱✱✱

REVIEW OF THE CENTRAL LIMIT THEOREM

There are many versions of the Central Limit Theorem. Some allow for dependent random variables, some allow for random variables that have different distributions, and some do not require the existence of a finite variance. The most general Central Limit Theorem is stated in terms of a triangular array of random variables and the concept of "uniform asymptotic negligibility."

We will not consider such general statements of the Central Limit Theorem. It will suffice for our purposes to consider the most basic statement of the Central Limit Theorem. This is the version which is best known and most frequently applied in practice.

Consider a situation in which simple random sampling is employed from a population with finite variance. Regardless of the underlying distribution of each observation, the sample mean tends to become more and more normally distributed as the sample size increases.

We already know, from the previous section on sampling theory, the parameters of the normal distribution to which the distribution of the sample mean is converging. The mean of this limiting normal distribution is simply the population mean of each observation, since

$$E[X^*(n)] = E[X] = M,$$

and the variance of the limiting normal distribution is

$$V[X^*(n)] = V(X)/n,$$

where n is the sample size.

This is one of the most profound results in all of probability theory, and it accounts for a great deal of the popularity of the normal distribution. A tremendous theory has been built up for dealing with the normal distribution (for example, simple linear regression, multiple regression, the analysis of variance, the analysis of covariance, the repeated measures analysis of variance, split-plot analysis of variance, and multivariate analysis of variance). Many of these methods are applied in practice with full knowledge that the underlying distribution is not normal, even though the methods require normality. This application of these methods can be justified through the Central Limit Theorem.

As an example, suppose that a sample of 36 people is taken, and the height of each is measured. If the mean height in the population is 66 inches, and the variance is nine inches, then what is the probability that the sample mean height will exceed 68 inches?

Since the variance is nine, the standard deviation is

$$SD = 9^{0.5}$$

$$= 3,$$

and the standard error (the standard deviation of the sample mean) is

$$SE = SD/n^{0.5}$$

$$= 3/36^{0.5}$$

$$= 3/6$$

$$= 1/2$$

We write

$$P\{X^*(36) > 68\} = P\{[X^*(36) - 66]/(1/2) > [68 - 66]/(1/2)\}.$$

By the Central Limit Theorem, we may re-express this as

$$P\{X^*(36) > 68\} = P\{Z > [68 - 66]/(1/2)\}$$

$$= P\{Z > [2]/(1/2)\}$$

$$= P\{Z > 4\}$$

$$= 0$$

Thus, it is nearly impossible that the sample mean will exceed 68 inches. We only know this by appealing to the Central Limit Theorem. Had we not used normality, we would have had to use Chebyshev's Inequality, which is far more crude.

We know that the variance of the sample mean is

$$V[X*(36)] = 9/36$$

$$= 1/4$$

$$= 0.25,$$

so by Chebyshev's Inequality we could find a bound for

$$P\{\,|\,X*(36) - 66\,|\, > 2\},$$

which still does not allow the calculation of

$$P\{X*(36) > 68\},$$

unless symmetry is assumed.

One of the most common applications of the Central Limit Theorem is to the case of the binomial distribution. If the parameters of a binomial distribution are n and p, then the variance is

$$V(X) = np(1 - p),$$

which is certainly finite. Therefore, the Central Limit Theorem applies.

The idea is to approximate the binomial distribution with an appropriate normal distribution. The mean of this normal distribution would be the mean of the binomial distribution, or

$$E[X] = np,$$

and the variance of this normal distribution would be the variance of the binomial distribution, or

$$V(X) = np(1 - p).$$

The approximation is useful because it is computationally intensive to compute exact binomial probabilities when n is large. However, the approximations are readily available in the normal tables.

One feature of the approximation of a binomial random variable (or any discrete random variable) with a normal random variable (or any continuous random variable) is the discrepancy in the distinction between "$\leq$" and "$<$". In the continuous case, these two have no distinction, since the probability that a continuous random variable actually equals any given value is zero. Of course, this is not the case when dealing with discrete random variables.

If X is continuous and one asks for $P\{X > k\}$ or $P\{X \geq k\}$, the same answer will result. But if X is discrete, then $P\{X \geq k\} = P\{X > k\} + P\{X = k\}$, which could turn out to be larger than $P\{X > k\}$ (if k is in the range of X).

The convention is to add a correction for continuity when approximating a discrete random variable with a continuous one. Now if X is a discrete random variable and we wish to appeal to the Central Limit Theorem, then

$$P\{X > k\}$$

will be treated as

$$P\{X > k + 0.5\},$$

while $P\{X \geq k\}$

will be treated as

$$P\{X > k - 0.5\}.$$

Likewise,

$$P\{X < k\}$$

will be treated as

$$P\{X < k - 0.5\},$$

while $P\{X \leq k\}$

will be treated as

$$P\{X < k + 0.5\}.$$

The term 0.5 is added as the correction for continuity, and guarantees that $P\{X > k\}$ and $P\{X \geq k\}$ will not turn out the same numerically for discrete random variables.

√ • PROBLEM 8-39

Suppose that a sample of size 64 is taken from a population with mean six and variance 25. What is the probability that the sample mean exceeds 7.875?

SOLUTION:

First, compute the standard error as

$SE = SD/n^{0.5}$

$\quad = V(X)^{0.5}/64^{0.5}$

$\quad = 25^{0.5}/8$

$\quad = 5/8$

$\quad = 0.625$

We use the Central Limit Theorem and write

$P\{X^*(49) > 7.875\}$

$\quad = P\{[X^*(49) - 6.000]/0.625 > [7.875 - 6.000]/0.625\}$

$\quad = P\{Z > 1.875/0.625\}$

$\quad = P\{Z > (15/8)/(5/8)\}$

$\quad = P\{Z > 15/5\}$

$\quad = P\{Z > 3\}$

$\quad = 0$

√ • PROBLEM 8-40

Suppose that a basketball player takes 100 foul shots during a basketball season. If the results of these 100 shots are all independent, and the probability of any one of them being successful is 0.8, then what is the probability that the player will score at least 76 shots? Do not use the correction for continuity.

SOLUTION:

First, compute the standard deviation of the number of shots made as

$$SD = V(X)^{0.5}$$

$$= [np(1 - p)]^{0.5}$$

$$= [(100)\,(0.8)\,(1 - 0.8)]^{0.5}$$

$$= [(100)\,(0.8)\,(0.2)]^{0.5}$$

$$= [16]^{0.5}$$

$$= 4$$

Also, the expected number of shots made is

$$E[X] = np$$

$$= (100)\,(0.8)$$

$$= 80$$

We use the Central Limit Theorem and write

$$P\{X > 76\} = P\{(X - 80)/4 > (76 - 80)/4\} \quad \text{why there is no } \sqrt{n}\ ?$$

$$= P\{Z > -4/4\}$$

$$= P\{Z > -1\}$$

$$= 0.8413$$

This is one approximate probability that at least 76 shots are successful.

✓• **PROBLEM 8–41**

Suppose that a basketball player takes 100 foul shots during a basket-ball season. If the results of these 100 shots are all independent, and the probability of any one of them being successful is 0.8, then what is the probability that the player will score at least 76 shots? Use the correction for continuity.

SOLUTION:

First, compute the standard deviation of the number of shots made as

$$SD = V(X)^{0.5}$$
$$= [np(1-p)]^{0.5}$$
$$= [(100)\,(0.8)\,(1-0.8)]^{0.5}$$
$$= [(100)\,(0.8)\,(0.2)]^{0.5}$$
$$= [16]^{0.5}$$
$$= 4$$

Also, the expected number of shots made is

$$E[X] = np$$
$$= (100)\,(0.8)$$
$$= 80$$

We use the Central Limit Theorem and write

$$P\{X \geq 76\} \text{ is approximately } P\{X > 76 - 0.5\}$$
$$= P\{X > 75.5\}$$
$$= P\{(X-80)/4 > (75.5-80)/4\}$$
$$= P\{Z > -4.5/4\}$$
$$= P\{Z > -9/8\}$$
$$= P\{Z > -1.125\}$$
$$= 0.87$$

This is another approximate probability that at least 76 shots are successful.

• PROBLEM 8–42

Suppose that a basketball player takes 100 foul shots during a basketball season. If the results of these 100 shots are all independent, and the probability of any one of them being successful is 0.9, then what is the probability that the player will score at least 84 shots? Do not use the correction for continuity.

SOLUTION:

First, compute the standard deviation of the number of shots made as

$$SD = V(X)^{0.5}$$

$$= [np(1 - p)]^{0.5}$$

$$= [(100)\,(0.9)\,(1 - 0.9)]^{0.5}$$

$$= [(100)\,(0.9)\,(0.1)]^{0.5}$$

$$= [9]^{0.5}$$

$$= 3$$

Also, the expected number of shots made is

$$E[X] = np$$

$$= (100)\,(0.9)$$

$$= 90$$

We use the Central Limit Theorem and write

$$P\{X > 84\} = P\{(X - 90)/3 > (84 - 90)/3\}$$

$$= P\{Z > -6/3\}$$

$$= P\{Z > -2\}$$

$$= 0.9772.$$

This is one approximate probability that at least 84 shots are successful.

● PROBLEM 8–43

Suppose that a basketball player takes 100 foul shots during a basket-ball season. If the results of these 100 shots are all independent, and the probability of any one of them being successful is 0.9, then what is the probability that the player will score at least 84 shots? Use the correction for continuity.

SOLUTION:

First, compute the standard deviation of the number of shots made as

$$SD = V(X)^{0.5}$$

$$= [np(1-p)]^{0.5}$$

$$= [(100)\,(0.9)\,(1-0.9)]^{0.5}$$

$$= [(100)\,(0.9)\,(0.1)]^{0.5}$$

$$= [9]^{0.5}$$

$$= 3$$

Also, the expected number of shots made is

$$E[X] = np$$

$$= (100)\,(0.9)$$

$$= 90$$

We use the Central Limit Theorem and write

$$P\{X \geq 84\} \text{ is approximately } P\{X > 84 - 0.5\}$$

$$= P\{X > 83.5\}$$

$$= P\{(X - 90)/3 > (83.5 - 90)/3\}$$

$$= P\{Z > -6.5/3\}$$

$$= P\{Z > -2.1667\}$$

$$= 0.9850$$

This is another approximate probability that at least 84 shots are successful.

CHAPTER 9

FAMOUS RESULTS OF PROBABILITY THEORY

Basic Attacks and Strategies for Solving Problems in this Chapter. See pages 673 to 721 for step-by-step solutions to problems.

This chapter will highlight some of the most famous results in probability theory. The first section deals with Jensen's Inequality (Billingsley, 1986, page 283).

Jensen's Inequality is a result from mathematics, and in particular from convex analysis. Nevertheless, Jensen's Inequality has found enough application in probability theory that it is included in this book for completeness.

The second section concerns the Borel-Cantelli Lemmas, which dictate the probabilities with which certain events occur infinitely often. The third section concerns the famous Zero-One Law of Kolmogorov, who is perhaps the most famous of all probabilists, as well as other Zero-One Laws (the Borel Zero-One Criterion, the Hewitt-Savage Zero-One Law, and Paul Levy's Zero-One Law). Kolmogorov's version of this law states that certain events, known as "tail events," can only occur with probability zero or with probability one. That is, they are either certain to occur or certain not to occur. It is quite remarkable that even armed with this knowledge it is often quite difficult in practice to determine if the probability is, in fact, zero or one.

The fourth section concerns generating functions and characteristic functions (Chow and Teicher, 1988, page 268). Technically speaking, these are tools, and not results. They are included in this chapter because so many results may be proven with these tools. For example, one of the most streamlined proofs of the Central Limit Theorem makes use of these functions. In addition, utilization of these functions is a method of choice for recognizing certain distributions which are derived from complicated operations. The key is the one-to-one correspondence between generating functions and distribution functions.

This chapter is of a more theoretical nature than most of the previous chapters of the book. This is because the results presented apply to general situations, and to specialize to particular cases would not do them justice.

Jensen's Inequality concerns expected values of convex functions of random variables. Before we can study Jensen's Inequality, therefore, we must define convex functions.

The simplest way to understand a convex function is to think of it as a function whose graph holds water. For example, the function

$$Y = X^2$$

is convex. If its graph is plotted, the result will be a parabola facing upwards, with a global (and local) minimum at $X = 0$. This parabola will hold water by its shape. It is shaped like a cup. On the other hand, consider the function

$$Y = -X^2.$$

The graph of this function is also a parabola, but this parabola faces down. It is shaped like a cup which has been turned upside down. Clearly, then, this cup will not hold water. Thus, this function is not convex.

The water test is not always accurate at characterizing functions as convex or not convex. To be convex, the graph of the function would need to hold water everywhere. But holding water everywhere is not sufficient for a function to be convex.

Consider the function

$$Y = -X \text{ for } X < -1,$$

$$Y = X^2 \text{ for } -1 < X < 1,$$

and $\quad Y = X \text{ for } X > 1,$

with Y defined by continuity at $X = -1$ and $X = 1$. That is,

$$Y = 1 \text{ when } X = -1$$

and $\quad Y = 1 \text{ when } X = 1.$

While the graph of this function holds water everywhere, the function is not convex. A general definition of a convex function is beyond the scope of this book, but we will present an operational definition.

It is not the case that every function is differentiable. Furthermore, not every function which is differentiable has a second derivative. Nevertheless, we will define convexity only for functions which have a second derivative (that is, we define when a twice differentiable function is convex).

If the second derivative of a function is non-negative, then this function is convex. This is essentially equivalent to requiring that the first derivative be non-decreasing. Notice that for the function

$$Y = -X \text{ for } X < -1,$$

$$Y = X^2 \text{ for } -1 < X < 1,$$

and $\quad Y = X \text{ for } X > 1,$

with Y defined by continuity at $X = -1$ and $X = 1$

is not convex because the first derivative of this function is

$$f'(X) = -1 \text{ for } X < -1,$$

$$f'(X) = 2X \text{ for } -1 < X < 1,$$

and $\quad f'(X) = 1 \text{ for } X > 1,$

while the derivative is not defined at $X = -1$ or $X = 1$. Clearly the derivative decreases at $X = -1$. This is why the function is not convex.

Now consider the second derivative. This is

$$f''(X) = 0 \text{ for } X < -1,$$

$$f''(X) = 2 \text{ for } -1 < X < 1,$$

and $\quad f''(X) = 0 \text{ for } X > 1.$

It would seem that this function is convex by virtue of the second derivative being non-negative. However, we already saw that this function is not convex. What went wrong?

This function is neither differentiable nor twice differentiable. Therefore, according to our definition, we will not even consider this function for convexity.

Common examples of convex functions are

$$Y = k \text{ for any constant } k,$$

$$Y = X^2,$$

$$Y = X^4,$$

$$Y = X^k \text{ for even integer-valued } k,$$

and $\quad Y = e^X.$

Jensen's Inequality states that if f is a convex function, then

$$E[f(X)] \geq f(E[X]).$$

We will not offer a proof of this profound statement. Interested readers are referred to Billingsley (1986), page 283.

Step-by-Step Solutions to Problems in this Chapter, "Famous Results of Probability Theory."

• PROBLEM 9–1

Is the function $Y = f(X) = |X|$ convex?

SOLUTION:

We first consider the second derivative of this function. If this second derivative exists and is non-negative, then the function is convex.

We write

$$f(X) = |X|,$$

so $\quad f(X) = -X$ for $X < 0,$

$$f(X) = X \text{ for } X = 0,$$

and $\quad f(X) = X$ for $X > 0.$

Then $\quad f'(X) = -1$ for $X < 0,$

$$f'(X) = 1 \text{ for } X > 0,$$

but $f'(X)$ is not defined for $X = 0.$

Thus, $f'(X)$ does not exist, and therefore $f''(X)$ cannot exist either.

The second approach to determining if $f(X)$ is convex or not is to consider the first derivative, and in particular, to determining if it is increasing or not. This will not work either, because the first derivative is undefined at $X = 0$.

Finally, we resort to our working definition. The graph of $f(X) = |X|$ does hold water, so we declare $f(X) = |X|$ to be convex. As it turns out, this function is also convex according to the more rigorous definition too.

• PROBLEM 9–2

Prove that X^k is convex if k is a positive even integer.

SOLUTION:

First consider the first derivative,

$$f'(X) = kX^{k-1} \text{ for all } X.$$

Now the second derivative is

$$f''(X) = k(k-1)X^{k-2} \text{ for all } X.$$

Since k is a positive even integer, we know the following seven facts:

    1. $k > 0$,

    2. $k - 1 > 0$,

    3. $(k)(k-1) > 0$,

    4. $k - 2 \geq 0$,

    5. $k - 2$ is a non-negative even integer,

    6. $X^{k-2} \geq 0$,

and finally

    7. $k(k-1)X^{k-2} \geq 0$.

The third statement follows from the first two. The sixth statement follows from the fifth. The seventh statement follows from the third and sixth, and establishes that

$$f''(X) \geq 0 \text{ for all } X.$$

Thus, $f(X) = X^{k-2}$ is convex for positive even integer k.

• PROBLEM 9-3

Is $f(X) = X^k$ convex if k is an odd positive integer? Is $f(X) = X^k$ concave if k is an odd positive integer?

SOLUTION:

First consider the first derivative,

$$f'(X) = kX^{K-1} \text{ for all } X.$$

Now the second derivative is

$$f''(X) = k(k-1)X^{k-2} \text{ for all } X.$$

Since k is a positive odd integer, we know the following seven facts:

1. $k > 0$,

2. $k - 1 \geq 0$,

3. $(k)(k-1) \geq 0$,

4. $k - 2$ can be either positive or negative,

5. $k - 2$ can be either positive or negative, but is an odd integer,

6. X^{k-2} can be positive, negative, or zero,

and finally

7. $k(k-1)X^{k-2}$ can be positive, negative, or zero.

The third statement follows from the first two. The sixth statement follows from the fifth. The seventh statement follows from the third and sixth, and establishes that $f''(X)$ need not be non-negative for all X. Thus, $f(X) = X^{k-2}$ is not convex for positive odd integer k.

Now consider the negative of $f(X)$ to determine if $f(X)$ is concave. This is given by

$$-f(X) = -X^k.$$

The first derivative is given by

$$-f'(X) = -kX^{k-1} \text{ for all } X.$$

The second derivative is

$$-f''(X) = -k(k-1)X^{k-2} \text{ for all } X.$$

Since k is a positive odd integer, we know the following seven facts:

1. $k > 0$,

2. $k - 1 \geq 0$,

3. $-(k)(k-1) \leq 0$,

4. $k - 2$ can be either positive or negative,

5. $k - 2$ can be either positive or negative, but is an odd integer,

6. X^{k-2} can be positive, negative, or zero,

and finally

7. $-k(k-1)X^{k-2}$ can be positive, negative, or zero.

The third statement follows from the first two. The sixth statement follows from the fifth. The seventh statement follows from the third and sixth, and establishes that $f''(X)$ need not be non-negative for all X. Thus, $f(X) = X^{k-2}$ is not concave for positive odd integer k.

• **PROBLEM 9–4**

Prove that $Y = f(X) = e^x$ is a convex function.

SOLUTION:

The first derivative of $f(X)$ is

$$f'(X) = e^x,$$

and the second derivative is

$$f''(X) = e^x.$$

Since $e^x > 0$, $f''(X)$ exists and is non-negative, so $f(X) = e^x$ is a convex function.

• **PROBLEM 9-5**

Is $Y = f(X) = e^{-x}$ convex? Is it concave?

SOLUTION:

The first derivative of $f(X)$ is

$$f'(X) = -e^{-x},$$

and the second derivative is

$$f''(X) = -f'(X)$$
$$= -[-e^{-x}]$$
$$= e^{-x}$$

Since $e^{-x} > 0$, $f''(X)$ exists and is non-negative, so $f(X) = e^{-x}$ is a convex function.

To determine if $f(X) = e^{-x}$ is also a concave function, consider $-f(X) = -e^{-x}$. The first derivative of $-f(X)$ is

$$f'(X) = -(-1)e^{-x}$$
$$= e^{-x},$$

and the second derivative is

$$f''(X) = -e^{-x}.$$

Since $e^{-x} > 0$, $-e^{-x} < 0$ and $f''(X)$ exists and is non-positive. But it is not non-negative, so $f(X) = -e^{-x}$ is not a convex function, and $f(X) = e^{-x}$ is not a concave function.

• **PROBLEM 9-6**

Let X be an arbitrary random variable. Prove that $V(X) \geq 0$.

SOLUTION:

Consider the function

$$f(X) = X^2.$$

This function is twice-differentiable, and

$$f'(X) = 2X$$

and $f''(X) = 2 > 0.$

Therefore, f is a convex function. By Jensen's Inequality

$$E[f(X)] \geq f(E[X]),$$

or $E[X^2] \geq (E[X])^2.$

Now

$$V(X) = E[X^2] - (E[X])^2 \geq 0$$

by Jensen's Inequality.

• PROBLEM 9–7

Let X be an arbitrary random variable, and let $Y = f(X)$, where f is not a convex function. Can $V(Y)$ be negative?

SOLUTION:

No. Problem 9–6 states that the variance of any random variable is non-negative. The manner in which the random variable is derived is inconsequential.

• PROBLEM 9–8

A function f is said to be concave if $-f$ is convex. What would be the extension of Jensen's Inequality to concave functions?

SOLUTION:

Since $-f$ is convex,

$$E[-f(X)] \geq -f(E[X]),$$

by Jensen's Inequality. But

$$E[-f(X)] = -E[f(X)].$$

Therefore,

$$-E[f(X)] = E[-f(X)] \geq -f(E[X]).$$

Multiplying both sides of the equation by -1 reverses the direction of the inequality, resulting in

$$E[f(X)] \leq f(E[X]).$$

This is the extension of Jensen's Inequality to concave functions of random variables.

• PROBLEM 9–9

Use both Jensen's Inequality and the extension of Jensen's Inequality (as illustrated in Problem 98) to prove that the expected value is a linear operator.

SOLUTION:

Let f be a linear function. That is,

$$f(X) = aX + b$$

for some constants a and b. Then we need to show that

$$E[f(X)] = f(E[X]).$$

This is a property which we used a great deal in Chapter 4, and now we are in a position to prove it using both Jensen's Inequality and the extension to Jensen's Inequality.

First notice that if we define $g(X)$ as

$$g(X) = -f(X)$$
$$= -[a + bX]$$
$$= c + dX,$$

where $c = -a$

and $d = -b,$

then $g(X)$ is also a linear function. Now the derivative of f exists and is given by

$$f'(X) = b.$$

The second derivative of f also exists and is given by

$$f''(X) = 0.$$

Of course, zero is non-negative. Since

$$f''(X) \geq 0$$

for all X, f is a convex function. Therefore, Jensen's Inequality applies. We know, then, that

$$E[f(X)] \geq f(E[X]),$$

or $\quad E[a + bX] \geq a + bE[X].$

Recall that we are trying to prove that these two quantities are equal, so we cannot assume it, as we would have in Chapter 4. That is, until we prove that the expected value is a linear operator, we cannot replace $E[a + bX]$ by $a + bE[X]$.

Now consider $g(X) = -f(X)$. This function is also twice-differentiable, and

$$g'(X) = d,$$

and $\quad g''(X) = 0$

for all X. Again, zero is non-negative, so

$$g''(X) \geq 0$$

for all X, and g is a convex function. But this means that $-g$ is a concave function. Since $f = -g$, we know that f is a concave function (in addition to being a convex function). By the extension to Jensen's Inequality given in Problem 9–8,

$$E[f(X)] \leq f(E[X]),$$

or $\quad E[a + bX] \leq a + bE[X].$

Combining this inequality with the previous inequality,

$$E[a + bX] \geq a + bE[X],$$

proves that

$$E[a + bX] = a + bE[X].$$

This is true for all linear functions, f, since we placed no constraints on the constants a or b. Allowing these constants to vary freely accounts for all linear functions. Therefore, we have proved that the expected value of any linear function of a random variable is equal to that function applied to the expected value of the random variable.

******

REVIEW OF THE BOREL-CANTELLI LEMMAS

There are two famous Borel-Cantelli Lemmas. We will consider both. Both deal with infinite sequences of events. One deals with convergence of the probabilities of these events, and one deals with the divergence of the probabilities of these events.

Prior to studying the Borel-Cantelli Lemmas it is important to become familiar with the concepts of limit supremum and limit infimum (see, for example, Billingsley, 1986, page 46). Consider, then, an infinite sequence of events, say $A_1, A_2, \ldots$ The limit supremum of this sequence of events is defined as

$$LS(A) = \cap_{m = 1 \text{ to infinity}} \cup_{n = m \text{ to infinity}} A_n,$$

and the limit infimum of this sequence of events is defined as

$$LI(A) = \cup_{m = 1 \text{ to infinity}} \cup_{n = m \text{ to infinity}} A_n.$$

These definitions require some explanation. After some thought it should, hopefully, become clear that $LS(A)$ is the event that A_n occurs infinitely often and $LI(A)$ is the event that after some point A_n occurs thereafter.

To see this, study the definitions. $LS(A)$ is a union of an intersection. Recall that a union is analogous to "or," while an intersection is analogous to "and." This is particularly useful when considering only two events. When considering more than two events, a union is analogous to "for some" or "there exists," while an intersection is analogous to "for all."

Thus the intersection in the definition of $LS(A)$ should be interpreted as "for all m between one and infinity." Now the union in the definition of $LS(A)$ should be interpreted as "there exists a number n between m and infinity." Putting it all together, we have "for all m between one and infinity there exists a number n between m and infinity such that the event A_n occurs."

What does this mean? It means that no matter how large a number one considers, there is always a larger number which is the index n for which A_n occurs. This means that as a process, A_n never stops occurring. Put another way, A_n (again viewed as a process) occurs infinitely often.

Consider the converse. If A_n occurs only finitely often (that is, for only a finite number of indices n), then there is some largest such index, say N. That is, A_N occurs, but A_n does not occur for any $n > N$. This would be a violation of the definition of $LS(A)$, because the definition of $LS(A)$ requires that for all N there exists an n larger than N such that A_n occurs. We have shown that $LS(A)$ is exactly the event that infinitely many of the A_n occur.

Now $LI(A)$ is a bit different from $LS(A)$. By definition, $LI(A)$ is a union of intersections. The union should again be interpreted as "there exists," while the intersection should be interpreted as "for all." Then

$$LI(A) = \cup_{m = 1 \text{ to infinity}} \cap_{n = m \text{ to infinity}} A_n$$

is the event that there exists a number m between one and infinity such that for all n between m and infinity A_n occurs. That is, for some number m we know that A_n occurs for all n larger than m. This means that $A_n{}^c$ only occurs finitely often. Thus,

$$LI(A) = [LS(A^c)]^c,$$
and $\quad LS(A) = [LI(A^c)]^c.$

There are three points of note:

1. $LS(A)$ is a (proper) subset of $LI(A)$,

2. $LS(A)$ does not depend on the order of $\{A_n\}$ (that is, if the set of $\{A_n\}$ is permuted arbitrarily, then $LS(A)$ will remain intact),

and

3. $LS(I)$ does not depend on the order of $\{A_n\}$ (that is, if the set of $\{A_n\}$ is permuted arbitrarily, then $LS(I)$ will remain intact).

We are now in a position to state the two Borel-Cantelli Lemmas. The first Borel-Cantelli Lemma (Rozanov, 1969, page 21) states that if the infinite sum of the probabilities of the events $\{A_n\}$ is finite, then $P\{LS(A)\} = 0$. That is, if

$$\Sigma_{n = 1 \text{ to infinity}} P\{A_n\}$$

is finite, then

$$P\{LS(A)\} = 0.$$

This is because

$$P\{LS(A)\} = P\{\cap_{m = 1 \text{ to infinity}} \cup_{n = m \text{ to infinity}} A_n\}.$$

We know that

$$P\{A \cup B\} \le P\{A\} + P\{B\},$$

since this is one of the axioms of probability. Likewise,

$$P\{\cup_{n = m \text{ to infinity}} A_n\} \le \Sigma_{n = m \text{ to infinity}} P\{A_n\}.$$

But if

$$\Sigma_{n = 1 \text{ to infinity}} P\{A_n\} < \text{infinity},$$

then

$$\Sigma_{n = m \text{ to infinity}} P\{A_n\} \text{ tends to zero}$$

as m tends to infinity. Therefore,

$$P\{\cup_{n = m \text{ to infinity}} A_n\}$$

also tends to zero. Now the probability of an intersection is no larger than the probability of any of the individual events comprising the intersection. Therefore,

$$0 \le P\{LS(A)\}$$

$$= P\{\cap_{m = 1 \text{ to infinity}} \cup_{n = m \text{ to infinity}} A_n\}$$

$$\le P\{\cup_{n = m \text{ to infinity}} A_n\},$$

which tends to zero as m gets large. Thus, $P\{LS(A)\}$ must be zero.

The second Borel-Cantelli Lemma (Rozanov, 1969, page 33) states that if the infinite sum of the probabilities of the events $\{A_n\}$ is infinite, then $P\{LS(A)\} = 1$ provided that the events $\{A_n\}$ are independent (or at least pairwise independent). That is, if

$$\Sigma_{n = 1 \text{ to infinity}} P\{A_n\}$$

is infinite, then

$$P\{LS(A)\} = 1$$

if the events $\{A_n\}$ are independent or pairwise independent. The proof of this statement is more complicated than the proof of the first Borel-Cantelli Lemma, and is omitted. Interested readers are referred to Rozanov (1969), page 34.

• PROBLEM 9–10

Suppose that we are considering events A_n which specify that the nth toss of a coin results in heads. What is $LS(A)$?

SOLUTION:

By definition, $LS(A)$ is the event in which at each toss there will be a subsequent toss for which the coin will land heads. Thus, $LS(A)$ is the event that the coin will land heads infinitely often.

• PROBLEM 9–11

For the events in Problem 9–10, what is $LS(A^c)$?

SOLUTION:

By definition, $LS(A^c)$ is the event in which at each toss there will be a subsequent toss for which A_n^c occurs, or the coin will not land heads. That means that the coin will land tails. Thus, $LS(A)$ is the event that the coin will land tails infinitely often.

• PROBLEM 9–12

For the events in Problem 9–10, what is $LI(A)$?

SOLUTION:

By definition, $LI(A)$ is the event in which at some toss N A_n will occur for all $n > N$. That means that the coin will land heads every toss beyond a certain point. Thus, $LI(A)$ is the event that the coin will land tails only finitely often.

• PROBLEM 9–13

For the events in Problem 9–10, what is $LI(A^c)$?

SOLUTION:

By definition, $LI(A^c)$ is the event in which at some toss N A_n^c will occur for all $n > N$. That means that the coin will never land heads beyond a certain point. Thus, $LI(A^c)$ is the event that the coin will land heads only finitely often.

• PROBLEM 9–14

What is the connection between $LI(A)$ and $LS(A)$ in terms of the process of complementation?

SOLUTION:

As seen in Problem 9–10, Problem 9–11, Problem 9–12, and Problem 9–13,

$LS(A)$ is the event that the coin lands heads infinitely often,

$LS(A^c)$ is the event that the coin lands tails infinitely often,

$LI(A)$ is the event that the coin lands tails only finitely often,

and $LI(A^c)$ is the event that the coin lands heads only finitely often.

Thus,

$$LS(A) = [LI(A^c)]^c,$$

and

$$LI(A) = [LS(A^c)]^c.$$

• PROBLEM 9–15

Construct an example of a sequence of events which illustrates the importance of the requirement in the second Borel-Cantelli Lemma that the events be independent. That is, construct a sequence of events such that

$$\Sigma_{n = 1 \text{ to infinity}} P\{A_n\}$$

is infinite, yet

$$P\{LS(A)\} < 1.$$

SOLUTION:

Let A be the event that a single fair coin lands heads. Now define A_n as the same event, namely that the fair coin lands heads. Since each of these events is the same, they clearly are not independent (or even pairwise independent). We see that

$$\Sigma_{n = 1 \text{ to infinity}} P\{A_n\} = \Sigma_{n = 1 \text{ to infinity}} P\{A\}$$

$$= \Sigma_{n = 1 \text{ to infinity}} P\{H\}$$

$$= \Sigma_{n = 1 \text{ to infinity}}(0.5),$$

which is infinite. But

$$P\{LS(A)\} = P\{A_n \text{ occurs infinitely often}\}.$$

Now infinitely many of the $\{A_n\}$ occur if and only if A occurs. In fact, every single one of the $\{A_n\}$ occurs if and only if A occurs. Thus,

$$P\{LS(A)\} = P\{A_n \text{ occurs infinitely often}\}$$

$$= P\{A\}$$

$$= P\{H\}$$

$$= 0.5$$

$$< 1$$

• PROBLEM 9–16

Consider tossing a coin an infinite number of times. Assume that the result of each toss is independent of the result of each other toss. Under what conditions would it be true that

$P\{A_n \text{ infinitely often}\} < 1,$

where A_n is the event that the nth toss results in heads? That is, under what conditions would you be less than certain to obtain an infinite number of heads?

SOLUTION:

Since the same coin is being tossed, the probability of heads is the same on each toss. Denote this probability by p. That is

$P\{A_n\} = p$

for each n. Now

$\Sigma_{n = 1 \text{ to infinity}} P\{A_n\} = \Sigma_{n = 1 \text{ to infinity}} p.$

This is infinite if $p > 0$, and is zero if $p = 0$. Now the Borel-Cantelli Lemma states that

$P\{LS(A)\} = 0$

if $p = 0$

and $P\{LS(A)\} = 1$

if $p > 0$. Thus, the only conditions under which $P\{LS(A)\} < 1$ is $p = 0$.

• PROBLEM 9-17

Construct another example of a sequence of events which illustrate the importance of the requirement in the second Borel-Cantelli Lemma that the events be independent. That is, construct a sequence of events such that

$$\sum_{n=1 \text{ to infinity}} P\{A_n\}$$

is infinite, yet not only is

$$P\{LS(A)\} < 1,$$

but also

$$P\{LS(A)\} = 0.$$

SOLUTION:

Notice that the example in Problem 9–15 did satisfy

$$P\{LS(A)\} < 1,$$

but it would not suffice for this problem because

$$P\{LS(A)\} = 0.5 > 0.$$

Let X be a continuous random variable with a uniform distribution with range $[0, 1]$. Define A_n as the event that $nX < 1$. Now

$$P\{A_n\} = P\{nX < 1\}$$
$$= P\{X < 1/n\}$$
$$= 1/n,$$

and by the theory of infinite sums,

$$\sum_{n=1 \text{ to infinity}} P\{A_n\} = \sum_{n=1 \text{ to infinity}} 1/n$$
$$= \text{infinity}.$$

Of course the events $\{A_n\}$ are not independent (or even pairwise independent), because if A_n occurs, then $nX > 1$, so for all $m > n$, mX must also exceed one, and therefore A_m must also occur. Therefore, we cannot apply the Borel-Cantelli Lemma. We see, in fact, that

$$P\{LS(A)\} = P\{A_n \text{ occurs infinitely often}\}$$
$$= P\{nX < 1 \text{ for infinitely many values of } n\}$$

$$= P\{X < 1/n \text{ for infinitely many values of } n\}.$$

Now if X is positive, then there is some largest value of n such that $nX > 1$, and for any value of m larger than this n, $mX > 1$. Thus, for such positive X, $nX < 1$ only finitely often, so A_n can occur only finitely often. On the other hand, if $X = 0$, then $nX = 0 < 1$ for all X, so A_n occurs for all n (and in particular, it occurs infinitely often). Thus,

$$P\{LS(A)\} = P\{X < 1/n \text{ for infinitely many values of } n\}$$

$$= P\{X = 0\}$$

$$= 0,$$

because X is a continuous random variable, and the probability of a continuous random variable taking on any given value is zero.

• PROBLEM 9-18

Let X be a random variable with variance $V(X)$. Let X_n be an infinite simple random sample from the distribution of X. Prove that $P\{X_n \text{ converges}\} = 0$ if $V(X) > 0$ and $P\{X_n \text{ converges}\} = 1$ if $V(X) = 0$.

SOLUTION:

The convergence referred to in this problem is convergence of a sequence of numbers, because the observed values of these random variables are simply numbers. We may define convergence of a sequence of numbers as

X_n converges to a limit L if and only if for all positive numbers k | $X_n - L$ | $> k$ only finitely often.

Now suppose that $V(X) = 0$. Then there is a value, say x, such that

$$P\{X_n = x\} = 1$$

and $P\{X_n = k\} = 0$ for k other than x.

Then with probability one each X_n will equal x, so the sequence $\{X_n\}$ will converge to x with probability one.

On the other hand, if $V(X) > 0$, then there exists a positive number k such that

$$P\{ \, |X - L| > k \} > 0.$$

But since each X_n has the same distribution as X,

$$P\{ \, |X_n - L| > k \} > 0.$$

Since these random variables are independent, we may apply the Borel-Cantelli Lemma, using A_n as the event that $|X_n - L| > k$. Let $p = P\{A_n\} = P\{ \, |X_n - L| > k \}$. Then

$$P\{A_n\} = P\{ \, |X_n - L| > k \}$$

$$= p$$

$$> 0$$

Now $P\{LS(A)\} = 1$

by the Borel-Cantelli Lemma and the independence of the A_n, which we may deduce from the independence of the X_n. Since $P\{LS(A)\} = 1$, the probability is one that A_n occurs infinitely often. Thus,

$$1 = P\{A_n \text{ occurs infinitely often}\}$$

$$= P\{ \, |X_n - L| > k \text{ infinitely often}\}$$

$$= P\{X_n \text{ does not converge}\}$$

Thus, $P\{X_n \text{ converges}\} = 1 - P\{X_n \text{ does not converge}\}$

$$= 1 - 1$$

$$= 0$$

We have shown that the probability of convergence of a sequence of independent random variables is either zero or one. This is a modification of a result known as the Borel Zero-One Criterion, which is one of the Zero-One Laws (Chow and Teicher, 1988, page 61). We will learn more about this type of result when we study the Zero-One Laws.

• PROBLEM 9-19

If the random variables are allowed to be dependent, must the probability of their convergence still be zero or one?

SOLUTION:

No. Consider, for example, the situation in which

$$P\{X_n = 0 \text{ for all } n\} = 0.5$$

and $P\{X_n = 0 \text{ for all even } n \text{ and } X_n = 1 \text{ for all odd } n\} = 0.5.$

If $X_n = 0$ for all n, then the sequence $\{X_n\}$ will converge to zero. This event occurs with probability 0.5. If, on the other hand, $X_n = 0$ for all even n and $X_n = 1$ for all odd n, then the sequence $\{X_n\}$ will not converge. This event also occurs with probability 0.5. Thus,

$$P\{X_n \text{ converges}\} = 0.5,$$

which is clearly neither zero nor one. Notice that the Borel-Cantelli Lemma does not apply, because in the situation described the random variables are not independent, or even pairwise independent.

To see this, consider that if $X_1 = 1$, then we know that the second event has occurred, and therefore X_3 must also be equal to one, as must X_5, X_7, and all other random variables with an odd index number.

A slight modification of the example presented proves that not only need the probability of convergence not be zero or one, but that in fact it can be any number between zero and one (that is, any number which is a valid probability). To see this, consider the situation in which

$$P\{X_n = 0 \text{ for all } n\} = p$$

and $P\{X_n = 0 \text{ for all even } n \text{ and } X_n = 1 \text{ for all odd } n\} = 1 - p,$

for p between zero and one. Then as shown previously, convergence will occur with probability p, which can be any number between zero and one.

✳✳✳✳✳✳

REVIEW OF THE ZERO-ONE LAWS

The Zero-One Laws are among the most striking results of probability theory. These laws are quite counter-intuitive, but the proofs are most instructive. The most well-known version of the Zero-One Law is the Kolmogorov Zero-One Law (Chow and Teicher, 1988, page 64) for independent random variables. There is also a Borel Zero-One Criterion (which we saw in the last section), a Hewitt-Savage version of the Zero-One Law (Chow and Teicher, 1988, page 230) for exchangeable random variables (Berger, 1985, page 104), and Levy's Zero-One Law (Chung, 1974, page 341).

Just as we needed to define convex functions prior to beginning our study of Jensen's Inequality, and we needed to define the limit supremum and limit infimum of an infinite sequence of events to properly study the Borel-Cantelli Lemmas, we must also postpone our study of the Zero-One Laws until three other concepts are defined and explored. These concepts are those of a tail event of an infinite sequence of random variables (Chow and Teicher, 1988, page 63), of measurability of an event with respect to a set of random variables (Billingsley, 1986, page 182), and of the permutable events (Chung, 1974, page 253).

There is a technical term known as measurability which is quite important in the study of probability theory. Much of the modern approach to probability theory is based on measure theory. In fact, some would say that probability theory is just measure theory when the spaces studied have total measure one.

We will not precisely define measurability here, but we will provide a working definition. A more formal definition is provided in Billingsley (1986), page 182.

For our purposes, an event is said to be measurable with respect to a set of random variables if and only if the occurrence or non-occurrence of this event depends only on these random variables. That is, for any observed values of the random variables we would know if the event has or has not occurred.

As an example, consider random variables X and Y, and events

1. $X < 0$,

2. $Y > 14$,

3. $X > Y$,

and

4. $X^2 > Y > 2$.

The first event is measurable with respect to (X, Y), since if we observe the actual values of both X and Y, then we will surely know if X takes on a negative value or not. In fact, we would know this even if we had not observed the value of Y, so the first event is also measurable with respect to X alone. However, had we observed only Y, then we would not know if $X < 0$ or not, so the first event is not measurable with respect to Y.

The second event is measurable with respect to (X, Y), since if we observe the actual values of both X and Y, then we will surely know if Y exceeds 14 or not. In fact, we would know this even if we had not observed the value of X, so the first event is also measurable with respect to Y alone. However, had we observed only X, then we would not know if $Y > 14$ or not, so the first event is not measurable with respect to X.

The third event is measurable with respect to (X, Y), since if we observe the actual values of both X and Y, then we will know if X takes on a larger value than Y does or not. However, had we observed only Y, then we would not know if $X > Y$ or not, so the first event is not measurable with respect to Y. Also, had we observed only X, then we would similarly not know if $X > Y$ or not, so the first event is not measurable with respect to X either.

The fourth event is measurable with respect to (X, Y), since if we observe the actual values of both X and Y, then we will know if $X^2 > Y > 2$ or not. However, had we observed only X, then we would not know if $X^2 > Y > 2$ or not, so the first event is not measurable with respect to X. Likewise, had we observed only Y, then we would not know if $X^2 > Y > 2$ or not, so the first event is not measurable with respect to Y either.

Sometimes it is not so clear-cut to determine whether or not a given event is measurable with respect to a given set of random variables. For a good example, see Example 4.9 of Billingsley (1986), page 53.

We will consider only events which have the property that they are relatively simple to classify as measurable or not measurable with respect to the set of random variables under consideration.

We are now in a position to define tail events (Billingsley, 1986, page 57). Consider an infinite sequence of random variables X_1, X_2, ... Let F_n be the set of events which are measurable with respect to the set of random variables indexed by n onward. That is, F_n is the set of events which are measurable with respect to $\{X_n, X_{n+1}, ...\}$. Now let F be the intersection of all of these sets. That is,

$$F = \bigcap_{n = 1 \text{ to infinity}} F_n.$$

Then a tail event of the sequence of random variables $\{X_1, X_2, \ldots\}$ is an event which is in F, or is measurable with respect to each set of terminal random variables $\{X_n, X_{n+1}, \ldots\}$. The Kolmogorov Zero-One Law states that any tail event of a sequence of independent random variables must have either probability zero or probability one.

An outline of the proof goes like this. For any n, X_n is independent of $E_n = \{X_{n+1}, X_{n+2}, \ldots\}$. Any tail event, A, must be measurable with respect to $\bigcap_{n = 1 \text{ to infinity}} E_n$. But this means that this event, A, must be independent of X_n for each n. It must therefore be independent of $\bigcup_{n = 1 \text{ to infinity}} X_n$. But since the event A is defined in terms of the sequence of random variables $\{X_n\}$, it must be measurable with respect to $\bigcup_{n = 1 \text{ to infinity}} X_n$. We see that A is measurable with respect to two sets of random variables, and that these two sets of random variables are independent of each other. Then A must be independent of itself. This means that

$$P\{A\} = P\{A, A\}$$

$$= P\{A\}P\{A\}$$

$$= P\{A\}^2$$

The only numbers which are equal to their own squares are zero and one. Therefore either

$$P\{A\} = 0$$

or $\qquad P\{A\} = 1.$

This is true for all tail events of sequences of independent random variables. A more formal proof is offered in Chung (1974), page 254.

We now consider the Hewitt-Savage Zero-One Law. We first must define the permutable events. An event is permutable if it remains invariant to any finite permutation of the order in which the random variables appear. For example, given the infinite sequence of random variables $\{X_n\}$, define the infinite sequence of events $\{A_n\}$, where

$$A_n = \{X_n > 0\}.$$

Then the limit supremum of $\{A_n\}$, $LS(A)$, is a permutable event because re-ordering the random variables (and consequently the events) does not affect the occurrence or non-occurrence of the limit supremum of $\{A_n\}$, which specifies only that an infinite number of these events occur.

A process is merely an infinite sequence of random variables. An independent process is an infinite sequence of independent random variables. A stationary independent process is an infinite sequence of independent random variables each of which has the same distribution. See Chung (1974), page 254.

The Hewitt-Savage Zero-One Law states that any permutable event of a stationary independent process has either probability zero or probability one. No proof is offered. Interested readers are referred to Chung (1974), page 255.

• PROBLEM 9-20

Let X and Y be random variables, and let

$$W = X + Y,$$

$$Z = X - Y,$$

and $R = X^2 - Y^2$.

Define the event A as

$$A = \{R > 0\}.$$

There are five random variables $(X, Y, W, Z,$ and $R)$, and consequently there are $2^5 = 32$ sets of random variables. With respect to which of these sets is A measurable?

SOLUTION:

Since A is defined exclusively in terms of R, any set which contains R will have the property that A is measurable with respect to this set. We therefore restrict attention to sets not containing R. This leaves four random variables $(X, Y, W,$ and $Z)$, and consequently $2^4 = 16$ more sets of random variables to consider. These sets are

1. X:

$$A = \{R > 0\}$$

$$= \{X^2 - Y^2 > 0\}$$

$$= \{X^2 > Y^2\}$$

is not measurable with respect to X alone.

2. Y:

$$A = \{R > 0\}$$
$$= \{X^2 - Y^2 > 0\}$$
$$= \{X^2 > Y^2\}$$

is not measurable with respect to Y alone.

3. W:

$$A = \{R > 0\}$$
$$= \{X^2 - Y^2 > 0\}$$
$$= \{X^2 > Y^2\}$$

is not measurable with respect to $W = X + Y$ alone.

4. Z:

$$A = \{R > 0\}$$
$$= \{X^2 - Y^2 > 0\}$$
$$= \{X^2 > Y^2\}$$

is not measurable with respect to $Z = X - Y$ alone.

5. X, Y:

$$A = \{R > 0\}$$
$$= \{X^2 - Y^2 > 0\}$$
$$= \{X^2 > Y^2\}$$

is measurable with respect to (X, Y), because it can be expressed in terms of X and Y.

6. X, W:

$$A = \{R > 0\}$$
$$= \{X^2 - Y^2 > 0\}$$
$$= \{X^2 > Y^2\}$$
$$= \{X^2 > (W - X)^2\}$$

is measurable with respect to (X, W), because it can be expressed in terms of X and W. Notice that

$$W = X + Y,$$

so $\quad Y = W - X.$

7. X, Z:

$$A = \{R > 0\}$$
$$= \{X^2 - Y^2 > 0\}$$
$$= \{X^2 > Y^2\}$$
$$= \{X^2 > (X - Z)^2\}$$

is measurable with respect to (X, Z), because it can be expressed in terms of X and Z. Notice that

$$Z = X - Y,$$

so $\quad Y = X - Z.$

8. Y, W:

$$A = \{R > 0\}$$
$$= \{X^2 - Y^2 > 0\}$$
$$= \{X^2 > Y^2\}$$
$$= \{(W - Y)^2 > Y^2\}$$

is measurable with respect to (W, Y), because it can be expressed in terms of W and Y. Notice that

$$W = X + Y,$$

so $\quad X = W - Y.$

9. Y, Z:

$$A = \{R > 0\}$$
$$= \{X^2 - Y^2 > 0\}$$
$$= \{X^2 > Y^2\}$$
$$= \{(Y + Z)^2 > Y^2\}$$

is measurable with respect to (Y, Z), because it can be expressed in terms of Y and Z. Notice that

$$Z = X - Y,$$

so $\quad X = Y + Z.$

10. W, Z:

$$A = \{R > 0\}$$

$$= \{X^2 - Y^2 > 0\}$$

$$= \{(X + Y)(X - Y) > 0\}$$

$$= \{WZ > 0\}$$

is measurable with respect to (W, Z), because it can be expressed in terms of W and Z.

11. X, Y, W:

Since A is measurable with respect to (X, Y), it must also be measurable with respect to any set of random variables which contains (X, Y), including (X, Y, W).

12. X, Y, Z:

Since A is measurable with respect to (X, Y), it must also be measurable with respect to any set of random variables which contains (X, Y), including (X, Y, Z).

13. X, W, Z:

Since A is measurable with respect to (X, Z), it must also be measurable with respect to any set of random variables which contains (X, Z), including (X, W, Z).

14. Y, W, Z:

Since A is measurable with respect to (Y, Z), it must also be measurable with respect to any set of random variables which contains (Y, Z), including (Y, W, Z).

15. X, W, Y, Z:

Since A is measurable with respect to (Y, Z), it must also be measurable with respect to any set of random variables which contains (Y, Z), including (X, Y, W, Z).

and

16. the empty set:

Clearly A is not measurable with respect to the empty set, because at least one random variable is required in order to determine whether A has occurred or not.

• **PROBLEM 9-21**

> Is the convergence of an infinite sequence of random variables, $\{X_n\}$, a tail event? Is it a permutable event?

SOLUTION:

The convergence of an infinite sequence of numbers, X_n, to a limit, L, can be expressed as follows:

For each $k > 0$ there exists an index, n, which may depend on k, such that for all $m > n \, | \, X_n - L \, | < k$.

An analogous characterization of convergence is possible for random variables. But to simplify the expression, we will restrict k to a countable set. That is, we will restrict k to $\{1, 1/2, 1/3 ,...\}$. Let A be the event that $\{X_n\}$ converges to L. Then

$$A = \cap_{k = 1 \text{ to infinity}} \cup_{n = 1 \text{ to infinity}} \cap_{m = n \text{ to infinity}} | X_m - L | < 1/k.$$

Since this expression for A may be written in terms of X_m for $m = n$ to infinity, no initial segment of the sequence is involved. This shows A to be a tail event of the sequence $\{X_n\}$.

Since arbitrary permutation of the indices of the random variables would not affect the convergence or non-convergence of the sequence, this is a permutable event.

• **PROBLEM 9-22**

> Let $A_n = (X_n > 0)$. Is $LS(A)$ a tail event of the sequence $\{X_n\}$? Is it a permutable event?

SOLUTION:

We may write

$$LS(A) = \cap_{m = 1 \text{ to infinity}} \cup_{n = m \text{ to infinity}} A_n.$$

Since this expression for $LS(A)$ may be written in terms of X_m for $m = n$ to infinity, no initial segment of the sequence is involved. This shows $LS(A)$ to be a tail event of the sequence $\{X_n\}$.

Since arbitrary permutation of the indices of the random variables would not affect the occurrence or non-occurrence of this event, this is a permutable event.

• PROBLEM 9–23

Let $A_n = \{X_n > 0\}$. Is $LI(A)$ a tail event of the sequence $\{X_n\}$? Is it a permutable event?

SOLUTION:

We may write

$$LI(A) = \cup_{m = 1 \text{ to infinity}} \cup_{n = m \text{ to infinity}} A_n.$$

Since this expression for $LI(A)$ may be written in terms of X_m for $m = n$ to infinity, no initial segment of the sequence is involved. This shows $LI(A)$ to be a tail event of the sequence $\{X_n\}$.

Since arbitrary permutation of the indices of the random variables would not affect the occurrence or non-occurrence of this event, this is a permutable event.

• PROBLEM 9–24

Is the event

$$A = \{X_1 > 0\}$$

a tail event relative to the sequence $\{X_n\}$? Is it a permutable event?

SOLUTION:

Since we would know whether or not A occurred after observing only the first random variable, X_1, A cannot be a tail event of the infinite sequence of random variables $\{X_n\}$.

Any permutation which switches X_1 with any other random variable in this sequence will potentially change the occurrence of A. Therefore, A is not a permutable event.

• PROBLEM 9–25

Problems 9–21, 9–22, and 9–23 may have given the impression that all tail events are permutable events and all permutable events are tail events. This is not the case. To see this, consider the sequence of random variables $\{X_n\}$, and let A be the event that at least one of these random variables is positive.

SOLUTION:

The first time we see a positive random variable A will have occurred. This may be realized after only finitely many random variables are observed. Thus, A is not a tail event relative to this sequence of random variables.

On the other hand, if at least one of these random variables is positive, then this will continue to be true no matter how the random variables are permuted. Thus, A is a permutable event.

• PROBLEM 9–26

Consider an infinite sequence of random variables, $\{X_n\}$. Split this sequence into the odd sequence, $\{X_{2k+1}\}$, and the even sequence, $\{X_{2k}\}$. Now define the event A as an infinite number of the even random variables being positive. If A_n is the event that $X_n > 0$, then

$$A = LS(A_{2k}).$$

SOLUTION:

As shown in Problem 9–22, then, A is a tail event of the even sequence. This means that the occurrence or non-occurrence of A is not known with only finitely many of the even random variables. Clearly the odd random variables contribute no information concerning the occurrence or non-occurrence of A, so no finite initial segment of the entire sequence, $\{X_n\}$, will be sufficient to determine if A has or has not occurred. Thus, A is not only a tail event of the even sequence, but also of the entire sequence, $\{X_n\}$.

On the other hand, suppose that for each k we have

$$X_{2k} > 0$$

and $X_{2k+1} < 0.$

Then A will occur for the original sequence, but if the order is permuted so that each even-numbered random variable becomes odd-numbered and each odd-numbered random variable becomes even-numbered, then A will no longer occur. Thus, A is not a permutable event of the sequence $\{X_n\}$, even though it is a permutable event of the even sequence, as shown in Problem 9–22.

• PROBLEM 9-27

Show that a tail event need not have probability zero or one if we do not insist on independence of the random variables.

SOLUTION:

Problem 9–19 of the previous section shows that the probability of convergence need not be either zero or one if the random variables are not independent. Problem 9–21 of the present section shows that the convergence of a sequence of random variables is a tail event of this sequence of random variables. Combining these two results provides an example of a tail event whose probability is neither zero nor one.

******

REVIEW OF CHARACTERISTIC FUNCTIONS

Moment generating functions were considered in Chapter 4. It was stated there that if the moment generating function exists, then the moments are sufficient to characterize the entire distribution of the random variable. The problem is that the moment generating function does not always exist.

This is in contrast to the characteristic function, which does always exist. The preliminary material required for the study of characteristic functions is the basis of complex analysis.

The number i is said to be imaginary. It is defined as the square root of -1. Multiples of i are also called imaginary numbers. Linear combinations of real and imaginary numbers are called complex numbers. For an excellent account of imaginary and complex numbers, see Strang (1988), page 183.

For example, 4, -3, π, and e are real numbers (but π and e are irrational), while $3i$, $6i$, and $29.5i$ are imaginary numbers. Numbers such as $4 - 3i$, $2.9 + 5.2i$, and $66.8^2 - 2i$ are called complex numbers. When adding, subtracting, or multiplying complex numbers, the real part is treated separately from the imaginary part. Thus,

$$(1 + i) + (2 + 2i) = (1 + 2) + (i + 2i)$$

$$= 3 + 3i,$$

$$(2 + 2i) - (1 + i) = (2 - 1) + (2i - i)$$

$$= 1 + i,$$

and

$$(2 + 2i)(1 + i) = [(2)(1) + (2)(i) + (2i)(1) + (2i)(i)]$$

$$= [2 + 2i + 2i + 2i^2]$$

$$= 2 + 4i + 2(-1)$$

$$= 2 + 4i - 2$$

$$= 4i,$$

which is imaginary.

The importance of complex numbers will become clear when we define characteristic functions. It should be noted at the outset that despite the name, complex (and imaginary) numbers are not fake or artificial. They play a prominent role in much of mathematics, including in probability theory. The use of complex numbers in probability theory is not limited to their use in defining characteristic functions, but this is the only use we shall have for them in this text. Complex numbers are solutions to polynomial equations with real coefficients (see Strang, 1988, page 183). For example,

$$X^2 = 1$$

has as its solutions i and $-i$. Complex numbers can also be eigenvalues of matrices with real entries (see Strang, 1988, page 184).

Let X be a random variable with probability density function (or probability mass function if X is discrete) $f_X(k)$, and cumulative distribution function

$$F_X(k) = P\{X \le k\}.$$

Then the characteristic function of X is defined to be

$$\phi_X(t) = E[e^{itX}].$$

The remarkable formula

$$e^{itX} = e^{i(tX)}$$

$$= \cos(tX) + (i)\sin(tX)$$

(Strang, 1988, page 185) shows that

$$\phi_X(t) = E[e^{itX}]$$

$$= E[\cos(tX) + (i)\sin(tX)].$$

Since both the sine and cosine are bounded functions, the expected value of the absolute value of the term $\cos(tX) + (i)\sin(tX)$ has a finite integral, and therefore this expectation exists. This is in contrast to the moment generating function, which need not exist because its integral may be infinite.

Suppose that a random variable X has characteristic function $\phi_X(t)$. Now define a new random variable, Y, as

$$Y = aX + b.$$

Then the characteristic function of Y is given by

$$\phi_Y(t) = \phi_{aX + b}(t)$$

$$= E[e^{iYt}]$$

$$= E[e^{i(aX + b)t}]$$

$$= E[e^{iaXt + ibt}]$$

$$= E[e^{iaXt}e^{ibt}]$$

$$= e^{ibt}E[e^{iX(at)}]$$

$$= e^{ibt}\,\phi_X(at)$$

Thus, if the characteristic function of a certain random variable is known, then it is a relatively simple matter to compute the characteristic function of all linear functions of this random variable by the above formula.

Another formula worthy of note is the formula for independent random variables. Suppose that X and Y are independent random variables, and that the characteristic functions of X and Y are $\phi_X(t)$ and $\phi_Y(t)$, respectively. Then the characteristic function of the sum of these random variables, $X + Y$, is given by

$$\phi_{X+Y}(t) = E[e^{i(X+Y)t}]$$

$$= E[e^{iXt + iYt}]$$

$$= E[e^{iXt}\,e^{iYt}]$$

$$= E[e^{iXt}]E[e^{iYt}]$$

$$= \phi_X(t)\phi_Y(t)$$

If we have a simple random sample of size n from a population with characteristic function $\phi_X(t)$, then the characteristic function of the sum of these independent and identically distributed random variables is

$$\phi_S(t) = E[e^{iSt}]$$

$$= E[e^{i(\Sigma X)t}]$$

$$= E[e^{\Sigma iXt}]$$

$$= E[\pi_{i=1\text{ to }n}\,e^{iXt}]$$

$$= \pi_{i=1\text{ to }n}\,E[e^{iXt}]$$

$$= \pi_{i=1\text{ to }n}\phi_X(t)$$

$$= [\phi_X(t)]^n$$

Suppose that X is a degenerate random variable, so that

$$P\{X = k\} = 1 \text{ if } k = a,$$

and $P\{X = k\} = 0$ for other values of k.

Then the characteristic function of X is given by

$$\phi_X(t) = E[e^{iXt}]$$

$$= \Sigma_k e^{ikt} P\{X = k\}$$

$$= e^{iat} P\{X = a\} + \Sigma_{k \text{ other than } a} e^{ikt} P\{X = k\}$$

$$= e^{iat}(1) + \Sigma_{k \text{ other than } a} e^{ikt}(0)$$

$$= e^{iat} + (0)$$

$$= e^{iat}$$

As would be expected, the calculation of characteristic functions will often be more complicated than the example just illustrated. We will have a chance to practice computing characteristic functions in the problems. The first set of problems will first serve to familiarize the reader with imaginary numbers and complex numbers.

• PROBLEM 9-28

What is $(4 + 3i) + (2 - 6i)$?

SOLUTION:

The arithmetic of complex numbers is quite similar to that of real numbers. Each component adds separately. Thus,

$$(4 + 3i) + (2 - 6i) = (4 + 2) + (3i - 6i)$$

$$= 6 + (3 - 6)i$$

$$= 6 - 3i$$

• PROBLEM 9-29

What is $(5 + i) - (8 - 9i)$?

SOLUTION:

Again, we treat the imaginary part separately from the real part. Thus,

$$(5 + i) - (8 - 9i) = (5 - 8) + (i + 9i)$$

$$= (-3) + (10i)$$

$$= 10i - 3$$

• PROBLEM 9-30

What is $(6 + 2i) (7 - 3i)$?

SOLUTION:

Again, we treat the imaginary part separately from the real part. Thus,

$$(6 + 2i) (7 - 3i) = [(6) (7) + (6) (-3i) + (2i) (7) + (2i) (-3i)]$$

$$= [42 - 18i + 14i - 6i^2]$$

$$= 42 - 4i - 6(-1)$$

$$= 42 - 4i + 6$$

$$= 48 - 4i$$

• PROBLEM 9-31

Can the square of a real number be imaginary? Can the square of an imaginary number be real? Can the square of a complex number be real?

SOLUTION:

Any real number can be written as

$$k = a + bi.$$

But because the number is real, there is no imaginary component. Thus,

$$b = 0,$$

so $k = a + bi$

$$= a + (0)i$$

$$= a$$

Thus,

$$k^2 = a^2$$

$$= a^2 + 0i,$$

which has no imaginary component. Thus, the square of a real number must also be real.

Now consider an imaginary number. This can be written as

$$k = a + bi,$$

but because k is imaginary there is no real component, so

$$a = 0.$$

Thus,

$$k = a + bi$$

$$= 0 + bi$$

$$= bi,$$

and $\quad k^2 = (bi)^2$

$$= b^2 i^2$$

$$= b^2(-1)$$

$$= -b^2$$

This number has a real component ($-b^2$) but no imaginary component. Thus, the number is real. That is, not only can the square of an imaginary number be real, but the square of an imaginary number must be real.

Finally, let k be complex. Then

$$k = a + bi,$$

and both a and b are arbitrary. Now

$$k^2 = (a + bi)^2$$

$$= a^2 + (bi)^2 + 2(a)(bi)$$

$$= a^2 + b^2 i^2 + 2abi$$

$$= a^2 + b^2(-1) + 2abi$$

$$= a^2 - b^2 + 2abi$$

This number is quite interesting. It can take different forms depending on the values of a and b. There are four cases to consider. These are:

1. $k^2 = 0$ if both a and b are zero,

2. k^2 is real if $ab = 0$ and $a^2 + b^2 > 0$ (that is, if either a or b is zero but not both),

3. k^2 is imaginary if neither a nor b is zero, and $|a| = |b|$,

and

4. k^2 is complex if neither a nor b is zero, and $|a|$ does not equal $|b|$.

To see this, note that if $a = b = 0$, then $k = 0$ and

$$k^2 = 0^2$$

$$= 0$$

If either $a = 0$ or $b = 0$, then k is either real or imaginary. As seen in the first two parts of this problem, the square of a real number is real, and the square of an imaginary number is also real. Thus, k^2 must be real.

If $|a| = |b| > 0$, then

$$k^2 = a^2 - b^2 + 2abi$$

$$= |a|^2 - |b|^2 + 2abi$$

$$= 2abi,$$

which is imaginary.

If $|a| > 0$, $|b| > 0$, and $|a|$ does not equal $|b|$, then

$$k^2 = a^2 - b^2 + 2abi$$

$$= |a|^2 - |b|^2 + 2abi$$

$$= (|a|^2 - |b|^2) + (2ab)i,$$

which is seen to be complex because neither the real component nor the imaginary component is zero.

Many students know that the quantity

$$a^2 - b^2$$

can be factored as

$$a^2 - b^2 = (a + b)(a - b).$$

It is often said that the quantity

$$a^2 + b^2$$

cannot be factored. This is a true statement if we confine ourselves to real numbers. If, on the other hand, we allow complex numbers as factors, then this quantity can be factored. What are the factors?

SOLUTION:

We write

$$a^2 + b^2 = (a + bi)(a - bi),$$

since

$$(a + bi)(a - bi) = a^2 + abi - abi - (bi)^2$$
$$= a^2 - b^2 i^2$$
$$= a^2 - b^2 (-1)$$
$$= a^2 + b^2,$$

as stated.

What is i^{399}?

SOLUTION:

It may seem, at first appearance, that the solution to this problem would require a great deal of time, as well as paper. But actually there is a short-cut which obviates the need to perform 399 multiplications.

Notice that

$i^0 = 1,$

$i^1 = i,$

$i^2 = -1,$

$i^3 = -i,$

$i^4 = 1,$

$i^5 = i,$

$i^6 = -1,$

$i^7 = -i,$

and $i^8 = 1.$

This cyclical pattern repeats itself, so

$i^{399} = i^{396 + 3}$

$= i^{396}i^3$

$= i^{(4)\,(99)}\,(-i)$

$= (i^4)^{99}\,(-i)$

$= (1)^{99}\,(-i)$

$= (1)\,(-i)$

$= -i$

• PROBLEM 9–34

Since imaginary numbers were defined to handle quadratics involving reals, such as

$X^2 = 1,$

it is conceivable that new types of numbers could be defined to handle quadratics involving complex numbers, such as

$X^2 = i.$

Show that doing so is unnecessary, since the above quadratic has two complex solutions.

SOLUTION:

Let

$$X_1 = (i + 1)/2^{0.5},$$

and let

$$X_2 = (-i - 1)/2^{0.5}.$$

Then

$$X_1^2 = [(1 + i)/2^{0.5}]^2$$
$$= [1^2 + i^2 + (2)(1)(i)]/2$$
$$= [1 - 1 + 2i]/2$$
$$= 2i/2$$
$$= i.$$

$$X_2^2 = [(-1 - i)/2^{0.5}]^2$$
$$= [(-1)^2 + (-i)^2 + (2)(-1)(-i)]/2$$
$$= [1 - 1 + 2i]/2$$
$$= 2i/2$$
$$= i.$$

• PROBLEM 9–35

Let X have a Bernoulli distribution with parameter p. Then what is the characteristic function of X?

SOLUTION:

Recall that the probability mass function of a Bernoulli distribution with parameter p is given by

$$P\{X = 1\} = p,$$
$$P\{X = 0\} = 1 - p,$$

and $P\{X = k\} = 0$ for other k.

We write

$$\phi_X(t) = E[e^{iXt}]$$

$$= e^{i(1)t}P\{X = 1\} + e^{i(0)t}P\{X = 0\}$$

$$= e^{it}p + e^0(1 - p)$$

$$= e^{it}p + (1)(1 - p)$$

$$= e^{it}p + (1 - p)$$

$$= 1 + p(e^{it} - 1)$$

• PROBLEM 9–36

Let X have a binomial distribution with parameters n and p. Then what is the characteristic function of X?

SOLUTION:

We know that a binomial random variable with parameters n and p can be considered as the sum of a simple random sample of size n from a Bernoulli population with parameter p. Therefore, we may use the result that if $\phi_X(t)$ is the characteristic function of X, and if S is the sum of n independent observations, each with the same distribution as X, then the characteristic function of S is given by

$$\phi_S(t) = [\phi_X(t)]^n,$$

as shown in the text preceding the problems. From Problem 9–35 we know that the characteristic function of the Bernoulli random variable with parameter p is given by

$$\phi_X(t) = 1 + p(e^{it} - 1).$$

Therefore, the characteristic function of S, a binomial random variable with parameters n and p, is given by

$$\phi_S(t) = [1 + p(e^{it} - 1)]^n.$$

• PROBLEM 9–37

Let X have a geometric distribution with parameter p. Then what is the characteristic function of X?

SOLUTION:

Recall that the probability mass function of the geometric distribution with parameter p is given by

$$P\{X = k\} = p(1 - p)^n \text{ for } k \text{ a non-negative integer,}$$

and $P\{X = k\} = 0$ otherwise.

Therefore, the characteristic function of a geometric random variable with parameter p is given by

$$\phi_X(t) = E[e^{iXt}]$$

$$= \Sigma_{n=0 \text{ to infinity}} P\{X = n\} e^{int}$$

$$= \Sigma_{n=0 \text{ to infinity}} (1 - p)^n p e^{int}$$

$$= p\Sigma_{n=0 \text{ to infinity}} (1 - p)^n [e^{it}]^n$$

$$= p\Sigma_{n=0 \text{ to infinity}} [(1 - p)e^{it}]^n$$

$$= p/[1 - (1 - p)e^{it}],$$

since the sum of a geometric series is the reciprocal of the ratio of consecutive terms.

• PROBLEM 9–38

Let X have a Poisson distribution with parameter L. Then what is the characteristic function of X?

SOLUTION:

Recall that the probability mass function of the Poisson distribution with parameter L is given by

$$P\{X = k\} = e^{-L} L^X / X! \text{ for } k \text{ a non-negative integer,}$$

and $P\{X = k\} = 0$ otherwise.

Therefore, the characteristic function of a Poisson random variable with parameter L is given by

$$\phi_X(t) = E[e^{iX_t}]$$

$$= \Sigma_{n=0 \text{ to infinity}}[P\{X=n\}][e^{int}]$$

$$= \Sigma_{n=0 \text{ to infinity}}[e^{-L}L^n/n!][e^{int}]$$

$$= e^{-L}\Sigma_{n=0 \text{ to infinity}}[L^n/n!][e^{it}]^n$$

$$= e^{-L}\Sigma_{n=0 \text{ to infinity}}[Le^{it}]^n/n!$$

$$= exp(-L)exp(Le^{it}),$$

because the infinite sum in the previous expression is the Taylor expansion of the exponential function. Now

$$\phi_X(t) = exp(-L)exp(Le^{it})$$

$$= exp(Le^{it} - L)$$

is the characteristic function of the Poisson distribution with parameter L.

• PROBLEM 9–39

Let X have an exponential distribution with parameter L (that is, mean $1/L$). Then what is the characteristic function of X?

SOLUTION:

Recall that the probability density function of the exponential distribution with parameter L (mean $1/L$) is given by

$$f_X(k) = Le^{-Lk} \text{ for } k > 0$$

and $f_X(k) = 0$ otherwise.

Therefore, the characteristic function of an exponential random variable with parameter L (mean $1/L$) is given by

$$\phi_X(t) = E[e^{iX_t}]$$

$$= I_{k=0 \text{ to infinity}}[f_X(k)][e^{ikt}]dk$$

$$= I_{k=0 \text{ to infinity}}[Le^{-Lk}][e^{ikt}]dk$$

$$= (L)I_{k=0 \text{ to infinity}}[e^{ikt-Lk}]dk$$

$$= (L)I_{k\,=\,0\text{ to infinity}}[e^{k(it\,-\,L)}]dk$$

$$= (L)[e^{k(it\,-\,L)}/(it - L)]_{k\,=\,0\text{ to infinity}}$$

$$= [L/(it - L)][e^{-\text{ infinity}} - e^{0(it\,-\,L)}]$$

$$= [L/(it - L)][0 - e^0]$$

$$= [L/(it - L)][0 - 1]$$

$$= [L/(it - L)][-1]$$

$$= [-L/(it - L)]$$

$$= L/(L - it)$$

• PROBLEM 9–40

Let X have a continuous uniform distribution with range $[a, b]$. Then what is the characteristic function of X?

SOLUTION:

Recall that the probability density function of the continuous uniform distribution with range $[a, b]$ is given by

$$f_X(k) = 1/(b - a) \text{ for } a < k < b$$

and $\quad f_X(k) = 0$ otherwise.

Therefore, the characteristic function of a continuous uniform random variable with range $[a, b]$ is given by

$$\phi_X(t) = E[e^{iXt}]$$

$$= I_{k\,=\,a\text{ to }b}[f_X(k)][e^{ikt}]dk$$

$$= I_{k\,=\,a\text{ to }b}[1/(b - a)][e^{ikt}]dk$$

$$= I_{k\,=\,a\text{ to }b}[e^{ikt}]dk/(b - a)$$

$$= [e^{ikt}]_{k\,=\,a\text{ to }b}/[(it)(b - a)]$$

$$= [e^{ibt} - e^{iat}]/[(it)(b - a)]$$

• PROBLEM 9–41

Let X have a standard normal distribution (with mean zero and variance one). Then what is the characteristic function of X?

SOLUTION:

The probability density function of the standard normal distribution is given by

$$f_X(k) = exp(-k^2/2)/(2\pi)^{0.5} \text{ for all } k.$$

Therefore, the characteristic function of the standard normal distribution is given by

$$\phi_X(t) = E[e^{iXt}]$$

$$= I_{k=-\text{infinity to infinity}}[f_X(k)][e^{ikt}]dk$$

$$= I_{k=-\text{infinity to infinity}}[exp(-k^2/2)/(2\pi)^{0.5}][e^{ikt}]dk$$

$$= (2\pi)^{-0.5}I_{k=-\text{infinity to infinity}}[exp(-k^2/2)][exp(ikt)]dk$$

$$= (2\pi)^{-0.5}I_{k=-\text{infinity to infinity}}[exp(2ikt-k^2)/2]dk.$$

Notice that

$$(k-it)^2 = k^2 + (it)^2 - 2kit$$

$$= k^2 + i^2t^2 - 2kit$$

$$= k^2 + (-1)t^2 - 2kit$$

$$= k^2 - t^2 - 2kit$$

Therefore,

$$-t^2 - (k-it)^2 = -t^2 - [k^2 - t^2 - 2kit]$$

$$= -t^2 - k^2 + t^2 + 2kit$$

$$= 2ikt - k^2$$

Plugging this into the integral results in

$$\phi_X(t) = E[e^{iXt}]$$

$$= (2\pi)^{-0.5}I_{k=-\text{infinity to infinity}}[exp(2ikt-k^2)/2]dk$$

$$= (2\pi)^{-0.5}I_{k=-\text{infinity to infinity}}exp\{[-t^2-(k-it)^2]/2\}dk$$

$$= (2\pi)^{-0.5}I_{k=-\text{infinity to infinity}}exp\{[-t^2/2]\}$$

$$exp\{[-(k-it)^2]/2\}dk$$

$$= exp(-t^2)\ (2\pi)^{-0.5}I_{k\ =\ -\ \text{infinity to infinity}}exp\{[-(k-it)^2]/2\}dk$$

$$= exp(-t^2)I_{k\ =\ -\ \text{infinity to infinity}}exp\{[-(k-it)^2]/2\}/(2\pi)^{0.5}dk.$$

This is a product of a term, $exp(-t^2)$, and an integral. But the integral is the integral over the entire range of a probability density function. In fact, it is the integral of the probability density function of a random variable with a normal distribution with mean 0 and variance one. We know that the integral over the entire range of any probability density function is one. Therefore, we see that

$$\phi_X(t) = E[e^{iXt}]$$

$$= exp(-t^2).$$

• PROBLEM 9-42

Let X be a dichotomous random variable, but not necessarily a Bernoulli random variable. That is,

$$P\{X = a\} = p,$$

$$P\{X = b\} = 1 - p,$$

and $P\{X = k\} = 0$ if k is neither a nor b.

Note that if $a = 1$ and $b = 0$, then X is a Bernoulli random variable. Find the characteristic function of X in two different ways.

SOLUTION:

The characteristic function of X is given by

$$\phi_X(t) = E[e^{iXt}]$$

$$= e^{iat}P\{X = a\} + e^{ibt}P\{X = b\}$$

$$= e^{iat}(p) + e^{ibt}(1 - p)$$

The second way to solve this problem is to recall that if X has characteristic function $\phi_X(t)$, and if $Y = aX + b$, then Y has characteristic function $\phi_X(at)e^{itb}$. Now we know from Problem 9–35 that the characteristic function of a Bernoulli random variable with parameter p is given by

$$\phi_{\text{Bernoulli}(p)} = 1 + p(e^{it} - 1).$$

If W has a Bernoulli distribution with parameter p, then we can define X as

$$X = (a - b)W + b.$$

We see that

$$
\begin{aligned}
P\{X = a\} &= P\{(a - b)W + b = a\} \\
&= P\{(a - b)W = a - b\} \\
&= P\{W = (a - b)/(a - b)\} \\
&= P\{W = 1\} \\
&= p,
\end{aligned}
$$

and

$$
\begin{aligned}
P\{X = b\} &= P\{(a - b)W + b = b\} \\
&= P\{(a - b)W = b - b\} \\
&= P\{(a - b)W = 0\} \\
&= P\{W = 0/(a - b)\} \\
&= P\{W = 0\} \\
&= 1 - p
\end{aligned}
$$

Thus, defining X as $(a - b)W + b$ gives X the dichotomous distribution we are studying. We know, then, that the characteristic function of X is

$$
\begin{aligned}
\phi_X(t) &= \phi_{(a - b)W + b}(t) \\
&= \phi_W[(a - b)t]e^{itb} \\
&= [1 + p(e^{i(a - b)t} - 1)]e^{itb} \\
&= e^{itb}[1 + pe^{iat - ibt} - p] \\
&= e^{itb}(1 - p) + pe^{iat - ibt}e^{itb} \\
&= e^{itb}(1 - p) + pe^{iat - ibt + ibt} \\
&= e^{itb}(1 - p) + pe^{iat} \\
&= e^{iat}(p) + e^{itb}(1 - p),
\end{aligned}
$$

which agrees with the earlier answer.

Let X have a normal distribution with mean M and variance V. What is the characteristic function of X?

SOLUTION:

Let Z have a standard normal distribution. That is, Z has a normal distribution with mean zero and variance one. We saw in Problem 4–41 that the characteristic function of Z is given by

$\phi_Z(t) = exp(t^2/2)$.

If we let $S = V^{0.5}$, then we may define X as

$X = SZ + M$.

Clearly X still has a normal distribution, because any linear function of a normal random variable is also a normal random variable. The moments of X are

$$E[X] = E[SZ + M]$$
$$= SE[Z] + M$$
$$= (S)(0) + M$$
$$= 0 + M$$
$$= M,$$

and $\quad V(X) = V(SZ + M)$

$$= S^2 V(Z)$$
$$= S^2(1)$$
$$= S^2$$
$$= V$$

Thus, $X = SZ + M$ has the normal distribution with mean M and variance V, which we are currently considering. Then the characteristic function of X is given by

$$\phi_X(t) = \phi_{SZ + M}(t)$$
$$= \phi_Z(St)e^{itM}$$
$$= exp[-(St)^2/2]e^{itM}$$

$$= exp[-S^2t^2/2]exp(itM)$$

$$= exp[itM - Vt^2/2]$$

• PROBLEM 9-44

Problem 9–38 showed that

$$exp(Le^{it} - L)$$

is the characteristic function of the Poisson distribution with parameter L. Use this and the uniqueness of the characteristic function to prove that a sum of n independent random variables, each of which has a Poisson distribution with parameter L, also has a Poisson distribution, but with parameter nL.

SOLUTION:

Let S be the sum of the n independent Poisson random variables, and let these random variables be $X_1, X_2, ..., X_n$. Then

$$\Sigma = \phi_{k = 1 \text{ to } n} X_k,$$

and the characteristic function of S is

$$\phi_S(t) = E[e^{iSt}]$$

$$= E[e^{i(\Sigma X)t}]$$

$$= E[e^{\Sigma X_i t}]$$

$$= E[\pi_{k = 1 \text{ to } n} e^{X_i t}]$$

$$= \pi_{k = 1 \text{ to } n} E[e^{X_i it}]$$

$$= \pi_{k = 1 \text{ to } n} \phi_x(t)$$

$$= \pi_{k = 1 \text{ to } n} exp(Le^{it} - L)$$

$$= exp[\Sigma(Le^{it} - L)]$$

$$= exp[(nL)e^{it} - (nL)],$$

which, by Problem 9–38, is the characteristic function of a Poisson random variable with parameter nL. By the uniqueness of the characteristic function, S is seen to have a Poisson distribution with parameter nL.

CHAPTER 10

MARKOV STOCHASTIC PROCESSES

> **Basic Attacks and Strategies for Solving Problems in this Chapter. See pages 732 to 786 for step-by-step solutions to problems.**

Among the most widely used stochastic processes in practice are those with the Markov property. This includes Markov chains as special cases.

A stochastic process is a collection of random variables indexed by some parameter. For our purposes, all stochastic processes will be indexed by time. In this context, time may be either continuous or discrete.

The Markov property can be summarized by stating that all information concerning the past, for the purpose of predicting the future, is summarized in the present. More formally, a stochastic process has the Markov property if the conditional distribution of the random variable (the process) at Time T_3, given the value of the process at Time T_2, is independent of the process at time T_1 for all times T_1, T_2, and T_3 such that $T_1 < T_2 < T_3$.

Some examples may clarify this concept. Consider a soccer game. Let the stochastic process under consideration be the score of the game. This is a stochastic process indexed by time, and here time is continuous. Given that one team has scored X goals by a given time in the game and the other team has scored Y goals, there are only three possible scores for a time right after the time at which the score is X goals to Y goals. These possible scores are

1. $X + 1$ goals to Y goals,

2. X goals to $Y + 1$ goals,

and

3. *X* goals to *Y* goals.

If we assume that the probabilities of each team scoring a goal are independent of the score of the game, and in fact independent of the entire history of scores, then this is a Markov process. This is because all that matters in determining the future scores of the game is the present score, and not the scores previous to it. If the game is now tied at two, then it does not matter if the score was 2 – 0 at one point or not (at least according to the model we are considering). It should be pointed out that there is far from universal agreement concerning the applicability of the Markov property to sporting events, as psychological factors such as momentum and the perceived probability of victory for the players involved may influence quality of play, and may in turn be influenced by the entire history of the sporting event.

To clarify what a Markov process is it may help to give several examples of processes which are not Markov processes. Consider, then, the following examples.

First consider drawing without replacement from an urn which has four white balls and four black balls. The process is the color of the last ball selected, and the process is indexed by time. Here time is discrete (in fact finite), and takes the values $\{1, 2, 3, 4, 5, 6, 7, 8\}$. For example, if the third ball drawn is white, then $X(3) = W$, and if the fifth ball drawn is black, then $X(5) = B$. Now if this process were a Markov process, then it would be true that

$$P\{X(t) = B \mid X(1), X(2), \ldots, X(t-1)\} = P\{X(t) = B \mid X(t-1)\}$$

and $P\{X(t) = W \mid X(1), X(2), \ldots, X(t-1)\} = P\{X(t) = W \mid X(t-1)\}.$

But this is not true. For example, let t be three in the above equalities. Then we would require that both

$$P\{X(3) = B \mid X(1), X(2)\} = P\{X(3) = B \mid X(2)\}$$

and $P\{X(3) = W \mid X(1), X(2)\} = P\{X(3) = W \mid X(2)\}.$

But in reality,

$$P\{X(3) = B \mid X(1) = B, X(2) = B\} = \frac{2}{6}$$

since there are two black balls left of the six remaining balls,

$$P\{X(3) = B \mid X(1) = B, X(2) = W\} = \frac{3}{6}$$

since there are three black balls left of the six remaining balls,

$$P\{X(3) = B \mid X(1) = W, X(2) = B\} = \frac{3}{6}$$

since there are three black balls left of the six remaining balls,

$$P\{X(3) = B \mid X(1) = W, X(2) = W\} = \frac{4}{6}$$

since there are four black balls left of the six remaining balls,

$$P\{X(3) = W \mid X(1) = B, X(2) = B\} = \frac{4}{6}$$

since there are four white balls left of the six remaining balls,

$$P\{X(3) = W \mid X(1) = B, X(2) = W\} = \frac{3}{6}$$

since there are three white balls left of the six remaining balls,

$$P\{X(3) = W \mid X(1) = W, X(2) = B\} = \frac{3}{6}$$

since there are three white balls left of the six remaining balls,

and $\quad P\{X(3) = W \mid X(1) = W, X(2) = W\} = \frac{2}{6}$

since there are two white balls left of the six remaining balls.

In contrast,

$$P\{X(3) = B \mid X(2) = B\} = \frac{3}{7}$$

since there are three black balls left of the remaining seven balls,

$$P\{X(3) = B \mid X(2) = W\} = \frac{4}{7}$$

since there are four black balls left of the remaining seven balls,

$$P\{X(3) = W \mid X(2) = B\} = \frac{4}{7}$$

since there are four white balls left of the remaining seven balls,

and $\quad P\{X(3) = W \mid X(2) = W\} = \dfrac{3}{7}$

since there are three white balls left of the remaining seven balls.

Now it is seen that, for example,

$$P\{X(3) = B \mid X(2) = B\} = \frac{3}{7}$$

is not equal to $\dfrac{3}{6}$

$$= P\{X(3) = B \mid X(1) = W, X(2) = B\},$$

so this process cannot be a Markov process.

As a second example, consider a health-conscious person who has heard from the latest studies that red meat should be consumed no more than twice per week. In an attempt to follow this policy, the person eats whatever he feels like on Monday and Tuesday, but then modifies this approach so that he will consume whatever he wants on the following days provided that this will not bring him over the limit of having red meat twice per week. Define a process as

$\qquad X(t) = M$ if red meat is consumed on Day t

and $\quad X(t) = N$ if no red meat is consumed on Day t.

Suppose that on any given day this person is as likely to want meat as to not want meat. Then for $t > 2$ (that is, Wednesday through Sunday) the probabilities of consuming meat are given by

$$P\{X(t) = M \mid X(1) = M, X(2) = M, X(3), \ldots, X(t-1)\} = 0$$

since meat was already consumed on Monday and Tuesday.

In fact,

$$P\{X(t) = M \mid X(1), X(2), X(3), \ldots, X(t-1)\} = 0$$

if meat was consumed at least twice previously, and

$$P\{X(t) = M \mid X(1), X(2), X(3), \ldots, X(t-1)\} = 0.5$$

if meat was not consumed at least twice previously.

Just looking at $X(t - 1)$ would not suffice to indicate if meat had or had not been consumed twice previously during this week. Therefore this is not a Markov process.

Despite these last two examples, Markov processes have found tremendous applicability in a great number of observable everyday processes. The most common types of Markov processes are Markov chains.

Markov chains have denumerable (finite or countably infinite) state space (set of possible values that each random variable can take on) and denumerable time. The probabilities of moving from one state at a given time to another state at the "next" time (the concept of "next" is well-defined when the time axis is finite but not when the time axis is continuous, and it may or may not be when the time axis is countably infinite) are known as transition probabilities. These transition probabilities are typically arranged in a matrix, known as the transition matrix, or more accurately, as the one-step transition matrix.

One may also consider the probability of moving from a given state to another state in several steps, and the governing higher-order transition probabilities are arranged in higher-order transition matrices. As will be seen, it is necessary when deriving these higher-order transition matrices to raise a matrix to a power.

A Markov chain is simply a Markov process with denumerable (finite or countably infinite) state space and denumerable time axis. Good references for Markov chains are Ross (1983), page 100; Sveshnikov (1978), page 231; Rozanov (1969), page 83; Feller (1966), Volume 1, page 372; Feller (1966), Volume 2, pages 93 and 205; and Lipschutz (1965), page 126. Unless otherwise noted, we will consider Markov chains with finite state spaces. The states need not be numbers, but consider as an example n states labelled S_1, S_2, ..., S_n. For $1 \leq i \leq n$ and $1 \leq j \leq n$ and both i and j integers (that is, both i and j are states of the process) let $p(i, j)$ be the probability that a process which is at state i at time t goes to state j at time $t + 1$. We will assume (unless otherwise noted) that these transition probabilities are homogeneous (that is, independent of the time, t). Then

$$P\{X(t + 1) = j \mid X(1), X(2), ..., X(t) = i\} = P\{X(t + 1) = j \mid X(t) = i\}$$

$$= p(i, j),$$

regardless of the values of $X(1), X(2), ..., X(t - 2)$. That is, the probability of landing at state j at time $t + 1$ given all the previous history of the process depends only on the value of the process at time t. This is a restatement of the Markov property. We define this probability as $p(i, j)$ for all states i and j. This probability is known as a one-step transition probability, because it is the probability of going from state i to state j in one step.

The one-step transition matrix is an n-by-n matrix whose $(i, j)^{\text{th}}$ element is $p(i, j)$. This is a stochastic matrix, meaning that each of its rows sums to one and each of its columns also sums to one. Before proceeding, we will give a brief introduction to matrices and matrix algebra for the benefit of the reader who is unfamiliar with these concepts. Good references for most of the matrix manipulations which we will be using are Searle (1982), Stephenson (1986), and Pettofrezzo (1978).

A matrix is a rectangular array of numbers. Each number in the matrix is known as an element of the matrix. Each element of a matrix has a position in the matrix which is defined by its row and its column. This is similar to an address. If there are r rows and c columns in a matrix, then this matrix will have rc elements.

Just like numbers, matrices can be added and subtracted. This is performed element-by-element. Matrices can never be divided by anything other than a number (known as a scaler to distinguish it from a matrix or a vector). Matrices can by multiplied by a scaler, but they can also be multiplied by other matrices if the number of columns in the first matrix is equal to the number of rows in the second matrix. The order in which this multiplication is written does make a difference, in contrast to numbers, for which

$$ab = ba$$

for all numbers a and b. If A and B are matrices, then not only need AB not equal BA, but in fact it is possible that one is defined and the other is not defined! For example, if A has three rows and four columns, while B has four rows and seven columns, then AB is defined and has three rows and seven columns. This is because the number of columns of A, four, matches the number of rows of B, also four. But BA is not defined because B has seven columns and A only has three rows. It may be comforting to know that

$$A + B = B + A,$$

even for matrices. For example, let

$$A = \begin{matrix} 1 & 2 \\ 2 & 1 \end{matrix}$$

and $\quad B = 3 \quad 2$

$\quad\quad\quad 1 \quad 4.$

Then

$$A + B = (A + B)_{11} \quad (A + B)_{12}$$
$$(A + B)_{21} \quad (A + B)_{22}$$
$$= A_{11} + B_{11} \quad A_{12} + B_{12}$$
$$A_{21} + B_{21} \quad A_{22} + B_{22}$$
$$= 1 + 3 \quad 2 + 2$$
$$2 + 1 \quad 1 + 4$$
$$= 4 \quad 4$$
$$3 \quad 5$$
$$= 3 + 1 \quad 2 + 2$$
$$1 + 2 \quad 4 + 1$$
$$= B_{11} + A_{11} \quad B_{12} + A_{12}$$
$$B_{21} + A_{21} \quad B_{22} + A_{22}$$
$$= (B + A)_{11} \quad (B + A)_{12}$$
$$(B + A)_{21} \quad (B + A)_{22}$$
$$= B + A.$$

Because matrices can only be multiplied when the first matrix has the same number of columns as the second matrix has rows, it is seen that a matrix can only be multiplied by itself if it has the same numbers of rows and columns. Such a matrix is known as a square matrix. Only square matrices can be raised to powers (i.e., multiplied by itself repeatedly).

While matrices can never be divided by other matrices (except for scalers), some matrices do have inverses. Only certain square matrices have inverses, and matrices which are not square never have inverses. We will not pursue further the topic of which matrices have inverses beyond mentioning that a square matrix has an inverse if and only if its determinant (for a definition of determinant see Searle, 1982) is non-zero.

There is an identity matrix, *I*, with a special form. This identity matrix is square, and has as its elements zeros when the column number does not match the row number, and one when the column number does match the row number. For example, the identity matrix with three rows and three columns is given by

$$I = \begin{matrix} 1 & 0 & 0 \\ 0 & 1 & 0 \\ 0 & 0 & 1. \end{matrix}$$

The definition of an inverse is that if A^{-1} is the inverse of A, then

$$AA^{-1} = I$$

and $A^{-1}A = I.$

That is, if A^{-1} is the inverse of A, then A is also the inverse of A^{-1}.

Often matrices are expressed by giving a formula for the entries, in terms of the rows and the columns. For example, a four-by-four matrix, A, can be defined by writing

$$A = \{A_{ij}; i = 1, 2, 3, 4; j = 1, 2, 3, 4\},$$

where $A_{ij} = i + j.$

This matrix would be

$$A = \begin{matrix} 2 & 3 & 4 & 5 \\ 3 & 4 & 5 & 6 \\ 4 & 5 & 6 & 7 \\ 5 & 6 & 7 & 8, \end{matrix}$$

because, for example, the upper left entry would be the sum of its row number and its column number. Since this element occupies the first row and the first column, its row number is one and its column number is also one. Therefore the element must be

$$A_{1,1} = 1 + 1$$

$$= 2,$$

as shown in matrix A.

If A is an I-by-J matrix with elements $\{A_{ij}; i = 1, 2, ..., I; j = 1, 2, ..., J\}$, and B is a J-by-K matrix with elements $\{B_{nm}; n = 1, 2, ..., J; m = 1, 2, ..., K\}$, then $AB = \{AB_{nm}; n = 1, 2, ..., I; m = 1, 2, ..., K\}$ exists (since A has I columns and B has J rows), and AB is an I-by-K matrix with elements $\{AB_{im}\}$, where

$$AB_{im} = \Sigma_{j\,=\,1\ \text{to}\ J}\,A_{ij}B_{jm}.$$

That is, the elements of the product matrix are a sum of products of certain elements of the original matrices. For example, consider

$$A = \begin{matrix} 1 & 2 & 3 \\ 2 & 3 & 4 \\ 3 & 4 & 5 \end{matrix}$$

and

$$B = \begin{matrix} 2 & 3 & 4 \\ 3 & 4 & 5 \\ 4 & 5 & 6. \end{matrix}$$

Then

$$AB = \begin{matrix} AB_{11} & AB_{12} & AB_{13} \\ AB_{21} & AB_{22} & AB_{23} \\ AB_{31} & AB_{32} & AB_{33} \end{matrix}$$

$$= \begin{matrix} A_{11}B_{11} + A_{12}B_{21} + A_{13}B_{31} & A_{11}B_{12} + A_{12}B_{22} + A_{13}B_{32} & A_{11}B_{13} + A_{12}B_{23} + A_{13}B_{33} \\ A_{21}B_{11} + A_{22}B_{21} + A_{23}B_{31} & A_{21}B_{12} + A_{22}B_{22} + A_{23}B_{32} & A_{21}B_{13} + A_{22}B_{23} + A_{23}B_{33} \\ A_{31}B_{11} + A_{32}B_{21} + A_{33}B_{31} & A_{31}B_{12} + A_{32}B_{22} + A_{33}B_{32} & A_{31}B_{13} + A_{32}B_{23} + A_{33}B_{33} \end{matrix}$$

$$= \begin{matrix} (1)(2) + (2)(3) + (3)(4) & (1)(3) + (2)(4) + (3)(5) & (1)(4) + (2)(5) + (3)(6) \\ (2)(2) + (3)(3) + (4)(4) & (2)(3) + (3)(4) + (4)(5) & (2)(4) + (3)(5) + (4)(6) \\ (3)(2) + (4)(3) + (5)(4) & (3)(3) + (4)(4) + (5)(5) & (3)(4) + (4)(5) + (5)(6) \end{matrix}$$

$$= \begin{matrix} 2 + 6 + 12 & 3 + 8 + 15 & 4 + 10 + 18 \\ 4 + 9 + 16 & 6 + 12 + 20 & 8 + 15 + 24 \\ 6 + 12 + 20 & 9 + 16 + 25 & 12 + 20 + 30 \end{matrix}$$

$$= \begin{matrix} 20 & 26 & 32 \\ 29 & 38 & 47 \\ 38 & 50 & 62. \end{matrix}$$

The other kind of multiplication in which matrices may be involved is scaler multiplication. This simply means that each element of a matrix is multiplied by a given scaler. For example, we may multiply the matrix *A* by the scaler two, resulting in

$$2A = 2A_{21} \quad \begin{array}{ccc} 2A_{11} & 2A_{12} & 2A_{13} \\ 2A_{21} & 2A_{22} & 2A_{23} \\ 2A_{31} & 2A_{32} & 2A_{33} \end{array}$$

$$= \begin{array}{ccc} (2)(1) & (2)(2) & (2)(3) \\ (2)(2) & (2)(3) & (2)(4) \\ (2)(3) & (2)(4) & (2)(5) \end{array}$$

$$= \begin{array}{ccc} 2 & 4 & 6 \\ 4 & 6 & 8 \\ 6 & 8 & 10. \end{array}$$

To illustrate squaring of matrices, consider a two-by-two matrix, A. In particular, let A be

$$A = \begin{array}{cc} 1 & 2 \\ 2 & 1. \end{array}$$

Then

$$A^2 = AA$$

$$= \begin{array}{cc} 1 & 2 \\ 2 & 1 \end{array} \text{ times } \begin{array}{cc} 1 & 2 \\ 2 & 1 \end{array}$$

$$= \begin{array}{cc} A^2_{11} & A^2_{12} \\ A^2_{21} & A^2_{22} \end{array}$$

$$= \begin{array}{cc} A_{11}A_{11} + A_{12}A_{21} & A_{11}A_{12} + A_{12}A_{22} \\ A_{21}A_{11} + A_{22}A_{21} & A_{21}A_{12} + A_{22}A_{22} \end{array}$$

$$= \begin{array}{cc} (1)(1) + (2)(2) & (1)(2) + (2)(1) \\ (2)(1) + (1)(2) & (2)(2) + (1)(1) \end{array}$$

$$= \begin{array}{cc} 1 + 4 & 2 + 2 \\ 2 + 2 & 4 + 1 \end{array}$$

$$= \begin{array}{cc} 5 & 4 \\ 4 & 5. \end{array}$$

Any square matrix can be squared, because its number of rows matches its number of columns. In fact, a square matrix can be raised to any power (even if this power is not an integer, but this would require appeal to a Taylor series expansion, which is possible even for matrices).

Step-by-Step Solutions to Problems in this Chapter, "Markov Stochastic Processes."

• PROBLEM 10–1

Let A and B be three-by-three matrices such that

$$A = \begin{array}{ccc} 2 & 1 & -5 \\ 3 & 4 & 6 \\ 3 & 4 & 2 \end{array}$$

and

$$B = \begin{array}{ccc} 2 & 3 & 3 \\ 1 & 4 & 4 \\ -5 & 6 & 2. \end{array}$$

Find $A + B$ and $B + A$.

SOLUTION:

The matrix $A + B$ can be computed element-by-element, so $A + B$ is a three-by-three matrix with elements which are the sums of the corresponding elements of the matrix A and the matrix B. That is,

$$A + B = \begin{array}{ccc} (A+B)_{11} & (A+B)_{12} & (A+B)_{13} \\ (A+B)_{21} & (A+B)_{22} & (A+B)_{23} \\ (A+B)_{31} & (A+B)_{32} & (A+B)_{33} \end{array}$$

$$= \begin{array}{ccc} A_{11} + B_{11} & A_{12} + B_{12} & A_{13} + B_{13} \\ A_{21} + B_{21} & A_{22} + B_{22} & A_{23} + B_{23} \\ A_{31} + B_{31} & A_{32} + B_{32} & A_{33} + B_{33} \end{array}$$

$$
\begin{array}{ccc}
 & 2+2 & 1+3 & -5+3 \\
= & 3+1 & 4+4 & 6+4 \\
 & 3+(-5) & 4+6 & 2+2 \\
 & 4 & 4 & -2 \\
= & 4 & 8 & 10 \\
 & -2 & 10 & 4,
\end{array}
$$

and

$$
B+A = \begin{array}{ccc}
(B+A)_{11} & (B+A)_{12} & (B+A)_{13} \\
(B+A)_{21} & (B+A)_{22} & (B+A)^{23} \\
(B+A)_{31} & (B+A)_{32} & (B+A)_{33}
\end{array}
$$

$$
= \begin{array}{ccc}
B_{11}+A_{11} & B_{12}+A_{12} & B_{13}+A_{13} \\
B_{21}+A_{21} & B_{22}+A_{22} & B_{23}+A_{23} \\
B_{31}+A_{31} & B_{32}+A_{32} & B_{33}+A_{33}
\end{array}
$$

$$
= \begin{array}{ccc}
2+2 & 3+1 & 3+(-5) \\
1+3 & 4+4 & 4+6 \\
-5+3 & 6+4 & 2+2 \\
4 & 4 & -2 \\
4 & 8 & 10 \\
-2 & 10 & 4.
\end{array}
$$

This confirms that $A + B = B + A$.

• PROBLEM 10-2

Is a scaler a matrix?

SOLUTION:

Yes. A scaler is a matrix of dimension one-by-one. That is, considered as a matrix, any number has one row and one column.

• PROBLEM 10-3

Let A and B be as defined in Problem 1. Then what is the difference matrix $A - B$? What is $B - A$?

SOLUTION:

We write

$$A - B = \begin{matrix} (A-B)_{11} & (A-B)_{12} & (A-B)_{13} \\ (A-B)_{21} & (A-B)_{22} & (A-B)_{23} \\ (A-B)_{31} & (A-B)_{32} & (A-B)_{33} \end{matrix}$$

$$= \begin{matrix} A_{11} - B_{11} & A_{12} - B_{12} & A_{13} - B_{13} \\ A_{21} - B_{21} & A_{22} - B_{22} & A_{23} - B_{23} \\ A_{31} - B_{31} & A_{32} - B_{32} & A_{33} - B_{33} \end{matrix}$$

$$= \begin{matrix} 2-2 & 1-3 & -5-3 \\ 3-1 & 4-4 & 6-4 \\ 3-(-5) & 4-6 & 2-2 \end{matrix}$$

$$= \begin{matrix} 0 & -2 & -8 \\ 2 & 0 & 2 \\ 8 & -2 & 0, \end{matrix}$$

and

$$B - A = \begin{matrix} (B-A)_{11} & (B-A)_{12} & (B-A)_{13} \\ (B-A)_{21} & (B-A)_{22} & (B-A)_{23} \\ (B-A)_{31} & (B-A)_{32} & (B-A)_{33} \end{matrix}$$

$$= \begin{matrix} B_{11} - A_{11} & B_{12} - A_{12} & B_{13} - A_{13} \\ B_{21} - A_{21} & B_{22} - A_{22} & B_{23} - A_{23} \\ B_{31} - A_{31} & B_{32} - A_{32} & B_{33} - A_{33} \end{matrix}$$

$$= \begin{matrix} 2-2 & 3-1 & 3-(-5) \\ 1-3 & 4-4 & 4-6 \\ -5-3 & 6-4 & 2-2 \end{matrix}$$

$$
\begin{array}{ccc}
0 & 2 & 8 \\
= -2 & 0 & -2 \\
-8 & 2 & 0.
\end{array}
$$

Notice that $A - B$ does not equal $B - A$, but that $(A - B) + (B - A) = 0$.

• PROBLEM 10–4

Let A be as in Problem 1. Then what is $3A$?

SOLUTION:

We are here referring to scaler multiplication, so each element of A is to be multiplied by the scaler three. This results in

$$
3A = \begin{array}{ccc}
3A_{11} & 3A_{12} & 3A_{13} \\
3A_{21} & 3A_{22} & 3A_{23} \\
3A_{31} & 3A_{32} & 3A_{33}
\end{array}
$$

$$
= \begin{array}{ccc}
(3)(2) & (3)(1) & (3)(-5) \\
(3)(3) & (3)(4) & (3)(6) \\
(3)(3) & (3)(4) & (3)(2)
\end{array}
$$

$$
= \begin{array}{ccc}
6 & 3 & -15 \\
9 & 12 & 18 \\
9 & 12 & 6.
\end{array}
$$

• PROBLEM 10–5

Let A and B be as in Problem 10–1. What is the matrix product AB? What is the matrix product BA?

SOLUTION:

Here we are referring to matrix multiplication. Before we can proceed, we must make sure that the matrices are compatible for matrix multiplication. Since both A and B are three-by-three, each has the same number of rows as the other has columns. Therefore both AB and BA are defined. We may now proceed.

By the definition of matrix multiplication,

$$
AB = \begin{matrix}
AB_{11} & AB_{12} & AB_{13} \\
AB_{21} & AB_{22} & AB_{23} \\
AB_{31} & AB_{32} & AB_{33}
\end{matrix}
$$

$$
= \begin{matrix}
A_{11}B_{11} + A_{12}B_{21} + A_{13}B_{31} & A_{11}B_{12} + A_{12}B_{22} + A_{13}B_{32} & A_{11}B_{13} + A_{12}B_{23} + A_{13}B_{33} \\
A_{21}B_{11} + A_{22}B_{21} + A_{23}B_{31} & A_{21}B_{12} + A_{22}B_{22} + A_{23}B_{32} & A_{21}B_{13} + A_{22}B_{23} + A_{23}B_{33} \\
A_{31}B_{11} + A_{32}B_{21} + A_{33}B_{31} & A_{31}B_{12} + A_{32}B_{22} + A_{33}B_{32} & A_{31}B_{13} + A_{32}B_{23} + A_{33}B_{33}
\end{matrix}
$$

$$
= \begin{matrix}
(2)(2) + (1)(1) + (-5)(-5) & (2)(3) + (1)(4) + (-5)(6) & (2)(3) + (1)(4) + (-5)(2) \\
(3)(2) + (4)(1) + (6)(-5) & (3)(3) + (4)(4) + (6)(6) & (3)(3) + (4)(4) + (6)(2) \\
(3)(2) + (4)(1) + (2)(-5) & (3)(3) + (4)(4) + (2)(6) & (3)(3) + (4)(4) + (2)(2)
\end{matrix}
$$

$$
= \begin{matrix}
4 + 1 + 25 & 6 + 4 + (-30) & 6 + 4 + (-10) \\
6 + 4 + (-30) & 9 + 16 + 36 & 9 + 16 + 12 \\
6 + 4 + (-10) & 9 + 16 + 12 & 9 + 16 + 4
\end{matrix}
$$

$$
= \begin{matrix}
30 & -20 & 0 \\
-20 & 61 & 37 \\
0 & 37 & 29.
\end{matrix}
$$

Also,

$$
BA = \begin{matrix}
BA_{11} & BA_{12} & BA_{13} \\
BA_{21} & BA_{22} & BA_{23} \\
BA_{31} & BA_{32} & BA_{33}
\end{matrix}
$$

$$
= \begin{matrix}
B_{11}A_{11} + B_{12}A_{21} + B_{13}A_{31} & B_{11}A_{12} + B_{12}A_{22} + B_{13}A_{32} & B_{11}A_{13} + B_{12}A_{23} + B_{13}A_{33} \\
B_{21}A_{11} + B_{22}A_{21} + B_{23}A_{31} & B_{21}A_{12} + B_{22}A_{22} + B_{23}A_{32} & B_{21}A_{13} + B_{22}A_{23} + B_{23}A_{33} \\
B_{31}A_{11} + B_{32}A_{21} + B_{33}A_{31} & B_{31}A_{12} + B_{32}A_{22} + B_{33}A_{32} & B_{31}A_{13} + B_{32}A_{23} + B_{33}A_{33}
\end{matrix}
$$

$$
= \begin{matrix}
(2)(2) + (3)(3) + (3)(3) & (2)(1) + (3)(4) + (3)(4) & (2)(-5) + (3)(6) + (3)(2) \\
(1)(2) + (4)(3) + (4)(3) & (1)(1) + (4)(4) + (4)(4) & (1)(-5) + (4)(6) + (4)(2) \\
(-5)(2) + (6)(3) + (2)(3) & (-5)(1) + (6)(4) + (2)(4) & (-5)(-5) + (6)(6) + (2)(2)
\end{matrix}
$$

$$4 + 9 + 9 \qquad 2 + 12 + 12 \qquad (-10) + 18 + 6$$

$$= 2 + 12 + 12 \qquad 1 + 16 + 16 \qquad (-5) + 24 + 8$$

$$(-10) + 18 + 6 \qquad (-5) + 24 + 8 \qquad 25 + 36 + 4$$

$$22 \qquad 26 \qquad 14$$

$$= 26 \qquad 33 \qquad 27$$

$$14 \qquad 27 \qquad 65.$$

• PROBLEM 10–6

Let I be the identity matrix, and let A be as in Problem 10-1. Then what is the matrix product AI? What is IA?

SOLUTION:

By the definition of matrix multiplication

$$AI_{11} \qquad AI_{12} \qquad AI_{13}$$

$$AI = AI_{21} \qquad AI_{22} \qquad AI_{23}$$

$$AI_{31} \qquad AI_{32} \qquad AI_{33}$$

$$A_{11}I_{11} + A_{12}I_{21} + A_{13}I_{31} \qquad A_{11}I_{12} + A_{12}I_{22} + A_{13}I_{32} \qquad A_{11}I_{13} + A_{12}I_{23} + A_{13}I_{33}$$

$$= A_{21}I_{11} + A_{22}I_{21} + A_{23}I_{31} \qquad A_{21}I_{12} + A_{22}I_{22} + A_{23}I_{32} \qquad A_{21}I_{13} + A_{22}I_{23} + A_{23}I_{33}$$

$$A_{31}I_{11} + A_{32}I_{21} + A_{33}I_{31} \qquad A_{31}I_{12} + A_{32}I_{22} + A_{33}I_{32} \qquad A_{31}I_{13} + A_{32}I_{23} + A_{33}I_{33}$$

$$(2)(1) + (1)(0) + (-5)(0) \qquad (2)(0) + (1)(1) + (-5)(0) \qquad (2)(0) + (1)(0) + (-5)(1)$$

$$= (3)(1) + (4)(0) + (6)(0) \qquad (3)(0) + (4)(1) + (6)(0) \qquad (3)(0) + (4)(0) + (6)(1)$$

$$(3)(1) + (4)(0) + (2)(0) \qquad (3)(0) + (4)(1) + (2)(0) \qquad (3)(0) + (4)(0) + (2)(1)$$

$$2 + 0 + 0 \qquad 0 + 1 + 0 \qquad 0 + 0 + (-5)$$

$$= 3 + 0 + 0 \qquad 0 + 4 + 0 \qquad 0 + 0 + 6$$

$$3 + 0 + 0 \qquad 0 + 4 + 0 \qquad 0 + 0 + 2$$

$$2 \qquad 1 \qquad -5$$

$$= 3 \qquad 4 \qquad 6$$

$$3 \qquad 4 \qquad 2,$$

which means that $AI = A$.

Also,

$$
IA = \begin{array}{ccc}
IA_{11} & IA_{12} & IA_{13} \\
IA_{21} & IA_{22} & IA_{23} \\
IA_{31} & IA_{32} & IA_{33}
\end{array}
$$

$$
= \begin{array}{ccc}
I_{11}A_{11} + I_{12}A_{21} + I_{13}A_{31} & I_{11}A_{12} + I_{12}A_{22} + I_{13}A_{32} & I_{11}A_{13} + I_{12}A_{23} + I_{13}A_{33} \\
I_{21}A_{11} + I_{22}A_{21} + I_{23}A_{31} & I_{21}A_{12} + I_{22}A_{22} + I_{23}A_{32} & I_{21}A_{13} + I_{22}A_{23} + I_{23}A_{33} \\
I_{31}A_{11} + I_{32}A_{21} + I_{33}A_{31} & I_{31}A_{12} + I_{32}A_{22} + I_{33}A_{32} & I_{31}A_{13} + I_{32}A_{23} + I_{33}A_{33}
\end{array}
$$

$$
= \begin{array}{ccc}
(1)(2) + (0)(3) + (0)(3) & (1)(1) + (0)(4) + (0)(4) & (1)(-5) + (0)(6) + (0)(2) \\
(0)(2) + (1)(3) + (0)(3) & (0)(1) + (1)(4) + (0)(4) & (0)(-5) + (1)(6) + (0)(2) \\
(0)(2) + (0)(3) + (1)(3) & (0)(1) + (0)(4) + (1)(4) & (0)(-5) + (0)(6) + (1)(2)
\end{array}
$$

$$
= \begin{array}{ccc}
2 + 0 + 0 & 1 + 0 + 0 & -5 + 0 + 0 \\
0 + 3 + 0 & 0 + 4 + 0 & 0 + 6 + 0 \\
0 + 0 + 3 & 0 + 0 + 4 & 0 + 0 + 2
\end{array}
$$

$$
= \begin{array}{ccc}
2 & 1 & -5 \\
3 & 4 & 6 \\
3 & 4 & 2,
\end{array}
$$

which means that $IA = A$. Because $IA = AI = A$ for any square matrix A of the proper dimensions, I is known as the identity matrix.

• PROBLEM 10–7

Let A be as in Problem 10–1. What is A^2?

SOLUTION:

We write

$$A^2 = AA$$

$$\begin{array}{ccc} 2 & 1 & -5 \\ = 3 & 4 & 6 \\ 3 & 4 & 2 \end{array} \qquad \begin{array}{ccc} 2 & 1 & -5 \\ 3 & 4 & 6 \\ 3 & 4 & 2 \end{array}$$

$$\begin{array}{ccc} AA_{11} & AA_{12} & AA_{13} \\ = AA_{21} & AA_{22} & AA_{23} \\ AA_{31} & AA_{32} & AA_{33} \end{array}$$

$$\begin{array}{ccc} A_{11}A_{11} + A_{12}A_{21} + A_{13}A_{31} & A_{11}A_{12} + A_{12}A_{22} + A_{13}A_{32} & A_{11}A_{13} + A_{12}A_{23} + A_{13}A_{33} \\ = A_{21}A_{11} + A_{22}A_{21} + A_{23}A_{31} & A_{21}A_{12} + A_{22}A_{22} + A_{23}A_{32} & A_{21}A_{13} + A_{22}A_{23} + A_{23}A_{33} \\ A_{31}A_{11} + A_{32}A_{21} + A_{33}A_{31} & A_{31}A_{12} + A_{32}A_{22} + A_{33}A_{32} & A_{31}A_{13} + A_{32}A_{23} + A_{33}A_{33} \end{array}$$

$$\begin{array}{ccc} (2)(2) + (1)(3) + (-5)(3) & (2)(1) + (1)(4) + (-5)(4) & (2)(-5) + (1)(6) + (-5)(2) \\ = (3)(2) + (4)(3) + (6)(3) & (3)(1) + (4)(4) + (6)(4) & (3)(-5) + (4)(6) + (6)(2) \\ (3)(2) + (4)(3) + (2)(3) & (3)(1) + (4)(4) + (2)(4) & (3)(-5) + (4)(6) + (2)(2) \end{array}$$

$$\begin{array}{ccc} 4 + 3 + (-15) & 2 + 4 + (-20) & (-10) + 6 + (-10) \\ = 6 + 12 + 18 & 3 + 16 + 24 & (-15) + 24 + 12 \\ 6 + 12 + 6 & 3 + 16 + 8 & (-15) + 24 + 4 \end{array}$$

$$\begin{array}{ccc} -8 & -14 & -14 \\ = 36 & 43 & 21 \\ 24 & 27 & 13. \end{array}$$

• PROBLEM 10-8

What is $A + (I + A)^2$?

SOLUTION:

We may proceed, for a while, as if both I and A were numbers, and write

$$A + (I + A)^2 = A + (I + A)(I + A)$$

$$= A + II + IA + AI + AA$$

$$= A + I^2 + IA + AI + A^2.$$

Since I is the identity matrix,

$$I^2 = I,$$

$$IA = A,$$

and $\quad AI = A$

(see Problem 10–6). Thus

$$A + (I + A)^2 = A + I^2 + IA + AI + A^2$$

$$= A + I + A + A + A^2$$

$$= I + 3A + A^2.$$

But we know from Problem 10–4 that

	(3) (2)		(3) (1)		(3) (– 5)
$3A =$	(3) (3)		(3) (4)		(3) (6)
	(3) (3)		(3) (4)		(3) (2)
	6		3		– 15
$=$	9		12		18
	9		12		6.

From Problem 10–7 we know that

	– 8		– 14		– 14
$A^2 =$	36		43		21
	24		27		13.

Thus $A + (I + A)^2 = I + 3A + A^2$

	1	0	0		6	3	– 15		– 8	– 14	– 14
$=$	0	1	0	$+$	9	12	18	$+$	36	43	21
	0	0	1		9	12	6		24	27	13

$1 + 6 + (-8)$	$0 + 3 + (-14)$	$0 + (-15) + (-14)$
$= 0 + 9 + 36$	$1 + 12 + 43$	$0 + 18 + 21$
$0 + 9 + 24$	$0 + 12 + 27$	$1 + 6 + 13$

$$
= 45 \quad
\begin{matrix}
-1 & -11 & -29 \\
45 & 56 & 39 \\
33 & 39 & 20.
\end{matrix}
$$

******

REVIEW OF TRANSITION MATRICES

Our use of matrices in this subsection will be restricted to special matrices known as transition matrices. These matrices belong to a class of matrices known as stochastic matrices.

A matrix is a stochastic matrix if it satisfies three properties. These properties are

1. the matrix is square, or has as many rows as it has columns,

2. the sum of the elements in each row is one,

and

3. each element is non-negative.

The point of these definitions is to ensure that each row constitutes a probability distribution. For a transition matrix, the ith row gives the probability distribution of the state of the Markov process at time $t + 1$ given that the state of the Markov process is i at time t. Notice that these three properties jointly imply that no element of a transition matrix can exceed one (again in accordance with what we know about probabilities). This can be seen by assuming that an element in a transition matrix does exceed one. But each other element in its row must be non-negative, by Property 3. This means that the sum of the elements in that row is at least as large as the element which exceeds one. Therefore the sum of the elements in the row in question is larger than one. But this is a violation of Property 2. This contradiction shows that no element of a transition matrix can be larger than one.

As an example of a transition matrix and its usefulness, suppose that a patient visits his doctor every month for routine blood pressure monitoring. Each such visit is classified either as a normotensive visit (which we will code as state 1) or as a hypertensive visit (which we will code as state 2).

Now suppose that if the patient is normotensive at any given visit, then he is equally likely to be normotensive or hypertensive at the next visit (independent of the results of any visits prior to the current one, per the Markov property). But if he is hypertensive at a given visit, then he will be prescribed a beta blocker, he will exercise, and he will restrict his dietary intake of sodium. Doing so will give him a 70% chance of being normotensive at his next visit and only a 30% chance of remaining hypertensive at his next visit (again, independent of the results of any previous visits).

Let A be the two-by-two transition matrix for this Markov chain. Then A is given by

$$A = 0.5 \qquad 0.5$$
$$0.7 \qquad 0.3.$$

The states of this Markov chain are $\{1,2\}$. Given that the process is in state 1 at a given time, the probability is 0.5 that the process will remain in state 1 at the next time, and the probability is 0.5 that the process will go to state 2 at the next time. Given that the process is at state 2 at a given time, the probability is 0.7 that the process will go to state 1 at the next time, and the probability is 0.3 that the process will remain in state 2. In symbols, this is written as

$$P\{X(t+1) = 1 \mid X(1), X(2), \ldots, X(t) = 1\} = P\{X(t+1) = 1 \mid X(t) = 1\}$$
$$= 0.5,$$

$$P\{X(t+1) = 2 \mid X(1), X(2), \ldots, X(t) = 1\} = P\{X(t+1) = 2 \mid X(t) = 1\}$$
$$= 0.5,$$

$$P\{X(t+1) = 1 \mid X(1), X(2), \ldots, X(t) = 2\} = P\{X(t+1) = 1 \mid X(t) = 2\}$$
$$= 0.7,$$

and $\quad P\{X(t+1) = 2 \mid X(1), X(2), \ldots, X(t) = 2\} = P\{X(t+1) = 2 \mid X(t) = 2\}$
$$= 0.3.$$

At this point this process can be studied without any further reference to doctor's offices, patients, or blood pressure. The medical expertise was called into play in three capacities. These are

1. determining that the process is, indeed, a Markov chain (that is, that the blood pressure at a given visit has a distribution which, given all the past results, depends only on the most recent results),

2. determining the probabilities of being normotensive and hypertensive at a given visit given the that results of the previous visit were a normotensive reading,

and 3. determining the probabilities of being normotensive and hypertensive at a given visit given that the results of the previous visit were a hypertensive reading.

Having made these medical determinations, all subsequent analysis can be made in complete generality without considering the process which generated the transition matrix. That is, it suffices to restrict attention to the transition matrix. This is, perhaps, most easily understood by stating that two different Markov chains with the same transition matrices have the identical probabilistic properties.

Suppose that we see that the patient is hypertensive at a given visit, and our interest is not in the next visit, but rather the visit after that. What can we say about this subsequent visit? We compute

$$P\{X(t + 2) = 1 \mid X(1), X(2), \ldots, X(t) = 2\} = P\{X(t + 2) = 1 \mid X(t) = 1\}$$

$$= P\{X(t + 2) = 1 \cap \text{the universal event} \mid X(t) = 1\},$$

since the universal event has probability one, every set is a subset of the universal set, and consequently any intersection between any set A and the universal set results in the original set A. Therefore,

$$P\{X(t + 2) = 1 \mid X(1), X(2), \ldots, X(t) = 1\} = P\{X(t + 2) = 1$$

$$\cap \text{the universal event} \mid X(t) = 1\}$$

$$= P\{X(t + 2) = 1 \cap [X(t + 1) = 1 \cup X(t + 1) = 2]$$

$$\mid X(t) = 1\},$$

because at time $t + 1$ the Markov chain must either be at state 1 or at state 2, so consequently the union $[X(t + 1) = 1 \cup X(t + 1) = 2]$ is the universal event. Then

$$P\{X(t + 2)$$

$$= 1 \mid X(1), X(2), \ldots, X(t) = 1\} = P\{X(t + 2) = 1 \cap [X(t + 1) = 1$$

$$\cup X(t + 1) = 2] \mid X(t) = 1\}$$

$$= P\{[X(t+2) = 1 \cap X(t+1) = 1] \cup [X(t+2) = 1$$

$$\cap X(t+1) = 2] \mid X(t) = 1\}$$

$$= P\{[X(t+2) = 1 \cap X(t+1) = 1] \mid X(t) = 1\}$$

$$+ P\{[X(t+2) = 1 \cap X(t+1) = 2] \mid X(t) = 1\},$$

because disjoint unions of conditional probabilities are additive. We now recall the definition of condition probability and re-express the last expression as

$$P\{X(t+2)$$

$$= 1 \mid X(1), X(2), ..., X(t) = 1\}$$

$$= P\{[X(t+2) = 1 \cap X(t+1) = 1] \mid X(t) = 1\}$$

$$+ P\{[X(t+2) = 1 \cap X(t+1) = 2] \mid X(t) = 1\}$$

$$= P\{X(t+1) = 1 \mid X(t) = 1\}P\{X(t+2) = 1 \mid X(t+1) = 1,$$

$$X(t) = 1\} + P\{X(t+1) = 2 \mid X(t) = 1\}P\{X(t+2) =$$

$$1 \mid X(t+1) = 2, X(t) = 1\}$$

$$= P\{X(t+1) = 1 \mid X(t) = 1\}P\{X(t+2) = 1 \mid X(t+1) = 1\}$$

$$+ P\{X(t+1) = 2 \mid X(t) = 1\}P\{X(t+2) = 1 \mid X(t+1) = 2\}$$

by the Markov property. Finally, we may compute the numerical value of this last expression by making use of the transition matrix. We obtain

$$P\{X(t+2) = 1 \mid X(1), X(2), ..., X(t) = 1\}$$

$$= P\{X(t+1) = 1 \mid X(t) = 1\}P\{X(t+2) = 1 \mid X(t+1) = 1\}$$

$$+ P\{X(t+1) = 2 \mid X(t) = 1\}P\{X(t+2) = 1 \mid X(t+1) = 2\}$$

$$= (0.5)(0.5) + (0.5)(0.7)$$

$$= 0.25 + 0.35$$

$$= 0.6.$$

Thus the probability of being normotensive two visits after a visit during which the patient was seen to be normotensive is 0.6. We may compute the other two-step transition probabilities in a similar fashion. Doing so, we obtain

$$P\{X(t+2)$$

$$= 2 \mid X(1), X(2), ..., X(t) = 1\} = P\{X(t+2) = 2 \mid X(t) = 1\}$$

$= P\{X(t+2) = 2 \cap \text{the universal event} \mid X(t) = 1\}$

$= P\{X(t+2) = 2 \cap [X(t+1) = 1 \cup X(t+1) = 2] \mid X(t) = 1\}$

$= P\{[X(t+2) = 2 \cap X(t+1) = 1] \cup [X(t+2) = 2$

$\cap X(t+1) = 2] \mid X(t) = 1\}$

$= P\{[X(t+2) = 2 \cap X(t+1) = 1] \mid X(t) = 1\}$

$+ P\{[X(t+2) = 2 \cap X(t+1) = 2] \mid X(t) = 1\}$

$= P\{X(t+1) = 1 \mid X(t) = 1\}P\{X(t+2) = 2 \mid X(t+1) = 1,$

$X(t) = 1\} + P\{X(t+1) = 2 \mid X(t) = 1\}P\{X(t+2) = 2 \mid$

$X(t+1) = 2, X(t) = 1\}$

$= P\{X(t+1) = 1 \mid X(t) = 1\}P\{X(t+2) = 2 \mid X(t+1) = 1\}$

$+ P\{X(t+1) = 2 \mid X(t) = 1\}P\{X(t+2) = 2 \mid X(t+1) = 2\}$

$= (0.5)\,(0.5) + (0.5)\,(0.3)$

$= 0.25 + 0.15$

$= 0.4,$

$P\{X(t+2)$

$= 1 \mid X(1), X(2), \ldots, X(t) = 2\} = P\{X(t+2) = 1 \mid X(t) = 2\}$

$= P\{X(t+2) = 1 \cap \text{the universal event} \mid X(t) = 2\}$

$= P\{X(t+2) = 1 \cap [X(t+1) = 1 \cup X(t+1) = 2] \mid X(t) = 2\}$

$= P\{[X(t+2) = 1 \cap X(t+1) = 1] \cup [X(t+2) = 1$

$\cap X(t+1) = 2] \mid X(t) = 2\}$

$= P\{[X(t+2) = 1 \cap X(t+1) = 1] \mid X(t) = 2\} + P\{[X(t+2) = 1$

$\cap X(t+1) = 2] \mid X(t) = 2\}$

$= P\{X(t+1) = 1 \mid X(t) = 2\}P\{X(t+2) = 1 \mid X(t+1) = 1,$

$X(t) = 2\} + P\{X(t+1) = 2 \mid X(t) = 2\}P\{X(t+2) = 1$

$\mid X(t+1) = 2, X(t) = 2\}$

$= P\{X(t+1) = 1 \mid X(t) = 2\}\,P\{X(t+2) = 1 \mid X(t+1) = 1\}$

$+ P\{X(t+1) = 2 \mid X(t) = 2\}P\{X(t+2) = 1 \mid X(t+1) = 2\}$

$= (0.7)\,(0.5) + (0.3)\,(0.7)$

$$= 0.35 + 0.21$$

$$= 0.56,$$

and $P\{X(t+2)$

$$= 2 \mid X(1), X(2), \ldots, X(t) = 2\} = P\{X(t+2) = 2 \mid X(t) = 2\}$$

$$= P\{X(t+2) = 2 \cap \text{the universal event} \mid X(t) = 2\}$$

$$= P\{X(t+2) = 2 \cap [X(t+1) = 1 \cup X(t+1) = 2] \mid X(t) = 2\}$$

$$= P\{[X(t+2) = 2 \cap X(t+1) = 1] \cup [X(t+2) = 2$$

$$\cap X(t+1) = 2] \mid X(t) = 2\}$$

$$= P\{[X(t+2) = 2 \cap X(t+1) = 1] \mid X(t) = 2\} + P\{[X(t+2) = 2$$

$$\cap X(t+1) = 2] \mid X(t) = 2\}$$

$$= P\{X(t+1) = 1 \mid X(t) = 2\} P\{X(t+2) = 2 \mid X(t+1) = 1,$$

$$X(t) = 2\} + P\{X(t+1) = 2 \mid X(t) = 2\} P\{X(t+2) = 2$$

$$\mid X(t+1) = 2, X(t) = 2\}$$

$$= P\{X(t+1) = 1 \mid X(t) = 2\} P\{X(t+2) = 2 \mid X(t+1) = 1\}$$

$$+ P\{X(t+1) = 2 \mid X(t) = 2\} P\{X(t+2) = 2 \mid X(t+1) = 2\}$$

$$= (0.7)(0.5) + (0.3)(0.3)$$

$$= 0.35 + 0.09$$

$$= 0.44.$$

We may summarize these results by presenting them in a two-step transition matrix. The $(i,j)^{th}$ element of this matrix is the probability of moving from state i to state j in two steps, without specifying the state of the Markov chain at the intermediate step. Based on our calculations, this matrix would be

$$A_{\text{two-step}} = \begin{matrix} 0.60 & 0.40 \\ 0.56 & 0.44. \end{matrix}$$

Fortunately there is a short-cut to computing this matrix based on the one-step transition matrix. The required operation is the squaring of the one-step transition matrix. To see this, recall that

$$A = \begin{matrix} 0.5 & 0.5 \\ 0.7 & 0.3. \end{matrix}$$

Then

$$A^2 = A^2_{11} \qquad\qquad A^2_{12}$$

$$A^2_{21} \qquad\qquad A^2_{22}$$

$$= A_{11}A_{11} + A_{12}A_{21} \qquad A_{11}A_{12} + A_{12}A_{22}$$

$$A_{21}A_{11} + A_{22}A_{21} \qquad A_{21}A_{12} + A_{22}A_{22}$$

$$= (0.5)\,(0.5) + (0.5)\,(0.7) \quad (0.5)\,(0.5) + (0.5)\,(0.3)$$

$$(0.7)\,(0.5) + (0.3)\,(0.7) \quad (0.7)\,(0.5) + (0.3)\,(0.3)$$

$$= 0.25 + 0.35 \qquad\qquad 0.25 + 0.15$$

$$0.35 + 0.21 \qquad\qquad 0.35 + 0.09$$

$$= 0.60 \qquad\qquad\qquad 0.40$$

$$0.56 \qquad\qquad\qquad 0.44,$$

in agreement with what we know to be the two-step transition matrix of probabilities. This proves that squaring the one-step transition matrix does, in fact, result in the two-step transition matrix, at least for the particular one-step transition matrix in this example.

Of course, we would like to be able to say more than just that a certain property holds only for this particular example. How can we generalize this result to the more general case of an arbitrary one-step transition matrix being squared to produce the two-step transition matrix? We reconsider the previous calculations as follows:

$$A^2 = A^2_{11} \qquad\qquad A^2_{12}$$

$$A^2_{21} \qquad\qquad A^2_{22}$$

$$= A_{11}A_{11} + A_{12}A_{21} \qquad A_{11}A_{12} + A_{12}A_{22}$$

$$A_{21}A_{11} + A_{22}A_{21} \qquad A_{21}A_{12} + A_{22}A_{22}$$

$$= P(1,1)P(1,1) + P(1,2)P(2,1) \quad P(1,1)P(1,2) + P(1,2)P(2,2)$$

$$P(2,1)P(1,1) + P(2,2)P(2,1) \quad P(2,1)P(1,2) + P(2,2)P(2,2)$$

$$= P(1,1,1) + P(1,2,1) \qquad\qquad P(1,1,2) + P(1,2,2)$$

$$P(2,1,1) + P(2,2,1) \qquad\qquad P(2,1,2) + P(2,2,2),$$

where

$$P(1,1,1) = P\{X(t+2) = 1,\ X(t+1) = 1 \mid X(t) = 1\},$$

$$P(1,2,1) = P\{X(t+2) = 1,\ X(t+1) = 2 \mid X(t) = 1\},$$

$$P(1,1,2) = P\{X(t+2) = 2, X(t+1) = 1 \mid X(t) = 1\},$$

$$P(1,2,2) = P\{X(t+2) = 2, X(t+1) = 2 \mid X(t) = 1\},$$

$$P(2,1,1) = P\{X(t+2) = 1, X(t+1) = 1 \mid X(t) = 2\},$$

$$P(2,2,1) = P\{X(t+2) = 1, X(t+1) = 2 \mid X(t) = 2\},$$

$$P(2,1,2) = P\{X(t+2) = 2, X(t+1) = 1 \mid X(t) = 2\},$$

and

$$P(2,2,2) = P\{X(t+2) = 2, X(t+1) = 2 \mid X(t) = 2\}.$$

Now

$$A^2 = \begin{matrix} P(1,1,1) + P(1,2,1) & P(1,1,2) + P(1,2,2) \\ P(2,1,1) + P(2,2,1) & P(2,1,2) + P(2,2,2). \end{matrix}$$

But notice that

$$P(1,1,1) + P(1,2,1) = P\{X(t+2) = 1, X(t+1) = 1 \mid X(t) = 1\}$$
$$+ P\{X(t+2) = 1, X(t+1) = 2 \mid X(t) = 1\}$$
$$= P\{X(t+2) = 1, [X(t+1) = 1 \cup X(t+1) = 2] \mid X(t) = 1\}$$
$$= P\{X(t+2) = 1, \text{universal set} \mid X(t) = 1\}$$
$$= P\{X(t+2) = 1 \mid X(t) = 1\},$$

$$P(1,1,2) + P(1,2,2) = P\{X(t+2) = 2, X(t+1) = 1 \mid X(t) = 1\}$$
$$+ P\{X(t+2) = 2, X(t+1) = 2 \mid X(t) = 1\}$$
$$= P\{X(t+2) = 2, [X(t+1) = 1 \cup X(t+1) = 2] \mid X(t) = 1\}$$
$$= P\{X(t+2) = 2, \text{universal set} \mid X(t) = 1\}$$
$$= P\{X(t+2) = 2 \mid X(t) = 1\},$$

$$P(2,1,1) + P(2,2,1) = P\{X(t+2) = 1, X(t+1) = 1 \mid X(t) = 2\}$$
$$+ P\{X(t+2) = 1, X(t+1) = 2 \mid X(t) = 2\}$$
$$= P\{X(t+2) = 1, [X(t+1) = 1 \cup X(t+1) = 2] \mid X(t) = 2\}$$
$$= P\{X(t+2) = 1, \text{universal set} \mid X(t) = 2\}$$
$$= P\{X(t+2) = 1 \mid X(t) = 2\},$$

and

$$P(2,1,2) + P(2,2,2) = P\{X(t+2) = 2, X(t+1) = 1 \mid X(t) = 2\}$$

$$+ P\{X(t+2) = 2, X(t+1) = 2 \mid X(t) = 2\}$$
$$= P\{X(t+2) = 2, [X(t+1) = 1 \cup X(t+1) = 2] \mid X(t) = 2\}$$
$$= P\{X(t+2) = 2, \text{universal set} \mid X(t) = 2\}$$
$$= P\{X(t+2) = 2 \mid X(t) = 2\}.$$

Then

$$A^2 = \begin{matrix} P(1,1,1) + P(1,2,1) & P(1,1,2) + P(1,2,2) \\ P(2,1,1) + P(2,2,1) & P(2,1,2) + P(2,2,2). \end{matrix}$$

$$= \begin{matrix} P\{X(t+2) = 1 \mid X(t) = 1\} & P\{X(t+2) = 2 \mid X(t) = 1\} \\ P\{X(t+2) = 1 \mid X(t) = 2\} & P\{X(t+2) = 2 \mid X(t) = 2\}, \end{matrix}$$

which is exactly the two-step transition matrix.

This result is quite remarkable. Consider that matrix multiplication was defined without consideration of transition matrices, Markov chains, or indeed of any probabilities. Yet the squaring of a transition matrix, the elements of which are the one-step transition probabilities of a Markov chain, results in a new matrix which is interpretable as the two-step transition matrix, the elements of which are the two-step transition probabilities of the Markov chain. It seems remarkable enough that squaring the one-step transition matrix of a Markov chain results in a stochastic matrix of any sort, let alone that it is the two-step transition matrix of the same Markov chain.

As one might guess, the one-step transition matrix may be raised to any integer power and the resulting matrix will not only be a stochastic matrix, but it will also be the multi-step transition matrix appropriate to govern the probabilities of shifting from one state to another in the number of steps dictated. This result can be proven using induction, but this will be deferred until the next subsection.

Let A be a three-by-three matrix given by

$$A = \begin{matrix} 0.1 & 0.3 & 0.2 \\ 0.3 & 0.3 & 0.3 \\ 0.4 & 0.4 & 0.4. \end{matrix}$$

Is A a transition matrix?

SOLUTION:

No. While all the elements of A are non-negative, the sums of these elements are not one in each row. The sum of the first row is

$$0.1 + 0.3 + 0.2 = 0.6,$$

the sum of the second row is

$$0.3 + 0.3 + 0.3 = 0.9,$$

and the sum of the third row is

$$0.4 + 0.4 + 0.4 = 1.2.$$

Let A be a four-by-three matrix given by

$$A = \begin{matrix} 0.5 & 0.3 & 0.2 \\ 0.4 & 0.3 & 0.3 \\ 0.2 & 0.4 & 0.4 \\ 0.3 & 0.6 & 0.1. \end{matrix}$$

Is A a transition matrix?

SOLUTION:

No. While all the elements of A are non-negative, and the sums of these elements are one in each row, A is not a square matrix. If A is not a square matrix, then it cannot serve as a transition matrix, because the states of the process are the same at one time as they are at the next. Thus there must be the same number of states at each time. The number of rows is the number of states at time t, and the number of columns is the number of states at time $t + 1$. These must be equal.

• PROBLEM 10–11

Let A be a four-by-four matrix given by

$$A = \begin{array}{cccc} 0.5 & 0.3 & 0.2 & 0.0 \\ 0.4 & 0.3 & 0.2 & 0.1 \\ 0.2 & 0.4 & -0.4 & 0.8 \\ 0.3 & 0.6 & 0.1 & 0.0. \end{array}$$

Is A a transition matrix?

SOLUTION:

No. While the sums of these elements are one in each row, and A is a square matrix, it also contains a negative element. Since each element of a transition matrix is interpreted as the probability of moving from one state (the state corresponding to the row) to another state (the state corresponding to the column), each element must be non-negative (since a probability cannot be negative).

• PROBLEM 10–12

Let A be a four-by-four matrix given by

$$A = \begin{array}{cccc} 0.5 & 0.3 & 0.2 & 0.0 \\ 0.4 & 0.3 & 0.2 & 0.1 \\ 0.2 & 0.4 & 0.1 & 0.3 \\ 0.3 & 0.6 & 0.1 & 0.0. \end{array}$$

Is A a transition matrix?

SOLUTION:

Yes. Each property of a transition matrix is satisfied, since A is a square matrix with non-negative elements which sum to one in each row.

• PROBLEM 10-13

Let A be the four-by-four transition matrix given in Problem 10–12,

$$A = \begin{matrix} 0.5 & 0.3 & 0.2 & 0.0 \\ 0.4 & 0.3 & 0.2 & 0.1 \\ 0.2 & 0.4 & 0.1 & 0.3 \\ 0.3 & 0.6 & 0.1 & 0.0. \end{matrix}$$

If the Markov process is in state 2 at time t, then what is the probability that it will go to state 3 at time $t + 1$?

SOLUTION:

Since A is a one-step transition matrix, we know that

$$A_{23} = P\{X(t + 1) = 3 \mid X(t) = 2\}.$$

But $A_{23} = 0.2$.

Therefore

$$P\{X(t + 1) = 3 \mid X(t) = 2\} = 0.2.$$

• PROBLEM 10-14

Let A be the four-by-four transition matrix given in Problem 10–12,

$$A = \begin{matrix} 0.5 & 0.3 & 0.2 & 0.0 \\ 0.4 & 0.3 & 0.2 & 0.1 \\ 0.2 & 0.4 & 0.1 & 0.3 \\ 0.3 & 0.6 & 0.1 & 0.0. \end{matrix}$$

If the Markov process is in state 3 at time t, then what is the probability that it will go to state 2 at time $t + 1$?

SOLUTION:

Since A is a one-step transition matrix, we know that

$$A_{32} = P\{X(t + 1) = 2 \mid X(t) = 3\}.$$

But

$$A_{32} = 0.4.$$

Therefore

$$P\{X(t + 1) = 2 \mid X(t) = 3\} = 0.4.$$

• PROBLEM 10–15

Let A be the four-by-four transition matrix given in Problem 10–12,

$$A = \begin{array}{cccc} 0.5 & 0.3 & 0.2 & 0.0 \\ 0.4 & 0.3 & 0.2 & 0.1 \\ 0.2 & 0.4 & 0.1 & 0.3 \\ 0.3 & 0.6 & 0.1 & 0.0. \end{array}$$

If the Markov process is in state 3 at time t, then what is the probability that it will stay in state 3 at time $t + 1$?

SOLUTION:

Since A is a one-step transition matrix, we know that

$$A_{33} = P\{X(t + 1) = 3 \mid X(t) = 3\}.$$

But

$$A_{33} = 0.1.$$

Therefore

$$P\{X(t + 1) = 3 \mid X(t) = 3\} = 0.1.$$

• PROBLEM 10–16

Using the one-step transition matrix from Problem 10–12, calculate the two-step transition matrix.

SOLUTION:

We recall that the two-step transition matrix of a Markov chain is given by

$$
A_2 = \begin{matrix}
A_{2;11} & A_{2;12} & A_{2;13} & A_{2;14} \\
A_{2;21} & A_{2;22} & A_{2;23} & A_{2;24} \\
A_{2;31} & A_{2;32} & A_{2;33} & A_{2;34} \\
A_{2;41} & A_{2;42} & A_{2;43} & A_{2;44}
\end{matrix}
$$

$$= A_1^2$$

$$= A_1 A_1$$

$$
= \begin{matrix}
0.5 & 0.3 & 0.2 & 0.0 \\
0.4 & 0.3 & 0.2 & 0.1 \\
0.2 & 0.4 & 0.1 & 0.3 \\
0.3 & 0.6 & 0.1 & 0.0
\end{matrix}
\quad \text{times} \quad
\begin{matrix}
0.5 & 0.3 & 0.2 & 0.0 \\
0.4 & 0.3 & 0.2 & 0.1 \\
0.2 & 0.4 & 0.1 & 0.3 \\
0.3 & 0.6 & 0.1 & 0.0.
\end{matrix}
$$

When multiplying a four-by-four matrix, A, by another four-by-four matrix, B, the (i,j) element of the resulting product matrix, AB, is

$$AB_{ij} = \Sigma_{k=1 \text{ to } 4} A_{ik} B_{kj}$$

$$= A_{i1} B_{ij} + A_{i2} B_{2j} + A_{i3} B_{3j} + A_{i4} B_{4j}.$$

When squaring a four-by-four matrix, A and B are equal, and therefore the (i,j) element of the squared matrix, A^2, is

$$A^2_{ij} = \Sigma_{k= \text{ to } 4} A_{ik} A_{kj}$$

$$= A_{i1} A_{ij} + A_{i2} A_{2j} + A_{i3} A_{3j} + A_{i4} A_{4j}.$$

We can use this expression to explicitly write the 16 elements of A^2. Doing so, we obtain

$$A^2 = \{A^2_{ij}\}$$

$$= \{A_{i1} A_{ij} + A_{i2} A_{2j} + A_{i3} A_{3j} + A_{i4} A_{4j}\}.$$

The first column of A^2 is

$$A_{11}A_{11} + A_{12}A_{21} + A_{13}A_{31} + A_{14}A_{41}$$

$$A^2{}_{\text{Column 1}} = \begin{array}{l} A_{21}A_{11} + A_{22}A_{21} + A_{23}A_{31} + A_{24}A_{41} \\ A_{31}A_{11} + A_{32}A_{21} + A_{33}A_{31} + A_{34}A_{41} \\ A_{41}A_{11} + A_{42}A_{21} + A_{43}A_{31} + A_{44}A_{41} \end{array}$$

$$= \begin{array}{l} (0.5)\,(0.5) + (0.3)\,(0.4) + (0.2)\,(0.2) + (0.0)\,(0.3) \\ (0.4)\,(0.5) + (0.3)\,(0.4) + (0.2)\,(0.2) + (0.1)\,(0.3) \\ (0.2)\,(0.5) + (0.4)\,(0.4) + (0.1)\,(0.2) + (0.3)\,(0.3) \\ (0.3)\,(0.5) + (0.6)(0.4) + (0.1)(0.2) + (0.0)(0.3) \end{array}$$

$$= \begin{array}{l} 0.25 + 0.12 + 0.04 + 0.00 \\ 0.20 + 0.12 + 0.04 + 0.03 \\ 0.10 + 0.16 + 0.02 + 0.09 \\ 0.15 + 0.24 + 0.02 + 0.00 \end{array}$$

$$= \begin{array}{l} 0.41 \\ 0.39 \\ 0.37 \\ 0.41. \end{array}$$

The second column of A^2 is

$$A_{11}A_{12} + A_{12}A_{22} + A_{13}A_{32} + A_{14}A_{42}$$

$$A^2{}_{\text{Column 2}} = \begin{array}{l} A_{21}A_{12} + A_{22}A_{22} + A_{23}A_{32} + A_{24}A_{42} \\ A_{31}A_{12} + A_{32}A_{22} + A_{33}A_{32} + A_{34}A_{42} \\ A_{41}A_{12} + A_{42}A_{22} + A_{43}A_{32} + A_{44}A_{42} \end{array}$$

$$= \begin{array}{l} (0.5)\,(0.3) + (0.3)\,(0.3) + (0.2)\,(0.4) + (0.0)\,(0.6) \\ (0.4)\,(0.3) + (0.3)\,(0.3) + (0.2)\,(0.4) + (0.1)\,(0.6) \\ (0.2)\,(0.3) + (0.4)\,(0.3) + (0.1)\,(0.4) + (0.3)\,(0.6) \\ (0.3)\,(0.3) + (0.6)\,(0.3) + (0.1)\,(0.4) + (0.0)\,(0.6) \end{array}$$

$$0.15 + 0.09 + 0.08 + 0.00$$
$$= 0.12 + 0.09 + 0.08 + 0.06$$
$$0.06 + 0.12 + 0.04 + 0.18$$
$$0.09 + 0.18 + 0.04 + 0.00$$

$$0.32$$
$$= 0.35$$
$$0.40$$
$$0.31.$$

The third column of A^2 is

$$A^2\text{Column 3} = \begin{matrix} A_{11}A_{13} + A_{12}A_{23} + A_{13}A_{33} + A_{14}A_{43} \\ A_{21}A_{13} + A_{22}A_{23} + A_{23}A_{33} + A_{24}A_{43} \\ A_{31}A_{13} + A_{32}A_{23} + A_{33}A_{33} + A_{34}A_{43} \\ A_{41}A_{13} + A_{42}A_{23} + A_{43}A_{33} + A_{44}A_{43} \end{matrix}$$

$$(0.5)\,(0.2) + (0.3)\,(0.2) + (0.2)\,(0.1) + (0.0)\,(0.1)$$
$$= (0.4)\,(0.2) + (0.3)\,(0.2) + (0.2)\,(0.1) + (0.1)\,(0.1)$$
$$(0.2)\,(0.2) + (0.4)\,(0.2) + (0.1)\,(0.1) + (0.3)\,(0.1)$$
$$(0.3)\,(0.2) + (0.6)\,(0.2) + (0.1)\,(0.1) + (0.0)\,(0.1)$$

$$0.10 + 0.06 + 0.02 + 0.00$$
$$= 0.08 + 0.06 + 0.02 + 0.01$$
$$0.04 + 0.08 + 0.01 + 0.03$$
$$0.06 + 0.12 + 0.01 + 0.00$$

$$0.18$$
$$= 0.17$$
$$0.16$$
$$0.19.$$

The fourth column of A^2 is

$$A^2_{\text{Column 4}} = \begin{matrix} A_{11}A_{14} + A_{12}A_{24} + A_{13}A_{34} + A_{14}A_{44} \\ A_{21}A_{14} + A_{22}A_{24} + A_{23}A_{34} + A_{24}A_{44} \\ A_{31}A_{14} + A_{32}A_{24} + A_{33}A_{34} + A_{34}A_{44} \\ A_{41}A_{14} + A_{42}A_{24} + A_{43}A_{34} + A_{44}A_{44} \end{matrix}$$

$$= \begin{matrix} (0.5)\,(0.0) + (0.3)\,(0.1) + (0.2)\,(0.3) + (0.0)\,(0.0) \\ (0.4)\,(0.0) + (0.3)\,(0.1) + (0.2)\,(0.3) + (0.1)\,(0.0) \\ (0.2)\,(0.0) + (0.4)\,(0.1) + (0.1)\,(0.3) + (0.3)\,(0.0) \\ (0.3)\,(0.0) + (0.6)\,(0.1) + (0.1)\,(0.3) + (0.0)\,(0.0) \end{matrix}$$

$$= \begin{matrix} 0.00 + 0.03 + 0.06 + 0.00 \\ 0.00 + 0.03 + 0.06 + 0.00 \\ 0.00 + 0.04 + 0.03 + 0.00 \\ 0.00 + 0.06 + 0.03 + 0.00 \end{matrix}$$

$$= \begin{matrix} 0.09 \\ 0.09 \\ 0.07 \\ 0.09. \end{matrix}$$

Thus

$$A^2 = \begin{matrix} 0.41 & 0.32 & 0.18 & 0.09 \\ 0.39 & 0.35 & 0.17 & 0.09 \\ 0.37 & 0.40 & 0.16 & 0.07 \\ 0.41 & 0.31 & 0.19 & 0.09. \end{matrix}$$

Notice this is a stochastic matrix.

• **PROBLEM 10–17**

Let A be the four-by-four transition matrix given in Problem 10–12,

$$A = \begin{matrix} 0.5 & 0.3 & 0.2 & 0.0 \\ 0.4 & 0.3 & 0.2 & 0.1 \\ 0.2 & 0.4 & 0.1 & 0.3 \\ 0.3 & 0.6 & 0.1 & 0.0. \end{matrix}$$

If the Markov process is in state 3 at time t, then what is the probability that it will stay in state 3 at time $t + 2$?

SOLUTION:

In Problem 10–16 we found the two-step transition matrix to be

$$A^2 = \begin{matrix} 0.41 & 0.32 & 0.18 & 0.09 \\ 0.39 & 0.35 & 0.17 & 0.09 \\ 0.37 & 0.40 & 0.16 & 0.07 \\ 0.41 & 0.31 & 0.19 & 0.09, \end{matrix}$$

so

$$A^2_{33} = P\{X(t + 2) = 3 \mid X(t) = 3\}.$$

But

$$A^2_{33} = 0.16.$$

Therefore

$$P\{X(t + 2) = 3 \mid X(t) = 3\} = 0.16.$$

• **PROBLEM 10–18**

Let A be the four-by-four transition matrix given in Problem 10–12,

$$A = \begin{matrix} 0.5 & 0.3 & 0.2 & 0.0 \\ 0.4 & 0.3 & 0.2 & 0.1 \\ 0.2 & 0.4 & 0.1 & 0.3 \\ 0.3 & 0.6 & 0.1 & 0.0. \end{matrix}$$

If the Markov process is in state 4 at time t, then what is the probability that it will go to state 1 at time $t + 2$?

SOLUTION:

In Problem 10–16 we found the two-step transition matrix to be

$$A^2 = \begin{matrix} 0.41 & 0.32 & 0.18 & 0.09 \\ 0.39 & 0.35 & 0.17 & 0.09 \\ 0.37 & 0.40 & 0.16 & 0.07 \\ 0.41 & 0.31 & 0.19 & 0.09, \end{matrix}$$

so

$$A^2{}_{41} = P\{X(t + 2) = 1 \mid X(t) = 4\}.$$

But

$$A^2{}_{41} = 0.41.$$

Therefore

$$P\{X(t + 2) = 1 \mid X(t) = 4\} = 0.41.$$

• PROBLEM 10-19

Let A be the four-by-four transition matrix given in Problem 10–12,

$$A = \begin{matrix} 0.5 & 0.3 & 0.2 & 0.0 \\ 0.4 & 0.3 & 0.2 & 0.1 \\ 0.2 & 0.4 & 0.1 & 0.3 \\ 0.3 & 0.6 & 0.1 & 0.0. \end{matrix}$$

If the Markov process is in state 4 at time t, then what is the probability that it will go to state 2 at time $t + 2$?

SOLUTION:

In Problem 10–16 we found the two-step transition matrix to be

$$A^2 = \begin{matrix} 0.41 & 0.32 & 0.18 & 0.09 \\ 0.39 & 0.35 & 0.17 & 0.09 \\ 0.37 & 0.40 & 0.16 & 0.07 \\ 0.41 & 0.31 & 0.19 & 0.09, \end{matrix}$$

so

$$A^2{}_{42} = P\{X(t + 2) = 2 \mid X(t) = 4\}.$$

But

$$A^2{}_{42} = 0.31.$$

Therefore

$$P\{X(t + 2) = 2 \mid X(t) = 4\} = 0.31.$$

✳✳✳✳✳✳

REVIEW OF INDUCTION

Since induction is actually quite useful in the study of Markov chains and other denumerable stochastic processes, we will explore it as a general method of proof. Induction can be used to prove far more about Markov chains than that the multi-step transition matrix can be obtained by raising the one-step transition matrix to the appropriate power.

The goal of induction is to prove that a certain statement is true for an entire set of indexed conditions. For our purposes the conditions will be indexed by positive integers. Thus we wish to prove that a certain statement is true for all positive integers. In this particular application of induction we wish to prove that the n-step transition matrix of a given Markov chain, say A_n, can be obtained by raising the one-step transition matrix or the Markov chain, A_1, to the nth power, or that

$$A_n = A_1{}^n$$

for all positive integer-valued n. We already have proved this result for $n = 2$, since

$$A_2 = A_1{}^2,$$

and this result is clearly true for $n = 1$, since

$$A_1 = A_1{}^1.$$

But now we want to appeal to induction to furnish a proof for $n = 3, 4,...$

The first step of a proof by induction is to prove the statement for the first case. We wish to prove that

$$A_n = A_1{}^n$$

for $n = 1, 2, 3, ...$ The first case is, therefore, $n = 1$. We have already established that the statement is true for $n = 1$.

The second step of a proof by induction is to assume that the result is true for $n = k$. The third step of a proof by induction is to then prove that the statement is true for $n = k + 1$.

Why do you suppose that this series of steps will lead to a valid proof that the statement is true for $n = 1, 2, 3,...$? Of course the statement was proved true for $n = 1$. We know that if the statement is true for $n = k$, then it must also be true for $n = k + 1$.

Let $k = 1$. Then the statement is true for $n = k = 1$, so it must also be true for $n = k + 1 = 1 + 1 = 2$. Now let $k = 2$. Since the statement is true for $n = k = 2$, it must also be true for $n = k + 1 = 2 + 1 = 3$. This logical process can be repeated indefinitely, and it would then be seen that the statement would have to be true for all positive integers. Hopefully you can see this without going through the process for an infinitely long time!

We wish to use induction to prove that

$$A_n = A_1{}^n,$$

for all n, where A_1 is the one-step transition matrix and A_n is the n-step transition matrix. We will offer two different yet similar proofs, both making use of induction. The first proof conditions on the state of the Markov chain at time $t + 1$, and the second proof conditions on the state of the Markov chain at time $t + k$.

The first step of either proof is to prove the statement for $n = 1$. We have already proven the statement for both $n = 1$ and $n = 2$. That is, we have proven that

$$A_2 = A_1{}^2,$$

and it holds true for $n = 1$ by definition of the one-step transition matrix A_1.

Now we assume that for $n = k$ it is true that

$$A_k = A_1{}^k,$$

and we endeavor to prove that for $n = k + 1$

$$A_{k+1} = A_1{}^{k+1}.$$

For the first proof of this we condition on the state of the Markov chain at time $t + 1$. Suppose that there are S states of the Markov chain, and for convenience we label these S states by 1, 2, 3, ..., S. Now to go from state i at time t to state j at time $t + k + 1$ the Markov chain must be at one of the S states at time $t + 1$. So there are S different paths connecting state i at time t to state j at time $t + k + 1$, and these S paths correspond to the S different states that the Markov chain may be in at time $t + 1$. Since these S paths are mutually exclusive events (the Markov chain can only be at one state at a given time), we know that

$$A_{k+1;ij} = P\{X(t + k + 1) = j \mid X(t) = i\}$$

$$= P\{X(t + k + 1) = j \cap \text{the universal set} \mid X(t) = i\}$$

(since any set, A, intersected with the universal set is the original set A)

$$= P\{X(t + k + 1) = j \cap [\cup_{s = 1 \text{ to } S} X(t + 1) = s] \mid X(t) = i\}$$

(since the S states at time $t + 1$ are exhaustive and mutually exclusive, and hence their union is the universal set)

$$= P\{[\cup_{s\,=\,1\ to\ S}X(t + k + 1) = j \cap X(t + 1) = s] \mid X(t) = i\}$$

(follows from set theory)

$$= \Sigma_{s\,=\,1\ to\ S}P\{X(t + k + 1) = j \cap X(t + 1) = s \mid X(t) = i\}$$

(because the S sets are mutually exclusive, so their probabilities are additive)

$$= \Sigma_{s\,=\,to\ S}[P\{X(t + 1) = s \mid X(t) = i\}$$
$$\times P\{X(t + k + 1) = j \mid X(t + 1) = s,\ X(t) = i\}]$$

(by the definition of conditional probability)

$$= \Sigma_{s\,=\,1\ to\ S}[P\{X(t + 1) = s \mid X(t) = i\}$$
$$\times P\{X(t + k + 1) = j \mid X(t + 1) = s]$$

(by the Markov property)

$$= \Sigma_{s\,=\,1\ to\ S}[P\{X(t + 1) = s \mid X(t) = i\}$$
$$\times P\{X(t + k) = j \mid X(t) = s]$$

(because the transition probabilities are homogenous in time, meaning they do not change over time, so the probability of going from state s at time $t + 1$ to state j at time $t + k + 1$ is the same as the probability of going from state s at time t to state j at time $t + k$)

$$= \Sigma_s = 1\ to\ S[A_{1;i}s\ times\ A_{k;sj}]$$

(by the definition of the one-step transition matrix, A_1, and the k-step transition matrix, A_k)

= the (i,j) element of the product of the matrix A_1 multiplied by the matrix A_k

(by the definition of matrix multiplication)

= the (i,j) element of the product of the matrix A_1 multiplied by the matrix $A_1{}^k$

(by the induction assumption that $A_k = A_1{}^k$)

= the (i,j) element of the matrix $A_1{}^{k+1}$

(since $A_1 A_1{}^k = A_1{}^{k+1}$).

This proves the result. The second proof is essentially the same, but it is, nevertheless, instructive to consider it anyway. This time, instead of conditioning on the state of the Markov chain at time $t + 1$, we condition on the state of the Markov chain at time $t + k$. Once again,

$$A_{k+1;ij} = P\{X(t+k+1) = j \mid X(t) = i\}$$

$$= P\{X(t+k+1) = j \cap \text{the universal set} \mid X(t) = i\}$$

(since any set, A, intersected with the universal set is the original set A)

$$= P\{X(t+k+1) = j \cap [\cup_{s=1 \text{ to } s} X(t+k) = s] \mid X(t) = i\}$$

(since the S states at time $t + 1$ are exhaustive and mutually exclusive, and hence their union is the universal set)

$$= P\{[\cup_{s=1 \text{ to } s} X(t+k+1) = j \cap X(t+k) = s] \mid X(t) = i\}$$

(follows from set theory)

$$= \Sigma_{s=1 \text{ to } s} P\{X(t+k+1) = j \cap X(t+k) = s \mid X(t) = i\}$$

(because the S sets are mutually exclusive, so their probabilities are additive)

$$= \Sigma_{s=1 \text{ to } s}[P\{X(t+k) = s \mid X(t) = i\}$$
$$\times P\{X(t+k+1) = j \mid X(t+k) = s, X(t) = i\}]$$

(by the definition of conditional probability)

$$= \Sigma_{s=1 \text{ to } s}[P\{X(t+k) = s \mid X(t) = i\}$$
$$\times P\{X(t+k+1) = j \mid X(t+k) = s]$$

(by the Markov property)

$$= \Sigma_{s=1 \text{ to } s}[P\{X(t+k) = s \mid X(t) = i\} \times P\{X(t+1) = j \mid X(t) = s]$$

(because the transition probabilities are homogenous in time, meaning they do not change over time, so the probability of going from state s at time $t + k$ to state j at time $t + k + 1$ is the same as the probability of going from state s at time t to state j at time $t + 1$)

$$= \Sigma_{s=1 \text{ to } s}[A_{k;is} \times A_{1;sj}]$$

(by the definition of the one-step transition matrix, A_1, and the k-step transition matrix, A_k)

= the (i,j) element of the product of the matrix A_k multiplied by the matrix A_1

(by the definition of matrix multiplication)

= the (i,j) element of the product of the matrix $A_1{}^k$ multiplied by the matrix A_1

(by the induction assumption that $A_k = A_1{}^k$)

$\quad$ = the (i,j) element of the matrix $A_1{}^{k+1}$

(since $A_1{}^k A_1 = A_1{}^{k+1}$).

• PROBLEM 10-20

Prove, by induction, that for all positive integers n

$\quad n^2 > 0.$

SOLUTION:

Notice that this proof does not require induction, since a simple proof can be offered without induction. Namely, if n is positive, then n^2 is a product of positive terms, which we all know must be positive. But rarely is a legitimate proof of this assertion actually provided.

To introduce induction as a general method of proof we use induction to prove this statement. First, is the statement true for $n = 1$? Since

$\quad 1^2 = 1$

$\quad\quad > 0,$

the statement is true for $n = 1$.

Next assume that this is a true statement for $n = k$. Then is the statement also true for $n = k + 1$? We write

$\quad (k + 1)^2 = k^2 + 2k + 1.$

We know that

$\quad k^2 > 0$

by the assumption that the statement

$\quad n^2 > 0$

is true for $n = k$. Since

$\quad k > 0$

(also part of the assumption),

$2k > 0$.

Finally

$1 > 0$.

So $(k + 1)^2$ can be expressed as a sum of three positive terms, so it must also be positive. The proof is complete.

Prove by induction that every positive integer is either even or odd. That is, prove that if n is a positive integer, then for some other positive integer m either

$n = 2m$

or

$n = 2m - 1$.

SOLUTION:

We first check this statement for $n = 1$. Since

$1 = 2(1) - 1$,

one is odd. Now assume that the statement is true for $n = k$, or that k is either even or odd. First consider the case in which k is even. Then

$k = 2m$,

so $k + 1 = 2m + 1$

$= 2(m + 1) - 1$,

and $k + 1$ is odd.

On the other hand, if k is odd, then

$k = 2m - 1$

so $k + 1 = (2m - 1) + 1$

$= 2m$,

and k is even. This completes the proof.

• **PROBLEM 10–22**

Prove, by induction, that if X_1, x_2, ..., X_n are mutually exclusive events, then

$$P\{X_1 \cup X_2 \cup ... \cup X_n\} = \Sigma_{i=1 \text{ to } n} P\{X_i\}$$

for all positive integers n.

SOLUTION:

We know from a previous chapter that this statement is true for $n = 2$. Namely, if X_1 and X_2 are mutually exclusive events, then

$$P\{X_1 \cup X_2\} = P\{X_1\} + P\{X_2\}.$$

This is the first step of the proof by induction. Now for the second step, assume that the statement is true for $n = k$. Now to prove that the statement is true for $n = k + 1$,

$$P\{\cup_{i=1 \text{ to } k+1} X_i\} = P\{X_1 \cup X_2 \cup ... \cup X_{(k+1)}\}$$

$$= P\{A \cup B\}$$

(letting $A = X_1 \cup X_2 \cup ... \cup Xk$ and $B = X_{(k+1)}$, for simplicity)

$$= P\{A\} + P\{B\}$$

(because as defined, A and B are still mutually exclusive)

$$= P\{X_1 \cup X_2 \cup ... \cup X_k\} + P\{X_{(k+1)}\}$$

(by definition of A and B)

$$= \Sigma_{i=1 \text{ to } k} P\{X_i\} + P\{X_{(k+1)}\}$$

(by the induction assumption that the statement is true for $n = k$)

$$= \Sigma_{i=1 \text{ to } k+1} P\{Xi\}$$

(by simple addition).

This completes the proof.

• **PROBLEM 10–23**

Prove, by induction, that if X_1, X_2, ..., X_n are mutually independent events, then

$$P\{X_1 \cap X_2 \cap ... \cap X_n\} = \pi_{i=1 \text{ to } n} P\{Xi\}$$

for all positive integers n.

SOLUTION:

We know from a previous chapter that this statement is true for $n = 2$. Namely, if X_1 and X_2 are mutually independent events, then

$$P\{X_1 \cap X_2\} = P\{X_1\}P\{X_2\}.$$

This is the first step of the proof by induction. Now for the second step, assume that the statement is true for $n = k$. Now to prove that the statement is true for $n = k + 1$,

$$P\{\cap_{i=1 \text{ to } k+1}X_i\} = P\{X_1 \cap X_2 \cap ... \cap X_{(k+1)}\}$$

$$= P\{A \cap B\}$$

(letting $A = X_1 \cap X_2 \cap ... \cap X_k$ and $B = X_{(k+1)}$, for simplicity)

$$= P\{A\}P\{B\}$$

(because as defined, A and B are still mutually independent)

$$= P\{X_1 \cap X_2 \cap ... \cap X_k\}P\{X_{(k+1)}\}$$

(by definition of A and B)

$$= \pi_{i=1 \text{ to } k}P\{X_i\} \times P\{X_{(k+1)}\}$$

(by the induction assumption that the statement is true for $n = k$)

$$= \pi_{i=1 \text{ to } k+1}P\{X_i\}$$

(by simple multiplication).

This completes the proof.

• PROBLEM 10-24

Prove, by induction, that if X_1, X_2, ..., X_n are events which are not necessarily mutually exclusive, then

$$P\{X_1 \cup X_2 \cup ... \cup X_n\} \leq \Sigma_{i=1 \text{ to } n} P\{Xi\}$$

for all positive integers n.

SOLUTION:

We know from a previous chapter that this statement is true for $n = 2$. Namely, if X_1 and X_2 are not necessarily mutually exclusive events, then

$$P\{X_1 \cup X_2\} \leq P\{X_1\} + P\{X_2\}.$$

This is the first step of the proof by induction. Now for the second step, assume that the statement is true for $n = k$. Now to prove that the statement is true for $n = k + 1$,

$$P\{\cup_{i=1 \text{ to } k+1} X_i\} = P\{X_1 \cup X_2 \cup ... \cup X_{(k+1)}\}$$

$$= P\{A \cup B\}$$

(letting $A = X_1 \cup X_2 \cup ... \cup X_k$ and $B = X_{(k+1)}$, for simplicity)

$$\leq P\{A\} + P\{B\}$$

(we know the statement is true for $n = 2$)

$$= P\{X_1 \cup X_2 \cup ... \cup X_k\} + P\{X_{(k+1)}\}$$

(by definition of A and B)

$$\leq \Sigma_{i=1 \text{ to } k} P\{X_i\} + P\{X_{(k+1)}\}$$

(by the induction assumption that the statement is true for $n = k$)

$$= \Sigma_{i=1 \text{ to } k+1} P\{X_i\}$$

(by simple addition).

This completes the proof.

✶✶✶✶✶✶

REVIEW OF MARKOV CHAINS

Having familiarized ourselves with transition matrices, the key tools in studying and analyzing Markov chains, we are well prepared to pursue this topic. In most cases a real-world problem will be given. The task will be to decide on whether or not the Markov property can reasonably be expected to hold for the particular application under study, and, if so, to determine the one-step transition matrix. This would be sufficient to determine all higher-order transition matrices.

First we must define some concepts which are related to Markov chains. A state of a Markov chain, say state i, is said to be an absorbing state if

$$A_{1;ii} = 1$$

and $A_{1;ij} = 0$ for all j not equal to i.

This definition says that once the Markov chain lands in state i, it will remain in state i thereafter, since the probability is zero that the chain will move to a different state, and the probability is one that it will remain in state i.

States i and j are said to be commutable if there exists a positive integer n such that $A_{n;ij} > 0$ and there exists a positive integer m such that $A_{m;ji} > 0$. This definition says that if the Markov chain is in state i, then there is a positive probability that the Markov chain will go to state j (but it may take a while), and that if the Markov chain is in state j, then there is a positive probability that the Markov chain will go to state i (but it also may take a while).

Two states which are commutable are said to be in the same class. It is true that if states i and j are commutable and states j and k are commutable, then states i and k must also be commutable. This is because under the assumptions the Markov chain can go from state i to state j with positive probability (p_1) in a finite number (n) of steps, and likewise the Markov chain can go from state j to state k with positive probability (p_2) in a finite number (m) of steps. But then

$$P\{X(t + n + m) = k \mid X(t) = i\}$$

$$= P\{X(t + n + m) = k, \text{ universal set} \mid X(t) = i\}$$

(since any set intersected with the universal set is the original set)

$$= P\{X(t + n + m) = k, \cup_{s = 1 \text{ to } s} X(t + n) = s \mid X(t) = i\}$$

(since $\cup_{s = 1 \text{ to } s} X(t + n) = s$ is the universal set)

$$= \Sigma_{s = 1 \text{ to } s} P\{X(t + n + m) = k, \ X(t + n) = s \mid X(t) = i\}$$

(since these sets are mutually exclusive)

$$\geq P\{X(t + n + m) = k, \ X(t + n) = j \mid X(t) = i\}$$

(since the sum of non-negative quantities cannot be less than any one of these quantities)

$$= P\{X(t + n) = j \mid X(t) = i\} \times P\{X(t + n + m) = k \mid X(t + n) = j, \ X(t) = i\}$$

(by the definition of conditional probability)

$$= P\{X(t + n) = j \mid X(t) = i\} \times P\{X(t + n + m) = k \mid X(t + n) = j\}$$

(by the Markov property)

$$= P\{X(t + n) = j \mid X(t) = i\} \times P\{X(t + m) = k \mid X(t) = j\}$$

(because the transition probabilities are time-homogeneous)

$$= A_{n;ij} \times A_{m;jk}$$

(by definition of the transition matrices)

$$> 0$$

(by assumption).

We can likewise show that the Markov chain can go from state k to state i in finitely many steps with positive probability. Thus if states i and j commute, and if states j and k commute, then states i and k also commute.

A state of a Markov chain is said to be persistent if the chain will, with probability one, return to that state infinitely often. Otherwise the state is said to be transient. Let

$$B_{n;i} = P\{X(t + n) = i, \ X(t + j) \text{ is not } i \text{ for } j = 1,2,\ldots,n - 1 \mid X(t) = i\}.$$

That is, $B_{n;i}$ is the probability, conditional on the fact that the Markov chain is in state i at time t, that the Markov chain will return to state i for the first time after n steps. It turns out that state i is persistent if $\Sigma_{n = 1 \text{ to } \infty} B_{n;i} = 1$, because

$$P\{\text{return to state } i \text{ at some time} \mid X(t) = i\} =$$

$$P\{\text{first return to state } i \text{ at time } t + n \mid X(t) = i\}$$

$$= \Sigma_{n = 1 \text{ to } \infty} P\{X(t + n) = i, \ X(t + j)$$

$$\text{is not } i \text{ for } j = 1,2,\ldots n - 1 \mid X(t) = i\}$$

(mutually exclusive events)

$$= \Sigma_{n = 1 \text{ to infinity}} B_{n;i}.$$

It is also true that state i is persistent if $\Sigma_{n = 1 \text{ to infinity}} A_{n;ii} = $ infinity, and state i is transient otherwise. If a Markov chain has only finitely many states, then at least one of these states must be persistent (because otherwise there would be a positive probability of visiting each state only finitely often, which is clearly impossible). If state i is commutable with state j, and state j is a persistent state, then state i must also be a persistent state (because the Markov chain will, with probability one, visit state j infinitely often, and each time it does it has a positive probability of visiting state i, so it must, with probability one, visit state i infinitely often).

Using these results, it is seen that a Markov chain with finitely many states and only one class must have all persistent states. This is because at least one state must be persistent (since there are only finitely many states). Since there is but one class, all states commute. Any state which commutes with a persistent state must also be persistent. Therefore, all states must be persistent.

As an example of a Markov chain, suppose that three soccer players kick around a soccer ball. Suppose that the players are standing in a triangle, and that each player will pass to the player on his left with probability 0.3, and will pass to the player on his right with probability 0.7. These probabilities are independent of any previous patterns of passing the soccer ball. Label the players as #1, #2, and #3. These are the three states of the stochastic process. Is this a Markov chain? If so, then what is the transition matrix?

This stochastic process is, in fact, a Markov chain. This is because the probability distribution of the state of the process at a given time, conditionally on the previous history of the stochastic process, depends only on the state at the most recent time. The transition matrix is

$$A_1 = \begin{matrix} 0.0 & 0.7 & 0.3 \\ 0.3 & 0.0 & 0.7 \\ 0.7 & 0.3 & 0.0. \end{matrix}$$

Any row of the one-step transition matrix can be viewed as a conditional probability distribution. That is, the ith row of the one-step transition matrix is the probability distribution of the state of the Markov process at time $t + 1$ conditional on the fact that the state of the Markov process at time t is i. What would happen if the state of the Markov chain at any given time is independent of the past of this Markov chain? In this case, the conditional probability distribution of the state of the Markov chain at the present time would not depend on the past, so in particular it would not depend on the most recent state. This state is the row of the one-step transition matrix. Therefore, such independence would entail that the one-step transition matrix, and hence all higher-order transition matrices, would have all identical rows.

• PROBLEM 10–25

Let i and j be absorbing states of a Markov chain. What can you say about the commutability of states i and j?

SOLUTION:

Since both states i and j are absorbing, we know that once the Markov chain goes to state i it must stay there forever after, and hence it cannot go to state j. The converse is true as well. Therefore states i and j cannot be commutable.

• PROBLEM 10–26

Let i and j be non-absorbing states of a Markov chain. What can you say about the commutability of states i and j?

SOLUTION:

Nothing can be said about the commutability of states i and j. Consider, for example, a Markov chain with one-step transition matrix

$$A_1 = 0.5 \qquad 0.5$$
$$0.5 \qquad 0.5.$$

Clearly neither state 1 nor state 2 is absorbing. It is also clear that these two states are commutative. Now consider a Markov chain with one-step transition matrix

$$A_1 = 0.0 \qquad 1.0 \qquad 0.0$$
$$0.0 \qquad 1.0 \qquad 0.0$$
$$0.0 \qquad 1.0 \qquad 0.0.$$

Clearly neither state 1 nor state 3 is absorbing. But state 2 is absorbing, and with probability one the Markov chain will go to state 2, and stay there forever after that, from either state 1 or state 3. Therefore there is no chance that the Markov chain will ever return to state 1 once it goes to state 3, nor can it ever return to state 3 from state 1. In this example states 1 and 3 are not absorbing yet are not commutative.

• PROBLEM 10–27

Let i be an absorbing state and let j be a non-absorbing state of a Markov chain. What can you say about the commutability of states i and j?

SOLUTION:

Since i is an absorbing state of the Markov chain, the Markov chain can never reach state j from state i. Therefore states i and j are not commutative.

• PROBLEM 10–28

Let a Markov chain have one-step transition matrix

$$0.2 \qquad 0.3 \qquad 0.3 \qquad 0.2$$
$$A_1 = 0.0 \qquad 1.0 \qquad 0.0 \qquad 0.0$$
$$0.4 \qquad 0.4 \qquad 0.1 \qquad 0.1$$
$$0.0 \qquad 1.0 \qquad 0.0 \qquad 0.0.$$

Classify each state as either absorbing or non-absorbing.

SOLUTION:

Since

$$A_{1;11} = 0.2$$

$$< 1.0,$$

state 1 is non-absorbing. Since

$$A_{1;22} = 1.0,$$

state 2 is absorbing. Since

$$A_{1;33} = 0.1$$

$$< 1.0,$$

state 3 is non-absorbing. Since

$$A_{1;44} = 0.0$$

$$< 1.0,$$

state 4 is non-absorbing.

• PROBLEM 10-29

Which pairs of states from the Markov chain described in Problem 10–28 are commutative?

SOLUTION:

There are

$$C(4,2) = 4! / [2!2!]$$

$$= 24 / [(2) (2)]$$

$$= 24 / 4$$

$$= 6$$

pairs of states. Considering each of these six pairs of states reveals that states 1 and 2 do not commute because state 2 is absorbing. States 1 and 3 do commute because

$$A_{1;13} = 0.3$$

> 0.0

and

$$A_{1;31} = 0.4$$

$> 0.0.$

States 1 and 4 do not commute because once the Markov chain is in state 4, it will go directly to state 2, since $A_{1;42} = 1.0$, and it will then stay in state 2 forever after. Thus it can never return to state 1.

States 2 and 3 do not commute because state 2 is absorbing. Likewise, states 2 and 4 do not commute.

States 3 and 4 do not commute because once the Markov chain is in state 4, it will go directly to state 2, since $A_{1;42} = 1.0$, and it will then stay in state 2 forever after. Thus it can never return to state 3.

• PROBLEM 10-30

Consider the Markov chain whose transition matrix appears in Problem 10–28. What are the classes of this Markov chain?

SOLUTION:

Since state 2 is absorbing, it cannot commute with any other state, so it must form its own class. Since state 4 does not commute with any other state, it also forms its own class. Finally, since states 1 and 3 do commute, they combine to form a class. Thus the three classes are $\{1,3\}$, $\{2\}$, and $\{4\}$.

• PROBLEM 10-31

Consider the transition matrix in Problem 10–28. Is state 2 transient or persistent?

SOLUTION:

Since

$$A_{1;22} = 1,$$

it is also true that

$$A_{n;22} = 1 \text{ for all } n.$$

Therefore

$$\Sigma_{n = 1 \text{ to infinity}} A_{n;22} = \Sigma_{n = 1 \text{ to infinity}} 1 = \text{infinity},$$

so state 2 is persistent. In fact, any absorbing state is persistent.

• PROBLEM 10-32

Consider a stochastic process in which the state of the process is the current down of a football game. Now there are four downs, and at any given down the choices are (excluding the possibility of a turn-over, a touchdown, a safety, or a punt) a first down or an increment of one to the current down. That is, if it is first down, then the next down can either be a first down or a second down. The probabilities governing this stochastic process are as follows:

$P\{\text{first down} \mid \text{first down}\} = 0.2,$

$P\{\text{first down} \mid \text{second down}\} = 0.3,$

$P\{\text{first down} \mid \text{third down}\} = 0.4,$

and $P\{\text{first down} \mid \text{fourth down}\} = 0.5.$

After fourth down, if the first down is not made, then the ball goes over to the other team. Call this state 5. Assume that the other team, if they get the ball, will not turn the ball over.

Assume also that this stochastic process is a Markov chain. What is the one-step transition matrix?

SOLUTION:

The transition matrix is given by

$$A_1 = \begin{array}{ccccc}
0.2 & 0.8 & 0.0 & 0.0 & 0.0 \\
0.3 & 0.0 & 0.7 & 0.0 & 0.0 \\
0.4 & 0.0 & 0.0 & 0.6 & 0.0 \\
0.5 & 0.0 & 0.0 & 0.0 & 0.5 \\
0.0 & 0.0 & 0.0 & 0.0 & 1.0.
\end{array}$$

● **PROBLEM 10-33**

Suppose that a basketball player shoots six foul shots, and that the success probability of each shot is 0.6, independent of any previous results. Let the state of a stochastic process be defined as

$X(t) = 0$ if the tth shot misses

and $X(t) = 1$ if the tth shot scores,

for $t = 1, 2,..., 10$. Is this stochastic process a Markov chain? If so, then what is its one-step transition matrix? What is its two-step transition matrix?

SOLUTION:

The current state of the stochastic process is independent of the past states of the stochastic process. This means that conditionally on the past of this stochastic process the present state does not depend on any of this past, including any part of the past prior to the most recent state. In fact,

$$P\{X(t + 1) = 1 \mid X(1), X(2), ..., X(t)\} = 0.6$$

$$= P\{X(t + 1) = 1 \mid X(t)\},$$

and $P\{X(t + 1) = 0 \mid X(1), X(2), ..., X(t)\} = 0.4$

$$= P\{X(t + 1) = 0 \mid X(t)\}.$$

Thus this stochastic process is a Markov chain.

The one-step transition matrix of this Markov chain is

$$A_1 = \begin{matrix} 0.4 & 0.6 \\ 0.4 & 0.6, \end{matrix}$$

since

$$P\{X(t+1) = 1\} = 0.6$$

regardless of the value of $X(t)$. The two-step transition matrix of this Markov chain is

$$A_2 = \begin{matrix} 0.4 & 0.6 \\ 0.4 & 0.6, \end{matrix}$$

since

$$P\{X(t+2) = 1\} = 0.6$$

regardless of the value of $X(t)$. We could also compute the two-step transition matrix directly as follows:

$$A_2 = A_1{}^2$$

$$= A_1 \text{ times } A_1$$

$$= \begin{matrix} 0.4 & 0.6 \\ 0.4 & 0.6 \end{matrix} \quad \text{times} \quad \begin{matrix} 0.4 & 0.6 \\ 0.4 & 0.6 \end{matrix}$$

$$= \begin{matrix} (0.4)\,(0.4) + (0.6)\,(0.4) & (0.4)\,(0.6) + (0.6)\,(0.6) \\ (0.4)\,(0.4) + (0.6)\,(0.4) & (0.4)\,(0.6) + (0.6)\,(0.6) \end{matrix}$$

$$= \begin{matrix} 0.16 + 0.24 & 0.24 + 0.36 \\ 0.16 + 0.24 & 0.24 + 0.36 \end{matrix}$$

$$= \begin{matrix} 0.4 & 0.6 \\ 0.4 & 0.6. \end{matrix}$$

• PROBLEM 10–34

Suppose that a basketball player shoots six foul shots, and that the success probability of each shot depends on the result of the previous shot. In particular, if the previous shot was successful, then the success probability of the next shot is 0.7, independent of the results of any shots before the most recent one. If the previous shot was not successful, then the success probability of the next shot is 0.5, independent of the results of any shots before the most recent one. Let the state of a stochastic process be defined as

$X(t) = 0$ if the tth shot misses

and $X(t) = 1$ if the tth shot scores,

for $t = 1, 2, \ldots, 10$. Is this stochastic process a Markov chain? If so, then what is its one-step transition matrix? What is its two-step transition matrix?

SOLUTION:

We note that

$$P\{X(t+1) = 1 \mid X(1), X(2), \ldots, X(t) = 1\} = 0.7$$
$$= P\{X(t+1) = 1 \mid X(t) = 1\},$$
$$P\{X(t+1) = 1 \mid X(1), X(2), \ldots, X(t) = 0\} = 0.5$$
$$= P\{X(t+1) = 1 \mid X(t) = 0\},$$
$$P\{X(t+1) = 0 \mid X(1), X(2), \ldots, X(t) = 1\} = 0.3$$
$$= P\{X(t+1) = 0 \mid X(t) = 1\},$$

and $$P\{X(t+1) = 0 \mid X(1), X(2), \ldots, X(t) = 0\} = 0.5$$
$$= P\{X(t+1) = 0 \mid X(t) = 0\}.$$

Thus this stochastic process is a Markov chain.

The one-step transition matrix of this Markov chain is

$A_1 = 0.5 \qquad 0.5$

$\qquad\quad 0.3 \qquad 0.7.$

The two-step transition matrix of this Markov chain is

$A_2 = A_1{}^2$

= A_1 times A_1

= 0.5	0.5	times	0.5	0.5
0.3	0.7		0.3	0.7

= (0.5) (0.5) + (0.5) (0.3)   (0.5) (0.5) + (0.5) (0.7)

   (0.3) (0.5) + (0.7) (0.3)   (0.3) (0.5) + (0.7) (0.7)

= 0.25 + 0.15	0.25 + 0.35
0.15 + 0.21	0.15 + 0.49
= 0.40	0.60
0.36	0.64.

• PROBLEM 10–35

For the Markov chain described in Problem 10–33, define an associated stochastic process whose state is the cumulative number of shots scored. Is this a Markov chain? If so, then what is its one-step transition matrix?

SOLUTION:

The state of the process at any given time depends, given the entire past, only on the present state of the system. Therefore this stochastic process is a Markov chain. There are seven possible states, because there are six shots. These seven states are {0, 1, 2, 3, 4, 5, 6}. The one-step transition matrix is given by

0.4	0.6	0.0	0.0	0.0	0.0	0.0
0.0	0.4	0.6	0.0	0.0	0.0	0.0
0.0	0.0	0.4	0.6	0.0	0.0	0.0
0.0	0.0	0.0	0.4	0.6	0.0	0.0
0.0	0.0	0.0	0.0	0.4	0.6	0.0
0.0	0.0	0.0	0.0	0.0	0.4	0.6
0.0	0.0	0.0	0.0	0.0	0.0	1.0.

• PROBLEM 10–36

For the Markov chain considered in Problem 10–35, which pairs of states commute? Which state are absorbing?

SOLUTION:

From any state the Markov chain can move to the next state (and will do so with probability 0.6) with a successful shot. That is, if the shot scores, then the total number of successful shots will increment by one. But having incremented, it can never go back. There is no process by which successful shots are removed. Since this is essentially a one-way process (the process is non-decreasing), no two states can commute.

Any state can lead to the next state, except that state 6 has no next state, since only six shots are taken. Therefore once there are six successful shots, there will always be six successful shots. The Markov chain will remain indefinitely at state 6, so this state is absorbing. No other state is absorbing.

• PROBLEM 10–37

For the Markov chain described in Problem 10–34, define an associated stochastic process whose state is the cumulative number of shots scored. Is this a Markov chain? If so, then what is its one-step transition matrix?

SOLUTION:

This is not a Markov chain. Given the present state of the system (that is, the number of shots made to this point in time), the state of the system at the next time will increment by one if the present shot is made, and will remain unchanged if the present shot is missed. Conditioned on the past, the probabilities of these events depend on the success or failure of the most recent shot. But this information is not, in general, available from knowledge only of the most recent state.

For example, suppose that two of the first three shots are made. Letting a success be denoted by 'S' and a failure by 'F', the three possibilities are

    1.   *SSF,*

    2.   *SFS,*

and

    3.   *FSS.*

Let Y be a variable which summarizes the entire past of the Markov chain. In particular,

$$Y(SSF) = 1,$$

$$Y(SFS) = 2,$$

and $Y(FSS) = 3.$

Now this stochastic process is a Markov chain if and only if for all times t, for all states i, and for all states j

$$P\{X(t + 1) = j \mid X(1), X(2), \ldots, X(t) = i\} = P\{X(t + 1) = j \mid X(t) = i\}.$$

Let $t = 3$, $i = 2$, and $j = 3$. Now

$$P\{X(3 + 1) = 3 \mid X(1), X(2), X(3) = 2\}$$

$$= P\{X(4) = 3 \mid X(1), X(2), X(3) = 2\}$$

$$= P\{X(4) = 3 \mid Y, X(3) = 2\}.$$

To be a Markov chain we require

$$P\{X(4) = 3 \mid Y, X(3) = 2\} = P\{X(4) = 3 \mid X(3) = 2\},$$

or that

$$P\{X(4) = 3 \mid Y, X(3) = 2\}$$

not depend on Y. But this is not the case, since

$$P\{X(4) = 3 \mid Y = 1, X(3) = 2\} = P\{X(4) = 3 \mid SSF\}$$

$$= P\{\text{fourth shot successful given third shot not successful}\}$$

$$= 0.5,$$

$$P\{X(4) = 3 \mid Y = 2, X(3) = 2\} = P\{X(4) = 3 \mid SFS\}$$

$$= P\{\text{fourth shot successful given third shot successful}\}$$

$$= 0.7,$$

and $P\{X(4) = 3 \mid Y = 3, X(3) = 2\} = P\{X(4) = 3 \mid FSS\}$

= P\{fourth shot successful given third shot successful\}

= 0.7.

Thus this probability does depend on Y, so this stochastic process cannot be a Markov chain.

● PROBLEM 10-38

Suppose that a soccer game is played and we consider the times t_0, t_1, t_2, ..., where t_0 is the start of the game (at which time the score is 0 – 0), t_1 is the time at which the first goal is scored, t_2 is the time at which the second goal is scored, and so on. The game stops when one team takes the lead by five goals. The team which has scored five more goals has won the game. Let a stochastic process be defined as the number goals by which either team leads the other. That is, if the score at time t_3 is 2 = 1, then

$$X(t3) = |\, 2 - 1 \,|$$

$$= |\, 1 \,|$$

$$= 1.$$

Suppose that one team is better than the other so that, given that a goal is scored, the probability is p that one team scores and the probability is $1 - p$ that it was the other team which scored. Let p be greater than $1 - p$. Is this stochastic process a Markov chain? If so, then what is its one-step transition matrix?

SOLUTION:

This is not a Markov chain. Suppose, for example, that

$$X(t_3) = 1.$$

Then either the better team is ahead 2-1 or the weaker team is ahead 2-1. Either way the state of the system is

$$X(t_3) = |\, 2 - 1 \,|$$

$$= |\, 1 \,|$$

$$= 1.$$

In the former case

$$P\{X(t_4) = 2 \mid \text{the better team is ahead}\}$$

$$= P\{\text{better team scores next goal}\}$$

$$= p.$$

But in the latter case

$$P\{X(t_4) = 2 \mid \text{the weaker team is ahead}\}$$

$$= P\{\text{weaker team scores next goal}\}$$

$$= 1 - p.$$

Thus the probability distribution of the stochastic process at the next time depends on more than just the state at the current time, so this cannot be a Markov chain.

• PROBLEM 10–39

Consider the set-up of Problem 10–38, except let $X(t)$ be the number of goals by which the better team is ahead at time t. If the better team is losing at time t, then $X(t) < 0$. Now is this a Markov chain? If so, then what is its one-step transition matrix?

SOLUTION:

This is a Markov chain, because given the current state is i, and that $|i| < 5$, the next state will be $i + 1$ with probability p, and will be $i - 1$ with probability $1 - p$. The states are $\{-5, -4, -3, -2, -1, 0, 1, 2, 3, 4, 5\}$. The one-step transition matrix is therefore

$$A_1 = \begin{array}{ccccccccccc}
1.0 & 0.0 & 0.0 & 0.0 & 0.0 & 0.0 & 0.0 & 0.0 & 0.0 & 0.0 & 0.0 \\
1{-}p & 0.0 & p & 0.0 & 0.0 & 0.0 & 0.0 & 0.0 & 0.0 & 0.0 & 0.0 \\
0.0 & 1{-}p & 0.0 & p & 0.0 & 0.0 & 0.0 & 0.0 & 0.0 & 0.0 & 0.0 \\
0.0 & 0.0 & 1{-}p & 0.0 & p & 0.0 & 0.0 & 0.0 & 0.0 & 0.0 & 0.0 \\
0.0 & 0.0 & 0.0 & 1{-}p & 0.0 & p & 0.0 & 0.0 & 0.0 & 0.0 & 0.0 \\
0.0 & 0.0 & 0.0 & 0.0 & 1{-}p & 0.0 & p & 0.0 & 0.0 & 0.0 & 0.0 \\
0.0 & 0.0 & 0.0 & 0.0 & 0.0 & 1{-}p & 0.0 & p & 0.0 & 0.0 & 0.0 \\
\end{array}$$

$$
\begin{array}{cccccccccc}
0.0 & 0.0 & 0.0 & 0.0 & 0.0 & 0.0 & 1{-}p & 0.0 & p & 0.0 & 0.0 \\
0.0 & 0.0 & 0.0 & 0.0 & 0.0 & 0.0 & 0.0 & 1{-}p & 0.0 & p & 0.0 \\
0.0 & 0.0 & 0.0 & 0.0 & 0.0 & 0.0 & 0.0 & 0.0 & 1{-}p & 0.0 & p \\
0.0 & 0.0 & 0.0 & 0.0 & 0.0 & 0.0 & 0.0 & 0.0 & 0.0 & 0.0 & 1.0.
\end{array}
$$

Notice that both 5 and − 5 are absorbing states, and therefore recurrent states. No other states are absorbing. The states {− 4, − 3, − 2, − 1, 0, 1, 2, 3, 4} all commute, and therefore form a single class. None of these states are recurrent (all are transient). The three classes are, therefore,

    1.   {− 5},

    2.   {− 4, − 3, − 2, − 1, 0, 1, 2, 3, 4},

and

    3.   {5}.

CHAPTER 11

RANDOM WALKS AND MARTINGALES

Basic Attacks and Strategies for Solving Problems in this Chapter. See pages 794 to 839 for step-by-step solutions to problems.

There are many stochastic processes which are encountered in everyday life (although they may not be recognized as stochastic processes by people not well-versed in probability theory). Some of these stochastic processes have the Markovian property, others do not. Even within the rich class of Markovian stochastic processes there are many processes which are so well-known in their own right that special attention has been granted to these processes, and they have even been given their own name. The random walk is one prominent example of such a Markovian stochastic process.

A stochastic process is a collection of random variables indexed by some variable, most often time. So if we define a random variable at each time t in the range $t = 0, 1, 2, \ldots$, then we have defined a stochastic process.

As a simple example, suppose that at time t the variable $X(t)$ has a Bernoulli distribution with parameter 0.5, and that each of these random variables is independent of all other such random variables. This is an infinite sequence of Bernoulli random variables, or a binomial process. This example is not a particularly interesting one because there is no dependence among the random variables involved. Typically the study of stochastic processes focuses on the relationship that the process at one time has with the process at other times. If this process is Markovian, then it would suffice to consider only the most recent prior time, since the distribution of the current state of the process, conditional on the entire past, depends only on the most recent time.

Unlike random walks, martingales need not satisfy the Markovian property (although they are not prohibited from doing so). The defining property of a martingale is that it has no systematic tendency to rise or fall. Martingales are therefore quite useful for modelling what may, under some conditions or assumptions, be taken to be a fair game. Such applications include gambling (for example, the famous Gambler's Ruin problem), stock prices, bond prices, daily temperature, or (possibly standardized) grades of a student of consecutive exams. In fact, martingales have recently found their way into the literature dealing with survival analysis (Fleming and Harrington, 1991). See, in particular, Chapters 1, 2, and 5 of this book.

The application of martingales to survival analysis is not so obvious, because survival analysis deals with failure-time distributions (that is, the time until some event takes place, often the failure of a particular component or the death of a patient enrolled on a clinical trial). What distinguishes these failure-time distributions from other distributions is the possible presence of censoring. That is, some patients may live beyond the time when the analysis is to be performed. In such a case, the time of this patient's death is known only to exceed the time which the patient has already been alive, but there is no numerical value which can reasonably be assigned to the duration of this patient's life. Nowhere in this formulation is there any mention of a fair game, yet martingales still are quite applicable to this situation.

＊＊＊＊＊＊

REVIEW OF RANDOM WALKS

A random walk is a particular case of a Markovian stochastic process. Let X_i, $i = 1, 2, \ldots$, be a set of random variables which are independent and identically distributed. Let

$$S_n = \Sigma_{i\,=\,1\,\text{to}\,n}\,X_i.$$

Then $\{S_n\}$ is a random walk.

We will define the symmetric Bernoulli distribution with parameter p as the distribution of

$$Y = 2X - 1$$

when X has a Bernoulli distribution with parameter p. Notice that when $X = 0$,

$$Y = 2(0) - 1$$
$$= 0 - 1$$
$$= -1,$$

and when $X = 1$,

$$Y = 2(1) - 1$$
$$= 2 - 1$$
$$= 1.$$

Therefore,

$$P\{Y = -1\} = P\{2X - 1 = -1\}$$
$$= P\{2X = 1 - 1\}$$
$$= P\{2X = 0\}$$
$$= P\{X = 0\}$$
$$= 1 - p,$$
$$P\{Y = 1\} = P\{2X - 1 = 1\}$$
$$= P\{2X = 1 + 1\}$$
$$= P\{2X = 2\}$$
$$= P\{X = 1\}$$
$$= p,$$

and $P\{Y = k\} = 0$ for k other than -1 and 1.

The most common random walk in the literature has as the distribution of X_i the symmetric Bernoulli distribution with parameter 0.5. This is a symmetric random walk. It is also quite common to let the distribution be symmetric Bernoulli but with a parameter other than 0.5.

Sometimes barriers are imposed on a random walk. There may be reflecting barriers (the object taking the random walk bounces off the walls) or absorbing barriers (the object taking the random walk sticks to the walls and remains there forever). The Gambler's Ruin problem is a famous example of absorbing barriers in random walks.

The distribution of the random variables, $\{X_i\}$, need not be one-dimensional. There are random walks in all dimensions. If the distribution of the $\{X_i\}$ is one-dimensional, then the random walk takes place on the line. For example, if the distribution is symmetric Bernoulli, then each step is either one unit to the right ($X_i = 1$, which occurs with probability p) or one unit to the left ($X_i = -1$, which occurs with probability $1 - p$). Even though this is a one-dimensional random walk, it is still most easily visualized in two dimensions (otherwise the path one would draw would correspond only to the range of the random walk, and not to the entire path of the random walk).

To construct a two-dimensional representation of a one-dimensional random walk, plot on the two-dimensional Cartesian plane points (n, S_n), where $S_0 = 0$, for example, so the first point would always be the origin. Still considering the symmetric Bernoulli distribution, we would plot a line from (n, S_n) to $(n + 1, S_n + 1)$ if the variable assumes the value one, and we would plot a line from (n, S_n) to $(n + 1, S_n - 1)$ if the variable assumes the value negative one. Many relevant probabilities can be computed for such a random walk.

The most basic probability in which one may be interested would be $P\{S_n = k\}$ for various values of n and k. Suppose that, of the first n steps of a random walk, c result in a step up, and $n - c$ result in a step down. Then $S_n = c + (n - c) = n - 2c$. By applying the binomial distribution, even though the distribution of S_n is symmetric binomial instead of binomial, the probability of this outcome may be found to be

$$P\{S_n = n - 2c\} = P\{c \text{ steps up}, n - c \text{ steps down}\}$$

$$= C(n, c)\,(0.5)^c(0.5)^{n-c}$$

$$= C(n, c)\,(0.5)^n.$$

Thus $P\{S_n = k\}$ can be found as follows. For S_n to be k, there must have been c steps up and $n - c$ steps down, with $2c - n = k$. Then

$$2c = n + k,$$

so $c = (n + k)/2.$

This means that

$$P\{S_n = k\} = 0$$

unless $(n + k)$ is even, which is the case when both n and k are even or when both n and k are odd. This should not be surprising, because if n is even, then one could use induction to show that S_n must be even and hence cannot be k unless k is also even. Likewise, if n is odd, then one could use induction to show that S_n must be odd and hence cannot be k unless k is also odd. If both n and k are even or both n and k are odd, then

$$P\{S_n = k\} = C(n, c) \, (0.5)^n$$

with $c = (n + k)/2,$

so $P\{S_n = k\} = C(n, (n + k)/2) \, (0.5)^n.$

For example,

$$P\{S_4 = 2\} = C(4, (4 + 2)/2) \, (0.5)^4$$

$$= C(4, 6/2) \, (0.5)^4$$

$$= C(4, 3) \, (0.5)^4$$

$$= 4!/[3!(4 - 3)!](1/2)^4$$

$$= 4!/[3!(1!)](1/2)^4$$

$$= \{24/[(6) \, (1)]\}/2^4$$

$$= \{24/6\}/16$$

$$= 4/16$$

$$= 0.25.$$

If we wish to generalize this formula to the case of the asymmetric random walk, then let us call p the probability of a step up and $1 - p$ the probability of a step down. Using this notation, we see that $S_n = k$ if there are c steps up and $n - c$ steps down if and only if $c - (n - c) = k$. That is,

$$2c - n = k,$$

so $c = (n + k)/2.$

Then

$$P\{S_n = k\} = P\{(n + k)/2 \text{ steps up}, n - (n + k)/2 \text{ steps down}\}$$
$$= P\{(n + k)/2 \text{ steps up}, 2n/2 - (n + k)/2 \text{ steps down}\}$$
$$= P\{(n + k)/2 \text{ steps up}, [2n - (n + k)]/2 \text{ steps down}\}$$
$$= P\{(n + k)/2 \text{ steps up}, [n - k]/2 \text{ steps down}\}$$
$$= C(n, (n + k)/2)p^{(n + k)/2}(1 - p)^{(n - k)/2}.$$

Notice that if $p = 0.5$, then $1 - p = 0.5$ and this formula reduces to

$$= C(n, (n + k)/2) \, 0.5^{(n + k)/2}(1 - 0.5)^{(n - k)/2}$$
$$= C(n, (n + k)/2) \, 0.5^{(n + k)/2}(0.5)^{(n - k)/2}$$
$$= C(n, (n + k)/2) \, 0.5^{(n + k + n - k)/2}$$
$$= C(n, (n + k)/2) \, 0.5^{(n + n)/2}$$
$$= C(n, (n + k)/2) \, 0.5^{2n/2}$$
$$= C(n, (n + k)/2)0.5^n,$$

as was given by the treatment of the symmetric random walk.

Just like with general Markov chains, the states of a random walk can be classified as being either recurrent (that is, if the walk starts at this state, then with probability one it will return to this state) or transient (that is, if the walk starts at this state, then the probability is less than one that it will return to this state). When considering the symmetric random walk with unit increments and unit decrements (that is, $P\{S_{n + 1} = S_n + 1\} = P\{S_{n + 1} = S_n - 1\} = 0.5$), the origin (state zero) is of particular interest. It turns out that in one dimension the origin is recurrent. When we consider two dimensions, then each unit shift can be up, down, left, or right, and each occurs with probability 0.25. In this case, the origin, which is now the state $(0, 0)$, is still recurrent. But things change when we move to three dimensions.

In three or more dimensions, the origin is transient. In three dimensions, each unit shift can be up, down, left, right, in, or out, and each occurs with probability $1/6$. Here the origin is the state $(0, 0, 0)$.

One of the most striking results in all of statistical theory is that an estimator as well-known as the sample mean is inadmissible (that is, there exist uniformly better estimators) in three or more dimensions. These so-called shrinkage estimators (see Lehmann, 1983, page 299) dominate the sample mean precisely because of the transience of the origin in three or more dimensions. This connection should not be obvious to you, but if it is, then you should certainly consider a career in probability!

It turns out that in one dimension, for the symmetric random walk with unit increments and unit decrements, not only is the origin recurrent, but in fact all states are recurrent. This fact can be used to prove a most remarkable result, which can be found in Ross (1983), page 224. Let Y_k be the number of times the random walk is at state k before it first returns to the origin. Thus if the random walk takes the path $\{0, 1, 2, 1, 2, 3, 4, 5, 4, 3, 4, 3, 2, 1, 2, 1, 0\}$, then $Y_1 = 4$ (because the path hits state 1 four times between consecutive visits to the origin), $Y_2 = 4$ (because the path hits state 2 four times between consecutive visits to the origin), $Y_3 = 3$ (because the path hits state 3 three times between consecutive visits to the origin), $Y_4 = 3$ (because the path hits state 4 three times between consecutive visits to the origin), $Y_5 = 1$ (because the path hits state 5 once between consecutive visits to the origin), and $Y_k = 0$ (because the path hits state k no times between consecutive visits to the origin) for $k > 5$. Then for any state k,

$$E[Y_k] = 1.$$

That is, the expected number of visits to state k between consecutive visits to the origin is one for all states k. To fully understand this result, consider a rock which lies in the gutter, ready to be kicked about by those who encounter it as they pass by. Suppose that

1. those who walk north to south will kick the rock south,

2. those who walk south to north will kick the rock north,

3. each kick is the exact same distance (say one unit),

and

4. an equal number of people walk north to south as do south to north.

Now think about the frequency with which you would expect the rock to travel a block before it returns to its initial location. Then think about the frequency with which you would expect the rock to travel a mile before it returns to its initial location. Think about the frequency with which you would expect the rock to travel clear out of the county before it returns to its initial location.

If the rock starts in New York, then, on average, it will be expected to travel a block north one time before it returns to its "home", but it will also be expected to travel to Miami once before it returns to its home. In fact, being that rocks do not require passports, it would also be expected to travel to Nova Scotia once before it returns to its starting location.

This result is obviously counter-intuitive. Problem 11–9 will provide a partial explanation for this phenomenon. In reality, it is probably not true that the expected number of trips to Miami between visits home is equal to the expected number of visits up the block between visits home. But this is because one or more of the four assumptions is not applicable.

For example, the first two assumptions may be violated if not every kick is perfectly straight. And then once the rock has veered off to the side, it may never get back on track because buildings would block it from going directly north or directly south. The third assumption is hard to believe, because not everyone will kick the rock an equal distance. The fourth assumption also may not be warranted, because there are natural blocks, such as rivers or mountain ranges. One can walk to these blocks, but not through them. When one approaches such a block, one must turn around. Thus if the rock is kicked into the river or off the mountain, then nobody will kick it again (until the next stone age evaporates the river).

The point is, though, that if one is prepared to believe the four assumptions, then the result holds true, fantastic though it may be.

Step-by-Step Solutions to Problems in this Chapter, "Random Walks and Martingales."

• PROBLEM 11–1

Prove that a random walk has the Markovian property.

SOLUTION:

A random walk is a stochastic process, $\{S_n\}$, where

$$S_n = \Sigma_{i\,=\,1\ \text{to}\ n} X_i,$$

and the X_i are independent with identical distributions. Then

$$P\{S_{n\,+\,1} = k \mid S_1, S_2, \ldots, S_{n\,-\,1}, S_n = c\}$$

$$= P\{X_{n+1} = k - c \mid S_1, S_2, \ldots, S_{n-1}, {}_n S_n = c\}$$

(by definition of the random walk process)

$$= P\{X_{n+1} = k - c \mid X_1, X_1 + X_2, \ldots, X_1 + \ldots + X_{n-1}, X_1 + \ldots + X_n = c\}$$

(by definition of the S_i)

$$= P\{X_{n+1} = k - c\}$$

(by the independence of X_{n+1} and the other n random variables, and the fact that this implies independence of X_{n+1} and all functions of the other n random variables)

$$= P\{X_{n+1} = k - c \mid X_1 + \ldots + X_n = c\}$$

(by the independence of X_{n+1} and the other n random variables, and the fact that this implies independence of X_{n+1} and all functions of the other n random variables)

$$= P\{X_{n+1} = k - c \mid S_n = c\}$$

(by definition of S_n)

$$= P\{S_{n+1} = k - c + c \mid S_n = c\}$$

(by definition of S_{n+1})

$$= P\{S_{n+1} = k \mid S_n = c\}.$$

This proves that the future of a random walk, conditioned on the present and the past of the random walk, is independent of the past of the random walk. In other words, every random walk is a Markov chain.

• PROBLEM 11–2

Is every Markov chain a random walk?

SOLUTION:

No. While it is true that a Markov chain has certain similarities with a random walk, there is no reason why a Markov chain could fail to be a random walk. For example, consider the Markov chain whose one-step transition matrix is given by

$$A_1 = 0.5 \qquad\qquad 0.5$$
$$0.5 \qquad\qquad 1.0.$$

If this Markov chain is at state 2, then it will stay there forever, because state 2 is absorbing. This means that the random variable to add to the state at one time to get to the state at the next time would need to be zero (the difference between two and two). But if the Markov chain is at state 1, then it can stay there (with probability 0.5) or move to state 2 (with probability 0.5). Therefore, the random variable to be added to one state to get to the next state would need to be Bernoulli with parameter 0.5 (that is, zero, or one minus one, with probability 0.5, and one, or two minus one, with probability 0.5). These random variables are not the same. Therefore, this stochastic process cannot be a random walk.

• PROBLEM 11-3

Consider a random walk based on the symmetric Bernoulli distribution. Suppose that we monitor this random walk for 10 time periods (after time zero), and find that the jumps are given by $X_1 = 1$, $X_2 = 1$, $X_3 = -1$, $X_4 = 1$, $X_5 = -1$, $X_6 = 1$, $X_7 = -1$, $X_8 = -1$, $X_9 = 1$, and $X_{10} = -1$. Then what is S_4?

SOLUTION:

We compute

$$S_4 = X_1 + X_2 + X_3 + X_4$$
$$= (1) + (1) + (-1) + (1)$$
$$= 2.$$

Thus we would plot the point $(4, 2)$.

• PROBLEM 11-4

For the sample random walk given in Problem 11–3, what is the highest this path ever attains? What is the lowest this path ever attains?

SOLUTION:

We compute

$$S_1 = X_1$$
$$= 1,$$
$$S_2 = X_1 + X_2$$
$$= 1 + 1$$
$$= 2,$$
$$S_3 = X_1 + X_2 + X_3$$
$$= 1 + 1 + (-1)$$
$$= 2 - 1$$
$$= 1,$$
$$S_4 = X_1 + X_2 + X_3 + X_4$$
$$= 1 + 1 + (-1) + 1$$
$$= 3 - 1$$
$$= 2,$$
$$S_5 = X_1 + X_2 + X_3 + X_4 + X_5$$
$$= 1 + 1 + (-1) + 1 + (-1)$$
$$= 3 - 2$$
$$= 1,$$
$$S_6 = X_1 + X_2 + X_3 + X_4 + X_5 + X_6$$
$$= 1 + 1 + (-1) + 1 + (-1) + 1$$
$$= 4 - 2$$
$$= 2,$$

$$S_7 = X_1 + X_2 + X_3 + X_4 + X_5 + X_6 + X_7$$
$$= 1 + 1 + (-1) + 1 + (-1) + 1 + (-1)$$
$$= 4 - 3$$
$$= 1,$$

$$S_8 = X_1 + X_2 + X_3 + X_4 + X_5 + X_6 + X_7 + X_8$$
$$= 1 + 1 + (-1) + 1 + (-1) + 1 + (-1) + (-1)$$
$$= 4 - 4$$
$$= 0,$$

$$S_9 = X_1 + X_2 + X_3 + X_4 + X_5 + X_6 + X_7 + X_8 + X_9$$
$$= 1 + 1 + (-1) + 1 + (-1) + 1 + (-1) + (-1) + 1$$
$$= 5 - 4$$
$$= 1,$$

and $\quad S_{10} = X_1 + X_2 + X_3 + X_4 + X_5 + X_6 + X_7 + X_8 + X_9 + X_{10}$
$$= 1 + 1 + (-1) + 1 + (-1) + 1 + (-1) + (-1) + 1 + (-1)$$
$$= 5 - 5$$
$$= 0.$$

Thus the largest value ever attained is two, and the smallest value ever attained is zero.

● PROBLEM 11-5

Prove, by induction, that if n is even and k is odd, or if n is odd and k is even, then $P\{S_n = k\} = 0$.

SOLUTION:

If $n = 0$, then $S_n = 0$. Here n is even and S_n must be zero, which is also even. Now assume that if n is even, then S_n must be even (with probability one). Then S_{n+2} is the next state of the random walk with an even index (i.e., $n + 2$). There are four possible paths from S_n to S_{n+2}. These are

1. {up, up},

2.   {up, down},

3.   {down, up},

and

4.   {down, down}.

The values of S_{n+2} will be, respectively, $S_n + 2$ (even), S_n (even), S_n (even), and $S_n - 2$ (even). Thus if S_n is even, then S_{n+2} must also be even. This completes the proof for even n.

If $n = 1$, then S_n can either be one or negative one. Here n is odd and S_n must also be odd. Now assume that if n is odd, then S_n must be odd (with probability one). Then S_{n+2} is the next state of the random walk with an odd index (i.e., $n + 2$). There are four possible paths from S_n to S_{n+2}. These are

1.   {up, up},

2.   {up, down},

3.   {down, up},

and

4.   {down, down}.

The values of S_{n+2} will be, respectively, $S_n + 2$ (odd), S_n (odd), S_n (odd), and $S_n - 2$ (odd). Thus if S_n is odd, then S_{n+2} must also be odd. This completes the proof for odd n.

• PROBLEM 11–6

Consider the symmetric random walk. Find $P\{S_8 = 0\}$.

SOLUTION:

If $S_8 = 0$, then four of the eight steps were steps up, and the other four of the eight steps were steps down. There are 2^8 possible paths, each of which is equally likely for the symmetric random walk. That is, each path has probability $1/2^8 = 2^{-8}$. Of these 2^8 paths, exactly $C(8, 4)$ lead to the event $\{S_n = 0\}$. Therefore,

$$P\{S_n = 0\} = C(8, 4)/2^8$$

$$= 8!/[4!4!2^8]$$

$$= [(5) (6) (7) (8)]/[(1) (2) (3) (4) (2^8)]$$

$$= 70/2^8$$

$$= (70) (0.0039)$$

$$= 0.2734.$$

• PROBLEM 11-7

Consider the asymmetric random walk with

$$p = P\{\text{step up}\}$$

$$= 0.6.$$

Find $P\{S_8 = 0\}$.

SOLUTION:

If $S_8 = 0$, then four of the eight steps were steps up, and the other four of the eight steps were steps down. There are 2^8 possible paths, but these are not equally likely since we are no longer dealing with the symmetric random walk. But we can still use the binomial formula to compute

$$P\{S_n = 0\} = C(8, 4)p^4(1 - p)^{8 - 4}$$

$$= \{8!/[4!4!]\}p^4(1 - p)^4$$

$$= 70 \, (0.6)^4(1 - 0.6)^4$$

$$= 70 \, (0.6)^4(0.4)^4$$

$$= 70 \, (0.6 \times 0.4)^4$$

$$= 70 \, (0.24)^4$$

$$= (70) \, (0.0033)$$

$$= 0.23.$$

• PROBLEM 11-8

Let

$$p = P\{\text{step up}\}$$

and $\quad 1 - p = P\{\text{step down}\}.$

For what value(s) of p is $P\{S_{2n} = 0\}$ maximized? For what value(s) of p is $P\{S_{2n} = 0\}$ minimized?

SOLUTION:

We calculate

$$P\{S_{2n} = 0\} = C(2n, n)p^n(1 - p)^n,$$

because for S_{2n} to be zero, we require n steps up and n steps down. The binomial distribution then show the above calculation to be correct. We may re-express this as

$$P\{S_{2n} = 0\} = C(2n, n)[p(1 - p)]^n.$$

Let $T = p(1 - p)$. Then

$$P\{S_{2n} = 0\} = C(2n, n)T^n.$$

As a function of T, $P\{S_{2n} = 0\}$ is monotonically increasing in T, since its derivative is

$$d/dT\ P\{S_{2n} = 0\} = d/dT\ C(2n, n)T^n$$

$$= C(2n, n)nT^{n-1},$$

which is non-negative for non-negative values of T, and positive for positive values of T. But T is always non-negative, because both p and $1 - p$ are non-negative. In fact, T is always positive unless $p = 0$ or $1 - p = 0$.

Because $P\{S_{2n} = 0\}$ is an increasing function of T, we can maximize and minimize $P\{S_{2n} = 0\}$ by maximizing and minimizing T. Now

$$d/dp\ T = d/dp\ p(1 - p)$$

$$= d/dp\ p - p^2$$

$$= 1 - 2p.$$

This derivative starts at one when $p = 0$, decreases to zero when $p = 0.5$, and then decreases further to negative one when $p = 1$. This means that T is maximized at $p = 0.5$, and its minimums are at $p = 0$ and $p = 1$. That is,

$P\{S_{2n} = 0\}$ has its maximum value when $p = 0.5$ (that is, for the symmetric random walk), and decreases monotonically as p moves away from 0.5 in either direction. When $p = 0$ or $p = 1$, $P\{S_{2n} = 0\} = 0$.

• PROBLEM 11–9

It may seem that if $k_1 > k_2 > 0$, then $Y_{k1} \leq Y_{k2}$, because for the path to travel to k_1, it would need to go through k_1 first. But if $Y_{k1} \leq Y_{k2}$, then $E[Y_{k1}] \leq E[Y_{k2}]$, with strict inequality unless the random variables are identically distributed. This may suggest that the result that $E[Y_{k1}] = E[Y_{k2}] = 1$ is false. Explain why this logic fails.

SOLUTION:

It is true that for the path to travel to k_1, it would need to go through $k1$ first. But this only means that $Y_{k2} > 0$ whenever $Y_{k1} > 0$. It does not imply that $Y_{k1} \leq Y_{k2}$. Consider, for example, the path $\{0, 1, 2, 3, 2, 3, 2, 3, 2, 3, 2, 1, 0\}$. For this path, $Y_1 = 2$ (because the path hits state 1 twice between consecutive visits to the origin), $Y_2 = 5$ (because the path hits state 2 five times between consecutive visits to the origin), $Y_3 = 4$ (because the path hits state 3 four times between consecutive visits to the origin), and $Y_k = 0$ (because the path hits state k no times between consecutive visits to the origin) for $k > 3$. So while it is less likely that the path will ever travel to a further point, once it does so, it would be expected to visit this further point more often than it would a less distant point.

******

REVIEW OF STOPPING TIMES

A stopping time is a "knowable" random time. Perhaps the best way to explain this is to give some examples of "unknowable" random times.

A quarterback would often like to hold off on passing the ball until just before he gets sacked. Unfortunately, the time just before he gets sacked is not knowable until he actually gets sacked. Then he knows that he waited too long.

The best time to buy a stock is just before its price increases. Unfortunately, the time just before the stock price increases is not knowable until the price actually increases. Then the investor knows that he waited too long.

The best time to sell a stock is just before its price decreases. Unfortunately, the time just before the stock price decreases is not knowable until the price actually decreases. Again, the investor knows that he waited too long.

None of the above random times are stopping times, precisely because they are not predictable until they occur. The time until a quarterback gets sacked is a stopping time, because at the moment that he gets sacked, it is known that the time has come. The time when a stock price either increases or decreases is also a stopping time, because at the time that this event occurs, it is known to be occurring.

A more formal definition is now in order. A stopping time is associated with a stochastic process, $\{S_n, n = 0, 1, 2,...\}$. We say that N is a stopping time of the stochastic process $\{S_n, n = 0, 1, 2,...\}$ if and only if the event $\{N = k\}$ is a function of $\{S_1, S_2,..., S_k\}$. That is, N is a stopping time of the stochastic process $\{S_n, n = 0, 1, 2,...\}$ if and only if knowledge of $\{S_1, S_2,..., S_k\}$ would suffice to determine whether or not $N = k$.

Let $\{S_n, n = 0, 1, 2,...\}$ be a symmetric random walk with unit increments and unit decrements. Let N be the last time, prior to time $n = 10$, that the path is at the origin. Thus if the path is $\{0, 1, 2, 1, 0, -1, 0, 1, 2, 3, 2\}$, then $N = 6$, because $S_6 = 0$ and S_n is not at the origin for $n > 6$. As defined, N is not a stopping time. This is because had we only known $\{S_n, n = 0, 1, 2, 3, 4, 5, 6\}$, then we would not have known that $N = 6$. At this point it would have been possible that $S_8 = 0$, in which case N is not six. Of course, if S_6 is not zero, then we know that N cannot be six. This does not mean, however, that N is a stopping time with respect to this stochastic process. The occurrence or non-occurrence of the event $\{N = n\}$ would need to be known for all possible outcomes, not just for certain outcomes.

As a trivial example, let N be the time when a symmetric random walk first hits the origin. Since the random walk begins at the origin at time 0, $S_0 = 0$, and consequently $N = 0$. This is known with or without knowledge of any other S_n, so this is a stopping time. Other examples of stopping times, as well as some examples of random times which are not stopping times, will be given in the problems.

• PROBLEM 11–10

Let M be a known number. Is $\{n = M\}$ a stopping time?

SOLUTION:

For any number n we know if $\{n = M\}$ has occurred or not. For $n < M$, the event $\{n = M\}$ has not occurred. For $n = M$, it has occurred. If we know the set $\{S_1, S_2, ..., S_n\}$, then we know n (because we can count the number of such random variables). Therefore with knowledge of $\{S_1, S_2, ..., S_n\}$, we would know n, and, in turn, we would know if $\{M = n\}$ has occurred or not. Thus $\{M = n\}$ is a stopping time for any number M.

• PROBLEM 11–11

Let N be a stopping time, and let M be a known number. Let T be the smaller of N and M. Is T a stopping time?

SOLUTION:

Having observed $\{S_1, S_2, ..., S_n\}$, we know if $\{n = N\}$ has occurred or not (because N is a stopping time). Obviously, we also know if $\{n = M\}$ has occurred (this event has occurred if and only if $M < n$). If either one of these events has occurred, then we have observed the smaller of the two stopping times. This would, of course, be known. Therefore the smaller of a stopping time and a fixed time is also a stopping time.

• PROBLEM 11–12

> Let N be a stopping time, and let M be a known number. Let T be the larger of N and M. Is T a stopping time?

SOLUTION:

Having observed $\{S_1, S_2, ..., S_n\}$, we know if $\{n = N\}$ has occurred or not (because N is a stopping time). Obviously, we also know if $\{n = M\}$ has occurred (this event has occurred if and only if $M < n$). If both of these events has occurred, then we have observed the larger of the two stopping times. This would, of course, be known. Therefore the larger of a stopping time and a fixed time is also a stopping time.

• PROBLEM 11–13

> Let N_1 and N_2 be stopping times, and let T be the smaller of N_1 and N_2. Is T a stopping time?

SOLUTION:

Having observed $\{S_1, S_2, ..., S_n\}$, we know if $\{n = N_1\}$ has occurred or not (because N_1 is a stopping time). We also know if $\{n = N_2\}$ has occurred or not (because N_2 is a stopping time). If either one of these events has occurred, then we have observed the smaller of the two stopping times. This would, of course, be known. Therefore the smaller of two stopping times is also a stopping time.

• PROBLEM 11–14

> Let N_1 and N_2 be stopping times, and let T be the larger of N_1 and N_2. Is T a stopping time?

SOLUTION:

Having observed $\{S_1, S_2, ..., S_n\}$, we know if $\{n = N_1\}$ has occurred or not (because N_1 is a stopping time). We also know if $\{n = N_2\}$ has occurred or not (because N_2 is a stopping time). If both of these events has occurred, then we have observed the larger of the two stopping times. This would, of course, be known. Therefore the larger of two stopping times is also a stopping time.

• PROBLEM 11–15

Use induction and the previous problems to prove that the maximum of a finite number of stopping times is a stopping time, and the minimum of a finite number of stopping times is a stopping time.

SOLUTION:

We have already shown, in the previous problems, that the maximum and minimum of two stopping times is itself a stopping time. For the induction hypothesis, suppose that the maximum of k stopping times is a stopping time, and the minimum k stopping times is a stopping time. Then we need to show that the maximum of $k + 1$ stopping times is a stopping time, and the minimum $k + 1$ stopping times is a stopping time.

The minimum of $k + 1$ quantities, say N_1, N_2, ..., $N_{k + 1}$, can be expressed as the minimum of T_1 and T_2, where

$$T_1 = \min_{i = 1 \text{ to } k} N_i,$$

and $\quad T_2 = N_{k + 1}.$

By the induction hypothesis, T_1 is a stopping time. By assumption, T_2 is also a stopping time. Therefore, $\min_{i = 1 \text{ to } k + 1} N_i$ must be a stopping time.

The maximum of $k + 1$ quantities, say N_1, N_2,..., $N_{k + 1}$, can be expressed as the maximum of T_1 and T_2, where

$$T_1 = \max_{i = 1 \text{ to } k} N_i,$$

and $\quad T_2 = N_{k + 1}.$

By the induction hypothesis, T_1 is a stopping time. By assumption, T_2 is also a stopping time. Therefore, $\max_{i = 1 \text{ to } k + 1} N_i$ must be a stopping time.

• PROBLEM 11-16

Let $\{S_n\}$ be a symmetric random walk with unit increments and unit decrements. Define N as the time at which the random walk first reaches state 1. Is N a stopping time?

SOLUTION:

If we know the path taken by this random walk up to and including time n, then we know if the path has ever reached state 1. If it has not, then $N > n$. If it has, then we know the first such time. This time is N. Thus N is a stopping time.

• PROBLEM 11-17

Let $\{S_n\}$ be a symmetric random walk with unit increments and unit decrements. Define N as the time at which the random walk first reaches state 1 after having reached state -2. Is N a stopping time?

SOLUTION:

If we know the path taken by this random walk up to and including time n, then we know if the path has ever reached state 1. We also know if the path has ever reached state -2. If the path has not reached both of the states in the proper order (i.e., -2 first, then 1), then $N > n$. If the path has reached these states in the proper order, then we know the first such time. This time is N. Thus N is a stopping time.

• PROBLEM 11-18

Let $\{S_n\}$ be a symmetric random walk with unit increments and unit decrements. Define N as the third time at which the random walk reaches state 5 after having reached state -5. Is N a stopping time?

SOLUTION:

If we know the path taken by this random walk up to and including time n, then we know if the path has reached state 5 and state -5 three times each (at least). If the path has not reached both of the states at least three times in the proper order (i.e., -5 first, then 5, three times), then $N > n$. If the path has reached these states in the proper order, then we know the first such time. This time is N. Thus N is a stopping time.

• PROBLEM 11-19

> If a military leader tells his troops not to fire until they see the whites of the eyes of the enemy, then is this a stopping time?

SOLUTION:

At each time one knows if one has or has not seen the whites of the eyes of the enemy. The first such time is N. This would be known with knowledge of the process $\{S_n\}$, where at each time n

$S_n = 0$ if the whites of the eyes are not seen

and $S_n = 1$ if the whites of the eyes are seen.

Thus this is a stopping time.

• PROBLEM 11-20

> It is common among some business people to assign a project and then to tell the person to whom the project was assigned that the project is due yesterday. Is this a stopping time?

SOLUTION:

As a random time, this time would be the day before the project is assigned. Thus $N = n$ if the project is assigned on day $n + 1$. But on day n one would not know if the project is to be assigned on day $n + 1$ or not. Thus on day n one would not know if $N = n$ or not. Therefore this is not a stopping time.

• PROBLEM 11-21

In a routine performed by a particular comedian, the comedian in-
structs one of his subordinates to let him know as soon as another
colleague of theirs doesn't show up. Is this a stopping time?

SOLUTION:

To know the exact time when somebody doesn't show up would,
presumably, involve knowing that the person never shows up at all. But
this, of course, would not be known until far later than the first time at
which the person is not present. Thus based only on the knowledge available at a given time, it would not be known if, in fact, this was the time at
which the person did not show up. Therefore this cannot be a
stopping time.

$$\ast\ast\ast\ast\ast\ast$$

REVIEW OF MARTINGALES

Martingales are among the most famous of all stochastic processes.
Martingales are the model of choice to represent a fair game, or a stochastic process which, on average, neither increases nor decreases. This is in
contrast to a submartingale, which increases on the average, and a
supermartingale, which decreases on the average.

More formally, a stochastic process, $\{X_n\}$, is a martingale if

$$E[X_{n+1} \mid X_n = k] = k$$

for all n and k. A stochastic process, $\{X_n\}$, is a submartingale if

$$E[X_{n+1} \mid X_n = k] \geq k$$

for all n and k. A submartingale is a favorable game. That is, you expect
your earnings to increase when the process directing your earnings is a
submartingale. A stochastic process, $\{X_n\}$, is a supermartingale if

$$E[X_{n+1} \mid X_n = k] \le k$$

for all n and k. A supermartingale is an unfavorable game. That is, you expect your earnings to decrease when the process directing your earnings is a supermartingale.

If $\{X_n\}$ is a martingale, then

$$E[X_{n+1} \mid X_1, X_2, \ldots, X_n = k] = k,$$

so it may appear as though a martingale is necessarily a Markov chain. This is not the case. While it is true that the expected value of a martingale, conditional on the entire past of the martingale, is equal to the most recent value of the martingale (and thus depends only on this most recent value), the distribution may depend on the entire past.

As an example, let X_n be your age on your n^{th} birthday. Clearly, then,

$$X_n = n$$

for all n. Then

$$E[X_{n+1} \mid X_n = n] = n + 1$$

$$= X_n + 1$$

$$> X_n.$$

This stochastic process is therefore a submartingale.

As an example of a martingale, consider the symmetric random walk with unit increments and unit decrements. For such a stochastic process,

$$S_{n+1} = S_n + 1 \text{ with probability } 0.5$$

and $\quad S_{n+1} = S_n - 1 \text{ with probability } 0.5,$

so $\quad E[S_{n+1} \mid S_n = k] = (k+1)(0.5) + (k-1)(0.5)$

$$= (k + 1 + k - 1)(0.5)$$

$$= (2k)(0.5)$$

$$= k$$

$$= S_n$$

for all n and k. This process is, therefore, a martingale.

As an example of a submartingale, consider the asymmetric random walk with unit increments and unit decrements. Let the probability of a unit increment, p, be larger than the probability of a unit decrement, $1 - p$.

For such a stochastic process,

$$S_{n+1} = S_n + 1 \text{ with probability } p$$

and $\quad S_{n+1} = S_n - 1 \text{ with probability } 1 - p,$

so $\quad E[S_{n+1} | S_n = k] = (k + 1)(p) + (k - 1)(1 - p)$

$$= kp + p + (k - 1) - p(k - 1)$$

$$= kp + p + k - 1 - pk + p$$

$$= k + 2p - 1$$

$$> k$$

$$= S_n$$

for all n and k. This process is, therefore, a submartingale.

As an example of a supermartingale, consider the asymmetric random walk with unit increments and unit decrements. Let the probability of a unit increment, p, be smaller than the probability of a unit decrement, $1 - p$. For such a stochastic process,

$$S_{n+1} = S_n + 1 \text{ with probability } p$$

and $\quad S_{n+1} = S_n - 1 \text{ with probability } 1 - p,$

so $\quad E[S_{n+1} | S_n = k] = (k + 1)(p) + (k - 1)(1 - p)$

$$= kp + p + (k - 1) - p(k - 1)$$

$$= kp + p + k - 1 - pk + p$$

$$= k + 2p - 1$$

$$< k$$

$$= S_n$$

for all n and k. This process is, therefore, a supermartingale. Notice that if we substitute in $p = 0.5$, then

$$E[S_{n+1} | S_n = k] = k + 2p - 1$$

$$= k$$

$$= S_n$$

and again we have a martingale, agreeing with our previous result.

For another example of a martingale, suppose that X_n has a normal distribution with mean one and variance one, and let

$$S_n = \pi_{i=1 \text{ to } n} X_i.$$

Then $E[S_{n+1} \mid S_n = k] = E[\pi_{i=1 \text{ to } n+1} X_i \mid S_n = k]$

(by definition of S_{n+1})

$$= E[X_{n+1} S_n \mid S_n = k]$$

(by definition of S_n)

(conditionally on $S_n = k$, S_n is known, and not random, so it may pulled out of the expectation as its value, which in this case is k)

$$= k E[X_{n+1} \mid S_n = k]$$

(conditionally on $S_n = k$, S_n is known, and not random, so it may pulled out of the expectation as its value, which in this case is k)

$$= k E[X_{n+1}]$$

(because all the Xs are independent, functions of independent random variables are independent, and S_n is a function of $\{X_1, \dots, X_n\}$)

$$= (k)(1)$$

(because $E[X_{n+1}] = 1$, as given)

$$= k$$

$$= S_n.$$

We have verified that this stochastic process is a martingale.

One of the most famous results concerning martingales (and random walks) is the reflection principle. Any symmetric random walk is a martingale (see Problem 11–24), whether or not is has unit increments and unit decrements. There is a natural symmetry of the paths of such a symmetric random walk. That is, if we consider the X-axis to be a large mirror, then for any path of this symmetric random walk there is a corresponding path defined as its mirror reflection. Each time the first path increases, its corresponding mirror reflection decreases by the same amount, and each time the first path decreases, its corresponding mirror reflection increases by the same amount. But because the random walk is symmetric, each path has the same probability as its mirror reflection. It should be noted that the mirror reflection of the mirror reflection of a given path is just that path.

If a path of length N is given by

$$S_n = k_n \text{ for } n = 1, 2, \dots, N,$$

then its mirror reflection is given by

$$S^*_n = -k_n \text{ for } n = 1, 2, \ldots, N.$$

This can be proven by mathematical induction (see Problem 11–28). There are quite a few results which can be derived by this reflection principle. We will only consider the most basic of these results. For a good reference to a more complete development, see Feller (1968), Volume I, page 68.

The first result is as follows. Let $n_2 > n_1$, and $C > B > A$. Then the number of paths from $\{S_{n1} = B\}$ to $\{S_{n2} = C\}$ for which $S_n = A$ for some n satisfying $n_1 < n < n_2$ is equal to the number of paths from $\{S_{n1} = 2A - B\}$ to $\{S_{n2} = C\}$. This is primarily because any path from $\{S_{n1} = 2a - B\}$ to $\{S_{n2} = C\}$ must pass through A, so for any such path $S_n = A$ for some n satisfying $n_1 < n < n_2$. This result can immediately be reworded in terms of probabilities of these events.

The second result which stems from the reflection principle is as follows. Let $A < B$. Then

$$P\{S_n = A, \max_{i = 1 \text{ to } n} S_i \geq B\} = P\{S_n = 2B - A\}.$$

Any path satisfying either condition must have a maximum, in the first n time points, which exceeds B (non-strictly). From this point on the reflection principle provides a one-to-one correspondence between paths leading to $P\{S_n = 2B - A\}$ and paths leading to $P\{S_n = A\}$.

As an example, if $\{S_n\}$ is a symmetric random walk with unit increments and unit decrements, then

$$P\{S_4 = 2, \max_{i = 1 \text{ to } 4} S_i \geq 3\} = P\{S_4 = 4\}.$$

This follows from the last application of the reflection principle. But we know that

$$P\{S_4 = 4\} = C(4, 4) \, (0.5)^4$$

$$= \{4!/[4!(4 - 4)!]\}/16$$

$$= \{24/[(24) \, (0!)]\}/16$$

$$= \{24/(24) \, (1)]\}/16$$

$$= 1/16.$$

Two other properties of martingales are most useful in certain applications. First, under some conditions martingales have limits. This has to do with the so-called "martingale upcrossing theorem". The idea is that the probability that a martingale goes under A infinitely often and over B infinitely often, where $A < B$, is zero. Since this is true for all pairs of A and B satisfying $A < B$, all subsequences of the martingale must converge. Therefore, the martingale itself must converge.

The second property involves optional stopping and stopping times. If $\{S_n\}$ is a martingale and N is a stopping time, such that

$E[N]$ is finite,

then the stopped martingale process, defined as $\{S*_n\}$, where

$S*_n = S_n$ for $n \leq N$

and $\quad S*_n = S_N$ for $n > N$,

is also a martingale. This implies, for example, that if you are betting in a fair game, and if your decision to stop is based only on your prior results, then your expected earnings (and your expected losses) are still zero. That is, optional stopping cannot help you to beat the system. See Problem 11–32 to see how to beat the system if you have plenty of time on your hands.

• PROBLEM 11-22

Is it possible for a stochastic process not to be a martingale, not to be a submartingale, and not to be a supermartingale?

SOLUTION:

Yes. Consider, for example, a Markov chain with three states, 1, 2, and 3, and a one-step transition matrix given by

$$
A_1 = \begin{matrix} 0 & 1 & 0 \\ 0 & 1 & 0 \\ 0 & 1 & 0. \end{matrix}
$$

Now if the Markov chain is at state 1, then the next state will, with probability one, be two. Thus

$$E[X_{n+1} | X_n = 1] = (1)\,(0) + (2)\,(1) + (3)\,(0)$$

$$= 0 + 2 + 0$$

$$= 2$$

$$> 1,$$

so this Markov chain appears to be a submartingale.

If the Markov chain is at state 2, then the next state will, with probability one, be two. Thus

$$E[X_{n+1} | X_n = 2] = (1)(0) + (2)(1) + (3)(0)$$
$$= 0 + 2 + 0$$
$$= 2,$$

so this Markov chain appears to be a martingale.

If the Markov chain is at state 3, then the next state will, with probability one, be two. Thus

$$E[X_{n+1} | X_n = 3] = (1)(0) + (2)(1) + (3)(0)$$
$$= 0 + 2 + 0$$
$$= 2$$
$$< 3,$$

so this Markov chain appears to be a supermartingale. But since it is not consistently fair, it cannot be a martingale. Since it is not consistently increasing, it cannot be a submartingale. Since it is not consistently decreasing, it cannot be a supermartingale.

• PROBLEM 11–23

Give an example of a martingale which is not a Markov chain.

SOLUTION:

Consider a stochastic process X for which there are three states, 1, 2, and 3, and the probabilities are

$$P\{X_{n+1} = 1 | X_{n-1} = 1, X_n = 1\} = 1.0,$$
$$P\{X_{n+1} = 2 | X_{n-1} = 1, X_n = 1\} = 0.0,$$
$$P\{X_{n+1} = 3 | X_{n-1} = 1, X_n = 1\} = 0.0,$$
$$P\{X_{n+1} = 1 | X_{n-1} = 1, X_n = 2\} = 0.5,$$

$$P\{X_{n+1} = 2 \mid X_{n-1} = 1, X_n = 2\} = 0.0,$$

$$P\{X_{n+1} = 3 \mid X_{n-1} = 1, X_n = 2\} = 0.5,$$

$$P\{X_{n+1} = 1 \mid X_{n-1} = 1, X_n = 3\} = 0.0,$$

$$P\{X_{n+1} = 2 \mid X_{n-1} = 1, X_n = 3\} = 0.0,$$

$$P\{X_{n+1} = 3 \mid X_{n-1} = 1, X_n = 3\} = 1.0,$$

$$P\{X_{n+1} = 1 \mid X_{n-1} = 2, X_n = 1\} = 1.0,$$

$$P\{X_{n+1} = 2 \mid X_{n-1} = 2, X_n = 1\} = 0.0,$$

$$P\{X_{n+1} = 3 \mid X_{n-1} = 2, X_n = 1\} = 0.0,$$

$$P\{X_{n+1} = 1 \mid X_{n-1} = 2, X_n = 2\} = 0.0,$$

$$P\{X_{n+1} = 2 \mid X_{n-1} = 2, X_n = 2\} = 1.0,$$

$$P\{X_{n+1} = 3 \mid X_{n-1} = 2, X_n = 2\} = 0.0,$$

$$P\{X_{n+1} = 1 \mid X_{n-1} = 2, X_n = 3\} = 0.0,$$

$$P\{X_{n+1} = 2 \mid X_{n-1} = 2, X_n = 3\} = 0.0,$$

$$P\{X_{n+1} = 3 \mid X_{n-1} = 2, X_n = 3\} = 1.0,$$

$$P\{X_{n+1} = 1 \mid X_{n-1} = 3, X_n = 1\} = 0.0,$$

$$P\{X_{n+1} = 2 \mid X_{n-1} = 3, X_n = 1\} = 0.0,$$

$$P\{X_{n+1} = 3 \mid X_{n-1} = 3, X_n = 1\} = 1.0,$$

$$P\{X_{n+1} = 1 \mid X_{n-1} = 3, X_n = 2\} = 0.5,$$

$$P\{X_{n+1} = 2 \mid X_{n-1} = 3, X_n = 2\} = 0.0,$$

$$P\{X_{n+1} = 3 \mid X_{n-1} = 3, X_n = 2\} = 0.5,$$

$$P\{X_{n+1} = 1 \mid X_{n-1} = 3, X_n = 3\} = 0.0,$$

$$P\{X_{n+1} = 2 \mid X_{n-1} = 3, X_n = 3\} = 0.0,$$

and $\quad P\{X_{n+1} = 3 \mid X_{n-1} = 3, X_n = 3\} = 1.0.$

Now this stochastic process is a martingale because

$$E[X_{n+1} \mid X_{n-1} = 1, X_n = 1] = (1)\,(1.0) + (2)\,(0.0) + (3)\,(0.0)$$

$$= 1.0 + 0.0 + 0.0$$

$$= 1$$

$$= X_n,$$

$$E[X_{n+1} \mid X_{n-1} = 1, X_n = 2] = (1)\,(0.5) + (2)\,(0.0) + (3)\,(0.5)$$
$$= 0.5 + 0.0 + 1.5$$
$$= 2$$
$$= X_n,$$

$$E[X_{n+1} \mid X_{n-1} = 1, X_n = 3] = (1)\,(0.0) + (2)\,(0.0) + (3)\,(1.0)$$
$$= 0.0 + 0.0 + 3.0$$
$$= 3$$
$$= X_n,$$

$$E[X_{n+1} \mid X_{n-1} = 2, X_n = 1] = (1)\,(1.0) + (2)\,(0.0) + (3)\,(0.0)$$
$$= 1.0 + 0.0 + 0.0$$
$$= 1$$
$$= X_n,$$

$$E[X_{n+1} \mid X_{n-1} = 2, X_n = 2] = (1)\,(0.0) + (2)\,(1.0) + (3)\,(0.0)$$
$$= 0.0 + 2.0 + 0.0$$
$$= 2$$
$$= X_n,$$

$$E[X_{n+1} \mid X_{n-1} = 2, X_n = 3] = (1)\,(0.0) + (2)\,(0.0) + (3)\,(1.0)$$
$$= 0.0 + 0.0 + 3.0$$
$$= 3$$
$$= X_n,$$

$$E[X_{n+1} \mid X_{n-1} = 3, X_n = 1] = (1)\,(1.0) + (2)\,(0.0) + (3)\,(0.0)$$
$$= 1.0 + 0.0 + 0.0$$
$$= 1$$
$$= X_n,$$

$$E[X_{n+1} \mid X_{n-1} = 3, X_n = 2] = (1)\,(0.5) + (2)\,(0.0) + (3)\,(0.5)$$
$$= 0.5 + 0.0 + 1.5$$
$$= 2$$
$$= X_n,$$

and $\quad E[X_{n+1} | X_{n-1} = 3, X_n = 3] = (1)\ (0.0) + (2)\ (0.0) + (3)\ (1.0)$

$$= 0.0 + 0.0 + 3.0$$

$$= 3$$

$$= X_n.$$

But this stochastic process is not a Markov chain, because, for example,

$$P\{X_{n+1} = 2 | X_{n-1} = 2, X_n = 2\} = 1.0$$

and $\quad P\{X_{n+1} = 2 | X_{n-1} = 3, X_n = 2\} = 0.0.$

For this stochastic process to be a Markov chain, these two probabilities would need to be equal, as would all other pairs of probabilities so related.

• PROBLEM 11-24

We have seen that the symmetric random walk with unit increments and unit decrements is a martingale. Generalize this to state that any symmetric random walk, with or without unit increments and unit decrements, is a martingale. That is,

$$S_n = \Sigma_{i=1 \text{ to } n}\ X_i,$$

with $\{X_i\}$ independent with the identical distribution, and

$$P\{X_i = k\} = P\{X_i = -k\}.$$

Show that $\{S_n\}$ is a martingale.

SOLUTION:

We write

$$E[S_{n+1} | S_n = k] = E[\Sigma_{i=1 \text{ to } n+1}\ X_i | S_n = k]$$

(by the definition of S_{n+1})

$$= E[S_n + X_{n+1} | S_n = k]$$

(by the definition of S_n)

$$= k + E[X_{n+1} | S_n = k]$$

(since we are conditioning on S_n being known, and consequently its expected value is equal to its known value)

$$= k + E[X_{n+1}]$$

(by independence of X_{n+1} and $\{X_1, X_2,..., X_n\}$, the fact that S_n is a function of $\{X_1, X_2,..., X_n\}$, and the fact that functions of independent random variables are also independent random variables)

$$= K + \Sigma_{j=1 \text{ to infinity}}[jP\{X_{n+1}=j\} + (-j)P\{X_{n+1}=-j\}]$$

(by the definition of the expected value in terms of the probability mass function of X_{n+1})

$$= K + \Sigma_{j=1 \text{ to infinity}}[jP\{X_{n+1}=j\} + (-j)P\{X_{n+1}=j\}]$$

(by the symmetry of the distribution of X_{n+1})

$$= K + \Sigma_{j=1 \text{ to infinity}}[(j-j)P\{X_{n+1}=j\}]$$

(combining like terms)

$$= K + \Sigma_{j=1 \text{ to infinity}}[(0)P\{X_{n+1}=j\}]$$

$$= K + \Sigma_{j=1 \text{ to infinity}}[0]$$

$$= k$$

$$= S_n,$$

thus establishing that this random walk is a martingale. If the distribution of X_{n+1} had been continuous, then the same result would hold true, only we would replace the sum with an integral, and replace the probability mass function with the probability density function.

• PROBLEM 11–25

Generalize Problem 11–24 to the case in which a random walk is a sum of independent and identically distributed random variables which need not be symmetric but do have mean zero.

SOLUTION:

We write

$$E[S_{n+1} \mid S_n = k] = E[\Sigma_{i=1 \text{ to } n+1}X_i \mid S_n = k]$$

(by the definition of S_{n+1})

$$= E[S_n + X_{n+1} \mid S_n = k]$$

(by the definition of S_n)

$$= k + E[X_{n+1} \mid S_n = k]$$

(since we are conditioning on S_n being known, and consequently its expected value is equal to its known value)

$$= k + E[X_{n+1}]$$

(by independence of X_{n+1} and $\{X_1, X_2, \ldots, X_n\}$, the fact that S_n is a function of $\{X_1, X_2, \ldots, X_n\}$, and the fact that functions of independent random variables are also independent random variables)

$$= k + 0$$

(because $E[X_{n+1}] = 0$, as given)

$$= k$$

$$= S_n,$$

thus establishing that this random walk is a martingale. It does not matter if the distribution of X_{n+1} is continuous, discrete, singular, or a combination of the three types of distribution.

• PROBLEM 11–26

Suppose that S_n is a product of independent and identically distributed random variables, each of which has mean one. Prove that this is a martingale.

SOLUTION:

We write

$$E[S_{n+1} \mid S_n = k] = E[\pi_{i=1 \text{ to } n+1} X_i \mid S_n = k]$$

(by the definition of S_{n+1})

$$= E[(S_n)(X_{n+1}) \mid S_n = k]$$

(by the definition of S_n)

$$= (k)\, E[X_{n+1} \mid S_n = k]$$

(since we are conditioning on S_n being known, and consequently its expected value is equal to its known value)

$$= (k)\, E[X_{n+1}]$$

(by independence of X_{n+1} and $\{X_1, X_2,..., X_n\}$, the fact that S_n is a function of $\{X_1, X_2,..., X_n\}$, and the fact that functions of independent random variables are also independent random variables)

$$= (k)\, (1)$$

(because $E[X_{n+1}] = 1$, as given)

$$= k$$

$$= S_n,$$

thus establishing that this random walk is a martingale. It does not matter if the distribution of X_{n+1} is continuous, discrete, singular, or a combination of the three types of distribution.

• PROBLEM 11-27

Let $\{X_i\}$ be an infinite sequence of independent continuous uniform random variables, each with range $[0, 1]$. Define

$$S_n = c^n \pi_{i=1\ \text{to}\ n} X_i.$$

For what value of c is $\{S_n\}$ a martingale?

SOLUTION:

To be a martingale, we require

$$c^n \pi_{i=1\ \text{to}\ n} X_i = S_n$$

$$= k$$

$$= E[S_{n+1} \mid S_n = k]$$

$$= E[c^{n+1} \pi_{i=1\ \text{to}\ n+1} X_i \mid S_n = k]$$

$$= cE[c^n \pi_{i=1\ \text{to}\ n+1} X_i \mid S_n = k]$$

$$= cE[S_n X_{n+1} \mid S_n = k]$$

(by definition of S_n)

$$= ckE[X_{n+1} \mid S_n = k]$$

(since we are conditioning on S_n being known, and consequently its expected value is equal to its known value)

$$= ckE[X_{n+1}]$$

(by independence of X_{n+1} and $\{X_1, X_2,..., X_n\}$, the fact that S_n is a function of $\{X_1, X_2,..., X_n\}$, and the fact that functions of independent random variables are also independent random variables)

$$= ck/2$$

(since the mean of a continuous uniform random variable is the unweighted average of the two endpoints of its range, which, in this case, implies that $E[X_{n+1}] = 0.5$).

Now we know that

$k = ck/2$ for all values of k.

Letting k be any value besides zero allows us to divide by k, thereby obtaining the equality

$1 = c/2$,

so $c = 2$.

This problem could also have been solved by appealing to the result of Problem 11–26. We recognize that

$$S_n = \pi_{i=1 \text{ to } n} Y_i,$$

where $Y_i = cX_i$,

because $\pi_{i=1 \text{ to } n} Y_i = \pi_{i=1 \text{ to } n} cX_i$

$$= c^n \pi_{i=1 \text{ to } n} X_i$$

$$= S_n.$$

Thus $\{S_n\}$ is a martingale if $E[Y_i] = 1$. But

$$E[Y_{ix}] = E[cX_i]$$

$$= cE[X_i]$$

$$= c\,(0.5)$$

$$= c/2.$$

Therefore

$$c/2 = 1$$

and $c = 2,$

as before.

• PROBLEM 11-28

Prove, using mathematical induction, that if $\{S^*_n\}$ is the mirror reflection of $\{S_n\}$, then

$$S^*_n = -S_n.$$

SOLUTION:

We start by proving this result for the case of $n = 1$. When $n = 1$, the state of the random walk is the first jump, so we see that

$$S^*_n = S^*_1$$

(because $n = 1$)

$$= X^*_1$$

(by definition of S^*_n)

$$= -X_1$$

(because $X^*_n = -X_n$ for all n, per the definition of mirror reflection)

$$= -S_1$$

(by definition of S_1).

Now we assume that

$$S^*_n = -S_n$$

for $n = 1, 2, \ldots, k$, and try to prove that

$$S^*_{k+1} = -S_{k+1}.$$

We see that

$$S^*_{k+1} = \Sigma_{n=1 \text{ to } k+1} X^*_n$$

(by definition of S^*_{k+1})

$$= \Sigma_{n=1 \text{ to } k} X^*_n + X^*_{k+1}$$

$$= S^*_k + X^*_{k+1}$$

(by definition of S^*_k)

$$= -S_k + X^*_{k+1}$$

(by the induction hypothesis)

$$= -S_k - X_{k+1}$$

(because X^* is the mirror reflection of X)

$$= -S_{k+1}$$

(by definition of S_{k+1}).

This completes the proof.

• PROBLEM 11-29

Given that $\{S_n\}$ is a symmetric random walk and that $S_2 = 2$, find

$P\{S_4 > 2 \mid S_4 \text{ does not equal } 2\}$.

SOLUTION:

By the reflection principle, there are as many paths for which $S_4 > S_2 = 2$ as there are for which $S_4 < S_2 = 2$, and there is a correspondence of probabilities between corresponding paths. Since we are conditioning on the event that S_4 is not two, these two possibilities are equally likely and exactly one must occur. Thus the probability of each is 0.5.

• PROBLEM 11-30

Let $\{S_n\}$ be a martingale. Prove that $\{S^*_n\}$ is a submartingale, where

$$S^*_n = [S_n]^2,$$

and prove that $\{T_n\}$ is a supermartingale, where

$$T_n = \ln[S_n].$$

SOLUTION:

We write

$$E[S^*_{n+1} \mid S^*_n = k] = E[S_{n+1}^2 \mid S_n^2 = k]$$

(by definition of S^*_{n+1})

$$= E[S_{n+1}^2 \mid S_n = k^{0.5}]$$

(by definition of S^*_n)

$$\geq E[S_{n+1} \mid S_n = k^{0.5}]^2$$

(by Jensen's inequality applied to $f(X) = X^2$, which is a convex function)

$$= [k^{0.5}]^2$$

(because $\{S_n\}$ is a martingale)

$$= k$$

$$= S^*_n.$$

Thus $\{S^*_n\}$ is a submartingale process.

Also,

$$E[T_{n+1} \mid T_n = k] = E[\ln(S_{n+1}) \mid \ln(S_n) = k]$$

(by definition of T_{n+1})

$$= E[\ln(S_{n+1}) \mid S_n = e^k]$$

(because the natural logarithmic function is the inverse function of the exponential function)

$$\leq \ln(E[S_{n+1} \mid S_n = e^k])$$

(by the extension of Jensen's inequality applied to $f(X) = \ln(X)$, which is a concave function)

$$= \ln(e^k)$$

(because $\{S_n\}$ is a martingale)

$$= k$$

$$= T_n.$$

Thus $\{T_n\}$ is a supermartingale process.

• PROBLEM 11–31

Let $\{S_n\}$ be a symmetric random walk with unit increments and unit decrements. Find $P\{S_6 = 0, \max_{i = 1 \text{ to } 6} S_i \geq 3\}$.

SOLUTION:

We recall the formula

$$P\{S_n = A, \max_{i = 1 \text{ to } n} S_i \geq B\} = P\{S_n = 2B - A\}.$$

If we apply this formula with

$n = 6,$

$A = 0,$

and $\quad B = 3,$

then we obtain

$$
\begin{aligned}
P\{S_6 = 0, \max_{i = 1 \text{ to } 6} S_i \geq 3\} &= P\{S_6 = 2(3) - 0\} \\
&= P\{S_6 = 6 - 0\} \\
&= P\{S_6 = 6\} \\
&= C(6, 6)\,(0.5)^6 \\
&= 6!/[6!(6 - 6)!2^6] \\
&= 6!/[6!(0!)2^6] \\
&= 6!/[6!(1)2^6] \\
&= 1/2^6 \\
&= 1/64.
\end{aligned}
$$

• PROBLEM 11–32

Suppose that you gamble in a fair game (a martingale) and decide to stop as soon as you have won \$1000. Does this application of optional stopping lead to a martingale?

SOLUTION:

No. Let N be defined as the first time that you have won $1000. Then

$$E[S_N \mid S_{N-1}] = 1000$$

no matter what the value of S_{N-1} (but if we are still considering the symmetric random walk with unit increments and unit decrements, then necessarily $S_{N-1} = 999$). This is not a martingale. The result given earlier on optional stopping does not apply because the expected waiting time until your fortune hits $1000 is infinite. That is, you can beat the system, but you have no way of bounding the number of lifetimes it may take. If the casino closes, then you are out of luck!

✳✳✳✳✳✳

REVIEW OF WALD'S EQUATION

Wald's Equation is an important application of stopping times to martingales. Basically Wald's Equation expands on the result given earlier on optional stopping.

In particular, suppose that N is a stopping time with finite expected value. Also suppose that $\{X_n\}$ are identically distributed (they may or may not be independent). Let

$$S_n = \Sigma_{i=1 \text{ to } n} X_i.$$

Then Wald's Equation says that

$$E[S_N] = E[N]E[X_i].$$

This is obvious if we let N be a fixed time. This is because if $N = n$, then

$$E[S_N] = E[S_n]$$

(because $N = n$)

$$= E[\Sigma_{i=1 \text{ to } n} X_i]$$

(by definition of S_n)

$$= \Sigma_{i=1 \text{ to } n} E[X_i]$$

(because the expected value operator is a linear operator)

$$= nE[X_i]$$

(because each X has the same expected value)

$$= E[N]E[X_i]$$

(because $E[N] = n$).

But when N is a stopping time which need not be a fixed value, this result is far from being obvious. Let us see where the previous discussion breaks down in this case. We write

$$E[S_N] = E[\Sigma_{i=1 \text{ to } N} X_i]$$

(by definition of S_N),

but this is not equal to

$$\Sigma_{i=1 \text{ to } N} E[X_i],$$

because N is now a random variable, and thus it cannot be taken out of the expression whose expected value is to be determined. This is why Wald's Equation is harder than it may first appear.

As a very simple application of Wald's Equation, let us consider a gambler with $50. He bets $1 per game, and decides to play until he either goes broke or doubles his money. Suppose that each bet is a fair game (martingale). That is, he wins $1 with probability 0.5, and he loses $1 with probability 0.5. What is the probability that he goes broke?

This can be formulated once again as the symmetric random walk with unit increments and unit decrements. But instead of starting at the origin, $S_0 = 50$. Let N be the stopping time as defined in the problem. That is, N is the first time n at which either $S_n = 0$ or $S_n = 100$.

To use Wald's Equation, we must first show that N is a stopping time and that $E[N]$ is finite. Given the path taken by this symmetric random walk, it would be immediately apparent at time n if $N = n$ or not. If $0 < S_i < 100$ for $i < n$ and $S_n = 0$ or $S_n = 100$, then $N = n$. Therefore N must be a stopping time.

Now to show that $E[N]$ is finite, consider that at any state between (but not including) 0 and 100, it would be possible, within 99 steps, to get to either 0 or 100. For example, at state 1 it would be possible to get to state 0 within 1 step (if \$1 is lost at this one step), but it would require 99 steps to have a positive probability of getting to state 100 (in particular, it would require 99 \$1 wins, which occurs with probability 0.5^{99}, which is, of course, positive). But it is true that for any state k between 0 and 100,

$$P\{S_{n+99} = 0 \mid S_n = k\} \geq 0.5^{99}$$

$$> 0,$$

and $\quad P\{S_{n+99} = 100 \mid S_n = k\} \geq 0.5^{99}$

$$> 0.$$

Since these two possibilities are mutually exclusive,

$$P\{N = n+99 \mid S_n = k\} = P\{S_{n+99} = 0 \cup S_{n+99} = 100 \mid S_n = k\}$$

$$= P\{S_{n+99} = 0 \mid S_n = k\} + P\{S_{n+99} = 100 \mid S_n = k\}$$

$$\geq 0.5^{99} + 0.5^{99}$$

$$= 0.5^{98}.$$

Now define Y as follows. If $N < 99$, then $Y = 1$. If $98 < N < 198$, then $Y = 2$. If $197 < N < 297$, then $Y = 3$. That is,

$$Y = [N/99] + 1,$$

where $[X]$ is the greatest integer function of X, or the largest integer not greater than X. For example,

$$[1] = 1,$$

$$[0.5] = 0,$$

$$[2.3] = 2,$$

and $\quad [-3.7] = -4.$

The key is that

$$X - 1 < [X] \leq X$$

for all X.

Now Y is stochastically smaller than a geometric random variable with parameter $p = 0.5^{98}$, meaning that for all c,

$$P\{Y > c\} \leq P\{Z > c\},$$

where Z is a geometric random variable with parameter $p = 0.5^{98}$. This follows because

$$P\{Y = n + 1 \mid Y > n\} \geq 0.5^{98}$$

$$= P\{Z = n + 1 \mid Z > n\}.$$

Now we use the alternate definition of the expected value to find

$$E[Y] = \Sigma_{i = 0 \text{ to infinity}} P\{Y > i\}$$

$$\leq \Sigma_{i = 0 \text{ to infinity}} P\{Z > i\}$$

$$= E[Z]$$

$$= 1/p$$

$$= 1/[0.5^{98}]$$

$$= 2^{98}$$

$$< \text{infinity}.$$

But since

$$Y = [N/99] + 1,$$

we know that

$$N/99 < Y \leq (N/99) + 1.$$

Now

$$E[N/99] < E[Y]$$

$$< \text{infinity},$$

so $E[N] < 99E[Y]$,

which must also be finite. Now we can apply Wald's Equation. It is more convenient to let S_n be the amount won (or lost) up to time n, rather than the amount of money held. Thus $S_0 = 0$ and we stop as soon as either $S_n = -50$ or $S_n = 50$. We find that

$$E[S_N] = E[N]E[X_i]$$

$$= E[N]\{(-1)(0.5) + (1)(0.5)\}$$

$$= E[N]\{-0.5 + 0.5\}$$

$$= E[N]\{0\}$$

$$= 0.$$

But

$$E[S_N] = (-50)P\{-50\} + (50)P\{50\}$$

$$= (-50)P\{-50\} + (50)(1 - P\{-50\})$$

$$= 50 + (-50)P\{-50\} - (50)P\{-50\}$$

$$= 50 + (-100)P\{-50\},$$

and we know that

$$E[S_N] = 0.$$

Therefore,

$$0 = 50 + (-100)P\{-50\},$$

or $$100P\{-50\} = 50,$$

so $$P\{-50\} = 50/100$$

$$= 0.5.$$

Likewise, then

$$P\{50\} = 1 - P\{-50\}$$

$$= 1 - 0.5$$

$$= 0.5.$$

The chances are equal that the gambler will win or lose. This is the simplest example of the Gambler's Ruin problem.

• PROBLEM 11-33

Suppose that a gambler has an arbitrary amount of money and decides to play until he either goes broke or doubles his money. If the game is fair and he either wins $1 or loses $1 at each play, then what is his eventual probability of doubling his money?

SOLUTION:

Let M be the initial amount of money the gambler has, and let N be the time when the gambler either goes broke or doubles his money. To use Wald's Equation, we must first show that N is a stopping time and that $E[N]$ is finite. Given the path taken by this symmetric random walk, it would be immediately apparent at time n if $N = n$ or not. If $0 < S_i < 2M$ for $i < n$ and $S_n = 0$ or $S_n = 2M$, then $N = n$. Therefore N must be a stopping time.

Now to show that $E[N]$ is finite, consider that at any state between (but not including) 0 and $2M$, it would be possible, within $2M - 1$ steps, to get to either 0 or $2M$. For example, at state 1 it would be possible to get to state 0 within 1 step (if \$1 is lost at this one step), but it would require $2M - 1$ steps to have a positive probability of getting to state $2M$ (in particular, it would require $2M - 1$ \$1 wins, which occurs with probability 0.5^{2M-1}, which is, of course, positive). But it is true that for any state k between 0 and 100,

$$P\{S_{n+2M-1} = 0 \mid S_n = k\} \geq 0.5^{2M-1}$$

$$> 0,$$

and $\quad P\{S_{n+2M-1} = 2M \mid S_n = k\} \geq 0.5^{2M-1}$

$$> 0.$$

Since these two possibilities are mutually exclusive,

$$P\{N = n + 2M - 1 \mid S_n = k\}$$

$$= P\{S_{n+2M-1} = 0 \cup S_{n+2M-1} = 2M \mid S_n = k\}$$

$$= P\{S_{n+2M-1} = 0 \mid S_n = k\} + P\{S_{n+2M-1} = 2M \mid S_n = k\}$$

$$\geq 0.5^{2M-1} + 0.5^{2M-1}$$

$$= 0.5^{2M-2}.$$

Now define Y as

$$Y = [N/(2M - 1)] + 1,$$

where $[X]$ is the greatest integer function of X, or the largest integer not greater than X. Again,

$$X - 1 < [X] \leq X$$

for all X.

Now Y is stochastically smaller than a geometric random variable with parameter $p = 0.5^{2M-2}$, meaning that for all c,

$$P\{Y > c\} \leq P\{Z > c\},$$

where Z is a geometric random variable with parameter $p = 0.5^{2M-2}$. This follows because

$$P\{Y = n + 1 \mid Y > n\} \geq 0.5^{2M-2}$$

$$= P\{Z = n + 1 \mid Z > n\}.$$

Now we use the alternate definition of the expected value to find

$$E[Y] = \Sigma_{i = 0 \text{ to infinity}} P\{Y > i\}$$

$$\leq \Sigma_{i = 0 \text{ to infinity}} P\{Z > i\}$$

$$= E[Z]$$

$$= 1/p$$

$$= 1/[0.5^{2M - 2}]$$

$$= 2^{2M - 2}$$

$$< \text{infinity.}$$

But since

$$Y = [N/(2M - 1)] + 1,$$

we know that

$$N/(2M - 1) < Y \leq \{N/(2M - 1)\} + 1.$$

Now $\quad E[N/(2M - 1)] < E[Y]$

$$< \text{infinity,}$$

so $\quad E[N] < (2M - 1)E[Y],$

which must also be finite. Now we can apply Wald's Equation. Again, it is more convenient to let S_n be the amount won (or lost) up to time n, rather than the amount of money held. Thus $S_0 = 0$ and we stop as soon as either $S_n = - M$ or $S_n = M$. We find that

$$E[S_N] = E[N]E[X_i]$$

$$= E[N]\{(- 1) (0.5) + (1) (0.5)\}$$

$$= E[N]\{- 0.5 + 0.5\}$$

$$= E[N]\{0\}$$

$$= 0.$$

But $\quad E[S_N] = (- M)P\{- M\} + (M)P\{M\}$

$$= (- M)P\{- M\} + (M)(1 - P\{- M\})$$

$$= M + (- M)P\{- M\} - (M)P\{- M\}$$

$$= M + (- 2M)P\{- M\},$$

and we know that

$$E[S_N] = 0.$$

Therefore,

$$0 = M + (-2M)P\{-M\},$$

or $\quad 2MP\{-M\} = M,$

so $\quad P\{-M\} = M/(2M)$

$$= 0.5.$$

Likewise, then

$$P\{M\} = 1 - P\{-M\}$$

$$= 1 - 0.5$$

$$= 0.5.$$

The chances are equal that the gambler will win or lose. This is independent of the initial sum of money brought to the casino.

Problem 11–32 mentioned that the expected time until your fortune hits $1000, when starting at $0 and playing a martingale, is infinite. In fact, in such a case, even the expected waiting time until you go ahead by $1 is infinite. This is what is meant by the persistence of bad luck. Feller (Volume 2, 1966), page 15, presents a nice account of the persistence of bad luck in terms of waiting on line.

The famous Gambler's Ruin problem is a particular application of Wald's Equation to gambling. In particular, a gambler starts with a given amount of money and decides to continue to bet until he either attains a pre-determined objective (in terms of earned winnings) or goes broke. There is a nice solution to the probability of each possibility. In this subsection we will generalize to the more realistic case in which the game need not be fair and the gambler may choose to stop when his fortune is other than twice his initial fortune.

The direct approach to finding the probability of ruin is by the method of difference equations. This approach is based on a conditioning argument, with the conditioning being on the first step. In particular, let N be the time at which either the gambler is ruined ($S_N = -A$) or the gambler has attained his goal ($S_N = B$). Then it follows that

$$P\{S_N = -A\} = P\{S_N = -A \cap \text{the universal set}\}$$

(because any set intersected with the universal set will result in the original set)

$$= P\{S_N = -A \cap (s_1 = 1 \cup S_1 = -1)\}$$

(because for the random walk with unit increments and unit decrements S_1 must either be 1 or -1)

$$= P\{[S_N = -A \cap S_1 = 1] \cup [S_N = -A \cap S_1 = -1]\}$$

(by basic set manipulation)

$$= P\{S_1 = 1\}P\{[S_N = -A \mid S_1 = 1]\} + P\{S_1 = -1\}$$
$$P\{S_N = -A \mid S_1 = -1\}$$

(by the definition of conditional probability)

$$= pP\{[S_N = -A \mid S_1 = 1]\} + (1-p)P\{S_N = -A \mid S_1 = -1\}$$

(the probabilities of each event for this asymmetric random walk)

$$= pP\{[S_N = -A \mid S_n = 1]\} + (1-p)P\{S_N = -A \mid S_n = -1\}$$

for any $n < N$

(because random walks satisfy the Markovian property).

Now if

$$P(k) = P\{S_N = -A \mid S_n = k\},$$

then we have shown that

$$P(0) = pP(1) + (1-p)P(-1)$$
$$= pP(1) + P(-1) - pP(-1)$$
$$= p[P(1) - P(-1)] + P(-1),$$

so $\quad P(0) - P(-1) = p[P(1) - P(-1)].$

This difference equation, in conjunction with certain boundary conditions, would provide a solution to the Gambler's Ruin problem. We will make use of martingales and Wald's Equation, however, to arrive at the same solution differently. This will be done through the problems.

• **PROBLEM 11-34**

Let $\{S_n\}$ be an asymmetric random walk with unit increments and unit decrements such that

$$S_n = \Sigma_{i = \text{to } n} X_i,$$

where $P\{X_i = 1\} = p$

and $\quad P\{X_i = -1\} = 1 - p.$

Show that $\{Y_n\}$ is a martingale, where

$$Y_n = [(1 - p)/p]^{S_n}.$$

SOLUTION:

Let $q = 1 - p$. We write

$$E[Y_{n+1} \mid Y_n = k] = E[(q/p)^{S_n + 1} \mid (q/p)^{S_n} = k]$$

(by definition of S_n)

$$= E[(q/p)^{X_n + 1}(q/p)^{S_n} \mid (q/p)^{S_n} = k]$$

(since $S_{n+1} = S_n + X_{n+1}$)

$$= (k)E[(q/p)^{X_n + 1}(q/p)^{S_n} = k]$$

(we may pull the constant out of the expectation)

$$= (k)E[(q/p)^{X_n + 1}]$$

(by independence)

$$= (k)[(q/p)P\{X_{n+1} = 1\} + (p/q)P\{X_{n+1} = -1\}]$$

(by definition of the expected value)

$$= (k)[(q/p)(p) + (p/q)(q)]$$

$$= (k)[q + p]$$

$$= k.$$

Thus this stochastic process is a martingale.

• PROBLEM 11–35

Apply Problem 11–34 and Problem 11–33 to solve the Gambler's Ruin problem. That is, find the probability of ruin.

SOLUTION:

Letting N be the time of ruin or victory, we know, from Problem 11–33, that N is a stopping time and that $E[N]$ is finite. Thus Wald's Equation applies. Consider the martingale $\{Y_n\}$ from Problem 11–34. Then

$$E[Y_N] = P\{\text{ruin}\}(q/p)^{-A} + P\{\text{win}\}(q/p)^B$$

$$= P\{\text{ruin}\}(q/p)^{-A} + (1 - P\{\text{ruin}\})(q/p)^B$$

$$= P\{\text{ruin}\}[(q/p)^{-A} - (q/p)^B] + (q/p)^B.$$

But, as can be shown by induction,

$$E[Y_N] = E[Y_1]$$

$$= 1.$$

Thus $1 = P\{\text{ruin}\}[(q/p)^{-A} - (q/p)^B] + (q/p)^B,$

so $P\{\text{ruin}\}[(q/p)^{-A} - (q/p)^B] = 1 - (q/p)^B,$

or $P\{\text{ruin}\} = 1 - (q/p)^B/[(q/p)^{-A} - (q/p)^B].$

This is the solution, except that when $p = 0.5$, then

$$q = 1 - p$$

$$= 1 - 0.5$$

$$= 0.5,$$

and the denominator of the final expression for $P\{\text{ruin}\}$ is zero. This is, of course, unacceptable. Fortunately, there is a solution when $p = 0.5$ as well. The solution above is valid whenever p is not 0.5.

When $p = 0.5$, then $\{S_n\}$ itself is a martingale. This means that we can define N as before, and use Wald's Equation (we have already proven that N is a stopping time and that $E[N]$ is finite). Then

$$E[S_N] = (-A)P\{\text{ruin}\} + BP\{\text{win}\}$$

$$= (-A)P\{\text{ruin}\} + B(1 - P\{\text{ruin}\})$$

$$= (-A - B)P\{\text{ruin}\} + B.$$

But by Wald's Equation,

$$E[S_N] = E[N]E[X_i]$$

$$= E[N](0)$$

$$= 0.$$

Thus

$$0 = (-A - B)P\{\text{ruin}\} + B,$$

or $(A + B)P\{\text{ruin}\} = B,$

and $P\{\text{ruin}\} = B/(A + B).$

• PROBLEM 11–36

When $p = 0.5$, what happens to the probability of ruin as the initial capital of the gambler goes to infinity?

SOLUTION:

In this case, the limit of $P\{\text{ruin}\}$ is

$\lim_{A \text{ to infinity}} B/(A + B) = 0.$

With enough capital it is highly likely that one will win B dollars, assuming that B does not increase as A does. That is, the amount you want to win must stay constant (not increase).

• PROBLEM 11–37

If you start with $100 and decide to quit when you are broke or when you have $150, then what are your chances of attaining your goal of $150?

SOLUTION:

We compute

$$P\{\text{ruin}\} = B/(A + B)$$

$$= 50/(100 + 50)$$

$$= 50/150$$

$$= 1/3,$$

so $\quad P\{\text{win}\} = 1 - P\{\text{ruin}\}$

$$= 1 - 1/3$$

$$= 2/3.$$

CHAPTER 12

GLOSSARY AND REFERENCES

GLOSSARY

$\lvert X \rvert$	absolute value of X
A^c	complement of event A
$E[X\lvert Y = k]$	conditional expected value of X given that $Y = k$
$P\{A \mid B\}$	conditional probability of A given that B has occurred
$F_X(x)$	cumulative distribution function of random variable X evaluated at x
$I[a, b]\, f(x)\, dx$	definite integral of $f(x)$ as x ranges from a to b
$E[X]$	expected value of the random variable X
e^X	exponential function applied to X
$\exp(X)$	exponential function applied to X
$[f(X)]_{X = a\ \text{to}\ b}$	$f(b) - f(a)$
I	identity matrix
$A \cap B$	intersection of events A and B
A^{-1}	inverse of the square, invertible matrix A
M_4	kurtosis
$\lim$	limit
$LI(A)$	limit infimum of the set of events $\{A_n\}$
$LS(A)$	limit supremum of the set of events $\{A_n\}$
$P\{X\}$	probability of X
$f_X(x)$	probability density (or mass) function of random variable X evaluated at x

840

$X^*(n)$	sample mean based on n observations
n	sample size
N_p	size of a finite population
M_3	skewness
$\{S_n\}$	stochastic process indexed by n
$A \cup B$	union of events A and B
$V(X)$	variance of the random variable X

REFERENCES

1. Berger, J. O., 1985, *Statistical Decision Theory and Bayesian Analysis,* Second Edition, Springer-Verlag, New York.

✓2. Billingsley, P., 1986, *Probability and Measure,* Second Edition, John Wiley and Sons, New York.

3. Chow, Y. S. and Teicher, H., 1988, *Probability Theory, Independence, Interchangeability, Martingales,* Second Edition, Springer-Verlag, New York.

4. Chung, K. L., 1974, *A Course in Probability Theory,* Second Edition, Academic Press, Orlando, Volume 21, Probability and Mathematical Statistics Monographs.

✓5. Feller, W., 1968, *An Introduction to Probability Theory and its Applications,* Volume 1, Third Edition, John Wiley and Sons, New York.

✓6. Feller, W., 1966, *An Introduction to Probability Theory and its Applications,* Volume 2, Third Edition, John Wiley and Sons, New York.

7. Fleming, T. R. and Harrington, D. P., 1991, *Counting Processes and Survival Analysis,* John Wiley and Sons, New York.

8. Lehmann, E. L., 1983, *Theory of Point Estimation,* John Wiley and Sons, New York.

9. Lipschutz, S., 1965, *Schaum's Outline Series, Theory and Problems of Probability,* McGraw-Hill, New York.

10. Pettofrezzo, A. J., 1978, *Matrices and Transformations,* Dover, New York.

11. Ross, S. M., 1983, *Stochastic Processes,* John Wiley and Sons, New York.

12. Rozanov, Y. A., 1969, *Probability Theory: A Concise Course,* Dover, New York.

13. Searle, S. R., 1982, *Matrix Algebra Useful for Statistics,* Wiley, New York.

14. Stephenson, G., 1986, *An Introduction to Matrices, Sets, and Groups for Science Students,* Dover, New York.

15. Strang, G., 1988, *Linear Algebra and its Applications,* Third Edition, Harcourt Brace Jovanovich, San Diego.

16. Sveshnikov, A. A., 1978, *Problems in Probability Theory, Mathematical Statistics, and Theory of Random Functions,* Dover, New York.

Numbers on this page refer to <u>PROBLEM NUMBERS</u>, not page numbers.

INDEX

Numbers on this page refer to **PROBLEM NUMBERS**, not page numbers.

Numbers on this page refer to <u>PROBLEM NUMBERS</u>, not page numbers.

Numbers on this page refer to <u>PROBLEM NUMBERS</u>, not page numbers.

Numbers on this page refer to **PROBLEM NUMBERS**, not page numbers.

ADDITIONAL TABLES

Left P(X≥x)		Cumulative Binomial Probabilities n = 4									Right P(X≤x)

x	π=	01	02	03	04	05	06	07	08	09	10	
1		0394	0776	1147	1507	1855	2193	2519	2836	3143	3439	3
2		0006	0023	0052	0091	0140	0199	0267	0344	0430	0523	2
3				0001	0002	0005	0008	0013	0019	0027	0037	1
4										0001	0001	0
x		99	98	97	96	95	94	93	92	91	90 =π	x

n = 4

x	π=	11	12	13	14	15	16	17	18	19	20	
1		3726	4003	4271	4530	4780	5021	5254	5479	5695	5904	3
2		0624	0732	0847	0968	1095	1228	1366	1509	1656	1808	2
3		0049	0063	0079	0098	0120	0144	0171	0202	0235	0272	1
4		0001	0002	0003	0004	0005	0007	0008	0010	0013	0016	0
x		89	88	87	86	85	84	83	82	81	80 =π	x

n = 4

x	π=	21	22	23	24	25	26	27	28	29	30	
1		6105	6298	6485	6664	6836	7001	7160	7313	7459	7599	3
2		1963	2122	2285	2450	2617	2787	2959	3132	3307	3483	2
3		0312	0356	0403	0453	0508	0566	0628	0694	0763	0837	1
4		0019	0023	0028	0033	0039	0046	0053	0061	0071	0081	0
x		79	78	77	76	75	74	73	72	71	70 =	x

n = 4

x	π=	31	32	33	34	35	36	37	38	39	40	
1		7733	7862	7985	8103	8215	8322	8425	8522	8615	8704	3
2		3660	3837	4015	4193	4370	4547	4724	4900	5075	5248	2
3		0915	0996	1082	1171	1265	1362	1464	1596	1679	1792	1
4		0092	0105	0119	0134	0150	0168	0187	0209	0231	0256	0
x		69	68	67	66	65	64	63	62	61	60 =π	x

n = 4

x	π=	41	42	43	44	45	46	47	48	49	50	
1		8788	8868	8944	9017	9085	9150	9211	9269	9323	9375	3
2		5420	5590	5759	5926	6090	6252	6412	6569	6724	6875	2
3		1909	2030	2155	2283	2415	2550	2689	2831	2977	3125	1
4		0283	0311	0342	0375	0410	0448	0488	0531	0576	0625	0
x		59	58	57	56	55	54	53	52	51	50 =π	x

NORMAL PROBABILITY FUNCTIONS AND DERIVATIVES

x	$P(x)$	$Z(x)$	$Z^{(1)}(x)$
1.00	0.84134 47460 68543	0.24197 07245 19143	-0.24197 07245 19143
1.02	0.84613 57696 27265	0.23713 19520 19380	-0.24187 45910 59767
1.04	0.85083 00496 69019	0.23229 70047 43366	-0.24158 88849 33101
1.06	0.85542 77003 36091	0.22746 96324 57386	-0.24111 78104 04829
1.08	0.85992 89099 11231	0.22265 34987 51761	-0.24046 57786 51902
1.10	0.86433 39390 53618	0.21785 21770 32551	-0.23963 73947 35806
1.12	0.86864 31189 57270	0.21306 91467 75718	-0.23863 74443 88804
1.14	0.87285 68494 37202	0.20830 77900 47108	-0.23747 08806 53704
1.16	0.87697 55969 48657	0.20357 13882 90759	-0.23614 28104 17281
1.18	0.88099 98925 44800	0.19886 31193 87276	-0.23465 84808 76986
1.20	0.88493 03297 78292	0.19418 60549 83213	-0.23302 32659 79856
1.22	0.88876 75625 52166	0.18954 31580 91640	-0.23124 26528 71801
1.24	0.89251 23029 25413	0.18493 72809 63305	-0.22932 22283 94499
1.26	0.89616 53188 78700	0.18037 11632 27080	-0.22726 76656 66121
1.28	0.89972 74320 45558	0.17584 74302 97662	-0.22508 47107 81008
1.30	0.90319 95154 14390	0.17136 85920 47807	-0.22277 91696 62150
1.32	0.90658 24910 06528	0.16693 70417 41714	-0.22035 68950 99062
1.34	0.90987 73275 35548	0.16255 50552 25534	-0.21782 37740 02216
1.36	0.91308 50380 52915	0.15822 47903 70383	-0.21518 57149 03721
1.38	0.91620 66775 84986	0.15394 82867 62634	-0.21244 86357 32434
1.40	0.91924 33407 66229	0.14972 74656 35745	-0.20961 84518 90043
1.42	0.92219 61594 73454	0.14556 41300 37348	-0.20670 10646 53034
1.44	0.92506 63004 65673	0.14145 99652 24839	-0.20370 23499 23768
1.46	0.92785 49630 34106	0.13741 65392 82282	-0.20062 81473 52131
1.48	0.93056 33766 66669	0.13343 53039 51002	-0.19748 42498 47483
1.50	0.93319 27987 31142	0.12951 75956 65892	-0.19427 63934 98838
1.52	0.93574 45121 81064	0.12566 46367 89088	-0.19101 02479 19414
1.54	0.93821 98232 88188	0.12187 75370 32402	-0.18769 14070 29899
1.56	0.94062 00594 05207	0.11815 72950 59582	-0.18432 53802 92948
1.58	0.94294 65667 62246	0.11450 48002 59292	-0.18091 75844 09682
1.60	0.94520 07083 00442	0.11092 08346 79456	-0.17747 33354 87129
1.62	0.94738 38615 45748	0.10740 60751 13484	-0.17399 78416 83844
1.64	0.94949 74165 25897	0.10396 10953 28764	-0.17049 61963 39173
1.66	0.95154 27737 33277	0.10058 63684 27691	-0.16697 33715 89966
1.68	0.95352 13421 36280	0.09728 22693 31467	-0.16343 42124 76865
1.70	0.95543 45372 41457	0.09404 90773 76887	-0.15988 34315 40708
1.72	0.95728 37792 08671	0.09088 69790 16283	-0.15632 56039 08007
1.74	0.95907 04910 21193	0.08779 60706 10906	-0.15276 51628 62976
1.76	0.96079 60967 12518	0.08477 63613 08022	-0.14920 63959 02119
1.78	0.96246 20196 51483	0.08182 77759 92143	-0.14565 34412 66014
1.80	0.96406 96808 87074	0.07895 01583 00894	-0.14211 02849 41609
1.82	0.96562 04975 54110	0.07614 32736 96207	-0.13858 07581 27097
1.84	0.96711 58813 40836	0.07340 68125 81657	-0.13506 85351 50249
1.86	0.96855 72370 19248	0.07074 03934 56983	-0.13157 71318 29989
1.88	0.96994 59610 38800	0.06814 35661 01045	-0.12810 99042 69964
1.90	0.97128 34401 83998	0.06561 58147 74677	-0.12467 00480 71886
1.92	0.97257 10502 96163	0.06315 65614 35199	-0.12126 05979 55581
1.94	0.97381 01550 59548	0.06076 51689 54565	-0.11788 44277 71856
1.96	0.97500 21048 51780	0.05844 09443 33451	-0.11454 42508 93565
1.98	0.97614 82356 58492	0.05618 31419 03868	-0.11124 26209 69659
2.00	0.97724 98680 51821	0.05399 09665 13188	-0.10798 19330 26376
	$\left[\dfrac{(-5)1}{10}\right]$	$\left[\dfrac{(-6)9}{10}\right]$	$\left[\dfrac{(-5)2}{10}\right]$

$$Z(x) = \frac{1}{\sqrt{2\pi}} e^{-\frac{1}{2}s^2} \quad P(x) = \int_{-\infty}^{x} Z(t)\,dt \quad Z^{(n)}(x) = \frac{d^n}{dx^n} Z(x) \quad He_n(x) = (-1)^n Z^{(n)}(x) / Z(x)$$